FINANCE FOR LAWYERS

■ ■ ■

Steven J. Willis
Professor of Law
University of Florida College of Law

Member, Florida Bar Association
Member, Louisiana Bar Association (in-active)
Certified Public Accountant (Louisiana, in-active license)

WEST
ACADEMIC
PUBLISHING

© 2021 LEG, Inc. d/b/a West Academic
    444 Cedar Street, Suite 700
    St. Paul, MN 55101
    1-877-888-1330

West, West Academic Publishing, and West Academic are trademarks of West Publishing Corporation, used under license.

Printed in the United States of America

ISBN: 978-1-68467-568-5

SUMMARY OF CONTENTS

TABLE OF CONTENTS

PART II. FINANCIAL TERMINOLOGY, RULES, AND GUIDELINES

PART III. CALCULATIONS

TABLE OF CASES

The principal cases are in bold type.

FINANCE FOR LAWYERS

PART I

INTRODUCTION

■ ■ ■

LESSON ONE

WHY LAWYERS NEED TO UNDERSTAND FINANCE

■ ■ ■

Lesson Objectives

1. Student will learn what this course concerns.

2. Student will learn some brief examples of financial calculations used by lawyers involving:

    a. Family Law.

    b. Tort Law.

    c. Corporate Law and Corporate Finance.

    d. Tax Law.

    e. Estate Planning and Estates and Trust Law.

    f. General Law/Property/Contract Law.

    g. Environmental Law.

    h. Bankruptcy Law.

    i. Competition and Anti-trust Law.

    j. Employment Law.

    k. Government Planning and Policy.

    l. Your own Life.

3. Student will learn some instances in which everyone needs to know some basic finance:

    a. Buying a Car.

    b. Buying a House.

    c. Saving for Retirement.

    d. Saving for a Child's Education.

    e. Valuing Lottery Winnings.

4. Student should end the lesson convinced of the _practical_ need for this course.

———————

Many areas of law require a working knowledge of finance, and financial calculations. Lawyers ignore this truism at their peril. If one side of a transaction or negotiation understands finance (to say nothing of accounting and tax law) but the other does not, the situation is inherently unfair and potentially heavily weighted to the knowledgeable side.

Life, however, is often unfair, as is law. Natural Law and morality may implore an attorney to educate an opponent; legal ethics, however, do not. Indeed, legal ethics may preclude an attorney from educating an opponent; alas, it may require an attorney to take advantage of others. Resolving that problem—if one views it as a problem—is for another time and place. Hence, you should proceed with caution.

Unfortunately, many law students arrive in law school without the basic tools of finance. This course aims to alleviate that problem. The course is not a complete course in finance, let alone a substitute for a degree in finance: a basic undergraduate introductory finance course generally constitutes three semester hours, while this course consumes either one or two semester hours. A degree in finance typically takes four years to complete; furthermore, many law students and lawyers have a master's degree in finance. Those with accounting degrees generally will have completed five years of study (resulting in a master's degree), which will have included substantial training in the intricacies of finance.

This course aims to arm you with the basic tools of how finance relates to law. You should then be able to communicate effectively with lawyers and clients who have greater expertise in the area. You should also be able to recognize when you need additional help.

The GLOSSARY file/appendix includes terms you should know. While it is not a comprehensive financial dictionary (such things exist and you may want one), it includes terms used in this course. Many such terms are "terms of art" in that they have a single acceptable definition; however, many others are open to differing meanings. You must know the difference and you must learn to define terms about which experts disagree. Use the GLOSSARY for terms used in the TEXT and the LESSONS. You should also read through the GLOSSARY, as it includes many other useful terms from both finance and accounting. If you do not know the vocabulary of others, they can take advantage of you, so be careful. In addition, the GLOSSARY also has a list of ACRONYMS which business-educated lawyers will often use. Once again, you should read through them to learn the vocabulary of business.

Read the GLOSSARY and ACRONYMS

The world of business has its own vocabulary. If you do not know it, you are at a disadvantage. Use the files for terms you do not understand; however, you should also read through it fully.

The various COURSE CALCULATORS, written in Java Script™, will compute what you need. In this basic course you will learn *how* to use them. More importantly, you will learn *when* to use them. In addition, the course will teach you how to use a commonly available hand-held financial calculator—the HP 10Bii™.

This TEXT is a more traditional linear analysis—and explanation—of the material covered in the lectures. You should read it in addition to listening to the lectures.

For example, tort law practice often involves calculating the present value of lost future wages. Family law practice involves valuing a stream of future income or a deferred compensation plan. Tax law practice necessitates an understanding of the Internal Revenue Code time value of money sections, which themselves require a working knowledge of financial calculations.

Inexpensive calculators have alleviated the need for lawyers to understand the actual formulas; however, because the calculators and their respective manuals are often complicated, lawyers lacking an accounting or finance background may shy away from this important area of law. Later LESSONS (chapters) include the formulas underlying the calculations. Understanding the formulas is not essential for a lawyer; however, you may someday find them useful.

This TEXT serves three purposes:

1. It provides a basic explanation—with lawyers as the intended audience—of the use and application of a typical hand-held financial calculator, the Hewlett Packard HP 10Bii™.

2. It discusses the legal system's use of financial terminology.

3. It links to workable COURSE FINANCIAL CALCULATORS that solve most of the problems faced by lawyers.

My first advice is "read the manual." Most financial calculator manuals explain the various types of calculations and provide understandable examples. This TEXT does not preempt or replace those manuals for other calculators. Rather, it supplements them with explanations and examples geared toward lawyers.

For users who rely solely on the COURSE CALCULATORS, this TEXT serves as the instruction manual.

While financial calculators can compute many things, six types of calculations are fundamental:

1. Future Value of a Sum.

2. Present Value of a Sum.

3. Present Value of an Annuity.

4. Future Value of an Annuity.

5. Sinking Fund.

6. Amortization.

LESSON ONE illustrates that knowledge of finance is important for all lawyers, not simply those who practice tax law or corporate law. For example:

1. FAMILY LAW

Much of family law involves allocating limited resources. This may arise in the division of property, the awarding of alimony, or the determination of child support.

If faced with any of those issues, the lawyer must know the value of various assets. Some—such as marketable securities—are easily valued. Others—such as real estate—require specialize appraisers. Still others, particularly those which produce regular income stream—such as leases, bonds, annuities, mineral interests, lottery winnings, structured settlements—require financial calculations. Each of those will involve the present value of an annuity. Also, in many jurisdictions, courts examine the entire arrangement, the property, alimony, and child support together. To do so, one must use a common viewpoint, such as the present value of each. That, too, would require the use of the present value of an annuity calculation.

2. TORT LAW

Although the study of torts often focuses on liability, the actual practice is often a function of value. Liability may be stipulated or already determined; what then matters is the amount of the award. Perhaps the matter involves the loss of wages for a period of time, or even for life. That requires the present value of an annuity calculation, with special attention paid to choosing the correct interest rate. As you will learn in later lessons, often the interest rate used it the most important issue in a tort matter, as it can easily affect the award amount by hundreds of thousands, if not millions of dollars. Many law students (and lawyers) not trained in finance, often find the interest rate choice counter-intuitive. As you will learn, the tortfeasor will seek a high rate and the victim a low rate—the opposite of what you might expect. Choosing wrong can be very costly.

Tort, as well as family and corporate law, may also require the valuation of a small business. Perhaps, the tortfeasor destroyed the business, or in a divorce, a spouse wants an amount equal to the present value, or in a corporate matter, one must determine value for a buy-out or merger. In any event, each requires financial calculations.

3. CORPORATE LAW AND CORPORATE FINANCE

Corporate law and corporate finance involve financial calculations in rather obvious ways. Each involves the valuation of assets and liabilities over time. That includes use of each of the main financial calculators: Present Value of a Sum, Future Value of a Sum, Present and Future Value of Annuities, Sinking Funds, and Amortizations. For example, dividends on preferred stock are generally a fixed annuity. Interest obligations on bonds require Amortization of the instruments. Balloon payments and similar obligations often necessitate Sinking Funds. And, for proper comparison and analysis, many items must be stated in either Present Value or Future Value terms.

4. TAX LAW

For tax lawyers, each of the listed calculations is relevant to one or more Internal Revenue Code provisions. Section 7872[1]—dealing with below market loans—requires the use of Present Value of a Sum and Present Value of an Annuity functions. Sections 1272[2] through 1274[3] deal with original issue discount loans and what is essentially a Sinking Fund. Section 1272 deals with the amortization of acquisition premium,[4] while sections 1275–76[5] deal with market discount,[6] which is essentially another

---

[1]   IRC § 7872 imputes interest on below-market loans, using the applicable federal rate (*AFR*). For gift and demand loans, it imputes a transfer from lender to borrower and a re-transfer characterized as interest. For term loans, it separates the nominal loan into two parts: a transfer of the nominal loan amount less the present value (for whatever reason motivated the below-market aspect) and then a semi-annual accrual of interest income and deductions for each party (subject to various limitations).

[2]   IRC §§ 1272–73 deal with original issue discount loans—those with interest deferred at the original issue date. They require knowledge of a constant yield to maturity, a term later defined herein.

[3]   IRC § 1274 covers the transfer of property for a deferred payment. Subject to large *de minimis* rules, it treats the cost (amount realized by the seller and the basis for the purchaser) as the present value of the future payments, discounted at the appropriate *AFR*. It then prompts the difference between the nominal price and the imputed price as original issue discount (OID) per sections 1272/163(e).

[4]   If interest rates fall, bond prices rise and buyers must pay a premium. Section 1272 and the related Treasury Regulations provide two methods for amortizing the premium.

[5]   IRC §§ 1275–76.

[6]   If interest rates rise, bond prices fall and buyers purchase at a discount. The code provides four methods for accruing the discount.

sinking fund. They also require solving for an interest rate—a constant yield to maturity. Section 467[7]—dealing with prepaid or deferred rent and non-qualified deferred compensation—involves the use of a Sinking Fund, as well as an Amortization. Future Value of an Annuity, as well as Sinking Fund calculations are relevant to deferred compensation and retirement planning. Analyzing deferred but incurred expenses (sections 461(h),[8] 468,[9] 468A,[10] and 468B[11]), deferred payments (*e.g.*, section 467(a)), and pre-paid items (*e.g.*, the *Schlude*[12] controversy as well as section 467(f)) each involve present values, annuities, and sinking funds.

5. ESTATE PLANNING AND ESTATES AND TRUST LAW

Estate planning and estates and trust law each involve financial calculations regarding the value of assets. In particular, trust law would involve the rights of a principal beneficiary, which is essentially a variable annuity. Estate planners use each of the six primary financial calculations. For example, they use sinking funds to plan for future needs, amortization to plan for extinguishment of current obligations, future value of a sum to calculate what current assets will be worth in the future, present value of a sum to calculate the remainder value of an asset, Future Value of an Annuity to evaluate a savings plan, and present value of an annuity to value an income legacy.

---

[7] IRC § 467(a) deals with deferred rent in contracts involving more than $250,000. It effectively requires the parties to use a sinking fund to determine the level payments (in many cases) that would produce the deferred amount. A portion of each accrued amount is interest and a portion is principal. Section 467(f) deals with pre-paid rent in excess of $250,000 and uses an amortization process to accrue the appropriate interest and rental amounts (principal) over the term.

[8] IRC § 461(h) requires the deferral of incurred but deferred expenses until "economic performance." Application of the section does not require knowledge of finance; however, determining the economic impact of it does. Because the section defers otherwise accrued deductions, it essentially deprives the taxpayer of a measurable portion of the deduction. Property financial analysis can justify contractual modifications which can reduce or eliminate the deprivation.

[9] IRC § 468 deals with solid waste reclamation costs (*e.g.* mining operations). It permits accrual of the present value of future costs, but oddly does not permit a deduction for the discount portion upon accrual or payment. Thus it effectively deprives the taxpayers of a significant portion of the deduction.

[10] IRC § 468A deals with nuclear power decommissioning costs. It permits accrual of the present value of future costs and requires funding of the amounts involved. It then excludes income earned by the fund, which effectively allows economically appropriate tax consequences. Why it uses a financial formula so different from that of solid waste costs is a mystery, but one with real-life consequences.

[11] IRC § 468B deals with some tort structured settlements. Effectively, it over-rides the harshness of section 461(h)(2)(C), but at the cost of depriving the victim of his/her section 103 exclusion. Almost certainly, it is useful only for class actions in which no known plaintiff exists to object.

[12] Schlude v. Comm'r, 372 U.S. 128 (1963). *See*, Steven J. Willis, *It's Time For Schlude to Go*, 93 TAX NOTES 127 (2001); *Show Me the Numbers, Please* 93 TAX NOTES 1321 (2001); IRC § 451(c) (2018) (adopting the *Schulde* accounting method which requires accrual method taxpayers to include amounts received or due prior to the amounts being earned).

6. GENERAL LAW

General practitioners and real estate attorneys will find the amortization calculations particularly useful, as they compute the needed payments on a home loan. The PRESENT VALUE CALCULATORS are relevant for contracts requiring advance payments; similarly, the FUTURE VALUE CALCULATORS are relevant for contracts involving deferred payments. Property law involves sales and financing, which necessarily involves the use of Amortization schedules, as well as interest rate terminology. Necessarily, attorneys practicing property law must understand how to convert from one statement of an interest rate to another, which involves the INTEREST RATE CONVERSION CALCULATOR and the YIELD CALCULATOR. They must also fully understand the legal significance (and financial insignificance) of the annual percentage rate calculation and disclosure.

7. ENVIRONMENTAL LAW

Environmental law involves evaluating the costs and benefits of existing or proposed activities. This necessarily involves financial computations to convert streams of costs and benefits to Present Value or Future Value terms. The computations may involve sums or Annuities. Further, Environmental Law may result in required Sinking Funds for future clean-up, decommissioning, or dismantling costs for mining, nuclear power plants, oil drilling rigs, and similar items.

8. BANKRUPTCY LAW

Bankruptcy law involves the valuation of assets and liabilities, each of which inherently involves financial calculations, including both the Present and Future Values of both Sums and Annuities. It also involves Amortization calculations for loan adjustments, Interest Rate Conversion Calculations for the proper statement of terms, and possibly Sinking Fund analysis for planned restructuring.

9. COMPETITION LAW AND ANTITRUST LAW

Competition law or antitrust law necessarily involves financial calculations to facilitate the comparison of entities and to evaluate competitiveness. The proper comparison of entities requires common factors, such as Present Value or Future Value.

10. EMPLOYMENT LAW

Employment law involves valuing lost future wages, as well as analyzing an employer's financial status (which requires accounting knowledge in addition to finance knowledge). The lost wages computation involves the present value of an annuity. Sinking fund calculations may be useful for negotiations involving future benefits.

11. YOUR OWN LIFE

Many students have student loans. Planning for them requires knowledge of amortizations to determine the payment needed for various pay-off terms. Future value of a sum is necessary to determine the amount owed after a period of deferred interest. Also, many graduates want to purchase a new car, or house, and need to again understand amortizations, as well as "points"—an important topic of LESSON FIVE-C.

Eventually, many of you will have children or grandchild and you will want to save for their education. To do so, you will need to understand several lessons, particularly LESSON FOURTEEN on *Sinking Funds*, plus LESSON SIX on *Why People Charge Interest*. The reason is the critically important interest rate assumption. None of you will have a crystal ball, but all of you will need to predict the future, be it for a child's education account or for your own retirement savings. And, yes, even if you are only in your early twenties, you very much need to start planning for your own retirement.

12. GOVERNMENT PLANNING AND POLICY

Much of governing involves planning for the future: the need for schools, roads, medical resources, housing, and general infrastructure. It also often involves choices, or a cost-benefit analysis. Each of those requires finance and calculations. One may need to predict future costs, future population numbers, future births (and thus the need for more or fewer teachers and schools), aging (and the need for medical care, as well as the type of medical care needed). One may also need to project the costs of a desired project to determine whether benefits outweigh the costs.

Part of this course—*an important part*—also involves the understanding of some statistics, particularly death rates and longevity. For government to plan, it needs to have some understanding of future population, ages, and deaths. For you to value a wrongful death matter, you need to understand how long people live. For you to plan for your own retirement, you need to understand how long *you* will likely live.

QUESTIONS

1. List the six basic calculations a financial calculator performs.

2. List ten areas of law that utilize financial calculations.

Lesson Two

Type of Calculators

■ ■ ■

Lesson Objectives

1. Student will learn the types of electronic calculators available:

   a. Simple.

   b. Scientific.

   c. Financial.

2. Student will learn some functions of the common calculators.

3. Student will learn that lawyers will commonly need a financial calculator.

4. Students will learn that an HP 10Bii™. is a highly recommended handheld calculator.

Terminology Introduced

- Reverse Polish Notation

Lesson Two is brief, but very important. It continues the introduction to finance with a focus on the types of *calculators* available.

The point of this lesson is to aid those new to financial calculations. It requires some understanding of the unfortunate nature of humans and some lawyers (as well as the odd humor of some "friends"). I've taught the course many years, and I've been in many situations involving lawyers, bankers, real estate agents and others. Many, perhaps most, are kind and well-meaning. Some are not.

As you will learn below, some calculators are easy to use, while others are cumbersome, if not difficult. Two stories illustrate my point (further elucidated below):

Story One: Many of my students want a hand-held calculator in addition to the ones I provide for use on a laptop. Indeed, I recommend everyone have one. Most telephones have inexpensive apps which mimic different calculators and thus moot the need for a separate device. More than a few students, unfortunately, have sought the advice of an experienced friend who "recommended" a calculator wholly unsuitable for someone new to finance. I suspect such suggestions were meant as a "joke," however frustrating it became. You are free to choose what you want: when I was in school we used slide rules, tables, and pencil/paper and the formulas. Do so if you want, but I will make much easier-to-use suggestions. Others insist Excel™ or some other program is best; indeed, they may be if you know how to use them. But, if you are taking this course, you likely do not, at least not at the level needed.

<u>Story Two</u>: Many times, I've been in a meeting in which some people were well-versed in finance and also in the use of calculators, while others were not. All-too-often, I've seen and heard the "well-versed" speak in "finance language" using terms and acronyms known to them and some others, but not to all. To help resolve this unfortunate, but all-too-common attempt at intimidation, I include a GLOSSARY as well as a list of ACRONYMS. Study them. Similarly, in such meetings, I've often seen the need for a quick calculation. All-too-often, the person who happens to have a calculator, has chosen one very difficult to use. Then, when another asks to borrow it to check the calculation, the borrower quickly realizes his/her inability to add two plus two, let alone compute the amount being discussed. I have often believed such behavior to be deliberate . . . I've seen it too often. Inevitably, the one-with-the-calculator has an HP 12C™ or something similar. I suspect they choose that one knowing if someone borrows it, they will not know how to use it. That will be intimidating, and, in my opinion, too much of negotiations and lawyering is about intimidating others.

Three types of calculators are commonly available:

1. Simple

2. Financial

3. Scientific

Simple. Every lawyer probably owns a Simple Calculator and uses it frequently. These inexpensive machines add, subtract, multiply, and divide. They often compute square roots as well as several other common calculations. While in the 1970s such machines were very expensive— costing hundreds of dollars (in terms of 2020 prices), they are now insignificant in price. While useful, they are not helpful in most financial calculations. Almost certainly, your cell phone has a simple calculator. Use it for simple calculations; however, it is insufficient for this course.

Scientific. Lawyers typically do not use scientific calculators. These machines compute various trigonometric functions such as sine, cosine, tangent, and cotangent. Useful for engineers, these calculations do not arise often in the practice of law. Be careful in purchasing a handheld calculator, as many of the most readily available are scientific calculators. Because these are useful in high school and college math courses, most households have one. A typical scientific calculator, however, will not solve for common financial functions. Some such calculators have a function which allows it to shift into a financial calculator, rather than a scientific one. You may use one; however, the calculator likely has many extra buttons or labels you will not use in this course (or in the practice of law). Thus, you may want to avoid these.

Financial. The subject of this course is financial calculations. Many hand-held and electronic financial calculators are available. They range in price from about $25 to several hundred dollars. The more expensive hand-held machines are typically programmable for more exotic financial functions. Lawyers rarely need such things. The Hewlett Packard HP 10Bii™ financial calculator is widely available and will serve nearly all needs of an attorney. Sharp and Texas Instruments also produce readily available, inexpensive calculators.

This course contains all the calculators you need for this course, although it does not include one which will solve for an interest rate in all cases. That calculation is beyond this course, though the topic will arise. For this, you will need a handheld. A telephone app simulating the HP 10Bii™ is more than adequate and should cost less than ten dollars. Some of the lessons describe how to use that calculator.

If you choose a hand-held or cell-phone app other than the HP 10Bii™, be sure to obtain the manual. While the basic calculations are the same, some significant functions differ. For example, they differ in how to clear numbers previously inputted—a critical function than prompts a huge number of mistakes. Also, they often differ in their cash flow assumption. In finance, cash flows out and then back in. If you view the out-flow as a negative (perhaps you are the lender), then the ultimate in flow must be a positive number (when the borrower pays you back). The reverse is correct for the other party to the transactions. HP calculators all require you to input numbers with the correct positive or negative sign. Other calculators—including the COURSE CALCULATORS—use "absolute values" with build-in (hidden) functions that adjust for the cash flow. I believe those are easier to use for someone new to finance, though they are not "pure" in the statement of cash flows. In my experience, Texas Instruments, Sharp, and most other manufacturers use absolute values. Thus, whatever you choose, you must know what you have.

When choosing a handheld calculator, be sure it has function keys for *PV*, *FV*, *PMT*, and *P/YR*. These cover Present Value, Future Value, Payment, and Payments per Year. Ideally, these will be the primary keys on the machine. Some scientific calculators have a shift function under which the calculator converts to a financial calculator. Be wary of these. The keys likely serve at least three, if not four functions, depending on whether the key is in normal mode, upward shift, downward shift, or even some other mode. This can be very confusing.

Because handheld calculators are fairly inexpensive, lawyers should have at least two: a financial calculator for financial calculations and a separate scientific calculator for the rare occasions they need to use trigonometry. Almost certainly they will have several simple calculators as well.

Lawyers should also be wary of calculators that use Reverse Polish Notation (*RPN*). This is behind **Story Two** above. In *reverse polish notation,* the mathematical operation follows the operands. For example, to add the numbers 3 and 5 in normal notation, one computes:

$$(3 + 5) = 8$$

To be specific, one presses the 3 key, then the + key, then the 5 key and then the = key. The screen then shows 8 as the answer.

But in *reverse polish notation,* one would perform:

$$3,5 +$$

To be specific, one presses the 3 key, then the enter key, then the 5 key, and then the + key. The screen then shows 8 as the answer.

The calculator would have no equal sign, so one would not have that extra function. Early computers and calculators used this format. The HP 12C™ calculator still uses it and continues to be popular. Because the format does not require parenthesis and similar symbols, it can calculate some very complex functions more efficiently than standard notation.

Simple *polish notation* is the opposite: the operator appears first:

$$+ 3,5$$

The term *Polish* dates from the creation of *Polish notation* by a famous Polish mathematician, Jan Łukasiewicz. The reverse method first appeared commonly in the 1960s.

Typically, lawyers have little use for *RPN*. They should be generally familiar with it because they will encounter many people—economists, real estate agents, and others—who use the HP 12C™ or similar calculators. As these people may be expert witnesses, a lawyer needs to understand their terminology and methodology. If, as explained in **Story Two**, you find yourself in a meeting with someone who offers you the use of his/her *RPN* calculator without explaining what it is, be wary. That person is likely trying to intimidate you. Useful knowledge, indeed.

QUESTIONS

1.   List the three most common types of calculators.

2.   Have you examined the COURSE CALCULATORS to be certain they work for you?

3.   Have you obtained a hand-held financial calculator or a cellphone app simulator?

LESSON THREE

TYPES OF CALCULATIONS

■ ■ ■

Lesson Objectives

1. Student will learn the eight basic calculations are:

   a. Present Value of a Sum.

   b. Future Value of a Sum.

   c. Present Value of an Annuity.

   d. Future Value of an Annuity.

   e. Sinking Fund.

   f. Amortization.

   g. Interest Rate Conversion.

   h. Yield Computation.

2. Student will learn generally why a Lawyer would use each calculation. Later LESSONS cover each in greater depth.

3. Student will see the formulas for each calculation, but need not master them.

Terminology Introduced

- Present Value
- Future Value
- Annuity
- Annuity Due
- Annuity in Arrears
- Sinking Fund
- Amortization
- Nominal Annual Interest Rate (*NAI*)
- Effective Interest Rate (*EFF*)
- Internal Rate of Return (*IRR*)
- Real Rate of Return (*RRR*)

- Yield

- Yield to Maturity (*YTM*)

LESSON THREE is brief, but also very important. It continues the introduction to finance with a focus on the types of calculations you need to understand. Eight types of Financial Calculations are fundamental to a lawyer's practice:

1. Future Value of a Sum

2. Present Value of a Sum

3. Present Value of an Annuity

4. Future Value of an Annuity

5. Sinking Fund

6. Amortization

7. Interest Rate Conversion

8. Yield Computation

The COURSE CALCULATORS include separate calculators for each type.[1] In contrast, a handheld calculator performs all eight functions using a single screen. I designed the calculators separately so as to avoid some common mistakes people make in using handheld calculators. With a handheld, a single machine has to be able to compute all eight functions, which are variations of the same formula. With a computer, however, one has the luxury of linking separate calculators for each primary calculation and thus making the operations much easier to use.

Trust me, I've taught this course for four decades. I've seen six very common mistakes made by those using a handheld calculator. I programmed the COURSE CALCULATORS to eliminate the possibility of you making those mistakes. Some of the mistakes, as you will see, are subtle and not obvious in the result, though they may still be material.

For example, if you have $100,000 in student loans with a <u>nominal annual interest rate</u> (*NAI*)[2] of 6.5% compounded monthly and you intend

---

[1]   They do not include a calculator that will always compute a yield, which is a very complex computation if the instrument has payments and a value that differs from the redemption price (other than zero). For such instruments, this course covers how to compute the yield using a handheld device

[2]   The *NAI* is the *periodic interest* rate times the number of periods in one year. It is an uncompounded rate. Abbreviated as *NAI*, the nominal rate is an important key on all financial calculators. The rate itself serves no purpose in computations; however, because humans tend to think in terms of one year, they typically multiply periodic rates times the number of periods in one year. The resulting *NAI* is a useful, albeit misleading, term for comparing financial instruments.

to pay them off monthly over ten years, you must decide whether to start today or a month from now. Starting today (using begin mode) results in a payment of $1,129.31.[3] In contrast, starting a month from now (using end mode) results in a payment of $1,135.43.[4] The $6.12 difference is not much, but it is the cost of a couple gallons of gasoline per month, a glass of "house wine," or perhaps a decent beer. The amount, however, is not huge and would not be obviously incorrect. It is an easy mistake to make with a hand-held, but much more difficult with the COURSE CALCULATORS (though not impossible).

Other common mistakes _should_ be obvious, but having graded thousands of finals, alas, I find they are not. Setting the compounding period incorrectly could change an answer from a few hundred thousand to tens of millions (and sometimes billions or trillions) of dollars. One would think all users would detect a billion-dollar error, but, trust me, not all do. People legitimately plan to save different amounts for their retirement or for their child's education; however, when I see someone planning to save $100,000,000 for a child or $10,000,000,000 for themselves, I typically conclude they made a simple, _albeit very costly mistake_, rather than conclude they are merely optimistic about their ability to save or pessimistic about how much education their child will require.

A billion-dollar error on a final will hurt your grade. But a billion-dollar error with a client will cost you your job and will get you sued for malpractice. Thus, be careful: _**calculators are themselves stupid: they only know what you tell them!**_

> **Good News!**
>
> Although the formula for _each_ computation appears, you _**do not**_ need to use them: the calculators do that for you. When I was in school, the formula (plus pencil and paper) was all we had. Calculators and computers were rudimentary.

The formula for converting an _effective interest_ rate to an _NAI_ is:

$$\left[\, 100py \left(\left(1 + \frac{eff}{100} \right)^{\frac{1}{py}} - 1 \right) \right]$$

where _eff_ = the _effective interest_ rate and _py_ = the number of periods per year.

LESSON FIVE-B: CONVERTING INTEREST RATES introduces a calculator which will convert an _EFF_ to an _NAI_ or to a periodic rate.

[3]   Using the AMORTIZATION CALCULATOR, as covered in LESSON THIRTEEN. Using an HP 10Bii™ calculator, the payment is $1,129.36. The difference results because of differing rounding assumptions.

[4]   Using the AMORTIZATION CALCULATOR, as covered in LESSON THIRTEEN. Using an HP 10Bii™ calculator, the payment is $1,135.48.

1. THE FUTURE VALUE OF A SUM

Figure 1 illustrates the FUTURE VALUE OF A SUM CALCULATOR. LESSON NINE explains how to use it. This calculation computes the future amount or value of a *current* deposit. The formula for the *FV* is:

$$FV = PV \left(1 + \frac{i}{100} \right)^n$$

where *PV* =present value, *i* = nominal annual interest rate, and *n* = number of periods per year.

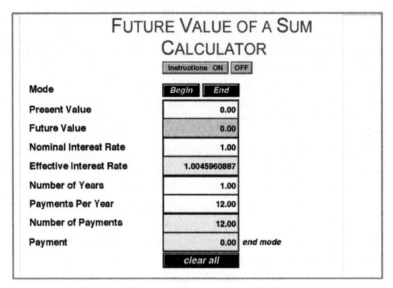

Figure 1: Future Value of a Sum Calculator

For example, $1,000 deposited today, earning 10% ***nominal*** interest compounded annually (*NAI*)—a.k.a., 10% ***effective*** interest (*EFF*)[5]—will

---

[5]   Sometimes labeled an *EIR*, the effective interest rate is a compounded rate of interest. It is the *periodic* rate compounded for one year. It differs from the *nominal annual interest rate* (*NAI*) in that the *effective* rate is compounded while the nominal rate is not. All financial calculators have an *effective rate* function, as well as a nominal rate function. For financial calculations, a calculator uses the periodic rate; hence, the nominal rate—which is the *periodic* rate times the numbers of periods in one year—is useful. Given an *effective rate*, one can convert it to the equivalent nominal annual rate for a given compounding frequency; then, one can divide by the frequency to produce the needed periodic rate.

An effective rate (*EFF*) differs substantially from an *Annual Percentage Rate* (*APR*), which is mostly a non-compounded rate. Federal law defines the *APR*, which generally is the nominal annual rate plus points and some other closing costs amortized for the stated life of the loan. In contrast, the *EFF* treats points as principal rather than interest and then produces a number different from the *APR* (assuming the loan includes points).

An *EFF* is arguably inapplicable to most consumer loans, which require current periodic interest payments. As such, they do not internally compound interest because the borrower pays all interest currently to the lender. But, externally, the funds for interest payments come from somewhere and end up somewhere. Hence, from the borrower's perspective, interest compounds to the extent the funds used to pay current interest are no longer available for other uses. Similarly, from the perspective of the lender, interest compounds to the extent the funds received

increase to $1,100 in one year. In two years it will increase to $1,210. In five years, it will be $1,610.51 and in 100 years it will be $13,780,612.34. The year two amount includes not only the $100 interest earned each year on the principal of $1,000, but it also includes an additional $10 interest earned on the first year's interest of $100: ten percent of $100 is $10.

> The distinction between an ***effective*** interest rate and a ***nominal*** interest rate is critical to understanding this course.
>
> LESSON FIVE covers this in greater depth. You should also consult the GLOSSARY.

This illustrates the effect of compounding: interest accelerates over time as it compounds . . . or, as it earns interest on interest.

Why would a lawyer want to perform this calculation? Several examples come to mind:

a.   If you deposit money into an account, you can compute what it will be worth in the future. This is useful if:

- You want to save for a child's education.

- You are saving for retirement.

- You are saving for a large purchase.

b.   If population growth rates continue at a constant rate, you can compute the population of an area after a given length of time. This is useful if:

- You are dealing with growth management.

- You are dealing with environmental issues, increasing at a constant rate.

c.   If your client was owed a specific amount—such as a debt or a judgment—as of a prior date, you can compute what he is owed today. The amount owed originally would be the present value and the amount today would be the future value.

---

in payment of current interest are either deposited elsewhere or expended (whereby they free-up other funds which are deposited or they relieve the need for other borrowing).

The formula for the *effective* interest rate:

$$eff = \left[\, 100\left(\left(1 + \frac{pr}{100}\right)^{py} - 1\right)\right]$$

where *eff* = effective interest rate, *pr* = periodic rate and *py* = number of periods per year.

LESSON FIVE-C: CONVERTING INTEREST RATES introduces a calculator which will convert an *EFF* to an *NAI* or to a periodic rate.

d.   If a budget item or cost increases at a particular rate, you can compute the amount for a future period.

e.   In a tort case, perhaps your client suffered damages three years ago. You will want to compute the value today of that amount. Today is the present, but it is also the future of the past. Thus the amount claimed today is the future value of the past loss.

2.   THE PRESENT VALUE OF A SUM

Figure 2 illustrates the PRESENT VALUE OF A SUM CALCULATOR. LESSON TEN explains how to use it. This calculation computes the present amount of a *future* deposit or debt. The formula for the *PV* is:

$$PV = \left(FV \left(1 + \frac{i}{100} \right)^{-n} \right)$$

where i = nominal annual interest rate, n = number of periods per year, and FV = the future value.

PRESENT VALUE OF A SUM CALCULATOR

	Instructions ON	OFF
Mode	Begin	End
Present Value	0.00	
Future Value		
Nominal Interest Rate	1.00	
Effective Interest Rate	1.0041924075	
Number of Years	1.00	
Payments Per Year	12.00	
Number of Payments	12.00	
Payment	0.00	end mode
	clear all	

Figure 2: Present Value of a Sum Calculator

For example, $1,100 to be received in *one* year, *discounted* at a 10% **effective interest rate** (*EFF*), has a present value of $1,000 today. In comparison, $1,100 in *two* years has a present value of $909.09. Discounting $1,100 for *five* years produces a value of $683.01. Discounting $1,100 for *100* years at 10% produces a value of only $ 0.0798.

Thus, if you owe $1,100 *100 years* from now, you should be able to *pay off* the obligation today with only 8¢, assuming the appropriate **effective interest rate** is 10%.

Why would a lawyer want to know how to compute the present value of a sum? Several reasons come to mind:

a. If you owe money in the future, you can compute what it equals in current value.

b. If you want a discount for an advance payment for goods or services, you would compute the present value of the future obligation.

c. If you know the amount you need at a future time—such as for retirement or college entrance—you can compute the present value needed to produce that future amount.

d. For tax or accounting purposes, a lawyer may suggest his client deduct the present value of a future cost if possible. While IRC section 461(h) of the may not permit this in many situations, alternative contractual relationships may make such a present value current deduction possible. For a lawyer to compare the after-tax consequences of a present deduction versus a future deduction of a larger amount, he must first be capable of computing the present value.

3.   THE PRESENT VALUE OF AN ANNUITY

PRESENT VALUE OF AN ANNUITY CALCULATOR

Instructions	ON	OFF

Mode	Begin	End	
Present Value		0.00	end mode
Future Value		0.00	
Nominal Interest Rate		1.00	
Effective Interest Rate	1.0041924075		
Number of Years		1.00	
Payments Per Year		12.00	
Number of Payments		12.00	
Payment			
	clear all		

Figure 3: Present Value of an Annuity Calculator

Figure 3 illustrates the PRESENT VALUE OF AN ANNUITY CALCULATOR. LESSON ELEVEN explains how to use it. This calculation computes the present value of a series of equal payments made at *regular* intervals, earning a *constant* interest rate. The formula for the *PVA* is:

$$PVA = \left[\frac{\left[PMT \left(1 - \left(1 + \frac{i}{100} \right)^{-n} \right) \right]}{\frac{i}{100}} \right]$$

where i = nominal annual interest rate, n = number of periods or payments per year, and PMT = periodic payment or deposit.

For example, $1,000 deposited at the **_end_** of each year for ten years, earning 10% _effective_ interest, has a present value today of $6,144.57.

> This is an example of an _annuity in arrears_: one in which the payments occur at the _end_ of each period.
>
> LESSON FOUR will define the term _annuity in arrears_. You may also consult the GLOSSARY.

Similarly, $6,144.57 deposited today, earning 10% _effective_ interest will produce a fund **_from which_** $1,000 could be withdrawn for ten consecutive years, beginning **_one year from today_**. This is an amortization.

> This is the _amortization_ of the present value: it creates the annuity.

> Each of the above examples—the _annuity in arrears_ and the _amortization_—use the **_end mode_** function. In contrast, the next example involves an _annuity due_, which uses the **_begin mode_** function. LESSON FOUR will discuss the Mode function.

In another example, $1,000 deposited at the **beginning of each year** for ten years, earning 10% _effective_ interest, has a present value today of $6,759.02. This is an example of an _annuity due_: one in which the payments occur at the _beginning_ of each period.

The 10-year, 10% _annuity due_ has a present value of $6,759.02. The _annuity in arrears_ has a present value of $6,144.57. The _annuity due_ has a _greater_ present value because it starts earlier: today (for the _annuity due_) and one year from now (for the _annuity in arrears_).

> LESSON FOUR will define the term **_annuity due_**. You may also consult the GLOSSARY.

Why would a lawyer want to know how to compute the present value of an annuity? Several reasons come to mind:

a. If you owe money at regular intervals in the future, you can compute what it equals in current value. This is useful if:

- You owe money on a loan. The present value would be the payoff amount.

- In a family law case, you owe alimony. The present value would be the lump sum amount to replace the periodic payments.[6]

b. If you want a discount for an advance payment for goods or services which will be provided at regular intervals, you would compute the present value of the future obligation. This is useful if:

- You need to compute the discount amount on an insurance or rental contract.

c. In a tort case, the victim may have lost future wages or suffer regular future medical expenses. The present value of such an amount would be the tortfeasor's obligation.

d. If you have won a state lottery. The present value of the future payments would be the alternative amount that might be elected.

e. You might need to compute the value of a bond or similar financial instrument. The regular interest payments would be an annuity. The present value of them added to the present value of the final payment would be the current value of the bond.

4. THE FUTURE VALUE OF AN ANNUITY

Figure 4 illustrates the FUTURE VALUE OF AN ANNUITY CALCULATOR. LESSON TWELVE explains how to use it. This calculation computes the future value of a series of <u>equal</u> payments made at <u>*regular*</u> intervals, earning a <u>*constant*</u> interest rate. The formula for the *FVA* is:

---

[6] You would want to further discount the lump sum because of risk changes, which affect the interest rate used for the discount. Under state law, the periodic payments likely end on the death of either party or the remarriage of the recipient. Also, state law likely provides for modification of periodic payments due to a substantial change in circumstances. The lump sum would not be subject to those risks and thus would likely be the result of a higher than typical discount rate.

$$FVA = \left[\frac{\left[PMT \left(1 + \frac{i}{100} \right)^{n} - 1 \right]}{\frac{i}{100}} \right]$$

where i = nominal annual interest rate, n = number of periods per year, and PMT = periodic payment or deposit.

We will mostly deal with <u>level</u> annuities: *e.g.,* $1,000 per month for ten years. An *un-level annuity*—*e.g.,* $1,000/month sometimes and $1,500/month other times—is generally beyond this course, though we will deal with growth annuities—those at increase at a constant rate. We also deal with regular payments: *e.g.,* every month or every quarter. An irregular annuity—*e.g.,* one that skips some otherwise regular payments— is beyond this course. Further, although an annuity can have a varying interest rate, we will deal with one involving level payments. Hence, by definition, it will have a constant *internal rate of return* (*IRR*).[7] When we compute the present value of the annuity, we will typically use a *current interest rate*[8] (which we project to be valid for the annuity period).

---

[7] The *internal rate of return* calculation can be very complex. It represents the *discount rate* at which the *net present value* of all cash flows (inward and outward) equals zero. If an investment has cash flows in only one direction (other than the initial deposit or final withdrawal), the computation of an *IRR* is the same as the computation of the PRESENT VALUE OF AN ANNUITY, the FUTURE VALUE OF AN ANNUITY an AMORTIZATION, or a SINKING FUND, none of which is particularly difficult.

However, if the direction of cash flows varies—and particularly if the periods and amounts vary substantially, the computation is difficult. Most calculators which compute an *IRR*, do so through an iteration method: they guess at the answer, test it, re-guess, and continue until an answer of acceptable precision is achieved.

The formula for an *IRR* is:

$$NPV = \left[\sum_{t=0}^{n} \frac{C_t}{(1 + r)^t} \right] = 0$$

where NPV = net present value, n = number of periods, C = cash flow, t = time or a particular period, and r = periodic interest rate.

Most lawyers will never need to compute an *IRR* other than the basic annuities, amortization, and sinking fund. Those involved with $M \& A$, however, will need to understand the computation of an *IRR*.

[8] As explained in LESSONS FIVE through SEVEN, interest rates change constantly in the marketplace of buying/selling financial instruments. The internal rate for the instrument typically does not change (although some are adjustable). Thus, as covered in later lessons, as market rate rise, the present value of financial instruments falls, and *vice versa*.

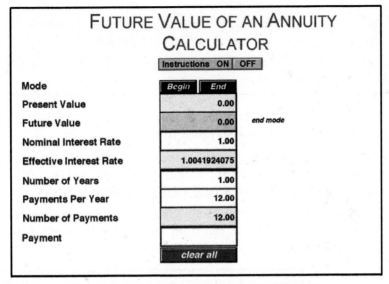

Figure 4: Future Value of an Annuity Calculator

For example, $1,000 deposited annually *beginning one year from now*, earning a 10% *effective* interest rate, will increase to $15,937.42 in ten years.

Similarly, if you need $15,937.42, in ten years, and you can earn 10% *effective* interest, you must deposit $1,000 annually **beginning one year from today**. This is the *sinking fund* of the future value: it creates the *annuity*.

> This is an example of an *annuity in arrears*: one in which the payments occur at the *end* of each period.
>
> LESSON FOUR will define the term *annuity in arrears*. You may also consult the GLOSSARY.

The future value of an annuity and a sinking fund are related. The sinking fund is the series of payments (the annuity) that equals the future value. For example, the annual deposit of $1,000 (the sinking fund/ annuity), at a 10% *effective* interest rate, beginning in one year, has a Future Value of $15,937.42.

In an alternate example, $1,000 deposited at the **beginning of each year** for ten years, earning 10% *effective* interest has a future value in ten years of $17,531.17. The 10-year, 10% *annuity due* has a future value of $17,531.17. In contrast, the *annuity in arrears* has a future value of $ 15,937.42. The *annuity due* has a *greater* future value because it starts earlier: today (for the *annuity due*) and one year from now (for the *annuity in arrears*).

> This is an example of an *annuity due*: one in which the payments occur at the *beginning* of each period.
>
> LESSON FOUR will define the term *annuity due*. You may also consult the GLOSSARY.

Why would a lawyer want to know how to compute the future value of an annuity? Two common reasons come to mind:

a. If you save money for a retirement plan at regular intervals, you can compute what it will be worth in the future, particularly if you use a **real rate of return** (*RRR*).[9]

b. If you save money for a child's education at regular intervals, you can compute what the fund will be worth in the future, particularly if you use a real rate of return (*RRR*).

As explained in LESSONS SIX, SEVEN, and TWELVE, the future value of an annuity is stated in future dollars, which are ***not comparable*** to current values. ***Thus the answer might not be useful***; however, two methods can be used to convert the answer to a useful number:

- Convert the amount to a present value.

- Modify the interest rate to reflect a "real rate of return" rather than the actual predicted rate.

---

[9] This is *not* a term of art, so lawyers should be careful with it. Generally, a *real rate of return* refers to the actual return on an investment adjusted for actual *inflation*. One should also adjust for taxes. But, even that definition is imprecise because the definition of *inflation* is itself imprecise. The *CPI* and other *inflation* measures represent broad segments of the economy, but they may not represent the individual.

The following formula is an *acceptable* representation of a *RRR*; however, *it is **not** the only acceptable formula*:

$$RRR = \left[\left(\frac{1 + \mathit{eff}}{1 + \mathit{inf}} \right) - 1 \right]$$

where *RRR* = real rate of return, *eff* = effective interest rate, and *inf* = actual past inflation.

5. AMORTIZATION

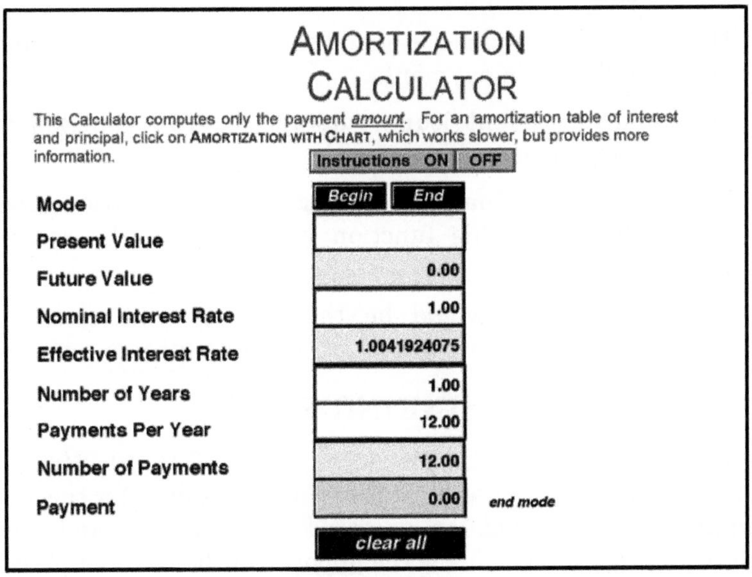

Figure 5: Amortization Calculator

Figure 5 illustrates the AMORTIZATION CALCULATOR. LESSON THIRTEEN explains how to use it. This calculation solves for the amount of the regular payment needed, at a stated interest rate and period, to pay off a present value. This is the opposite of the calculation involving the present value of an annuity. The formula for an *amortization* is:

$$PMT = \left[\frac{\left(PV \left(\frac{i}{100} \right) \right)}{1 - \left(1 + \frac{i}{100} \right)^{-n}} \right]$$

where i = nominal annual interest rate, n = number of periods per year, and FV = the future value.

For example, if you were to borrow $100,000 today and agreed to make 360 equal monthly payments at an interest rate of eight percent *nominal annual interest* (NAI), each payment would need to be $733.76, beginning one month from now. In contrast, if you were to begin payments immediately, the monthly payment would be $728.90.

LESSON FIVE defines *nominal annual interest*. You may also want to consult the GLOSSARY.

Why would a lawyer want to know how to compute an amortization? Several reasons come to mind:

a.   If you want to purchase a home, this function will determine your monthly loan payments.

b.   If you have student loans outstanding, this function will determine your monthly payments.

c.   If you need to re-finance a loan or to combine various credit card obligations, this function will compute the monthly payments.

d.   The amortization would be the annuity equivalent (the structured settlement) of a lump sum amount in a tort case.

6. SINKING FUND

Figure 6 illustrates the SINKING FUND CALCULATOR. LESSON FOURTEEN explains how to use it. This calculation solves for the amount of the regular deposit needed, at a stated interest rate and period, to accumulate a *future* value. This is the *opposite* of the calculation involving the future value of an annuity.

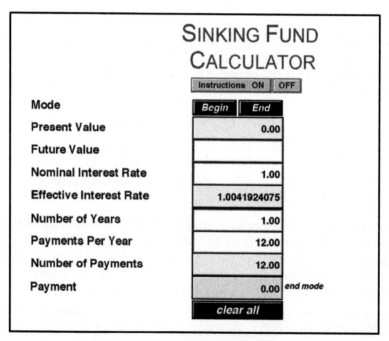

Figure 6: Sinking Fund Calculator

The formula for the sinking fund is:

$$SF = \left[\frac{\left(FV \left(\frac{i}{100} \right) \right)}{\left(1 + \frac{i}{100} \right)^{n} - 1} \right]$$

where i = nominal annual interest rate, n = number of periods per year, and FV = the future value.

You should remember: the term "sinking fund" is another term for an "annuity." The sinking fund is the series of deposits (the annuity) that accumulates to a desired future value.

> The term "Sinking Fund" is another term for an "Annuity."

For example, if you want to accumulate $25,000 in ten years and are willing to make ten equal annual deposits, _beginning today_, at an _effective interest_ rate of ten percent, each deposit would need to be $1,426.03. Similarly, if you annually deposit $1,426.03, beginning today, and you can earn 10% _effective_ interest, the FUTURE VALUE OF AN ANNUITY CALCULATOR will tell you that in ten years, you will have $25,000. This is the _future value_ of the _sinking fund_. The fund is itself an annuity.

In an alternative example, If you want to accumulate $25,000 in ten years and are willing to make ten equal annual deposits, _beginning one year from now_, at an _effective interest_ rate of ten percent, each deposit would need to be $1,568.63. The 10-year, 10% _annuity due_ Sinking Fund requires $1,426.03 to produce $25,000. The _annuity in arrears_ Sinking Fund requires $1,568.63 to produce the same $25,000. The _annuity due_ has a _lesser current_ value because it starts earlier: today (for the _annuity due_) and one year from now (for the _annuity in arrears_).

Why would a lawyer want to know how to compute a sinking fund? Several reasons come to mind:

a. If you need to save for a child's education and know the future amount needed.

b. If you need to save for retirement and know the future amount needed.

c. You need to pay off a bond or debenture in the future and want to save the principal necessary for the "balloon payment."

7. INTEREST RATE CONVERSION

Figure 7 illustrates the INTEREST RATE CONVERSION CALCULATOR. LESSON FIVE-B explains how to use it. LESSONS FOUR through SEVEN also cover the terminology used by the calculator.

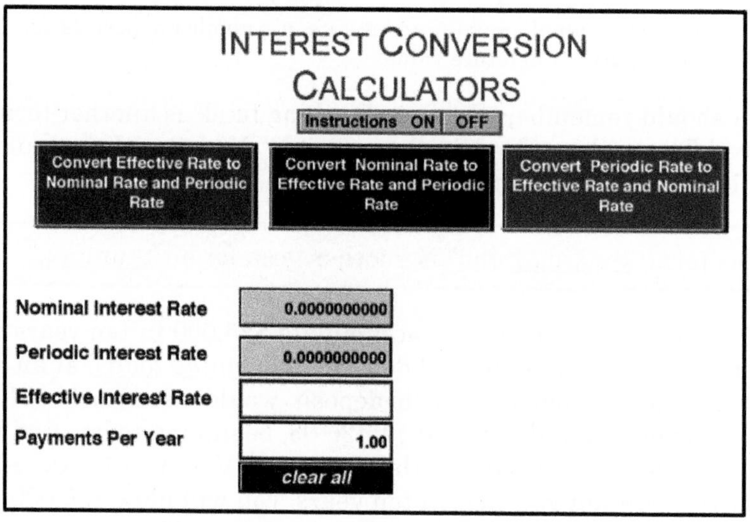

Figure 7: Interest Rate Conversion Calculator

As explained in subsequent lessons, the term interest rate is itself meaningless. All calculations use a periodic rate—the interest rate for the relevant compounding or payment period, be it a day, month, quarter, half-year, or year. Contracts, loan papers, and such, however, tend use annual rates. As a result, lawyers must be able to convert a periodic rate to the equivalent nominal (uncompounded) annual rate for a stated compounding or payment period. They also should be able to convert the nominal rate to the equivalent effective rate, which is compounded.

Also, as explained in LESSON FIVE-C, lawyers must be able to convert a periodic, nominal, and effective rate to an annual percentage rate (*APR*), as defined in federal statutes. The *APR* is a legal term of art in the United States, as well as in the European Union (with a different definition) but is not a financial term. Neither the COURSE CALCULATORS nor a typical handheld calculator contain a function to compute it. LESSON FIVE-C, however, explains how to compute it using interpolation.

8. YIELD COMPUTATION

Figure 8 illustrates the YIELD CALCULATOR. LESSON FIVE-E explains how to use it. LESSONS FOUR through SEVEN also cover the terminology used by the calculator. This calculator will compute a simple, periodic, and compounded yield, but only if the instrument is not self-amortizing and only if it also has a constant value. LESSON FIVE-A will introduce another calculator for discount instruments which defer interest to maturity.

As explained in the GLOSSARY, the term "*yield*" is not a term of art. Neither is the commonly used term "*yield to maturity*." Computing a missing yield is not a common calculation for many lawyers (though it is common for some) and is mostly beyond this course. We will cover it, but not in depth.

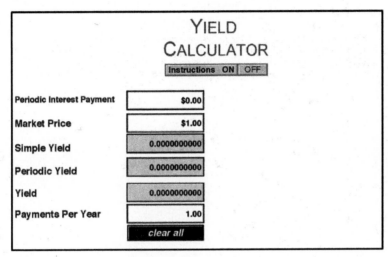

Figure 8: Yield Calculator

QUESTIONS

1. Define an annuity. Distinguish it from a life annuity.

2. When would a lawyer need to compute the present value of an annuity?

3. Define a sinking fund. When would a lawyer need to calculate a sinking fund?

4. Define the term amortization as used in finance. When would a lawyer need to amortize something?

LESSON FOUR

CALCULATOR TERMINOLOGY AND COMMON MISTAKES

■ ■ ■

Lesson Objectives

1. Student will learn the function keys on a calculator:

   a. Present Value (*PV*).

   b. Future Value (*FV*).

   c. Payment (*PMT*).

   d. Interest (*I/YR*).

   e. Number of Periods (*N*).

   f. Payments per Year (*P/YR*) (*aka* Periods per Year).

   g. Mode.

2. Student will learn where to find these functions on:

   a. an HP 10Bii™ calculator.

   b. the COURSE CALCULATORS.

3. Student will learn that he/she will know five of the first six functions (a through f above) and that the calculator will solve for the single missing function.

4. Student will learn that if he/she lacks factual information on two or more functions, he/she must nevertheless infer, deduce, or otherwise "make-up" the missing functions until only one is unknown.

5. Student will learn the importance (*or lack thereof*) of rounding and precision.

6. Student will be introduced to a basic law of finance:

   • **The compounding period (periods per year) and the payment period (payments per year) must either be identical or be 1.**

Terminology Introduced

• Present Value

• Future Value

- Compounding Period
- Payment Period
- Annuity
- Mode

LESSON FOUR is the end of the introduction. It emphasizes essential terminology in LESSON FOUR-A and common mistakes in LESSON FOUR-B.

A. ESSENTIAL TERMINOLOGY (LESSON FOUR-A)

Each calculation relies on the same basic formula, involving six factors, with the typical key label. The COURSE CALCULATORS use the words for each function. In contrast, handheld calculators use keys with abbreviations.

Financial calculators have seven *basic* function keys:

1. Present Value (*PV*)
2. Future Value (*FV*)
3. Payment (*PMT*)
4. Interest (*I*) or (*I/YR*)
5. Number of Periods (*N*)
6. Payments per Year (*P/YR*)
7. Mode

For purposes of this course, you will almost always know the mode. You must then know five of the remaining six functions. The calculator will solve for the remaining function. That is the point of a financial calculator: to solve for _one_ missing function. If you only know _four_ of the _six_ functions, you must nevertheless estimate, logically deduce, or "make up" one of the two missing functions. ***No calculator can solve for two missing functions.***

For example, if you know:

- how much you borrowed for your home loan (*PV*),
- the interest rate (*I/YR*),
- that you intend to pay it off to zero (*FV*) and
- that you want monthly payments (*P/YR*),

you cannot solve for _both_ the time period _and_ the payment amount. You _may_ tell the calculator the time period—perhaps 30 or 15 years—and it will tell you the needed payment. Or, you may tell the calculator that you want to pay $1,500 monthly (*PMT*), and it will tell you how long that will take

(*N*). But, you must tell it one of those functions: either the time period or the payment amount (assuming you know the other four functions).

On a handheld calculator—such as an HP 10Bii™ shown in **Figure 9**—the six functions are found along the top row of keys. All keys serve two functions with the orange (sometimes green) key serving as the shift key to change a key from one function to another.

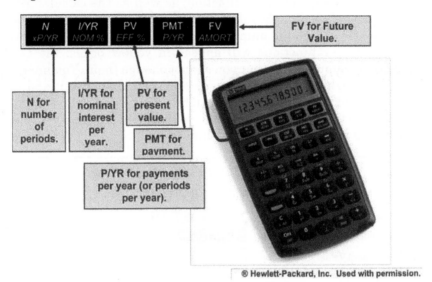

® Hewlett-Packard, Inc. Used with permission.

Figure 9: HP 10Bii™ Calculator

Figure 10 shows a cellphone app simulating a handheld calculator. It has the additional feature of showing values for the various variables.

Figure 10: Cellphone App Simulator

As shown in **Figure 11**, on the COURSE CALCULATORS provided in this course, all function keys are always displayed clearly. The seven critical function keys *always* appear. Also, several other important, but less critical, function keys always appear. Plus, the values for each function *always* appear. Each of the blue functions in the calculators has a "pop-up" function with a definition. Simply let your cursor hover over the word and the definition will appear. [That function, as well as the calculators work within the calculators, but they do not work within this TEXT]. As you will see, the value you seek—the number you are solving for—will always be in a green box. Other functions will appear in yellow boxes: the COURSE CALCULATORS compute them, but you cannot change them. You must input numbers in the white boxes and you must (except for present and future value of a sum calculations) set the mode by clicking on Begin or End, each of which appear in a black box. The calculator will then display **end mode** or **begin mode** next to the payment number.

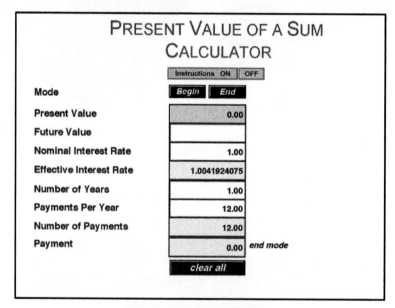

Figure 11: Course Calculator

The seven main function keys are:

1. PRESENT VALUE (*PV*)

This function inputs *or* solves for the value today of either a sum in the future or a series of payments in the future. Thus it is useful in both the present value of a sum calculation as well as the present value of an annuity calculation.

For example, if you know the future value (*FV*), the interest rate (*I/YR*) and the time period (*N*), then you *solve for the present value* of the future amount. Perhaps you know you will owe $25,000 in two years (the future value with no other payments (*PMT*)) and you also know the creditor will give you a 5% *NAI* discount if you pay early—today. You thus need to compute the present value, using the PRESENT VALUE OF A SUM CALCULATOR. The *PV* would be $22,675.74.

If, instead, you *know the present value*, then you must be solving for another function, such as the future value or the series of withdrawal payments that the present value can generate—an amortization.

2.   FUTURE VALUE (*FV*)

This function inputs *or* solves for the value in the future of either a present sum or a series of payments in the future. Thus it is useful in both the future value of a sum calculation as well as the future value of an annuity calculation.

For example, if you know the present value, the interest rate and the time period, then you *solve for the future value* of the present amount. Perhaps you know you have $22,675.4 to invest for two years and your borrower will pay 5% *NAI* compounded annually. You then, using the FUTURE VALUE OF A SUM CALCULATOR to solve for *FV*, which is $25,000.

If, instead, you *know the future value*, then you must be solving for another function, such as the present value or the series of payments needed to generate the future value—a sinking fund.

3.   PAYMENT (*PMT*)

This function inputs *or* solves for the value of a regular deposit or withdrawal. It is useful in the present and future value of an annuity calculation (the payment is the regular annuity amount). It is the function solved for in both the amortization and sinking fund calculations.

For example, if you know the present or future value and the interest rate and time period, then you *solve for the payment amount* that the present sum would generate or the needed deposit to result in the future value. Perhaps you know you owe $100,000 in student loans and must begin paying them back today (begin mode). You also know the lender charges 6.5% *NAI* compounded monthly and expects monthly payments for ten years. You would use the AMORTIZATION CALCULATOR to solve for the *PMT* of $1,129.31.[1]

---

[1]   An HP 10Bii™ computes the *PMT* as $1,129.36, using a nine digit rounding assumption. The course AMORTIZATION CALCULATOR uses a ten-digit rounding assumption. It produces a *PMT* of $1,129.31, but has a 121st payment of $8.85. The HP adds 5 cents to each payment and produces a smaller 120th payment. The difference is immaterial.

Or, if you *know the payment value*, then you must be solving for another function, such as the present or future value of the series of deposits.

4.   INTEREST (*I/YR*)

This function inputs *or solves* for the nominal annual interest rate. It is essential in all the various calculations.

> LESSON FIVE-A focuses on interest rate terminology. It distinguishes nominal rates from periodic rates, from effective rates, and from an annual percentage rate.

The COURSE CALCULATORS require you to input the nominal annual interest rate, which is the uncompounded interest per year. In contrast, the HP 10Bii™ has an *I/YR* button that acts as the nominal rate. The HP 10Bii™ also has a *NOM%* button, which *also* acts as the nominal rate.[2] Some calculators, such as the HP 12C™ use only a periodic interest rate, which is actually the critical information for all the formulas. The COURSE CALCULATORS and the HP 10Bii™ use the nominal rate (*I/YR* or *NAI*) divided by the periods or payments per year (*P/YR*) to compute the periodic rate. Neither permits the user to input the periodic rate directly.

For example, if you know the present and future value, the payment amount and the time and frequency period, then you *solve for the interest rate*. Or, if you *know the interest rate*, then you must be solving for another function, such as the present or future value of the series of deposits.

5.   NUMBER OF PERIODS (*N*)

This function inputs *or* solves for the total number of periods. It is essential in all calculations.

For example, if you know the present and future value, the payment amount and the frequency and interest rate, then you *solve for the number of periods*. Or, if you *know the number of periods*, then you must be solving for another function, such as the present or future value of the series of deposits or for the interest rate.

The COURSE CALCULATORS require you to input the *Number of Years* as well as the number of *payments per year* or *periods per year*. They then compute the total Number of Periods or Payments (*N*), which you *do not enter*. In contrast, the *N* function on an HP 10Bii™ is a function *you must enter*. It stands for the total number of periods or payments. You may enter it in two ways. For example, suppose you have 12 payments per year for

---

2   For some calculations, such as interest conversion, the *NOM%* function is necessary as opposed to the *I/YR* function, even though they represent the same factor.

ten years, which is a total of 120 payments. You can enter 120 as the *N* or you can use the shift function to enter 10 and the number of years times the *P/YR* Thus, on the HP 10Bii™, you *do not* enter the number of years. Some calculators, such as the HP 12C™, use only a periodic interest rate and thus the total number of years is not used, although for some calculations, you must enter dates.

120

or

10

6. PAYMENTS PER YEAR (OR, PERIODS PER YEAR) (*P/YR*)

This function inputs *or* solves for the total number of periods or payments per year. Another way of defining this is as the compounding period: the nominal annual interest rate compounds at this *frequency*. On both the COURSE CALCULATORS and on the HP 10Bii™, the *P/YR* function acts as both periods per year or payments per year. The HP 12C™ calculator does not use the periods or payments per year function; however, it relies on dates for some calculations. Use of a HP 12C™ is beyond the scope of this course. Many people, including many lawyers and real estate agents, use that calculator; hence, some familiarity with it is important.

For example, if you know the present and future value, the payment amount, the total time period and interest rate, then you *solve for the number of periods per year*. Or, if you *know the number of periods per year*, then you must be solving for another function, such as the present or future value of the series of deposits or for the interest rate.

CAUTION

As Explained in LESSON FIVE

The compounding period (periods per year) and the payment period (payments per year) *must* either be identical or be 1.

7. MODE

This function defines the timing of the initial payment in a sinking fund, an amortization, or in an annuity. *Begin Mode* occurs when the first payment is at the beginning of each period. _End Mode_ occurs when the first payment is at the end of each period. The COURSE CALCULATORS always display the mode next to the payment amount. On an HP 10Bii™, the display will indicate Begin Mode if you set the calculator to that mode. It will remain in begin mode until you re-set it (or change the battery). If you set the calculator to End Mode, the display will not indicate the mode. Many HP 10Bii™ simulators, however, _always_ indicate the mode.

When using the COURSE CALCULATORS, you may always highlight one of the function words—such as Present Value or Mode—using your cursor. This will cause a definition to appear. The definition will disappear when you move your cursor away.

Be Careful with Mode

The mode matters, _but not a great deal_. Thus, if you set the mode incorrectly, your answer will be incorrect, but not obviously so. In contrast, some other mistakes—such as setting the number of payments incorrectly—could cause your answer to appear ridiculous (a 30-year loan versus a 3-year loan is a huge difference, but begin versus end mode is much less so).

B. COMMON MISTAKES IN USING A CALCULATOR (LESSON FOUR-B)

Six Calculator Rules

1. Clear the machine's memory when starting a new calculation.
2. Set the cash flows with the proper sign.
3. Set the mode correctly.
4. Set the interest rate to compound for each payment period.
5. Set the periods per year correctly.
6. Set the display to the appropriate number of decimal places.

Unless the calculator is defective, which is unlikely, it will produce the correct answer if given the correct information. Nevertheless, many users, at one time or another, exclaim "This thing doesn't work!" Usually, they have violated one of the following six rules.[3] Users of all handheld calculators risk making these mistakes.

1.   FIRST, CLEAR THE MACHINE— AND DO SO CORRECTLY

A calculator knows only what you tell it and it does not forget until you tell it to forget, typically *even if you turn off the machine*. Thus, be certain to clear all functions and memory when beginning a new calculation. This is particularly important for hand-held calculators, such as the HP 10Bii™: the display shows only one function at a time, creating the risk that the user will not remember to clear all other functions. Many of the cell phone apps which mimic the HP 10Bii™:, however, show the values for multiple functions, which helps resolve this mistake. The images, however, are often very small, so be careful.

The COURSE CALCULATORS minimize this risk because the display shows all function values at all times; hence, users are unlikely to forget to set a function correctly. In contrast, with a hand-held calculator, users can only see (or can only easily see) one function display at a time; as a result, they often forget to set one or more functions which retain settings from prior calculations.

All calculators have a *clear* key, usually denominated with a C or the word clear. In addition, many calculators have a function key by which merely the last information entered can be cleared, and a different function key by which all information can be cleared.

a.   Course Calculators

All COURSE CALCULATORS have a Clear All button. Pressing it sets all functions to the default value—often zero or 1.

clear all

You *need not* clear all the values to work alternative functions, as long as you insure the ones displayed are correct. Clearing them all, however, will reduce mistakes until you are adept at using the calculators.

Your computer's Back Space key will erase individual digits and the delete key will erase an entire highlighted number.

---

[3]   I recall one student many years ago who could not get the right answer with her calculator—and neither could I. I asked if it had gotten wet or been dropped. She answered, "No, but I did throw it against the wall a few times!" Indeed, this material can sometimes be frustrating. Try to relax and take it slowly. I check all my answers and find that I, too, make all of these mistakes. Plus, I've also wanted to throw the calculator across the room a few times. If that happens, it is best to take a deep breath, do something else and come back to it later. You can also contact your Professor.

The calculators also have different colored fields: green, white, yellow, and black. **Green** is always the answer to the problem you are working. **Black** always sets the mode. The default mode is End. If you set the mode to Begin, it will appear in **Red**. **Yellow** boxes are calculated by the calculator: you must _NEVER_ change a yellow box. White **_boxes are the ones into which you input information_**. Because the COURSE CALCULATORS display all function values at all times, the risk of a user failing to clear some values in white boxes—and thus computing a wrong value—is largely eliminated. To test the two clear functions, type a number in the white box below. Use the _backspace_ key or _delete_ key to erase it. Or, click on the **_Clear All_** key illustrated above to clear the box.

b.   HP 10Bii™ Calculator

The HP 10Bii™ Calculator has three levels for the clear function.

1.   The C key—when pressed in un-shifted mode—will clear the _entire_ displayed number; however, it leaves the memory intact. _See_ **Example 1** for the **_un_**-shifted use.

2.   The back arrow key will clear single digits, one at a time. See **Example 2.**

EXAMPLE 1

Clearing an HP 10Bii™

If you input 50 + 20 + 30 but intended 50 + 20 + 40, press C erasing the 30 but leaving the 70 in memory. You can then press 40 and =. The display will then read 110. Press the following keys:

50 + 20 + 30

  The display will read 110.

EXAMPLE 2

Clearing an HP 10Bii™

If you input 523 but intended 524, you may use the backward arrow key to erase the 3. Then simply enter the number 4. The display will read 524. In contrast, the C key will clear the entire number 523. Press the following keys:

523   4 The display will read 524.

3. The *C ALL* key when pressed in the "shifted mode" will clear the entire memory, as well as the displayed number. To perform this function on an HP 10Bii™ calculator, press the orange downshift key and then press *C ALL*. These strokes shift the function to *C ALL* (clear all) rather than C (clear). Before working a new problem, you should press these keys:

The *C ALL* function does *not* reset the number of periods per year. If you change this setting, it will remain—*even if you turn off the calculator* until you manually change it or remove the battery.

Also, the *C ALL* function does *not* change the mode. Thus if you reset the mode from end to begin, or *vice versa*, it will remain—*even if you turn off the calculator*—until you re-set it manually through the procedure described below or remove the battery.

CAUTION

To Summarize

The HP 10Bii™ **clear all button does not clear everything, so be careful!** In contrast, the clear all button on the course calculators will clear everything except the mode.

2. SET THE CASH FLOWS WITH THE PROPER SIGN

Many, but not all, calculators require that cash flows be directional.[4] This means that one set of cash flows must be positive and the other must be negative. This is true of the HP 10Bii™ Calculator. It is not true the COURSE CALCULATORS.

As explained earlier, if you lend money, you view the cash flow as a negative. The borrower views it as a positive. But, you view the repayment of the loan as a positive and the borrower views it as a negative.

a. Course Calculators

The COURSE CALCULATORS eliminate the need to input cash-flows directionally. Hence, all numbers[5] should be entered as positive numbers. The calculator then converts them, as appropriate. Thus the COURSE CALCULATORS thus eliminate the second most common difficulty faced by users of many handheld calculators.

b. HP 10Bii™ Calculator

The HP 10Bii™ Calculator requires cash flows to be entered with opposite signs. As shown in **Example 3**, failure to do so will prompt the display **no SoLution** or **inf**. You may enter a negative number in two ways.

For example, to input the number (1000), first enter the positive number 1000, and then press the "plus/minus" key:

1000   The display will show a negative 1000.

This will change the sign from positive to negative or back from negative to positive. _In the alternative_, press the minus sign first and then the number. With some older calculators, you may need to press the equal sign following the number. Please experiment with your calculator, if you have one.

---

[4] Many other calculators—such as those manufactured by Texas Instruments—do not require opposite signs between present value and future value.

[5] I did not design the calculators with negative interest rates in mind. Negative rates have become common in many countries, which may prompt me to re-design them. At the time of publication, negative rates are rare in the United States.

EXAMPLE 3

Negative Numbers on HP 10Bii™

Suppose you want to compute the Effective Interest rate inherent to a Present Value of 500, a Future Value of 1000 and a period of 10 years. The correct answer is 7.177346254. This process solves for an unknown interest rate.

To achieve this, either the 500 or the 1000 must be expressed as a negative number while the other must be positive. From the lender's point of view, the 500 loan is negative and the 1000 repayment is positive. From the borrower's viewpoint, the opposite is true.

To enter 500 as a negative number, press the following keys:

500

The display will read −500. If you wish to complete the problem, enter or press the following:

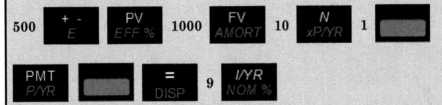

The display will read 7.177346254, which is the missing interest rate you just solved for. If, instead, you entered both numbers—the 500 Present Value and the 1000 Future Value as positive numbers, the display would read:

no SoLution or inf

3.   SET THE MODE CORRECTLY

Calculations involving annuities, sinking funds and amortizations, require a "mode" setting: either **Begin Mode** or **End Mode**. This is true of all calculators, including the HP 10Bii™ as well as the COURSE CALCULATORS.

Begin Mode applies if payments (or deposits or withdrawals) occur at the beginning of each period. End Mode applies if payments occur at the end of each period.

Typically, a sinking fund uses the Begin Mode because the depositor wants to begin immediately. Typically, an amortization—such as the repayment of a loan—uses the End Mode because loan payments do not begin on the date of the loan. Instead, loan payments begin at the end of each period. For example, payments on a car loan typically start one month after the purchase. Using Begin Mode for a loan amortization makes little sense: a payment on the date of the borrowing merely collapses to a lower amount borrowed, resulting in end mode.

Future value of a sum and present value of a sum calculations are not affected by the mode setting.

a. Course Calculators

The COURSE CALCULATORS have **black** keys labeled **Begin** and **End** to designate the mode. Click on Begin to set the Calculator in Begin Mode; or, click on End to set it in End Mode. Also, when in Begin Mode, the words *begin mode* appear in red. Similarly, in End Mode, the words *end mode* appear in black. Hence you are unlikely to forget to set the mode correctly. This effectively eliminates the third most common difficulty with using hand-held calculators.

b. HP 10Bii™ Calculator

To set the mode on an HP 10Bii™ calculator, first press the orange shift key and then press the BEG/END key to operate the mode function.

Most calculators are preset at the factory in end mode. Pressing these two keys will change it to begin mode, which the display will note with the word BEGIN. To revert to end mode, press the two keys again. *The display may no longer indicate the mode*. If you change the setting to begin mode, it will remain, even if you turn off the calculator or utilize the clear all (*C ALL*) function. To revert to end mode, you must do so manually by repeating the above steps. In many cell phone apps, the display will indeed show *End* for end mode.

The display on <u>most</u> hand-held calculators does not indicate End Mode. Instead, it only indicates mode when the Calculator is in Begin Mode. As a result, users often fail to notice the mode and thus obtain an incorrect answer.

A common mistake among calculator users involves begin mode annuities, sinking funds, or amortizations. Because the HP 10Bii™ display *may not* indicate end mode, the user may forget to change the mode to begin, thus producing significant (but not obvious) incorrect results. The default setting is for end mode because that is consistent with most amortizations, a common calculation involving mode. However, sinking funds and annuities commonly use begin mode, necessitating a different calculator setting.

For example, if you were saving for a child's education and desired to make monthly deposits, a sinking fund calculation can tell you the necessary monthly deposit to make, depending on the child's age and the expected interest rate. If you were to begin the deposits today, you would use begin mode. Or, if you want to begin making the deposits at the end of the first month, you would use end mode.

For example, new parents who desire to accumulate $100,000 for their child's 18th birthday and who expect to earn 4% nominal annual interest compounded monthly, must deposit $316.91[6] monthly if they begin making deposits at the *end* of month 1. Or, they need deposit only $315.86[7] if they *begin immediately*. Although the differences may seem slight in this problem, they can be material in many other situations.

4. SET THE INTEREST RATE TO COMPOUND FOR EACH PAYMENT PERIOD

A basic law of finance is that the compounding period and the payment period must be the same. Thus, if the facts provide for annual payments, the interest rate must be stated as an annual rate. If, instead, the facts provide for semi-annual payments, then the interest rate must be stated as a semi-annual rate. Likewise, monthly payments call for a monthly interest rate. Setting the *P/YR* to the correct amount to correspond with payments requires the user to have the correct information. This, in turn, necessitates that the interest rate be stated using correct terminology. As a result, common practice involves stating interest rates using a nominal annual uncompounded format along with a statement of the compounding period. LESSON SIX covers this in greater depth. LESSON FIVE-B introduces the INTEREST CONVERSION CALCULATOR which will make the conversions for you.

If, however, the facts—such as a contract—do not state the interest rate in such a format, *you must convert them* to a nominal annual

---

[6] Using the SINKING FUND CALCULATOR, which rounds all internal calculations to 10 decimals. The HP 10Bii™ produces $316.86, but rounds to 9 decimals. The difference is immaterial.

[7] Using the SINKING FUND CALCULATOR, which rounds all internal calculations to 10 decimals. The HP 10Bii™ produces $315.81, but rounds to 9 decimals. The difference is immaterial.

uncompounded format or the equivalent. Otherwise, no calculator will produce the correct answer. LESSON FIVE-B covers how to convert interest rates to equivalent rates with different compounding periods.

A Basic Law of Finance

The compounding period and the payment period must be the same.

This is not something you directly set for this purpose; instead, you must be sure the interest rate you use corresponds with the periods (or payments) per year.

a. Course Calculators

The COURSE CALCULATORS require you to input a nominal interest rate (*NAI*) as well as the number of periods or payments per year. The calculator will automatically convert the rate to the correct effective rate (*EFF*). In most problems we will work, these have the same value; hence, the same input box controls both. The calculator labels it payments per year, but it also stands for periods per year. If you have a set of facts in which the payment frequency and the compounding frequency differ, you will need to convert the nominal interest rate to a compounding frequency equal to the payment period. LESSON FIVE-B will explain how to do this. LESSONS FOUR-A and FIVE cover the terms "nominal interest rate" and "effective interest rate," as well as "periodic rate."

Because you will always enter a nominal rate, you will not make this mistake, assuming you set the period consistent with the given facts.

b. HP 10Bii™ Calculator

Confusing as it is, the HP 10Bii™ calculator has two ways to enter a nominal interest (uncompounded) rate, plus a method to enter an effective (compounded) rate.

For example, to enter a nominal rate of 10 percent compounded monthly, enter or press the following:

10 12

The calculator is factory set at 12 *P/YR* or 12 payments (periods) per year. Hence, you need to enter the 12 shift button *P/YR* only if you previously set the periods to another value. Remember, pressing the shift **clear all** button *does not re-set the periods per year.*

The *I/YR* button acts as the nominal rate button. But, as you should see, it also has a shift function to act as the nominal rate button. Confusing, yes, because it appears redundant.[8] But that is the design chosen by HP. The second method (below) is useful, as described in LESSON FIVE-B for converting an effective rate to a nominal rate and vice versa. Thus, to enter a nominal rate of 10 percent compounded monthly, you may, if you wish, enter or press the following:

An HP 10Bii™ calculator also allows you to enter an effective rate, which it will internally convert to the equivalent nominal rate using the payment or period frequency you enter. In contrast, the COURSE CALCULATORS eliminate this possibility. Thus, if all you know is the effective rate, you must use the INTEREST CONVERSION CALCULATOR (covered in LESSON FIVE-B) to convert the effective rate to the correct nominal rate. You must do this because all the formulas actually use the periodic rate—*never* the effective rate nor the nominal rate (unless the period is annual). Few calculators other than the HP 12C™ allow the user enter a periodic rate. The COURSE CALCULATORS as well as most hand-held calculators internally convert the nominal rate to the proper periodic rate (by diving the nominal rate by the periods per year). If you enter an effective rate on a hand-held, the machine will convert it to the equivalent nominal rate and also to the correct periodic rate. The process will seem instantaneous. To enter a 10 percent effective rate with monthly compounding, press or enter:

5.   SET THE PERIODS PER YEAR CORRECTLY

a.   Course Calculators

On the COURSE CALCULATORS, the periods per year are always displayed. The calculator labels it as "payments per year," which, as explained earlier, is the same thing as periods per year. To change it, simply insert the correct number: 2 for semi-annual; 4 for quarterly; 12 for monthly, or 365 for daily.

---

[8]   It is not redundant, as covered in LESSON FIVE.

b.   HP 10Bii™ Calculator

On the HP 10Bii™ calculator, the default factory setting is 12. To change it to 2 for semi-annual press 2, the shift key and the *P/YR* key:

2

The shift key uses the *P/YR* function of the  key rather than the *PMT* or payment function. The calculator will remain set at 2 periods per year (semi-annual compounding) until you either re-set it or you remove the battery (which causes it to revert to the factory default when you replace the battery). Users commonly re-set the *P/YR* to work a problem, but then forget to re-set it for the next problem. That mistake is unlikely with the COURSE CALCULATORS because they always display the number of Periods Per Year (or Payments Per Year). Setting the number of periods incorrectly can cause enormous mistakes, as demonstrated in later lessons.

6.   SET THE DISPLAY TO THE APPROPRIATE NUMBER OF DECIMAL PLACES

a.   Course Calculators

On the COURSE CALCULATORS, the setting occurs in several ways, which you cannot change. First, the display typically shows two decimals for most functions, such as dollar amounts. The calculator automatically rounds to those two decimals. If you place your cursor on the function, it will display the number to 16 decimals. Internally, the calculators round computations to ten decimals. You cannot change this.

b.   HP 10Bii™ Calculator

On the HP 10Bii™, the calculator internally rounds to nine or ten decimals (models vary). You cannot change this. The display comes from the factory to show two decimals; however, you can change that to display up to nine. To do so press the shift key, the equal sign and then the number of desired decimals to be displayed:

 9

Example 3 included this function of setting the display to nine decimals. *Note*: if you do this, you ***have not*** changed how the calculator computes internally: it always rounds to nine (or ten) decimals, regardless of what you set the display to be.

Because the HP 10Bii™ (and most hand-held calculators) internally round to nine decimals, they will produce a slightly different answer for some problems than will the COURSE CALCULATORS (which round to ten). For example, some numbers terminate their decimal representation quickly, some do so after many decimals, and some repeat. Irrational numbers, such as pi, never repeat and never terminate.

> ### Rounding
>
> Calculators round using different conventions: some round to nine decimals, some to ten, and some at some other level. Thus, for numbers with repeating or otherwise non-terminating decimal representations, different calculators may produce slightly different answers.
>
> For engineers, this could be significant; however, for lawyers, it is not. ***Do not worry about non-material differences in answers.***

Consider a 12 percent nominal annual interest rate that compounds monthly. The periodic rate will be 12 divided by 12 or 1.000000000. Whether we round to nine or ten or one-hundred decimals is irrelevant. Similarly, a 6 percent *NAI* compounded monthly would be 0.5000000 percent periodic: again, rounding beyond one decimal is irrelevant. A third example would involve 9 percent *NAI* compounded monthly: that would be 0.750000 percent periodic. Rounding beyond two decimals is irrelevant.

In contrast, 8 percent *NAI* compounded monthly would be 0.33333333333 as a repeating decimal. The HP 10Bii™ calculator will round that to 0.333333333, while the COURSE CALCULATORS will use 0.3333333333. The difference will likely be immaterial.

Many problems in the various lessons round the answer to two decimals, while others round the answer to more. In almost all cases, two or three decimals is best for legal matters. Indeed, nearly all payments will round to two decimals. For federal tax purposes, many forms permit rounding to the nearest dollar.

Property taxes in many jurisdictions, however, use a millage rate,[9] which is 1/10th of a cent. In my home jurisdiction, my property tax bill is a function of four decimals. For example, the rate may be 21.4673 mills per $1,000 of property value. Because 1 mill is 1/10th of a cent, 21 mills is 2.1 cents. Thus 21.4673 mills is 2.14673 cents or $0.0214673. The mill is 1/1000th of a dollar. The fourth decimal on the property tax millage rate is 1/10,000,000th of a dollar. Thus the property tax assessor where I live

---

[9] The term mill or millage rate comes from the Latin word millesimum, which is 1/1000th.

rounds to 7 decimals in terms of each dollar, at least for computation. The bill, of course, rounds to the nearest cent, or two decimals on the dollar. When I was much younger, some states produced mill coins for sales taxes. Each coin was 1/10th of a cent. Today, stores often do not bother with cents, so times have changed.

On a related subject, lawyers need to understand *__materiality__* and *__the false sense of precision__*. Materiality is a fundamental principal of accounting: if something matters, it must be accounted for and reported. But, if something does not matter, it may be ignored. In your own life, you surely know this. Surely no reader would fret over losing a penny, a nickel, and likely not a dollar. $100 may be material to you as a student, but to many people it is irrelevant. If you receive a job offer of $100,000 per year and another of $100,500, would you really base your choice on the $500? Of course you would not, because undoubtedly a great many other variables are also involved. In law—except for property taxes—pennies rarely matter and often dollars do not, which raises the other issue: *precision*.

The calculators will provide *precise* answers, but that does not mean you must use the level of precision calculated. Indeed, if you set the display to nine decimals, it will show tiny fractions of a cent. As explained above, the fourth decimal in a millage rate represents 1/10,000/000 of a dollar. The ninth decimal in a millage rate, if it were used, would represent one-trillionth of a dollar. The COURSE CALCULATORS will display up to 16 decimals. In a millage rate, that would be 1 quintillionth of a dollar. Just because we *can* compute to that level, does not mean we *must*.

As you use the calculators, you may enjoy examining that type of precision, but you must remember, it probably does not matter. Were you an engineer and were you planning to send a ship to land on Mars, 100 or perhaps 1,000 decimals might make a difference (I really do not know); however, as a lawyer, typically three decimals in an interest rate is the most that is material. In most cases, governments and businesses round to two decimals for interest, if not to the nearest dollar or often 1,000 dollars for values.

Some of the problems you encounter with this course provide very precise answers—largely because I, the author, enjoy doing so. But, if I grade your exam, *__I do not care about such precision__* (except when I do, and part of the exam is for you to know the difference). Indeed, precision can be misleading because, as you will quickly learn, many calculations involve estimates or assumptions. Hence, they are merely approximations. Other times, such as with a property tax bill, precision to the penny matters: I owe what I owe.

For example, when I've testified as an expert witness in a tort case, I've often wanted to round the answer. Suppose lost wages were $10,000 per month, work-life expectancy was 40 years, and I used a 3.5% *EFF* discount rate, the present value of the loss computes to $2,603,504.8557813577.[10] Of course, I round immediately to 86 cents because no one cares about the fractions of a penny. But, I always wanted to round to $2.6 million. The $3,504.86 is not relevant because the interest rate I chose was an opinion. Had I chosen 3.5% *NAI*, my answer would have been justifiable, but it would have been $2,581,506.6844815775—a smaller number because 3.5% *NAI* translates to a bit over 3.557% *EFF*. I would likely have rounded the second number to $2.6 million as well.

But—*and this is a critical point*—every single time I've testified, the attorney who called me asked that I present the precise answer to the jury: $2,603,504.86. Each attorney—*and they were admittedly far more experienced with juries and human nature than I*—insisted juries would view the precision as confidence and greater accuracy and thus give it more weight. In my opinion, that is false because I could not possibly be confident to the penny, let alone the nearest thousand dollars regarding the present value of 40 years of lost wages. Indeed, the 40 years is an estimate (the victim might have died tomorrow or might have worked until age 100), as is the interest rate, the way we project inflation, and the way we project productivity, each of which enters the expert's calculation. I complied with each attorney's wish, testifying the results of my calculation, which was accurate because that is what the calculator generated. I've never had a cross-examiner question the precision or mock it, as I've always feared. Perhaps they did not understand how ridiculous the precision appeared, *at least to me*.

Precision

Precision matters sometimes: if you are building a bridge or marking the boundaries of property. ***But in finance, precision often looks silly.***

Also to emphasize the point, as explained in a footnote above, the COURSE CALCULATOR produces $2,603,504.86 while an HP 10Bii™ computes $2,603,461.86 for the same set of facts. Over the past couple decades, I've had many students fret about that difference. Seriously? Would you really view two experts whose calculations differed by $43 out of over $2.6 million as disagreeing? Surely not.

On exams, I've often asked students to calculate a reasonable offer in a similar tort case—from the perspective of the plaintiff and from the

---

[10] Using the PRESENT VALUE OF AN ANNUITY CALCULATOR. An HP 10Bii™ computes $2,603,461.86. The $43 difference is immaterial.

defense. Later LESSONS explain how to compute this. But, if the defense expert calculated $2,603,504.86, would anyone actually use that in an initial offer? I really doubt it. I can see asking for $2.6 million or $2.7 million or $2.5 million to settle. But precise to 86 cents? Surely without a jury present, that would seem absurd. To press the point, suppose you are buying a house that is priced at $350,000. You might offer $325,000 or $330,000, but would you ever offer $328,566.17? Surely not (unless you were attempting to be humorous). Thus if asked for a reasonable offer on an exam or by an employer, compute the amount precisely, but consider rounding so as not to appear silly.

QUESTIONS

1.   Define the term Mode as used in finance.

2.   Distinguish an annuity due from an annuity in arrears. Which uses begin mode and which uses end mode?

3.   What does the term "cash flows" mean in finance? Provide an example.

4.   Discuss the importance of precision in legal financial calculations.

5.   To how many decimals would a lawyer normally round an interest rate?

6.   Do you know how to clear the display as well as the memory on the COURSE CALCULATORS? On your hand-held calculator or app?

7.   Distinguish a present value from a future value.

PART II

FINANCIAL TERMINOLOGY, RULES, AND GUIDELINES

■ ■ ■

LESSON FIVE

INTEREST TERMINOLOGY

■ ■ ■

Lesson Objectives

1. Student will learn more about the following terms:
   a. Interest rate.
   b. Nominal Annual Interest Rate (*NAI*).
   c. Periodic rate.
   d. Compounding period.
   e. Effective Interest Rate (*EFF*).

2. Student will learn how to input information regarding these terms on:
   a. an HP 10Bii™ calculator.
   b. the COURSE CALCULATORS.

3. Student will learn that the term "interest" without further definition is legally misleading and/or meaningless.

4. Student will learn to convert (though the actual process of conversion is in LESSON FIVE-B).
   a. A nominal rate to an effective rate.
   b. An effective rate to a nominal rate.
   c. A nominal rate to a periodic rate.

Terminology Introduced

- Interest Rate
- Nominal Annual Interest Rate (*NAI*)
- Periodic Rate
- Compounding Period
- Effective Interest Rate (*EFF*)
- Simple Interest

LESSON FIVE has five parts:

A.   Interest Terminology.

B.   Interest Rate Conversion.

C.   Annual Percentage Rate (*APR*).

D.   Annual Percentage Yield (*APY*).

E.   Yield.

Each is complex. ***The LESSON FIVE group is the most difficult part of this course.*** LESSONS FIVE-A and FIVE-C are the most important. LESSON FIVE-D is the *least* important. The complexity of FIVE-C is important for lawyers, particularly those who deal with real estate or banking: the calculation must be correct and can have serious consequences if it is not. Because lawyers likely prepare or present the disclosure documents, they must understand the *APR* computation sufficiently to check its accuracy. The complexity of LESSON FIVE-D, in contrast, is important to the extent it convinces the reader it exists: the terms are not terms of art and alternative acceptable definitions can matter a great deal. If all you learn from it is to define the terms, that may be sufficient.

A. INTEREST TERMINOLOGY (LESSON FIVE-A)

You should read the GLOSSARY and the list of ACRONYMS. Those files include terms from finance and from accounting that lawyers should be familiar with. Many terms are "terms of art" in that they have consistent definitions. Many other terms, however, are not terms of art: respected experts disagree on how to define them. As a result, lawyers must be very careful to define non-terms-of-art in any legal document. Failure to do so will present problems and potential liability for malpractice. As the author, I am not the arbiter of alternative definitions: my job is to present acceptable alternatives, particularly if they are material. Even if you have a degree in finance, please read the GLOSSARY: terms you may believe you understand often have competing definitions.

We consider the following terms in LESSON FIVE-A:

1.   Interest rate

2.   Nominal rate

3.   Periodic rate

4.   Compounding period

5.   Effective rate

6.   Simple interest

Interest is the price charged for the use of money over time. LESSON SIX explains *Why People Charge Interest*. The major components are liquidity, expected inflation or deflation, and risk.

For tax purposes, some *interest* is deductible, subject to limitations.[1] Because (for tax purposes) the character of *interest* income differs from that of capital gain or service income, measuring what portion of a payment is *interest* as opposed to *principal* or service income can be very important.[2]

At least one famous Ninth Circuit opinion[3] defined—for some tax purposes—compensation for the use of money over time as something other than interest. The decision was both widely applauded and widely ridiculed.[4] Those who ridicule it have the better argument.[5]

1. INTEREST RATE

For finance, we must define ***interest rate***. Standing alone, this term has no meaning. To describe interest *correctly*,[6] one *must* state it in one of three ways:

1) as a *periodic rate* for a stated period;

2) as a *nominal annual interest rate* to be compounded at a stated frequency; or

3) as an *effective rate*.

Interest Rate

Standing alone, this term has ***no meaning***. Be very careful how you state an interest rate in a legal document.

---

[1] IRC § 163.

[2] Capital gains are subject to special rates and limitations. IRC §§ 1, 1211–1212. Service income is subject to employment taxes such as social security and Medicare. Interest income/deductions might be passive, IRC § 469, subject to at-risk limitations, IRC § 465, or excluded, IRC §§ 103, 512(b)(1).

[3] Albertson's v. Commissioner, 42 F. 3d 537 (9th Cir. 1994).

[4] Edward A. Zelinsky, *The Ninth Circuit's Albertsons Decision: Right for 1983, Wrong for Today*, 63 TAX NOTES 231 (1994); Steven J. Willis, *Leave Albertson's Alone*, 63 TAX NOTES 1481 (1994); Daniel Halperin, *Albertson's: More Outrage*, 63 TAX NOTES 1771 (1994); Steven J. Willis, *Albertson's: A Little Less Emotion, Please*, 64 TAX NOTES 961 (1994).

[5] As one who ridiculed it, I have some bias. But, extra money paid on a principal sum because payment of the sum was delayed is interest. If that is not interest, what is? But, twenty-five years after the decision, people still disagree regarding whether it was correct.

[6] As covered in LESSON FIVE-B, federal law often requires the statement of an annual percentage rate of interest (*APR*), which is not a financial term and which is flawed. Failure to state it, however, has serious consequences.

All three are _identical_ ways of saying the same thing and are inter-changeable (*subject to rounding*).[7] Each of these methods includes the effect of compounding and the frequency of compounding. The term interest rate standing alone, however, does not; hence, it is inherently non-specific and thus meaningless (or at least dangerous because of vagueness). Using the term interest rate without modifiers reflecting the compounding frequency is malpractice (or it should be). Consider two examples from my own experience.

Story Three: I borrowed money from my father for the purchase of a house. I drafted the loan as well as the mortgage.[8] My father suggested the interest rate. Armed with both the COURSE CALCULATORS and multiple financial calculators, particularly a HP 10B™ (precursor to the ii), I asked him to be more specific. Although well-educated, he did not immediately understand. I felt conflicted because I knew our interests were adverse. I showed him the calculator and pointed out I could enter the chosen number as a nominal annual rate or as an effective rate. I explained _we_ had to choose—we knew the loan amount (the present value), the ultimate balance (a zero future value), the payment frequency (monthly), the mode (end), and the term (15 years). We needed to solve for the monthly payment and then produce an amortization schedule. But to do so, we had to enter the interest rate—*no calculator can solve for two variables . . .* only one. But, each calculator (well, not the HP 12C™, but I did not want to use that very good but confusing-to-the-uninitiated machine) required me to enter the interest rate as either a nominal rate or as an effective rate. He said "you choose." I explained, that was not appropriate because the amount mattered, at least a little. Entering it as a nominal rate produced a payment $10.64 greater per month than entering it as an effective rate. Not a lot of money, but at the time the equivalent of about five gallons of gas or a modest bottle of wine—every month for fifteen years. That is 900 gallons of gas or 15 cases of wine. Ultimately, I asked him where he got the suggested interest rate. He answered "I based it on what I otherwise would earn on a

---

[7]   Typically, documents round to two decimals. For federal tax purposes, two decimals is also the norm. In my opinion, three decimals can be significant, but more precision is unlikely material. The effective rate is identical to the periodic rate and to the nominal rate if the instrument has no payments during the year. If it has payments, the effective rate is identical only if one assumes the periodic rate as the cost of payments made as well as the return on payments received.

[8]   One of my pet-peeves (which I believe has real legal consequences) involves those to refer to paying a mortgage or owing a mortgage. One pays debts or obligations. A mortgage is a security device, not all that different from a pawn or a pledge. One cannot "own" a mortgage or pay it or owe it. A mortgage is not property and is not an asset. It secures a debt or obligation and thus affects the value of that debt or obligation. The debt is a liability in the view of the debtor. It is an asset for the creditor. The mortgage grants the creditor preference rights upon default, but it is not the obligation.

certificate of deposit. I increased it above that amount but kept it below what banks are now charging for home loans." That helped a little, _but not much_. Banks advertise and pay an effective rate on deposits, but routinely advertise a nominal rate on loans: the two are not comparable (as further explained in LESSON FIVE-C). I explained, as impartially as I could "If you are thinking more in terms of what you would otherwise earn, you are thinking in terms of an effective rate; however, if you are thinking more in terms of what I would otherwise pay to a bank, you are thinking in terms of a nominal rate." I showed him the calculator buttons and entered it both ways. Defining the chosen interest rate as an effective rate favored me—I got the 900 gallons of gas or the 15 cases of wine. Defining the rate as a nominal rate favored him— he got the gas or the wine. I no longer recall which we chose, but I learned an important lesson about how non-lawyers and non-financial experts use terms without defining them. But that leads to another story.

Story Four: Within the next year, another family member also sought a similar loan from my father (though larger in amount). They asked me—the family lawyer—to draft the documents. That was a simple task until I got to the interest rate description. Once again, all I received from them was something like "6 percent interest." Once again, I brought up the question of whether it was a nominal rate or an effective rate (it was way too much to be a periodic rate). I explained I could not choose, as I was ostensibly representing both and could not favor one over the other. The family member discussed it with a bank officer whom she quoted as saying "It does not make any difference: they are the same thing." Well, that was troubling because of course it makes a difference. In that case it was closer to $20 per month—still not a huge deal, but still frustrating when I was trying to do it correctly. The lesson to me was: very well-educated people often do not have a clue regarding what they are talking about, including some bank officers. Plus, they often do not listen to family members who are lawyers and who know what they are doing. For a bank officer not to understand how to state an interest rate was the most troubling lesson. But it indeed happened. I fear it is common; indeed, I have examples in later lessons that involve much greater consequences to lawyers and bankers who refused to listen to things and who insisted they were absolutely right when they were actually wrong . . . unfortunately very wrong in one case.

See below in this lesson for a discussion of the three ways of stating an interest rate. Also, see LESSON FIVE-B: _Interest Rate Conversion_ for a discussion of how to convert from one statement of an interest rate to another. The INTEREST CONVERSION CALCULATOR will perform this function automatically.

2.   NOMINAL ANNUAL INTEREST RATE (*NAI*)

This is the *periodic interest* rate times the number of periods in one year. Thus is it is more properly called the Nominal Annual Interest Rate (*NAI*). It is an uncompounded rate. Abbreviated as *NAI*, the nominal rate is an important key on all financial calculators. The rate itself serves no purpose in computations, which use the periodic rate; however, because humans tend to think in terms of one year, they typically multiply periodic rates times the number of periods in one year. The resulting *NAI* is a useful, *albeit misleading*, term for comparing financial instruments.

The formula for converting an *effective interest* rate to an *NAI* is:

$$\left[\, 100py \left(\left(1 + \frac{eff}{100} \right)^{\frac{1}{py}} - 1 \right) \right]$$

where *eff* = effective interest rate and *py* = number of periods or payments per year.

LESSON FIVE-B: *Interest Rate Conversion* introduces a calculator that will easily convert an *EFF* to an *NAI* or to a periodic rate.

The COURSE CALCULATORS include a place for you to input the nominal annual interest rate. An HP 10Bii™ calculator automatically considers the *I/YR* to be the nominal annual rate; however, the calculator also includes a button for *NOM%*, which stands for the nominal annual interest rate. The calculator operates the same regardless of which method you use to input the rate in most cases.

3.   PERIODIC INTEREST RATE

This is the rate of interest earned in one period. The periodic rate is critical in all financial calculations. For simplicity, we often multiply the *Periodic Rate* times the number of periods per year—the *P/YR*—to produce the Nominal Annual Interest Rate (*NAI*):

$$pr = \left(\frac{NAI}{P/YR} \right)$$

where *pr* = periodic interest rate, *NAI* = nominal annual interest rate, and *P/YR* = number of periods or payments per year.

LESSON FIVE-B: INTEREST RATE CONVERSION introduces a calculator that will easily convert an *EFF* to an *NAI* or to a periodic rate.

The formulae for computing present or future values, amortizations, and sinking funds all use a periodic rate. As a result, you must always convert the nominal rate to the periodic rate. To save you the trouble, the HP 10Bii™ calculator automatically divides the *NAI* by the *P/YR*. It does not display the periodic rate. The COURSE CALCULATORS do not permit you to input the periodic rate; instead, they, too, automatically divide the *NAI* by the *P/YR*. They also do not display the periodic rate.

4. COMPOUNDING PERIOD (*P/YR*)

This refers to the frequency of compounding for interest. For example, the period may be a month, which would result in twelve instances of compounding per year. Or, the period could be a day, which would result in 365/66 compounds per year. Many institutions use a 360 day year for compounding.

A critical rule of finance is: *the compounding period and the payment period must be the same or it must be annual*. The mathematical formulae for determining present and future values for sums and annuities require this rule. Of course, if the two are not the same, one can easily adjust the compounding period—and the resulting nominal interest rate—to reflect compounding consistent with the payment period.

Compounding is the process of paying or charging interest on interest. For example, if interest compounds monthly at 1%, then after one-month a $100.00 deposit would be worth $101.00. After two months, it would be worth $102.01. In the second month, the deposit would earn 1% interest on the original $100.00 deposit plus 1% interest on the first month's $1.00 of interest.

All interest compounds, which helps explain the term effective interest rate. The *EFF* reflects the result of compounding the periodic rate for one year.

Arguably, interest on an *amortizing* loan does not compound because the borrower pays it regularly (typically monthly). This is correct when viewed solely as it affects the borrower and lender together. Individually, however, the interest necessarily compounds because it either goes somewhere or came from somewhere. The lender who receives the $1.00 interest at the end of the first month does not later receive any additional interest on the $1.00 of interest from that particular borrower because the borrower has paid the $1.00 interest. The lender, however, may then lend the $1.00 to someone else—and thus effectively earn compounded interest; or, the lender will spend the $1.00. In the latter case, the lender receives no compounded interest; however, s/he reduces what would otherwise be borrowing costs or reduces what would otherwise be income from his *capital* and thus experiences the same effect.

> ### "All Interest Compounds"
> This "rule" is correct, ***depending on one's perspective***. We cover it in several Lessons. Be careful: if you are comparing different perspective, you risk drawing incorrect conclusions.

The same analysis applies to the borrower who pays his $1.00 interest obligation at the end of the first month. S/he does not owe or pay any additional compounded interest on that interest to that lender; however, the $1.00 paid came from somewhere. If s/he took it from a deposit, s/he earns less interest. If s/he borrowed it from someone else, s/he pays additional interest. Thus, the effective cost expressed in terms of a year necessarily involves compounded interest.

5. EFFECTIVE INTEREST RATE (*EFF*)

Sometimes labeled an *EIR*, this is a compounded rate of interest. It is the *periodic* rate compounded for one year. It differs from the *nominal annual interest rate* (*NAI*) in that the *effective* rate is compounded while the nominal rate is not. All financial calculators have an *effective rate* function, as well as a nominal rate function. For financial calculations, a calculator uses the periodic rate; hence, the nominal rate—which is the *periodic* rate times the numbers of periods in one year—is useful. Given an *effective rate*, one can convert it to the equivalent nominal annual rate for a given compounding frequency; then, one can divide by the frequency to produce the needed periodic rate.

An effective rate (*EFF*) differs substantially from an *Annual Percentage Rate* (*APR*), which is mostly a non-compounded rate, and the subject of LESSON FIVE-B. Federal law defines the *APR*, which generally is the nominal annual rate plus points and some other closing costs amortized for the stated life of the loan. In contrast, the *EFF* treats points as principal rather than interest and then produces a number different from the *APR* (assuming the loan includes points).

An *EFF* is arguably inapplicable to most consumer loans, which require current periodic interest payments. As such, they do not internally compound interest because the borrower pays all interest currently to the lender. But, externally, the funds for interest payments come from somewhere and end up somewhere. Hence, from the borrower's perspective, interest compounds to the extent the funds used to pay current interest are no longer available for other uses. Similarly, from the perspective of the lender, interest compounds to the extent the funds received in payment of current interest are either deposited elsewhere or expended (whereby they free-up other funds which are deposited or they relieve the need for other borrowing).

The formula for the *effective* interest rate:

$$EFF = \left[100 \left(\left(1 + \frac{pr}{100} \right)^{py} - 1 \right) \right]$$

where EFF = effective interest rate, pr = periodic rate and py = the number of periods per year.

LESSON FIVE-B: *Interest Rate Conversion* introduces a calculator that will easily convert an EFF to an NAI or to a periodic rate.

The COURSE CALCULATORS will not allow you to enter the EFF; instead, you must enter the NAI. The calculators will then convert the NAI to an EFF for you and will display the amount. An HP 10Bii™ calculator allows you to enter an EFF. To do so, press the numbers reflecting the interest amount, the shift key, and the EFF key:

12

This term EFF has the same general meaning as the annual percentage yield or the yield to maturity[9] and a similar meaning to the term internal rate of return. The four similar terms, however, have their own uses and are not precisely inter-changeable. Analysis of an EFF may vary depending on viewpoint: lender (deposits) or borrower (loans).

a. Deposits

For deposits with no withdrawals, the four terms will typically be the same (though some experts define APY and YTM differently, so be careful). The effective interest rate will be the annual compounded rate of interest: the actual amount of interest earned for a particular year divided by the amount on deposit at the beginning of the year. Financial institutions generally quote this rate compounded for the appropriate number of periods for an entire year. This is the most useful number for purposes of comparing one deposit with another.

For example, one financial institution may offer 10% nominal annual interest compounded semiannually, while another offers 9.9% nominal annual interest compounded quarterly, and a third offers 9.8% compounded daily. A comparison of those three rates is difficult because of the differing com-pounding periods. Stating each in terms of an effective annual rate eliminates any confusion. The first institution is actually offering 10.25% effective interest. The second is offering 10.273639392% effective interest, slightly more than the first even those it offers a lower

---

[9]   Be careful with the YTM, as experts differ widely regarding its meaning. Thus you should always define it.

nominal rate. The third institution is offering 10.294827704, more still even though it offers the lowest of the three nominal rates.

TIP

Because the nominal annual interest rate for a deposit is lower than the effective interest rate, financial institutions will often prominently quote the effective interest rate or annual percentage yield on a deposit. They may most prominently quote the lower nominal rate for a loan.

The nominal annual interest rate for a deposit will always be lower than the effective interest rate. As a result, financial institutions will often quote, in the most prominent language, the effective interest rate or annual percentage yield on a deposit.

Accounts that have occasional withdrawals or additional deposits will have the same effective interest rate and annual percentage yield or yield to maturity; however, they may have a different internal rate of return. Sales of a debt instrument subsequent to issue and prior to maturity—or offers to sell it—may result in a different yield to maturity and internal rate of return, because of the changing present value as a result of market forces.

b. Loans

Discount loans with no payments prior to maturity and no points have an effective interest rate equal both to the annual percentage yield and the nominal annual rate. They also have an annual percentage rate equal to the nominal rate. Installment loans and loans with points, however, have differing effective interest rates, nominal rates, and annual percentage rates.

Both the nominal interest rate and the annual percentage rate [*APR*] on an installment loan will *always* be lower than the effective rate.

Thus financial institutions rarely, if ever, prominently disclose or otherwise advertise the effective rate of a loan.

TIP

From the lender's viewpoint, interest compounds. Thus a lender should compare an installment loan's effective rate to the lender's cost of funds.

The effective rate on an installment loan with no points will be the interest rate that would accrue annually if the interest on the loan compounded. In actuality, interest on an installment loan without negative amortization does not compound; instead, the installments pay the interest due plus, usually, a portion of the principal. As a result, no interest is charged on interest. In a sense, the effective interest rate on such a loan is not representative of reality: while the effective rate is a compounded rate, the actual interest on the loan does not compound.

The effective rate reflects what would happen *if* the interest compounded. In reality, the interest _does_ compound, though not specifically with regard to the loan instrument and not necessarily at the same rate as the loan. This is true both from the standpoint of the lender and the borrower. From the lender's perspective, he receives installment payments, including all interest due and typically some principal. Those amounts do not earn additional interest from this borrower with regard to this loan; however, the lender must do something with the funds. If deposited or loaned elsewhere, they will earn additional interest. If expended, they will free up other funds that can earn interest, or they will reduce the need for borrowing, which will reduce other interest costs. Thus, effectively, the funds earn interest for the entire year (unless the applicable currency is stuffed in a mattress or some other unproductive investment).

CAUTION

Comparing either the nominal rate or *APR* of an installment loan to the lender's cost of capital would be misleading. ***This is an example of comparing a different perspective***.

Stating the uncompounded periodic rate on the particular loan as a compounded effective rate reflects the reality that the funds will earn interest from some source for the entire year; however, it reflects reality _only if_ the lender happens to re-invest the funds immediately and at the exact internal rate for the loan. That is a big IF; however, stating the *EFF* nevertheless provides a better approximation of reality than pretending the lender fails to re-invest or otherwise benefit from the timing of the receipt.

TIP

From the borrower's viewpoint, interest on an installment loan compounds. Thus a borrower should compare an installment loan's effective rate to his cost of funds.

Comparing either the nominal interest rate or the annual percentage rate (*APR*) of an installment loan to the borrower's effective rate or annual percentage yield (*APY*) on a savings account would be misleading. ***This is another example of a different perspective.***

From the borrower's viewpoint, the installment payments include all interest due and some principal. As a result, the borrower does not owe additional interest on those funds to that lender with regard to that loan; however, the borrower must have a source of funds to make the payments. That source of funds itself has a cost, which reflects its own interest rate. If borrowers use other available funds to make the payments, the they are then unable to earn interest elsewhere on those funds. Or, if a borrower must borrow the funds to make the payments, the borrower must pay additional interest on such additionally borrowed funds. Thus, effectively, the funds cost interest for the entire year (unless the borrower steals or prints the currency, it has a cost). Stating the uncompounded periodic rate on the particular loan as a compounded effective rate reflects the reality that the funds cost interest for the entire year.

The nominal annual interest rate and the annual percentage rate on an installment loan will *always* be lower than the effective rate. As a result, financial institutions rarely, if ever, prominently disclose or otherwise advertise the effective rate of a loan. This contrasts with their eagerness to advertise the effective rate on a deposit. Federal law does not require disclosure of the effective rate. In fact, it expressly requires prominent disclosure of the annual percentage rate (*APR*), which is always a lower number on an installment loan and which does not reflect the above-described reality.

Also, federal law expressly require the disclosure of an effective interest rate[10], though with a very different definition than used herein.

6. SIMPLE INTEREST, USURY, AND INVERTED CURVES

Some contracts refer to "*simple interest*," which is not a financial term of art. Be wary of that term. Users probably refer to the nominal, uncompounded rate, but you should not assume that: *make them define it*, particularly with regard to whether unpaid interest compounds, *i.e.,* becomes principal. Neither the COURSE CALCULATORS nor the HP 10Bii™ have a way to enter a simple interest rate. Thus, for those calculators, it is not a defined term. That said, one can convert a statement of simple interest to useful terms, albeit with some difficulty.

CAUTION

Simple Interest

This is not a term of art. If someone uses it, *make them define it*. If a statute uses it, read carefully.

Many state statutes unfortunately refer to "*simple interest*."[11] One particularly unusual statute (from a finance perspective at least) is a Tennessee provision defining interest:

(8) "Interest" is compensation for the use or detention of, or forbearance to collect, money over a period of time, and does not include compensation for other purposes, including, but not limited to, time-price differentials, loan charges, brokerage commissions, or commitment fees. For example, when you borrow

---

[10] 12 CFR 617.1730, dealing with farm credit, but it has little resemblance to the finance term.

[11] *E.g.,* F.S. § 687.02 (defining usury) (emphasis added); Mich. St. § 438.41: "A person is guilty of criminal usury when, not being authorized or permitted by law to do so, he knowingly charges, takes or receives any money or other property as interest on the loan or forbearance of any money or other property, at a rate exceeding 25% at *simple interest* per annum or the equivalent rate for a longer or shorter period. Any person guilty of criminal usury may be imprisoned for a term not to exceed 5 years or fined not more than $10,000.00, or both." (emphasis added); Maryland 12–103(a)(3): "If a loan made under paragraph (1) of this subsection is secured by the pledge of collateral which is other than a savings account or if such loan is unsecured, the lender may charge a rate of interest not in excess of 18 percent. However, on a loan made on or after July 1, 1982, a lender may charge an *effective rate of simple interest* not in excess of 24 percent per year on the unpaid principal balance. . . ." (emphasis added). *See also,* Ga. S. § 7–4–2: "(a)(1)(A) The legal rate of interest shall be 7 percent per annum *simple interest* where the rate percent is not established by written contract." (emphasis added).

money, you pay the lender *simple interest* (which is like rent) for the use of the money. The amount of interest you pay depends on:

(A) The principal, which is the amount you borrow;

(B) The rate, which is a percent based on a period of time, usually one (1) year; and

(C) The number of periods of time that you have the use of the money.

Thus, interest equals principal × rate × time. Accordingly, to determine the interest charged for borrowing five hundred dollars ($500) for three (3) years if the rate of interest is nine percent (9%) per year, first calculate the interest for one (1) year using the proportion rate equal percent/base, or 9/100 equals I/500; where I stands for interest, interest equals 9 × 500/100 equals forty-five dollars ($45.00). For three (3) years, the interest equals 3 × $45.00 equals $135; or you can combine steps 1 and 2 so that interest for three (3) years equals (9% × $500) × 3 equals one hundred thirty-five dollars ($135), presuming that no payment is made toward the principal of the loan during the three-year period.[12]

The Tennessee statute also defines "effective interest rate" in an unusual manner:

(6) "Effective rate of interest" is the simple rate of interest, i.e., the ratio between the interest payable on an obligation and the principal for a period of time, *including the result of converting compound, discount, add-on, or other nominal rates of interest into simple rates of interest*;[13]

Consider what the Tennessee statute requires: it defines the effective rate as the equivalent "simple interest" rate determined after converting compounding into an uncompounded rate. Although the term "simple interest" sounds as if it is "simple" or easy to compute, it is anything but. As demonstrated below in relation to the Florida statute, one must remove the effect of compounding, which results in an inverted curve for multi-year loans.

Also, consider the Tennessee statutory example: 9% interest on $500 for three years. The statute clearly presumes no principal payment, but is less than clear regarding interest payments. If, in the example, the borrower pays the interest annually, the computation is both clear and correct; however, if the borrower pays the interest upon maturity—at the end of the three years—the phraseology is, at best, confusing because it fails to compound the interest. If the statute applies to deferred interest

---

[12] Tenn. Code § 47–14–102(8) (emphasis added).

[13] Id. at (6).

(and it does not address the issue), the $135 interest on $500 principal is 8.293% *EFF*, not the stated 9%. If so, converting that to simple interest involves only division—135/500 = 9%. The point of requiring the conversion is unclear. *All financial calculators compound interest, which is the fundamental nature of the time value of money*. States, as many do, can certainly re-define financial terms as they wish and can require lenders and borrowers to convert financial terminology into artificially-defined state terms, but one must wonder the purpose for such requirements.

Compound Interest

All financial calculators compound interest, which is the fundamental nature of the time value of money.

Interpreting such statutes can be daunting. For example, the Florida Usury[14] statute as well as the Florida Consumer Finance[15] statute each use the term, but facially as an uncompounded rate. Each also has both civil[16] and criminal[17] consequences for violation: possible forfeiture of all interest plus up to five years imprisonment. That said, one wonders how either statute could result in a crime, considering they so poorly drafted. The usury statute provides:

> [I]t shall be usury and unlawful for any person . . . to reserve, charge, or take for any loan . . . a rate of interest greater than the *equivalent* of 18 percent per annum *simple interest*, either directly or indirectly, . . . whereby the debtor is required or obligated to pay a sum of money greater than the *actual principal sum received*, together with interest at the rate of the *equivalent* of 18 percent per annum *simple interest*.[18]

---

[14] F.S. 687.02.

[15] F.S. 516.031.

[16] F.S. 516.23; 687.147.

[17] Violation of F.S. 516 is a first degree misdemeanor, punishable with up to one year in jail. Violation of chapter 687 (usury) is a third-degree felony, punishable with up to five years in prison.

[18] F.S. 687.03. The consumer finance statute provides:

A person who is engaged in the business of making loans of money, except as authorized by this chapter or other statutes of this state, may not directly or indirectly charge, contract for, or receive any interest or consideration greater than 18 percent per annum upon the loan, use, or forbearance of money, goods, or choses in action, or upon the loan or use of credit, of the amount or value of $25,000 or less.

F.S. 516.02(2)(a).

Chapter 560 covers "money services businesses," "check cashing," and "deferred presentment" (commonly known as payday loans) transactions.

That contains many words, but little clarity. Let's take them slowly: "per annum," "principal sum," and "equivalent."

Per annum. A Florida Attorney General opinion suggests "*per annun*" means per year;[19] hence, the use of a 360-day convention is risky. Thus, the maximum daily rate must be .049315068%, which is 18/365, at least in non-leap years.

Equivalent. The word "equivalent" must refer to a portion of a year having a rate that would generate 18% if the amount earned interest for the entire year. But, how to compute the rate is not facially clear in the statute. At least one Florida Appellate Court[20], however, used simple division to determine the equivalent rate. Thus, using a 365-day year, or a 12-month year, or a 52.14 week year, the equivalent rates must be .049315068% per day, 1.8888903567% per week, 1.5% per month, 4.5 % per quarter, and 9% per six months. While that may seem clear, it presents some difficulty regarding the statement of the rate for roll-over loans.

The actual principal sum received. This is problematic. Facially, it seems clear: the amount the borrower received. But, practically, it should—along with the word equivalent—refer to the daily amount outstanding; otherwise, an amount outstanding for a single day could bear interest for the entire year, frustrating the statute's purpose.

Consider some examples. **Example 4** is not usurious. The amount loaned is $1,000, and the interest is $180, which is exactly 18% of the amount loaned. If, instead, A loaned B $1,000 for six months, A could

---

F.S. 687.071(g) covers loansharking:

(g) "Loan sharking" means the act of any person as defined herein lending money unlawfully under subsection (2), subsection (3), or subsection (4).

(2) Unless otherwise specifically allowed by law, any person making an extension of credit to any person, who shall willfully and knowingly charge, take, or receive interest thereon at a rate exceeding 25 percent per annum but not in excess of 45 percent per annum, or the equivalent rate for a longer or shorter period of time, whether directly or indirectly, or conspires so to do, commits a misdemeanor of the second degree, punishable as provided in s. 775.082 or s. 775.083.

(3) Unless otherwise specifically allowed by law, any person making an extension of credit to any person, who shall willfully and knowingly charge, take, or receive interest thereon at a rate exceeding 45 percent per annum or the equivalent rate for a longer or shorter period of time, whether directly or indirectly or conspire so to do, commits a felony of the third degree, punishable as provided in s. 775.082, s. 775.083, or s. 775.084.

[19] "It is a violation of Ch. 687, F. S., for a lender, except those lenders, loans, or securities specifically excepted or exempted by law, to calculate interest on the basis of a 360-day year instead of a 365-day year when an individual is charged the maximum rate of 10 percent interest per annum. The term "per annum" means "by the year" which in its ordinary meaning is understood to mean a period of time of 365 days." Florida Attorney General Opinion 75–269 (October 29, 1975).

[20] Saralegui v. Sacher, Zelman, Van Sant Paul, Beily, Hartman & Waldman, P.A., 19 So. 3d 1048 (Fla. 3d DCA 2009). The court considered a 30-day loan of $300,000 with a repayment of $450,000 and calculated the interest as 600% per year. It also considered a 25-day loan of $200,000 with a repayment of $280,000 and calculated the interest rate as in excess of 580% per year. Clearly the court must have viewed the first loan as 50% per month and the second loan period as 1/14.6th of a year with a rate of approximately 40%. Thus, it used simple division to determine the periodic rate and did not compound.

charge $90 interest. A problem, however, arises if at the end of six months B cannot pay the loan and A lends B the 1090 for another six months. Based on a strict statutory reading, the second loan would bear interest of $98.10, which is exactly 9% of $1,090 and thus not usurious. But if the two loans were viewed as one, the amount loaned would be $1,000 and the amount repaid in one year would be $1,188.10. That is an annual interest rate[21] of 18.81%, which would be usurious. Cases tend not to combine loans for the usury statute.

EXAMPLE 4

Simple Usury Example

A lends B $1,000 for one year. B agrees to pay back $1,180 in one year.

EXAMPLE 5

More Complex Usury Example

A lends B $1,000. B agrees to pay $180 for the year. B actually pays back $900 of principal after one day and $280 in one year.

Based on the initial loan in **Example 5**, the annual simple interest on the "actual principal sum" received is 18% and not usurious. But the daily rate should be a maximum of 0.049%. Viewed fairly, this is two loans: one of $900 for one day, and a second loan of $100 for one year. The maximum interest should be 44 cents for the $900 for one day and an additional $18 for the remaining $100 for the entire year, for a total of $62.38. But, unless a court were to split it into two loans, the single loan would not be usurious. The statute provides:

> For the purpose of this chapter, the rate of interest on any loan, advance of money, line of credit, forbearance to enforce the collection of a debt, or other obligation to pay interest shall be determined and computed *upon the assumption that the debt will be paid according to the agreed terms*, whether or not said loan, advance of money, line of credit, forbearance to enforce collection of a debt, or other obligation is paid or collected by court action prior to its term . . . .[22]

---

[21] Because the hypothetical loan has no payments and last for one year, the *NAI, EFF,* and simple interest amounts are the same.

[22] F.S. 687.03(3).

If, in **Example 5**, B voluntarily pre-pays a portion of the loan early, the loan appears non-usurious. If, instead, the agreement required the early payment, it probably would be usurious. The interest rate on the $100 loan would be 180% (simple, *NAI* or *EFF*). What constitutes a contractual requirement and thus a single loan versus multiple or serial loans is not clear. The issue involves the meaning of "the actual principal sum received."

Litigation regarding "the actual principal sum received" fits into two different categories—neither focusing on timing, as discussed in the prior paragraph. The two categories are:

- Discount loans.

- Serial loans.

a. Discount Loans and Simple Interest

Discount loans—generally those with interest payments deferred to maturity—present interesting situations in usury situations, as well as in tax law. Although a full discussion is beyond this course, some coverage is essential. **Example 5** presented a simple example: $1,000 loaned with $1,180 due in one year: the interest was not due or paid monthly, but was deferred to maturity.

A more complex example involves the treatment of points[23] or other finance charges[24] which the statute considers interest. The Florida usury statute (unlike the federal *APR* statute discussed below and unlike tax laws, discussed briefly below) allocates discount interest oddly. It also calculates the interest rate oddly. Consider a 1982 Florida Supreme Court decision.[25] Under the then-existing usury statute, the maximum rate on secured loans of the type involved was 10% simple interest. The stated loan amount was $290,000 and the various charges were $5,800. The stated interest rate was 9% per year, with all the interest deferred until maturity. The amount due in two years was $342,200. Putting aside whether the charges were interest and assuming they were, the Florida Supreme Court computed the rate as exactly 10% and thus approved the loan, reversing the Second District Court of Appeals, which computed the rate as 10.204% *effective* (using a statutory[26] rather than financial definition of *EFF*). The courts differed on the amount loaned. Admittedly, the statute is not well-drafted. Paragraph (1) of the statute currently reads:

---

[23] A "point" is one percent of the amount loaned and is often considered "pre-paid" interest.

[24] What constitutes interest per the statute is beyond this course. How to calculate the interest rate, however, is within the confines of the course.

[25] St. Petersburg Bank & Trust v. Hamm, 414 So. 2d 1071 (Fla. 1982), reversing Hamm v. St. Petersburg Bank & Trust Co., 379 So. 2d 1300 (Fla. 2d DCA 1980).

[26] F.S. 687.03(3).

(1) *Except as provided herein*, it shall be usury ... to reserve, charge, or take for any loan ... either directly or indirectly, by way of ... *discounts* ... or by any contract, contrivance, or device whatever whereby the debtor is required or obligated to pay a sum of money greater than the *actual principal sum received*, together with interest at the rate of *the equivalent of 18 percent per annum simple interest* ... .[27]

Following that provision, the DCA netted the nominal loan amount ($290,000) with the finance charges (either paid immediately or withheld from the loan) to produce a "principal amount loaned" of $284,200. The court relied on numerous Florida cases similarly netting and referred to the gross or "stated" amount loaned as "fictitious."[28]

The Supreme Court, instead, viewed the "stated amount loaned" as $290,000, relying on a 1977 amendment which added paragraph (3) to the statute:

(3) ... [T]he rate of interest on any loan ... shall be ... computed upon the assumption that the debt will be paid according to the agreed terms, whether or not said loan ... is paid or collected by court action prior to its term, and any payment or property charged, reserved, or taken as an advance or forbearance, which is in the nature of ... interest shall be valued as of the date received and shall be spread over the *stated* term of the loan ... for the purpose of determining the rate of interest. The spreading of any such advance ... for the purpose of computing the rate of interest shall be calculated by first computing the advance ... as a percentage of *the total stated amount of such loan*. ... This percentage shall then be divided by the number of years ... without regard to early maturity in the event of default. The resulting annual percentage rate shall then be added to the *stated* annual percentage rate of interest to produce the effective rate of interest *for purposes of this chapter*.[29]

The Court insisted it must read the statute "literally" and thus found the paragraph (3) usage of "stated amount of such loan" altered the paragraph (1) reference to the "actual principal sum received." Rejecting the DCA's opinion, the Court held the 1977 Legislature intended to change a longstanding rule, which dated to 1906. The Court added: "It is up to the legislature to determine how best to protect the unwary or foolish consumer."[30]

---

[27] F.S. 687.03(1) (2020) (emphasis added).

[28] *Hamm, supra* note 25 at 1304.

[29] F.S. 687.03(3) (2020) (emphasis added).

[30] 414 So 2d at 1074.

Hamm is a disturbing case for many reasons, including the "yield inversion" described below. Other critical observations include:

- Calculating simple interest is anything but simple.

- Calculating simple interest on a discount loan is particularly complex.

- The *Hamm* loan *EFF* was only 9.73065354%, which was less than the 10% simple interest cap.

- F.S. 687.03(3) arguably applies only if a loan is paid or collected early (or so held the DCA). That at least appears to be the issue prompting the 1977 amendment.

- F.S. 687.03(3) uses the term "annual percentage rate" in referring to the paragraph (3) spread calculation. That usage differs from the federal definition of "annual percentage rate" discussed in LESSON FIVE-C.

- F.S. 687.03(3) defines the "effective rate of interest for purposes of this Chapter." That definition of "effective rate" differs substantially from the financial definition of *EFF*.

- Chapter 687 uses the phrase "effective rate of interest" only in 687.03(3), although F.S. 687.125 uses the term "effective yield."

- F.S. 687.03(1) (the general usury rule) is a function of the "equivalent" rate of interest (taking into account direct or indirect "contrivances") rather than the "effective" rate, making the paragraph (3) 4th sentence *superfluous*, if read literally (*as the Court insisted upon doing*) at least for the paragraph (1) operative rule.

Thus Hamm appears incorrectly decided. At the very least, the usury statute is unclear because of its inconsistent definitions (paragraphs (1) and (3) are quite differ in how they calculate interest). Further the dangling use of "effective rate" in paragraph (3) is something that would seem to command Legislative attention.

Consistent with the statute, both courts spread the "finance charge" as well as the stated interest *evenly* over the two-year term. This is odd for two reasons: how both courts described the loan as well as how they calculated the interest rate. The actual financial effective rate on the loan was 9.73% *EFF*, which was below the statutory cap of 10% simple interest per annum or the "equivalent." Part of the problem deals with defining the "amount loaned" and part with the lack of compounding under the statute. Effectively, it results in under-stating the rate in loans of one year or less and over-stating the rate in multi-year loans.

Consider **Example 6**, based on the 1982 decision. Per the usury treatment of discount loans, the amount loaned is $290,000. In reality, it is $287,100 because B either "paid" the $2,900 finance charge immediately or it was withheld from the loan. In any event, B had the use of $287,100 for one year. B had to repay $316,100, which is 109% of $290,000. The Court divides the $2,900 charge by the $290,000 nominal loan amount to compute 1%, which it adds to the stated interest rate of 9%—stated as a percentage of the nominal amount loaned—to calculate a 10% effective rate (as defined in the statute). That was not usurious under the 1982 statute. The DCA, in contrast, divided the 2,900 (plus 9% interest on 2,900) by the actual amount received of $287,100 to obtain an additional charge of 1.1%, which, when added to the stated 9% produced a then usurious rate of 10.101%. In reality, B borrowed $287,100 and repaid $316,100 in one year. That is an interest rate of 10.101% *EFF* (or *NAI* or simple). Thus, for a one-year period, the DCA was financially correct, though arguably statutorily incorrect. The statutory method, as construed by the Supreme Court, under-stated the interest. Interestingly, in the actual case—which involved two years and twice the finance charge—both methods (the Supreme Court's and the DCA's) over-stated the true financial interest rate. Thus the Second DCA method only works correctly (in financial, as opposed to statutory terms) for loans of one year.

EXAMPLE 6

Discount Usury Example

A nominally lends B $290,000 with a finance charge (statutorily interest) of $2,900 and nominal interest stated of 9%.

Computing the financial (true economic) rate on a discount loan with no payments is a fairly simple process. It becomes complex under usury statutes which use "simple interest," which is somewhat ironic. The "simple" method is supposed to be simpler, but is actually very complex and fraught with bizarre consequences (as illustrated further below).

To compute the rate in **Example 6**, open the OID COURSE CALCULATOR. This calculator is actually one I use in an LL.M. tax course, but I include it here because it will solve for a missing interest rate if the loan has no payments (a true discount loan).

ORIGINAL ISSUE DISCOUNT CALCULATOR

Term (years)	1.0	Periodic Interest Rate	4.929028%
Issue Price	$287,100.00	NAI (semi-annual)	9.858057%
Redemption Price	$316,100.00	Effective Interest Rate	10.101010%

Figure 12: Example 6 Effective Rate

To work **Example 6** using an HP 10Bii™ calculator, follow these steps:

The display will read 10.1010101.

Figure 13 illustrates the correct financial rate in *Hamm* (a two-year loan) using the OID CALCULATOR.

ORIGINAL ISSUE DISCOUNT CALCULATOR

Term (years)	2.0	Periodic Interest Rate	4.752400%
Issue Price	$284,200.00	NAI (semi-annual)	9.504800%
Redemption Price	$342,200.00	Effective Interest Rate	9.730654%

Figure 13: Correct Financial Rate in *Hamm*

To work it using a HP 10Bii™, follow the procedure above but substitute 284,200 as the present value and −342,200 as the future value. The answer will be 9.730653541% *EFF* (or *NAI* because it compounds annually). The OID CALCULATOR is set to compound semi-annually because that is what section 1272[31] of the Internal Revenue Code requires.

F.S. § 687.03 describes usury in a way that generally appears to forbid compounding, with a limit of 18% "*simple interest*" in most cases. For a one-year loan in which the initial principal was outstanding for the entire year, that would equal 18% *NAI* compounded annually,[32] or 18% *EFF*. One could also state it as 16.555% *NAI* compounded daily or 16.666% *NAI* compounded monthly. Those stated rates would compound, but would

---

[31] IRC § 1272. Treasury Regulations permit taxpayers to use annual compounding, but the default is semi-annual.

[32] The statute forbids a charge of more than 18% of the initial principal times the number of years outstanding.

produce an effective rate (using the financial as opposed to statutory definition) of 18%.

But for a two-year discount loan (with the initial principal as well as all interest outstanding for the entire two years) the equivalent *EFF* would be 16.619%. Consider **Example 7**. The usury statute permits 18% simple interest, which does not compound for unsecured loans. Thus the maximum permitted interest would be $18,000 (18% of $100,000) each year for two years or $36,000. As a result, the loan to B would not be usurious, but the loan to C would be usurious because under the statute, it has an effective interest rate of 19.62% (39.204 divided by 2). Financially, the loan to B has an interest rate of 16.619% *EFF*, which is thus the statutory usurious rate for a two-year loan. The loan to C has a true interest rate of 18% *EFF*, but the statutory definition of a multi-year effective rate differs. **Figure 14** demonstrates the rate for the loan to B.

EXAMPLE 7

Discount Usury Example

A nominally lends B and C each $100,000 <u>unsecured</u> for two years with all interest deferred to maturity. B must re-pay $136,000 in two years. C must re-pay $139,240 in two years.

Is either loan usurious?

For a five-year loan, the maximum non-usurious *EFF* for a loan with all payments (interest and principal deferred to maturity) is 13.697%. The maximum *NAI* would be the same 13.697% *NAI* compounded annually, 12.906% *NAI* compounded monthly, or 12.839% *NAI* compounded daily (ignoring leap years which appear to affect usury!). **Example 8** considers alternative five-year discount loans. The loan to B is non-usurious because the total interest ($90,000) divided by the number of years (5) is $18,000, which is exactly 18% of the amount loaned. The loan to C, however, is usurious because, using the statutory definition of an effective rate, the interest rate is 25.76%.

ORIGINAL ISSUE DISCOUNT CALCULATOR

Term (years)	2.0	Periodic Interest Rate	7.990295%
Issue Price	$100,000.00	NAI (semi-annual)	15.980590%
Redemption Price	$136,000.00	Effective Interest Rate	16.619038%

Figure 14: Financial Rate for Example 7

EXAMPLE 8

Discount Usury Example

A nominally lends B and C each $100,000 <u>*unsecured*</u> for five years with all interest deferred to maturity. B must re-pay $190,000 in five years. C must re-pay $228,775.78 in five years.

Is either loan usurious?

But, financially, the loan in **Example 8** to B has an interest rate of 13.679% as shown in **Figure 15**. The loan to C, as shown in **Figure 16**, has an interest rate of 18% *EFF*.

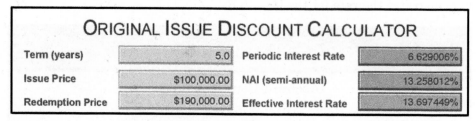

ORIGINAL ISSUE DISCOUNT CALCULATOR

Term (years)	5.0	Periodic Interest Rate	6.629006%
Issue Price	$100,000.00	NAI (semi-annual)	13.258012%
Redemption Price	$190,000.00	Effective Interest Rate	13.697449%

Figure 15: Example 8 Loan B Effective Rate

ORIGINAL ISSUE DISCOUNT CALCULATOR

Term (years)	5.0	Periodic Interest Rate	8.627805%
Issue Price	$100,000.00	NAI (semi-annual)	17.255610%
Redemption Price	$228,775.78	Effective Interest Rate	18.000000%

Figure 16: Example 8 Loan C Effective Rate

If all that seems un-duly complex, you are in the right place, because it is absurdly complex, if not bizarre. Why? The answer is because interest compounds, not only on principal, but also on interest. That is the only logical method of computing an investment yield. Capping annual interest rates using usury laws is understandable at some level of consumer protection. But capping it as a function of the term of the loan, with such a declining permitted effective rate seems at best very strange. One wonders whether the drafters actually understood what they were doing. Assuming they did, one wonders why they failed to use traditional financial terminology. They could have simply said, interest compounds continuously during the loan period on the outstanding balance. The maximum effective rate is 18% for a loan of one year or less, 16.619% for a loan greater than one-year but less than two, etc. Had they done so, anyone with a financial calculator and a clear definition of "interest" (*e.g.*, do we include application fees, points, closing costs, and such) could then compute the effective rate and compare it to the statute.

The unfortunate use of the term "simple interest" however, creates a sliding scale of maximums and far more complexity than is needed. In financial terms, it creates an inverted yield curve, which economically is quite strange. Short term interest rates typically are below those of longer terms because they involve less risk.

If the loan is secured by a mortgage, the statute permits compounding and thus becomes feasible: the maximum rate for a secured loan is thus 18% effective or 16.555 *NAI* with daily compounding. With scheduled monthly payments, I would be comfortable with 16.666% *NAI* compounded monthly; but, on an unsecured loan, I would state it in terms of daily compounding and specifically exclude interest compounding from year to year.

b. Serial Loans

Serial loans—in which the borrower uses a new loan to pay-off the prior loan—present interesting legal issues. Many are covered by Chapter 560 of the Florida Statutes which covers, inter alia, payday loans. Treatment of those covered by the usury statute has been inconsistent.

A complicated, but fairly common, 1985 appellate case is worth reading as it illustrates the problem. Note it is a summary judgment, which means the court found no disputed issues of material fact. I find the decision particularly noteworthy for two reasons. First, it refuses to combine loans (at least the first two) which strike me as effectively a single loan, particularly when applying a statute "for substance" and a statute that should protect consumers. Second, the court mis-calculates the interest rates—which is the point of this course. It stated Loan One charged a rate of 14%, but it actually charged 15.893% *EFF*. It stated Loan Two charged 15.5%, but it actually charged 16.58% if one believes the difficult-to-believe form of the loan. Substantively, Loan Two charged 20.64% *EFF*. Together the two loans charged 18.24% *EFF*. The Third Loan just made things worse. That the bank won this case on summary judgement is at best disturbing. Most disturbing is the following statutory language defining usury as a loan which:

> either *directly or indirectly*, by way of commission for advances, *discounts*, or exchange, or by any contract, *contrivance*, or device whatever whereby the debtor is required or obligated to pay a sum of money greater than the actual principal sum received, together with interest at the rate of the equivalent of 18 percent per annum simple interest . . .[33]

---

[33] F.S. 687.03(1).

If the series of loans and "escrow" accounts is not a "contrivance," then one wonders what would be.

REBMAN V. FLAGSHIP FIRST NAT'L BANK

472 So. 2d 1360 (Fla. 2d DCA 1985)
(emphasis and comments added)

DANAHY, JUDGE.

Loan One

$21,000 loaned with $24,337.53 owed at year-end, **charges 15.893%** *EFF*, *not* **the stated 14%.** Thus Loan One understated the interest rate and the Court did not comment on that fact.

The pay-off amount must have been $30,000 (loan two) less the extra $5,662.47, which equals $24,337.53.

This is an appeal from a **summary judgment** of mortgage foreclosure. The only issue involves usury. We affirm the judgment and the finding of the trial judge that the mortgagee bank did not charge the mortgagor, Virginia W. Rebman, a usurious rate of interest.

Loan Two

Loan Two was for $24,337.53 (loan one pay-off) with a balance due in one year of $29,360 (loan three amount).

It had a stated amount of 30,000 and "monthly payments of $430.19) but the $5,662.47 "holdback" was unavailable to the borrower (she had no signature card on Loan Two, unlike Loan Three). The lender held the amount at zero interest and used it nominally to make monthly payments to itself. I find it difficult to locate any substance to the "holdback" or to the "payments." For a court that claims to apply "substance" over "form," this is an odd structure to approve.

Loan Two thus charged 20.6367% *EFF*, which is usurious and significantly greater than the stated rate of 15.5%. Taken at face, a loan of $30,000 with monthly payments of $430.19 and an amount due of $29,360 in one year, the loan charged 16.58% *EFF* and 15.44% *NAI*.

The mortgage secured three loans evidenced by three promissory notes which were made at different times. The **first note** was for one year in the principal amount of $21,000 and carried an interest rate **of 14% per**

annum. The **second note**, executed a year later, was for a term of one year, in the principal amount of $30,000 with interest at the rate of 15 1/2% per annum. The proceeds of that note paid off the balance of the first note and the remaining $5,662.47 was deposited in the bank in a non-interest-bearing account entitled "Virginia W. Rebman Escrow Account, Mike Willingham."[1] According to Rebman's affidavit, **she signed no signature card and was not allowed to make withdrawals from this account because "the funds were there for the purpose of paying payments on the mortgage."** Bank records show that the only transactions involving this account were monthly withdrawals equal to Rebman's $430.19 monthly mortgage payment of principal and interest. These account transactions continued until the funds were depleted, approximately one year later. At about the same time, Rebman executed the **third promissory note** for $29,360 with interest at the rate of 17% per annum. A handwritten notation on the bottom of the second note indicates that the third note was a renewal of the second note. Each of the three notes contained the following clause:

In no event shall the interest charged hereunder be in excess of the legal maximum rate of interest (if any) allowed by applicable law as the law now exists or as the law may be changed in the future to allow higher rates of interest, and in the event that interest is charged at a rate in excess of the maximum rate allowed, any excess sums collected by the Bank shall be applied as a reduction to principal, it being the intent of the Maker hereof and the Bank that the Maker pay no more and the Bank collect no more than the sums allowed using a lawful rate of interest.

Two months later Rebman executed yet another promissory note, which was unsecured, for $2,762.40 with an interest rate of 15% per annum. [* * * *]

Rebman contends that since she did not have use of the funds in the escrow account, those funds should be treated as an "advance" or "forbearance" in computing the effective rate of interest under Florida's general usury law, chapter 687, Florida Statutes (1983). **The bank argues that there is no evidence that the opening or maintenance of the account was a requirement of the bank.** The trial court rejected Rebman's contention and in doing so stated:

By placing a portion of the principal amount in escrow to assure timely repayment, the bank placed itself in the position of escrow agent for the defendant vis-a-vis the escrowed money. Since the bank did not retain an ownership interest in the money and could use it only to make the monthly loan payments, the principal

---

[1] Mike Willingham was a bank officer.

amount was not thereby reduced. A usurious interest rate was not charged.

> This is a question of fact, which her affidavit and the lack of a signature card appear to dispute. Would the bank actually have allowed her to withdraw those funds? Doubtful.

We agree with the trial court and begin our discussion by noting the four requirements necessary to establish a usurious transaction. They are:

1. A loan, either express or implied.

2. An understanding between the lender and the borrower that the money must be repaid.

3. For such loan a greater rate of interest than is allowed by law shall be paid or agreed to be paid.

4. There must be a corrupt intent on the part of the lender to take more than the legal rate of interest for the use of the money loaned.

[* * * *] The burden to establish these elements of usury is on the borrower. [* * * *]

While we agree that Rebman did prove the first and second requirements, she did not prove the third and fourth. [* * * *]

This section thus requires interest to be calculated upon the "actual principal sum received." **Florida courts have defined that term to mean the actual money _distributed_ by the lender to the borrower at the time of closing.** [* * * *] In this regard, Rebman asks this court to treat the escrowed monies as a forbearance in the form of an interest reserve or alternatively as a compensating balance account. She therefore argues that the effective rate of interest should be computed according to the "spreading" formula set forth in section 687.03(3), Florida Statutes (1983), and approved in _St. Petersburg Bank & Trust Co. v. Hamm_, 414 So.2d 1071 (Fla. 1982).

A court should seek substance over form when it analyzes the amount of "actual principal sum received" for purposes of usury calculations. _See Mindlin._ Accordingly, any amounts advanced by a lender which directly or indirectly benefit the borrower—as well as any amounts directly received by a borrower—should be a part of the principal used for calculating interest under our usury law. That being so, **although the escrowed monies never passed through Rebman's hands, they were used exclusively to benefit her in the payment of her monthly principal and interest obligation.** Consequently, we find appellant's argument that the escrow accounts were in fact compensating balance or interest reserve accounts established for the bank's benefit is without merit. In its simplest form, a compensating balance is an amount a lender contractually requires a borrower to leave on deposit during the term of the loan; an interest reserve account is an express contractual designation of a portion of the loan to be used to pay interest that will accrue on that loan. These two practices are discussed in *Practice Under Florida Usury Law*, sections 4.33 and 4.34 at 114 through 116 (Florida Bar Continuing Legal Education Practice Manual, 1982).

> The lender held the money and paid itself. The borrower never had the funds and never had access to them. Describing this as substantively "distributed" to her is difficult to fathom.

In the case before us, the loan documents in evidence contain no bank requirement that either the operation or maintenance of the escrow account was a condition of the loan, and in her affidavit Rebman never stated that it was. Further, the bank records revealed that the deposited funds did not remain in either escrow account during the entire loan period but instead were used to pay monthly interest and principal on Rebman's obligation until these funds were depleted. This evidence is not refuted by Rebman's affidavit. Consequently, there are no facts to be found, nor inferences which remain, after the findings by the trial judge here that the escrow account was merely encouraged by the bank and that the escrow account was established as a convenience for Rebman. Additionally, it is not disputed that Rebman authorized the bank to make withdrawals from the subsequent escrow account, that she executed additional notes to obtain funds to make the accrued payments on the third note, that she made a subsequent deposit to one of the escrow accounts, and that the stated interest rate on the face of each note was within the legal limit. Therefore, there is no indication that the principal balance was or should be reduced by the amounts placed in the escrow accounts. The only conclusion to be reached in this case is that a greater rate of interest than is allowed by law was neither paid nor agreed to be paid.

> This appears to be a contrivance to charge more than the statutory rate.

Turning to the fourth necessary element, corrupt intent, we note that the statute imposes a penalty only on those lenders who "willfully" violate it. § 687.04, Fla. Stat. (1983). Generally, the question of intent is one of fact. However, in this particular instance where there is no conflict in material facts, that question is one of law for the court. *See Johnson v. Gulf Life Insurance Co.*, 429 So.2d 744 (Fla. 3d DCA 1983). The circumstances surrounding the entire transaction, together with the stated interest rate and the disclaimer clause found on the face of each note, conclusively show that the bank did not willfully or knowingly charge or accept excessive interest in connection with the loan. Moreover, Rebman made neither an allegation nor a showing that the bank had a purposeful intent to violate the law, as was her burden. Therefore we think the trial judge was correct in his finding that the loan is not usurious and that Rebman is not entitled to cancellation of her obligation. For these reasons, we affirm the summary judgment entered by the trial judge in favor of the bank.

> The "disclaimer clause" is _arguably_ sufficient to preclude criminal liability, but that sort of "fine print" seems to be a "contrivance."

BOARDMAN, EDWARD F., (RET.) J., concurs.

GRIMES, ACTING CHIEF JUDGE, dissenting.

My quarrel with the majority opinion is that it overlooks the fact that this case was decided on summary judgment.

According to 45 Am.Jur.2d _Interest and Usury_ § 113 (1969):

If as a condition of making a loan the borrower is required to leave part of the money on deposit with the lender, the transaction is usurious if the interest paid for the loan amounts to more than legal interest on the sum actually available for the use of the borrower.

As stated in the annotation at 92 A.L.R. 3d 769, 774 (1979), entitled "Leaving Part of Loan on Deposit With Lender as Usury":

It is generally recognized that if as a condition of making a loan, the borrower is required to leave part of the money on deposit with the lender, the transaction is usurious where the interest paid for the loan amounts to more than the legal interest on the balance left in the borrower's hands for his actual use.

For a case involving the application of this rule under Florida law, see _American Acceptance Corp. v. Schoenthaler_, 391 F.2d 64 (5th Cir. 1968), _cert. denied_, 392 U.S. 928, 88 S.Ct. 2287, 20 L. Ed. 2d 1387 (1968).

Significantly, in its brief the bank conceded that if the funds in the escrow account were considered as being taken as an advance or forbearance, the effective rate of interest computed according to the formula proved in _St. Petersburg Bank & Trust Co. v. Hamm_, 414 So.2d 1071 (Fla. 1982), would **approximate 23%.**[3] Therefore, the pivotal

---

[3] The bank may have conceded more than necessary because monies in the account were used to meet the interest payments under the loan as they became due. Therefore, even if the escrow account was a condition of the loan, the bank could logically argue that in computing the effective rate of interest, consideration should be given to the fact that appellant was only deprived

question is whether the bank required the establishment of the escrow account as a condition of the loan.

I find it difficult to believe that Rebman would voluntarily place a portion of the loan proceeds in a non-interest bearing account controlled entirely by the bank if she were not required to do so in order to obtain the loan. In any event, the bank presented no evidence that the opening of the escrow account was not a condition of the loan, and ***for purposes of summary judgment, the burden of proof was on the bank***.

Moreover, if the effective rate of interest was usurious, I cannot see how it can be said on summary judgment that there was no corrupt intent. It may be that the corrupt intent required for usury would be negated by the clause appearing in each note which provides that interest shall not exceed the maximum allowable rate of interest and that any excess shall be applied to the reduction of principal. However, this issue has not yet been argued by either side and **disclaimer clauses such as this have not always been effective to preclude a finding of usury.** *See Oklahoma Preferred Finance & Loan Corp. v. Morrow*, 497 P.2d 221 (Okla. 1972); Practice Under Florida Usury Law § 1.21 (Fla. Bar Continuing Legal Educ. Practice Manual, 1982).

I would reverse and remand for further proceedings in which these issues could be fully explored.

QUESTIONS

1. If someone uses the phrase "5% interest per year," what exactly do they mean?

2. Distinguish a nominal annual interest rate from an effective interest rate.

3. If a loan has monthly payments, can the compounding period be weekly when using a financial calculator?

4. What is a discount loan? Provide an example.

5. If the loan amount is $1,000, the term is two years, all interest is deferred to maturity and the effective interest rate is 10%, how much is owed in one year? In two years?

6. If the loan amount is $1,000, the term is two years, all interest is deferred to maturity and the interest rate is 10% simple interest, how much is owed in one year? In two years?

---

of the use of the escrow funds until they were applied to meet her interest payments on the loan. This record contains no such computations.

7.   If a bank is advertising the interest rate it pays on deposits, is it likely to emphasize the effective rate or the nominal rate and compounding period?

8.   If a bank is advertising rates on a loan, is it likely to emphasize the effective interest rate or the nominal rate and payment period?

9.   If a certificate of deposit accumulates interest compounded monthly, which is higher, the *EFF* or the *NAI*?

10.   Define a self-amortizing loan. Between the borrower and lender, does interest normally compound on such a loan, assuming all payments are timely? From the perspective of the borrower, does the interest compound? From the perspective of the lender does the interest compound? Are the two perspectives the same? If they differ, why do they differ?

B. INTEREST RATE CONVERSION
(LESSON FIVE-B)

Lesson Objectives

1.   Student will learn *how to* use the INTEREST CONVERSION CALCULATOR.

- How to locate the Instructions.

- How to find Definitions of each Function.

- How to jump from one calculator to another, depending on which conversion you need.

2.   Student will learn the *formulae* for the Interest Conversions:

Effective Rate:	Nominal Rate:
$$100\left(\left(1+\frac{pr}{100}\right)^{py} - 1\right)$$	$$100py\left(\left(1+\frac{eff}{100}\right)^{\frac{1}{py}} - 1\right)$$
pr = periodic rate	py = payments per year
py = payments per year	eff = effective rate

3.   Student will learn *when* a lawyer would need to convert an interest rate to an equivalent interest rate in a different form:

- **As a lawyer, you may be given an effective rate, but you need to know the period rate or the nominal, uncompounded rate; or, you may be given a periodic rate and you need to know the equivalent effective rate.**

4.   Student will *work* some practical examples of situations in which a lawyer would need to convert and interest rate.

5. Student will *learn* that the various forms of an interest rate are mathematical equivalents.

———

LESSON FIVE-B covers how to convert an interest rate from one of the three statements of a rate—effective, nominal, periodic—into the others. The INTEREST CONVERSION CALCULATOR accomplishes this. As explained in prior LESSONS, the proper statement of an interest rate is essential.

The INTEREST CONVERSION CALCULATOR contains three separate calculators in one:

- Converting a Known Effective Rate into the Equivalent Nominal and Periodic Rates.

- Converting a Known Nominal Rate into the Equivalent Effective and Periodic Rates.

- Converting a Known Periodic Rate into the Equivalent Effective and Nominal Rates.

Key to understanding the conversion involves the word *Equivalent*. These are three different ways of stating the same thing. The results are exactly the same (subject, of course, to rounding and the choice of how many decimals to use).

The 3 calculators appear below.

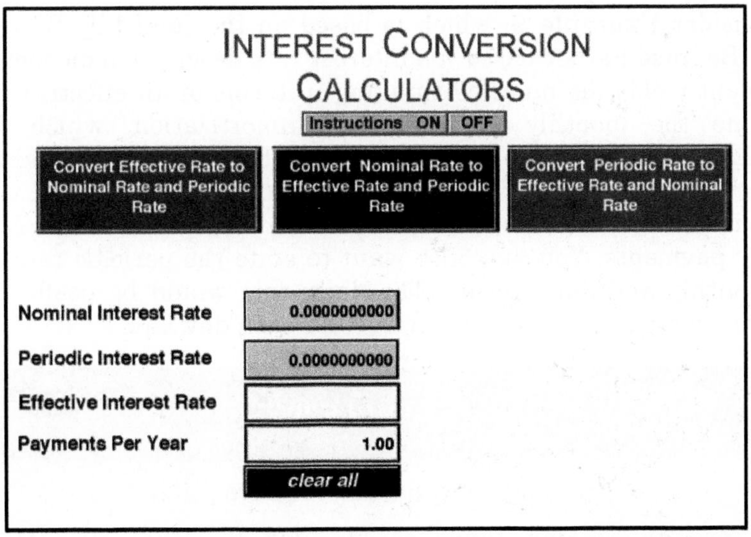

Figure 17: Converting Effective Rate to Nominal and Periodic Rates

Figure 17 illustrates the INTEREST CONVERSION CALCULATOR set for a known effective rate. To use it, open the INTEREST CONVERSION CALCULATOR and click on the ***brown*** button:

> **Convert Effective Rate to Nominal Rate and Periodic Rate**

This will set the Effective Interest Rate box as white and will allow you to enter that known rate. The Nominal Interest Rate and Periodic Interest Rate boxes will appear in green. You will not be able to change them, as they provide the solutions. The compounding period is the other information you must know. The calculator labels this as "Payments Per Year," but that term can also refer to "Periods Per Year." If the instrument has regular payments, the compounding period must be the same as the payment period. Thus monthly payments result in monthly compounding and 12 periods per year. Similarly, quarterly payments result in quarterly compounding and 4 periods per year.

As with all the calculators, you can click on the Instructions ON Button and some basic instructions will appear. Click on the OFF button and the instructions will disappear. If you forget the meaning of terms, let your cursor hover on the blue words and a definition of the term will appear. Move your cursor away and the definition will disappear.

Consider **Example 9**, which is based on the Real Life Story Three earlier. Because Father based his interest rate description on comparable investment yields, he must be thinking in terms of an effective rate. To determine the monthly payments (an amortization, which LESSON THIRTEEN covers in greater depth), you must know the Nominal Annual Interest Rate with monthly payments: the AMORTIZATION CALCULATOR will require it. The loan document should state the rate in terms of an *NAI* with monthly payments. You may also want to state the periodic rate with in both monthly and daily terms. The daily rate would be useful for late payments, which should accrue interest for each day late.

EXAMPLE 9

Known Effective Rate

Father wants to lend funds to Son for 15 years with monthly repayments. He described the interest rate as 6.5% per year. He based his choice on what similarly-sized savings accounts yielded annually.

You are asked to draft the loan and mortgage documents.

Figure 18 illustrates the initial conversion. Type 6.5 in the Effective Interest Rate box and 12 in the Payments Per Year box. The answers appear in the green boxes. A 6.314033% *NAI* with monthly payments is equivalent to 6.5% *EFF*. You would probably round this to 6.31 or 6.314% *NAI*. The equivalent monthly periodic rate is 0.5261694277%. But, that periodic rate is not particularly useful because both the COURSE CALCULATORS and the HP 10Bii™ use the *NAI* and internally convert it to the equivalent periodic rate, at least for the initial amortization and determination of the monthly payment. LESSON THIRTEEN covers this in greater depth. What you probably would want to know is the equivalent daily periodic rate so that you could apply it to late payments.

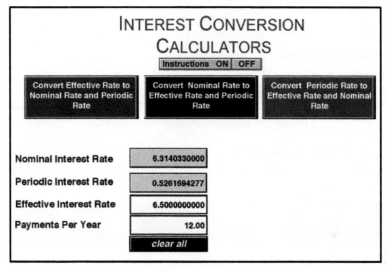

Figure 18: Example 9 Conversion to Monthly *NAI* and PIR

Figure 19 illustrates how to determine the equivalent daily periodic rate. Enter 365 into the Payments Per Year box, replacing the 12 used in **Figure 17**. The *NAI* changes to 6.298% and the Periodic Rate changes to 0.172548581%, which you would likely round to 0.173%. If the loan payments are due on the first of each month, you may want to provide they earn interest at the daily rate until paid. Typically a bank or other commercial lender will allow a five-day grace period before a payment is subject to a "late" charge, but it nevertheless typically will charge interest at the daily rate during the five days (as well as after, if the payment is very late). In a family situation, you may choose not to include such provisions, but you need to know how to compute them if needed. The loan should describe the interest rate as 6.31% nominal annual interest with monthly payments, but with a daily periodic rate of 0.173% for payments made after the first of each month (or whatever the due date is). For clarity, you may also want to disclose these rate are equivalent to 6.5% effective interest. If the loan is subject to disclosure of the *APR* (discussed in LESSON

FIVE-C), you would also describe that. For this particular loan, the *APR* would be 6.31%.

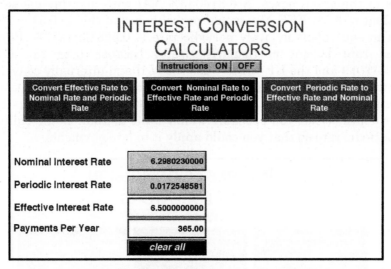

Figure 19: Example 9 Daily Periodic Rate

To convert the known effective rate to the equivalent nominal rate with monthly compounding (or payments) using a HP 10Bii™ calculator, follow these steps:

The display will read 6.314033132.

To compute the daily periodic rate, follow these steps:

The display will read 6.098023211. Divide this by 365 to obtain 0.1725%.

Example 10 continues the Real Life Story Three, but with a twist. In this scenario, Father based his interest rate choice by examining what commercial lenders charge for similar home loans. In this case, Father is clearly thinking in terms of a nominal rate with monthly payments. You could simply divide the 6.5 by 12 to determine the monthly rate; however, as explained earlier, the AMORTIZATION CALCULATOR and the HP 10Bii™ will do that for you internally. For drafting the loan, you do not require the equivalent effective rate; however, you may want to compute it. But to compute the equivalent daily rate, you should[34] know the effective rate. **Figure 20** illustrates the INTEREST CONVERSION CALCULATOR set to convert a known nominal rate to the equivalent effective and periodic rates.

EXAMPLE 10

Known Nominal Rate

Father wants to lend funds to Son for 15 years with monthly repayments. He described the interest rate as 6.5% per year. He based his choice on what lenders are currently charging for similarly-sized 15-year home mortgage loans.

You are asked to draft the loan and mortgage documents.

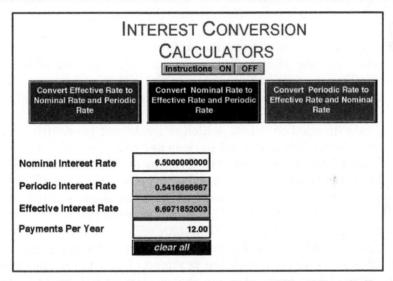

Figure 20: Example 10 Converting Known *NAI* to *EFF* and Periodic Rates

To work this, open the INTEREST CONVERSION CALCULATOR and press the Blue Button. That will open the Nominal Interest Rate box, which will appear white. The effective and periodic rate boxes will appear green and you will not be able to change them. For **Example 10**, enter 6.5 as the Nominal Interest Rate and 12 as the Payments Per Year. The monthly periodic rate is 0.54166666667%, which is 6.5 divided by 12. The equivalent effective rate is 6.6971852003%. By describing the 6.5% interest rate as nominal rather than effective, Father has actually increased the rate he is charging Son. In **Example 9**, the effective rate was 6.5%, but in **Example**

---

[34] Converting the *NAI* to an *EFF* and then converting that to a periodic rate with 365 periods is probably best. In the alternative, you could use the *NAI* as the *EFF* and set the number of periods as 30.

10, it is 6.697%. The difference is not huge, but it does make a difference. For example, if the loan amount is $250,000, **Example 9** produces a monthly payment of $2,141.03, while **Example 10** produces a monthly payment of $2,166.04. The difference is $25.01 per month for fifteen years. LESSON THIRTEEN explains how to compute the monthly payment amount.

> ### Convert Nominal Rate to Effective Rate and Periodic Rate

To draft the loan, you would state the interest rate as 6.5% nominal annual interest with monthly payments. If you also want to state a daily rate to apply for late payments, you will need to make another adjustment. **Figure 21** illustrates what to do. It uses the INTEREST CONVERSION CALCULATOR set to a known effective rate (by pressing the Brown Button). Before I did this, I put my cursor in the green Effective Interest Rate box from **Figure 17**. The rate appeared to fourteen decimals. I copied it and then clicked on the Brown Button to open the known effective rate calculator. Then I pasted the number in the Effective Interest Rate box, which appeared to 10 decimals on the screen and I entered 365 as the number of Periods Per Year (using the Payments Per Year box). The nominal rate dropped to 6.48%, which is irrelevant for drafting the loan because this is the *NAI* using 365 periods per year. For the loan, you need the *NAI* using 12 periods per year (6.5%). The daily periodic rate is 0.178% rounded to three decimals. If you entered 6.7 or 6.697 as the effective rate, you would show the same daily periodic rate, at least to three decimals, which is all that is significant. This is the number you would use in the loan for late payments. LESSON THIRTEEN will cover this in more depth. But, you should understand that for late payments, this is traditionally not interest due or to be paid with the payment. The monthly payment will stay the same; however, the portion that is interest will change, and thus the portion that is principal will change. This will essentially require a new amortization table, which LESSON THIRTEEN covers. Commercial lenders will do this. In a family situation as described in **Examples 9** and **10**, you may decide the re-computation of the amortization is not worth the trouble. If so, as further explained in LESSON THIRTEEN, you must then either charge the extra daily interest currently or forgo it and not charge it at all. Do not worry about that now, as we will cover it in due time. For now, just learn how to convert one statement of an interest rate to another.

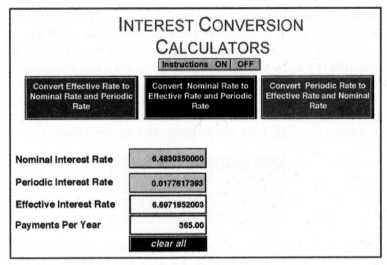

Figure 21: Example 10 Daily Periodic Rate

To work **Example 10** using a HP 10Bii™ calculator, follow these steps:

The display will show 6.697185200. Note you must enter the nominal rate using the shift key. If you do not use the shift key as shown, you may press the shift/*EFF*% twice to obtain the answer.

To compute the daily rate, enter:

The display will show 6.482861222. Divide this number by 365 to obtain 0.1776%.

EXAMPLE 11

Known Periodic Rate

A wants to lend funds to B one month and charge 1.5% interest.

You are asked to draft the loan and to calculate the *APR* as well as the effective rate and daily rate (in case of a late payment).

Example 11 posits a known monthly Periodic Rate and asks you to convert it to an *APR*, an *EFF* and to a daily periodic rate. Unfortunately, the example does not define a month, which is important for the daily rate: months vary from 28 to 31 days. Determination of the *APR* and the *EFF* does not require knowing which month is involved. As covered in LESSON FIVE-C, an *APR* is a nominal rate assuming the loan has not points or other finance charges treated as interest. Because **Example 11** states no such charge, the *APR* and the *NAI* must be the same. To compute these, as well as the *EFF*, open the INTEREST CONVERSION CALCULATOR and set it to convert a known periodic rate. To do this, click on the Green Button:

> **Convert Periodic Rate to Effective Rate and Nominal Rate**

The Periodic Interest Rate box will appear in white and will allow you to change the number. The Nominal Interest Rate and Effective Interest Rate boxes will appear in green and will not permit changes. As shown in **Figure 22**, type 1.5 as the periodic rate and 12 as the Payments Per Year.

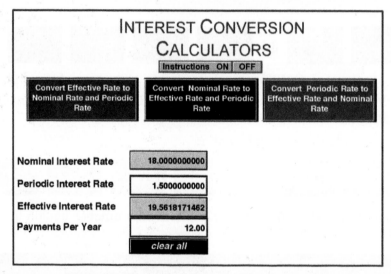

Figure 22: Example 11 Periodic Rate Conversion

The *NAI* will appear as 18, which is also the *APR* (because the loan lacked points or other charges treated as interest under the statute). The *EFF* is 19.56%. To determine the daily rate (using 365 days per year[35]) one must copy the *EFF* and then paste it into the effective interest rate box with the INTEREST CONVERSION CALCULATOR set to a known effective rate (the Brown Button). After inserting 19.56 as the effective rate and 365 as the Payments Per Year (redefined for this purpose as Periods Per Year),

---

[35] Leap years have 366 days. A common finance convention permits the assumption of a 360 day year and a 30 day month.

the new daily periodic rate will appear as 0.04896%. **Figure 23** illustrates this conversion.

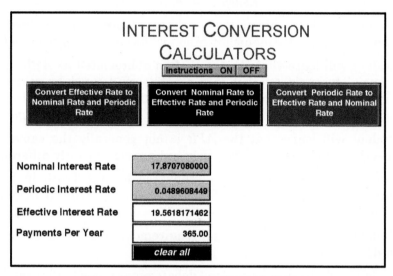

Figure 23: Example 11 Daily Periodic Rate

To work **Example 11** using a HP 10Bii™ calculator, follow these steps:

The display will read **19.561817146**, which you should round to **19.56%** *EFF*. Then, without clearing the calculator, input:

The display will show 17.870708390. Divide this by 365 to obtain 0.4896.

QUESTIONS

1. Convert 10% *EFF* to the equivalent *NAI* compounded monthly.

2. Convert 6% *NAI* compounded quarterly to the equivalent *EFF*.

3. Convert a periodic rate of 1% per month to the equivalent *NAI* and *EFF*.

C. ANNUAL PERCENTAGE RATE (LESSON FIVE-C)

Lesson Objectives

1. Student will learn about the legal term *"Annual Percentage Rate."* They will briefly distinguish it from an *"Annual Percentage Yield."*

2. Student will learn that the term, often abbreviated as **APR**, is not a financial term; instead, it is a legal term defined by statute and regulation. They will briefly learn about the **APY**, which is also a legal term and the subject of **LESSON FIVE-D**: *Annual Percentage Yield*.

3. Student will learn that the *APR* is not generally the same as the Effective Interest Rate. Often they two are significantly different.

4. Student will read and briefly study the federal Truth in Lending Statute creating the term *APR*, as well as the Federal Regulations defining the term.

5. Student will learn general legal requirements regarding disclosure of an *APR*.

6. Student will hear discussion and debate regarding whether the federal *APR* disclosure requirements favor banks over consumers. Arguably, the *APR* is a misleading rate in most cases; hence, it falsely lures consumers into believing loan rates are more favorable than they truly are. Whether this aspect of the "Truth in Lending Law" resulted from Congressional misunderstanding of finance or from intentional deception is left to the Student to decide. Some students may decide *APR* disclosure requirements actually help consumers; however, such students should review the mathematical calculations and economic impacts of the loans involved.

Terminology Introduced

- Annual Percentage Rate
- Annual Percentage Yield
- Point

We consider the term Annual Percentage Rate in LESSON FIVE-C. In credit transactions not involving *points* or some other fees, the *annual percentage rate* <u>formula</u> equals the *nominal annual interest rate* <u>formula</u>. The components may differ because the *APR* is mostly about the components of interest, rather than the computation. Assuming no fees or other costs of borrowing (e.g., closing costs, application fees), the *APR* and the *NAI* are the same.

However, transactions involving *points* and some other fees have an *annual percentage rate* that reflects both the *nominal* rate and the *compounded* amortized effect of the points or other fees. United States Federal Law requires disclosure of this rate law for most credit transactions. "*APR*" is the typical abbreviation. The legal definition appears in federal statute, 15 U.S.C. § 1606. Arguably—as explained in LESSON FIVE-B and below—the Truth in Lending Law requirement that lenders disclose the *APR* actually favors banks and misleads borrowers.

Of critical importance, the *APR* does not equal the *EFF* (*effective interest rate*) unless the obligation *compounds* annually. Financial Calculators always have an *EFF* function; however, they rarely have an *APR* function, as it is a legal rather than a financial term.

Other nations also use the term *Annual Percentage Rate* and abbreviate it as *APR*. Several of them define it differently than does U.S. law.[36] For example, the EU defines it as a compounded rate. The formula is complicated because it is a function of timing and compounding, with the possibility of cash-flow changes. The current general EU formula is:

$$\sum_{k=1}^{m} C_k \, (1 + X)^{-t_k} \; = \; \sum_{l=1}^{m'} D_l \, (1 + X)^{-S_l}$$

> Where $X = APR$, m is the number of the last "drawdown" (loan), k is the number of a drawdown (thus $1 \le k \le m$), C_k is the amount of drawdown k, t_k is the interval, expressed in years and fractions of a year, between the date of the first drawdown and the date of each subsequent drawdown, thus $t_1 = O$, m' is the number of the last repayment or payment of charges, l is the number of a repayment or payment of charges, D_l is the amount of a repayment or payment of charges, S_l is the interval, expressed in years and fractions of a year, between the date of the first drawdown and the date of each repayment or payment of charges.

Some member nations modify the definition; hence, be careful with international contracts. Lawyers must therefore be *very careful* when using the term contractually. They must define the meaning in relation to the law of a particular jurisdiction.

The COURSE CALCULATORS *do not* directly compute an *APR*, although the following explanation explains how you can use them indirectly. Neither does the HP 10Bii™, though with a few extra steps, one can do it. Some financial calculators have an *APR* button; however, at least some of them compute the value incorrectly,[37] so be very careful. This is a term-of-

---

[36] *E.g.,* F.S. 687.03(3). *But see,* Cal Fin. Code § 4970 (defining an *APR* by reference to the federal definition).

[37] I've only seen one hand-held with an inaccurate *APR* function. I have long forgotten the brand, but I clearly recall it computed it as a compounded rate—essentially, an *EFF*. Indeed, it was the only handheld I've owned that had an *APR* function. Various internet sites compute an *APR*. Some do so correctly, but some do not.

art for U.S. federal law purposes with a very technical definition, just as it is a term-of-art for EU purposes, with a very different and also very technical definition.

1.   COMPUTING AN *APR* WITH NO FEES OR POINTS

Computing the *APR* for a loan with no "points" or other amortizable closing costs is simple: it is merely the nominal annual interest rate. Hence, for a credit card loan with a monthly periodic rate of one percent, the *APR* is 12%. With a monthly periodic rate of 1.5%, the *APR* is 18. Those amounts are simply the *NAI*, which is uncompounded. Credit cards issuers, however, routinely compound interest on unpaid balances. Thus a 12% *APR* is more _akin_ to a 12.6825 *EFF* %. An 18% *APR* is _akin_ to a 19.5618% *EFF*. I use the word "akin" because the comparison holds only on amounts unpaid for the entire year.

Consider some examples. If you charge $100 on a credit card with no fees and if you pay the entire balance by the due date, you incur zero interest. Your actual rate—*vis a vis* you and the lender—is zero. If, instead, you pay the minimum amount due, carry over the remainder, and then pay the entire amount after one month, the interest charged is the periodic rate for the period outstanding (be careful about that definition). Both the *NAI* and the *APR* would be the same: the periodic rate times the number of periods in a year. If the period is one month and the rate is 1.5%, then the *NAI* and the *APR* are both 18. If, instead, you carry a $100 balance for the entire year, routinely making new charges and also minimum payments such that your principal balance remains $100, you will owe $119.56 at the end of the year. The *NAI* and the *APR* remain 18, but the *EFF*—between you and the borrower—is 19.56.

Computing an *EFF* on a credit card—or on any amortizing loan (one with payments)—requires assumptions. _As a result, it is not accurate._ Nevertheless, it is arguably more useful than the mere *APR*. Consider the first example: you borrowed $100 for one month, paid it off timely, and thus incurred no interest charge. From the point of view of the lender, the rate (ignoring charges to stores which use the card) is not zero as computed above. Indeed, it is zero _between you and the lender_, but the lender had opportunity costs: it could have invested the funds elsewhere or, if it borrowed the funds to lend to you, it need not have done so. As a result, from the point of view of the borrower, the rate was negative (again, ignoring the profit it made from the store).

Your point of view is similar. You charged the $100 for the month (or whatever the "interest-free" period was). Had you not done so, you would have used funds for the purchase that otherwise you could have invested or which you actually used to pay off another loan or spent elsewhere. Such lost opportunities are real. They are difficult to measure because they are personal to the borrower and to the lender. Possibly, you or the lender _used_ (the lender) or _could have used_ (you) idle currency which bore zero return. But, even that has a cost, as explained in LESSON SIX: the liquidity cost of money, which ranges from 1.5% to 3.5% _EFF_, depending on the authority.

EXAMPLE 12

Credit Card _APR_ Calculation

Typically, a credit card will have a monthly rate of interest, perhaps 1.5%.

To compute the _APR_, multiple 1.5 times 12 to get 18 as the _APR_.

Loans (ignoring application and other fees not labeled as interest) may have a weekly or daily rate. To compute the _APR_, multiple the weekly rate by 52 or the daily rate by 365.

An HP 12C™ only computes a periodic rate. It has no _EFF_ function. I respect that because if an instrument amortizes, the periodic rate is the only reality. We can convert it to an _NAI_ or an _EFF_, but that is not real because it did not and does not happen. But, the EU does it. Indeed it uses a daily rate to do so.

2. COMPUTING AN _APR_ WITH POINTS AND OTHER FEES

Computing the _APR_ for loans with "points," however, is not quite as simple. For our purposes, we will only consider "points" and will ignore other closing costs which federal law treats in the same manner as "points."

The short explanation is: points are non-refundable "pre-paid" interest. In reality, interest cannot be pre-paid: one simply borrows less. For example, if I were to lend you $100,000 for fifteen years at an _NAI_ of 5% compounded monthly, and you "pre-paid" $5,000 of interest, you would actually have borrowed $95,000. Consider how you would enter the cash flows in a financial calculator. On day one, you would have a cash inflow (the amount you borrowed) of $100,000. But, on the same day you would have a cash out flow (the points) of $5,000. The COURSE CALCULATORS have no way to enter this other than by combing them to a net inflow of $95,000.

EXAMPLE 13

Calculating Points

You have borrowed $100,000 to purchase a new house. The loan has a stated nominal annual interest rate (*NAI*) of 5%. The lender charges 5 points. The term of the loan is fifteen years and the payments are monthly, beginning one month from today.

In credit parlance, a "point" is equal to one percent of the principal amount loaned. Thus on a $100,000 loan, one point equals $1,000 and two points equals $2,000. In **Example 13**, the 5 points on a $100,000 loan equals $5,000. That is an unusually high number of points; however, some lenders permit the borrower to "buy-down" the interest rate by paying additional points. Thus, the number is often negotiable. Similarly, on a $200,000 loan, one point equals $2,000 and two points equals $4,000.

To compute the *APR* in **Example 13**, we would follow the steps illustrated below. The *APR* would be 5.787%.

Institutions charge points for three general reasons:

1. First, the points—which are actually discounted interest—are not reflected in the nominal annual interest rate. As a result, the nominal rate is understated. While a lender must prominently disclose the annual percentage rate, which reflects the points, it can do so along with disclosure of the nominal rate. Thus, lenders hope borrowers will visualize the nominal rate as the true rate, rather than the higher—and sometimes less prominent *APR*. Lenders in the U.S. are not required to disclose the effective rate, which is arguably the most accurate measure.

2. Second, the points—if attributable to a home loan—are generally deductible by the borrower for federal income tax purposes. As a result, borrowers may benefit from having more of the interest deductible in the first year of the loan.[38]

3. Third, the points are almost always nonrefundable. They are paid—either with separate funds or by being withheld from the loan proceeds—at the time of the loan transaction: If the loan is outstanding for its entire term, the points are effectively paid periodically over the life of the loan. However, if the borrower pays the loan prematurely, he must pay all

---

[38] Prior to 2018, this was a significant deduction and thus tax benefit. Changes to the standard deduction in 2018 make itemization less likely and thus the tax benefit of points less significant.

remaining principal, unreduced by the points. For example, a $100,000 loan with two points is the equivalent of a $98,000 loan because just as soon as the borrower receives the $100,000 he must pay back $2,000 as points. Nevertheless, the borrower is immediately liable for the entire $100,000 loan principal, even if he were to repay the loan the next day.

As a practical matter, most home loans are paid early because they contain a "due on sale" clause, accelerating them whenever the underlying security changes hands. Many purchasers of residential property sell the property—and thus pay off the respective loan early—prior to the end of the original loan term. As a result, the lender earns an extraordinary interest rate—higher even than the original effective interest rate. Often, it will be much higher.

EXAMPLE 14

Illustrating a Nightmare

You have borrowed $300,000 to purchase a new house. The loan has a stated nominal annual interest rate (*NAI*) of 5%. The lender charges 3 points. The term of the loan is thirty years and the payments are monthly, beginning one month from today.

LESSON THIRTEEN will cover how to amortize this loan. For now, accept that the monthly payments would be $1,610.46, the *APR* would be 5.269%, and the effective rate would be 5.398%. But, the *APR* and the *EFF* are accurate only if the borrower makes timely payments for the entire thirty years. Suppose, however, the borrower must sell the house a month after purchasing it. Perhaps his/her employer transferred him/her to another state or perhaps a family emergency required the move. While such a quick sale may be unlikely, it is certainly not impossible. People may move, on average, every seven years or so, but that means some stay longer and some much shorter periods. If the **Example 14** borrower sold the house after one month, the balance due on the loan would be $299,639.54. The stated amount loaned was $300,000, the borrower made a single payment of $1,610.46, of which $360.41 was principal and $1,250.00 was interest. LESSON THIRTEEN covers how to compute these amounts. But you should be able to do it fairly simply. The 5% *NAI* corresponds to a monthly periodic rate of 0.41666667%: simply divide 5 by 12. Multiplying that by the $300,000 loan principal produces the first month's interest of $1,250. Subtract the interest from the payment of $1,610.46 and you get the $360.41 principal payment.

Thus, the borrower owes $299,639.59 to pay off the loan in one month. But, the borrower will "feel" as if he/she only borrowed $291,000 because he/she paid $9,000 in points at the loan closing. Thus he/she borrowed $300,000, but actually received only $291,000. Borrower and lender may have exchanged checks, but the result is the same.

As a result, the borrower actually paid $10,250 to borrow $291,000 for a single month. That is a *periodic* rate—*admittedly in hindsight*—of 3.522337%. It translates to a *NAI* of 42.27% and an *EFF* of 51.50%—far, far, far greater than the stated nominal rate of 5% or the disclosed *APR* of 5.269%.

Let's move on to actually compute the *APR*. Consider **Example 15** for both the HP 10Bii™ and for the COURSE CALCULATORS.

EXAMPLE 15

Computing an *APR* with Points (Ignoring Other Fees)

You have borrowed $200,000 to purchase a new house. The loan has a stated nominal annual interest rate (*NAI*) of 7.5%. The lender charges one and one-half points. The term of the loan is thirty years and the payments are monthly, beginning one month from today.

---

a. Computing an *APR* with a HP 10Bii™

Computing the *APR* using a HP 10Bii™ calculator involves the following steps, which involve amortizing the loan, the subject of LESSON THIRTEEN. This method involves iterations, but so does a HP 12C™ calculator because the formula is so complex.

1. Input the stated *NAI* as the *I/YR*.

2. Input 12 as the *P/YR*.

3. Input the stated term times 12 as the *N* or input the term and shift N.

4. Input zero as the *FV* (you may ignore this as zero is the default).

5. Input the stated principal amount as the *PV*.

6. Solve for the payment amount (which will show as a negative number).

7. Subtract the points from the stated loan principal and input the difference as the *PV*.

8. Press *I/YR* and the display will show the *APR*.

The first six steps are (ignoring step four):

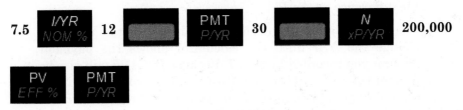

The display will read: −1,398.43, which is the amount of the monthly payment (be sure the calculator is in End Mode). As explained earlier, the negative sign indicates a cash flow outward from you to the lender.

Step 7 requires you first to compute the amount of the 1.5 points. That is 1.5% of the $200,000 principal, or $3,000. Then you must subtract 3000 from 200,000, to produce $197,000, which is the actual amount borrowed. You then input it:

197,000

Step 8 requires you to re-solve for the interest rate, but this time the display will show the *APR*:

I/YR
NOM %

The display will read: 7.655055419 (assuming you set it to 9 decimal places). You may round this to 7.66% as the *APR*.

b. Computing an *APR* Using the Course Calculators

Computing an *APR* using the COURSE CALCULATORS involves interpolation, but is just as accurate. In fact, the HP calculators also use interpolation in solving the very complex equation.

To use the Interpolation Method, follow these nine steps:

1. Open the AMORTIZATION CALCULATOR and press End Mode.

2. Input the stated *NAI*.

3. Input 12 as the *P/YR*.

4. Input the stated term as the *N*.

5. Input zero as the *FV* (you may ignore this as zero is the default).

6. Input the stated principal amount as the *PV*.

7. Record the payment amount.

8. Subtract the points from the stated loan principal and input the difference as the *PV*.

9. The payment amount will change on the calculator. You must change the *NAI* until the calculator shows the payment amount you recorded in Step 7. Because the *APR* will also be greater than the *NAI* (with positive points), you should input a number greater than the *NAI*. You should use an educated guess as to what it would be. When you input you guess, the payment amount will increase. If it remains smaller than the amount you recorded in Step 7, try again with a larger *NAI*. If, instead, it becomes larger than the Step 7 amount, try again with a smaller *NAI*. You should be able to guess the correct *NAI* within seven to ten attempts.

AMORTIZATION
CALCULATOR

This Calculator computes only the payment *amount*. For an amortization table of interest and principal, click on AMORTIZATION WITH CHART, which works slower, but provides more information.

	Instructions	ON	OFF
Mode	Begin	End	
Present Value		200,000.00	
Future Value		0.00	
Nominal Interest Rate		7.50	
Effective Interest Rate	7.7632598856		
Number of Years		30.00	
Payments Per Year		12.00	
Number of Payments		360.00	
Payment		1,398.43	end mode
	clear all		

Figure 24: Example 15 Payment Calculation

Using the numbers from **Example 15,** Steps 1 through 7 appear in **Figure 24.** Notice the payment amount is 1,398.43, the same as produced by the HP 10Bii™.

You must write this number so that you do not forget it. Step 8 requires you first to compute the amount of the 1.5 points. That is 1.5% of the $200,000 principal, or $3,000. Then you must subtract 3000 from 200,000, to produce $197,000, which is the actual amount borrowed. You then input it to begin the interpolation (guessing).

Figure 25 uses the AMORTIZATION CALCULATOR from Steps 1–7, but with the *PV* changed to 197,000. Notice the payment amount is now

$1,377.45. We must change the *NAI* until the payment amount shows. 1,398.43 (the number you wrote down from **Figure 24**).

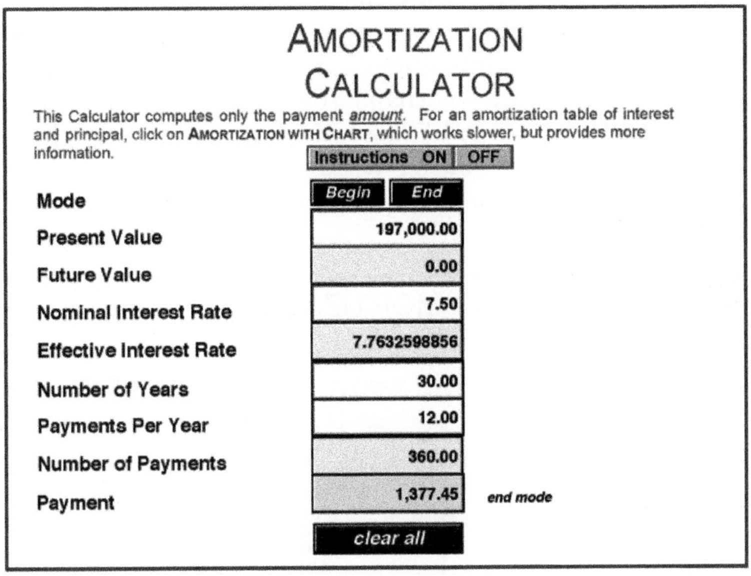

Figure 25: Step 8

The stated *NAI* in **Example 15** is 7.5%. We used that number to compute the monthly payment on the loan, which will not change in reality. We know the *APR* will be higher than the stated *NAI* (it *always* is), so we need to guess an *NAI* amount greater than 7.5%. A higher *NAI* will produce a higher payment amount. You must continually guess until the payment amount reads 1,398.43. The guess that produces that payment amount will be the *APR*. With a bit of practice, this should take no more than five to seven guesses, or a minute or two.

Aside

Think of this as similar to the guessing game of pick a number between 1 and 1000 and answer higher/lower when I try to guess it. Suppose you pick 729. I will guess 500 and you will say higher. I will then guess 750 and you say lower. I may guess 700 and you say higher. I'm getting close. Perhaps I guess 725 and you say higher, so I guess 730 and you say lower, so I guess 729 and have the answer. We are using the same principle. Indeed, the HP calculators, including the powerful 12C, interpolate through guess, as the HP manual explains. That is because the formula is very complex. I could program it using geometry (sines and arc sign and tangents and such), but even that would involve interpolation.

Your first guess can be any *NAI* greater than the stated amount of 7.5. **Figure 26** uses a guess of 8%. But, as shown, it produces a payment of $1,445.50, which is <u>*too high*</u>. Hence, the *NAI* <u>*must be lower*</u> than 8%. For a loan, the higher the interest rate, the higher the payment, which is something you almost certainly already know. If, instead, you guessed an even higher number than 8—perhaps 10% *NAI*—the resulting payment amount would be much higher: 1,728.83. Remember, you need the payment to be 1,398.43 (the number you wrote down after Steps 1–7 (**Figure 24**) above. That would suggest to drop your guess significantly below 10, but still above 7.5.

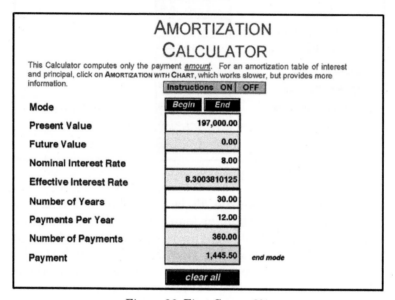

Figure 26: First Guess: 8%

Because I <u>*first guessed*</u> 8, which produced a too-high payment of 1,445.50, I know I must drop the guess below 8 but above 7.5. My advice is to split the difference and try 7.75. As shown in **Figure 27**, that <u>*second guess*</u> produces a still-too-high payment of 1,411.35.

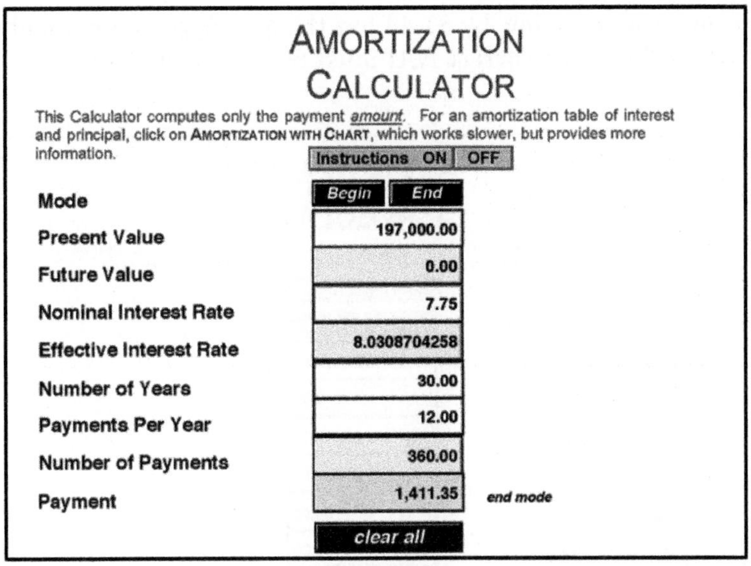

AMORTIZATION CALCULATOR

This Calculator computes only the payment *amount*. For an amortization table of interest and principal, click on AMORTIZATION WITH CHART, which works slower, but provides more information.

Instructions **ON** OFF

Mode	Begin	End
Present Value		197,000.00
Future Value		0.00
Nominal Interest Rate		7.75
Effective Interest Rate		8.0308704258
Number of Years		30.00
Payments Per Year		12.00
Number of Payments		360.00
Payment		1,411.35

end mode

clear all

Figure 27: Second Guess: 7.75%

Remember, we must get the payment amount down to 1,398.43; hence, we must next guess an amount between 7.5 and 7.75. Guessing 7.6 seems to make sense, so that is what I do in **Figure 28**, but that *third guess* produces a too-low payment of 1,390.99. But, we are getting close: the correct number must be between 7.6 and 7.75.

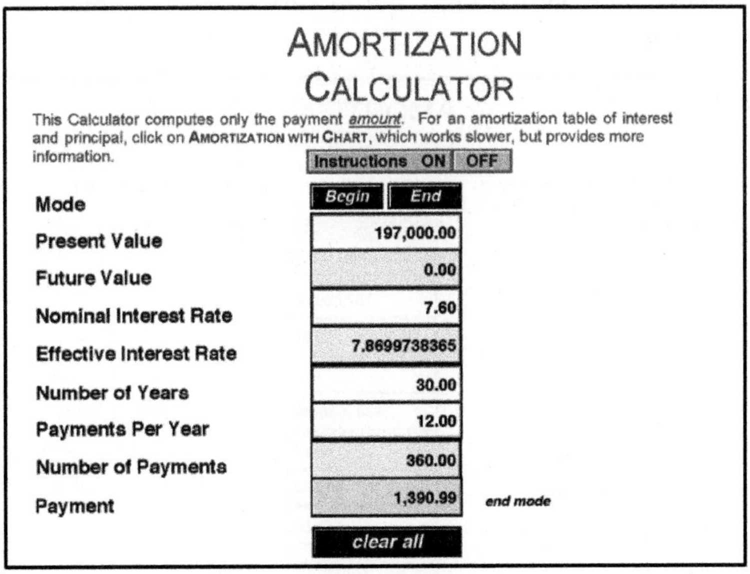

AMORTIZATION CALCULATOR

This Calculator computes only the payment *amount*. For an amortization table of interest and principal, click on AMORTIZATION WITH CHART, which works slower, but provides more information.

Instructions **ON** OFF

Mode	Begin	End
Present Value		197,000.00
Future Value		0.00
Nominal Interest Rate		7.60
Effective Interest Rate		7.8699738365
Number of Years		30.00
Payments Per Year		12.00
Number of Payments		360.00
Payment		1,390.99

end mode

clear all

Figure 28: Third Guess: 7.6%

For a *fourth guess*, I attempt 7.7% in **Figure 29**, but that produces a too-high payment of 1,404.51. If I'm paying attention, I notice the third guess payment was too low by \$7.44 but the _fourth guess_ payment was too high by \$6.08. Thus the correct _NAI_ must be a little closer to 7.7 than it is to 7.6.

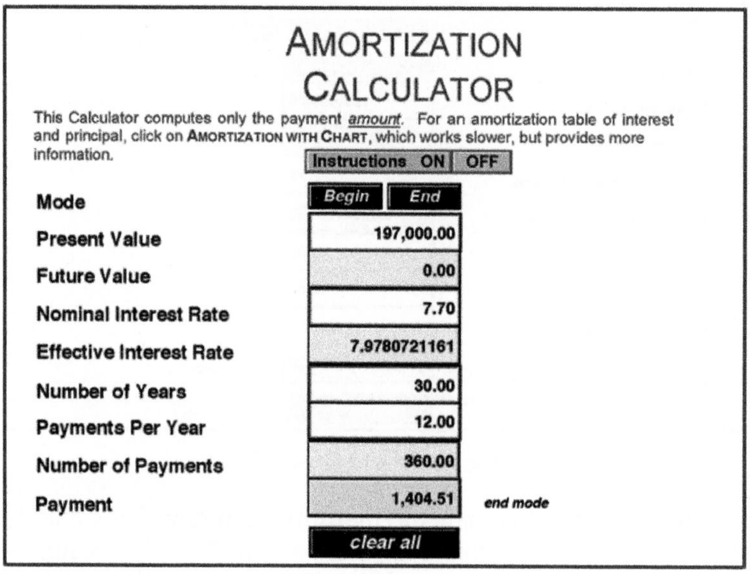

AMORTIZATION CALCULATOR

This Calculator computes only the payment _amount_. For an amortization table of interest and principal, click on AMORTIZATION WITH CHART, which works slower, but provides more information.

	Instructions ON OFF
Mode	_Begin_ **End**
Present Value	197,000.00
Future Value	0.00
Nominal Interest Rate	7.70
Effective Interest Rate	7.9780721161
Number of Years	30.00
Payments Per Year	12.00
Number of Payments	360.00
Payment	1,404.51 _end mode_
	clear all

Figure 29: Fourth Guess: 7.7%

Thus, in **Figure 30**, I attempt a _fifth guess_ of 7.66, which produces 1,399.12. That remains too high, but is very close. It is high by only 69 cents.

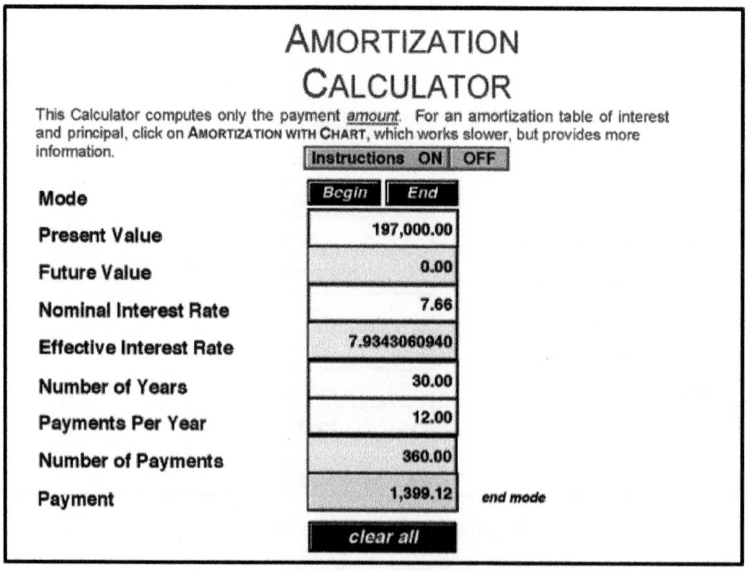

AMORTIZATION CALCULATOR

This Calculator computes only the payment _amount_. For an amortization table of interest and principal, click on AMORTIZATION WITH CHART, which works slower, but provides more information.

	Instructions ON OFF
Mode	_Begin_ **End**
Present Value	197,000.00
Future Value	0.00
Nominal Interest Rate	7.66
Effective Interest Rate	7.9343060940
Number of Years	30.00
Payments Per Year	12.00
Number of Payments	360.00
Payment	1,399.12 _end mode_
	clear all

Figure 30: Fifth Guess: 7.66%

But, if I were paying attention, as explained above, I know the *APR* is closer to 7.7 than to 7.6, but perhaps I was not paying that close attention, so for a *sixth guess*, I'll go with 7.65. Oops, that produces a payment of 1,397.74, which is 69 cents too low, as shown in **Figure 31**. But, since 7.66 was 69 cents too high and 7.65 is 69 cents too low, the answer must be exactly between them (or close to it).

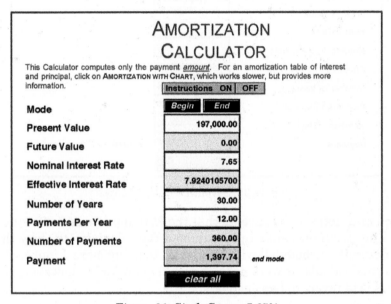

Figure 31: Sixth Guess: 7.65%

Thus in **Figure 32**, I make a *seventh guess* half-way between 7.66 and 7.65, which is 7.655. Bingo! The payment answer is correct: 1,398.43. thus the *NAI* shown is the correct *APR*.

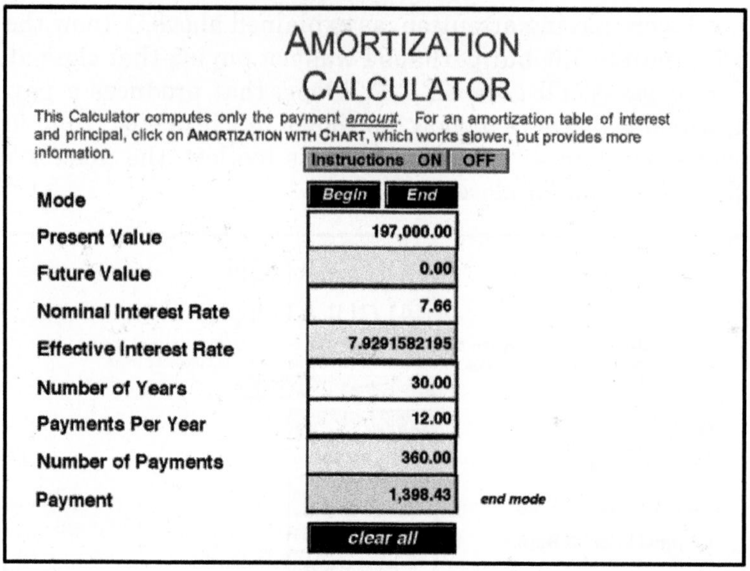

AMORTIZATION
CALCULATOR

This Calculator computes only the payment *amount*. For an amortization table of interest and principal, click on AMORTIZATION WITH CHART, which works slower, but provides more information.

| | Instructions | ON | OFF |

Mode	Begin	End
Present Value		197,000.00
Future Value		0.00
Nominal Interest Rate		7.66
Effective Interest Rate		7.9291582195
Number of Years		30.00
Payments Per Year		12.00
Number of Payments		360.00
Payment		1,398.43	end mode

clear all

Figure 32: Seventh Guess: 7.655%

You may notice in **Figure 32** that the *NAI* appears as 7.66 rather than 7.655. That occurs because I programmed the calculator to show the *NAI* to two decimals, although it will calculate it to many more. I inputted 7.655. If the actual calculator were open, it would show 7.655; however, printing it causes it to revert to two decimals.

Thus working **Example 15** with the AMORTIZATION COURSE CALCULATOR required seven interpolations, or guesses. If you practice, that is about the high end of how many guesses you will need. It should only take you a few minutes because it really boils down to three steps: determine the correct payment amount (using the stated *NAI* of 7.5) and you write that down, then change the *PV* to the amount loaned minus the points, and finally change the *NAI* until you see a payment equal to what you wrote down.

You may also notice that the *APR* as determined by the HP 10Bii™ calculator is 7.655055419%, assuming you set it to show nine decimals. The Interpolation Method produced a very slightly less precise *APR* of 7.655%. That is because if you put your cursor on the payment amount in the AMORTIZATION CALCULATOR, it shows the actual payment as $1,398.43090143276. Absent your cursor, the calculator payment was the correct $1,398.43 because it rounds to two decimals for the display unless you highlight it. The difference is not material: our guess was approximately 55/1,000,000ths of a percent off. If we wanted to achieve a more accurate *APR* through interpolation, we would merely need to take the payment amount to fractions of a cent. But, in the real world, we rarely deal with fractions of a cent, particularly for home mortgage loans, so the effort would not be worth the trouble.

QUESTIONS

1. A credit card charges 1.5% interest per month. What is the *APR*? What is the *EFF*?

2. A home loan with zero points and zero finance charges considered interest under federal law charges 5% nominal annual interest with monthly payments for thirty years. What is the *APR*? What is the *EFF*?

3. A home loan for $400,000 charges 5% *NAI* with monthly payments for fifteen years. It also charges 3 points (and no other charges defined as interest under the applicable federal statute). What is the *APR*? What is the monthly payment?

D. ANNUAL PERCENTAGE YIELD (LESSON FIVE-D)

The term *Annual Percentage Yield* (*APY*) and its legal consequences appear in federal statute.[39] Specifically, the statute defines it as "the total amount of interest that would be received on a $100 deposit, based on the annual rate of simple interest and the frequency of compounding for a 365-day period. . . ."[40] Advertisements for deposits generally must include a statement of the *APY*. The definition assumes re-investment of periodic interest at the stated interest rate and a maturity of at least one-year. For deposits for which those assumptions do not apply, the *APY* is not accurate; nevertheless, federal law generally requires its disclosure.

For example, an account with a maturity of less than one year would have an *APY* that assumes re-investment at the original rate. That assumption, however, is likely inaccurate, as interest rates continually change in the economy.

The COURSE CALCULATORS and the HP 10Bii™ compute an effective rate, which has the same meaning. Computing the *APY* is not a significant part of this course. Indeed, LESSON FIVE-D merely links to the relevant statute and regulations.

---

[39] 12 U.S.C. § 4302.

[40] Notice the interesting use of the term "simple interest" in the federal statute. For purposes of an *APY*, is has the same meaning as an *NAI*.

E. YIELD (LESSON FIVE-E)

Lesson Objectives

1. Students will learn more about the following terms:

    a.   Simple Yield.

    b.   Yield.

    c.   Yield to Maturity (*YTM*).

    d.   Internal Rate of Return (*IRR*).

2. Students will learn that the terms *Simple Yield* and *Yield* are not terms of art. They will also learn common formulas for the two terms.

$\dfrac{\textit{nominal annual interest rate}}{\textit{current market value}}$	$\dfrac{\textit{effective interest rate}}{\textit{purchase price}}$

Common <u>Simple Yield</u> Formula   **Common <u>Yield</u> Formula**

They will learn that some authorities substitute the current market value for the purchase price in the *Yield* Formula:

$\dfrac{\textit{effective interest rate}}{\textit{current market value}}$

Alternative <u>Yield</u> Formula

3. Students will learn that the terms *Yield to Maturity* and *Internal Rate of Return* are terms of art and are closely related. They will learn that some authorities, including federal law, interchange the terms *Yield* and *Yield to Maturity*. They will learn the definition of a **Yield to Maturity** as:

> **The nominal annual interest rate at which the price of an instrument minus the present value of the various cash flows equals zero.**

4. Students will learn to abbreviate *Yield to Maturity* as *YTM*. They will learn to abbreviate the *Internal Rate of Return* as the *IRR*.

5. Students will learn some basic principles of finance and economics, namely: *as interest rates fall, bond prices* (and present values) *rise*. Similarly, *as interest rates rise, bond prices* (and present values) *fall*.

Terminology Introduced

- Simple Yield

- Current Yield

- Yield

- Annualized Yield

- Yield to Maturity (*YTM*)

- Internal Rate of Return (*IRR*) (students are **not** responsible for this term)

––––––––––––

LESSON FIVE-E is complicated because it involves terms many people define differently. Tax lawyers may need to compute a yield; however, many, if not most, others do not. Familiarity with the terminology is important. Understanding the nuances is less so.

1.   GENERAL DEFINITION

The term *Yield* is <u>not</u> a term of art; hence, lawyers should use it only with an accompanying definition. Often it represents the following formula:

$$\left(\frac{EFF}{purchase\ price}\right)$$

where *EFF* = the effective interest <u>earned for the period</u> as opposed to the rate.

Thus the rate is a function of the <u>original cost</u> of the instrument. This itself, is not clear without a better understanding of the interest (or other return) on the investment. If the instrument (investment) does not make distributions, the numerator would be the compounded accumulation increase for the year. But if it makes distributions, an effective yield would need to account for the timing of the distributions, converting what would then be a periodic return to an effective return as a function of the original purchase price.

Others define it as:

$$\left(\frac{EFF}{market\ value}\right)$$

where *EFF* = the effective interest <u>earned for the period</u> as opposed to the rate

which results in a variable yield because it is a function of the <u>current value</u> of the instrument. Some users call this alternative definition the "*current yield.*" Both usages are common and neither is correct or incorrect. Both however, require clarification regarding whether they count distributions weighted for timing or not.

Still other users impose the *NAI* as the numerator in one or the other above formulas, which eliminates the timing issue above:

$$\left(\frac{NAI}{purchase\ price} \right) \quad \left(\frac{NAI}{market\ value} \right)$$

Such usage interchanges the term *yield* with the term *simple yield*. Again, neither is correct nor incorrect, although the latter two are less common. In each of the formulas using "market price" in the denominator, one must determine whether the user considers the "asked" or the "bid" price to be the "market price" if firmer quotations are unavailable.

2. OTHER RELATED IMPORTANT FINANCIAL TERMS

Several important terms arise in relation to interest rates and the term "yield." They include:

a.   Simple Yield

b.   Yield

c.   Yield to Maturity (*YTM*)

d.   Internal Rate of Return (*IRR*)

The first two of these terms—simple yield and yield—are not terms of art: their precise definitions may vary from user to user. Thus anyone using either of them in a legal context should provide a precise definition. Likewise, anyone coming across them in a legal context should demand a precise definition. The latter two terms—yield to maturity and internal rate of return—have generally accepted meanings.

a. Simple Yield

This is an easy-to-compute, but imprecise measure of the return on a debt instrument. As illustrated in **Example 16**, it is the nominal annual interest ($70 in the example) divided by the current market price of the instrument. It does not vary—at least not under most traditional definitions—as a function of the payment period. As a result, it does not reflect re-investment of any interest paid more frequently than annually. This computation would change constantly, as the market value of the instrument changed. The ease of computation justifies the use of the figure. It is, however, an inferior measure of the true return on the bond or similar investment. The actual yield for a stated period or the yield to maturity would be more accurate and thus more useful.

In the example, the stated return is 7%, which is the *NAI* times the face value. Bonds, however, change in price as interest rates change, hence the alternative purchase prices in the example. Notice, the lower the _price_ (not the face amount of $1,000, which does not change) the higher the interest rate. Also notice, this use of "simple yield" does not account for the market discount of $100 in the first alternative: you may have purchased the bond for $900, but the issuer will pay you $1,000 on maturity. That extra $100 is market discount interest and affects the yield to maturity, though not the simple yield as defined above. Similarly, in the third alternative, you paid a premium for the bond: $1,100, or an extra $100. You did so because market interest rates dropped, while the bond's rate remained the same—7% paid quarterly on the face value. Thus the person who sold it to you made a profit of $100 (assuming he/she bought it for its $1,000 face value). You will thus lose $100 over the life of the bond. That would also be reflected in a yield to maturity, but not in a simple yield.

Some users may interchange this term with the slightly different term "yield." Others might compound the quarterly payment to generate a more precise calculation. Neither use is wrong—they are merely different. As cautioned above, if someone uses the term "simple yield," request a definition.

EXAMPLE 16

Simple Yield

Compute the simple yield of a $1,000 (face amount) bond paying 7% nominal annual interest, paid quarterly. Assume that it sells, alternatively, for $900, $1,000, and $1,100.

$$\frac{70}{900} = \textbf{7.778\%}\ \textit{simple yield}$$

$$\frac{70}{1000} = \textbf{7.000\%}\ \textit{simple yield}$$

$$\frac{70}{1100} = \textbf{6.364\%}\ \textit{simple yield}$$

---

b.   Yield

This measure of the return on a debt instrument is sometimes interchanged slightly different term "simple yield." More commonly, however, it constitutes the actual yield on an instrument for a stated period of time, as a function of the purchase price. As explained earlier, some users define it as a function of the current market value.

Using one common definition, it would divide any periodic interest payment by the purchase price and then convert it to an annual rate, compounding the periodic rate for the number of periods. **Example 17** illustrates the computation of a Yield, using this definition:

$$\left(\frac{EFF}{purchase\ price}\right)$$

where *EFF* = the effective interest *earned for the period* as opposed to the rate.

To work **Example 17** you should open the INTEREST CONVERSION CALCULATOR, click on Convert Nominal Rate to Effective Rate, and enter the numbers in **Figure 33** which come from the example: an *NAI* of 7 and 4 payments per year.

EXAMPLE 17

Yield

Compute the yield of a $1,000 (face amount) bond paying 7% nominal annual interest, paid quarterly. Assume that it sells, alternatively, for $900, $1,000, and $1,100.

$$\frac{71.19}{1000} = 7.1859\%\ simple\ yield$$

Under the assumed definition, the current market price would be irrelevant; hence, the yield would not change as the market value changed. This definition, more properly, is called the *historic effective yield* or the *stated* effective yield.

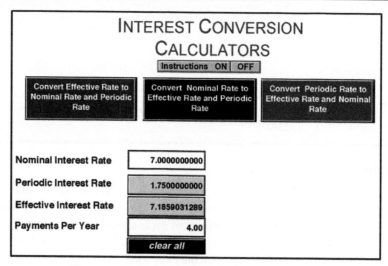

Figure 33: Interest Conversion for Example 17

This measure of the instrument differs from the "simple yield" in two respects. First, it adds the compounding feature, when appropriate; hence the yields are greater when the payment period is less than one year.

Second, it does not change constantly as the market price of the instrument changes; instead, it is fixed by the purchase or issue price of the instrument (depending on whose viewpoint is involved). Also, although the above definition describes a number which is more accurate and hence more useful than the number described as a "simple yield," this term—yield—does not present a true measure of an instrument's return. Two inaccuracies are inherent.

One, it relies on interest compounding, when, in fact, as far as the instrument is concerned the interest is paid and thus does not compound. This is less criticism of the calculation—and more mere observation, however, because that feature is inevitable.

For yields to be useful, they must generally be comparable to those of other instruments. For this to be possible, they must be based on a common standard—such as the year. Instruments that pay interest annually will thus present an accurate yield. In contrast, instruments which pay at periods other than a year will never present an accurate annual yield because they violate the rule stated earlier: the payment period and the compounding period must be the same. For instruments that pay interest other than annually, an annual yield will never be precise because it inherently requires an assumption that the interest paid continued to earn interest at the same internal rate. While useful, such an assumption is not perfect. As long as users understand this feature, the calculation of a yield can be very useful and generally accurate.

Annualized Yield

Instruments that pay interest more often than annually will have an "annualized" yield, which assumes a constant return. The assumption is the best one can do, but it is inherently inaccurate.

A second inaccuracy of the above "yield" calculation involves its common failure to consider the impact of changing values, *i.e.*, changing market interest rates. Another way of stating this somewhat obvious point is that the term—as defined above—ignores market discounts and premiums. While the point of the calculation is simply to look at paid returns for a particular period—and thus it accomplishes what its definition constrains it to do, the calculation nevertheless risks presenting a significantly inaccurate picture. To solve this problem, some users define a yield as:

$$\frac{EFF}{market\ value}$$

Still others, use this definition in relation to the term "current yield."

For example under the above definition, an instrument sold at a premium will have the same "yield," regardless of its life. In contrast, it will have a higher "yield to maturity" the longer the period until maturity. Similarly, an instrument sold at a discount will have the same "yield," regardless of its life, although it will have a lower "yield to maturity" the longer the period until maturity. Despite some inherent inaccuracies of its own, the "yield to maturity" calculation presents the most accurate and useful picture of a debt instrument. Hence a comparison of the yields of two instruments, ignoring the terms of the instruments, might (though not necessarily) present a distorted picture. A comparison of yields that considers the terms would indeed be mostly accurate; however, it would also be a comparison of "yields to maturity" and thus, by definition, not a comparison of mere yields.

c.   Yield to Maturity (*YTM*)

This is the most accurate measure of the return on a debt instrument. Comparable to—and sometimes interchanged with either the "effective interest rate" or the "internal rate of return"—it considers the instrument's actual cash flows. Thus it is the most realistic measure of an instrument's return. As illustrated in **Examples 18 through 21**, the yield to maturity calculation amortizes the premium or discount element of the issue price over the life of the instrument.

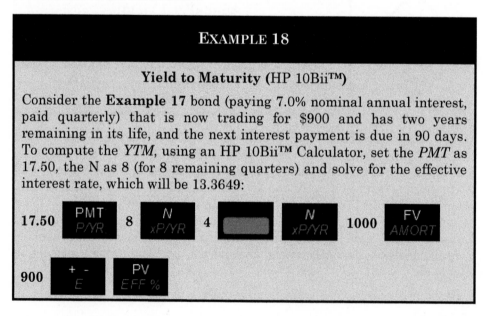

EXAMPLE 18

Yield to Maturity (HP 10Bii™)

Consider the **Example 17** bond (paying 7.0% nominal annual interest, paid quarterly) that is now trading for $900 and has two years remaining in its life, and the next interest payment is due in 90 days. To compute the *YTM*, using an HP 10Bii™ Calculator, set the *PMT* as 17.50, the N as 8 (for 8 remaining quarters) and solve for the effective interest rate, which will be 13.3649:

The display will read 12.742990875 as the *NAI*.

The display will read 13.364966 as the *EFF*.

The simple yield is 7.778% $\left(\dfrac{70}{900}\right)$.

The "current" yield is 7.984% using $\dfrac{EFF}{market\ value}$

as the definition $\left(\dfrac{71.859}{900}\right)$.

The yield to maturity is currently 13.365%.

This is more useful than the mere "yield" which, as defined above, ignores the premium or discount. Nevertheless, the term *Yield to Maturity* (*YTM*) is <u>not</u> a term of art; hence, lawyers should not use it without an accompanying definition. One statutory definition defines it in terms of a *yield*:

> *Definitions* (4) The <u>*yield to maturity*</u>, or <u>*yield*</u>, is the annualized rate of return to maturity on a fixed principal security expressed as a percentage.[41]

This particular definition has two problems. First, it assumes all interest received is re-invested at the stated rate: hence, the use of the word "*annualized*" rather than "*annual.*" Second, it is a *nominal* rather than a *compounded* rate. Many users define the term *Yield to Maturity* using an *effective* or compounded rate.

But, even that definition has problems, as explained below following **Example 19.**

EXAMPLE 19

Yield to Maturity (HP 10Bii™)

Consider the **Example 17** bond (paying 7.0% nominal annual interest, paid quarterly) that is now trading for $900 and has <u>ten</u> years remaining in its life, and the next interest payment is due in 90 days. To compute this figure, using a HP 10Bii™ Calculator, set the *PMT* as 17.50, the N

---

[41] 70 FR 57437 (discussing 31 CFR Parts 356, 357, and 363, sale of T-bills, bonds etc.).

as 40 (for 40 remaining quarters) and solve for the effective interest rate, which will be 8.7685:

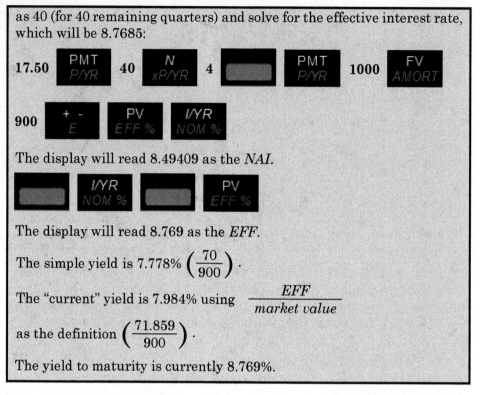

The display will read 8.49409 as the *NAI*.

The display will read 8.769 as the *EFF*.

The simple yield is 7.778% $\left(\dfrac{70}{900}\right)$.

The "current" yield is 7.984% using $\dfrac{EFF}{market\ value}$

as the definition $\left(\dfrac{71.859}{900}\right)$.

The yield to maturity is currently 8.769%.

First, it also assumes—as does the effective interest rate—that any payments continue to earn or cost the same constant interest rate. This is unlikely to be accurate; nevertheless, because no investor has a crystal ball with which to determine future investment returns, such an assumption is the best possible. It permits realistic comparisons between instruments. Nevertheless, it can result in some misunderstandings and thus should be fully understood. The assumption that all returns are reinvested at the same rate, while necessary mathematically can cause misunderstanding. An investor might assume that the two instruments in **Example 20** are interchangeable because they have the same original cost and the same yield to maturity. Because they have different cash flows, however, they are comparable only with the above assumption, which may—or may not— be realistic.

EXAMPLE 20

Yield to Maturity (HP 10Bii™)

Consider the **Example 17** bond (paying 7.0% nominal annual interest, paid quarterly) that is now trading for $1,100 and has *two* years remaining in its life, and the next interest payment is due in 90 days.

To compute this figure, using an HP 10Bii™ Calculator, set the *PMT* as 17.50, the N as 8 (for 8 remaining quarters) and solve for the effective interest rate, which will be 1.906:

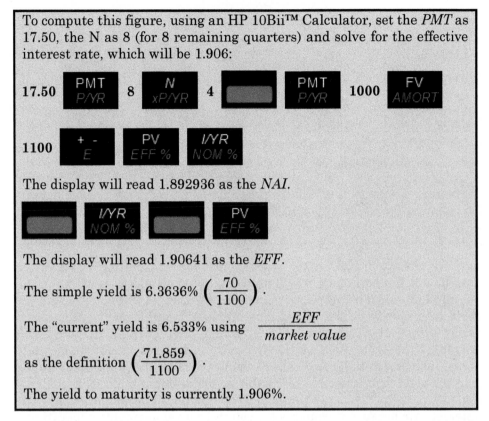

The display will read 1.892936 as the *NAI*.

The display will read 1.90641 as the *EFF*.

The simple yield is 6.3636% $\left(\dfrac{70}{1100} \right)$.

The "current" yield is 6.533% using $\dfrac{EFF}{market\ value}$

as the definition $\left(\dfrac{71.859}{1100} \right)$.

The yield to maturity is currently 1.906%.

The second potential inaccuracy involving the yield to maturity calculation involves the assumption that the instrument will be outstanding for its entire expected life. This, again, is a necessary assumption: to input a future maturity value one must know the future date. Because no crystal balls exist to foretell the future, the assumption becomes necessary that the instrument will continue to be outstanding for its entire scheduled life and will make all scheduled payments. Many instruments, however, have a put or call feature under which either the maker or purchaser—or both—may offer or demand payment early, respectively. In such cases, the statement of a yield to maturity should note the assumption regarding maturity.

EXAMPLE 21

Comparison of Instruments with the Same Yield

Instrument One with a face value of $100,000 issued for $96,000, *paying* 10% nominal annual interest with annual payments for five years will have a yield to maturity of 11.084585%.

Instrument Two involves $96,000 invested at 11.084585% nominal annual interest compounded annually for five years. It will generate $162,382.87 in five years. It, too, has a yield to maturity of 11.084585%.

But, Instrument One will generate approximately $162,382.87 _only if_ each $10,000 annual interest payment is itself reinvested at 11.084585%. The investor, however, will receive each annual payment and do something with it: spend it or invest it elsewhere. Money being fungible, the investor can never be certain what the annual payments generate in investment return. Even if spent, they free-up other funds for investment—or they reduce other debts—and thus effectively generate a return. But how much return can never be clear. Thus, comparing the two instruments and concluding they have the same _YTM_ is inaccurate, but an accurate comparison is not possible.

The YIELD CALCULATOR works only for the initial issue of an instrument issued at par: it will not compute the yield to maturity on an instrument issued below par or above par. Further, it will not compute the yield to maturity on an instrument purchased mid-stream (after initial issue) either at a discount or a premium. The OID CALCULATOR _will_ compute the yield or _YTM_ on discount or premium instruments if, and only if, the instrument has no current payments. Be careful: one cannot simply add the yield from the yield calculator to the discount yield from the OID CALCULATOR to achieve a proper _YTM_. Doing so would overstate the interest rate because it would not account for level payments generating a decreasing yield on an increasing principal. For now, you must use the HP 10Bii™ calculator to solve for a missing interest rate when the instrument has both current payments and either discount interest or acquisition premium (sold above par). The formula to solve for such a missing interest rate cannot be solved using algebra; instead, it is far more complicated. Most calculators, such as the HP series, use an interpolation (guessing) algorithm to solve for such a missing interest rate.

d.   Internal Rate of Return (_IRR_)

This is the effective interest rate at which the initial investment equals the present value of all future cash flows. If all cash flows are level and in the same direction, this computation is relatively simple and essentially parallels the computation of a yield to maturity. Uneven cash flows—and particularly those that change direction—present computational difficulties. Most calculators actually use a trial and error approach because the formula can be extremely complex.

Computation of an _IRR_ is beyond this course.

LESSON SIX

WHY PEOPLE CHARGE INTEREST

■ ■ ■

Lesson Objectives

1. Student will learn the following components of interest:

   a. Expected Inflation.

   b. Risk.

   c. Liquidity.

   d. Market Risk.

2. Student will learn the following terms:

   a. Real Rate of Return.

   b. Liquidity Component of Interest.

3. Student will learn that the risk component of interest varies from borrower to borrower. Until late 2008, everyone viewed U.S. securities as essentially having a zero risk component (although they could fluctuate as a function of short-term Fed actions). More recently, some risk component has begun to appear in U.S. and other sovereign debt securities. This phenomenon is disconcerting, to say the least. How it impacts the analysis of LESSON SIX is little understood.

4. Student will learn that the expected inflation component of interest varies from lender to lender. Until late 2008, inflation was a persistent but varying factor in the U.S. economy. More recently deflation has erupted, along with some negative interest rates. Whether it will continue is unknown (and unknowable). How it impacts the analysis of LESSON SIX is not clear.

5. Student will learn that the liquidity component of interest tends to average about 3% per year.

   a. But, for short periods, in the past twenty-five years, the real rate of return has been as high as seven percent.

   b. For short periods, in the past twenty-five years, the real rate of return has been as low as zero percent.

   c. Since late 2008, the real rate of return has been negative. Indeed, the actual rate of return on some U.S. securities has been negative at least for some short periods. That is a bizarre phenomenon, which has odd impacts on the LESSON SIX analysis. Traditional economics suggests such a situation foretells deflation. Probably, the 3 percent liquidity component of interest remains; however, combined with deflation, the apparent rate may be lower.

Terminology Introduced

- Real Rate of Return
- Liquidity Component of Interest
- Risk Component of Interest
- Expected Inflation Component of Interest
- Market Risk
- Mean
- Arithmetic Mean
- Geometric Mean
- Period Life Table
- Cohort Life Table
- Moving Average

———————

LESSON SIX has two parts:

- the components of interest
- a discussion of averages and life expectancies.

The second topic must go somewhere and this Lesson is as relevant as any. The discussion of averages—particularly the part regarding various definitions of a "mean" is very complex. Mostly, lawyers will only deal with the more simple types of a mean; however, the discussion includes more because they exist and it is better to know what you do not know than to not know the issues even exist. I include the formulas because I like formulas: do not let them distract you. If they help, use them. If they confuse you, ignore them (though you may someday require an expert to help you with them).

A. COMPONENTS OF INTEREST (LESSON SIX-A)

To understand how an economist, accountant, or other expert chooses the appropriate interest rate, consider why people charge interest. They do so for three (arguably four) reasons:

1. To compensate for inflation.

2. To compensate for lost liquidity.

3.   To compensate for risk.

4.   To compensate for market risk.

1.   TO COMPENSATE FOR INFLATION

In times of low inflation, this factor is small, while in times of high _expected_ inflation, this factor is correspondingly high. The key word here is "expected" inflation. Interest rates are often compared to past inflation—an interesting comparison that shows the market's ability or inability to predict the future. This comparison, however, is not itself important for the prediction of future interest rates, _which consider only future inflation_. Past inflation, to the extent it predicts the future, is relevant; however, it must be understood as a _predictor_ of a factor and not a factor itself.

Some financial instruments, are not subject to discount for this factor: those which bear interest in an amount that fully compensates for expected inflation. An example is a TIP: a Treasury Inflation Protected security.[1] In contrast, noninterest or low-interest bearing notes must be discounted to reflect their insufficient interest. This has very little to do with the instrument's marketability or the solvency of the obligor; instead, it merely reflects the nature of the contract. Because all instruments must ultimately produce an adequate return on investment, the market will price them to do so.

Three types of examples illustrate the relevance of this factor for valuations important in legal matters: one tax example, one personal injury example, and one family law example.

a.   Tax Law Example

Example 22 illustrates a tax law example. For federal tax purposes, income must be recognized upon the receipt of a "cash equivalent." The rule applies to all cash method taxpayers and to most accrual method taxpayers.

---

[1]   Issued in terms of 5, 10, and 30 years, "Treasury Inflation-Protected Securities, or TIPS, provide protection against inflation. The principal of a TIPS increases with inflation and decreases with deflation, as measured by the Consumer Price Index. When a TIPS matures, you are paid the adjusted principal or original principal, whichever is greater. TIPS pay interest twice a year, at a fixed rate. The rate is applied to the adjusted principal; so, like the principal, interest payments rise with inflation and fall with deflation." https://www.treasurydirect.gov/indiv/products/prod_tips_glance.htm.

EXAMPLE 22

Effect of Inflation Factor on the Tax Law Cash Equivalence Doctrine

Taxpayer received two notes. Note A pays 8% interest and Note B pays no interest. Expected inflation over the remaining note terms is 4%. The appropriate "risk factor" attributable to Note A is 10% and to Note B is 4%, *i.e.*, Note A is much more riskier.

Note A includes sufficient interest to compensate for future inflation and liquidity: 4 for inflation and 3 for risk. To value it correctly, it must be discounted by the under-stated risk factor: 9% (1% reflected and 9% not).

Note B pays no interest. To value it correctly, it must be discounted by all three factors: expected inflation, liquidity, and risk: a total of 11%.

Comparing the two, Note A is subject to a discount rate of 9% while Note B is subject to a discount rate of 11%. Viewed simply, Note B would appear to be more heavily discounted. But that is incorrect. The first 7% of discount on Note B (for expected inflation and liquidity) merely places it on the same terms as Note A—that discount has nothing to do with the creditworthiness of the maker. Only the additional "risk discount" matters.

Thus, in evaluating whether the instruments constitute "cash equivalents," a recipient would look only at the 10% and 4% risk factors. The legal question would be whether the risk discount was "significantly greater than the prevailing market rate."

Courts generally define a "cash equivalent" as an unconditional promise to pay, of a solvent obligor, assignable, not subject to setoff, readily marketable, and subject to a discount not substantially greater than the prevailing market rate.[2] Instruments that properly reflect expected inflation will not be subjected to a discount for this factor. In contrast, those that insufficiently reflect expected inflation will be subject to this discount. The factor itself, however, has nothing to do with whether the instrument is a cash equivalent, the relevant factor instead being "risk discount." If the risk component is "large," the instrument is not a cash equivalent and the recipient will not have income upon receipt; instead, he/she will have income upon collection or disposition. How "large" is large is debatable and beyond this course.

---

[2]   Cowden v. Comm'r, 289 F.2d 20 (5th Cir. 1961). No specific authority for this doctrine appears in the code or regulations other than very general language to the effect that taxpayers have income upon the receipt of cash or its equivalency. Treas. Reg. § 1.61–4.

As a result, per **Example 22**, the extent a particular note must be discounted to reflect the expected inflation factor should be irrelevant in determining whether it is a cash equivalent.

b.   Personal Injury Example

Example 23 illustrates a personal injury example. In a personal injury case, the "expected future inflation" factor would require an estimate of inflation that will occur over the remaining work-life or life of the injured person, depending on which period determines the loss. This speculative factor would enter the valuation computation twice: once as a factor in estimating future income and again as a discount factor. The two instances thus almost cancel each other, making the inflation factor largely irrelevant.

As demonstrated in **Example 23** the cancellation is not exact. Thus, the theoretically correct liquidity discount of 2.5% to 3.5% (the TEXT generally uses 3% hereafter) arguably should itself be reduced by the expected inflation rate. In times of no expected inflation, 3% remains the liquidity discount (or at least a popular one). For expected inflation of 5%, the liquidity discount becomes 2.85% and for expected inflation of 10%, the liquidity discount becomes 2.7%% Because the liquidity factor is itself subject to debate: it credibly ranges from 1.5% to 3.5% (pre-tax), adjusting it for the inflation effect is arguably unnecessary: arguably that element was built-into the factor determination. Still, **Example 23** illustrates how actual, _known_ inflation affects the factor.[3] For low inflation and short periods, the impact is likely immaterial. For high inflation and longer terms, the impact may be noteworthy. As a practical matter, clients receiving a present value will want to consider the impact, while clients paying a present value will not.

EXAMPLE 23

Effect of Inflation Factor on a Personal Injury Case

Plaintiff, earning $100,000 per year, was injured such that he cannot work for three years. Expected inflation over the next three years is 5% per year. The correct measure of the loss involves computing the present value of a three-year annuity equal to the lost future income. Ignoring the possibility of productivity increases, the expected loss would be $100,000 for year one, $105,000 for year two, and $110,250 for year three. Assuming (to simplify this example) that all wages are paid at the beginning of each year, the present value of the loss would be $100,000

---

[3]   When discounting a future loss, the inflation factor is unknown. When adjusting a past lost to the present, the inflation factor is known.

for year one, $97,222.22 for year two, and $94,521.60 for year three. The total would be $291,743.82. The discount rate would be 8%: 5% for expected inflation and 3% for liquidity.

Ignoring inflation, the wages would remain stable at $100,000 per year. The present value of a three-year annuity due of $100,000, at 3% nominal annual interest compounded annually would be $291,346.97.

The two computations differ because the present value must actually earn enough to compensate for both inflation and liquidity. With an inflation factor of 5%, the liquidity factor becomes overstated by 5% of 3% or approximately 0.15% (the effect compounds, so it is not precise). Thus a good approximation would use a liquidity discount of slightly less than 3%: the greater expected inflation, the lesser the discount.

In some jurisdictions, courts permit testimony regarding expected future inflation in a tort matter. If that is the case, computing the present value _should_ involve the same calculation. For example, if the accepted testimony is that the earnings would have inflated by 3% annually— because of inflation as opposed to productivity increases—the calculation should ignore the inflation increase but also remove it from the discount rate, which will _mostly_ cancel out the effect. As explained in **Example 23**, reducing the liquidity discount rate by the inflation rate will closely approximate the inflation wage increases. Omitting inflation from the discount rate, but realistically assuming the victim's investment will earn enough to compensate for inflation makes the victim whole assuming level wages. Further reducing the discount rate by the inflation rate percentage will approximate the wages increases that would have resulted from inflation.[4]

In reality, tort law follows three methods regarding the appropriate discount rate. The Court of Appeals for the Eleventh Circuit explained them succinctly in 1983. The Court's explanation follows with a few comments. A more detailed analysis of the three methods appears in LESSON ELEVEN, which covers the PRESENT VALUE OF AN ANNUITY CALCULATOR and use of the calculator. You should generally understand the three methods now, but be prepare for many more details and complications in LESSON ELEVEN. The court explained:

> In the **case-by-case method**, the fact-finder is asked to predict all of the wage increases a plaintiff would have received during each year that he could have been expected to work, but for his injury, **including those attributable to price inflation**. This

---

[4]   More discussion of this inflation modification appears in LESSONS ELEVEN and TWELVE, along with instructions on how to use an HP 10Bii™ calculator to modify for regular inflation increases. The actual modification would be the discount rate divided by 1 plus the inflation rate. In the example, that would be 3 divided by 1.05, which equals 2.875.

prediction allows the fact-finder to compute the income stream the plaintiff has lost because of his disability. The fact-finder then discounts that income stream to present value, using the estimated **after-tax market interest rate**, and the resulting figure is awarded to the plaintiff.

In the **below-market-discount method**, the fact-finder does not attempt to predict the wage increases the particular plaintiff would have received as a result of price inflation. Instead, the trier of fact estimates the wage increases the plaintiff would have received each year as a result of all factors **other than inflation**. The resulting income stream is discounted by a below-market discount rate. This discount rate represents the estimated market interest rate, adjusted for the effect of any income tax, and then offset by the estimated rate of general future price inflation.

The third method is the **"total-offset" method**. In this calculation, future wage increases, including the effects of future price inflation, are legally presumed to offset exactly the interest a plaintiff would earn by investing the lump-sum damage award. Therefore, the fact-finder using this method awards the plaintiff the amount it estimates he would have earned, and neither discounts the award nor adjusts it for inflation.[5]

Most calculations dealing with tort/wrongful death injuries in this and subsequent LESSONS use the _below-market-discount method_. The TEXT and LESSONS describe it as the liquidity factor of interest. This is the most commonly used method, though as described above and in greater detail in LESSONS ELEVEN and TWELVE, it has some small built-in flaws. Mostly, the longer the time period and the greater the actual inflation, the more likely the victim is arguably undercompensated (though that can be partially resolved as described above by adjusting the liquidity factor); however, that under-compensation is arguably offset by the likely risk premium the plaintiff will actually earn.

The _case-by-case method_ is complicated and very speculative, as it attempts to estimate future inflation. If we were omniscient and knew the future, it would be more accurate than the below-market-discount method (absent an adjustment for the liquidity factor as described in **Example 23**. The method require the expert to predict future inflation, assume wage increases exactly follow inflation, apply a pre-tax inflation factor to the lost wages (either before or after-tax), and then to discount the resulting un-level stream by the sum of the after-tax liquidity and after-tax predicted inflation factors. The Supreme Court, while permitting the method, has discouraged it:

---

[5] Culver v. Slater Boat Co., 722 F.2d 114, 118 (5th Cir. 1983), _cert. denied_, 469 U.S. 819, 0 (1984), quoted approvingly in Delta Air Lines v. Ageloff, 552 So. 2d 1089, 1092–93 (Fla. 1989).

"The average accident trial should not be converted into a graduate seminar on economic forecasting." *Doca v. Marina Mercante Nicaraguense, S. A.*, 634 F.2d, at 39. For that reason, both plaintiffs and trial courts should be discouraged from pursuing that approach.[6]

The *total-offset method* is simple, but not widely-used.[7] It ignores all financial calculations and merely multiplies the lost wages by the lost work life expectancy.

c. Family Law Example

Example 24 illustrates a family law example. In a family law case settling alimony or other liabilities, the factor would depend on the period for which the payments would otherwise be made. Computing the present value of the future obligations would provide a number with which the matter could be settled completely. To reach this number, the discount rate would likely include the expected inflation factor as well as the liquidity factor, but possibly not the risk factor. **Example 24** explains the reasoning behind this analysis. State laws vary regarding whether inflation is a factor that can, by itself, affect modifications in alimony or child support. If state law permits such modifications—and if they are realistic—then one could assume they will occur.[8] As a result, one would then eliminate the expected inflation component in the discount rate for determining the present value of future alimony or child support obligations.

Other factors, however, could be hugely important in family law, though they may be difficult to quantify. Typically, both alimony and child-support obligations end on the death of the payor, the recipient, or the child. State laws factor in two separate ways:

- Calculating a Lum-Sum Alternative.

- Viewing the Judgement/Settlement as a Whole.

EXAMPLE 24

Effect of *Inflation* Factor on a Family Law Case

Recipient Spouse has agreed to alimony equal to $2,000 per month for the remainder of his/her life (or until he/she remarries). To settle the

---

[6] Jones & Laughlin Steel Corp. v. Pfeifer, 462 U.S. 523, 548 (1983).

[7] Beaulieu v. Elliott, 434 P.2d 665 (Alaska 1967); Paducah Area Public Library v. Terry, 655 S.W.2d 19 (Ky. App. 1983); Estate of Andy Warhol, 1994 NYLJ LEXIS 7101 (1994); Delta Air Lines v. Ageloff 552 So. 2d 1089 (Fla. 1989) (declining to adopt any of the three methods and leaving the decision to the trier of fact). See also, Nesselrode v. Exec. Beechcraft, Inc., 707 S.W.2d 371, 385 n. 13 (Mo. 1986) (describing the total offset method as a "minority view").

[8] Modifications, however, may require a new petition, new court costs, attorneys' fees, and expert witness fees. Those may outweigh any resulting adjustment.

amount with a lump sum, the parties may wish to compute the present value of the $2,000 monthly annuity.

The period would be the shorter of three periods: payor's life, recipient's life and recipient's life until remarriage. The discount rate would *involve* the total of expected inflation, liquidity, and risk (the risk that payor could not or would not pay).

Handled properly, the risk factor can be partially ignored. This results because the parties could secure the payor's obligations with a life insurance policy, reducing the risk of non-payment. Still, the lump-sum should be discounted by the no-longer required insurance policy.

The inflation factor is problematic. Possibly, the parties considered inflation in settling the amount of the contracted payments. By not including an inflation adjustment they either concluded that payor's obligation lessened as time passed, or they relied on recipient's ability to seek a modification for changes resulting from inflation.

If the payments include expected inflation, the lump sum equivalent should include an expected inflation discount: the resulting lump sum will then earn the inflation factor over time, resulting in the equivalent payments. If, however, the agreement did not include an adjustment for inflation—perhaps state law permits recipients to seek a modification based on inflation—then the lump sum should still consider some inflation discount (adjusted due to the costs of modification). It will ultimately, when invested, earn an appropriate inflation factor, which will balance the modification rights.

1) Lump-Sum Alternatives

States typically permit the parties—or the court—to award a lump sum amount rather than periodic payments. The lump-sum resolves the matter such that the parties need not deal with each other, a factor many parties prefer. But it also substantially changes the valuation. Periodic payments are subject to the death of either party, the re-marriage of the recipient (and perhaps co-habitation), as well as other circumstances such as enforcement issues and economic changes affecting either party. To be fair, the lump sum amount should factor-in such differences, however difficult they may be to measure. Expected inflation is but one of the factors.

Sometimes, the lump sum is payable in a few installments, but nevertheless a far shorter period than the periodic payments, which could last for the shorter of the parties' remaining life expectancies. For example, a 40-year old male owing permanent periodic alimony to a 35-year old female following a 17 year marriage would likely owe payments for at least 17 years (the term of the marriage), if not for life. Such alimony would typically end on the death of either person. A 40-year old male in 2016[9] has a remaining life expectancy of 38.59 years, while a 35-year old female in the U.S. has a remaining life expectancy of 47.23 years. Using the shorter of the two[10] would provide the discount period. But, the life expectancy is based on an average (a mean typically). Many 40-year old men will live shorter lives and some will live longer. That is why people purchase life insurance. In the case of permanent alimony, the recipient may want to purchase life insurance on the payor because he might die early. If she were to accept a lump sum, she no longer need worry about the life insurance. Fairly, she should thus receive a lower amount equal to the present value of the now un-needed life insurance. Further, she also could die early, but she need not worry about that if she accepts a lump sum. Thus, the lump should also be discounted by the present value of a policy on her life: otherwise, she would have a windfall.

Those are the easy factors for the discount. Permanent alimony typically is modifiable by a substantial change in circumstances, such as the payor no longer being employable or the recipient winning the lottery or otherwise no longer needing the alimony. Settling on the lump sum removes those risks; hence, it should be discounted for them, as well. How great those risk are is personal to the parties, who might have information about employment risks or possible changes in wealth.

An even greater relevant discount would relate to the re-marriage (or typically co-habitation) of the recipient. The state may provide that either circumstance justified ending the permanent alimony. A lump sum settlement, however, removes that restriction. Valuing it, such that a lawyer or judge can properly value the lump sum alternative, is not easy. How likely is a 35-year old divorced female to re-marry or cohabit? That information is available, but it varies significantly by age, gender, and ethnicity. Whether that information applies to this particular recipient could be relevant to the court, or perhaps not. But clearly gaining the option to re-marry or co-habit in a manner that otherwise would cause the loss of permanent periodic alimony has value greater than zero. It thus should be reflected in a reduced lump-sum amount.

Thus, a family-law discount involves not just expected inflation, liquidity, and traditional risk, but also other more-difficult-to-quantify factors.

---

[9]   Using the latest available tables from the Social Security Administration.

[10]   One could find joint life tables, as well, but the text method is likely accurate.

2) *Viewing the Judgement as a Whole*

At least some jurisdictions[11] require courts to examine a divorce monetary award as a whole. This is certainly a useful exercise, albeit fraught with difficulties. Using the Florida cases, the process should involve stating each component of the judgment using the same terms; otherwise, they are not comparable. Thus one should view:

- Value of marital assets awarded to each spouse (ideally adjusted for potential tax effects).

- Debt awarded to each.

- Present value of alimony award.

- Present value of child support award.

Including child support in the award seems odd; however, that is what Florida Courts consistently demand. Another significant problem involves personal goodwill, earning capacity, and degrees, each of which are related. Florida—as is true of nearly all states—does not consider a degree earned during a marriage to be an asset. Similarly, Florida—consistent with many states—does not consider "personal" goodwill to be an asset. Earning capacity is a function of alimony, but is not an asset subject to valuation under Florida law. Despite those settled rules, degrees, personal goodwill, and earning capacity are valuable, as any doctor or lawyer already knows. Valuing them may be "speculative," but placing a zero value on them is certainly incorrect. Nevertheless, a zero value is what Florida courts place. Thus, the following discussion is itself flawed because it ignores degrees, personal goodwill, and earning capacity. That said, viewing the award components using consistent terms—present values—is unquestionably an improvement over viewing some as present values, others as future values, and others as annuities.

---

[11] Dorsey v. Dorsey, 266 So. 3d 1282, 1284–85 (1st DCA 2019), relying on Hamlet v. Hamlet, 583 So. 2d 654, 657 (Fla. 1991) which remarkably held:

> The judge possesses broad discretionary authority to do equity between the parties and has available various remedies to accomplish this purpose, including lump sum alimony, permanent periodic alimony, rehabilitative alimony, child support, a vested special equity in property, and an award of exclusive possession of property. As considered by the trial court, these remedies are interrelated; to the extent of their eventual use, the remedies are part of one overall scheme. It is extremely important that they also be reviewed by appellate courts as a whole, rather than independently.

The *Hamlet* Court even more remarkably stated:

> We find that the district court had no basis to hold that the trial judge abused his discretion without considering the judgment as a whole and, particularly, whether the trial judge utilized alimony to balance inequities.

Id.

How and under what authority a Florida court can use alimony to balance inequities is never explained. Statutorily, the court must first equitably divide marital assets and liabilities. Then—after that is done *equitably*—it may award alimony and child support as a function of the division. Viewing the judgment as a whole results in each award being a function of each other. F.S. § 61.08(2).

Consider the 1993 Schiller decision.[12] Following a 30-year marriage, the parties divorced. Ms. Schiller was 54 years old and "in poor health and unlikely to ever become self-supporting."[13] Mr. Schiller earned $52,000 annually and received employer-provided health insurance plus some employer-provided entertainment. The trial court awarded Husband property with a net value of $263,269 and Wife $274,153. It also awarded Wife $450 per week in permanent periodic alimony.

After considering various issues,[14] the appellate court remanded the case with instructions to view the judgment as a whole. It generally spoke of leaving the parties "in substantially equal financial circumstances."[15] How should the trial court do that? The matter involved only monetary awards. Neither party had significant separate property.

Viewing the matter "as a whole" would logically involve reducing all awards to their respective present values. That should have raised three questions for the trial court on remand:

1. What was the proper value of the partnership interest and other marital assets?

2. What was the present value of the alimony award?

3. What was the present value of Mr. Schilling's earning capacity?

Central to the valuations would be several factual and legal issues not addressed by the appellate court. First, in relation to the partnership valuation, the court included a substantial amount for "goodwill," which is unquestionably an important asset. Valuation of goodwill is generally beyond the scope of this course. It would include an inquiry into whether it was transferable, i.e., whether it was "personal goodwill" closely tied to the owners or whether it was more a function of non-personal factors. Generally, the value would be the present value of the future expected earnings to the extent they exceeded a typical rate of return for similar investments. If found to be personal, courts in many states (including Florida in which the case was decided), the goodwill would typically have a zero value.

Similarly, courts in most jurisdictions—New York[16] and Michigan[17] being prominent exceptions—have typically declined to value degrees or

---

[12] Schiller v. Schiller 625 So. 2d 856 (Fla. 5th DCA 1993).

[13] Id. at 861. The court found she "has had chronic health problems with her bladder and persistent back pain." Id at note 12.

[14] The primary issue involved the trial court's award of a partnership interest to Ms. Schiller. The appellate court found the partnership could not be divided; hence, it remanded with instructions to award Ms. Schiller a dollar amount equal to half the partnership interest value.

[15] Id. at 862.

[16] Mairs v. Mairs, 61 A.D.3d 1204 (N.Y. App. 2009).

[17] Wiand v. Wiand, 443 N.W.2d 464 (Mich. App. 1989).

earning capacity as an asset. That said, states tend to consider earning capacity in an award of alimony. That presents a quandary: the earning capacity would be relevant for an alimony award, but not for a property division award, which is presumptively equal and does not include personal goodwill or earning capacity. As a result, how a trial court can view the "judgment as a whole" when some aspects are relevant only in part is unclear.

With that general understanding, the trial court should reduce all items to present values and then compare the relevant totals.

<u>Marital asset valuation</u>. Apparently the net (reduced for debts) value of marital assets was $537,422, which included approximately $100,000 of goodwill.

<u>Alimony valuation</u>. Unfortunately, the reported decision did not include information regarding the life expectancy of the parties, including the age of Mr. Schiller. Assuming the parties were both 54, and assuming Ms. Schiller's back pain and bladder condition did not seriously reduce her life expectancy, they likely had a joint expectancy of about 25 years. As explained earlier, valuation of an alimony award involves many issues. Considering the valuable business of Mr. Schiller, he would seem unlikely to stop working until a normal retirement age. Considering Ms. Schiller's health, she would seem to be an unlikely candidate for re-marriage or cohabitation such that she would risk losing the permanent periodic alimony. Alimony is modifiable for inflation—which was low at the time of the decision and actually remained low for many years thereafter. Alimony is also modifiable upon the payor's retirement; however, considering the business valuation and her health, that would appear unlikely. Thus the $450 income stream probably had an expected period of 20 to 25 years. Discounting it at a 2.5%–3.5% *NAI* compounded weekly (because it was a weekly stream) would seem appropriate. At the low end, it had a present value of about $336,000 (using a 20-year period and 3.5% discount rate). At the higher end, it had a present value of about $435,000 (using a 25-year life and a 2.5% discount rate). This ignores the tax consequences of the alimony, which were significant in 1993, but arguably irrelevant in 2020.[18]

<u>Earning capacity</u>. Mr. Schilling earned $52,000 annually plus health insurance. The court did not place a value on the insurance and did not make findings regarding his tax liability. Mr. Schilling probably had after-tax income of about $36,000 annually. In 1993, his insurance was likely worth about $5,000 annually, for a total of about $41,000. But, he was employed by his partnership, which included substantial "goodwill." Were

---

[18] In 2017 (effective 2019) Congress repealed the long-existing tax provisions allowing an alimony payor to deduct alimony payments and requiring a recipient to include them (and thus pay tax on them). See, Steven J. Willis, *Naked Stripping for Alimony/Child-Support Tax Benefits*, 73 THE TAX LAWYER 861 (2020) (arguing that alimony payors can successfully assign income to recipients and thus exclude the income while the recipients include it, despite the nominal repeal).

he to sell the partnership to obtain that value, he would presumably lose his income and benefits; hence, valuing them separately is problematic, even assuming inclusion of "earning capacity" in the analysis is appropriate. Assuming Mr. Schilling was 54 years old and assuming he would have worked to age 65 and assuming his income would have kept up with inflation, the present value of his earnings, discounted at 3.5% *EFF* would be about $369,000. That valuation would require many more facts, particularly whether the value of the partnership and its goodwill included the employment that accompanied the partnership interest. Nothing in the decision indicates whether the court consider his earnings from the partnership as part of the value of the partnership. Typically, the two would be intertwined: a person typically will purchase a small business not just for its assets and customer base, but also with the expectation that he/she will work at the business and thus earn an income, rather than need to hire a manager. One would not discount the value fully for the expected earnings, but might do so if the expected earnings exceed the expected cost of a manager. In any event, the court had no apparent findings on this issue.

To summarize, the values were:

1. Net marital assets: $437,000–$537,000 (depending on the appropriateness of including goodwill).

2. Alimony: $336,000–$435,000.

3. Earning capacity: zero–$369,000.

Absent a modification in the amounts awarded, Ms. Schiller, received $274,000, including $112,385 for the partnership and about $162,000 in other assets. She also received alimony worth between $336,000 and $435,000. She thus received between $610,000 and $709,000.

Mr. Schiller received the partnership interest legally worth between $124,769 and $224,769 (including goodwill). He also received other net assets of about $151,000. But, he had an obligation to pay Ms. Schiller $112,385 for her share of the partnership interest. He incurred an alimony obligation of between $336,000 and $435,000. He kept his own ability to work which was legally worth between zero and $369,000. He thus received between ($271,616)[19] and $145,384.[20]

The assets to be allocated (alimony being a transfer payment and not a joint asset) were the partnership interest ($124,769–$224,769), other net

---

[19] Viewed in the worst light, the partnership had a value of $124,769, other assets were worth $39,000, his alimony obligation was $435,000 and his earning capacity was legally irrelevant and thus worth zero.

[20] Viewed in the best light, the partnership had a value of $224,769, other assets were worth $39,000, the alimony obligation was $336,000, and his earning capacity was worth $369,000.

assets ($313,000), and earning capacity (zero to $369,000). The total was thus $437,769 to $906,769.

Ms. Schiller thus received between 67% and 162% of the marital net assets. The 67% figure _includes_ the goodwill as well as the separate valuation of the earning capacity, each of which is financially and legally questionable. The trial court initially awarded attorney's fees and costs to be paid by Mr. Schiller; however, the appellate court stated that if the parties were generally in equal financial condition, the fees and costs would be inappropriate. One must wonder how the court could view the result as equal. Mr. Schiller's award included his having to work and Ms. Schiller's included her not working. The courts also did not factor in Social Security benefits each party would have received based on Mr. Schiller's earnings.

Consider, as well, the 1991 Florida case which created the "view it as a whole" doctrine. Unfortunately, some of the facts are unclear, particularly the property division award. The Court described the total marital property value as approximately $3,000,000, but said each spouse received in excess of $1,000,000. Unfortunately, the Court did not say more precisely how much each received.

The District Court of Appeals added some clarity: it accepted the distribution as essentially equal and stated each received "well in excess" of $1 million, though the dissent considered the facts much less clear.[21] The Supreme Court stated in note 2, the words "equally divided" appear in the DCA opinion, but not as reported. The Supreme Court was less convinced of the equal division; however, rather than remand for further findings of fact, it quashed the appellate reversal and upheld the judgment.

Assuming the DCA was correct that each spouse received approximately $1.5 million, viewing the decision as a whole would require the court to compute the present value of the $4,000 per month alimony award. Using a 25-year life and a discount rate of 2.5% to 3.5%,[22] the alimony annuity had a value between $700,000 and $900,000. Unlike the discussion above covering lump sum alimony _as an alternative to_ periodic alimony, this valuation is of what occurred. Ms. Hamlet apparently accepted the amount and periodic nature, lessening the importance of other discounts, particularly involving remarriage or cohabitation. Mr. Hamlet had sold his business; hence, his risk of unemployment did not exist. The facts described him as "self-employed" and as engaging in frequent investment activities. His financial affidavit suggests investments were his only income source. The file had no information regarding unusual life

---

[21] Hamlet v. Hamlet, 552 So. 2d 210, 211 (1989), Sharp, J. _dissenting._

[22] Ms. Hamlet proposed a permanent periodic alimony award in settlement negotiations and thus apparently already discounted the effect of re-marriage and similar issues relevant when considering lump sum alimony as an alternative.

expectancies; thus, a discount factor between 2.5% *NAI* and 3.5% *NAI* (with monthly payments) seems appropriate.

Ms. Hamlet thus received between $2,200,000 and $2,400,000, while Mr. Hamlet received between $600,000 and $800,000, assuming the division was equal, as described by the DCA. At the extreme—following the DCA dissent—he received a net of between $1,100,000 and $1,300,000 while she received between $1,700,000 and $1,900,000. Thus Ms. Hamlet may have received value equal to as much as 80% of the marital property. At worst, she received at least 57% of the value. Despite the enormous *possible* discrepancies—as well as the certain large discrepancies, the Court did not deem the matter deserving of remand for further facts, let alone for an explanation for her receiving an extra portion.

HAMLET V. HAMLET

583 So. 2d 654 (Fla. 1991)
(emphasis and comments added)

OVERTON, JUSTICE.

Karen Hamlet petitions this Court to review *Hamlet v. Hamlet,* 552 So. 2d 210 (Fla. 5th DCA 1989), in which the Fifth District Court of Appeal held that it was error for a trial court to award permanent periodic alimony in circumstances where there was equitable distribution of substantial assets to both parties. We find conflict with *Canakaris v. Canakaris,* 382 So. 2d 1197 (Fla. 1980). For the reasons expressed, we quash the decision of the Fifth District Court of Appeal and direct that the final judgment entered by the trial court be reinstated.

The Hamlets' marriage lasted approximately twenty-two years, the parties having been married on September 3, 1965, and separated in May of 1987. The record reflects that Karen Hamlet earned a college degree in business, but she did not pursue a business career after the marriage. Instead, she accepted the responsibility of running the household, raising the children, and participating in numerous civic activities. In the trial court proceeding, there was evidence that Mrs. Hamlet was having difficulty obtaining employment after the parties separated due to her lack of experience. The record also establishes that John Hamlet is a successful, self-employed businessman. He founded a computer software company which was subsequently purchased by a large insurance company, and he is regularly engaged in multiple stock transactions. His financial affidavit dated September 1, 1987, indicates an average monthly gross income of $41,136, and his March 31, 1988, affidavit indicates an average monthly gross income of $16,125. The parties had approximately $3,000,000 in assets for distribution, and each received in excess of $1,000,000 in marital assets as part of the equitable distribution in the final judgment.

The parties agreed to a summary hearing procedure instead of a traditional trial. Accordingly, each of the parties submitted evidence in the form of written proposals and arguments, followed by written rebuttals. Each party was then allowed to testify, after which counsel presented arguments to the court. The parties then submitted proposals to the court, which later entered its final judgment of dissolution of marriage.

The final judgment provided for the equitable distribution of the marital estate in paragraph 3, entitled *"EQUITABLE DISTRIBUTION."* In subparagraph 3.A. it identified the specific marital property awarded to the wife. In subparagraph 3.B. it identified the specific marital property awarded to the husband. In subparagraph 3.C. it distributed specifically identified, jointly owned personal property. In subparagraph 3.D. it awarded the coin collection *or* $292,371 to the wife, at the election of the husband. In subparagraphs 3.E. and 3.F. it explained how these distributions would be implemented. Paragraph 4 was entitled *"ALIMONY."* Subparagraph 4.A. directed the husband to pay to the wife $4,000 per month as permanent periodic alimony, and subparagraph 4.B. directed the husband to pay, as alimony for one year, an amount necessary to take care of the wife's reasonable and necessary medical, hospital, and dental expenses. The judgment further provided that each of the parties would pay his or her own attorney's fees.

John Hamlet appealed only that part of the judgment awarding monthly alimony of $4,000 to Karen Hamlet. The district court reversed the alimony award and stated:

> From the judgment entered below, it cannot be mathematically ascertained that the trial court equally divided those investments, since there were no specific findings in regard to the value of individual items. **Since the trial court found that there *was* an equitable distribution of these properties, and that finding is not challenged on appeal by either party, we must accept it.**

Hamlet, 552 So. 2d at 211. The district court then concluded that the trial court had no authority to award permanent periodic alimony, stating:

> From that point, it follows that it was error to award pure alimony to the wife in addition to the equitable distribution of the investment assets. . . .
>
> As argued in the husband's brief: "An award of alimony, where substantial assets have been equally divided between the two similarly situated spouses, giving them equal and complete ability

to provide for their support, constitutes an abuse of discretion and must be reversed."

Id. (citations omitted).[2]

In a dissent, Judge Sharp noted that "the distribution of marital assets and an award of permanent periodic alimony, *inter alia,* as remedies in a dissolution proceeding, are parts of an overall scheme that should be reviewed '*not piecemeal but as a whole.*'" *Id.* (Sharp, J., dissenting) (quoting *Thompson v. Thompson,* 546 So. 2d 99, 100 (Fla. 4th DCA 1989)). The dissent also noted that the record could support the conclusion that the amount of marital assets awarded to the wife differed from that awarded to the husband, and, consequently, periodic alimony could be considered a counterbalance to that asset distribution.

There are two legal principles that must be considered in light of the district court decision. The first is the authority of the trial court to award permanent periodic alimony when there has been a substantial distribution of assets to the spouse receiving the alimony. The second is the requirement that an appellate court review the overall scheme of a property and alimony distribution when considering whether or not the trial court abused its discretion in entering the judgment.

With regard to the first principle, in *Canakaris* we stated the following:

> Permanent periodic alimony is used to provide the needs and the necessities of life to a former spouse as they have been established by the marriage of the parties. The two primary elements to be considered when determining permanent periodic alimony are the needs of one spouse for the funds and the ability of the other spouse to provide the necessary funds. The criteria to be used in establishing this need include the parties' earning ability, age, health, education, the duration of the marriage, the standard of living enjoyed during its course, and the value of the parties' estates.
>
> . . . .
>
> While permanent periodic alimony is most commonly used to provide support, in limited circumstances its use may be appropriate to balance such inequities as might result from the allocation of income-generating properties acquired during the

---

[2] The words, "have been equally divided between the two," appear in the district court's opinion but were not published in the *Southern Reporter, Second Series. See* Hamlet v. Hamlet, 552 So.2d 210 (Fla. 5th DCA Aug. 31, 1989); *see also* Hamlet v. Hamlet, 552 So. 2d 210, 14 F.L.W. 2042 (Fla. 5th DCA Aug. 31, 1989).

marriage. Patterson v. Patterson, 315 So. 2d 104 (Fla. 4th DCA 1975).

382 So. 2d at 1201–02 (emphasis added). It is clear that we intended to allow permanent periodic alimony to be used by trial judges to appropriately balance inequities that might result from property disposition in the final judgment. We note that there is evidence in this record that could support the need for alimony, such as the disparity in the parties' earning abilities, attributable in part to Karen Hamlet's twenty-two-year absence from the work force during the marriage, and the parties' standard of living.

With regard to the second issue, we again emphasize that an appellate court, in reviewing a dissolution judgment, must examine the judgment as a whole in determining whether the trial court abused its discretion. In *Canakaris,* we stated:

> Dissolution proceedings present a trial judge with the difficult problem of apportioning assets acquired by the parties and providing necessary support. The judge possesses broad discretionary authority to do equity between the parties and has available various remedies to accomplish this purpose, including lump sum alimony, permanent periodic alimony, rehabilitative alimony, child support, a vested special equity in property, and an award of exclusive possession of property. As considered by the trial court, these remedies are interrelated; to the extent of their eventual use, the remedies are part of one overall scheme. It is extremely important that they also be reviewed by appellate courts as a whole, rather than independently.

Id. at 1202. The district court clearly did not do so in this instance. Its decision was based on its view that when there is a distribution of substantial assets to the parties, the trial court has no authority to award permanent periodic alimony. This view is both an application of an erroneous rule of law and a piecemeal approach to the consideration of a final judgment. We find that the district court had no basis to hold that the trial judge abused his discretion without considering the judgment as a whole and, particularly, whether the trial judge utilized alimony to balance inequities. A party seeking relief and claiming that the trial court abused its discretion has the burden of presenting a record that would justify a conclusion that the judgment was arbitrary or unreasonable. *See Canakaris.* The district court majority opinion concedes that "it cannot be mathematically ascertained that the trial court equally divided those investments." 552 So. 2d at 211. Further, this record does contain evidence that would justify a conclusion that there was a difference between the values of the assets distributed to each spouse, as noted in the dissent of Judge Sharp. In addition, the record also supports a conclusion that Karen

Hamlet's earning capacity had been diminished because of the twenty-two years she spent taking care of the couple's home and their two children.

John Hamlet, in the appeal before the district court, had the burden to show that the judgment entered by the trial court, when taken as a whole, constituted an abuse of the trial court's discretion. This record clearly does not support such a conclusion. Accordingly, we quash the decision of the Fifth District Court of Appeal with directions that the trial court judgment be affirmed.

It is so ordered.

2.   TO COMPENSATE FOR LIQUIDITY

Historically, people charge approximately 1% to 3% interest in times of no inflation and cases of no risk. This is to compensate lenders for their lack of liquidity. Human beings expect interest as compensation simply for giving up the use of money, even if inflation and risk are zero. The difference between 1% and 3% can be huge. This TEXT mostly uses 3%, but experts disagree.

As with the expected inflation factor, an instrument that reflects this liquidity factor will not be subject to a discount for the factor, though it may be discounted for expected inflation and risk. In contrast, an instrument that bears no interest will be subject to a discount reflecting liquidity, in addition to a discount reflecting the other two (or three) factors. Some experts may argue that this factor varies from time to time, or even that it has somehow shifted to a higher or lower number. Long-term evidence suggests considerable stability in this, a largely sociological factor. Short-term evidence may reflect periods of excessive interest rates, causing some commentators to suggest that the factor has somehow shifted upward. A closer look, however, indicates the market's inability to predict future inflation accurately over the short, or even mid-term. Other experts suggest a more recent shift downward, though that may reflect world-wide economic instability, capital flight to the U.S. dollar (bidding down real rates) or even deflation.

This TEXT refers to this factor as the liquidity factor. Others call it the "real rate of return" or the "natural rate of interest." Still others refer to "R-star,"[23] which is a related short-term liquidity factor. One could argue the liquidity factor increases, the longer the investment. Or, one could view it as stable, but add a factor for market risk or volatility drag.[24] Whatever one calls it, the zero-risk, zero-inflation return has been very stable for

---

[23] "R-star is what economists call the natural rate of interest; it's the real interest rate expected to prevail when the economy is at full strength. While a central bank like the Fed sets short-term interest rates, r-star is a result of longer-term economic factors beyond the influence of central banks and monetary policy." John C. Williams, *The Future Fortunes of R-star: Are They Really Rising?*, Speech to the Economic Club of Minnesota (May 15, 2018).

[24] Volatility drag is the difference between the arithmetic and geometric returns.

many years. A noted group of economics, writing for the St. Louis Federal Reserve Bank, stated in 2015:

> Although it is relatively straightforward to define the natural rate of interest, it is more challenging to pin it down quantitatively. If the natural rate were close to constant over time and there were no trend in the inflation rate, a reasonable estimate would be the sample mean of actual real interest rates. For example, the ex post real fed funds rate—defined as the nominal effective federal funds rate less the percent change in the personal consumption expenditures price index over the prior year—has averaged about 2% over the past 50 years. If history were a good guide, then one would expect real interest rates to return to 2% in the future. However, factors affecting supply and demand evolve over time, shifting the natural rate around. If these 4 movements are sufficiently large and persistent, the long-term average is a poor predictor of the natural rate of interest.[25]

Because they spoke of a rate which was a function of the federal funds rate, it was a short-term "natural rate." Thus the longer-term rate—which would be most relevant for lawyers—is arguably higher by 100–200 basis points, as argued below. That said, the study suggested a plausible permanent decrease in the natural rate. Consistent with that, in a 2018 speech, the Chairman of the San Francisco Federal Reserve Bank stated:

> My own view is that r-star today is around 0.5 percent. Assuming inflation is running at our goal of 2 percent, that means the typical, or normal short-term interest rate is 2.5 percent. When put into a historical context, r-star stands at an incredibly low level—in fact, a full 2 percentage points below what a normal interest rate looked like just 20 years ago. This trend is not unique to the United States: Averaging across Canada, the euro area, Japan, and the United Kingdom, a measure of global r-star is a bit below 0.5 percent.
>
> . . .
>
> Recently some economists and central bankers have pointed to signs that the fortunes of r-star are set to rise. I wish I could join in this optimism, but I don't yet see convincing evidence of such a shift. The longer-run drivers still point to a "new normal" of a low r-star and relatively low interest rates.[26]

---

[25] Thomas Laubach and John C. Williams (2016), *Measuring the Natural Rate of Interest Redux*, FINANCE AND ECONOMICS DISCUSSION SERIES 2016–011. Washington: Board of Governors of the Federal Reserve System, https://www.frbsf.org/economic-research/files/wp2015-16.pdf at 3–4.

[26] John C. Williams, *supra* note 23 at 2–3 (footnotes omitted).

He further explained the reasons for his predicted relatively permanent downward shift in the natural rate: aging demographics, slower productivity growth, and "heightened demand for safe assets."[27] While productivity and risk-taking may change, demographic changes are likely more permanent. As life expectancies increase, people tend to save more for retirement, which increases demand for investment assets and tends to push down interest rates.[28] As a result, the 3% liquidity factor typically used herein is arguably too high.

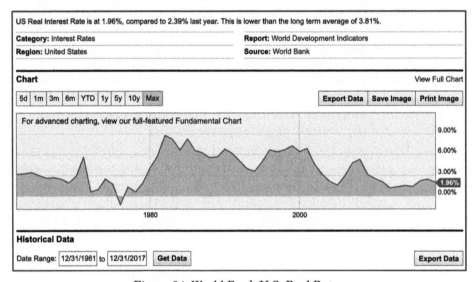

Figure 34: World Bank U.S. Real Rates

Figure 34 shows United States Real Interest Rates for the period 1962 to 2017, as determined by the World Bank. Yields were high during the period 1983 to 1987, tending to indicate market and Federal Reserve over-predictions of inflation. In contrast rates were very low in 1978–79 and for most years following 2008, periods during which the Federal Funds Rate was unusually low, coinciding with economic recessions. Over time, however, risk-free yields tended to range between two and four percent. According to the World Bank, the long-term average is 3.81%, as shown in **Figure 34**.

Figure 35 illustrates actual yields on 30-year U.S. inflation-protected securities from 2010 to 2019, as graphed by FRED—the Federal Reserve Bank of St. Louis. Such instruments were not widely available until the mid-1990s. Prior to that time, economists routinely argued about the appropriate "real" or liquidity factor for interest. Since 1997, however, investors can protect against both expected inflation and risk with TIPS

---

[27]   Id. at 4.

[28]   Id.

(Treasury Inflation Protected Securities).[29] This is possible because the instruments adjust their principal for immediately prior period inflation figures. Because they are U.S. government backed, the risk element is essentially zero. Although the yields on such instruments have varied over time, the *long-term* trend is consistent with the lower-end of the historical liquidity factor.

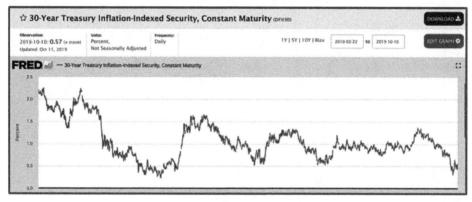

Figure 35: FRED on U.S. TIPS

In personal injury, wrongful death, family law, and other legal matters, three percent is probably the most appropriate number for this factor, although a strong case could be made for an amount anywhere between 1% and 4%.[30] Arguably, a case could be made for a much lower liquidity factor of perhaps even zero.[31] Indeed, a 2015 FRED study did precisely that.[32] I remain unconvinced, but the study should carry significant weight. A very long-term study,[33] as shown in **Figure 36** (*of short-term rates*) showed a much larger variance, but with an apparent average hovering around 3%. The difference can be quite substantial.

---

[29] Issued in terms of 5, 10, and 30 years, "Treasury Inflation-Protected Securities, or TIPS, provide protection against inflation. The principal of a TIPS increases with inflation and decreases with deflation, as measured by the Consumer Price Index. When a TIPS matures, you are paid the adjusted principal or original principal, whichever is greater. TIPS pay interest twice a year, at a fixed rate. The rate is applied to the adjusted principal; so, like the principal, interest payments rise with inflation and fall with deflation." https://www.treasurydirect.gov/indiv/products/prod_tips_glance.htm.

[30] The higher number would include some factor for risk-taking under the belief investment markets have historically outperformed the natural rate plus inflation despite the risk.

[31] Laubach and Williams, supra note 25 at 1.

[32] Id.

[33] Id. at 4.

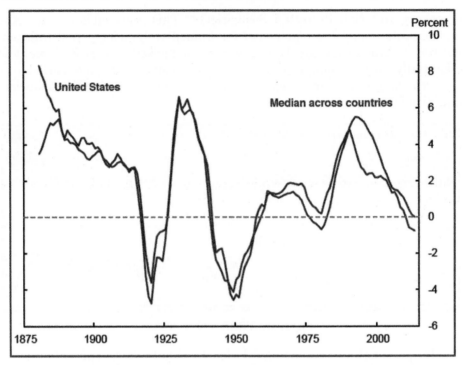

Figure 36: Very Long Study of Real Short-Term Rates

For example, the present value of a $10,000 30-year monthly annuity in arrears (paid at the end of the month)—assuming zero risk and zero inflation—is $3,600,000 using a zero liquidity rate, but only $2,094,504.11 using a 4% liquidity rate. Using a 2% liquidity rate, the present value is $2,705,879.83. Notice: the average of the two present values is $2,847,252.06; however, using the average of the interest rates produces a number $141,372.23 lower. *Thus **averaging** the dollar amounts testified to by experts is not at all the same as **averaging** the interest rates to which they testify.* Because a higher present value number favors the plaintiff in a tort case, the victim's lawyer would not want to merely split-the-difference between interest rate testimony.

Average Versus Average

Averaging the interest rates to which experts testify is not the same as averaging the present values. Averaging the rates will _always_ favor the defense in a tort case, assuming positive interest rates. Thus if one expert testifies to 0% and the other to 4%, 2% is not a fair average.

3.   TO COMPENSATE FOR RISK

This factor—unique to the maker—reflects the creditor's impression of the risk of default. Highly solvent makers are subject to little, if any, risk discount. In contrast, insolvent debtors will be subject to a very high risk-interest factor.

In personal injury, wrongful death, family law, and other legal matters, either zero or up to one percent is probably the most appropriate number for this factor. Arguably, plaintiffs should invest any award in a low risk instrument such that this factor is irrelevant. To the extent an award recipient can earn a greater return by accepting additional risk, he or she can also lose a portion of the principal.

In a free market, the risk of loss and the opportunity for an excess return will theoretically cancel each other over time. Empirical and anecdotal evidence, however, suggest that many persons earn excess returns. Hence some discount factor for risk may be appropriate in most legal matters. But any amount much greater than one percent is highly speculative, especially during short periods.

Many people appear to believe the risk return is worth taking. Perhaps so. But be very careful with how someone presents it to you. For example, **Figure 37** shows the annual returns on the S & P 500 from 1957 through 2018. The accompanying discussion claims the average annual return during the period was 7.96%. The average annual from the inception of the S & P was 10%, as stated in **Figure 37**. Both numbers, however, are arithmetic means. In finance, however, a geometric mean is more appropriate; indeed, use of an arithmetic mean is arguably fraudulent, as explained below.

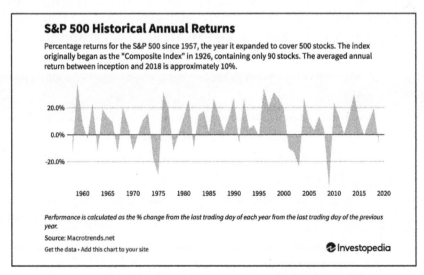

Figure 37: S & P 62-Year Return (Not Including Dividends)

From 1957 to 2018, using the numbers from **Figure 37**, the geometric mean annual return was approximately 6.65%. Consider the difference as illustrated in **Example 25**. The arithmetic mean is higher, but it is also *incorrect*. Consider a simple example, as in **Example 26**.

EXAMPLE 25

Arithmetic Versus Geometric S & P Return

Assume you invested $1,000 on 1/1/57 in a S&P index fund (assume it existed) with no distributions. Ignore all investment costs, inflation, and taxes. How much would you have on 12/31/18 using the arithmetic annual average return of 7.96% and how much would you have on 12/31/18 using the geometric annual average return of 6.65%.

Arithmetic Return: Per the FUTURE VALUE OF A SUM CALCULATOR, $1,000 invested for 62 years at a 7.96% *NAI* rate compounded annually produces $115,424.58.

Geometric Return: Per the FUTURE VALUE OF A SUM CALCULATOR, $1,000 invested for 62 years at a 6.65% *NAI* rate compounded annually produces $54.409.10.

In **Example 26**, the two-year return is exactly zero; hence, the *average* annual return must also be zero if honestly expressed. That simple example demonstrates how use of an annual arithmetic mean produces false information if any year has a negative return. In year one, the return is 100% of $1,000. In year two the loss is 50% of $2,000. The year-one $1,000 gain equals the year-two $1,000 loss, producing a two-year return of zero. Averaging the 100% with the −50% is misleading because they apply to different values. Yet, as shown in **Figure 37**, use of an arithmetic mean is not unusual in stating investment returns.[34]

EXAMPLE 26

Arithmetic Versus Geometric Return

Calculate the arithmetic and the geometric average return for the following investment:

On 1/1/19, you invest $1,000. On 1/1/20, your investment has a fair market value of $2,000. On 1/1/21, your investment has a fair market value of $1,000.

---

[34] The following source uses the same example, with similar comments. Both it and I created the example independently. http://www.moneychimp.com/features/market_cagr.htm.

> **Arithmetic Mean Return**: in 2019, the investment had an annual return of 100%. In 2020, it had an annual return of −50%. The arithmetic average annual return is thus 25% (100 − 50 = 50, divided by 2 years = 25%).
>
> **Geometric Mean Return**: zero.

Another problem with commonly-stated investment returns involves inflation, which is a separate component of interest. During the **Figure 37** period (1957 through 2018), U.S. inflation averaged 3.57%. Thus, even the 6.65% annual geometric mean return on investment is over-stated. Removing the inflation component is not a matter of simple subtraction because each of the interest components compound with each other. Determining the actual risk return on the S & P during the **Figure 37** period is beyond the scope of this course. But even crude subtraction suggests an un-inflated annual return of a little over 3%, which approximates the long-term liquidity return for the period. Viewed that way, the risk component was close to zero.

But, the **Figure 37** numbers are mis-leading for another reason: they ignore dividends.

Further, as covered in LESSON SEVEN, the United States (and most countries) tax inflation. In other words, although a component of interest or other investment returns is typically due to inflation rather than real economic value increases, the tax system applies to it anyway. Timing the tax is complicated, as it depends on the investor's method of accounting and many other factors—all of which beyond the scope of this course. But, you should at least realize the tax would apply to the full 6.65% annual return. Reducing the annual return by a modest 15% tax rate drops it by about one percentage point. Further reducing it by inflation drops it to about 2% annual return.

At this point, pay close attention. I've read a couple thousand exams in this course. Despite my argument that one should expect a long-term before tax return of about 3%, I've seen a great many students—often with degrees in finance—insist they can expect to earn 9% (and sometimes more) annually for 18 years (saving for a child's education) or annually for 40–50 years (saving for their own retirement). Perhaps they will. But, most will not: at least historically they have not. As explained in later lessons, planning an education or retirement account requires one to predict the future. Predicting future inflation and future risk returns is, well, risky. Look again closely at **Figure 37** and market volatility. If you invested at the bottom in 1975 and cashed-out at the top in 2000, your return would have been quite large. But, if you invested in 1977 and sold in 2009, your return would have been a great deal less. **Figure 37** has many more gain years than loss years, but both gains and losses have regularly occurred.

Predicting them is very difficult. If you could do that, then you probably could also predict the drop of a roulette ball, or dice on a crap table. Be careful. If you consistently invest and wisely reduce your risk the closer to the time you need the funds (e.g., don't wait until your child is a senior in high school to move to stable investments or until you are 65).

Arithmetic Mean

In Finance, if any returns are negative, an arithmetic mean will always over-state the true mean. You must use a geometric mean.

4. TO COMPENSATE FOR MARKET RISK

This factor is arguably a component of factors 2 or 3—liquidity and personal risk. It compensates the creditor for the risk of his experiencing temporary fluctuations in market liquidity or valuation of a particular instrument. Generally, the larger the market for a given instrument, the less the risk of price fluctuations unrelated to the main three factors; nevertheless, at any given point, short term fluctuations occur in any market, arguably justifying this additional factor of interest. Mostly, references to market risk refer to fluctuations outside the control of the investor. For example, some problems—perhaps wars or natural disasters—can affect the entire market, and often without much warning.

In personal injury, wrongful death, family law, and other legal matters, an amount close to zero is probably the most appropriate number for this factor. The longer the term, the lesser the risk as price and liquidity fluctuations tend to level overtime. In addition, the larger the sums involved, the greater the ability of the investor to hedge against unanticipated fluctuations through the use of varying investments or maturity dates.

Planning for retirement or a child's education, one must consider volatility, which is related to market risk. Over time, markets are volatile in unexpected ways. While diversified investments may generally trend upward, as is apparent in **Figure 37**, downturns occur with some regularity. As a result, if saving for a child's education, one probably should consider stable investments the closer the need for liquidity. The same is true in saving for retirement: if you expect to retire at age 70, you probably do not want to risk volatility in the few years prior to retirement. An unexpected market drop could otherwise result in delayed retirement. For example, in October 1987, the Dow Jones Industrial average fell about 22% in a single day. Look at **Figure 37**: at age 45, you would have plenty of time to recover from such an event. At age 69, you might not. This affects the choice of an interest rate in sinking funds—such as for education and retirement savings. Your choice may include modest or significant risk for much of the period, but likely will include little risk component for a material portion.

QUESTIONS

1. What are the factors of interest?

2. Is past inflation a factor of an interest rate?

3. Define the "natural rate of interest," the "real rate of return," and the liquidity factor of interest.

4. What are TIPS?

5. What is the most generally accepted range for the discount rate in personal injury cases involving lost wags?

6. What are the three general methods of determining the present value of lost wages?

B. AVERAGES (LESSON SIX-B)

Many financial calculations a lawyer faces involve averages, such as an average life expectancy or an average return on investment. Because the term "average" has many meanings, discussion of them is important. We cover this in three parts: the three types of averages, the application to life expectancy, and then the multiple types of means. Most readers will be familiar with the first discussion and fewer with the second or third. Each is important and has nuances lawyers must not over-look.

1. TYPES OF AVERAGES

Averages comes in three main types: the mean, the median, and the mode. Most people are familiar with each. The mean is the average of a group of numbers. The median is the middle-point of a list, with half being larger and half being smaller. The mode is the most common number in a group.

When to use which deserves some thought. Life expectancies and work-life expectancies provide good examples. Planning for retirement, one must consider how long the person will live. Valuing a tort claim, one typically must consider both the victim's life expectancy absent the tort as well as his/her work-life expectancy: how much longer would the victim likely have continued to work. At the very least, a lawyer must be aware of which type of average a statute or court requires, as well as which type a source or expert uses. For example, if one expert uses a mean life expectancy while another uses a median, the results are not fairly comparable, at least without full disclosure of the different measures. But, assuming all parties use the same measure, which is the best predictor remains an issue to consider.

2. LIFE EXPECTANCY

Lawyers must use life expectancy tables in many areas: *e.g.,* retirement planning, tort law (to measure and to value lost lives), and family law (to determine the present value of periodic alimony or child support). Not all tables are the same, however, just as not all averages are the same. Some aspects can be surprising. Other aspects are controversial. Two significant issues arise concerning life tables: the type of table and the type of average.

a. Table Types

Two types of life expectancy tables exist:

* Period Life
* Cohort Life

Most readily available tables are based of the period-life type. A study from the U.S. Social Security Administration explains the differences:

> A period life table is based on, or represents, the mortality experience of an entire population during a relatively short period of time, usually one to three years. Life tables based directly on population data are generally constructed as period life tables because death and population data are most readily available on a time period basis. Such tables are useful in analyzing changes in the mortality experienced by a population through time. If the experience study is limited to short periods of time, the resulting rates will be more uniformly representative of the entire period. This study presents period life tables by sex for decennial years 1900 through 2000 based on United States and Medicare data, and for decennial years 2010 through 2100 reflecting projected mortality.

> A cohort, or generation, life table is based on, or represents, mortality experience over the entire lifetime of a cohort of persons born during a relatively short period of time, usually one year. Cohort life tables based directly on population experience data are relatively rare, because of the need for data of consistent quality over a very long period of time. Cohort tables can, however, be readily produced, reflecting mortality rates from a series of period tables for past years, projections of future mortality, or a combination of the two. Such tables are superior to period tables

for the purpose of projecting a population into the future when mortality is expected to change over time, and for analyzing the generational trends in mortality.[35]

Another source explains the difference more bluntly:

> While the discussion about life expectancy and its projected further increase has finally reached policy makers and the public at large, more technical and political attention is needed on the selection of the estimates and their application. Analysis of 5 countries data suggest that *period life expectancy*, even projected, *substantially underestimates policy-relevant cohort life-expectancy by a margin of **30 and more percent***. This has main implications for signaling financial stability and for many recent reforms in which pension variables have been linked to period life expectancy measures[36]

Life Expectancy

All major countries use Period Life tables, which arguably understate life expectancies by up to 30%. This could be a serious problem in the near future.

That study consider the United States, Spain, Portugal, Australia, and the United Kingdom. Somewhat disturbingly, the authors noted:

> [F]or most countries, information on observed and projected life expectancy based on static calculations (typically jointly collected for different countries by international organizations such as the UN,3 the World Bank, 4 Eurostat, 5 and OECD6) can be found, and is systematically used in calculations related to pensions, health, log-term care, and welfare status; on the contrary, it is rare to find life expectancy estimates based on cohort tables.[37]

The differences can be profound and affect genders differently. According to the IZA study, using 2010 cohort versus period-life tables, U.S. men needed to increase retirement savings by 26.3% and women by 22.3%. Because both public and private plans tend to use shorter period-life

---

[35] *Felicitie C. Bell and Michael L. Miller,* ACTUARIAL STUDY NO. 120 (August 2005), https://www.ssa.gov/oact/NOTES/as120/LifeTables_Body.html#wp1168565.

[36] Mercedes Ayuso, Jorge Bravo, and Robert Holzmann, *Getting Life Expectancy Estimates Right for Pension Policy: Period versus Cohort Approach,* IZA INSTITUTE OF LABOR ECONOMICS (2018). (emphasis added).

[37] Id. at 11.

expectancies, benefits are likely too high based on funding, which risks shifting a substantial burden to younger workers:

> Translating these differences in life expectancy at age 65 (around the age of retirement) amounts to an implicit subsidy to the average retiree that can reach 30 percent or more of the pension wealth of the current working generation. That is, using period life expectancy to calculate the initial benefit at retirement offers a too-generous benefit level that is not consistent with actual financial sustainability. To address the implications at a later stage will require additional contributions or budget transfers by future working generations or a partial default for those currently working (i.e., future retirees).[38]

b.   Average Type

Most life tables—whether period life or cohort—use a mean life expectancy. Thus for a given age, they present the mean average remaining life. Early deaths, however, affect the mean in a manner than _may_ be distorting. "May" is the key word because why one is using the table is important.

If the use is for pricing a product, such as insurance or an annuity, the mean is probably best: early deaths matter very much. But, if the use is retirement planning, the median is probably a better choice. For example, if you are 25, your median life expectancy—the point at which half the people your age will remain alive—is about three years longer than your mean. Why? That occurs because of the weight given early deaths as compared to late deaths. At age 25, a male has a mean remaining life expectancy of 52.3 years and a female of 56.83 years. On average, he will live to age 77.3 and she to 81.83. But, some people of each gender will die much sooner ... perhaps tomorrow. They thus lose 52 to 57 years of expected life. None, however, will live an extra 52 to 57 years: men do not live to age 129.6 and women do not live to 138.6. Thus those who die early distort the mean average more than those who die late because the periods tend to be longer for early deaths.

If you are planning for your own retirement, the possibility you may die tomorrow is not a significant factor because your plan is to live until retirement age and then for whatever years you expect at that point. To modify a traditional table to find the approximate median, look at the "number of lives column." The commonly-used social security 2016 period life table suggests that at age 25, 98,055 of the males born 25 years earlier remain alive, and 98,861 of the females remain. An imperfect, but acceptable median results from examining the age at which that number reaches 50,000. For males, it is a little beyond age 80, and for females, it is

---

[38]   Id. at 25.

closer to 84.5. Thus of the boys born in 1991 (25 years prior to the 2016 tables), half are expected to be alive in 2071 and half the females in 2075. Both dates are materially beyond the mean expectations of 2068 and 2073. As explained earlier, a cohort table will predict even longer lives.

Another modification to consider is to examine the remaining life at your planned retirement age. To summarize, if you are 25, your expectations looking at age 25 in the table are you will live to age 77.3–80 if males, and to age 81.83–84.5 if female. However, if you plan to retire at age 70, you must be assuming you will live to age 70; hence, you may want to examine how long 70-year-olds expect to live. Again using the 2016 social security period life table, 70-year-old males have a mean expectancy of 14.4 years and a median of about the same. For females at age 70, the mean is 16.57 years and the median is closer to 17.

Median Versus Mean

At age 25, a person's median life expectancy is about three years longer than his or her mean life expectancy.

To summarize, if you are 25 and male, born in 1991, using the 2016 period-life tables, your mean expectancy is to live to 77.3 but if you assume you will make it to age 70, your mean jumps to 84.5. A cohort table will add a few years to that. If you are female, the period-life table at age 25 says you have a mean expectancy to live to 80, but if you assume you make it to 70, you have a 50% chance of also living to 87. Again, a cohort table will present even more years. Plus, even with the period-life table, of the males who actually live to age 84, half will live to 90. Of the females who life to 87, half will live to 93. Thus, be careful: you can easily underestimate your life expectancy by ten or more years.

3. TYPES OF MEANS

Means come in many flavors. Some are listed below. Lawyers will mostly deal with the first four, but being aware of others is important— when someone uses a term such as "mean" a lawyer always needs to understand the user's definition.[39]

---

[39] See, Daniel McNichol, *On Average, You're Using the Wrong Average: Geometric & Harmonic Means in Data Analysis*, https://towardsdatascience.com/on-average-youre-using-the-wrong-average-geometric-harmonic-means-in-data-analysis-2a703e21ea0.

- Arithmetic
- Weighted
- Moving
- Geometric
- Harmonic
- Quadratic
- Cubic

a. Arithmetic Mean

An arithmetic mean is one most people are familiar with. It is the sum of a set of numbers, divided by the number of numbers in the set. Mathematically, it is:

$$\left(\sum_{i=1}^{n} a_i \right) \frac{1}{n}$$

For a simple example, the average of (1, 3, 5) is $1 + 3 + 5 \div 3 = 9 \div 3 = 3$. In most legal matters, the arithmetic mean is the one used.

b. Weighted Mean

In many legal matters, an expert may want to weigh some numbers greater than others, but still use an arithmetic mean. For example, if valuing a going concern using the earnings from the past five years, one might give greater weight to the more recent years and less weight to the earlier years. An expert could accomplish this in many ways, but the sum-of-the year's digits might be acceptable. You would multiply year five earnings (the most recent) by 5, year four by 4, and so forth. You would then divide the total by 15—the sum of $5 + 4 + 3 + 2 + 1$.

c. Moving Average

Legal matters might also involve a moving average. For example, a contract or statutory provision could be triggered if an average number exceeds a specified amount. Perhaps your usage of a product must not generally exceed 8 hours daily, but occasional peaks are acceptable. If so, a moving average would smooth the peaks and valleys. In a simple case, consider a period of ten days with a three-day moving average provision. Suppose daily usage was 7, 2, 6, 4, 11, 7, 7, 7, 7, 8. Total usage is 66 and the average is 6.6—well under the limit of 8; however, one day had excessive use: 11. Using it plus the two prior days (6, 4, 11) produces a three-day average of 7. Using 11 as the middle day (dropping the 6, but adding the 7) produces an average of 7.3. Then using 11 as the first day

(11, 7, 7) produces a three-day average of 8.3, which exceeds the three-day permitted average of 8. To picture it, consider the highlighted days as the ones being averaged: you should see the average effectively moving across the page.

7, 2, 6, 4, 11, 7, 7, 7, 7, 8

7, 2, 6, 4, 11, 7, 7, 7, 7, 8

7, 2, 6, 4, 11, 7, 7, 7, 7, 8

7, 2, 6, 4, 11, 7, 7, 7, 7, 8

7, 2, 6, 4, 11, 7, 7, 7, 7, 8

7, 2, 6, 4, 11, 7, 7, 7, 7, 8

7, 2, 6, 4, 11, 7, 7, 7, 7, 8

7, 2, 6, 4, 11, 7, 7, 7, 7, 8

That is a moving average: the three-day average continually dropped the oldest day and added the most recent. The day 5 usage of 11 did not trigger the contract provision (perhaps a penalty or extra charge), but the 7th-day usage of 7 did trigger it. The user should have paid close attention once a single day of usage exceeded the limit: the moving average provision provided notice to limit usage during the next two days.

d. Geometric Mean

As explained earlier, in finance, the geometric mean is most useful because it property accounts for negative returns. **Figure 37** and **Example 26** illustrated this.

e. Harmonic Mean

Lawyers are less likely to encounter a harmonic mean, although measurements of average speed or average returns from differently sized/weighted investments will likely use it. Calculating it is beyond the scope of this course, but defining it and general familiarity with it are not. Lawyers must be familiar with multiple definitions for similar terms, else they risk comparing things which are not fairly comparable. In words, it is:

"the reciprocal of the arithmetic mean of the reciprocals of the dataset."[40]

The most likely financial involvement regards rates/returns different time lengths or different sizes. For example, you might have one investment of $10,000 and another of $100,000. An arithmetic mean—even a weighted arithmetic mean—of their returns will be overstated. The harmonic mean will resolve the issue. Or you may have one investment for

---

[40] Id.

three years and another for seven: again, using the harmonic mean produces a more accurate average, albeit beyond this course. Or, if you are a sports fanatic, arguably it produces greater accuracy in analyzing baseball players.[41] The formula is complex and certainly beyond this course:

$$\left[\left(\sum_{i=1}^{n} x_i^{-1}\right)\frac{1}{n}\right]^{-1}$$

f.   Quadratic Mean

In words, this is the square root of the mean of the squares:

$$\left[\left(\sum_{i=1}^{n} x_i^{2}\right)\frac{1}{n}\right]^{\frac{1}{2}}$$

This is not a mean lawyers will likely deal with directly; however, it is part of the equation for computing a standard deviation, which calculates distributions around a mean. One standard deviation will typically include 68.3% of the set, two standard deviations typically include 95.4%, and three include 99.7%. A large standard deviation indicates scattered data, while a small SD includes data clumped around the mean.

You may run across the term "Six Sigma" in manufacturing, or in a contract involving quality control. That is a perfection goal: one that seeks no defects within six standard deviations of the mean.

g.   Cubic Mean

Way beyond this course—except for having the vocabulary to known such a thing exists—the formula is:

$$\left[\left(\sum_{i=1}^{n} x_i^{3}\right)\frac{1}{n}\right]^{\frac{1}{3}}$$

It is useful in measuring the life of machinery parts.

———

QUESTIONS

1.   Is an arithmetic mean appropriate for calculating financial returns over a period of years?

---

[41] Tom Thress, PLAYER WON-LOSS RECORDS IN BASEBALL: MEASURING PERFORMANCE IN CONTEXT (McFarland Press, 2017) at 57.

2.   What is a moving average?

3.   What is your mean life expectancy using the Social Security Administration's period life tables?

4.   What is your approximately median life expectancy using the Social Security Administration's period life tables?

5.   What is your mean life expectancy using the Social Security Administration's cohort life tables?

LESSON SEVEN

CHOICE OF AN INTEREST RATE

■ ■ ■

Lesson Objectives

1. Student will *review* the following main components of interest:
   a. Inflation Expected (I).
   b. Risk (R).
   c. Liquidity (L).

2. Student will learn the following possible uses of interest rate factors:
   a. Market Rate of Interest = I + R + L.
   b. Modified Market Interest = R + L.
   c. Real Rate of Return = L.

3. Student will learn that for matters involving the purchase of a home or a car, he/she will typically use the Market Rate of Interest—I + R + L, with the R factor unique to the borrower.

4. Student will learn that for matters involving Personal Injury Litigation, he/she will typically use the Real Rate of Return—L, eliminating both the Inflation Factor and the Risk Factor from the equation. He will learn why this produces the best result and why it is sometimes controversial.

5. Student will learn that for matters involving Family Law, he/she will typically use a Modified Market Rate of Interest—R + L, eliminating the Inflation Factor. Student will cover a simple example of how an attorney may use financial analysis in valuing a stream of alimony.

6. Student will learn that for matter involving Business Valuations, he/she will typically use a Modified Interest Rate, eliminating the Inflation Factor; however, he/she will also learn that sometimes inclusion of the Inflation Factor is appropriate.

7. Student will learn that for matters involving Retirement or Education Planning and Savings, he/she will typically use a Modified Real Rate of Return, which will equal a Modified Liquidity Factor. He/she will learn why this is appropriate and how to modify the factor for *past* inflation, as opposed to *expected* inflation.

Terminology Introduced

- Real Rate of Return

- Liquidity Component of Interest

- Risk Component of Interest

- Expected Inflation Component of Interest

- Current Lost Wages

- Future Lost Wages

- Future Loss of Services

- Basis Points

LESSON SEVEN covers how one determines what interest rate to use. By definition, all financial calculations involving the time value of money require the use of an interest rate. The choice of the applicable interest rate is typically the most important factor in a legal valuation: small variations in the rate can have large consequences in the computed amount. The choice of rate is also arguably the least understood factor, the most subjective factor, and the one which varies the most in the testimony of "experts."

Example 27 illustrates how the choice of the interest rate can be the most important factor in a wrongful death matter. In a personal injury or wrongful death case involving future lost wages, the plaintiff will be entitled to the present value of the future loss. In addition to liability, the plaintiff must prove:

- the number of years of the loss, which equates with the N function

- the annual amount of loss, which equates with the *PMT* function

- the frequency of the lost, which equates with the *P/YR* function

- the timing of the loss, which equates with the Mode function

- the interest rate, which equates with the *I/YR* function

Typically, the number of years will be easily determined and may even involve a stipulation: it would be based on work or life expectancy. The annual loss will be a question of fact, but may be debated only within a range of numbers based on the plaintiff's income experience and the value of his or her personal services and consumption. Some jurisdiction allow testimony regarding future expected wage increases. To the extent those involve expected productivity changes, they are highly relevant. But, to the extent those involve expected future inflation, one must be careful not to double count: if one expands lost future wages by inflation, then one should also discount them by the same amount to produce the present value. LESSON ELEVEN will explain this in greater detail.

The frequency and timing of the loss also affect the calculation; however, they are largely inconsequential: a timing change will cause a corresponding number of years change, and a frequency change will cause a corresponding interest rate change. These are relevant to how one states the interest rate. Wages paid monthly should use a nominal interest rate with monthly compounding to determine the discount rate, as further explained in LESSON ELEVEN. One must not annualize the wages (multiply by 12) unless one also adjusts the interest rate to annual compounding. To be accurate, one should stick with the facts presented: if wages are weekly, use 52 periods per year. If they are monthly, use 12. Translating monthly wages to annual changes the facts and depending on the time period, can significantly distort the result.

The choice of the appropriate interest rate, however, will have both a large impact and little case-specific evidentiary support. Indeed much evidence exists regarding interest rate; however, very little of it has anything to do with a specific matter.

The choice of an interest rate is often the most significant issue in a personal injury case, but also often the least understood by both attorneys and the judiciary.

Experts often disagree sharply regarding the appropriate discount rate.

Example 27 illustrates a common variance in expert testimony for a wrongful death or tort matter involving lost wages. The victim's age will be known, as will be his/her earning history. If employed, the amount of the recent wages will often be uncontroversial, though it could involve issues such as over-time and expected promotions. The work-life expectancy will matter, though probably less than you expect. Many people expect to work until age 65 or 70. Some occupations (airline pilot) have a mandatory retirement age, while others (university professor or federal judge) do not. Typically, people are paid at the end of a work period, thus end mode would be most commonly used. The interest rate for discounting the lost annuity (the lost wages) will be the most controversial factor.

LESSON SIX argued the liquidity discount rate—the value humans traditionally pay for having money now rather than later (ignoring inflation, taxes, and risk) is about three percent. As you should recall, credible authorities have suggested a downward shift closer to one or one and one-half percent. We will explore the difference shortly. But, as covered in LESSON SIX, a credible case can also be made supporting a traditional investment return of about six percent, even ignoring inflation. Adding inflation and using a misleading, but commonly-available, arithmetic mean, one can find significant support suggesting a nine percent return.

The point of LESSON SEVEN is not to argue the correct interest rate as much as it is *to illustrate the importance of the choice*, as well as the risk of being misled. As explained in LESSON SIX, if future wages do not include expected inflation, the discount rate must also exclude expected inflation. Including risk is problematic. Traditionally, the United States investment markets have out-performed expected risk and thus have produced returns greater than liquidity plus inflation. Although the past is a good predictor of the future, it is far from a guaranty.

Did You Notice?

The choice of the interest rate caused the present value to vary by more than $2,000,000—a huge portion of the damages. This factor would be far more important than the number of years, the Mode, or even the amount of lost wages.

At this point, remember a truism regarding present values. *The higher the discount interest rate, the lower the present value.* Thus using a high number favors the tortfeasor or the insurance company ... **ALWAYS**. Using a low interest rate, favors the victim. **ALWAYS**. Thus expecting a victim or surviving spouse to take significant risk with a tort recovery can be troublesome. Undoubtedly, insurance companies will argue for a higher discount rate—and to some extent (such as traditional long-term success in U.S. markets) that is justifiable; however, victims and plaintiff's counsel must be wary of numbers too high.

EXAMPLE 27

The Effect of Interest Rates on Wrongful Death Valuations

John died with a work expectancy of 40 years. He was then earning $100,000 per year, at age 25 and expected to work until age 65. His work-life expectancy was thus 25 years.

Undiscounted, the loss would be $4,000,000–$100,000 per year for 40 years. However, because the present value would be paid by the tortfeasor, the court or parties would discount the 40-year annuity to the present.

Often, a plaintiff's expert will testify that the appropriate discount rate is one percent. Using that number (and end Mode), the present value would be $3,283,468.61. With Begin Mode, the *PV* would be $3,316,303.30.

Often, a defense expert will testify that the appropriate discount rate is 7.5%, or some similar number reflecting commonly-quoted long-term investment returns. Using that number (and End Mode), the present value would be $1,259,440.87. With Begin Mode, the *PV* would be $1,353,898.93. Notice how the change of mode made little difference when accompanied with a low discount interest rate; however, it made a material difference when accompanied with a higher discount rate.

Properly analyzed, (in the author's opinion) the correct discount rate should be between 2.5 and 4.0 percent. Using those numbers, the present value would be between $1,979,277.39 (using End Mode) and $2,573,034.44 (using Begin Mode). At 3.0% (and End Mode), the *PV* would be $2,311,477.20.

Pay close attention to **Example 27**. We will modify it below, but for now, use the facts given (including the annual rather than monthly income). A 1% discount rate—the low end of what is credible—produced a present value of up to $3,316,000 (admittedly with begin mode). The insurance company's 7.5% discount rate (and end mode)—at the very high end of credibility—produced $1,259,000. The difference is $2,060,000—an enormous discrepancy.

Next, let's look at the factors.

Work-Life Expectancy. Example 27 used 40 years: the intended retirement age of 65 less the current age of 40. But, closer examination of the 2016 social security period-life tables say 98,055 of the males born 25 years earlier remain alive, but only 79,893 remain alive of those born 65 years earlier. That is a static viewpoint, as is the case with a period-life table. But using those numbers, the tort victim—had he not died in the tort—had a 18.52 % chance of dying from some other cause prior to age 65. But, he also might have changed his plans and decided to work longer, as many people do. The 40-year term is probably thus best, but some experts may seek to shorten it slightly. The 1% discount rate produced $3,283,468.61 as the present value for 40 years. Reducing the work-life expectancy to 37 years—a reduction equal to roughly 40% the chance of dying anyway (some deaths would have been soon after the tort, but most would have been closer to 65)—produces a present value of $3,079,950.99, or $203,517.62 less. Thus, with a small discount rate (1%), a 12% reduction in work-life produces a 6.19% reduction in present value. Using the tortfeasor's expert's 7.5% discount rate, the present value drops from $1,259,440.87 to $1,241,536.95, a reduction of only 1.4% in present value despite the 12% reduction in life expectancy. Using a 3% discount rate (which the author generally recommends) produces $2,311,477.20 for a 40-year life and $2,216,723.54, a 4% reduction. Thus arguing about work-life expectancy matters because some victims would die anyway, but the impact is negligible at higher discount rates, and not large even at low rates.

EXAMPLE 28

Change in Work-Life for Younger Worker

Use the facts of **Example 27**, but make the victim 25 years old. Compute the present value of lost wages using a 45-year expectancy (work until 70) versus a 40-year expectancy (work until 65).

Using the numbers from **Example 28** ($100,000 annual income lost/end mode) produces the following table for alternative discount rates and work-life expectancies:

Table 1: Effect of Changing Work-Life Expectancy

EFF Discount Rate	45-Year Work Life	40-Year Work Life (11% less)
1	3,609,450.84	3,283,468.61 (9% less)
3	2,451,871.24	2,311,477.20 (6% less)
7.5	1,281,862.90	1,259,440.87 (2% less)

As you see in **Table 1**, reducing the work-life expectancy for a younger victim by 11%, reduces the present value by significantly less, especially at higher discount rates. Hence, arguing about whether a victim might have worked until age 65 or 70 matters, but the present value (and thus settlement or verdict) impact is far than changing the discount rate.

Payment Frequency. The example used $100,000 as the annual income. The victim, however, more likely earned $8,333.33 monthly. Using the plaintiff's 1% discount rate and 40-year work-life, the present value was $3,283,468.61. Changing the lost wages to monthly and also changing the 1% effective annual rate to a .99544% *NAI* compounded monthly produces a present value of $3,298,490.81. That is an increase of less than one-half of one percent. Using the tortfeasor's 7.5% effective rate produced $1,259,440.87, while using the equivalent monthly *NAI* and monthly salary produced $1,302,168.88. That is an increase of about 3.3%. Clearly, stating monthly wages as monthly rather than converting them to annual favors the victim. The difference, however, is not huge, though the higher the interest rate, the more it matters. Because the wage frequency should be an undisputed fact in most cases, stating it correctly (monthly if that is what it is) should be uncontroversial, although the impact is minimal.

Mode. As shown in the example, the mode mattered more at higher interest rates than at lower ones, but that was using an annual salary. But, in reality, it should be a determinable fact, as would be the payment frequency. Changes are high the victim was paid monthly, weekly, every two weeks, or twice monthly. LESSON ELEVEN will show more examples, but you will find the more frequent the payment, the less the mode matters. For the **Example 28** facts, you should know the date of death and the date of the last paycheck, as well as the date of the next expected check. The victim will be paid for time worked. In almost all cases, people are paid after they work, rather than in advance; hence, end mode will be the default.

Taxes. Taxes matter. They are the subject of LESSON EIGHT. The **Example 28** victim may have lost $8,333.33 per month in terms of his gross salary; however, he would have paid a significant portion of that in taxes. Including income tax and employment taxes, but ignoring state and local income taxes, the federal government would likely have taken about 25%, reducing his loss to $6,250 monthly. Using end mode, a monthly paycheck, 40-year work-life expectancy, the present values for 1, 3, and 7.5% effective discount rates are:

Did You Notice?

Reducing the payment amount by taxes favors the insurance company, but reducing the interest rate favors the victim.

Table 2: Various Discount Rates and Tax Effects

EFF Discount Rate	$8,333.33 (before tax)	$6,250 (after-tax)	Percentage *PV* Decrease
1	3,298,489.49	2,473,868.10	25%
3	2,343,089.45	1,757,317.80	25%
7.5	1,302,168.36	976,626.66	25%

As you see in **Table 2**, reducing the wage by taxes (or other items such as consumption) is *linear*: it reduces the present value proportionately. LESSON EIGHT will explore whether the reduction is appropriate and whether it should also apply to the discount rate, as well: *i.e.*, should the discount rate be reduced (or *increased*?) by taxes. But, at this point, you should understand two things. First, reducing the payment amount favors the insurance company, but reducing the interest rate favors the victim.

Interest Rates do not Produce Linear Results. Next, consider the $6,250 after-tax loss for various interest rates: 1, 2, 3, 4.25, 5.5, and 7.5. The 4.5 rate is the average of the 1 and 7.5: a temptation would be to "split the expert testimony." The 5.25 is the average of the 3 and the 7.5.

Table 3: Changing/Splitting Discount Rate

EFF Discount Rate	$6,250 (after-tax)
1	2,473,868.10
2 (split of 1 and 3)	2,070,400.59
3	1,757,317.80
4.25 (split of 1 and 7.5)	1,458,867.17
5.25 (split of 3 and 7.5)	1,273,721.03
7.5	976,626.66

Did You Notice?

Splitting the difference in discount rates *always* favors the tortfeasor and hurts the victim.

Suppose plaintiff's expert testifies as to a 1% discount rate and a present value of $2,473,868.10. Defense expert testifies as to a 7.5% discount rate and a present value of $976,626.66. If we split the present values, we get $1,725,247.38, which is roughly the result we get using a 3% discount rate. Splitting the rates—and thus using 4.25 as the discount rate (half of 7.5 plus 1)—produces a substantially lower number: $1,458,867.17. The same happens if plaintiff has me testify and I say 3%. Splitting the present values produces $1,366,972.23, but splitting the rates produces only $1,273,721.03. Or if defense called me and I testified the rate should be 3%, while plaintiff had an expert testify to 1%, splitting the present values produces $2,115,592.95. Again, splitting the rates produces a lower number of $2,070,400.59.

Thus, splitting the expert testimony as to the appropriate discount rate will always favor the insurance company (tortfeasor) and hurt the victim (plaintiff). Ultimately, it is a jury question. Chances are significant, the verdict form will include some questions: what is the work life expectancy, the payment amount, the interest rate, etc. If so, jurors may be tempted to split the expert testimony. That favors the defense significantly. Perhaps the plaintiff's counsel should seek a different jury form. Counsel could, of course, attempt to explain to the jury that splitting the difference in rates is not linear and thus does not split the outcome, but experience suggests that is difficult to communicate to the uninitiated.

EXAMPLE 29

Negotiating Both Work-Life and Discount Rate, Adjusted for Monthly Wages and Taxes

Using the facts of **Example 28**, suppose the parties disagree on the correct work-life expectancy for the victim and also on the correct discount rate, but agree on the tax rate and a monthly wage period. Compute the present values using 1, 3, 4.5, 7.5 and 9% discount rates and work-lives of 40, 50, 70, and 80 years. Thus the loss is $6,250 per month, after taxes.

Table 4: Solutions for Example 29

EFF Discount Rate	40-Year Work-Life	50-Year Work-Life	70-Year Work-Life	80-Year Work-Life
1	2,473,868.10	2,953,158.27	3,779,853.02	4,135,449.38
3	1,745,886.03	1,941,129.44	2,193,055.59	2,272,524.85
4.5	1,408,357.56	1,512,477.00	1,622,694.76	1,650,494.65
7.5	976,626.66	1,006,124.80	1,027,381.46	1,030,750.67
9	839,564.82	855,511.31	865,092.63	866,294.54

Notice several things in **Table 4**. The longer life matters considerably if we use a 1% *EFF* discount rate; however, the longer life—*even doubling it*—is almost irrelevant if we use a 7.5% *EFF* or 9% *EFF* discount rate. *If we assume* both sides are well-informed and have equal access to these computations, as well as equal understanding of them, negotiations will involve the present value. But, if we assume one side is better-informed than the other, shenanigans are possible.

For example, suppose Defense counsel offered "If you agree to a two-percentage point increase in the discount rate, we will double the work-life expectancy from 40 to 80 years!" Of course, the two-percentage point (200 basis points) increase in the discount rate from 1 to 3 is tripling the rate, compared to doubling the life; however, the language may not be so clear to all. Calling it a 2% discount rate increase compared to a 100% work-life increase is not altogether wrong, albeit mis-leading. In any event, the 1% discount rate with a 40-year life produced $2,473,868.10, while the 3% discount rate with an 80-year life produced substantially less: $2,272,524.85. Similarly, an 80-year life discounted at 4.5% *EFF* is better for the tortfeasor than a 40-year life discounted at 3%. In that case, we increased the discount rate by 50% (150 basis points or 1.5 percentage points) and increased the work-life by 100%.

Comparing two interest rates requires precise language. Rates are often properly quoted in **basis points**, with 100 basis points equaling one percentage point.

Thus a change from 1% to 3% is an increase of 200 basis points or 2 percentage points. _It is not an increase of 2%._ Increasing 1% by 2% equals 1.02%.

LESSON EIGHT considers the proper choice of an interest rate in family law and tort matters in greater depth, after factoring in the effect of taxes. It also considers the appropriate rate for retirement education savings.

QUESTIONS

1. If interest rates rise, what happens to bond prices?

2. In a wrongful death case, would the plaintiff prefer a higher or lower discount interest rate?

3. Loan A charges 4% *EFF*. Loan B charge 6.5% *EFF*. By how many basis points do the loans differ?

4. If one expert recommends a discount rate of 1% *EFF* and the other a rate of 6% *EFF*, would it be appropriate to average the two to get 3.5% *EFF*?

LESSON EIGHT

AFTER-TAX INTEREST RATE

■ ■ ■

Lesson Objectives

1. Student will learn the **importance** of an after-tax interest rate.

   Because interest is typically a component of income for tax purposes, most persons do not truly earn their stated effective rate of interest. Instead—because they pay income tax on the interest earned (or sometimes received), they actually accumulate only the after-tax interest rate. Thus:

   - A before-tax interest rate can be mis-leading.

   - An after-tax interest rate provides real economic information.

2. Student will learn the **formula** for an after-tax interest rate:

   - 1 minus the tax rate times the given interest rate.

3. Student will learn the **difficulty** of computing a fully accurate after-tax interest rate. Because interest compounds during the year at regular intervals, and because people generally pay taxes either at irregular intervals—or after the taxable year ends—a perfectly computed after-tax rate is complex. But, recognizing that perfection is often the enemy of the good, we will use an approximation.

Terminology Introduced

- Tax Rate
- Marginal Tax Rate
- After-Tax Interest Rate

LESSON EIGHT considers the effect of taxes on financial calculations. To be accurate, financial calculations need to reflect the tax consequences that apply to them—at least regarding the earning or receipt of interest over time. Most jurisdictions tax interest. Some apply the cash method of accounting, which results in tax due upon *receipt* of the interest. Others apply the accrual method of accounting, which results in tax due upon the *earning* of the interest. Some exclude some interest from income altogether.

Computation of an after-tax rate is simple, but speculative. The simple aspect exists because the calculation involves only multiplication. If the interest rate is 10% *EFF* and the applicable tax rate is 25%, then the after-tax interest rate is 7.5% (100% minus the 25% tax) of the effective rate. Ten percent times .75 is 7.5% *EFF*.

The computation of an after-tax interest rate is speculative, however, for many reasons. Fully understanding the computation is beyond this course; however, awareness of the major issues is not. They include:

- Tax Rates Change.

- Tax Brackets Change.

- Income is Fungible, but Rates are Not.

- Taxes are Annual, but Income is Often Periodic.

- Application of Employment Taxes is Controversial.

- State and Local Taxes can be Significant.

- Tax Consequences Compound.

- A Dollar Does not Always Equal a Dollar.

Tax Rates Change. Tax rates often change over time. For example, the highest marginal U.S. rate in 2020 is 37% at the federal level.[1] In 1952, the highest U.S. rate was 94%. In 1963, it was 70%, in 1982, it was 50%, and in 1988 it was 28%. Financial calculations, however, require speculation regarding the future. Speculation regarding future tax rates is clearly subject to error because tax laws frequently change, or at least historically they have. Probably, the best one can do is to use known rates (including already-enacted changes). That said, the risk that rates may increase or decrease is akin to market risk as part of an interest rate. It is real, albeit difficult to measure. Assuming both payor and payee are subject to tax, the risk affects both, though not necessarily equally.

Tax Brackets Change. Most jurisdictions apply various brackets to income taxpayers. Thus some taxpayers are subject to a zero tax rate (typically low-income persons), while others are subject to higher rates, with the rates increasing as the taxpayers' income increases. Thus speculating about future tax rates for an individual is not only difficult because the law may change, but also because the individual's income may change, which will change the saver's marginal tax rate.

---

[1]   IRC § 1.

In the United States, federal tax brackets on taxable income in 2020 are:

Table 5: 2020 U.S. Income Tax Brackets

Rate	For Single Individuals, Taxable Income Over	For Married Individuals Filing Joint Returns, Taxable Income Over	For Heads of Households, Taxable Income Over
10%	$0	$0	$0
12%	$9,875	$19,750	$14,100
22%	$40,125	$80,250	$53,700
24%	$85,525	$171,050	$85,500
32%	$163,300	$326,600	$163,300
35%	$207,350	$414,700	$207,350
37%	$518,400	$622,050	$518,400

Those are the rates and brackets for 2020. Different brackets will likely apply in future years. Also, notice, the brackets vary depending on the person's "filing status." A single person is subject to one set of brackets, while married persons have another, and "heads of households" to a third set.

Ignoring some exceptions beyond this course, consider a single person with $100,000 taxable income in 2020. The federal income tax would be 0% on the first $9,875, 12% of $30,250 ($40,125 minus $9,875), 22% of $45,400 ($85,525 minus $40,125), and 24% of $14,475 ($100,000 minus $85,525). The total would be $0 plus $3,630, plus $9,988, plus $3,474, which equals $17,092. The average tax rate is a bit over 17% (17,092/100,000), the marginal rate is 24%, but some income is taxed at 0%, some at 12%, some at 22%, and some at 24%. If the taxpayer suddenly earned another $75,000, most would be taxed at 24%, but some would be taxed at 32%. Thus defining the tax rate applicable to particular funds can be problematic, as explained below.

Income Is Fungible but Rates Are Not. For taxpayers subject to various rates—which would be most persons in the U.S.—one must determine which rate applied to which income. Arguably, one should use the highest marginal rate for the individual because *but for* the particular interest, the rate would be lower. But, arguably one should use a blended or average rate because money is fungible. Or, one could apply the lowest marginal rate in a FIFOesque[2] argument. While that might not be the most accurate, it is arguably correct, particularly if the savings program began which the saver was in a low bracket: arguably the savings being measured is thus always the first, with future changes in income being at the higher rates.

Taxes Are Annual, but Income Is Often Monthly. Most taxpayers pay taxes annually, though they often receive or earn interest monthly. As explained in LESSON FOUR, the for financial calculations, the compounding period must be the same as the payment or earning period. Monthly interest earned requires monthly, not annual, compounding. Because interest typically compounds at a different period than the taxing period (which is typically annual), one must adjust the estimated tax rate to the proper compounding period. In reality, some U.S. taxpayers pay income taxes on April 15th, which others pay earlier, and still others quarterly. In addition, people vary what they do over time.

Application of Employment Taxes Is Controversial. Quantifying the impact of Social Security[3]/Medicare[4] taxes is not simple. Those employment taxes take approximately 7.65% of wages. When computing the present value of lost wages, one must explore the impact of not having to pay those taxes. In terms of lost "take-home" pay, the victim does not suffer a loss to the extent of the employment taxes not paid. However, by not earning wages, the victim (or survivors) accumulate a reduced eligibility for Social Security or Medicare—benefits which have value. Probably the best method is to reduce the lost income by expect employment taxes, but separately value any loss of expected benefits.

State and Local Taxes Can Be Significant. Many state or local jurisdictions also tax income with rates ranging from zero in seven states to 13.3% in California.[5] Thus the after-tax interest rate varies from state to state.

---

[2] FIFO is a commonly-used accounting inventory method. It presumes the first inventory purchased was the first sold. Deciding what rate applied to particular income requires a choice of ordering assumptions each of which can be inaccurate. Posit someone who pays zero tax on some income, 15% on other income, then 20%, 25% and 35% on various brackets of income. One could average the rates and assume a particular source suffered that rate. Or, one could use a LIFO approach (last inventory purchased, first sold) and assume the income in question suffered the highest bracket. Or, one could assume the income suffered the lowest bracket, which is reminiscent of FIFO inventory accounting. Using the highest rate works if the analysis focuses only on that source of income and the client is considering not having the income, depending on the analysis: then a "but for" test is appropriate. Real life, however, often involve many inter-related choices such that any of the three assumptions could provide inaccurate results. In any event, the three possible assumptions produce different answers; hence, lawyers need to aware of them even if no "correct" answer exists.

[3] IRC § 3101(a) imposes a 6.2% tax on wages.

[4] IRC § 3101(b) imposes a 1.45% tax on wages.

[5] https://taxfoundation.org/state-individual-income-tax-rates-brackets-2019/.

Tax Consequences Compound. Changing an interest rate over time is not linear: it has a compounding effect.

A Dollar Does Not Always Equal a Dollar. This is particularly complicated because it involves tax law, which is beyond the scope of this course. Nevertheless, for the following examples to be realistic, one must include tax consequences.

To illustrate these points, consider three legal categories:

1.   Saving for Retirement or Education.

2.   Valuing a Personal Injury Award.

3.   Valuing Alimony or Child Support.

1.   SAVING FOR RETIREMENT OR EDUCATION

Three examples illustrate the last two points. **Example 30** is simplified to illustrate the both points, while **Example 31** is more complicated (though beyond this course in some respects). It includes future tax consequences as well as the likely _annuity_ aspect of the examples. **Example 32** is even more complicated and significantly beyond the scope of the course; however, it is much more realistic than are **30** and **31**. It incorporates the tax impact on the deposits, as well as the withdrawals. Even if you do not fully understand it, you should look at it because it is closer to the reality you will face in your personal life, as well as your professional life.

Example 30 involves the future value of a sum, covered in LESSON NINE. The **Example 31** and **32** calculations involve the future value of an annuity, covered in LESSON TWELVE. These examples focus on the answer, as opposed to the process: they illustrate the consequences of an after-tax interest rate. Later LESSONS focus on the process: how to work the example using the COURSE CALCULATORS or an HP 10Bii™. If you have difficulty understanding, move on to the later LESSONS and then return to this one.

EXAMPLE 30

Comparing Taxable and Non-Taxable Investments: _Simple_ Version

Saver One deposits $100,000 today for 18 years in a _taxable investment_, planning to save for a child's education.

Saver Two deposits $100,000 today for 18 years in a non-taxable investment, planning for a child's education.

Saver Three deposits $100,000 today for 18 in a tax-deferred investment, planning for his/her own retirement.

Calculate how much each will have in 18 years assuming a constant flat income tax rate of 20% (paid annually) and a 6% *NAI* compounded annually.

Let's first focus on the Future *Nominal* Values, which is the easier focus. Then we will focus on the Future *After-Tax* Values.

Table 6: Example 30 Results

Saver	Future *Nominal* Value	Future *After-Tax* Value
One (Taxable Account)	$232,542.90	$232,542.90
Two (Section 529 Plan)	$285,433.92	$285,433.92
Three (Retirement Plan)	$285,433.92	$228,347.13

The *future nominal values* in **Table 5** are the amounts that will be available in 18 years at the assumed interest and tax rates. Focus first on those, as they illustrate the *compounding* nature of the after-tax interest rate. Saver One nominally will have $52,891.02 less money in 18 years than will Savers Two and Three. Saver One will have accumulated $132,542.90 in interest, but Two and Three will have accumulated the extra $52,891.02, which is an increase of 39.9% (ignoring the original principal of $100,000 for each). This illustrates the compounding benefit of a non-taxable account (or of a tax deferred account). The assumed tax rate was 20%, but the accumulated increase was almost 40% more (this will vary by time and rate in a non-linear fashion). Saver One had a 6% *NAI* compounded annually or a 4.8% after-tax rate. Savers Two and Three each had a 6% *NAI* compounded annually both before and after tax because their chosen investments were either tax-free or tax deferred. Thus Two and Three had a rate that was 120 basis points higher (1.2 percentage points higher) and 25% higher by degree (6 is 25% larger than 4.8). Thus, using similar terminology, a 25% increase in the interest rate (tax-free rather than taxable) resulted in a 39.9% increase in the nominal future value. Thus the future value increased by a larger percentage than the nominal interest rate. That occurred because it compounded, as is the nature of interest.

The *future after-tax values* in **Table 5** are the real spending value of the accounts, assuming each Saver wanted to spend the amounts in 18 years. Saver One has real dollars: each dollar will be worth whatever a dollar is worth in 18 years. That occurs because Saver One already paid tax on the interest accumulated and need not pay tax again upon withdrawal. Saver Two likewise has real "educational" dollars: each dollar will be worth whatever a dollar is worth in 18 years, although that is true only if the dollar are spent for qualified educational purposes.[6] Saver Two could spend the funds on non-educational purposes, but would then owe income tax on the amounts, which would reduce the amount available. Thus Saver One's dollars each have more valuable than Saver Two's dollars because Saver One has more options on how to spend them. Still, Saver Two has significantly more dollars. Saver Three appears to be an anomaly (though he/she is not, that is merely the appearance from this *simple-but-flawed* **Example 30**). Three's dollars are pre-tax dollars. To be useful, those dollars must first be subjected to the 20% assumed tax. Thus for spending purposes, each nominal dollar is really only worth 80 cents. Hence, Saver Three effectively has only $228,347.13 to spend (80% of the nominal amount). He/she thus appears worse off than Saver One. That is an incorrect observation, but it is an easy mistake to make.

At this point, you should understand that the compounding nature of interest impacts the after-tax interest rate. How much it impacts depends on the perspective. The prior explanation described this by comparing how much more Savers Two and Three had: 39.9% more interest accumulation because of a 25% interest rate increase. Another way of viewing it is from the opposite *perspective*. Saver One had $52,891.02 less than Savers Two and Three, which was 28.52% less compared to a 20% reduction in the rate because of taxes.

Perspective Matters

Changing the perspective changes the percentage change, so be careful in comparing perspectives. For example, if a store normally sells an item for $100, but has it on sale for $60, the sale price is 40% off; however, the regular price is 66.7% greater than the sale price.

Before we move to the most realistic example, let's change **Example 30** to make it partially more realistic: make the deposits an annuity rather than a lump sum. While some people may have a lump sum to invest for education savings or retirement (perhaps a gift or an inheritance), most will save periodically. Thus the **Example 31** annuity savings plan is more realistic.[7] As before, we are focusing on the results, rather than the

---

[6]   IRC § 529.

[7]   To keep the examples somewhat comparable, I stated the interest rate as an effective rate in **Example 31**, as compared to a nominal rate compounded annually in **Example 30**. The two rates are the same, as explained in LESSON FIVE-B. I could have stated the **Example 30** rate as a 6% *NAI* or the **Example 31** rate as 5.841060678% *NAI* compounded monthly.

computation. LESSON TWELVE covers the mechanics of the computation using the FUTURE VALUE OF AN ANNUITY CALCULATOR.

EXAMPLE 31

Comparing Taxable and Non-Taxable Investments: Moderate Version

Saver One deposits $1,000 monthly, beginning today, for 18 years in a *taxable investment*, planning to save for a child's education.

Saver Two deposits $1,000 monthly, beginning today, for 18 years in a non-taxable investment, planning for a child's education.

Saver Three deposits $1,000 monthly beginning today for 18 in a tax-deferred investment, planning for his/her own retirement.

Calculate how much each will have in 18 years assuming a constant flat income tax rate of 20% (paid annually) and a 6% *EFF*.

Analyzing the **Example 31** results is essentially the same as analyzing **Example 30.** Be careful comparing the numbers between examples because they reflect very different savings: **Example 30** involved a lump sum of $100,000 and **Example 31** involved an 18-year monthly sinking fund of $1,000. I used those number for two reasons. First, they are round numbers. Second, they will help illustrate a later point regarding savings for education or retirement and how to equate future and present values to determine the appropriate sinking fund deposit. We cover that in LESSON FOURTEEN.

The *future nominal values* in **Table 6** are the amounts that will be available in 18 years at the assumed interest and tax rates. Each saver will have deposited $216,000 over the course of 18 years (12 months times $1,000/month equals $216,000). Savers Two and Three will have accumulated an extra $42,902.91 in interest because their accounts are either non-taxable or tax-deferred. That is an extra 34.62% accumulation of interest compared to an increased after-tax effective interest rate of 25%. The compounding impact appears less than that of **Example 30**because the weighted time-period is shorter: in **30**, all the funds were available to earn interest for the full 18 years.

The *future after-tax values* in **Table 5** are the real spending value of the accounts, assuming each Saver wanted to spend the amounts in 18 years. The Saver Three amount is lower because he/she would owe tax upon withdrawal. That is correct, but also misleading.

It is correct because dollar-for-dollar, the Saver One's dollars have already been fully taxed—both when earned and also when they produced interest. Thus Saver One can spend the full $339,910.83 upon withdrawal. Saver Two's dollars were taxed when earned, but not taxed as they produced interest. Because they were in a Section 529 Plan, Saver Two can spend them on a family member's qualified education expenses without incurring any further tax liability. Thus Saver Two-A's dollars are real, plus they are more valuable than Saver One's because they are in a non-taxable account (though, at this point Saver One could decide to deposit his/her dollars into such an account to make them more valuable, though possibly with a fee); however, they are also arguably less valuable because they can only be spent on qualified educational expenses. Saver Three's dollars are not real because he/she must pay tax on them upon withdrawal. Thus each saver's dollars are different, as in **Example 30**.

Table 7: Example 31 Results for Sinking Fund Saving

Saver	Future *Nominal* Value	Future *After-Tax* Value
One (Taxable Account)	$339,910.83	$339,910.83
Two (Section 529 Plan)	$382,813.74	$382,813.74
Three (Retirement Plan)	$382,813.74	$306,250.96

Let that sink in. Finance itself is complicated. Tax law is complicated. Together they are more so because a dollar does not necessarily equal a dollar. Some dollars are taxed. Some are not. Some dollars can earn tax-free interest. Some cannot. This is not the course to teach you those differences (and many more); however, it is an appropriate course in which to teach you those differences exist. If you understand them, you are doing well. If you do not understand, you need to accept the reality that a dollar is not necessarily a dollar, and you should recognize you need further training in tax law as well as the inter-play between tax law and finance.

Example 31 is misleading, however, because the monthly $1,000 deposits were not equal. Savers One and Two would have been taxed prior to the monthly deposits, assuming they came from wages (which is the most likely scenario). Ignoring Social Security/Medicare employment taxes (which would apply to all three prior to deposit), Savers One and Two each had to earn $1,250 before tax to make the $1,000 deposit. Saver Three, to have an equal time-of-deposit result, could have deposited the entire $1,250 each month.

Example 32 uses the facts of **Example 31**, but changes the Saver Three deposit to $1,250. It remains less than fully realistic for two reasons. First, it uses a 6% *EFF*, which likely includes at least some inflation component. As explained in more detail in LESSON FOURTEEN, a more realistic savings would eliminate the inflation component of the interest rate, but adjust the deposit amount at least annually for actual inflation. Also, as explained in LESSON FOURTEEN, we would likely begin with the future amount and solve for the deposit (using the SINKING FUND CALCULATOR), rather than assume the deposit and solve for the future amount. We can thus eliminate inflation from the analysis and focus instead on liquidity and risk and taxes as factors in the interest rate.

EXAMPLE 32

Comparing Taxable and Non-Taxable Investments: More Realistic

Saver One deposits $1,000 monthly, beginning today, for 18 years in a _taxable investment_, planning to save for a child's education.

Saver Two deposits $1,000 monthly, beginning today, for 18 years in a non-taxable investment, planning for a child's education.

Saver Three deposits $1,250 monthly beginning today for 18 in a tax-deferred investment, planning for his/her own retirement.

Calculate how much each will have in 18 years assuming a constant flat income tax rate of 20% (paid annually) and a 6% _EFF_.

Once again, **Example 32** demonstrates the tax-free interest rate compounds such that the percentage extra interest earned is proportionately more than the percentage higher interest rate (because it is tax-free). Notice how the _future **after-tax** value_ is the same for both Saver Two and Saver Three. Saver Two must pay income tax at the time of each deposit and thus saves/earns less, but Saver Three must pay income tax on both the principal and the accumulated interest at the end. Mathematically, they rely on the same formula.

Table 8: Example 32 Results

Saver	Future _Nominal_ Value	Future _After-Tax_ Value
One (Taxable Account)	$339,910.83	$339,910.83
Two (Section 529 Plan)	$382,813.74	$382,813.74
Three (Retirement Plan)	$478,517.18	$382,813.74

2. VALUING A PERSONAL INJURY AWARD

LESSON ELEVEN, dealing with the present value of an annuity will contain more examples and explanation. But in this Lesson, we consider the effect of taxes on the award and on the valuation.

First, some background. Personal _physical_ injury awards are not taxable to the recipient,[8] regardless whether the victim receives funds in a lump sum or in installments (an annuity) over time. The tortfeasor (as opposed to an insurance company), however, cannot deduct (and thus receive tax benefits) until it pays the amount.[9] Insurance companies are subject to separate rules which permit the current deduction for discounted reserves[10] and discounted unpaid losses[11] in some matters.

Thus, proper analysis of a personal physical injury (or wrongful death) award varies depending on whether the defendant (the one who will pay) is an insurance company (as defined for U.S. tax purposes). First, let's assume the payor is an insurance company and second, it is not.

a. Insurance Company Payor

For this discussion, I _assume_ the insurance company suffers the appropriate after-tax economic cost for the obligation, whether it is a lump sum or an annuity. _Under that assumption_, the following analysis flows.

- The victim would prefer an annuity—a structured settlement in tort law terms—because s/he can exclude all receipts, including those which are economically interest or wage substitutes—from income for U.S. tax purposes.

- The insurance company would be indifferent between a structured settlement and a lump sum. Subchapter L of the Internal Revenue Code covers the tax liability of "insurance companies" and is beyond the reach of this course.

With those assumptions, lost wages should be reduced by projected income taxes and employment taxes. The victim, however, should be compensated for any loss of potential Social Security or Medicare benefits (including spousal benefits).

The interest rate used to discount the loss should be an after-tax interest rate because any earnings from the lump sum payment will be taxable. To equal the lost wages, the earnings must also be non-taxable—which is the theoretical result of the after-tax rate. Unfortunately, the United States taxes inflation, which presents a significant problem for tort

---

[8]   IRC § 102. The definition of a "personal" injury and of a "physical" injury is beyond this course.

[9]   IRC § 461(h)(2).

[10]   IRC §§ 807(b), 805(a) (generally dealing with life insurance and annuities).

[11]   IRC §§ 832(b)(5), 846 (dealing with non-life insurance companies).

awards. If we ignore the likelihood of wage increases due to inflation, we can cancel that by ignoring expected inflation in the discount rate. The lump sum received will actually earn more than the discount rate (which includes only liquidity and perhaps a small amount for risk) because it should, over-time, also earn enough to compensate for inflation. That extra portion, however, will be subject to tax; however, had the victim continued to work and had s/he received wage increases due to inflation, that, too, would have been taxed. Hence, the inflation issue falls away.

As a bottom line, plaintiffs should seek a discount rate—using the FRED study—of about 1%. Insurance companies will likely seek a discount rate of 6–8%, using historic returns from U.S. markets, such as the S & P. Independently, I believe both approaches are flawed—the FRED analysis is too low and the S & P is too high because it likely includes both risk and inflation. I would suggest an after-tax rate of about 2.5%, but anything between 2 and 4 is credible. Of course, if plaintiff can prove the likelihood of productivity wage increases beyond inflation, that would increase the award, at least in jurisdictions that permit such evidence.

Using an after-tax discount rate fairly compensates a victim; however, some jurisdictions will not permit testimony regarding the tax consequences of an award. That issue is beyond the scope of this course.

b.   Non-Insurance Company Payor

A non-insurance company tortfeasor should oppose a structured settlement because it cannot deduct the present value of the liability. Per section 461(h),[12] the tax deduction for tort and worker's compensation payments is deferred until actual payment. Thus a non-insurance payor has a strong incentive to pay a lump sum. In contrast, the victim has a strong incentive to seek a structured settlement: s/he can exclude all payments received for person physical injuries, including the interest component of deferred awards. Negotiating an award with an uninsured or self-insured tortfeasor is beyond the scope of this course. Suffice to say, a well-informed tortfeasor will insist on a structured settlement which has a present value less than the lump sum.

3.   VALUING ALIMONY OR CHILD SUPPORT

In a dissolution of marriage, both alimony and child support are common awards. Typically, a state will permit a lump sum alimony award in lieu of periodic payments. If so, the parties must be able to determine the present value of the periodic payments. Further, in at least some jurisdictions, an appeal of part of a monetary award results in the appellate court examining the judgment as a whole—alimony, child support, and property/debt division. In such cases, the only proper method would be to

---

[12]   IRC § 461(h)(2)(C) defers a deduction for tort obligations until payment.

reduce all awards to a present value; otherwise, one would be comparing present funds with future funds which are not comparable.

Choosing the appropriate interest rate for the present value of periodic alimony *to determine an alternative lump sum* involves many issues. Prior to 2018, alimony was generally taxable to the recipient and deductible by the payor. Thus, as with a tort award, the computation should have involved the after-tax alimony amount and the interest rate should have been after-tax as well. Post 2018, however, alimony is no longer taxable to the recipient and is not deductible by the payor.[13] As a result, the payment amount in the present value of an annuity calculation should be the full award, unreduced by taxes. Any lump sum received, however, will produce earnings subject to tax. To be fair to the recipient, the discount rate should continue to be an after-tax rate.

The impact of inflation is more difficult to analyze. In at least some states, inflation alone can justify a modification of periodic alimony. If that were automatic, then the inflation analysis would be simple: assume no modifications and exclude inflation from the discount. However, obtaining an alimony modification is not a simple matter. It often involves a new petition, with new court costs, new attorney's fees and likely new expert witness fees. Unless the inflation implications are sufficiently large to justify such expenses, the modification is unlikely. The solution may appear counter-intuitive. Assuming modification costs and inertia likely result in a recipient of a periodic award suffering a significant portion of future inflation, the recipient should seek a discount rate lower than the liquidity rate to compensate him/her for the expected loss. In contrast, the payor might view the modification costs as simply part of the system chosen by the legislature and thus would argue for including at least some inflation component in the discount rate to equalize, in practical terms, the lump sum with the alternative periodic payments.

Other, even more difficult issues, also arise. Typically, periodic alimony ends on the death of either the payor or the payee. An alternative lump sum award, however, would not end. Thus, to be fair, the lump sum amount should be discounted by a factor determined in relation to the joint life expectancies of the parties. If they are young, that might be small, but nevertheless material. Also, typically periodic alimony can be modified upon a substantial change in circumstances. Predicting the future is not easy, but the payor has a built-in incentive to earn less if s/he believes it will result in reduced alimony obligations. Likewise, perversely, the recipient also has an incentive to earn less for the same reason. Thus the lump sum alternative award should be reduced by a factor related to the payor losing his/her employment or suffering an injury or other event

---

[13] But see, Steven J. Willis, *Naked Stripping for Alimony/Child-Support Tax Benefits*, 73 THE TAX LAWYER 861 (2020) (explaining how, despite statutory changes effective in 2019, most taxpayers continue to have tax benefits available from alimony and child support payments).

justifying a reduced alimony obligation (tempered by the cost of seeking a modification).

Unfortunately, many alimony payors simply do not pay what they owe. Despite various programs to help with unpaid alimony or child-support, default in the payment of periodic alimony is real. That is a risk factor that cannot be ignored. A lump sum paid does not have that risk; hence, the alternative lump sum should be reduced by a factor relating to the risk of default.

Most significantly perhaps, periodic alimony typically ends if the recipient re-marries or cohabits in a "marriage-like" situation. How valuable the opportunity to remarry or cohabit is to the recipient is an individually specific matter. Some recipients are unlikely to remarry, while others—at least statistically—are very likely to do so. Receiving a lump sum award rather than periodic payments eliminates the statutory restrictions on re-marriage or co-habitation. That is perhaps very valuable, particularly for someone who is young.

The above discussion considers a situation in which the parties are negotiating (or a judge is considering) a lump sum award rather than a periodic award. Cases in which a court must examine a judgment as a whole, however, present a very different analysis. In those cases—if they include periodic alimony—the alternative for a lump sum does not exist: the decision has already been made for the periodic award. Still, one cannot reasonably compare future dollars with current dollars. Thus, to view the judgment as a whole, one must reduce any periodic alimony and child support to a comparable present value. One would then add the amount to the recipient's net property division award (assets less liabilities) and would also subtract it from the payors net property award.

To determine the present value of alimony or child support in such a matter, an after-tax liquidity interest rate is probably best. Arguably, if the amounts are significant, a small risk factor would be appropriate because history tells us people do tend to earn more than liquidity plus inflation. How to factor inflation is more difficult and is subject to the above analysis. Ignoring it is probably best.

Unfortunately, despite searching through a very large number of cases, I have yet to find one in which the court initially or on remand actually reduced periodic alimony and child support awards to a present value and then added them to the recipient's property award and subtracted them from the payor's award. As a result, cases in which one former spouse—in present value terms—received a negative amount and the other received more than 100% of the available value are common. To be fair, states typically do not value degrees earned during a marriage and often ignore "personal goodwill" which can be valuable.

QUESTIONS

1. Are personal physical injury awards taxable to the recipient?

2. Can a person invest in a tax-free educational savings account?

3. Can a person invest in a tax-deferred retirement plan?

PART III

CALCULATIONS

■ ■ ■

LESSON NINE

FUTURE VALUE OF A SUM

■ ■ ■

Lesson Objectives

1. Student will learn how to use the FUTURE VALUE OF A SUM CALCULATOR.

   a. How to locate the Instructions.

   b. How to find Definitions of each Function.

2. Student will learn when a lawyer would need to compute the Future Value of a Sum:

   • **As a lawyer, you would use this calculation if you or a client needs to pay a debt or other obligation late. . . . *i.e.*, if you want to defer paying an obligation; or, you would use it if you have money saved and need to know what it will be worth in the future.**

LESSON NINE begins the calculations part of the course. As explained in LESSON THREE, eight types of Financial Calculations are fundamental to a lawyer's practice:

1. Future Value of a Sum
2. Present Value of a Sum
3. Present Value of an Annuity
4. Future Value of an Annuity
5. Sinking Fund
6. Amortization
7. Interest Rate Conversion
8. Yield Computation

LESSON NINE covers the future value of a sum. This calculation computes the future amount or value of a current deposit. As a lawyer, you would use this calculation if you or a client needs to pay a debt or other obligation late. For example, you may want to *defer* paying an obligation. Perhaps you owe $1,000 today, but wish to pay it five years from now. If so, you need to determine the future value in five years of $1,000 today. Or, perhaps you have $1,000 currently saved and would like to know what it will be worth in five or ten years at an assumed interest rate. Again, that would be the future value of a sum.

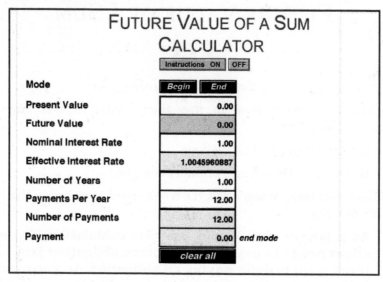

Figure 38: Future Value of a Sum Calculator

Figure 38 illustrates the FUTURE VALUE OF A SUM COURSE CALCULATOR. LESSON THREE also listed multiple uses for the calculator, which we should explore further with examples.

a.   If you deposit money into an account, you can compute what it will be worth in the future. This is useful if:

  • You want to save for a child's education.

  • You are saving for retirement.

  • You are saving for a large purchase.

b.   If population growth rates continue at a constant rate, you can compute the population of an area after a given length of time. This is useful if:

  • You are dealing with growth management.

  • You are dealing with environmental issues, increasing at a constant rate.

c.   If your client was owed a specific amount—such as a debt or a judgment—as of a prior date, you can compute what he is owed today. The amount owed originally would be the present value and the amount today would be the future value.

d.   If a budget item or cost increases at a particular rate, you can compute the amount for a future period.

e.   In a tort case, perhaps your client suffered damages three years ago. You will want to compute the value today of that amount. Today is the present, but it is also the future of the past. Thus the amount claimed today is the future value of the past loss.

But, first, let's look at the calculator again and its features. If you do not have it open, you should open it. Notice the button to turn Instructions ON or OFF. Click on it and you will see these instructions, which appear on *each* of the course calculators. They disappear if you click OFF.

---

1.   Press "Clear All" prior to working a problem.

2.   Type appropriate numbers in the white boxes.

3.   Do not change the numbers in the yellow boxes.

4.   The answer will appear in the green box.

5.   Place your cursor over terms for a definition of the term.

If the boxes have a bluish[1] tint over them, you need to change a setting in Adobe Reader. Open Reader/Preferences/Forms on a MAC or Edit/Preferences/Forms on a PC. You should see a box with a default setting: "Show border hover color for fields." If checked, that puts a tint over all the boxes, which eliminates the color scheme. Why Adobe has this annoying feature as a default setting is unclear, but it has for several years. Uncheck the box if checked and then click on OK to save it.

Clearing the COURSE CALCULATORS before working a problem is not essential, but is probably good practice as it will help avoid mistakes. As you saw in **Figure 1**, the white boxes are the Present Value, the Nominal Interest Rate, the Number of Years, and the Payments per Year. You must type number into each box. The numbers need not be whole numbers. For example, you could use 1.5 years. *Do not use dollar signs*. Also, *do not use commas*. Thus, to enter $115,000 you type 115000. The calculator will insert the comma. To enter cents, use the period. Thus $5.15 is 5.15.

TIP

You may enter the various values *in any order*. For example, you could enter the Nominal Interest Rate prior to entering the Present Value .

---

[1]   Light blue is the default setting, so perhaps you see a different color. In any event, turn off this feature!

Also, you may change _any_ of the values in white boxes. Doing so will automatically cause re-calculation of other values.

Do not change numbers in yellow boxes. The effective interest rate appears in a yellow box. Once you enter the *NAI* (the nominal rate), the calculator will convert it to the appropriate effective rate. The number of payments (or sometimes the number of periods) is also a yellow box. Once you enter the number of years and the number of periods or payments per year, the calculator will display the total number of payments or periods. For the future value of a sum, payments are irrelevant; hence, this box represents the number of periods. The amount of the payment is also in a yellow box. For the FUTURE VALUE OF A SUM CALCULATOR, it is set to zero. You cannot change it. That is because you are computing the future value of a present amount with no additional payments or contributions other than interest.

Your answer will appear in the green box, which for this calculator is the Future Value. It will be rounded to two decimals; however, if you let your cursor hover over the number, it will display up to 14 decimals. You will rarely need that degree of precision.

Each of the boxes has a label using a dark blue font. If you let your cursor hover over the blue words, a definition of the term will appear. If you move your cursor away, it will disappear.

Consider **Example 33**, in which you have a present investment and you want to know the value in the future at alternative dates. The 1, 2, and 5 year periods are realistic. The 100 year period is for fun: to illustrate the impact of compounding over a long period. Why would you want to know this? Perhaps a relative gave you $10,000 upon the birth of a child. You place in an educational savings account and want to know what you will have in 18 years—that would use an 18-year period rather than 1, 2, or 5. Or perhaps you inherited $50,000 and you want to know how much you will have in 40 years when you expect to retire. Again, that uses the future value of a sum, but with a period of 40 years.

EXAMPLE 33

Future Value of a Sum

You deposit $1,000 today. You and the debtor agree that an appropriate interest rate would be 10% interest compounded _annually_.

You would like to know the value—alternatively—in one, two, five and 100 years.

To work the problem, open the FUTURE VALUE OF A SUM CALCULATOR. Type 1000 in the white box next to Present Value (or 10000 for the gift to your child or 50000 for the gift to you). Input the 10% *NAI* in the white box labeled Nominal Interest Rate. As discussed in LESSON SEVEN, this rate would combine liquidity, risk, and expected inflation. In **Example 33**, you and the borrower (bank, investment company, insurance company, private person) have negotiated a 10% *NAI* compounded annually. Or, perhaps, this is what you project you will earn annually for the term you choose.

Next, input 1 in the white box next to Payments (Periods) per Year. This is important because **Example 33** states a 10% *NAI* compounded annually. You will quickly see the calculator input 10 as the effective rate, as well. If you fail to change the periods per year, the calculator will compute a higher *EFF* and you will receive a wrong answer. The default mode is END; however, for the future value of a sum, the mode is irrelevant. You may change it to begin, but it will not affect your answer. With other course calculators—the Future Value of an Annuity, a Sinking Fund, an Amortization, or the Present Value of an Annuity—the mode matters.

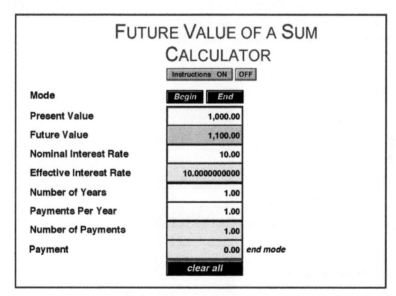

Figure 39: Example 33 for 1 Year

The default number of years is one; hence, you should see the answer for one year in the green box, as shown in **Figure 39**: $1,100.00. If you change the number of periods to 2, as shown in **Figure 40**, the Future Value answer changes to $1,210. You do not need to press Clear All between the calculations—just change one value and the others change with it.

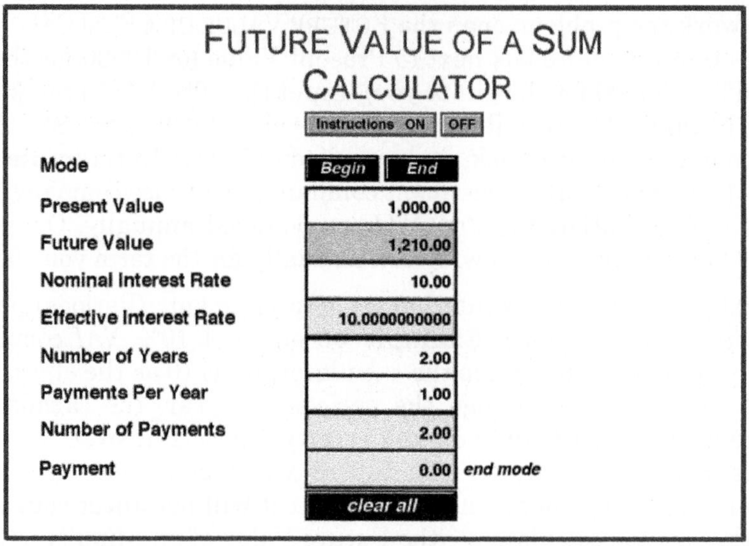

FUTURE VALUE OF A SUM CALCULATOR

Instructions	ON OFF
Mode	Begin End
Present Value	1,000.00
Future Value	1,210.00
Nominal Interest Rate	10.00
Effective Interest Rate	10.0000000000
Number of Years	2.00
Payments Per Year	1.00
Number of Payments	2.00
Payment	0.00 *end mode*
	clear all

Figure 40: Example 33 for 2 Years

In **Figure 41**, the number of years appears as 5, which changes the future value to $1,610.51. Then in **Figure 42**, the number of years is 100, which produces a future value of $13,780,612.34.

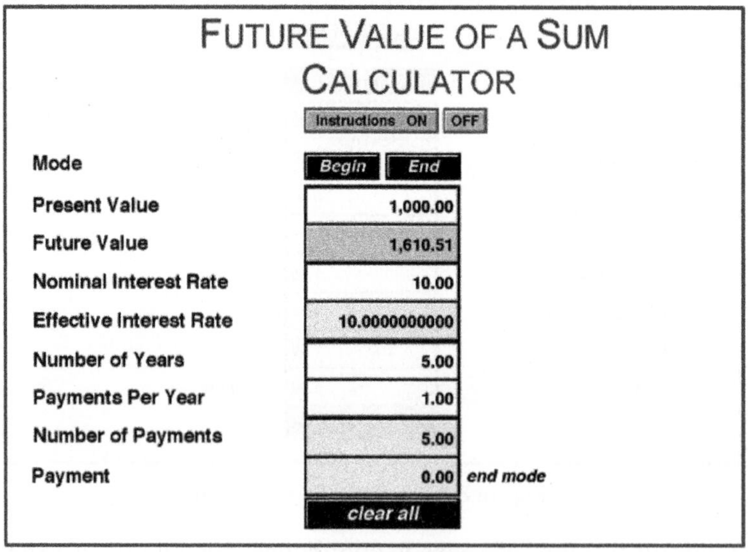

FUTURE VALUE OF A SUM CALCULATOR

Instructions	ON OFF
Mode	Begin End
Present Value	1,000.00
Future Value	1,610.51
Nominal Interest Rate	10.00
Effective Interest Rate	10.0000000000
Number of Years	5.00
Payments Per Year	1.00
Number of Payments	5.00
Payment	0.00 *end mode*
	clear all

Figure 41: Example 33 for 5 Years

In each of these calculations, we used an interest rate of 10% *NAI* compounded annually. If this were invested in a tax-deferred account (as covered in LESSON EIGHT) and if we could reliably earn 10% *EFF*, the answers produced are correct. If the savings were for a child's education, opportunities exist for tax deferral, though the time period would likely be

18 years. Similarly, if the savings were for retirement, tax deferral opportunities also exist, but the time frame could be 40 years or more. In most other cases, the annual interest would be taxable. Thus, as explained in LESSON EIGHT, you should consider using an after-tax interest rate. Also, as explained in LESSON SEVEN, inflation is a substantial component of interest, as well as other investment returns. You might very well earn 10% *EFF* on investments during some five year periods (or perhaps more as illustrated in LESSON SEVEN); however, the future value calculated would not likely have the purchasing power of that same amount today. To correct for this, you would need to adjust the interest rate downward to remove the expected inflation component. Thus, after removing taxes and inflation, that 10% return may actually be four or five, of which some would reflect risk—both risk of default by the borrower and market risk, as covered in LESSON SEVEN. Some investors would suffer no defaults and would time the market such that fluctuations did not matter. Others, however, would not be so lucky and could lose the entire amount. As covered in LESSON SEVEN, if we consider a large number of investors and a medium to long period of time, the likely return, after taxes, will more likely be two or three percent *EFF*.

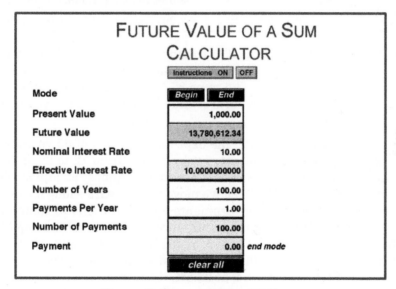

Figure 42: Example 33 for 100 Years

Another problem with **Example 33** is the annual compounding. Most investments and loans with have monthly compounding, if not more frequent, such as daily. Thus consider the same example with a present value of $1,000, but change the annual compounding monthly. LESSON FIVE-B covered this in greater depth, but the FUTURE VALUE OF A SUM CALCULATOR will also do this for you. Input 10 as the *NAI*, but change the Payments (Periods) per Year to 12 to reflect the 12 months in a year. To make the example interesting, let's use periods of 5, 10, 65 and 100 years. Five and ten years are common periods human face in borrowing money. Sixty-five years is likely the remaining life expectancy of many readers. One hundred years is quite long, but a nice round number.

Also, to be realistic for a debt scenario, use common credit card rates of 12%, 18%, 21%, and 22.5% *NAI* with monthly compounding. To make the example even more interesting, though admittedly unrealistic, make the additional assumption that you make no payments at any point and you suffer no late payment fees. Notice before we work the problem, the low rate of 12% is less than half of the high rate of 22.5%. But as you will soon see, an increase from 12 to 22.5, or even from 21 to 22.5 can make a massive change in the result over a long period of time.

Table 9: Comparison of Compounding Periods

	5 YEARS	10 YEARS	65 YEARS	100 YEARS
12% *NAI*	1,816.70	3,300.39	2,347,856.51	153,337,556.81
18% *NAI*	2,443.22	5,969.32	110,538,334.09	57,444,797,117.12
21% *NAI*	2,831.82	8,019.18	753,088,403.05	1,099,768,983,384.10
22.5% *NAI*	3,048.30	9,292.12	1,962,207,645.13	4,798,948,514,202.90

Look at **Table 9**.[2] Changing the *NAI* (compounded monthly) from 12 to 22.5 was an increase of 87.5%. The future value, however, increased by only 67.8% over a five-year period. The same 87.5% increase in the interest rate, however, resulted in a 181.5% future value increase over ten years, as the compounding accelerated.

But then look at a common life expectancy period of 65 years. Again, we increased the nominal interest *rate* by 87.5% (from 12 to 22.5), but the future value increased from about $2.3 million to almost $2 billion. That is an increase of almost 835%. When we move to 100 years—long for humans, but perhaps not so long for governments or corporations to contemplate, the 87.5% jump in the interest rate produced a future value jump of over 31,000%. At 12% *NAI* compounded monthly for 100 years, that $1,000 turned into over $153 million. But compounded at 21%, it became approximately $1.1 trillion. And, at 22.5%, it became $4.8 trillion. Thus the seemingly modest interest rate increase from 21 to 22.5 (150 basis points or about a 2.4% increase in the rate) produced a result 336% larger.

The highest credit card *APR* I've seen was a department store card that had a 196.6% *APR*. Although I recall it compounded daily, to be consistent with **Figure 36**, assume it was monthly. Also assume the initial balance was one cent. Neither the COURSE CALCULATORS nor an HP

---

[2] I used an HP 10Bii™ calculator for these numbers, while the LESSON NINE calculations use the COURSE CALCULATOR. The difference is immaterial.

10Bii™ can handle the rate for longer than twenty years, at which point it produces a future value of over $90 trillion. And that was not starting at $1,000: it was starting at one cent. If we start with a truly tiny sum of $0.00000001, which is 1/1,000,000th of a cent and use an *EFF* of 517.57 (approximately the *EFF* from the 196.6 *NAI*), over 100 years we get:

$117,000,000,000,000,000,000,000,000,000,000,000,000,000,000, 000,000,000,000,000,000,000,000,000,000.

An issue many students have had trouble with involves computing the value of a tort loss. LESSON TWELVE will consider this in more detail because typically it involves the Present Value of an Annuity. But, the issue is also relevant to LESSON ELEVEN involving the future value of an annuity, and this lesson, as well. Consider **Example 34**.

EXAMPLE 34

Future Value of a Sum

Your client's property was destroyed two years ago. At the time, it had a value of $115,000. You are in settlement negotiations today. What is the value of the loss?

States vary regarding whether pre-judgment interest is appropriate. Often, it is available at least for "out-of-pocket" costs, but not for unliquidated damages. In **Example 34**, the value of the property two years ago would be a question of fact. Once determined, the amount can be inflated to the current date of settlement. That would be the future value of a sum because today is the future of the past lost. Assuming the inflated value—the loss in terms of the value today—is recoverable, the appropriate interest rate would be whatever the plaintiff likely would have earned had he/she had the $115,000 two years ago. That would include a liquidity amount—perhaps 2–3%—plus an actual past inflation amount—whatever inflation was for the prior two years. That, too, would be a question of fact. Whether a risk factor should be included would depend on the victim, his/her cost of capital and other information outside the fact pattern. Using 5.5% *NAI* compounded monthly (5.64% *EFF*), the future value would be $128,339.72. If such interest is not permitted, the defense has an incentive to delay settling or to delay litigation, as some states have begun to realize. What seems to confuse many people is that the present value—the value today—is actually the future value. That is because the loss was in the past.

In LESSONS ELEVEN and TWELVE, we will consider more complex tort cases involving lost wages. In such examples, inevitably part of the damages are in the past and part are in the future. That occurs because few cases settle immediately after the injury; often, they take two or more years to reach serious negotiations or litigation. Thus, past lost wages require the use of the FUTURE VALUE OF AN ANNUITY CALCULATOR, while future lost wages require the use of the PRESENT VALUE OF AN ANNUITY CALCULATOR. Again, today (the date of settlement negotiations) is the future of the past.

To work **Examples 33** and **34** with an HP 10Bii™ calculator follow the following steps:

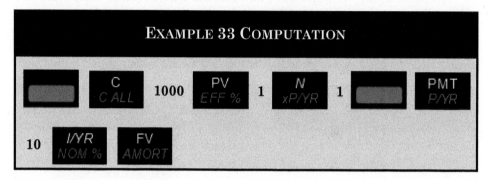

The answer will appear as −1,100. The mode is irrelevant. **Example 33** posited 10% interest compounded annually; hence, you must either enter the 10% rate as a nominal rate (as shown) with the number of periods per year as 1 (as shown) and the number of periods (N) also as 1.

In the alternative, you could enter the 10% rate as 10 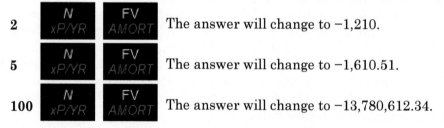. That enters it as an effective rate. If you leave the periods per year as 1, the answer will be the same. Or, you could set the periods per year as 12 (which is the default); however, you would then need to enter 12 as the number of periods (N). Again, the answer will be −1,100.

To work the alternative values at 2, 5, and 100 years, you do not need to start over. Instead, using the initial method (1 period per year), input:

2 **N** **FV** The answer will change to −1,210.

5 **N** **FV** The answer will change to −1,610.51.

100 **N** **FV** The answer will change to −13,780,612.34.

As explained in LESSON THREE, the HP 10Bii™ answer appears as a negative because of the cash flow. You deposited 1000, which you might view as a positive number. If so, you withdraw 1,100, which must be a negative. If, instead, you inputted −1,000 as the deposit, the withdrawal (future value) would be 1,100—a positive number.

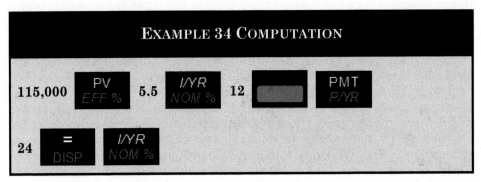

EXAMPLE 34 COMPUTATION

The answer will appear as −128,339.72. As above, we chose a 5.5% *NAI* compounded monthly; hence, we had to change the number of periods per year to 12 and the total number of periods (N) to 24.

QUESTIONS

1.   You borrowed $10,000 today and agreed to defer all interest and principal payments for 5 years. Interest accrues at a rate of 5% *EFF*. How much will you owe in 5 years?

2.   You and your employer agreed your bonus, which you have earned, should be $100,000 today. Prior to offering it to you, your employer gave you the option of deferring receipt for twenty years. How much will the amount be if you agree upon an interest rate of 3% *EFF*? How much will it be if you agree upon an interest rate of 7.5% *EFF*? *Ignore any U.S. tax consequences.*

3.   You have $10,000 received from a grandparent for your newborn's education. You deposited it into a section 529 account, which accumulates money tax-free. You expect to begin to use the funds in 18 years. You also assume you can earn 8% per year in stock index funds consistently for the entire 18 years. How much will you nominally have in 18 years under your assumption? How much will you have if you assume inflation will be zero and you can consistently earn 4% per year? [Hint: this gives you an idea of what the future funds will be worth in current dollars.]

4.   The community in which you live has a population of 500,000. You project the population to grow at an annual rate of 2.5% for the foreseeable future. How many people do you expect in five years, ten years, and twenty-five years?

5.   An invasive species has entered your area. You estimate 1000 of the creatures (snake/rodent/fish/insect/plant) currently exist. You estimate that unchecked (the creatures have no known predators in the area), the species will double in population every year for the foreseeable future. How many will

exist in your area in five, ten, twenty-five, or thirty years if neither you nor nature do anything to check the population? In the alternative, suppose the things double in population every three months but there are currently only 2 of them. How many will exist, if unchecked, in one, five, ten, or eleven years?

6. You have two people who just wed and who plan to have a large family (as was common 100 years ago). They expect 8 children to reach adulthood and they predict each will marry and produce another 8 who reach adulthood. How many great-grand-children will the initial two people have, assuming all survive? (Note, the children are siblings, the grand-children are first cousins, and the great-grand-children are second cousins). Suppose, in the alternative the couple expects to have two children and expects future generations to have the same. You might contemplate this in a few ways. The family structure: how many members of the extended family will exist? Two, suppose the initial couple have a net worth of $100,000,000,000 (100 years ago there were several such families, as there are today). Suppose they expect (ignoring taxes) to keep the wealth in the family. Suppose the wealth grows (ignoring inflation and taxes) at a rate of 3% *EFF* (after consumption) annually and is equally divided among the great-grandchildren in 75 years.

7. A new virus has begun to spread rapidly. The WHO reports 10,000 identified cases, which it says are increasing by 25% per day. Assuming the information is correct and assuming the spread rate continues, how many days will pass before it reaches the entire world population of about 7.6 billion?

LESSON TEN

PRESENT VALUE OF A SUM

■ ■ ■

Lesson Objectives

1. Student will learn *how to* use the PRESENT VALUE OF A SUM CALCULATOR.

    • How to locate the Instructions.

    • How to find Definitions of each Function.

2. Student will learn the *formula* for the Present Value of a Sum:

$$PV = \left(FV \left(1 + \frac{i}{100} \right)^{-n} \right)$$

    where i = nominal annual interest rate, n = number of periods per year, and FV = the future value.

3. Student will learn **when** a lawyer would need to compute the Present Value of a Sum:

    • **As a lawyer, you would use this calculation if you or a client needs to pay a _debt_ or other obligation _early_. . . . i.e., if you want to pre-pay an obligation; or, you would use it if you have money saved and need to know what it will be worth in the future.**

4. Student will learn how to use the COURSE CALCULATORS for a period other than one involving full years.

———————————

LESSON TEN covers the present value of a sum. This calculation computes the present amount or value of a future obligation. As a lawyer, you would use this calculation if you or a client desire to pay a debt or other obligation _early_: a pre-payment. For example, you may want to pre-pay an obligation because doing so results in a discount, or lower payment; or perhaps the creditor demands payment in advance.

Figure 43 (Figure 2 from LESSON THREE) illustrates the PRESENT VALUE OF A SUM CALCULATOR. LESSON THREE also raised several reasons why would a lawyer want to know how to compute the present value of a sum:

a. If you owe money in the future, you can compute what it equals in current value.

b. If you want a discount for an advance payment for goods or services, you would compute the present value of the future obligation.

c. If you know the amount you need at a future time—such as for retirement or college entrance—you can compute the present value needed to produce that future amount.

d. For tax or accounting purposes, a lawyer may suggest the client deduct the present value of a future cost if possible. While IRC section 461(h) of the Internal Revenue Code may not permit this in many situations, alternative contractual relationships may make such a present value current deduction possible. For a lawyer to compare the after-tax consequences of a present deduction versus a future deduction of a larger amount, he must first be capable of computing the present value.

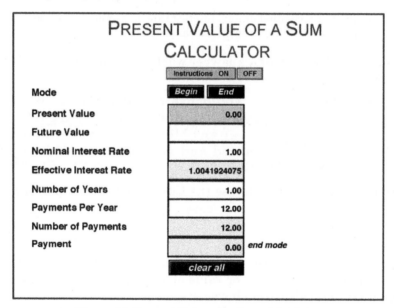

Figure 43: Present Value of a Sum Calculator

For general instructions regarding use of the PRESENT VALUE OF A SUM CALCULATOR, see the discussion above under LESSON NINE. The same instructions apply for each of the COURSE CALCULATORS.

Consider **Example 35**, which is the opposite of **Example 33**. You owe money in the future and you want to know the present value—the "payoff" amount if you pay early—in using alternative dates for the debt. The 1, 2, and 5 year periods are realistic. The 100 year period is for fun: to illustrate the impact of compounding over a long period, As in LESSON NINE. Why would you want to know this? Perhaps you want to have $100,000 when your child turns 18, and you want to fully fund the educational account today. That would use an 18-year term, rather than 1, 2, or 5. Or perhaps you believe you need $5,000,000 to retire in 40 years and would like to know (unrealistically) what would be required to fund the account today. That would use a 40-year term and a $5,000,000 future value. Otherwise, it is the same problem as **Example 35**.

EXAMPLE 35

Present Value of a Sum

You owe $1,000 in the future. You and the creditor agree that an appropriate discount rate for early payment would be 10% interest compounded _annually_.

You would like to know the value—alternatively—in one, two, five and 100 years.

To work the problem, open the PRESENT VALUE OF A SUM CALCULATOR. Type 1000 in the white box next to Future Value (or 100000 for the educational savings or 5000000 for the retirement plan), as shown in **Figure 44**. Input the 10% *NAI* in the white box labeled Nominal Interest Rate. As discussed in LESSON SEVEN, this rate would combine liquidity, risk, and expected inflation. In **Example 35**, you and the creditor (bank, investment company, insurance company, private person) have negotiated a 10% *NAI* discount for early payment, compounded annually. Or, you may want to experiment with alternative discount rates—whatever you believe the creditor might agree to (perhaps 5% *EFF* or 3% ... use your judgement).

Next, input 1 in the white box next to Payments (Periods) per Year, as also shown in **Figure 44**. This is important because **Example 35** states a 10% *NAI* compounded annually. You will quickly see the calculator input 10 as the effective rate, as well. If you fail to change the periods per year, the calculator will compute a higher *EFF* and you will receive a wrong answer. The default mode is END; however, for the present value of a sum, the mode is irrelevant. You may change it to begin, but it will not affect your answer. With other course calculators—the FUTURE VALUE OF AN ANNUITY, a SINKING FUND, an AMORTIZATION, or the PRESENT VALUE OF AN ANNUITY—the mode matters.

The default number of years is one; hence, you should see the answer for one year in the green box, as shown in **Figure 44**: $909.09. If you change the number of periods to 2, as shown in **Figure 45**, the present value answer changes to $826.45. You do not need to press Clear All between the calculations—just change one value and the others change with it.

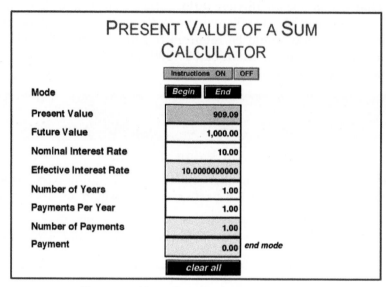

Figure 44: Example 35 for 1-Year Discount

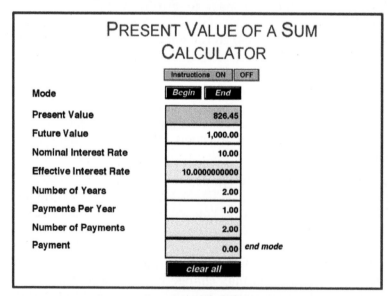

Figure 45: Example 35 for 2-Year Discount

In **Figure 46**, the number of years appears as 5, which changes the present value to $620.92. Then in **Figure 47**, the number of years is 100, which produces a present value of merely $0.07.

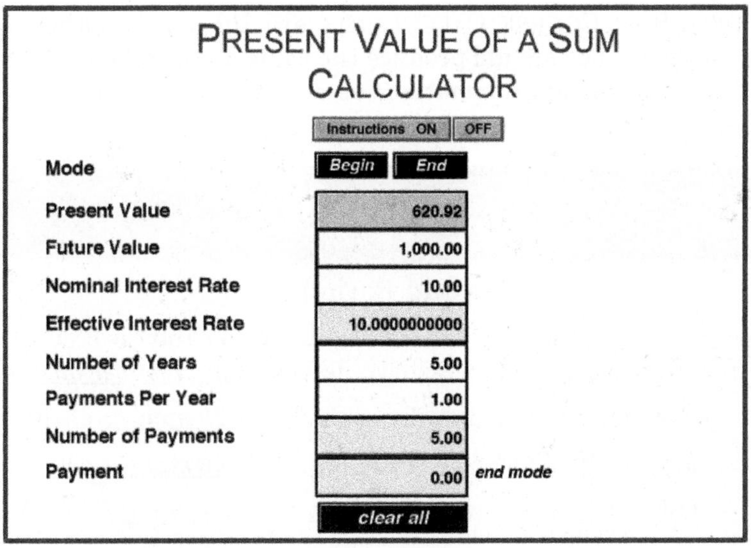

Figure 46: Example 35 for 5-Year Discount

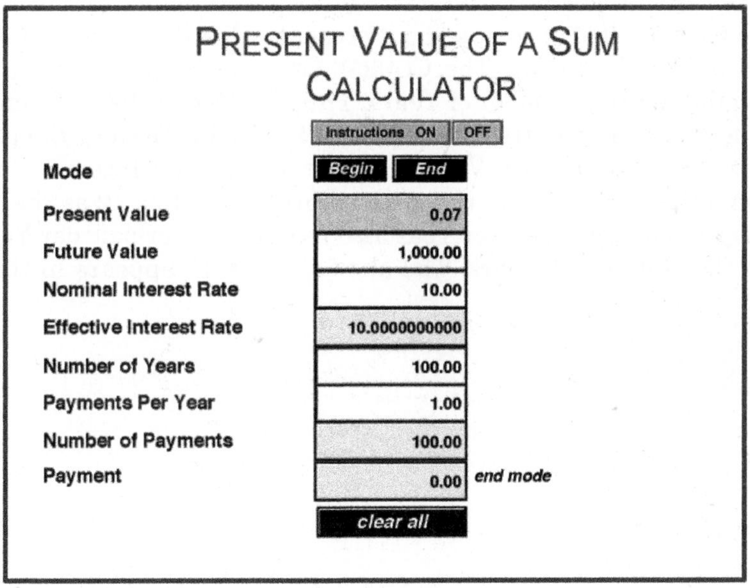

Figure 47: Example 35 for 100-Year Discount

Example 36 presents scenarios with periods involving partial years. Solving such problems—which are likely common—can take two different approaches. Notice **Example 36** states a periodic rate of interest. If the period involves a number of months, that would be the correct way of stating the interest rate. If, instead, the agreement involves an effective rate, the rate would have to be converted to the equivalent *NAI* compounded monthly and, in turn, to the appropriate periodic rate. LESSON FIVE-B covers such conversions. The two methods for the PRESENT

VALUE OF A SUM COURSE CALCULATOR are the easy method and the periodic method. They should produce the same answer; however, the easy method involves an approximation, so it could vary from the periodic method slightly.

EXAMPLE 36

Odd Periods

You owe $10,000 in the future at a given date. You and the creditor agree that an appropriate discount rate would be *1% interest per month*.

- How much do you owe if you pay it off *18 months* early?

- How much do you owe if you pay it off *36 months* early?

- How much do you owe if you pay it off *37 months* early?

---

1. EASY METHOD

The easy method of computing a present value for a non-even number of years is just that: easy. The COURSE CALCULATORS do not require an even number for the Number of Years. Thus for 18 months, you simply use 1.5 as the Number of Years, as shown in **Figure 48**. To work the problem, input 10000 as the Future Value, 12 as the Nominal Interest Rate (the stated monthly periodic rate times 12 months per year), 12 as the Periods Per Year (recall Payments Per Year also represents Periodic per Year) and 1.5 and the Number of Years. The answer 8,360.17 appears in the green box.

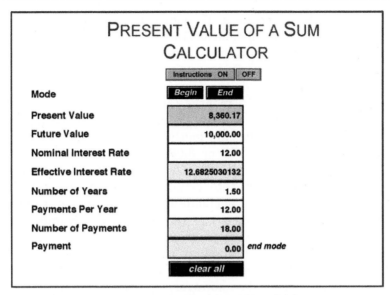

Figure 48: Example 36 with 1.5-Year Discount

This method will work easily for any example involving 12 months or more. The calculator is not programmed for periods of less than 12 months; hence, for those problems, you will need the periodic approach discussed below.

Example 36 next posits a 36-month period, which of course is back to an even number of years. **Figure 49** shows the solution obtain by merely changing the Number of Years to 3: 6,989.25.

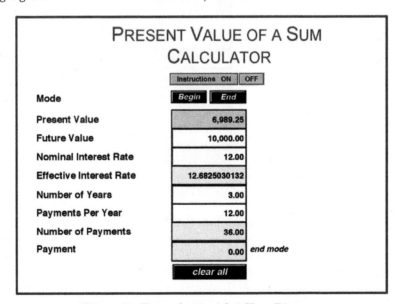

Figure 49: Example 36 with 3-Year Discount

Then **Example 36** posits a 37-month period, which presents some difficulty. Periods such as 18 months (1.5 years) or 15 months (1.25 years) are easily converted to their decimal equivalents. Thirty-seven, however, is not so simple. You may want to use a simple calculator (your cell phone almost certainly has one) to do the conversion. For 18 months, divided 18 by 12 to produce 1.5. For 15 months, divide 15 by 12 to produce 1.25 months. But if you divide 37 by 12, you get a repeating number: 3.0833333333. Thus to use the easy method, you must round that result at some point. You could use 3.08 or 3.083. **Figure 50** uses 3.08333. As illustrated below, using more decimals does not change the present value (which is necessarily rounded to cents) unless you are interested in fractions of a cent. Using fewer decimals changes the present value, though not by much. **Figure 50** appears to use 3.08 as the Number of Years; however, that is because the calculator rounds the Number of Years to 2 decimals for the display, although it uses up to 10 decimals for the calculation. If you open the calculator and input 3.08333 as the Number of Years, that is what will display; however, as soon as you move your cursor and click anywhere else, the display will revert to two decimals. You can click again on the white box showing 3.08 and it will again display 3.08333.

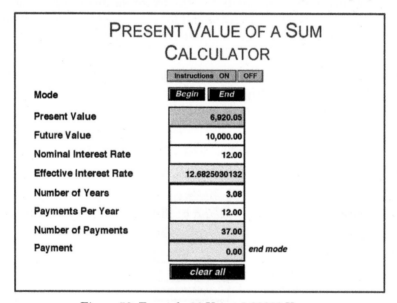

Figure 50: Example 36 Using 3.08333 Years

Figure 51 inputs merely 3.08 as the Number of Years. It computes a present value of 6,922.80, which is $2.75 too much. That is not a large error, but it is an error. You must decide how large an error you are willing to tolerate. Again, notice the image shows 3.08 as the Number of Years, which is the same as in **Figure 50**; however, the actual calculation is using 3.08333 in **Figure 50** but merely 3.08 in **Figure 51**. If you change the statement of years to one additional decimal—3.083—the present value changes to 6,920.32, an error of only 27 cents. Using a fourth decimal—3.0833—produces a present value of 6,920.08, an error of 3 cents. The fifth decimal—3.08333—produces the correct answer of 6,920.05. To be more precise, placing your cursor on the green box, you will see the answer as 6920.05176048211, which the display rounds to 6,920.05. If you add a sixth decimal—3.083333—the green box (with cursor clicked on it) will display a slightly more precise answer of 6920.04928163759. Both round to 6,920.05. The difference, to be precise, is slightly more than 1/4th of a cent. Adding additional decimals will produce continually more precise answers; however, they are not legally significant.

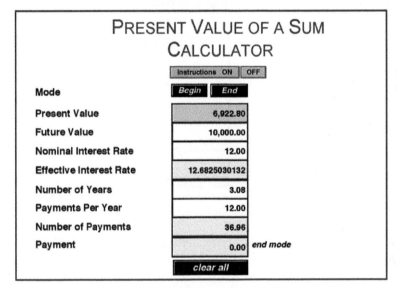

Figure 51: Example 36 with 3.08 Years

Before we move on to the periodic method, let's work one more problem. Suppose the period is 18.5 months. That partial month presents another problem because the interest rate compounds monthly but the period is no longer monthly. To be correct, we cannot use the easy method; however, as demonstrated later, we also cannot use the periodic method, at least not without some modification and additional information. The difference, however, may not be great. To obtain an approximate answer using the easy method, we would divide 18.5 by 12 to determine the number of years as 1.541666667. Inputting 1.54666 produces a present value of 8,313.72. Additional decimals do not change that answer, but fewer decimals change it slightly.

2. PERIODIC METHOD

The periodic method uses the periodic interest rate as the *NAI*, re-defines the Payments (Periods) per Year as one, and re-defines the Number of Years as the Number of Periods (here, months). **Figure 52** illustrates the solution, which is 8,360.17—the same number produced by the easy method. Notice the Number of Years is 18 because under this method, Years actually means months (periods to be exact). Also Payments (Periods) per Year is set to 1, which would always be the case under this method.

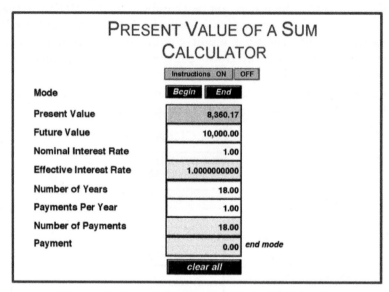

Figure 52: Example 36 Periodic Method 18 Months

Figure 53 uses the periodic method for 36 months and produces the same answer as shown in **Figure 49** using the easy method. Instead of 3 years and 12 periods per year, **Figure 53** uses 36 periods and 1 period per period (with the above-described re-definition of year and period).

Figure 54 shows the periodic method for the 37-month problem. As with the easy method (using five decimals), the answer is 6,920.05—the same as **Figure 50**. Using the periodic method for periods not evenly divided by 12 actually turns out to be simpler because we need not experiment with the number of decimals. It requires, however, the understanding of the changed definitions. Basically, years become months (or whatever the period happens to be).

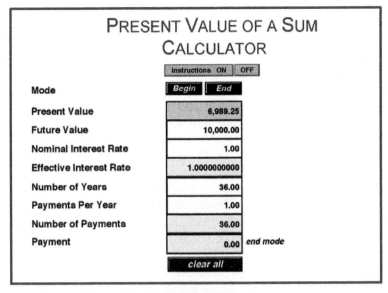

Figure 53: Periodic Method for 36 Months

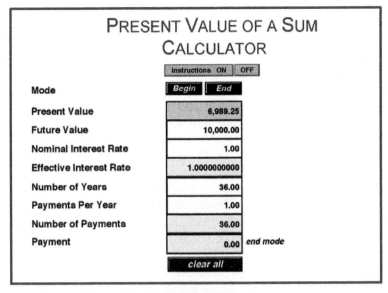

Figure 54: Periodic Method for 37 Months

That brings us back to the hypothetical posed above under the easy method: what if the period turns out to involve a portion of a month? The correct answer would be to blame the contract, which should have anticipated the scenario. Any agreement should state a daily interest rate if days are potentially significant to the answer. This is particularly true when one recognizes that some months have 31 days, some have 30 and some 28 or 29. In the financial world, contracts may stipulate a convention in which all months have 30 days and all years have 360. But if that is not the agreement, then the number of days matters (though often, not by much).

To approach the scenario of 18.5 months using the periodic method, we would need to re-state the interest rate as a daily rate rather than a monthly one. That, however, changes the facts because it will treat months differently: March with 31 days will no longer have the same rate as April with 30 days. Thus the calculation would no longer fit the contract. A better approximation would be to work the problem using 18 months first. Then calculate the daily rate and, using the answer for 18 months, re-work the problem for the 15 days in the half month (or 14 if February). We thus use the answer from **Figure 52** for 18 months: 8,360.17. We then need to discount it further by 15 days. Divide the 1% monthly periodic rate by 30 to produce a daily rate of .033333333. That is not exact because not every month has 30 days, but for such a short period (15 days) it cannot matter much. As shown in **Figure 55**, this produces a present value of 8,318.52. In the alternative, we could approximate the answer, using 18.5416666 as the number of years. That produces a present value of 8,315.23, which is $3.29 less. As explained above, using the easy method and 1.541666 years produced a present value of 8,313.72, which is an additional $1.51 lower. None of these answers is "correct" because the facts given were incomplete: they failed to state a daily rate if a daily rate mattered. Thus, we had to interpret what the parties intended. From high to low, the difference is quite small in terms of percentage. Thus, even if we added many zeros to the future value, the percentage difference would remain quite tiny. For example, if we added five zeros such that the future value was $1 billion rather than $10 thousand, the difference between the highest and lowest present value would be about $500,000. That may seem like a great deal of money; however, if you suddenly had $999,500,000. Rather than $1,000,000,000, would you really care? Assuming the receipt is taxable and the governments (federal, state, local) took up to 50%, the difference is only $250,000 (with the understanding that "only" modifying "$250,000" is relative).

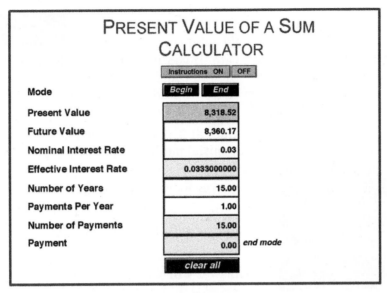

Figure 55: Periodic Method for 15 Days

The bottom line you need to understand from the scenario is a rule stated in LESSON FOUR: the payment (or interest accruing) period must be the same as the compounding period. Stating an interest rate as monthly is correct only if the period involves a period of full months. If it involves partial months, the rate must be stated as weekly or daily or whatever period is or might be involved, at least if precision is the goal. If *approximation* is acceptable, then a monthly rate is acceptable even for daily periods.

To work **Examples 35** and **36** with an HP 10Bii™ calculator follow the following steps:

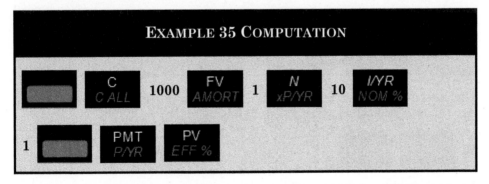

The answer will appear as −909.09. The mode is irrelevant. **Example 25** posited 10% interest compounded annually; hence, you should either enter the 10% rate as a nominal rate (as shown) with the number of periods per year as 1 (as shown) and the number of periods (N) also as 1.

In the alternative, you could enter the 10% rate as 10 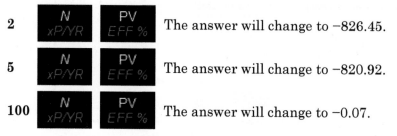. That enters it as an effective rate. If you leave the periods per year as 1, the answer will be the same. Or, you could set the periods per year as 12 (which is the default); however, you would then need to enter 12 as the number of periods (N). Again, the answer will be −909.09.

To work the alternative values at 2, 5, and 100 years, you do not need to start over. Instead, using the initial method (1 period per year), input:

2 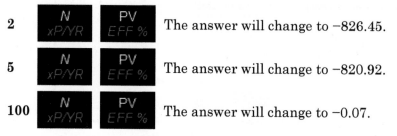 The answer will change to −826.45.

5 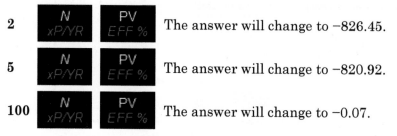 The answer will change to −820.92.

100 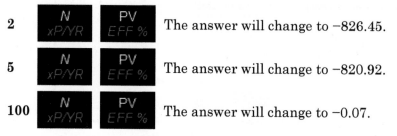 The answer will change to −0.07.

As explained in LESSON THREE, the HP 10Bii™ answer appears as a negative because of the cash flow. You owe 1000, which you might view as a positive number. If so, you currently could pay 909.09, which must be a negative. If, instead, you inputted −1,000 as the future value, the current payment/deposit (present value) would be 909.09—a positive number.

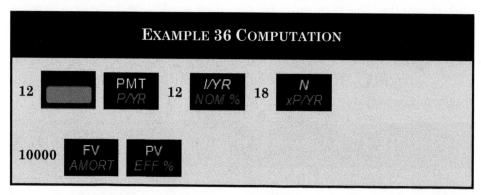

EXAMPLE 36 COMPUTATION

The answer will appear as −8,360.17. To compute the amount for 36 months, you need not clear the calculator. Simply press:

36 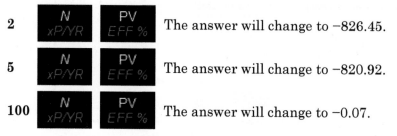 The answer will appear as −6,989.25.

To compute the amount for 37 months, press:

37 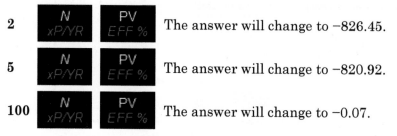 The answer will appear as −6,920.05.

QUESTIONS

1. You owe $5,000 in three years. You and the creditor agree an appropriate discount rate for early payment is 5% *EFF*. What should you pay today to discharge the loan?

2. You want to have $100,000 saved for your child's education in 15 years when the child graduates from high school, but you also want to have a sufficient amount today without having to make future deposits. How much should have invested today if you believe you can consistently earn 8% *EFF*? How much do you need if you believe you will consistently earn 3.5% plus inflation?

3. You want to have $3,000,000 in 45 years for your retirement. You want the money to be able to purchase what $3,000,000 could purchase today; hence, you are thinking in terms of un-inflated dollars. You believe you can save the lump sum amount tax-deferred (whether that is correct is beside the point: you believe it). You believe you can earn 4% *EFF* plus inflation consistently for 45 years. How much do you need to save today if you save a lump sum? How much do you need if you believe you can consistently earn 3% *EFF* plus inflation for 45 years? How much if you believe you can consistently earn 10% plus inflation?

LESSON ELEVEN

PRESENT VALUE OF AN ANNUITY

■ ■ ■

Lesson Objectives

1. Student will learn *how to* use the PRESENT VALUE OF AN ANNUITY CALCULATOR.

   - How to locate the Instructions.

   - How to find Definitions of each Function.

2. Student will learn the *formula* for the Present Value of an Annuity:

   PV of an Annuity:

   $$\frac{\left[PMT \left(1 - \left(1 + \frac{i}{100} \right)^{-n} \right) \right]}{\frac{i}{100}}$$

   PMT = payment

   N = number of periods

   i = nominal annual interest rate

   PV = present value

   ---

3. Student will learn *when* a lawyer would need to compute the Present Value of an Annuity:

   - **As a lawyer, you would use this calculation if you or a client needs to pay or receive a series of <u>obligations</u> <u>early</u> ... *i.e.,* if you (or the other party) want to pre-pay the obligations. . . .**

4. Student will *work* some practical examples of situations in which a lawyer would need to compute the Present Value of an Annuity.

5. Student will *see* dramatic examples of the incredible potential results from compound interest over significant time. They will learn that small changes in the rate of interest can result in huge changes in the present value.

LESSON ELEVEN covers the present value of an annuity. This calculation computes the present amount or value of a future series of obligations. As a lawyer, you would use this calculation if you or a client desire to pay an amortizing debt or other obligation _early_: a pre-payment. For example, you may want to pre-pay a loan for a house or car because doing so results in a discount, or lower payment; or perhaps the creditor has called the debt due. The following discussion has five parts:

- A General Explanation of the Calculation.

- Examples Using Lottery Winnings.

- Examples using non-wrongful death Tort Settlements.

- Wrongful Death Discussion.

- Calculations Involving the Transfer of Lottery Winnings or Structured Settlements.

1. GENERAL EXPLANATION

Figure 50 (**Figure 3** from LESSON THREE) illustrates the PRESENT VALUE OF AN ANNUITY CALCULATOR. LESSON THREE also raised several reasons why a lawyer would want to know how to compute the present value of an annuity: If you owe money at regular intervals in the future, you can compute what it equals in current value. This is useful if:

- You owe money on a loan. The present value would be the payoff amount.

- In a family law case, you owe alimony. The present value would be the lump sum amount to replace the periodic payments.[1]

- If you want a discount for an advance payment for goods or services which will be provided at regular intervals, you would compute the present value of the future obligation. This is useful if:

  o You need to compute the discount amount on an insurance or rental contract.

- In a tort case, the victim may have lost future wages or suffer regular future medical expenses. The present value of such an amount would be the tortfeasor's obligation.

---

[1] You would want to further discount the lump sum because of risk changes, which affect the interest rate used for the discount. Under state law, the periodic payments likely end on the death of either party or the remarriage of the recipient. Also, state law likely provides for modification of periodic payments due to a substantial change in circumstances. The lump sum would not be subject to those risks and thus would likely be the result of a higher than typical discount rate.

- If you have won a state lottery. The present value of the future payments would be the alternative amount that might be elected.

- You might need to compute the value of a bond or similar financial instrument. The regular interest payments would be an annuity. The present value of them added to the present value of the final payment would be the current value of the bond.

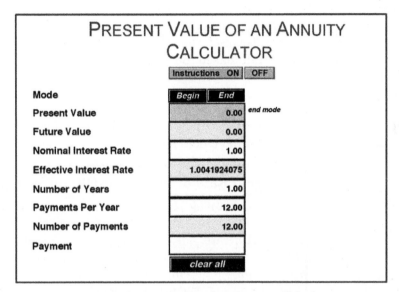

Figure 56: Present Value of an Annuity Calculator

For Lawyers, this is one of the most useful of the various calculations, as it has significant applications in tort and family law. Consider **Example 37**. The example assumes a loan secured by a mortgage on an automobile.

EXAMPLE 37

Present Value of an Annuity

You owe $500 monthly for a car loan. The interest rate on the account is stated as an 8% annual percentage rate (*APR*).

Compute the amount you owe if, alternatively, you have 12, 24 or 37 months left to pay. For this example, assume the stated rate for the loan is the appropriate discount rate.

The loan *APR* is 8%. As discussed in LESSON SEVEN, rates fluctuate with inflation and other factors. Eight percent may seem high in 2020 (year of publication), but is not historically high for automobile loans, which vary greatly by borrower risk, as well as whether the vehicle is new or used. As covered in LESSON FIVE-B, the *APR* (at least in the United States) is an uncompounded rate, except for points, which would not be typically "charged" for many automobile loans. Thus, without further information, I would conclude the interest rate is 8% *NAI* with monthly payments. In reality, the internal stated rate on the loan would be irrelevant for computing the present value of an annuity—the payoff amount on the loan or the value of the paper.

Think about that for a moment. Why would the internal rate be irrelevant? LESSON SEVEN covered the answer: interest rates fluctuate regularly—they rise and fall based on market expectations of future inflation as well as measures of the maker's (the borrower's) individual risk. The likelihood the internal loan rate—the amount the lender charged in the loan contract papers—precisely reflects the current appropriate rate is very small. We will consider that in a later problem, so for now, make the unlikely assumption rates have not changed.

Internal Rate of Interest is Often *Irrelevant*

When measuring the present value of a stream of payments—an annuity—the obligation's (loan's) internal rate is typically irrelevant. The appropriate discount rate would reflect current conditions (current inflation expectations and current risk status of the obligor).

Before we can work the problem, we first must address the mode and the date of the last payment. If you borrowed the money today, the mode is necessarily end: one does not begin to pay off a loan the day one borrows the funds—that is called borrowing less. But, if you have been making payments regularly and now have twelve remaining, we need to know whether you just made a payment today and thus the next one is a month from now, or whether your last payment was other than today. To make this easier, let's conclude we investigated the issue and discovered the most recent payment was today or yesterday; hence, end mode makes sense. But, realize you must never assume this fact. While mode does not have a large impact, it still matters and is a factual question. If the facts presented do not provide the information, do not assume it: ask.

Figure 57 provides the COURSE CALCULATOR answer for **Example 37** with one year remaining in end mode. Discounted at 8% *NAI* with monthly payments, the present value of the remaining payments is $5,748.17. Indeed, as we will learn in LESSON THIRTEEN, the present value of an annuity is related to an amortization. If we were to amortize a loan of

$5,748.17 for 12 months with an 8% *NAI*, the payment amount would be $500 per month. Or, as we will see, if we amortized some other loan amount at 8% *NAI* and the calculator produced a monthly payment of $500 and if we had 12 months remaining on the loan, we would find the current principal balance on the loan is $5,748.17 (give or take a penny, depending on rounding).

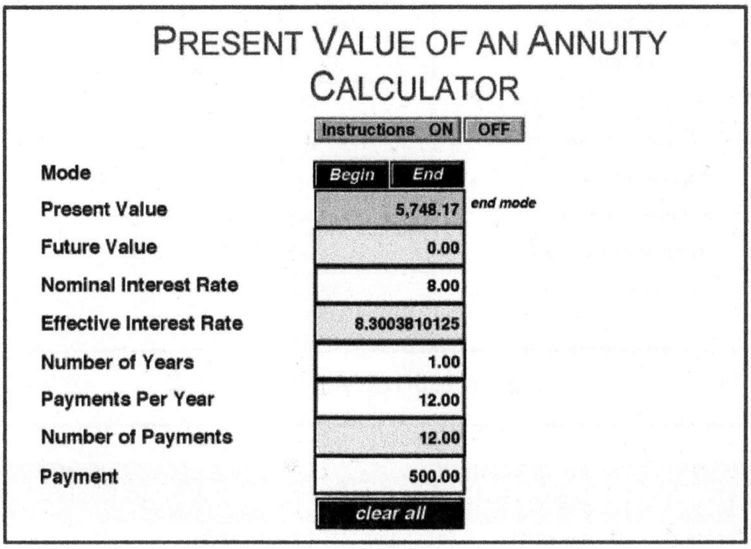

Figure 57: Example 37 for 1 Year Remaining

Indeed, to prove this, I amortized a loan of $24,660[2] for five years, using end mode, an 8% *NAI* and monthly payments. The AMORTIZATION CALCULATOR, as shown in **Figure 58**, computes a monthly payment of $500 per month for 60 months (though with a 60th payment of $501.47). With 48 months remaining, it has a principal balance remaining of $5,749.20, as shown in **Figure 59**. The extra $1.03 is because of the rounding assumptions build into the calculator (which also results in the extra $1.47 due in the last month).

---

[2] If you are wondering how I arrived at $24,660: I guessed. Or, I interpolated to be more precise—just as LESSON FIVE-B explained in relation to APR and points. I knew the payment had to be $500, but chose not to use the PRESENT VALUE OF AN ANNUITY CALCULATOR (I really wanted to be certain the ANNUITY CALCULATOR produced the same answer, or close enough). Thus I inputted 8% *NAI*, 5 years, 12 payments per year, end mode, and then kept changing the present value until the payment appeared as $500. It took about ten guesses. Another way, of course, is with the PRESENT VALUE OF AN ANNUITY CALCULATOR. Input 500 as the payment, end mode, 8% *NAI*, 12 payments per year and the present value answer is $24,660.22. Rounding assumptions explain the differing answers. My point is to help you understand all these calculators ultimately depend on the same formula, just with a different missing variable.

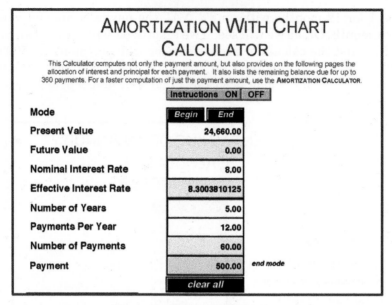

Figure 58: 5-Year Amortization

Amortization for Deferred Annuity (end mode)

Period	Payment	Interest	Principal	Balance
45	500.00	50.44	449.56	7,115.94
46	500.00	47.44	452.56	6,663.38
47	500.00	44.42	455.57	6,207.81
48	500.00	41.39	458.61	5,749.20
49	500.00	38.33	461.67	5,287.53
50	500.00	35.25	464.75	4,822.78
51	500.00	32.15	467.84	4,354.94
52	500.00	29.03	470.96	3,883.98
53	500.00	25.89	474.10	3,409.88
54	500.00	22.73	477.26	2,932.62
55	500.00	19.55	480.44	2,452.18
56	500.00	16.35	483.65	1,968.53
57	500.00	13.12	486.87	1,481.66
58	500.00	9.88	490.12	991.54
59	500.00	6.61	493.39	498.15
60	501.47	3.32	498.15	0.00
61	0.00	0.00	0.00	0.00

Figure 59: 5-Year Amortization

Figure 60 provides the answer for **Example 37** with two years remaining in end mode. Discounted at 8% *NAI* with monthly payments, the present value of the remaining payments is $11,055.78. That would reflect the principal balance due on the loan and the pay-off amount assuming interest rates have not changed.[3]

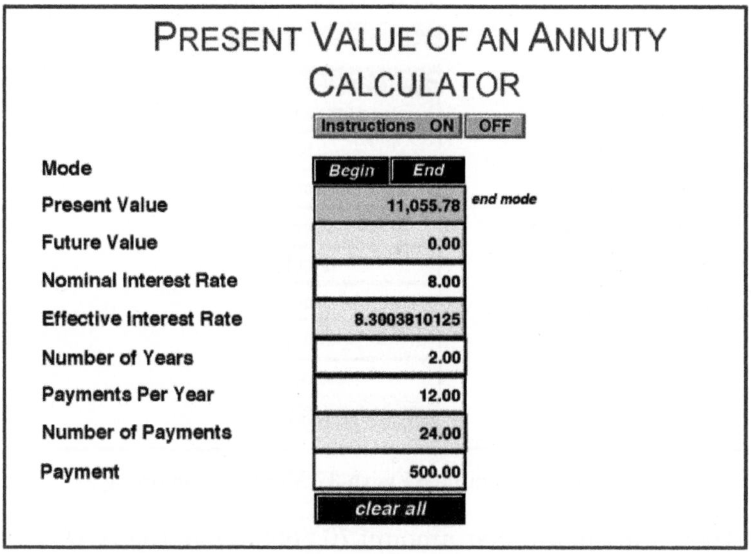

PRESENT VALUE OF AN ANNUITY
CALCULATOR

| Instructions | ON | OFF |

Mode	Begin	End	
Present Value		11,055.78	end mode
Future Value		0.00	
Nominal Interest Rate		8.00	
Effective Interest Rate		8.3003810125	
Number of Years		2.00	
Payments Per Year		12.00	
Number of Payments		24.00	
Payment		500.00	
		clear all	

Figure 60: Example 37 for 2 Years Remaining

To work **Example 37** with 37 months remaining, we must change how we use the COURSE CALCULATOR. But, this change differs from the LESSON TEN changes in **Example 36** because we already have a monthly payment period. What we need to determine is the periodic interest rate. LESSON FIVE-B explains the INTEREST CONVERSION CALCULATOR, which will convert an *NAI* to the equivalent periodic or effective rate, or an *EFF* to the equivalent periodic and *NAI*, or a periodic rate to the equivalent *NAI* and *EFF*. Or, we can simply divide 8% *NAI* by 12 months to get 0.666667 per month as the periodic interest rate.

---

[3]   Between the lender and the borrower, that would be the contractual payoff amount event if interest rates had changed; however, as demonstrated in a later example, the parties could negotiate different amount.

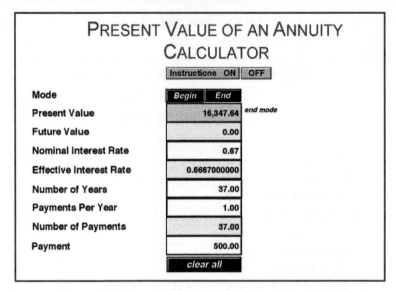

Figure 61: Example 37 with 37 Months Remaining

We then must enter that amount (0.666667) as the *NAI* (re-defining the *NAI* as a periodic rate). We also must re-define Payments Per Year as Payments Per Period and set it at 1 (the period becomes a month and one month has one month). We then enter 37 as the Number of Years (which we re-define as Number of Periods). **Figure 61** illustrates how to work the example.

In the alternative, as illustrated in **Figure 62**, we could have left the calculator definitions as they are. If so, we would put in 3.08 as the number of years (37 months divided by 12 months per year: 37/12 = 3.083333). To obtain the correct answer using this method, I had to enter the number of years to six decimals. As explained elsewhere, the calculator will show 3.08 as the Number of Years because it rounds the display to two decimals. The calculation, however, uses up to 10 decimals. Working the problem using three decimals (3.083 years) showed 37 months; however, the present value was 56 cents lower: 16,347.08. That is an immaterial difference: few people would quibble about 56 cents out of over $16 thousand.

PRESENT VALUE OF AN ANNUITY CALCULATOR

| Instructions ON | OFF |

	Begin	End	
Mode			
Present Value		16,347.64	*end mode*
Future Value		0.00	
Nominal Interest Rate		8.00	
Effective Interest Rate		8.3003810125	
Number of Years		3.08	
Payments Per Year		12.00	
Number of Payments		37.00	
Payment		500.00	

| clear all |

Figure 62: Example 37 for 3.083333 Years Remaining

Next, consider how to work **Example 37** using an HP 10Bii™ calculator. You would first determine the 8% *APR* is actually the *NAI* with monthly payments. You also would set the calculator in End Mode. Then you would input the following:

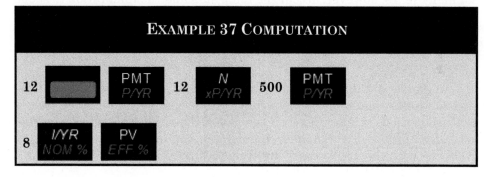

The answer is 5,747.89, which is 28 cents less than determined with the COURSE CALCULATOR—an immaterial difference.[4] To compute the amount for 24 months, maintain the above inputs (do not clear the calculator) and input:

---

[4] As of 12/12/19, I noticed the *EFF* computed in the PRESENT VALUE OF AN ANNUITY CALCULATOR differs slightly from the *EFF* computed in the INTEREST CONVERSION CALCULATOR. I am convinced the INTEREST CONVERSION CALCULATOR is correct; however, the slight error in the PRESENT VALUE OF AN ANNUITY CALCULATOR is irrelevant because the *EFF* is not part of the computation, which depends on the periodic rate. I will explore this error. The 28 cent difference between the PRESENT VALUE OF AN ANNUITY CALCULATOR and the HP 10Bii™, while immaterial, is sufficient to warrant further exploration. Likely, it results from different rounding: ten versus nine decimals.

24

The answer is 11,055.27, which is 51 cents less than determined with the COURSE CALCULATOR. To compute the amount for 37 months, maintain the above inputs (do not clear the calculator) and input:

37

The answer is 16,346.92, which is 74 cents less than with the COURSE CALCULATOR.

The display will produce each of these answers as a negative number because of the cash flow treatment HP uses; or, you could enter the present value as a negative number and the calculator answer will be positive.

2. LOTTERY EXAMPLE

Many factors should enter a lottery winner's decision regarding whether to accept the lump sum or the annuity. Most are beyond this course. But to mention a few, the age of the winner matters because it has significant tax implications.[5] Also, the savviness and self-control of the winner matters considerably: take the annuity and the winner has income for many years; however, accept the lump sum and the temptation to spend it arguably increases. Bankruptcy and creditor rights issues also should enter the evaluation because some jurisdictions may exempt the annuity (but not the lump sum) from the rights of creditors. But, for this course we focus on the interest rate.

In reality, the discount rate will not be negotiable between the winner and the lottery commission. Typically, the discount rate (or more clearly the cash option) is announced on the day of the winnings and is a market rate. In Florida, for example, the lottery commission purchases U.S. STRIPS[6] with the appropriate duration to fund the annuity pay-out, or it

---

[5]　If a person dies while owning a lottery annuity, the decedent's estate will include the present value of the annuity for estate tax purposes; however, the estate may lack sufficient funds to pay the tax. Thus, older lottery players may want to consider this factor in deciding whether to accept the lump sum or the annuity.

[6]　https://www.treasurydirect.gov/instit/marketables/strips/strips.htm. As explained by Treasury Direct:
- STRIPS is the acronym for Separate Trading of Registered Interest and Principal of Securities.
- STRIPS let investors hold and trade the individual interest and principal components of eligible Treasury notes and bonds as separate securities.
- STRIPS are popular with investors who want to receive a known payment on a specific future date.
- STRIPS are called "zero-coupon" securities. The only time an investor receives a payment from STRIPS is at maturity.

pays the equivalent amount as the cash option. Because the discount rate is a function of U.S. Treasury obligations, it is low.[7] **Example 38** uses 7.5% and 3% as the annual discount rates. **Figure 63** shows the lottery cash value (present value of the annuity) as $12,696,165.24. Notice it uses Begin Mode because the first payment would be today—the day you claimed the prize if you chose the annuity rather than the cash option.

EXAMPLE 38

Present Value of an Annuity: Lottery

You won the lottery. It will pay $1,000,000 per year for twenty years, beginning _today_. You are considering taking the lump sum instead.

You and the state discuss that an appropriate discount rate would be, in the alternative, 7.5% _NAI_ or 3% _NAI_, each compounded _annually_.

In the alternative, a prospective purchaser offers to buy the annuity from you and offers an interest rate of 15% _NAI_, compounded annually.

Which alternative do you prefer?

- STRIPS are not issued or sold directly to investors. STRIPS can be purchased and held only through financial institutions and government securities brokers and dealers.

[7] Rates vary, but U.S. Treasury obligations should have the lowest rate for dollar-denominated investments. STRIPs have a smaller market than more traditional Treasury obligations and thus should have a slightly higher rate for similar term obligations. The actual rate used by the lottery commission is thus a blended rate, with each of the 25 or thirty STRIPS being subject to a different rate because they have different maturities.

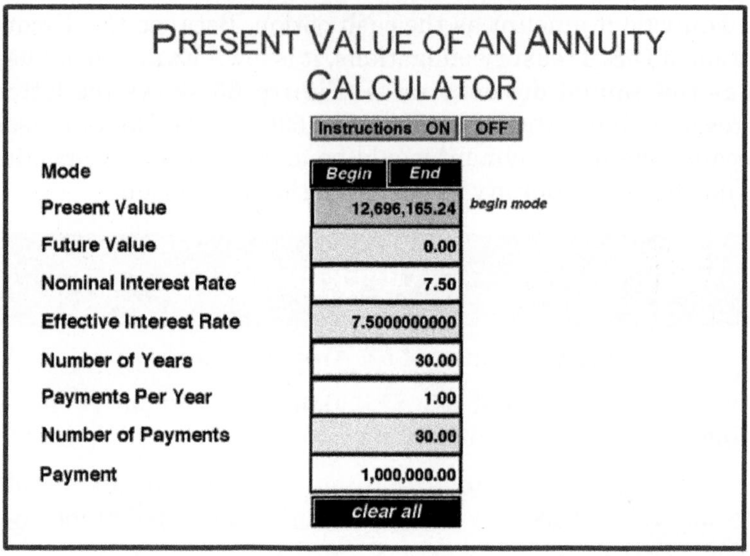

PRESENT VALUE OF AN ANNUITY CALCULATOR

Instructions ON	OFF

Mode	Begin	End	
Present Value	12,696,165.24		begin mode
Future Value	0.00		
Nominal Interest Rate	7.50		
Effective Interest Rate	7.5000000000		
Number of Years	30.00		
Payments Per Year	1.00		
Number of Payments	30.00		
Payment	1,000,000.00		
	clear all		

Figure 63: Example 38 with 7.5% Discount

Figure 64 shows the alternative cash value if the appropriate discount rate were 3%. The cash value _increases_ to $20,188,454.59. That occurs because of a basic law of finance: as interest rates fall, bond prices (present value of an annuity mostly) rise. As interest rates rise, bond prices (and annuity values) drop. _This is always the case_. As result, lottery winners and tort victims will always prefer a lower discount rate, while purchasers of existing annuities or tortfeasors (and insurance companies negotiating tort settlements) will always prefer a higher discount rate.

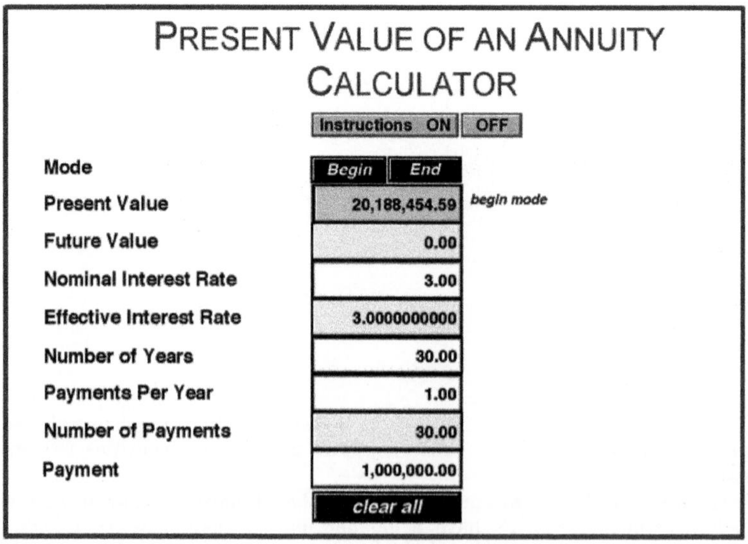

PRESENT VALUE OF AN ANNUITY CALCULATOR

Instructions ON	OFF

Mode	Begin	End	
Present Value	20,188,454.59		begin mode
Future Value	0.00		
Nominal Interest Rate	3.00		
Effective Interest Rate	3.0000000000		
Number of Years	30.00		
Payments Per Year	1.00		
Number of Payments	30.00		
Payment	1,000,000.00		
	clear all		

Figure 64: Example 38 with 3% Discount

Figure 65 considers the scenario in which you have chosen the annuity; however, you now wish to sell it.[8] The prospective purchaser offers a 15% discount rate. For this example, we make the admittedly unrealistic assumption you have not yet received the first payment. In reality, winners who sell the lottery annuities tend to do so a few years after winning and collecting a few payments; however, to more clearly compare the results, we assume the sale is soon after winning. As you see in **Figure 65**, with those assumptions, the value drops to $7,550,876.58. Once again, the higher the discount rate, the lower the present value. The third section of this LESSON considers the transfer of wining in greater depth.

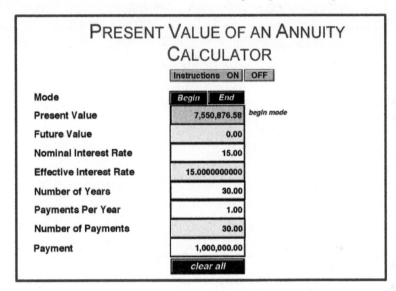

Figure 65: Example 38 Using 15% Discount Rate

To work **Example 38** using a HP 10Bii™, input the following after putting the calculator into Begin Mode for this example.

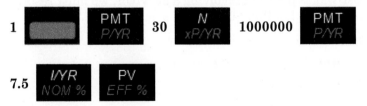

The answer is 12,696,165.24, which is exactly the same answer as computed by the COURSE CALCULATOR.

---

[8]   Nontransferable without court permission and cash equivalence.

The answer is 20,188,454.59, again exactly the same as computed by the COURSE CALCULATOR.

15

The answer is 7,550,876.58, again exactly the same as computed by the COURSE CALCULATOR.

3.   TORT EXAMPLE (NON-WRONGFUL DEATH)

EXAMPLE 39

Present Value of an Annuity: Tort

Your client was injured in an automobile accident. She was earning $50,000 annually. She is permanently disabled and cannot work again. Her work-life expectancy is 35 years.

Your expert witness testified that the appropriate discount rate is 0.5% for the next 35 years.

The insurance company's expert testified the appropriate discount rate is 7.5%.

I argued in LESSON EIGHT that the appropriate discount rate in a tort case would be between 2% and 4% (an admittedly wide range).

Tort cases involving lost wages take two formats: one in which the victim survived and is the plaintiff, and others involving wrongful death claims. The analysis is similar, but sufficiently different to merit separate treatment here.

For a _future_[9] lost-wages problem involving a survivor, we must resolve multiple issues unrelated to liability. The issues are:

- Lost income stream at the date of injury.
- Lost Future **_non-inflation_** wage increases.
- Work-life expectancy.
- Tax rate on lost income.
- Determine the discount rate, if any (including how to treat **_inflation-based_** wage increases).
- Adjust the discount rate for taxes.

---

[9]   Past lost wages involve other issues, such as the availability of pre-judgement interest. LESSON TWELVE covers that issue.

Step One: Lost income stream at the date of injury. We must know what the victim was earning at the time of injury.[10] That will be fact specific. In many cases, the injured person was employed and the parties stipulate as to the wages the victim earned. In other cases, the victim was self-employed or worked intermittently, in which case the trier of fact will need to determine the lost income based on evidenced produced reflecting earnings history and whatever other evidence the jurisdiction permits. Examples in this TEXT mostly provide the Step One information and presume that lost fringe benefits offset work-related costs.

Step Two: Lost future *non*-inflation caused income Increases. Jurisdictions vary regarding whether information about future earnings increases is admissible, but most appear to allow it. One must be careful to distinguish future increases due to expected inflation from future increases due to other causes, such as productivity increases and expected promotions. Such information is often not available. As explained by the Supreme Court (combining several of the steps into one):

> the first stage in calculating an appropriate award for lost earnings involves an estimate of what the lost stream of income would have been. The stream may be approximated as a series of after-tax payments, one in each year of the worker's expected remaining career. In estimating what those payments would have been in an inflation-free economy, the trier of fact may begin with the worker's annual wage at the time of injury. If sufficient proof is offered, the trier of fact may increase that figure to reflect the appropriate influence of individualized factors (such as foreseeable promotions) and societal factors (such as foreseeable productivity growth within the worker's industry).[11]

If this information is available and proven, it results in an un-level income stream. Neither the COURSE CALCULATORS nor the HP 10Bii™ are designed to deal with an unlevel stream of more than a few years—at least not easily[12]—unless the rate of increase is itself level. An HP 12C™ calculator will deal with changing increases, but using one is complex and beyond this course. Thus all examples ignore this factor, except for constant predicted increases.

Step Three: Work-life expectancy. People rarely work for their entire lives: they tend to retire. Thus if dealing with lost wages, one must

---

[10] The most obvious and most appropriate place to begin is with the worker's annual wage at the time of injury. Jones & Laughlin Steel Corp. v. Pfeifer, 462 U.S. 523, 534 (1983). This may be adjusted upward for fringe benefits (such as medical insurance and retirement plans) and downward for work-related costs (such as transportation and clothing). In many cases, the parties agree these adjustments offset each other. Id.

[11] Jones & Laughlin Steel Corp. v. Pfeifer, 462 U.S. 523, 534 (1983).

[12] As covered in LESSON TWELVE, the HP 10Bii™ will handle an annuity increasing at a regular rate, though the inputting is complex. For an annuity with payments changing at changing rates, a HP 12C™ is best.

determine the period for which the wages were lost. As demonstrated below, the longer the period, the less impact this factor has (the difference between 35 remaining years and 36 remaining years, for example is minor if the trier of fact using a discount to present value method). In many cases, the parties stipulate as to this factor, picking an age such as 65 or 70, considering the work involved and at what age workers in that job/industry tend to retire. As the Supreme Court explained:

> The lost stream's length cannot be known with certainty; the worker could have been disabled or even killed in a different, non-work-related accident at any time. The probability that he would still be working at a given date is constantly diminishing. Given the complexity of trying to make an exact calculation, litigants frequently follow the relatively simple course of assuming that the worker would have continued to work up until a specific date certain. In this case, for example, both parties agreed that the petitioner would have continued to work until age 65 (12 1/2 more years) if he had not been injured.[13]

Examples herein will mostly provide the remaining work-life expectancy.

Step Four: Tax rate on lost income. Taxes are a reality. As explained in LESSON EIGHT, one must often use an after-tax interest rate. Similarly, courts traditionally reduce lost earnings by the projected taxes the earning would have suffered.[14] Whether this should occur is debatable, but that it occurs is almost certain. If the award is for person physical injuries (as opposed to emotional) at least in part, the entire award is tax-free.[15] Arguably, Congress enacted the section 104 personal injury exclusion to benefit victims. Whether that actually occurs is mostly beyond this course, but a brief comment is appropriate. By reducing the lost wages by expected taxes, the victim can be made whole and does not receive a windfall; however, the government also does not receive the taxes that, but for the tort, it would have received. The tortfeasor, however, but for the injury would have (or someone else would have) continued to employ the victim and thus would have suffered the tax. Arguably, the exclusion thus benefits the tortfeasor, not the victim, and hurts the government. Counter to that argument, the tortfeasor likely will replace the victim with a new employee

---

[13] Id. at 533–34 (footnote omitted).

[14] Courts routinely reduce lost income by the estimated taxes the earner would have paid. See, Jones & Laughlin Steel Corp. v. Pfeifer, 462 U.S. 523, 534 (1983):

> [T]he injured worker's lost wages would have been diminished by state and federal income taxes. Since the damages award is tax-free, the relevant stream is ideally of *after-tax* wages and benefits. See *Norfolk & Western R. Co.* v. *Liepelt*, 444 U.S. 490 (1980).

Although the court only spoke of "income taxes," reduction for employment taxes would also be appropriate; however, one would then need to consider the value of lost Social Security and Medicare benefits, if any.

[15] IRC § 104.

and thus suffer the tax anyway. Still, the government loses because of the lost tax on the lost productivity, but that is the practical choice Congress made in enacting section 104.

Examples herein will provide the expected tax rate on lost income. In reality, it varies substantially by income level and by geography because of state and local taxes. But, this is a finance text, not a tax text.

Step Five: Determine the discount rate, if any. As explained in LESSON SIX, courts use one of three methods for discounting the lost income stream:

- Case-by-Case Method (which projects future inflation and then discounts for inflation plus liquidity).

- Below-Market Method (which discounts lost wages by the liquidity factor of interest times 1 minus the inflation rate, assuming inflation increases offset the inflation component of interest).

- Total-Offset Method (which ignores discounting completely).

Most examples herein use the below-market discount method. They use various rates to demonstrate the potentially enormous impact of a seemingly small change in discount rate. This TEXT suggests a *pre-tax rate* ranging between 2% and 4% *EFF*, as explained in LESSON SEVEN. The Supreme Court has declined to choose a rate, but significantly stated:

> Although we find the economic evidence distinctly inconclusive regarding an essential premise of those approaches [case-by-case and below-market discount methods], we do not believe a trial court adopting such an approach [* * * *] should be reversed if it adopts a rate between 1 and 3% and explains its choice.[16]

The Court was discussing an after-tax rate and a 1983 case involving an injury covered by the Longshoremen's and Harbor Workers' Compensation Act.[17] Tax rates were higher than currently. Comparable pre-tax rates would be approximately 1.5% to 4% *EFF*, consistently with the TEXT's recommendation.

Step Six: Adjust the discount rate for taxes. Whatever earnings the present value lump sum award produces in the future will be subject to tax, depending on the recipient's investment choices. Some investments, such as state and local bonds and educational savings accounts, are tax free. The state and local bonds, however, tend to earn less interest (after factoring risk) because of their tax-free nature. Some investments, such as retirement accounts are tax-deferred. Other investments produce capital gains which are subject to lower rates than ordinary income. Thus

---

[16] Id. at 548–49.

[17] 44 Stat. 1426, 33 U.S.C. § 904.

determining the likely tax rate on the lump sum's future earnings is not exact. But, failure to reduce the rate for likely taxes reduces the present value and thus hurt's the victim. To properly compensate the victim, the discount rate thus must be an after-tax rate, despite the uncertainty regarding the projected rate. To keep that in perspective, all the factors are speculative: future wages, future wage increases, future inflation and whether it will be reflected in future wages, work-life expectancy, and life-expectancy itself. Adjusting the discount rate for taxes is essentially. It is speculative, but probably less speculative than many of the other essential issues.

Once we have all that information from the six steps, we can work the problem. Thus, to work **Example 39**, we know <u>Step One</u> ($50,000 per year), we ignore <u>Step Two</u> (future productivity increases), and we know <u>Step Three</u> (35 years remaining work life). I am also ignoring pain and suffering, as well as medical expenses, each of which would involve a separate claim (albeit in the same case).

Next, we must adjust for taxes per <u>Step Four</u>. The example does not say whether the victim was married or had dependents; hence, I cannot be sure of her tax filing status. In real-life, you would have to know that. For this problem, I conclude she is unmarried and not a head-of-household and has no other significant income. As a result, I estimate her income and employment taxes as approximately 25%. I also recognize she would have a separate claim for lost Social Security and Medicare benefits. For now, we simply cover the lost wages. The after-tax loss is $37,500 per year for 35 years, or more accurately $3,125 per month.

We thus need to compute the present value of a 35-year annuity of $3,125 per month at the alternative rates of 0.5% *EFF*, 2% *EFF*, 4% *EFF*, and 7.5% *EFF*. For simplicity, let's assume away <u>Step Six</u> and assume these are already after-tax rates.

If her wage payment period was weekly, every two weeks, or twice monthly, we could also adjust for that, although the effect would be small. Also, notice **Example 39** did not state the rates as an *EFF*. We would have to ask the experts to further define them. In this case, I concluded they were an *EFF*, which is most likely. I thus used the INTEREST CONVERSION CALCULATOR (covered in LESSON FIVE-B) to convert the *EFF* rates to the equivalent *NAI* rates with monthly compounding. They are 0.498858%, 1.981898%, 3.928488%, and 7.253903%. I decided six decimals is sufficiently accurate.

Figure 66 shows the result for 0.5% *EFF* (0.498858% *NAI* compounded monthly) as $1,204,832.26. You should notice the image lists the *NAI* as 0.5; however, rest assured the calculator used the more precise number I typed. It also uses End Mode, which would be a question of fact: when the next paycheck would have been due.

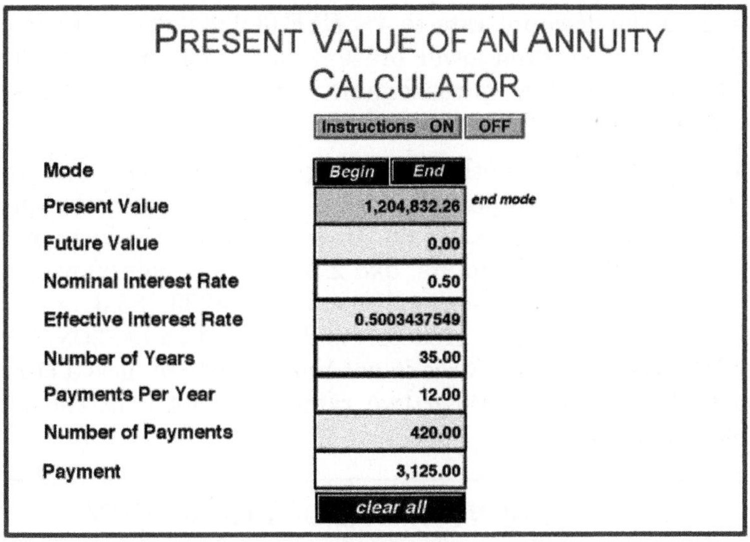

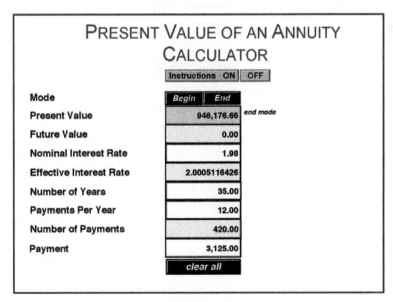

Figure 66: Example 39 Using 0.5% *EFF*

Figure 67 works **Example 39** using the 2% *EFF* discount rate (1.981898% *NAI* compounded monthly). This is at the lower end of what I believe would be reasonable. It computes the present value of the lost wages (again ignoring lost Social Security and Medicare benefits, pain & suffering, and medical or other care expenses) as $946,176.66. That is significantly lower, although the discount rate is only 150 basis points higher.

Figure 67: Example 39 Using 2% *EFF* Discount

Changing the discount rate to 4% *EFF* (3.928488% *NAI* compounded monthly) produces an even lower present value. This rate is at the high-end of what I would view as reasonable. The present value, as shown in **Figure 68** is $712,690.35.

You should notice something very significant. The change from 0.5% *EFF* to 2% *EFF* (150 basis points, *aka* 1.5 percentage points) resulted in a present value lower by $258,655.60. In comparison, the change from 2% *EFF* to 4% *EFF* (200 basis points, *aka* 2 percentage points) was not quite as large. It resulted in a present value lower by $233,486.31, even though the basis point increase was greater. As discussed in LESSON SEVEN, the impact of changing interest rates is not linear; instead, it is a curve. Thus splitting the difference between two rates does not split the difference between two present values.

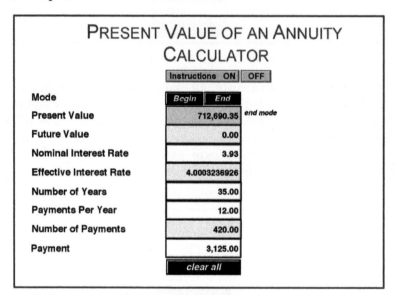

Figure 68: Example 39 Using 4% *EFF* Discount

But, look what happens when we use the insurance company's expert testimony for a 7.5% *EFF* discount rate (7.253903% *NAI*). The present value drops to $475,834.03, as shown in **Figure 69**. That is a decrease of $236,856.32—a substantial amount indeed, but notice it results from a whopping increase of 375 basis points (3.75 percentage points) in the discount rate! It is about the same decrease as occurred from the 200-basis-point increase between **Figures 67** and **68** and is significantly smaller than the consequences of the 150-basis-point increase between **Figures 67** and **68**.

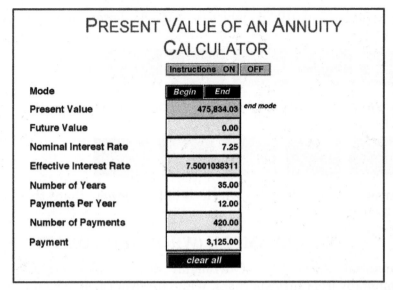

Figure 69: Example 39 Using 7.5% *EFF* Discount

The case would not be quite so simple in reality. Lawyers and experts do not determine the present value as of the date of the injury; instead, they determine the present value as of the date of settlement negotiations or litigation, each of which could be one to three years after the injury. As a result, the actual computation would likely involve the future value of an annuity for the past lost wages (today is the future of the past) using an interest rate that includes actual inflation. To that number, we would add the present value of the remaining lost wages, computed as above, but for the remaining lost work-life expectancy. But, unfortunately, even that aspect varies by jurisdiction.

To work **Example 39** using a HP 10Bii™, input the following with the calculator in End Mode:

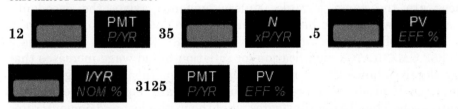

The answer is 1,204,076.99, which is $755.27 lower than the COURSE CALCULATOR.[18]

---

[18] This is immaterial as it is only 6/10,000ths of one percent different; however, as explained in note 4, the difference creates some concern and needs exploration.

The answer is 946,010.78, which is $165.88 lower than the COURSE CALCULATOR.

4

The answer is 712,664.05, which is $26.30 lower than the COURSE CALCULATOR.

7.5

The answer is 475,832.65, which is $1.38 lower than the COURSE CALCULATOR.

4. TORT EXAMPLE (WRONGFUL DEATH)

Financial evaluation of wrongful death cases arguably differ fundamentally from survivor cases. While survivor cases focus on the value of lost income (ignoring medical costs and pain and suffering, which are not the focus of this course), death cases often focus on lost "net accumulations."[19] Jurisdictions also vary regarding who has a cause of action to recover for a wrongful death. The discussion herein assumes a survivor with a cause of action. Also, wealth—such as existing assets (*e.g.*, investments, interests in a trust)—which continues following the death are not the focus herein: they continue after the death and thus are not lost.[20]

Two methods are available to measure the loss:

- Compute the present value of lost earnings, but subtract expected consumption by the decedent (but for the death).

- Compute the present value of the future value of what the decedent would have saved (but for the death).

These are the same formula, unless evidence exists the decedent's investments would have had a higher return in decedent's control than in the control of the survivors. **Table 12** in LESSON TWELVE illustrates a COURSE CALCULATOR modification for inflation-based wage increases that very closely mimics the more complicated HP method involving un-level annuities. It produces a present value essentially equal to the inflated future value. That **Table** illustrates what the victim lost and demonstrates the present value, properly amortized and adjusted for inflation, provides the correct compensation.

With that illustration (essentially a proof) in mind, consider the same issue in relation to a wrongful death. A surviving victim loses 100% of the

---

[19] Of the states, Florida uses the term most often.

[20] Some cases have considered the negative early tax consequences resulting from the death but have rejected them as compensatory. Zinn v. U.S., 835 F. Supp. 2d 1280 (S.D. Fla. 2011).

expected inflation-adjusted income. Reducing that to present value is the correct method. Although courts and litigants quibble regarding the correct discount _rate_, they do not quibble amount the method (see also the proof the case-by-case and discount methods are the same, as is the total offset, which merely uses a zero discount). The essential difference in a wrongful death case is that the victim (now deceased) would have consumed much of the lost earnings, which means they were not lost to the surviving plaintiff. But, that merely multiplies the payment amount in the formula by the savings rate; otherwise, it does not change the algebra.

For example, assume the victim would have saved 25% of the lost earnings annually. That means **Table 12** should use 250 as the payment amount rather than 1000. Otherwise, the computations are identical. Similarly, **Table 12** would work exactly the same if the victim lost 10,000 per period rather than 1000, or any other multiple. The same is true if the payments were monthly or weekly rather than annual—such changes alter the timing and thus the amount of the loss, but do not otherwise change the computation: the present value at the assumed adjusted rates will always amortize very closely into the loss. Thus, if the method works for the victim who loses 100% of the earnings, it would also work for a survivor in a wrongful death case who lost 25% of the earnings (the savings rate), or any other savings percentage. In algebraic terms, if $A = B$, then $2A = 2B$, or $.25A = .25B$.

The only other factor would be the possible extra investment return above the liquidity and projected inflation rates. Perhaps the victim would have earned an extra 1%, or even an extra 5% with wise investments. As discussed in LESSON SIX, investments often produce returns because of risk. In a _non-wrongful-death_ case, one would generally conclude the victim (who is alive) will earn a risk return on the present value awarded equal to whatever the victim would have earned had no tort occurred. As a result, the factor is irrelevant. Logically, in a wrongful-death case, one might also assume survivors can earn a risk return on the present value awarded also equal to whatever the victim would have received on savings had no tort occurred. If so, the factors cancel each other and are irrelevant.

But, that is the point at which the two wrongful-death methods can arguably differ. Evidence may exist proving the victim was a particularly talented investor. If so, then the survivors lost that investment skill and arguably deserve compensation for it. As a result, the net accumulations consider what the victim would have earned on savings over and above what a typical investor would earn. A full discussion of tort and wrongful death law is far beyond this course; however, logically such lost skills are compensable in all jurisdictions, assuming they are proved and properly argued. If so, the two methods are actually identical.

That said, logic does not always control legal matters and court decisions. Thus, consider two 1989 Florida Supreme Court decisions concerning the net-accumulations method. Both cases involved questions certified to the Court by the Eleventh Circuit Court of Appeals. The first decision—*Wilcox v. Leverock*[21]—involved only *passive* investments which continued after the death; however, the Court described its view of *active* investments, as well. The second decision—*Delta Airlines v. Ageloff*[22]—involved active investments on savings. In it, the Court appeared—*at least to your author*—to permit a double recovery, although the Court is very careful to insist it does not. You be the judge.

WILCOX V. LEVEROCK
548 So. 2d 1116 (Fla. 1989)
(emphasis and comments added)

[* * * *]

The facts which precipitated the question are set forth in the opinion of the court of appeals:

> [* * * *] **At the time of her death, the decedent's only source of income was the net income from these two trusts.** By the terms of the trusts, the decedent was entitled to receive the net income from these trusts for the remainder of her life. Upon the death of the decedent, the right to receive the income from one of the trusts passed to Edith Wilcox. Under the other trust, upon the death of the decedent, the right to receive the income devolved to Edith Wilcox's daughter, Susan Wilcox.

> Both sides moved for summary judgment on the net accumulations claim. Appellees contended that Wilcox was not entitled to recover the estate's loss of net accumulations because the estate's only source of income was from the two aforementioned passive trusts. Appellees contended that the definition of "net accumulations" contained in section 768.18(5), Fla. Stat. (1983) excluded income derived from such trusts, because the income was not generated by the skill or effort of the decedent. The district court granted appellee's motion for summary judgment on net accumulations and denied appellant's motion for summary judgment on that issue. Final judgment was entered on the parties' stipulation. This appeal followed.

Wilcox v. Leverock, No. 88–3248, slip op. at 3–4 (11th Cir. Oct. 17, 1988).

---

[21] Wilcox v. Leverock, 548 So. 2d 1116 (Fla. 1989).
[22] Delta Air Lines v. Ageloff, 552 So. 2d 1089 (Fla. 1989).

The certified question reads:

Whether the executrix of an estate is entitled to recover the loss of income received from a trust, pursuant to the definition of "net accumulations" contained in section 768.118(5), Fla. Stat. (1983), when said income has not resulted from the skill or effort of the decedent.

Id. at 5.

Under section 768.21(6)(a), Florida Statutes (1983), the personal representative in this suit was entitled to claim the "loss of the prospective net accumulations . . . which might reasonably have been expected but for the wrongful death, reduced to present money value." Net accumulations are defined in section 768.18(5) as follows:

(5) "Net accumulations" means the part of the decedent's expected net business or salary income, including pension benefits, that the decedent probably would have retained as savings and left as part of his estate if he had lived his normal life expectancy. "Net business or salary income" is the part of the decedent's probable gross income after taxes, *excluding income from investments continuing beyond death*, that remains after deducting the decedent's personal expenses and support of survivors, excluding contributions in kind.

The personal representative argues that by excluding from "probable gross income after taxes" only "income from investments continuing beyond death," the legislature did not intend to limit net accumulations to amounts of income earned by the skill or effort of the decedent. She further points out that gross income as defined by the Internal Revenue Code includes income from an interest in a trust. Appellees respond that the statute reflects an intent to limit the recovery of net accumulations to those investments depending upon the skill or effort of the decedent and point out that the act makes no reference to the Internal Revenue Code.

The words "net accumulations" first appeared as part of the comprehensive revision of the Wrongful Death Act accomplished in 1972. The 1972 revision to the act was largely the product of the Florida Law Revision Commission (FLRC). In analyzing the damages recoverable by a decedent's estate under current law, the FLRC report stated:

The <u>most popular theory</u> of loss to estate measurement is that monetary damages should represent the present value of decedent's probable future net earnings. **This figure is found by determining the probable future gross earnings of the decedent over his life expectancy and *deducting* therefrom**

his probable personal living expenses. The figure is then discounted to present value.

> How do these methods differ?
>
> Earnings less expenses = savings, doesn't it?

Another theory of recovery to the estate subscribed to by several states is to measure damages by the present value of decedent's probable future accumulations. This is the Florida position when there is no survivor in the three prior classes. Like the probable "net income" theory, this method of measurement relies solely on probable business income without regard to possible investment income. **The future accumulations theory, however, requires that the jury determine the amount of decedent's net earnings he would have *saved* and left at his death as part of his estate.** Though it is indeed a fine line which separates the "net earning" theory from the "future accumulations" theory, the latter seems more equitable since the jury must not only evaluate the decedent's propensity to earn but also his ***propensity to save***. In Florida, the jury is allowed to consider the habits, skill, age, and health of the decedent in determining his probable accumulations. This approach is probably more difficult to apply, however, since the jury must objectively evaluate the subjective personality traits of the decedent.

> How does "propensity to save" differ from "probable personal living expenses"?
>
> What you save is what you do not spend, isn't it?

Florida Law Revision Commission, Report on Proposed Revision of Florida Wrongful Death and Survival Statutes at 30–31 (included in Volume 2 of Record on Appeal in *Wilcox v. Leverock*, No. 88–3248 (11th Cir. Oct. 17, 1988)) (footnotes omitted). As part of recommendations for revision, the FLRC report stated:

> Although the act should contain an expanded "loss to survivors" theory of damages, a limited recovery should be allowed the estate for losses heretofore allowed under the survival statute, and lost accumulations should be recoverable to the estate under certain defined circumstances.

Id. at 44. The FLRC went on to recommend a definition of net accumulations which was adopted by the legislature with only minor revisions, and the statutory definition has remained unchanged.

With reference to net accumulations, it appears that the emphasis of the FLRC report was upon a decedent's propensity to earn and his subjective personality traits. By excluding investment income, it is evident that passive income which continues to accrue regardless of the skill or efforts of the decedent is not to be included. While the income from the trusts involved in this case did not derive from investments made by Ms. Jordan herself, the statute does not require that the investments be those of the decedent. However it is characterized, the trust income is undeniably passive income. As such, we believe that it is the constructive equivalent of investment income which is excluded from the term "net accumulations."

The obvious purpose of allowing a personal representative to recover net accumulations is to preserve what has been lost by the decedent's untimely death. Monies which would have accumulated as a result of the skill or efforts of the decedent are irretrievably lost upon death and are properly recoverable by the estate. **On the other hand, the income derived from the trusts in this case is no different than income received from a certificate of deposit purchased by Ms. Jordan before her death. In either instance, the income continues beyond the decedent's death.**

We note that in this case when Ms. Jordan died, the right to receive the income from one of the trusts passed to Edith Wilcox and the right to receive the income from the other trust passed to Edith Wilcox's daughter. Ms. Wilcox and her daughter are also the persons who will ultimately receive the proceeds of Ms. Jordan's estate. Thus, under the personal representative's interpretation of net accumulations, this would result in a double recovery. We do not suggest that these facts should control the interpretation of the statute, and we recognize that there could be circumstances where the residuals of the trusts might pass to persons unrelated to the decedent's estate. In either event, however, the income from the trusts continues to accrue even though the decedent has died.

We answer the certified question in the negative and return the record to the United States Court of Appeals for the Eleventh Circuit.

It is so ordered.

EHRLICH, C.J., and OVERTON, McDONALD, SHAW, BARKETT and KOGAN, JJ., concur.

Arguably, "propensity to save" differs from "probable personal living expenses," but as a practical matter it probably does not unless living expenses are merely a function of statistical averages as opposed to evidence tailored to the victim. For example, if the victim were a 40-year old male with a spouse and three children, an expert would likely testify regarding what portion of the family income is typically consumed by the adult male in such situations. Information proving the particular victim would seem admissible. If so, the portion "saved" would equal the lost income minus the portion consumed by all five persons. Typically, the four survivors would have a cause of action for lost support, which means they would be entitled to lost support plus lost savings under both methods. From that viewpoint, the two methods are the same.

Perhaps, the Florida Court referred to the possibility the victim was a strong-willed saver and without his influence, the survivors would be more wasteful. But, that seems unlikely to be compensable because survivors could always spend as they please. Essentially, if that were the approach, the survivors would be arguing "pay me more because I'm wasteful." That would not seem to be a compelling argument.

The next case provides a slightly different analysis, albeit from the same Court in the same year. Pay attention not only to how the Florida Supreme Court answered the certified questions, but also to the testimony of the three experts. The plaintiffs appear to argue "pay us more because the victim was a brilliant investor and we are incompetent."

DELTA AIR LINES V. AGELOFF
552 So. 2d 1089 (Fla. 1989)
(emphasis and comments added)

[T]he United States Court of Appeals for the Eleventh Circuit has certified to this Court certain questions concerning the Florida Wrongful Death Act. We have jurisdiction. [* * * *]

The joint statement of facts which was submitted together with the certified questions states:

> Scott Ageloff was a passenger who died in the crash of Delta Air Lines (hereinafter "Delta") Flight 191 at the Dallas-Ft. Worth Regional Airport on August 2, 1985. At the time of his death, the Decedent was twenty-nine years old and was employed by the Ageloff family-owned toy business, Harry's Kidsworld, Inc., (hereinafter "Kidsworld") in which he owned a 25% share.

> In January of 1986, Ageloff's parents, in their capacities as Personal Representatives of his estate, brought a wrongful death action against Delta Air Lines in the United States District Court for the Southern District of Florida. Subject matter jurisdiction was invoked based on the diversity of citizenship of the parties, pursuant to 28 U.S.C. § 1332. The parties stipulated that Delta would not contest liability for compensatory damages and that the Estate would waive all other claims for damages, including any claim for punitive damages. The case proceeded to a jury trial

solely on the issue of damages under the Florida Wrongful Death Act, *Fla. Stat.* § 768.16–768.27. **Since Ageloff was unmarried and had no dependents, the sole issue for the jury to determine was the loss of prospective net accumulations to his estate reduced to present money value.**

Prior to trial, Delta filed a Motion in Limine objecting to testimony of the Plaintiffs' experts regarding any investment return on Ageloff's future savings. The Defendant's position was that the investment yield on future savings was not a proper component of net accumulations as defined in *Fla. Stat.* § 768.18(5). That provision defines "net accumulations" as that portion of the Decedent's expected net business and salary income that probably would have been retained as savings and left as part of his estate if he had lived his normal life expectancy. "Net business and salary income" is further defined as "the part of the Decedent's probable gross income after taxes, excluding income from investments continuing beyond death, that remains after deducting the Decedent's personal expenses and support of survivors, excluding contributions in kind." Plaintiffs claimed that investment yield on future savings does not constitute "income from investments continuing beyond death" and was, therefore, a proper element of net accumulations, as defined in § 768.18(5). After hearing argument at trial, the District Court denied Delta's Motion in Limine.

At trial, the **Plaintiffs** presented expert testimony of Dr. Irving Goffman, an economist, and Dr. Jonathan Cunitz, a financial consultant, regarding the value of the Estate's net accumulations. Dr. Goffman began by postulating that in fiscal 1985 the amount of remuneration Ageloff earned, as opposed to the amount he actually received, had been $40,000. He utilized an annual growth rate for Ageloff's earnings of 19%, which consisted of an inflation rate of **6.5%** and a real growth rate of **3.5%**. Dr. Goffman then assumed that Ageloff would save **25%** of his gross earnings and reinvest it back into the family business, Kidsworld. Based on his analysis of the company's earnings, Dr. Goffman assumed that these reinvested savings would yield an annual return of **12.5%**. Based upon these assumptions, Dr. Goffman testified that the **prospective net accumulations of Ageloff's estate, unreduced to present value, were $38,730,300.** Utilizing a discount rate of 7%, **Dr. Goffman reduced the net accumulations to a present value of $1,974,190.**

> **This does not seem remotely credible.**
>
> The 6.5% predicted inflation for the next several decades seems excessive, *certainly in hindsight*. According to the Bureau of Labor Statistics, U.S. inflation in 1986 was merely 1.86% and from 1986 to 2016 it averaged 2.65%.
>
> The 3.5% "real growth rate" is unclear whether it refers to a "real rate of return" or to predicted productivity increases. In either case, it is excessive.
>
> The total 19% wages growth rate is nothing short of ridiculous. This "expert" testified the 29-year old single man working in a family business earning an average of less than $30,000 annually (based on tax returns) was actually earning $40,000 annually and likely would have been earning $7,387.012 annually by 2016.

The Plaintiffs' second expert witness, Dr. Cunitz, performed his calculations in substantially the same manner. Dr. Cunitz estimated Ageloff's annual earnings from Kidsworld at the time of his death at $41,250. He used an annual growth rate for Ageloff's earnings of 11.5%, consisting of an inflation rate of 6.5% and a real growth rate of 5%. Dr. Cunitz then assumed a savings rate beginning at 10% for 1986 and increasing gradually each year thereafter to 25% in the year 2016, after which it would remain constant. Like Dr. Goffman, Dr. Cunitz also predicted that Ageloff would have reinvested the saved portion of his income into Kidsworld. He estimated, however, that the annual return on these reinvested savings would be 18%. From these assumptions, Dr. Cunitz calculated that Ageloff's prospective net accumulations unreduced to present value were $55,540,850. He reduced that figure to present value by use of a 7% discount rate for a result of $2,829,688.

> Company sales in 1985 were about $1.84 million. Assuming sales growth at the same rate of the 18% projected annual profits growth (a not-unreasonable correlation), this expert predicted the Ft. Lauderdale toy stores would have had annual sales of over $600,000,000 in 2020. According to the Court, the business started in 1981, though it was incorporated in 1984 and dissolved in 1988.
>
> Effectively, the argument of the survivors was "the victim was a financial genius and we are incompetent, so pay us more." Perhaps it was true. In any event, it worked.

Delta's expert, Dr. Hartley Mellish, an economist, based his calculation of Ageloff's net accumulations on Ageloff's actual remuneration received from Kidsworld during the period from 1981 to 1985, i.e., Ageloff's income shown on his federal income tax return. Dr. Mellish annualized the income figure for the incomplete calendar year of 1985, then accounted for inflation by adjusting all figures to 1986 dollars. Finally, he averaged those adjusted figures to yield an estimated 1986 income of $29,688. He then took into account probable future increases in income in real terms in order to avoid predicting the future rate of inflation. Dr. Mellish predicted that Ageloff's "net accumulation rate" (rather than savings rate) would have been 25% of his gross income over the remainder of his life expectancy. According to Dr. Mellish, that 25% figure included both a savings rate and an increase in the value of assets in which those savings were placed. Dr. Mellish assumed that the Decedent would not reinvest his savings in Kidsworld, because, according to Dr. Mellish's calculations, such an investment would yield a negative rate of return.

This is far more credible. It allows for an extra 100 basis points for productivity/risk gains. The amount could be higher, such as 200 or even 300 basis points. It also properly accounts for post-retirement consumption.

Using $29,688 earnings (based on what the victim reported to the government), a generous 25% savings rate, a 36-year work life, 2.65% inflation growth (which is what actually occurred) and an inflation-adjusted discount rate of 2.434%, the present value would be $176,635. Even with annual productivity gains of several percent (higher than the U.S. average during the period) the jury verdict seems quite high. The Delta expert seems about right. Granted, according to news reports, the victim's father described him as a "business genius" who had led the business to grow from one store to five and who had worked in the business "for nine years" (although it was incorporated in 1984 and he died in 1985).

Dr. Mellish then assumed that, for the period between the Decedent's death and his retirement at age 65, the difference between the real growth rate and the real discount factor would average 1%. Dr. Mellish calculated the prospective net accumulations of Ageloff's Estate, reduced to present value, as $305,026. Dr. Mellish predicted that Ageloff's cost-of-living consumption between age 65 and the completion of his life expectancy nine years later, would have diminished the present value of the prospective net accumulations to $279,878 by the time of his death.

The jury returned a verdict in favor of the Plaintiffs for $1,000,000. The Defendant's Motion for New Trial was denied. Thereafter, Delta filed a timely Notice of Appeal in this Court.

Ageloff v. Delta Air Lines, Inc., 867 F.2d 1268, 1269–71 (11th Cir. 1989) (footnote omitted).

The court of appeals certified the following questions:

1.   Does the definition of Net Accumulations under *Fla. Stat.* § 768.18(5) of the Florida Wrongful Death Act:

> (a)   include investment income?
>
> (b)   exclude the investment return on future savings of a Decedent as constituting "income from investments continuing beyond death?"

2.   Under the Florida Wrongful Death Act, should determination of the future inflationary effects on prospective net accumulations be calculated upon the (i) below-market-discount method, (ii) the case-by-case method, (iii) the total offset method?

Id. at 7 (footnote omitted).

As worded, the answer to question 1(a) appears to be answered by the explicit language of the Wrongful Death Act. Section 768.18(5) provides:

> (5) "Net accumulations" means the part of the decedent's expected net business or salary income, including pension benefits, that the decedent probably would have retained as savings and left as part of his estate if he had lived his normal life expectancy. "Net business or salary income" is the part of the decedent's probable gross income after taxes, *excluding income from investments continuing beyond death*, that remains after deducting the decedent's personal expenses and support of survivors, excluding contributions in kind.

(Emphasis added.) As we recently explained in *Wilcox v. Leverock*, 548 So.2d 1116 (Fla.1989), income from investments in which the decedent had an interest at his death is passive income which continues to accrue regardless of his skill or efforts. The untimely death deprives neither the decedent's estate nor his survivors of the income from these investments. Thus, we answer question 1(a) in the negative.

Whereas we presupposed that question 1(a) involves investments that the decedent made before his death, question 1(b) involves a wholly different proposition: income from investments that the decedent would have made with his anticipated savings, had he lived. Ageloff contends that by excluding income on "investments continuing beyond death," the statute only intended to prevent the recovery of interest on the decedent's actual investments, and not those which could have been made had he not died. Delta argues that by excluding "income from investments continuing beyond death," the legislature meant to exclude income derived from acts of investing which continue beyond death. Delta further contends that if anticipated future investment income is computed in net accumulations, the survivors not only would receive the money the decedent would have earned by investing savings but would also have the ability to earn interest on those funds.

The logic of excluding from net accumulations the income from investments in which the decedent had an interest at the time of his death is evident. The income will continue to accumulate regardless of the decedent's efforts. Therefore, there has been no loss to the decedent's estate or his survivors. On the assumed facts of this case, however, the absence of the decedent makes a great deal of difference. Because of his death, there are no earnings from which funds can be saved with which to buy investments that would generate additional income. If the decedent had lived and acquired investments from savings on his earnings, the income from these investments would have enhanced the value of his estate had he lived his normal life span. Under these circumstances, the estate and the survivors are deprived of the income on these investments.

> This makes no sense. Of course the algebra is the same for the two methods.

In keeping with the legislative admonition that the Wrongful Death Act is remedial and shall be liberally construed, section 768.17, Florida Statutes (1987), _we hold that the investment return on future savings of a decedent is not excluded from net accumulations._ **Delta's argument relies on the faulty premise that the present value of net accumulations should be computed in the same manner as determining an award for impaired earning capacity on an annual basis. _However, the recovery of net accumulations does not occur on an annual basis, but only once at the end of the decedent's life expectancy._** Net accumulations are more than replacement salary. They are supposed to represent what the decedent's estate would have been worth at death. This sum is reduced to present value so that it can be reinvested by the survivors, with the intention that when the estimated natural death of the decedent occurs the estate will equal what it would have been worth had he not died. **_If it can be proved that the decedent would have earned income from savings, it is not a double recovery for the survivors to recover this lost income._** We answer question 1(b) in the negative.

> Surely the Court meant to include only the excess investment return the decedent would have earned over what the survivors can reasonably earn.

> This sentence is absurd.
>
> Of course the decedent would have earned income from savings, absent a negative interest rate. But so would the survivors; hence, of course it is a double recovery unless there is proof of special investment abilities of the decedent.

[* * * *]

It is so ordered.

OVERTON, ACTING C.J., and MCDONALD, SHAW and KOGAN, JJ., concur.

EHRLICH, C.J. and BARKETT, J., did not participate in this case.

———————

Several aspects of the *Delta Airlines* case are noteworthy. *First*, focus on the Court's description of the net accumulations method. To understand it, go back to *Wilcox*, in which the Court logically excluded, as required by the statute, income from existing investments which continued after the death. Wilcox involved an interest in a trust, presumably managed by a third party; however, the statute and case would logically exclude income from other existing investment accounts. For example, if the decedent owned $100,000 in a brokerage account containing stocks and bonds, the survivors would inherit the account. Had the victim lived, the account would have had earnings. But, it will also have earnings in the hands of the survivors. Nothing in the statute or cases suggest a recovery is available if the survivors argue they are less competent investors than was the decedent with regard to existing investments.

But, the Court in *Dela Airlines* treats future savings differently than past savings. Presumably the survivors inherited their son's interest in the family corporation, which actually dissolved about two years after his death. The case, however, did not involve lost income from that investment. Instead, the case focused on future investment income from future savings which would have resulted from future earnings. With regard to the future investments, the Court language includes all the investment income the decedent would have earned on his savings, not merely the portion he would have earned in excess of what his parents could earn on the present value award. Published reports regarding the case suggest the parents argued their son was a "financial genius" and they were far less competent. Perhaps they were able to prove those points; however, the Court holding appears to treat all survivors as essentially incompetent with regard to future investment earnings from future savings:

> If it can be proved that the decedent would have earned income from savings, it is not a double recovery for the survivors to recover this lost income.[23]

Taken at face value, that statement is difficult to accept. The Court was contemplating an enormous amount of savings over several decades: tens of millions of dollars. One would think—and surely the Court knows—that anyone would earn income from such savings, absent an economy in which everyone is losing. But, one would also think—and surely the Court knows—any survivor who received over a million dollars would also earn income from that amount. How the Court could claim its rule did not involve a double recovery is unclear.

Second, examine the testimony of the plaintiffs' economist. He projected an earnings growth rate of 19% over the following decades. He testified in 1985 when actually inflation was under 2% and real GNP growth was about 3%. The business apparently started in 1981, was incorporated in 1984, and was dissolved in 1988. Indeed, as do many new businesses, it grew rapidly in several of its early years; however, as do approximately half of all small enterprises, it ultimately failed. The projected growth rate seems almost ludicrous in hindsight, and difficult-to-defend at the time.

Part of the growth was undoubtedly due to projected inflation of 6.5%; however, actual inflation at the time was far lower and had been for several years. Indeed, it continued to be far lower for all the years since the date of the testimony. In hindsight, the "expert" was a very poor prognosticator.

The "real growth rate" of 3.5% likely referred to projected productivity gains. That number is defensible, albeit high. But, the 3.5% added to the 6.5% projected inflation comprises only 10% points of the projected 19% return. The extra 9% would seem to be from risk. That is arguably a proper measure of the risk factor in the business in question; however, extrapolating it to an expected return unadjusted for risk is not credible, at least not apparently so. Delta's expert testified the business would likely generate negative returns, as many young and rapidly expanding businesses ultimately do. The risk of failure would seem to balance the chance of greater-than-normal returns—the 9%—and thus should not have been part of the calculation. As explained earlier, the inflation component cancels itself in the calculations and is also best ignored. In addition, the expert recommended a 7% discount rate, which was presumably 6.5% for inflation and .5% for liquidity. In 1985, using cherry-picked data, such a low liquidity rate was justifiable; however, as explained in LESSON SIX, the

---

[23]   Delta Air Lines v. Ageloff, 552 So. 2d 1089, 1092 (Fla. 1989).

correct amount is likely higher. Thus, the expert would seem to justify, at best, 3.5% productivity gains and a meager .5% liquidity rate (high for the former and low for the latter). Still further, the expert considered the lost earnings to be $40,000, though the amount reported for taxes was less than $30,000.

Using the expert's aggressive testimony, $10,000 of savings for 36 years with regular 3.5% productivity gains and a low .5% discount rate, the present value of the annuity would be $627,000 from the time of expected retirement. As the Delta expert logically explained, the victim—had he lived—likely would have consumed considerable funds during retirement, which likely would have lasted about twenty years.

Using a more defensible $8,750 of savings (splitting the difference between the experts), 3% productivity gains and a 2.5% liquidity rate, the present value would be about $335,000. That is far more consistent with the Delta expert.

Third, the jury—which awarded $1,000,000 for lost accumulations—seems to have approximately averaged the testimony of the plaintiffs' economist ($1,974,190) and that of Delta's expert ($279,878), with perhaps a downward adjustment for the expected retirement consumption. It appears to have ignored the second expert from the plaintiffs ($2,829,688).

5. LEVEL PRODUCTIVITY INCREASES

The formula for the present value of an annuity increasing at a level rate is:

$$\frac{PMT_1}{i-g}\left[1-\left(\frac{1+g}{1+i}\right)^n\right]$$

Where PMT_1 = initial payment; i = discount rate; g = rate of increase; n = number of payments.

The COURSE CALCULATORS include a PRESENT VALUE OF A GROWTH ANNUITY CALCULATOR. It works only in End Mode, which is the most likely scenario lawyers will face. Also, it is set for annual payments. Realistically, a lawyer would mostly use this in a tort case involving evidence the victim would have received regular wage increases for productivity improvement. Such raises would likely be annual, as opposed to monthly. **Figure 64** shows the calculator. It works generally the same as the other COURSE CALCULATORS; however, it substitutes the term "Discount Rate" for the nominal interest rate used in other CALCULATORS. It also adds a box in which to input the expect Growth Rate: the amount of anticipated wage increases. Notice: the default Growth Rate differs from the default Discount Rate. If they were equal, the Calculator will not work because that would involve dividing by zero, which is forbidden.

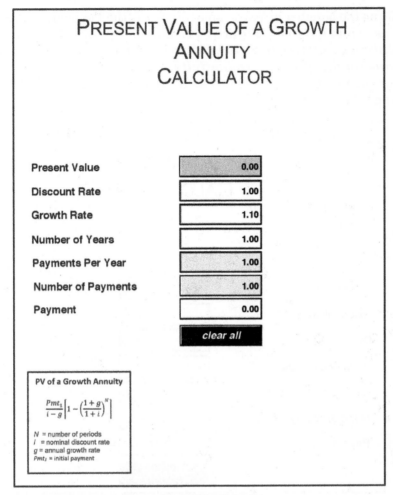

Figure 70: *PVGA* Calculator

Consider **Example 40** which contemplate a tort victim who has evidence of annual productivity wage increases.

EXAMPLE 40

Present Value of a Growth Annuity

Tort Victim was earning $100,000 annually at the date of injury, but can no longer work. Victim had a remaining work life expectancy of 30 years. Evidence suggests Victim would have received 3% annual wage increases due to productivity improvement.

To solve **Example 40** using the PRESENT VALUE OF A GROWTH ANNUITY CALCULATOR, input 2.5 as the Discount Rate, 3 as the Growth

Rate, 30 as the Number of Years, and 100,000 as the Payment. The present value is $3,143,592.56. **Figure 71** illustrates this solution. ***This calculation considers the $100,000 to be the wage for the first year and thus un-inflated by productivity.*** If the victim were to expect the raise for the first year, use 103,000 as the payment in this and also in the following calculations.

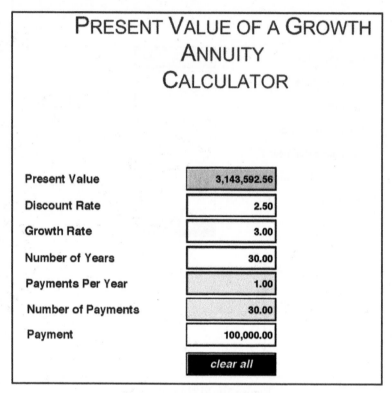

Figure 71: Example 40

Using the formula, the present value would be:

$$\frac{100,000}{-.005} \left[1 - \left(\frac{1.03}{1.025} \right)^{30} \right] \text{ which equals } \mathbf{-20,000[1 - (1.00487805)^{30}]}$$

That solves to 3,143,592.56.

To solve **Example 40** using the formula and a HP 10Bii™, input:

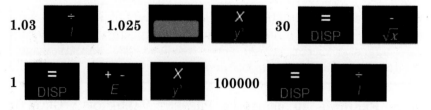

.005

The answer is 3,143,592.56.

To solve **Example 40** using the programmable features of a HP 10Bii™, input:

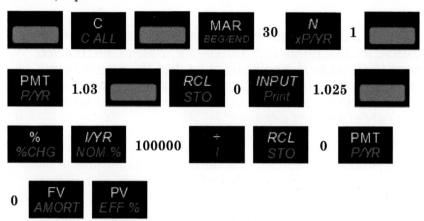

The answer is 3,143,592.56.

6.   TRANSFER OF LOTTERY AND TORT STRUCTURED SETTLEMENTS

A secondary market exists for annuities such as lottery winnings and tort structured settlements. Most states have a statute requiring court permission for the transfer of such annuities. The Florida statute on the transfer of structured settlements requires, among other items:

At least 10 days before the date on which the payee first incurred an obligation with respect to the transfer, the transferee provided to the payee a disclosure statement in bold type, no smaller than 14 points in size, which specifies:

a.   The amounts and due dates of the structured settlement payments to be transferred;

b.   The aggregate amount of the payments;

c.   The discounted present value of the payments, together with the discount rate used in determining the discounted present value;

d.   The gross amount payable to the payee in exchange for the payments;

e.   An itemized listing of all brokers' commissions, service charges, application fees, processing fees, closing costs, filing fees, referral fees, administrative fees, legal fees, and notary fees and other commissions, fees, costs, expenses, and charges payable by the payee or deductible from the gross amount otherwise payable to the payee;

　　f.　　The net amount payable to the payee after deducting all commissions, fees, costs, expenses, and charges described in sub-subparagraph e.;

　　g.　The effective annual interest rate, which must be disclosed in the following statement: "Based on the net amount that you will receive from us and the amounts and timing of the structured settlement payments that you are turning over to us, you will, in effect, be paying interest to us at a rate of percent per year"....[24]

The court must state:

　　The court has determined that the net amount payable to the payee is fair, just, and reasonable under the circumstances then existing.[25]

Key to that determination should be the highlighted provisions "c" and "g" of the statute. For purposes of determining the "discounted present value," the statute requires use of the current annuity[26] applicable federal rate [*AFR*][27] for the term involved. The internal revenue service issues that rate monthly for the following month and for short (under 3 years), medium (3 to 9 years), and long terms (more than 9 years). In November 2019, the rates were 1.68%, 1.59%, and 1.94%.[28] Those rates apply for various tax purposes. They reflect a minimum rate for many loans. Admittedly, they are low compared to market rates for secured home loans, let alone unsecured loans. But, they are an independent measure of a very low-risk rate. By comparison, the *AFR*s for November 2017 were 1.38%, 2.0%, and 2.6%. In November 2014, they were 0.38%, 1.90%, and 2.91%. Oddly, the statute for transfers of an annuity require the use of the *AFR* annuity rate, rather than the rate for the appropriate term. In November 2019, the annuity rate was 2.8%, which was significantly higher than the long-term rate.

---

[24]　F.S. § 626.99296(3).

[25]　F.S. § 626.99296(3)(a)6.

[26]　"Applicable federal rate" means the most recently published applicable rate for determining the present value of an annuity, as issued by the United States Internal Revenue Service pursuant to s. 7520 of the United States Internal Revenue Code, as amended." F.S. 626.99296(1)(b).

[27]　IRC § 1274 defines the *AFR*.

[28]　Rev. Rul. 2019–12. Notice the rates are inverted.

In addition to state statutes regulating the transfer of structured settlements, the internal revenue code also applies a 40% excise tax on the discount unless the transfer was approved by a "qualified order".[29]

Trial courts frequently must rule on the appropriateness of structured settlement dispositions. Some cases involve annuities which are life-dependent—they end if the victim dies. Those require very careful evaluation because the discount rate is a function of the particular annuitant's life expectancy, which requires clear knowledge of the individual. Thus the following analysis ignores cases which are life-dependent.

Many recent Florida cases involving approved transfers—which the court found to be "fair, just, and reasonable" have used discount rates ranging from 8% to 33%. These involved well-known, highly solvent insurance companies who issued the annuities or other deferred payments. Because the discount rates include all the major factors of interest—liquidity, expect inflation, risk, and market risk—one might argue the appropriate rate might be twice the *AFR (which includes all factors as well)*, although, frankly that seems quite high. But many courts have approved discounts that were 400% to over 2000% of the *AFR*, with nothing more than a conclusory finding of "fair, just, and reasonable."

Consider a few examples. In a 2016 Florida decision,[30] the court considered whether to allow the recipient of a 100-payment structured settlement annuity to J.G. Wentworth, a common purchaser of such products. The annuity sold—which the transferor's tort counsel presumably negotiated in the victim's best interest—provided for 100 payments of $544.73 beginning January 1, 2017.[31] The entire amount the victim was to receive would have been tax-free because it was based on personal physical injuries. Thus even the inherent interest component of each payment would be non-taxable. The victim, however, after consulting counsel,[32] agreed to transfer it for a lump sum of $30,599, which would also be tax free; however, any interest the victim earned on the proceeds would be taxable after the transfer. In addition, under Florida law, the annuity was free from most creditor claims, but the lump sum was not. Although the tort case was not reported, almost certainly the parties negotiated the structured settlement with the victim arguing for a low discount rate (perhaps 1–2%) and the tortfeasor/insurance company likely arguing for a higher rate (perhaps 6–8%). As argued in LESSON SIX, an appropriate

---

[29]   IRC § 5891.

[30]   In re Approval for Transfer of Payment Rights by Lutz, 2016 Fla. Cir. LEXIS 16149 (11/15/16).

[31]   Ms. Lutz also received $20,000 per year for 4 years beginning on 11/1/15 and the $544.73 for a total of 40 years. She apparently sold only 100 of the 480 monthly payments and none of the annual payments.

[32]   See the petition, exhibit C.

discount rate would likely have been between 2.5 and 4%. The payments were to be made by Metropolitan Life Insurance Company, a highly-rated entity.[33]

The court order approving the transfer specifically found:

5.   ***After holding a hearing*** on the Application, and upon the ***personal appearance*** of S. Lutz, the Court has determined that the transfer of S. Lutz's structured settlement payments rights is in S. Lutz's ***best interests***, taking into account the welfare and support of S. Lutz's ***dependents, if any***, and the transfer is necessary, reasonable or appropriate.

6.   S. Lutz **has received, or waived in writing his or her right to receive, independent professional advice** regarding the legal, fax and financial implications of the transfer.[34]

Consider several things about that order. *First*, the hearing was set for 10 minutes, although the court records are not available showing the exact time. *Second*, Ms. Lutz appeared by telephone, which is a "personal appearance," but unusual for an unrepresented party.[35] *Third*, Ms. Lutz had no dependents, but no one modified the "boiler-plate" order to indicate that fact; instead, it used the language "if any." *Fourth*, although Ms. Lutz signed a statement that she had received professional advice, nothing in the record indicated from whom, let alone the qualifications of the advisor. *Fifth*, the court found the transfer was fair, just, and reasonable under the circumstances and that the parties had established the reasons for it. The complaint summarily stated Ms. Lutz needed the funds for "business capital" and that she was 19 years old.

The disclosure date was September 26, 2016. It properly listed the *AFR* as 1.40%.[36] Using that rate, the present value would have been $51,465.66 on 1/1/2017 and 51,286.27 on 9/26/2016. The disclosure valued it at $50,981.14, a small discrepancy, but nevertheless a discrepancy.

---

[33]   https://www.metlife.com/about-us/corporate-profile/ratings/.

[34]   (emphasis added).

[35]   Although Ms. Lutz signed a statement that she consulted professional advice, no attorney appeared on her behalf. See the Order, but see the service.

[36]   Rev. Rul. 2016–20.

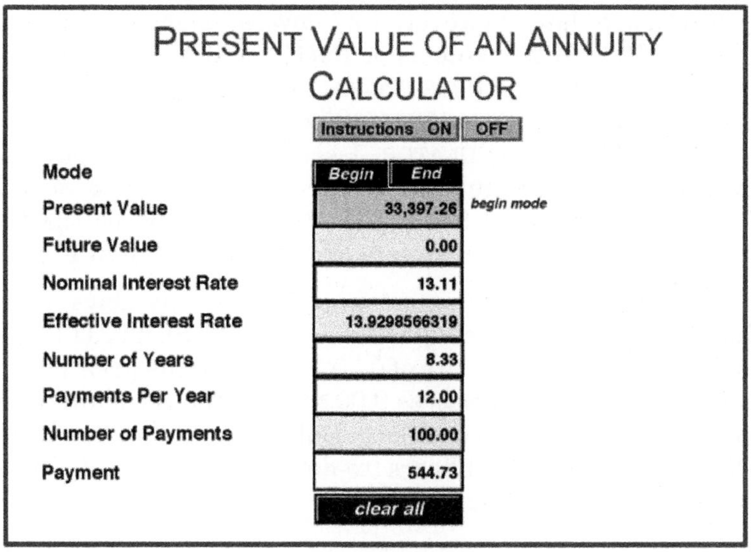

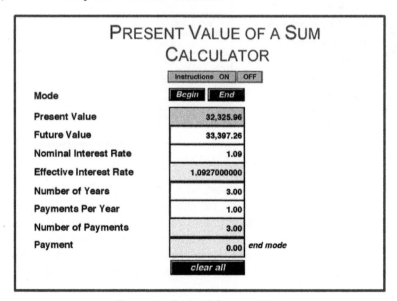

Figure 72: Lutz Value on 1/1/17

The disclosure also listed the effective discount interest rate as 13.93%. But, using that rate, the annuity was worth $33,397.26[37] on 1/1/17, as shown in **Figure 72**. I use Begin Mode because the first payment was due on that date. The nominal rate I use is very slightly below the equivalent of 13.93% *EFF*, but the difference is not material. I use 8.333333 years, which is very close to 100 months.

Figure 73: Lutz Value on 1/1/16

---

[37] Using an HP 10Bii™ calculator I determined a 1/1/17 present value of $33,397.44.

The disclosure date, however, was several months earlier. Thus I discounted the $33,397.26 value as of 1/1/17 for three months to produce the 10/1/17value. I used the PRESENT VALUE OF A SUM CALCULATOR and a periodic rate of 1.0927106011553445%, which is determined using the INTEREST CONVERSION CALCULATOR. I set the number of payments per period (year) as 1 and the number of periods (years being re-defined as periods) as 3. The answer is $32,325.96,[38] which would be the 10/1/2016 value using the disclosed effective rate of 13.93, as shown in **Figure 73**.

The disclosure date, however, was 9/25/16, six days earlier. To determine this, I again use the PRESENT VALUE OF A SUM CALCULATOR, but with a daily nominal interest rate of 0.002993728% (the prior periodic rate divided by 365). The rate appears as 0.00 because the calculator rounds the image to two decimals, but keeps the calculator set to ten; hence, the *EFF* is 0.003%. I set the Number of Years (re-defined as days) to 6. The answer, as shown in **Figure 74**, is $32,320.14.[39]

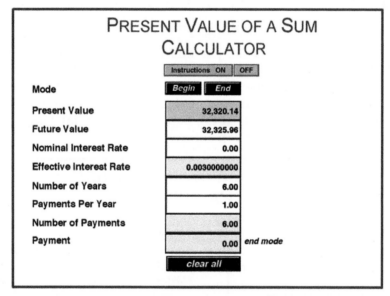

Figure 74: *Lutz* Value on 9/25/16

The payment amount, however, was only $30,599 and the disclosure stated it included no other fees or charges. Thus, the actual effective discount rate was 15.68%, which is 175 basis points greater than the amount stated in the disclosure statement: 13.93%. That is a substantial error, especially considering Ms. Lutz should have received interest from the disclosure date to the "funding date" which likely was after the court

---

[38] With an HP 10Bii™, I got 32,326.13.

[39] $32,321.29 with an HP 10Bii™.

order. As a result, both disclosures—the statutory present value using the *AFR* and the effective interest rate—appear mistaken.

Florida—as do many other states—provides for serious consequences for failing to follow the statute, assuming the error was not intentional and was due to a bona fide error:[40]

> A transferee or assignee is not liable for any penalty in any action brought under this section if the transferee or assignee establishes by a preponderance of evidence that the violation was not intentional *and* resulted from a bona fide error, notwithstanding the transferee's maintenance of procedures reasonably designed to avoid such errors.[41]

The calculations needed to compute the effective rate are not difficult. They are relatively simple using an HP 12C™ calculator. Using an HP 10Bii™, I interpolated. I knew the *EFF* was higher than the 13.93% disclosed. Thus I guessed until I produced the present value of $30,599. The process required about five guesses and took perhaps five minutes. Thus, if J.G. Wentworth maintained "procedures reasonably designed to avoid" such an error of 175 basis points, I find it difficult to consider this a "bona fide" error.

The statute provides for two remedies. For violating the discount and finance charges, the payee (Ms. Lutz) may void the transfer and recover any discount collected by the purchaser.[42] In addition, the payee may recover a penalty up to three times the discount. Further, for general violations of the statutory disclosure requirements, the payee may also recover a penalty equal to up to three times the discount, plus attorney's fees and costs.

In this case, the gross amount owed by Metropolitan Life was $54,473.00. The discount under the contract with Wentworth was $23,874. Seven times that amount equals a potential amount due Ms. Lutz (assuming my calculations are correct) of $167,118 plus attorney's fees and costs. Assuming my calculations are correct, the federal excise tax owed by Wentworth is $9,549.60. One should not, therefore, be surprised of multiple class actions against J. G. Wentworth in June, 2019.[43] The statute of limitations expires one year after the last payment, which would be May 1, 2025.

---

[40]   F.S. § 626.99296(6)(c).

[41]   Id.

[42]   Ms. Lutz signed an arbitration agreement, which would arguably affect her rights to litigate the validity of the sale; however, nothing in the agreement appears to affect her statutory rights regarding faulty disclosure.

[43]   *E.g.,* Dockery v. Heretick (2:17–cv–04114) District Court, E.D. Pennsylvania (2019); U.S. District Court for the Eastern District of Missouri case number 4:19–cv–02860–SRC (2019).

Many questions regarding the Lutz case come to mind:

1. Why did the court approve the transfer? Even if the disclosure were correct, the 13.93% *EFF* discount rate for an 8-year A+ rated annuity seems to be about twice the appropriate rate. The mid-term *AFR* at the time (the one generally applicable to obligations under 9 years) was 1.22% *EFF*. Because the statute requires an "express finding" of need, why did the court not state the payee's needs more clearly that refer to a conclusory allegation of a need for "business capital"?

2. Did Ms. Lutz or the court inquire as to what other buyers would have paid? Other reported decisions during the same time period but involving different purchasers used a much more reasonable (albeit high) discount rate of approximately 8% *EFF*.

3. After Met Life received notification, why did it not offer Ms. Lutz a discount of perhaps 8%, which would have been at the high end of what it likely offered during the tort negotiations (which likely occurred while he was a juvenile)? It would be purchasing its own obligation. During the years involved, one struggles to imagine how Met Life could have guaranteed a higher return for itself.

4. Who advised Ms. Lutz?[44] Even if she were desperate for the funds (and nothing in the record suggests that fact), the market for such paper is competitive. She should have received at least $10,000 more.[45]

QUESTION

Client suffered personal physical injuries. Pursuant to a structured settlement, Client received an annuity of $5,000 per month for twenty years. Another attorney represented Client in that matter. A major, highly rated insurance company issued the annuity, which is not life dependent.

Two years have passed and Client seeks your advice regarding selling the annuity for a lump sum. Client needs your help pursuant to the state Structured Settlement Protection Act.

---

[44] The Order was sent to Francisco J. Moro, Esq.; however, he never made an appearance in the record.

[45] Using a 6% *EFF* discount rate to the date of payment (rather than to the date of disclosure) produces a present value of approximately $43,000. I allow $400 for court costs, $600 for document preparation and investigation, and $1,000 for attorney fees for the 10-minute hearing. Even with those costs allocated to the seller, the buyer should have paid $41,000, which is $10,401 more than it paid.

LESSON TWELVE

FUTURE VALUE OF AN ANNUITY

■ ■ ■

Lesson Objectives

1. Student will learn *how to* use the FUTURE VALUE OF AN ANNUITY CALCULATOR.

    - How to locate the Instructions.

    - How to find Definitions of each Function.

2. Student will learn the *formula* for the Future Value of an Annuity:

> **FV of an Annuity:**
>
> $$\frac{\left[PMT \left(1 + \frac{i}{100} \right)^{n} - 1 \right]}{\frac{i}{100}}$$
>
> PMT = payment
>
> n = number of periods
>
> i = nominal interest rate
>
> FV = the future value

3. Student will learn **when** a lawyer would need to compute the Future Value of an Annuity:

    - **As a lawyer, you would use this calculation if you or a client plans to save or borrow a series of _payments_ . . . i.e., if you (or the other party) wants to _know what is owned or owed in the future_.**

4. Student will **work** some practical examples of situations in which a lawyer would need to compute the Future Value of an Annuity.

5. Student will **see** dramatic examples of the incredible potential results from compound interest over significant time. They will learn that small changes in the rate of interest can result in huge changes in the future value.

———————

LESSON TWELVE covers the future value of an annuity. This calculation computes the future amount or value of a future series of deposits or obligations. As a lawyer, you would use this calculation if you or a client desire to pay a recurring debt or other obligation *late*—a deferred-payment, or if you need to know the future value of regular savings. For example, you may want to defer rent or interest obligations until a future date.

Of the six main financial calculations, this is probably the *least useful* for lawyers. The related sinking fund calculation—the regular deposit needed to generate a future sum—is more useful: you are more likely to know the future amount required (perhaps for retirement or an education fund) and thus need to calculate the necessary deposit (the sinking fund) than you are to know the deposit and need to solve for the future amount. Nevertheless, the calculation is fundamental and potentially useful.

Figure 75 (Figure 4 from LESSON THREE) illustrates the FUTURE VALUE OF AN ANNUITY CALCULATOR. LESSON THREE also raised several reasons why a lawyer would want to know how to compute the present value of an annuity: If you owe money at regular intervals in the future, you can compute what it equals in current value. This is useful if you know or have planned the regular deposit or obligation and need to know what you owe or own in the future at a given interest rate.

FUTURE VALUE OF AN ANNUITY CALCULATOR

Instructions ON	OFF

Mode	Begin	End	
Present Value		0.00	
Future Value		0.00	end mode
Nominal Interest Rate		1.00	
Effective Interest Rate		1.0041924075	
Number of Years		1.00	
Payments Per Year		12.00	
Number of Payments		12.00	
Payment			
	clear all		

Figure 75: Future Value of an Annuity Calculator

Consider **Example 41**. The example assumes you are making a regular deposit at regular intervals and will earn a pre-determined interest rate in a tax-free or tax-deferred account. The tax-free nature is possible for educational savings accounts and the tax-deferred nature is possible for some deferred compensation or retirement plans. The fixed interest rate could be contracted, but realize it affects the inflation component of interest. Contracting for a fixed rate on savings (similar to a fixed rate on a loan or annuity) shifts risk of higher than expected inflation to the depositor and lower than expected inflation to the borrower. In **Example 41**, the fixed 5% *EFF* rate necessarily includes liquidity, risk, and expected inflation. Assuming liquidity is 2.5 and risk is a nominal 0.5% *EFF* (perhaps a federally insured account or a highly-rated insurance company borrower), the parties must anticipate 2% *EFF* inflation for the various periods. If, in fact, inflation is higher, the depositor (you) will lose purchasing power—your future amount will not purchase as much as you anticipated. Or, if inflation is lower than 2% *EFF*, you will earn an extra return and your funds will be more valuable than anticipated.

EXAMPLE 41

Future Value of an Annuity

You plan to deposit $500 monthly in a tax-free or tax-deferred account that will earn 5% *EFF*.

Compute the amount you will have saved in 12, 24, and 216 months (18 years).

Figure 76 provides the COURSE CALCULATOR answer for the 12-month period in **Example 41**, using Begin Mode. Before we could compute it, we had to determine whether the deposits began today (an annuity due) or one month from now (an annuity in arrears). The example did not provide that needed information. Let's work it both ways.

Figure 76 provides the Annuity Due answer as $6,161.08. As explained in prior LESSONS, type 500 as the Payment amount, 12 as the Payments Per Year, and 1 as the Number of Years (12 months). Because the COURSE CALCULATORS require the use of an *NAI*, you must first have converted the stated 5% *EFF* into the equivalent *NAI* for monthly compounding.

FUTURE VALUE OF AN ANNUITY CALCULATOR

	Instructions ON OFF	
Mode	Begin　End	
Present Value	0.00	
Future Value	6,161.08	*begin mode*
Nominal Interest Rate	4.89	
Effective Interest Rate	4.9998446656	
Number of Years	1.00	
Payments Per Year	12.00	
Number of Payments	12.00	
Payment	500.00	
	clear all	

Figure 76: Example 41 for $500 Deposit Beginning Today

As explained in LESSON FIVE-B on Interest Conversion, you would open the INTEREST CONVERSION CALCULATOR as shown in **Figure 77**. You would click on the Brown Button to convert an effective rate to a nominal rate and then insert the numbers as shown. The INTEREST CONVERSION CALCULATOR converted the 5% *EFF* to 4.888949. Type that number as the *NAI* in the FUTURE VALUE OF AN ANNUITY CALCULATOR as shown in **Figure 77**. It will show an *EFF* of 4.99984446656%, which is essentially 5% *EFF*. The rounding error is not material.

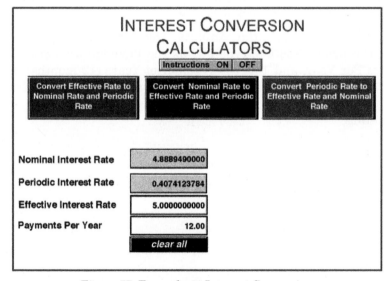

Figure 77: Example 41 Interest Conversion

As explained above, the **Figure 76** answer of $6,161.08 is useful with the contracted interest rate of 5% *EFF*, which likely included a projected inflation amount of 2%. Because the dollar amount is necessarily stated in future dollars (that is the nature of a future value calculation), it is not comparable to current dollars, assuming inflation of other than zero. Thus, the $6,161.08 will purchase whatever that amount will purchase in 12 months. Perhaps inflation will ultimately be zero, which would mean it would purchase what $6,161.08 would purchase today; or perhaps inflation will be rapid, in which case it may not purchase much. LESSON FOURTEEN will explore ways of compensating for this uncertainty. Predicting inflation (or deflation) is notoriously difficult, particularly for long periods. For the 12 months in the example, the prediction might be reasonably accurate because the period is so short.

Future Values Do Not Translate Directly to Present Values

Although present and future values are "equal" under the calculation conditions (interest rate, compounding, time period), they are not equal in purchasing power unless inflation/deflation is zero.

Figure 78 provides the answer to **Example 41** using an annuity in arrears (end mode). The answer of $6,136.10 is only $24.98 lower than the answer using an annuity due. The delay in making the deposit results in the loss of a month's interest, which is not significant for such a short period.

FUTURE VALUE OF AN ANNUITY CALCULATOR

Instructions	ON	OFF

	Begin	End	
Mode			
Present Value		0.00	
Future Value		6,136.10	*end mode*
Nominal Interest Rate		4.89	
Effective Interest Rate		4.9998446656	
Number of Years		1.00	
Payments Per Year		12.00	
Number of Payments		12.00	
Payment		500.00	
		clear all	

Figure 78: Example 41 for 12-Month Annuity in Arrears

Figure 79 provides the answer for an annuity due after 24 months: $12,630.22. **Figure 80** provides the answer for a 24-month annuity in arrears: $12,578.99. You can switch the calculators between begin and end mode without changing the other numbers: simply click on the black box that states ***Begin*** or ***End***.

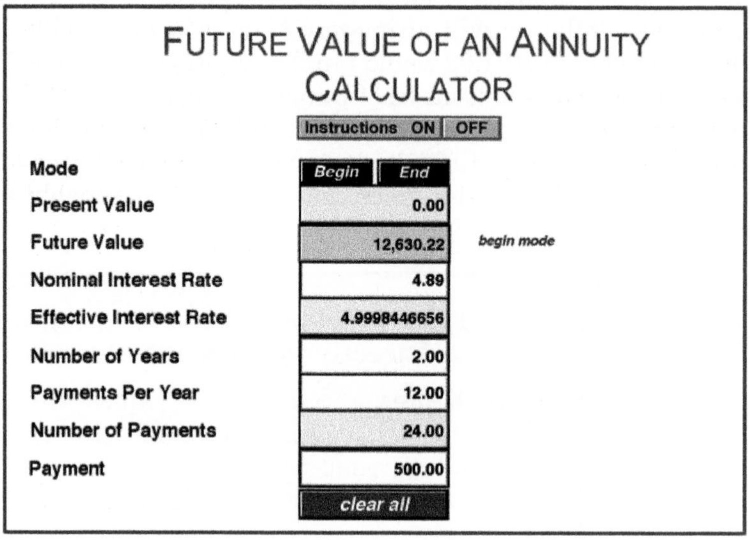

FUTURE VALUE OF AN ANNUITY
CALCULATOR

| Instructions | ON | OFF |

Mode		Begin	End	
Present Value			0.00	
Future Value			12,630.22	*begin mode*
Nominal Interest Rate			4.89	
Effective Interest Rate			4.9998446656	
Number of Years			2.00	
Payments Per Year			12.00	
Number of Payments			24.00	
Payment			500.00	

clear all

Figure 79: Example 41 with 24-Month Annuity Due

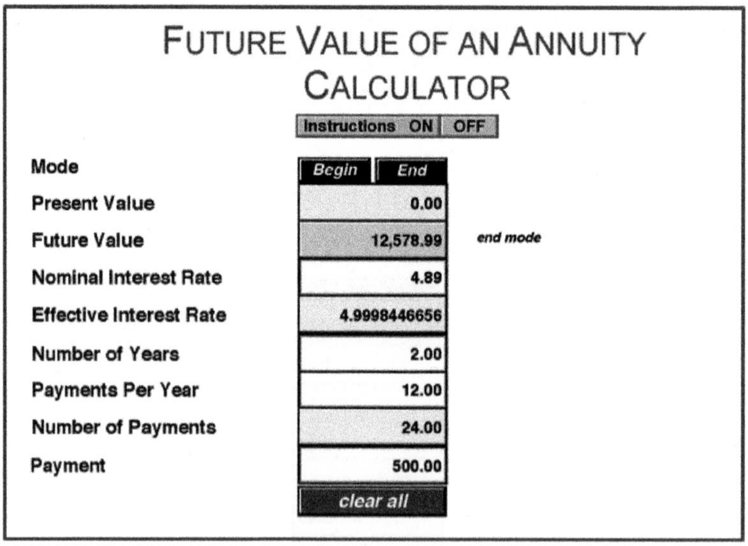

FUTURE VALUE OF AN ANNUITY
CALCULATOR

| Instructions | ON | OFF |

Mode		Begin	End	
Present Value			0.00	
Future Value			12,578.99	*end mode*
Nominal Interest Rate			4.89	
Effective Interest Rate			4.9998446656	
Number of Years			2.00	
Payments Per Year			12.00	
Number of Payments			24.00	
Payment			500.00	

clear all

Figure 80: Example 41 for 24-Month Annuity in Arrears

Figures 81 and **82** provide the answers for **Example 41** using 18 years (216 months) which is a common savings period for a child's education savings account. This problem assumes you know how much you want to save, which allows you to compute the future value when the child reaches age 18 (assuming you started at birth). As per the ***Caution*** above, the future value numbers are not particularly useful because they are not comparable in purchasing power to current dollars. The example is also flawed because it involves a level amount of savings for a long period. As explained in LESSON FOURTEEN, you would likely want to alter the deposit amount annually by the actual inflation amount (which you would know each year). Also, while the 12 and 24-month examples of a fixed interest rate were realistic because the periods were short, locking in an interest rate for 18 years is questionable: inflation predictions would be far too speculative. LESSON FOURTEEN explains how to adjust for this problem. The answers—$173,323.76 for the Annuity Due and $172,620,52 for the Annuity in Arrears—are correct under the calculation conditions. But, the cost of a college education 18 years from now is far too speculative for those numbers to be useful. They are arguably ample, if not generous in terms of 2020 costs, but one cannot know whether they are ample, generous or woefully inadequate in terms of 2038 costs, 18 years hence.

FUTURE VALUE OF AN ANNUITY CALCULATOR

Instructions	ON	OFF

	Begin	End	
Mode			
Present Value	0.00		
Future Value	173,323.76		*begin mode*
Nominal Interest Rate	4.89		
Effective Interest Rate	4.9998446656		
Number of Years	18.00		
Payments Per Year	12.00		
Number of Payments	216.00		
Payment	500.00		
clear all			

Figure 81: Example 41 for 18-Year Annuity Due

Note, once again, the fairly small difference between begin and end mode. Although the difference is quite small, especially considering the speculative nature of the calculation, the difference still exists. It is not so great as to be obviously wrong; thus, if you are seeking accuracy at that level of precision, you must be careful to set the mode correctly.

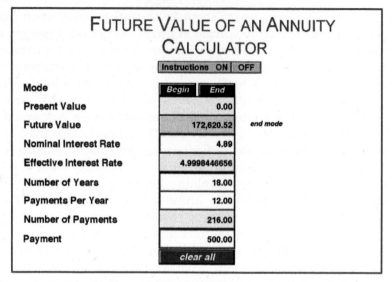

Figure 82: Example 41 for 18-Year Annuity in Arrears

Example 42 presents a second plausible scenario for using the future value of an annuity calculation. It involves a fixed obligation for a fairly short period at a fixed interest rate. Calculating the amount using the same process as used for **Example 41**. Two scenarios are common—a series of student loans[1] and deferred commercial rent.

EXAMPLE 42

Future Value of an Annuity

You plan to borrow $1,500 monthly beginning today. The lender has agreed to accept payment in 4 years (either as a lump sum or through an amortization). The negotiated interest rate is 6% *NAI*.

Compute the balance due in 4 years.

Figure 83 provides the answer: $81,552.48. Notice, the example provided an *NAI* and also stated the loan used begin mode. With the fixed interest rate, the answer is accurate. LESSON THIRTEEN will demonstrate how to amortize the loan if it is to be paid off over a ten or fifteen-year period, as is typical for student loans. If, instead, this involves deferred rent, the amount would likely be due at the end of the term. The tax consequences of deferred rent are fascinating, but mostly beyond this

---

[1] Some student loans do not accumulate interest during the education term because the government or some other entity pays the interest for the borrower. In **Example 42**, interest accumulates.

course. IRC section 467(f)[2] covers the issue. It involves the use of a sinking fund (covered in LESSON FOURTEEN) and a federally determined interest rate. Section 467 would not apply to **Example 42** because the dollar amounts are too small: it only applies if the total amount exceeds $250,000 for the rental term.

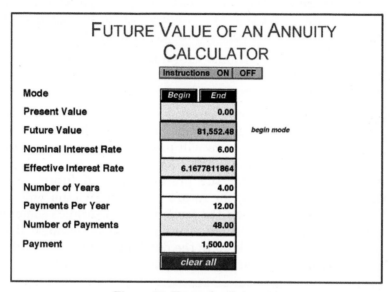

Figure 83: Example 42 Answer

Example 43 presents a more common use for the future value of an annuity calculation. It involves a tort case in which settlement negotiations are on-going for several years following the injury. In the example, four years have already past. The Client had a work-life expectancy of 35 years. As a result, Client lost four years of past wages and 31 years of future wages, at least from your point of view on the date of the settlement negotiations. The future lost wages involve the present value of an annuity, as covered in LESSON ELEVEN. The past lost wages, however present a different issue. An expert could plausibly view the past losses in terms of the future value of an annuity, with today (the date of settlement negotiations) being the future of the past. In such a case, one would know the past interest rates typical for a person such as the client, including past inflation rates.

---

[2]   IRC § 467(f).

EXAMPLE 43

Future Value of an Annuity

Your client was injured in an accident three years ago such that he/she can no longer work. At the time of the injury, Client was earning $10,000 monthly after taxes and had a work-life expectancy of 35 years.

Settlement negotiations continue, with a trial date set for next month. You are asked to compute the value of the lost wages.

Figure 84 uses an after-tax interest rate of 5% *NAI* to measure the past losses as of today. Be careful: for past losses (using the future value of an annuity calculation), the victim will prefer a higher interest rate and the tortfeasor or insurance company will prefer a lower rate, which is the opposite of the calculation for the present value of future losses. As explained in LESSON ELEVEN, for future losses, the victim will prefer a lower discount interest rate and the tortfeasor or insurance company will prefer a higher rate. The calculation uses end mode because the client would have been paid for work up to the date of the injury and otherwise, would likely have been paid at the end of each pay period.

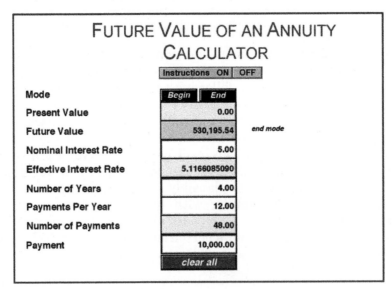

Figure 84: Example 43 Using Future Value of an Annuity

This a realistic way of computing the past lost wages; however, it is arguably flawed for two reasons. *First*, one might question whether it considers both the inflation effect on lost accumulations as well as the inflation component of lost wages. *Second*, it applies an interest rate to the past "pre-judgement" losses, which some jurisdictions arguably do not permit. Let's consider those issues carefully.

1. DOES THE MODEL ACCOUNT FOR INFLATION-BASED WAGE INCREASES, AS WELL AS NET ACCUMULATION INFLATION-BASED INCREASES?

The answer is _no_ as to inflation-based wage increases but yes as to accumulations.

The inflation impact on _accumulations_ is the easier to detect. The victim would have received the after-tax wages absent the injury—the $10,000 per month for four years. The rate used in the calculation includes the liquidity factor, which is appropriate because the victim lost the use of the funds for the four years, and that is what the loss of use is worth, ignoring risk and inflation. The rate also included an after-tax inflation factor because the victim likely would have earned this amount, if the funds had been available. Whether this is legally relevant is the subject of the second issue below: the relevance of pre-judgement interest.

The lack of an inflation impact on _past lost wages_ is less obvious and requires some proof. An example should suffice. Following the example, which proves the flaw, we must discuss two very complicated issues in greater depth:

- In LESSONS SIX and ELEVEN, the TEXT posited the correct discount rate for future lost wages which would increase by inflation was the liquidity rate time 1 minus the inflation rate. We must now prove that modification works satisfactorily.

- Although the above modification works for future wage inflation-based increases, it does not work (as illustrated in the Example) for past lost wages to the extent of inflation-based increases. Thus, we must cover two alternative methods of accounting for this issue.

Following that, we can return to the issue of pre-judgment interest and whether consideration of past inflation or liquidity interest is even legally admissible.

a. Example Proving the Flaw (the _Example 23_ Modification Does Not Work for Past Losses)

LESSON SIX **Example 23** posited the proper discount rate for _future_ losses should be the liquidity rate times 1 minus the expected after-tax inflation rate. That results in the victim being compensated as if the _future lost wages_ increased by inflation. We will prove that in part b. below. First, let's modify **Example 43** to be more like **Example 23**, which will illustrate that the modification does not work for past lost wages. We thus have **Example 44**:

EXAMPLE 44

Future Value of an Annuity

Your client was injured in an accident 4 years ago such that he/she can no longer work. At the time of the injury, Client was earning $120,000 annually after taxes, with all the wages due at the end of the year (however unrealistic). Had Client not been injured, Client would have received a paycheck either yesterday or today for the past year.

The parties agree the proper after-tax discount rate for liquidity (real rate of return or whatever they wish to call it) is 2.5% *EFF*. They also agree that inflation during the prior four years was 2.5% after-taxes. Further, they agree wages would have increased by 2.5% after taxes had Client not been injured. And, they stipulate the impact of inflation and the "real rate of return" is admissible and should apply.

You need to compute the value today of the prior losses.

Assume (slight change from **Example 23**) that all wages were to be paid at the end of each year and lets use 5% *EFF* as the rate (which is slightly lower than **Example 43**, which used 5% *NAI* compounded monthly).

Table 10 shows the nominal wages (increased by inflation) as well as the future value of each lost paycheck as of today. Note, using end mode and assuming four prior years, today is the fourth wage lost. For example, if today is January 1, 2024, the four prior years would be 2020, 2021, 2022, and 2023. The lost wages would have been due December 31 of each of the four years.

The total future value (today) of those four lost paychecks is $695,392.09. Essentially, this follows the "case-by-case" evaluation method described in LESSONS SIX and ELEVEN. It must be correct because it tediously accounts for the after-tax inflation impact plus the after-tax liquidity effect attributable to the deferred availability of the funds.

But, the calculation is anything but simple. It is tedious; hence, one might understand the fairly consistent criticism by courts of the "case-by-case" method. This should help you understand the search for a simpler, but also accurate, method to achieve the same or approximately the same result.

Table 10: Example 44 Case-by-Case Method

Year	Nominal Wage Earned (adjusted for inflation)	Future Value (Today)
0		
1	123,000[3]	142,387.88[4]
2	126,075[5]	138,997.69[6]
3	129,226.88[7]	135,688.22[8]
4	132,457.55[9]	132,457.55
Total Future Value		549,531.34

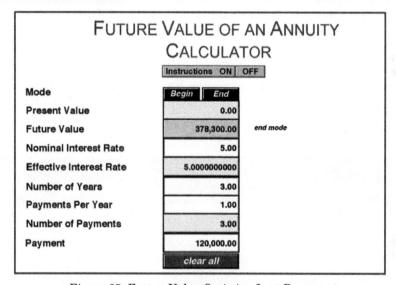

Figure 85: Future Value Omitting Last Payment

Figure 85 shows the future value of the lost wages excluding the last wage, which must be added separately. The $378,300.00 future value plus the last paycheck of $132,457.55 total $510,757.55, which is incorrect: it is

---

[3]   120,000 times 1.025 = 123,000.

[4]   I used the FUTURE VALUE OF A SUM CALCULATOR with 123,000 as the present value, 5% as the *NAI*, 3 as the number of years, and 1 as the payments per year. The HP 10Bii™ produces the same answer.

[5]   123,000 times 1.025 = 126,075.

[6]   I used the FUTURE VALUE OF A SUM CALCULATOR with 126,075 as the present value, 5% as the *NAI*, 2 as the number of years, and 1 as the payments per year. The HP 10Bii™ produces the same answer.

[7]   126,075 times 1.025 = 129,226.88.

[8]   I used the FUTURE VALUE OF A SUM CALCULATOR with 129,226.88 as the present value, 5% as the *NAI*, 1 as the number of years, and 1 as the payments per year. The HP 10Bii™ produces the same answer.

[9]   129,226.88 times 1.025 = 132,457.55.

low by almost $40,000, which reflects the increased wages adjusted for inflation. Altering the discount rate will not resolve the problem, which results because the annuity is not level—the same amount per year. Instead, the annuity increases each year by the after-tax inflation amount of 2.5% *EFF*.

To resolve the problem, one could use the tedious Case-by-Case method. **Table 10** illustrates it for 5 payments. Similar computations for monthly payments would be significantly more complicated because each year would have 12 payments (if not 26 if the paycheck were every two weeks). Adjusting the interest rate by a function of the inflation rate times the liquidity rate—as we did in **Example 23**, LESSON SIX—will not solve the problem because the problem is with the *unlevel annuity*. Before we actually find a solution for **Example 44**, we should first be certain the **Example 23** method works as stated for future lost wages.

b.   Proof the *Example 23* Modification Works for Future Losses

Consider a much simpler example: **Example 45**. It involves only four years. Adding years would not alter the computations significantly, just as adding zeros to the lost wages would not change the calculation other than by its magnitude.

EXAMPLE 45

Present Value of an Annuity

Client lost four years of *future* wages, with each wage due at the end of the year. At the date of injury Client earned, after-taxes, $1,000 per year. But for the injury, wages would have increased by an annual 10% inflation rate. The parties stipulate the appropriate liquidity rate is 2.5%.

Figure 86 shows the present value of the lost future wages discounted by 2.2727% *EFF* (the liquidity rate adjusted for inflation and taxes). To obtain this, divide the 2.5% discount rate by 1.1, which is 1 plus the projected inflation rate (stated as a decimal). The present value is $3,782.66.

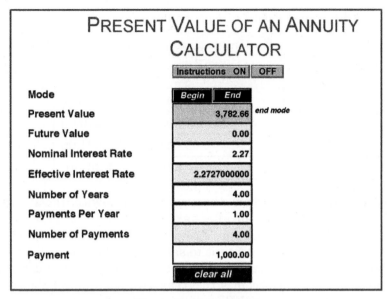

Figure 86: Example 45

To further illustrate the point, **Table 11** shows the unadjusted wages, adjusted wages, and the present value of each un-adjusted wage at a 2.2727% discount rate. The total present value adds to $3,784.74, as the PRESENT VALUE OF AN ANNUITY CALCULATOR showed.

Table 11: Proof of Figure 86

Year	Unadjusted Wage	Adjusted Wage	Present Value of Un-adjusted Wage
1	1000	1100.00	977.78
2	1000	1210.00	956.05
3	1000	1331.00	934.80
4	1000	1464.10	914.03
Total			3,782.66

Next, we need to amortize the present value to illustrate the cash flows that would result, after-taxes, using the assumed rates of 2.5% *EFF* for liquidity and 10% *EFF* for inflation, both after taxes. This proves the computed present value is correct, or at least sufficiently so. **Table 12** shows the beginning balance the Client could invest at the start of Year 1: $3,782.66, which is the present value of the level (unadjusted for inflation) annuity of $1,000 after taxes per year for four years, discounted at 2.2727% *EFF* (liquidity adjusted for inflation and taxes).

Table 12: Additional Proof of Figure 86

Year	Beginning Balance	Ending Balance Before Withdrawal	Withdrawal	Ending Balance
1	3,782.66	4,255.49	1,100.00	3,155.49
2	3,155.49	3,549.93	1,210.00	2,339.93
3	2,339.93	2,632.42	1,331.00	1,301.42
4	1,301.42	1,464.10	1,464.10	0.00

The second column show the year-end, pre-withdrawal, after-tax account balance assuming an after-tax interest rate of 12.5% (10% for inflation and 2.5% for liquidity). The amount is $4,255.49. Client could withdraw $1,100 from that account to satisfy the inflation-adjusted after-tax lost wage due at the end of year one, leaving a year-end balance of $3,155.49. That amount becomes the Year Two beginning balance, which would earn (after-tax) 12.5% *EFF* to produce $3,549.93, from which Client could withdraw $1,210 to replace the inflation-adjusted wage then due. That would leave $2,339.93, which would be the Year Three beginning balance. It would again earn the assumed 12.5% *EFF* to produce $2,632.42, from which Client could withdraw $1,331.00 to replace the Year Three inflation-adjusted lost after-tax wage, leaving $1,301.42. That would be the Year Four beginning balance and would again earn 12.5% *EFF* to produce $1,464.10, from which client could withdraw the lost inflation-adjusted after-tax wage due of $1,464.10.

Table 12 shows an ending balance of $0.00. Thus the adjustment works. It compensates for inflation-based future wage increases without the complications of the case-by-case method.

c.   Resolving the Inflation Impact for Past Lost Wages

As explained above, adjusting the discount rate adequately accounts for future inflation-based wage increases, but cannot similarly work for past lost wages. Two solutions are available—one using the COURSE CALCULATORS and another using an HP 10Bii™.

1)   *Course Calculator Method*

Support for the COURSE CALCULATOR method appear in a U.S. Supreme Court footnote from the 1983 *Jones & Laughlin Steel* decision:

> At one time it was thought appropriate to distinguish between compensating a plaintiff "for the loss of time from his work which has actually occurred up to the time of trial" and compensating him "for the time which he will lose in [the] future." C. McCormick, Damages § 86 (1935). This suggested that estimated future

earning capacity should be discounted to the date of trial, and a separate calculation should be performed for the estimated loss of earnings between injury and trial. *Id.*, §§ 86, 87. **It is both easier and more precise to discount the entire lost stream of earnings back to the date of injury—the moment from which earning capacity was impaired. The plaintiff may then be awarded interest on that discounted sum for the period between injury and judgment, in order to ensure that the award when invested will still be able to replicate the lost stream.** See *In re Air Crash Disaster Near Chicago, Illinois, on May 25, 1979*, 644 F.2d 633, 641–646 (CA7 1981); 1 Speiser § 8:6, p. 723.[10]

The method involves two steps:

- Discount the *past lost wages*[11] to the date of injury, using the inflation-adjusted after-tax liquidity rate and the PRESENT VALUE OF AN ANNUITY CALCULATOR.

- Copy the present value into the FUTURE VALUE OF A SUM CALCULATOR to determine the current value using an interest rate equal to the sum of the after-tax liquidity rate and the after-tax inflation rate.

Step One appears in **Figure 87** using the numbers from **Example 44**: $120,000 per year for four prior years with the first payment at the end of the period. The present value would be $452,101.05. The interest rate is the 2.5% *EFF* stipulated *divided by* 1 plus the past inflation rate of 2.5% (1.025), which equals 2.439. Because the facts contemplate one payment per year, the *EFF* and the *NAI* are the same. **Figure 86** shows the *NAI* as 2.44; however, the calculator uses the 2.439 inputted, but rounds to two decimals merely for the display, as opposed to the computation.

---

[10] Jones & Laughlin Steel Corp. v. Pfeifer, 462 U.S. 523, 538 (1983), at note 22 (emphasis added).

[11] The case suggests reducing all lost wages to a date-of-injury value and then inflating them to the judgment date. That is effectively the same as reducing future losses to date of judgement (using an inflation-adjusted liquidity rate) and then adding the result of reducing past losses to date of injury and inflating them to date of judgement. The difference would involve using two separate inflation rates: the one affecting past losses being based on what actually occurred and the one affecting future losses being based on predictions made at the date of judgment (or settlement). While what actually occurred during the past is helpful in predicting the future, better information may be available at the date of settlement or judgment; hence, the TEXT method would seem marginally superior.

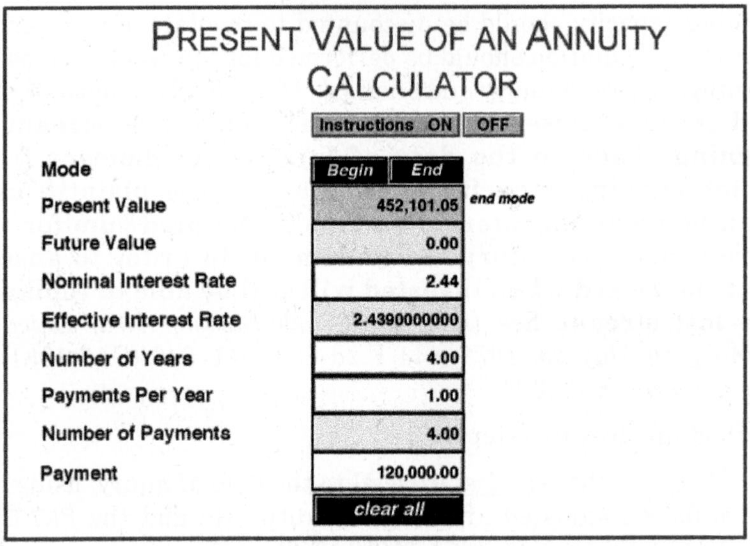

PRESENT VALUE OF AN ANNUITY CALCULATOR

Instructions ON OFF

Mode	Begin	End
Present Value		452,101.05	*end mode*
Future Value		0.00
Nominal Interest Rate		2.44
Effective Interest Rate	2.4390000000	
Number of Years		4.00
Payments Per Year		1.00
Number of Payments		4.00
Payment		120,000.00

clear all

Figure 87: Step One

Step Two computes the future value of that amount using 5% *EFF*. **Figure 88** shows that to be $549,531.65. That is a reasonable approximation of the case-by-case method demonstrated in **Table 11**: $549,531.34. Thirty-one cents out of over half of one million dollars is immaterial.

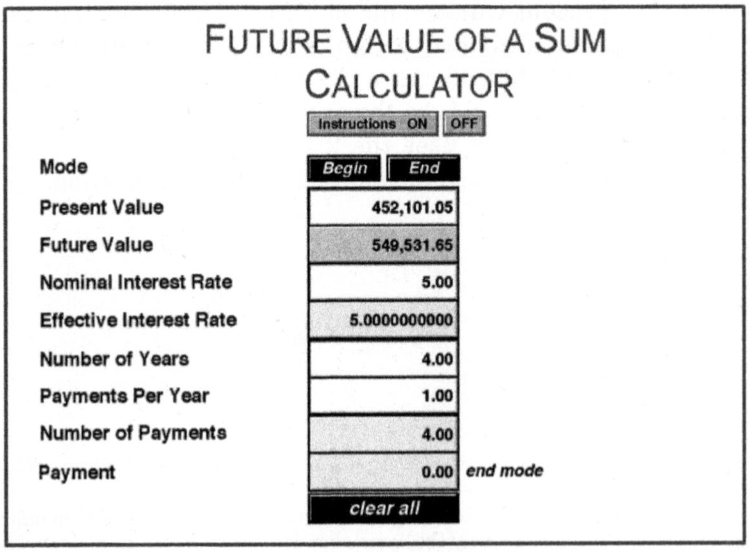

FUTURE VALUE OF A SUM CALCULATOR

Instructions ON OFF

Mode	Begin	End
Present Value		452,101.05
Future Value		549,531.65
Nominal Interest Rate		5.00
Effective Interest Rate	5.0000000000	
Number of Years		4.00
Payments Per Year		1.00
Number of Payments		4.00
Payment		0.00	*end mode*

clear all

Figure 88: Step Two

2) HP 10Bii™ Method

This is _very_ complicated. It involves using some programmable functions of the calculator. HP provides on-line explanations, but be careful with them: they are very complicated and contain at least three surprising errors.[12] It provides a slightly more precise answer than the COURSE CALCULATOR method; however, the complexity is probably not worth the trouble.[13]

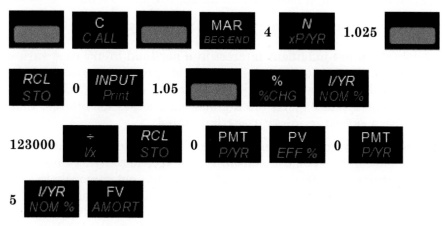

The first two steps below clear the memory and put the calculator into End Mode. The answer will be $549,531.33, which is within one cent of the case-by-case method (**Figure 11**) and within 32 cents of the COURSE CALCULATOR method. The HP method works the same way as the COURSE CALCULATOR method: it computes the present value of the increasing annuity and then the future value of the present value. But, notice the COURSE CALCULATOR method uses an inflation-adjusted discount rate and an un-inflated wage amount. The HP method uses an un-adjusted discount rate but an inflation-adjusted (for one year) wage amount. Why the methods differ in these aspects is beyond the level of this course.

The important lesson is that all three methods—tedious case-by-case, COURSE CALCULATOR two-step, and the complicated HP method—produce an answer of about $550,000. Unadjusted for inflation and the liquidity deferral, the loss is nominally $480,000.[14] One can easily defend $550,000, but $535,000 or $565,000 are also easily defensible given the uncertainly

---

[12] At least as of 12/10/19. The _PV_ of an increasing annuity (Begin Mode) instructions mistakenly say to use END mode in step 1. Step 5 says to press _PV_. Then, in step 6, the same instructions say to press _FV_ to calculate the present value. Clearly, one must use BEGIN mode and press _FV_ in step 5 and _PV_ in step 6. https://support.hp.com/us-en/document/bpia5027.

[13] I spent five days working examples and reading the HP manuals until I was confident I could correctly describe the method. For a 32-cent difference out of over a half million, I do not believe it is worth the trouble, especially considering the folly of seeking precision for a calculation involving so many assumptions, estimates, and educated guesses.

[14] $120,000 per year for four years.

of the required assumptions[15]; however, $480,000 is too low—*so pay close attention to the following discussion regarding relevance/admissibility of pre-judgment interest*.

Also, consider a wise statement from the Supreme Court:

> We do not suggest that the trial judge should embark on a search for "**delusive exactness**." It is perfectly obvious that the most detailed inquiry can at best produce an approximate result.[16]

2.   PREJUDGMENT INTEREST

Availability of pre-judgment interest in a personal injury case varies by jurisdiction, at least as a matter of law. Florida presents a good study in the issue, which appears to create considerable confusion. One 2017 commentator noted that experts often adjust past losses for interest that would have been earned in injury cases, but stated:

> This is unlikely to be permissible in Florida. Florida awards prejudgment interest on compensatory damages in contract cases at the statutory rate from the date of the loss but not generally in wrongful death and personal injury cases because the amount of the damages is at the jury's discretion (e.g., is too speculative) and is unliquidated at the time of the trial. A limited exception when prejudgment interest may be awarded in personal injury and wrongful death cases for actual "out-of-pocket" costs, such as medical and funeral expenses, likely does not apply to lost net accumulations, loss of support, and lost earnings capacity.[17]

The statement is arguably correct; however, it can also be easily misunderstood. Damages are a question of fact for the trier of fact. Prejudgment interest—at least in many jurisdictions—is a question of law. One should be careful, therefore, not to omit the issue, as well as not to count it twice. If it is part of the verdict, it thus should not also be awarded by the court as a matter of law. If, instead, it is not considered by the trier of fact and not part of the verdict, then the court should award it. At least, that seems to be the opinion of the Florida Supreme Court. In 1985, the Court explained the issue, though the case involved property damage rather than personal injury. The Court said:

---

[15] Whether the correct liquidity rate after-tax is 2.5 or 2 or 1.0 or 3 is not certain. Also, whether the inflation rate represented the victim's experience is unclear and will never be known. Plus, whether the victim would have earned the liquidity and inflation after-tax rates is likewise unknown: perhaps the victim would have earned a bit more or perhaps less. Thus quibbling about $535,000 versus $565,000 seems unwise. Certainly, quibbling about $549,531 versus $549,551 is ludicrous.

[16] Jones & Laughlin Steel Corp. v. Pfeifer, 462 U.S. 523, 552 (1983). Justice Holmes coined the phrase "delusive exactness." *Truax* v. *Corrigan*, 257 U.S. 312, 342 (1921) (Holmes, J., dissenting).

[17] Charles L. Baum II, *Computing Economic Damages in Florida Wrongful Death and Personal Injury Cases*, 91 FLA. BAR J. 8, 18 (2017) (citations omitted).

Once a verdict has liquidated the damages as of a date certain, computation of prejudgment interest is merely a mathematical computation. There is no "finding of fact" needed. Thus, it is a purely ministerial duty of the trial judge or clerk of the court to add the appropriate amount of interest to the principal amount of damages awarded in the verdict. **We conclude that the finder of fact should not consider the time-value of money in its consideration of damages.**

. . . .

In short, when a verdict liquidates damages on a plaintiff's out-of-pocket, pecuniary losses, plaintiff is entitled, as a matter of law, to prejudgment interest at the statutory rate from the date of that loss.[18]

Unfortunately, the Court recognized the traditional rule that prejudgment interest had been unavailable for personal injury awards.[19] But, in its explanation, the Court recognized the general factual issue of damages, which naturally (its terminology) includes interest. The Court disapproved of interest begin used as a penalty, but appeared to approve of it as part of damages. Exactly when it is a question of fact versus a question of law seems unclear. As a practical matter, that boils down to the interest rate used. If a matter of law, the statutory rate applies.[20] If a matter of fact, the trier of fact determines the rate—but, one would think the statutory rate would be strong evidence of the appropriate factual rate.

3. DOES PREJUDGMENT INTEREST EVEN MATTER?

Consider **Example 43** in totality. It modified **Example 33**, which contemplated not only past losses, but also substantial future losses. Using the past of four years from **Example 43**, the future losses were 31 years at 10,000 per month. Adjusted for inflation, the lost wage would have been $11,038 per month, after-tax at the date of settlement or trial. Discounted at 2.5%, the present value of future losses on settlement day would be nearly $2.9 million. At the very least, one would add the un-adjusted $480,000 past losses to that number to reach between $3.25 and $3.3 million. The pre-judgement interest involved is, as argued above, between $55,000 and $85,000. Each component is an approximation: the loss, the time period, whether wages would have increased by inflation, the future inflation rate, the discount rate, whether to apply the statutory rate to the past or whether to admit evidence of past inflation, and the tax rate. Further, if the past interest is a jury question, how will the jury react to evidence of one interest rate (the liquidity rate) for future losses and what

---

[18] Argonaut Ins. Co. v. May Plumbing Co., 474 So. 2d 212, 215 (Fla. 1985).

[19] Id. at note 19.

[20] F. S. § 687.01.

might be a substantially higher rate for past losses? While that may be correct, will the jury understand it? Or might the jury consider the two rates as contradictory and thus lose respect for whichever counsel argues for the differences? Is the difference between $3,250,000 and $3,350,000 really material? Or is it a search for more delusive exactness?

QUESTION

What is "pre-judgement" interest?

LESSON THIRTEEN

AMORTIZATION

■ ■ ■

Lesson Objectives

1. Student will learn **how to** use the AMORTIZATION CALCULATORS.

    *   How to locate the Instructions.

    *   How to find Definitions of each Function

    *   How and when to use the Begin and End Mode Calculators.

    *   How and when to use the simple AMORTIZATION CALCULATOR without a chart and how and when to use the AMORTIZATION CALCULATOR with a chart.

2. Student will learn the **formula** for Amortization of an amount:

    > **Amortization Payment:**
    >
    > $$\left[\frac{\left(PV\left(\frac{i}{100}\right)\right)}{1-\left(1+\frac{i}{100}\right)^{-n}}\right]$$
    >
    > n = number of periods
    > i = nominal interest rate
    > PV = present value

3. Student will learn **when** a lawyer would need to Amortize an amount:

    *   **As a lawyer, you would use this calculation if you or a client owes a current amount ... *i.e.*, if you (or the other party) wants to *how much to pay overtime to retire the debt*.**

4. Student will **work** some practical examples of situations in which a lawyer would need to Amortize an amount.

LESSON THIRTEEN covers the amortization of a debt. This calculation computes the amount needed in a series of payments to retire an obligation. As a lawyer, you would use this calculation if you or a client desire to pay a debt with level payments over a period of time. For example, you may want to pay of a house or car loan or a student loan. Of the six main financial calculations, this is probably the *most useful* for lawyers.

Figure 88 (**Figure 5** from LESSON THREE) shows the basic AMORTIZATION CALCULATOR. Two different AMORTIZATION CALCULATORS are available among the COURSE CALCULATORS. The one in **Figure 88** merely computes the level payment needed to amortize a present value over a period of time at a given interest rate and payment frequency. It works in the same fashion as the other calculators and with the same speed.

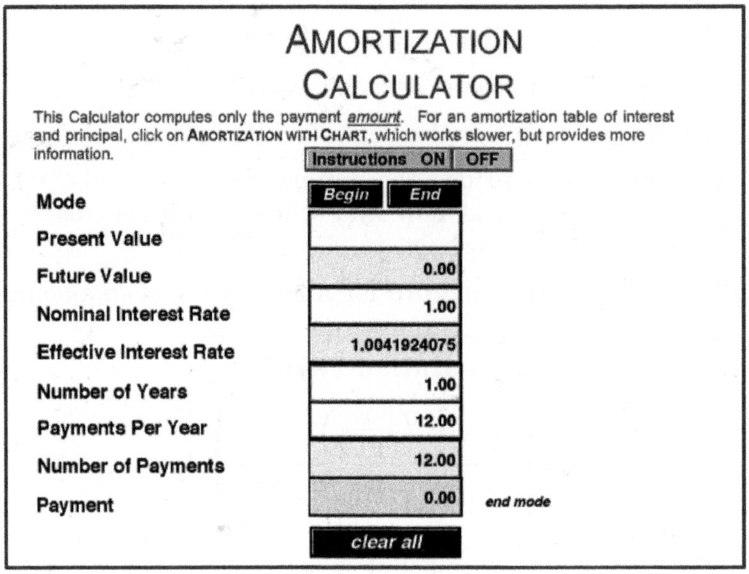

AMORTIZATION CALCULATOR

This Calculator computes only the payment *amount*. For an amortization table of interest and principal, click on AMORTIZATION WITH CHART, which works slower, but provides more information.

	Instructions ON	OFF
Mode	Begin	End
Present Value		
Future Value		0.00
Nominal Interest Rate		1.00
Effective Interest Rate	1.0041924075	
Number of Years		1.00
Payments Per Year		12.00
Number of Payments		12.00
Payment		0.00	end mode
	clear all	

Figure 89: Amortization Calculator

A separate AMORTIZATION WITH CHART CALCULATOR is also available. The first page of the CHART CALCULATOR is exactly the same as the basic AMORTIZATION CALCULATOR in **Figure 89**—it operates either in begin or end mode; however, it has nine additional pages of calculations showing the periodic effects of the amortization process. Those pages calculate and show the period, the payment amount, the portion of each payment allocable to principal, the portion allocable to interest, and the remaining balance due at the end of the period. It does this for up to 360 periods, which is useful for a thirty-year loan with monthly payments (360 total). Because the CHART CALCULATOR makes many additional calculations, it works a bit more slowly than do the others. You will find a brief delay of *a few seconds* after you enter each of the variables: the *NAI*, the Present Value, the Number of Years, and the Payments Per Year.

Consider **Example 46**. Use the basic AMORTIZATION CALCULATOR. Student loans, bearing 6% *NAI* are payable over 10, 15, or 20 years at the debtor's option. **Figure 90** shows the calculation for 20 years: a payment of $716.43 per month. Change the number of years to 15 and the monthly payment is $843.86. Change the number of years to 10 and the monthly payment is $1,110.21.

EXAMPLE 46

Amortization

Graduate owes $100,000 in student loans which charge 6% nominal annual interest with monthly payments. The first payment is due one month from today. What is the amount of each payment if Graduate selects, alternatively, a 10-year, 15-year, or 20-year payoff period?

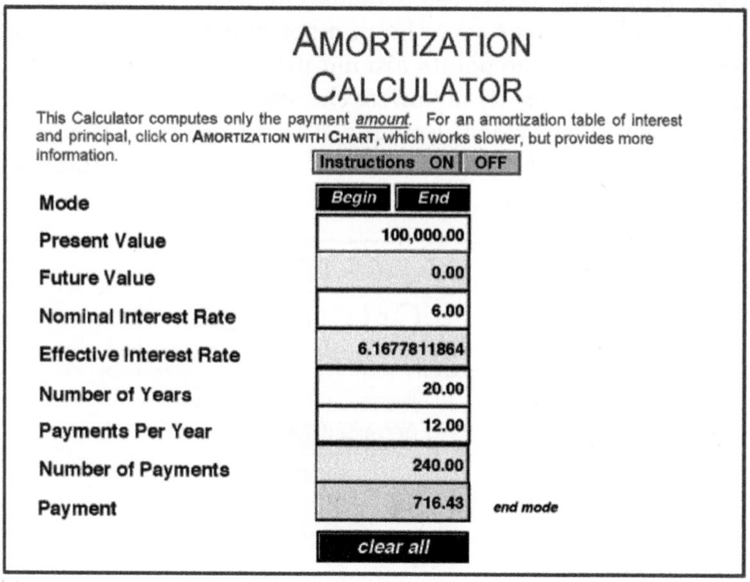

AMORTIZATION CALCULATOR

This Calculator computes only the payment *amount*. For an amortization table of interest and principal, click on **AMORTIZATION WITH CHART**, which works slower, but provides more information.
Instructions ON | OFF

Mode	Begin | End
Present Value	100,000.00
Future Value	0.00
Nominal Interest Rate	6.00
Effective Interest Rate	6.1677811864
Number of Years	20.00
Payments Per Year	12.00
Number of Payments	240.00
Payment	716.43 *end mode*

clear all

Figure 90: Student Loan for 20 Years

Recall **Example 14** from LESSON FIVE-C (now **Example 47**). You then had to accept that the monthly payments would be $1,610.41, the *APR* would be 5.269%, and the effective rate would be 5.398%. The nightmare involved having to pay off the loan a month after purchasing the property because your job moved to another state. Let's compute those numbers now.

EXAMPLE 47

Illustrating a Nightmare

You have borrowed $300,000 to purchase a new house. The loan has a stated nominal annual interest rate (*NAI*) of 5%. The lender charges 3 points. The term of the loan is thirty years and the payments are monthly, beginning one month from today.

Figure 91 shows the payment amount of $1,610.41. Recall from LESSON FIVE-C: points (and other closing costs) affect the federally-defined annual percentage rate on a loan (*APR*). Tax law and consumer finance law both treat points as pre-paid interest (despite the impossibility of pre-paying interest). As a result, the points (and other closing costs which statutorily figure into the *APR*) do not affect the payment amount. The payment amount is the amortized principal plus current interest needed to pay off the stated principal over the number of contracted periods (360 in **Example 47**). Because the points are not principal (at least not under the statute and contract), they do not affect the stated principal amount; hence, they cannot affect the payment amount. As a result, the payment amount, as shown in **Figure 84** is a function of the $300,000 stated principal amount—the present value.

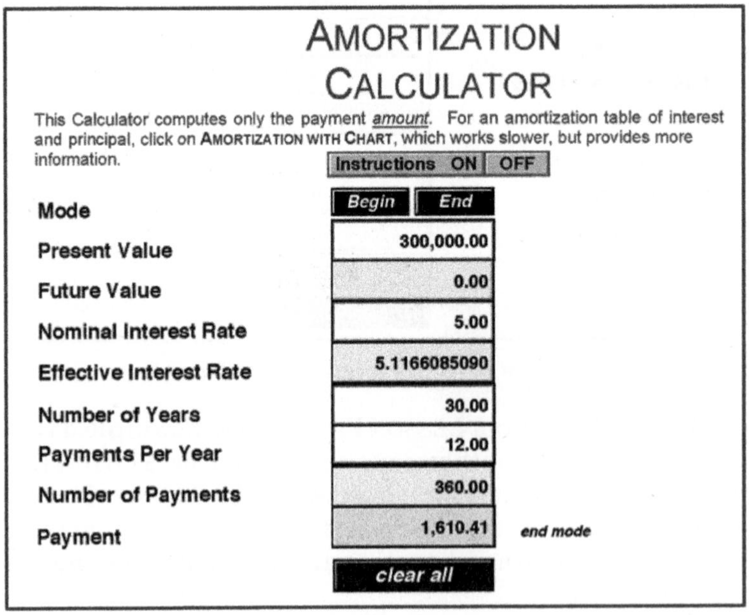

AMORTIZATION CALCULATOR

This Calculator computes only the payment *amount*. For an amortization table of interest and principal, click on AMORTIZATION WITH CHART, which works slower, but provides more information.

Instructions ON OFF

Mode	Begin	End
Present Value		300,000.00
Future Value		0.00
Nominal Interest Rate		5.00
Effective Interest Rate		5.1166085090
Number of Years		30.00
Payments Per Year		12.00
Number of Payments		360.00
Payment		1,610.41	*end mode*

clear all

Figure 91: Example 14

To compute the *APR*, as explained in LESSON FIVE-C, one must subtract the points (and other closing costs as listed in the *APR* statute) from the stated principal, but only for purposes of computing the *APR*. Three points on $300,000 would be $9,000; hence, the principal amount— solely for purposes of computing the *APR*—becomes $291,000. Because the payment amount must remain the same—$1,610.41—and because the loan term (monthly payments for thirty years) cannot change (that is the contract term), the only variable that can change is the interest rate. Thus the *APR*, as shown in **Figure 91** is higher than the stated interest rate of 5% *NAI*. **Figure 92** shows an interest rate of 5.27; however, if (using the AMORTIZATION CALCULATOR) you put your cursor on the interest rate white box, it would show 5.2693. As demonstrated in LESSON FIVE-C, the *APR* process would take about seven interest-rate guesses to produce the payment amount of $1,610.41.

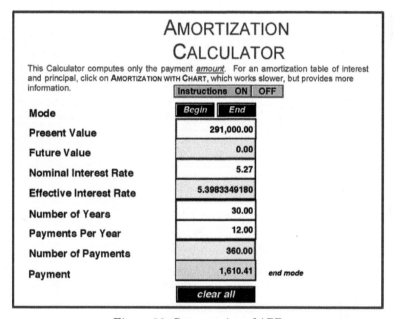

Figure 92: Computation of APR

Figure 93 shows the first page of the amortization schedule, which is page two on the AMORTIZATION WITH CHART CALCULATOR. Page one of the calculator is identical to **Figure 91** using the regular AMORTIZATION CALCULATOR. LESSON FIVE-C, **Example 14** explained the Nightmare Scenario: in which you borrowed the $300,000 at 5% *NAI* and 3 points, made the first payment and then sold the property (which triggered a due-on-sale clause) forcing you to pay off the loan. After the first payment of $1,610.41, the principal balance due would be $299,639.59, which would the amount you would have to pay to retire the loan. But, as explained in LESSON FIVE-C, you nominally "borrowed" $300,000, but you actually only borrowed $291,000. That occurred because of the points. At the closing, the lender transferred $300,000 to you and you immediately transferred $9,000 to the lender. The net transferred to you was merely $291,000. Effectively, the $9,000 became an amortizable pre-payment penalty: if you made all 360 payments, you would feel as if you borrowed $291,000 at 5.269% *NAI*. If, instead, you paid-off the principal balance any earlier, you would feel as if you borrowed $291,000 at a higher interest rate.

Amortization for Deferred Annuity (end mode)

Period	Payment	Interest	Principal	Balance
1	1,610.41	1,250.00	360.41	299,639.59
2	1,610.41	1,248.50	361.91	299,277.68
3	1,610.41	1,246.99	363.42	298,914.26
4	1,610.41	1,245.48	364.93	298,549.33
5	1,610.41	1,243.96	366.45	298,182.88
6	1,610.41	1,242.43	367.98	297,814.90
7	1,610.41	1,240.90	369.51	297,445.39
8	1,610.41	1,239.36	371.05	297,074.34
9	1,610.41	1,237.81	372.60	296,701.74
10	1,610.41	1,236.26	374.15	296,327.59
11	1,610.41	1,234.70	375.71	295,951.88
12	1,610.41	1,233.13	377.28	295,574.60
13	1,610.41	1,231.56	378.85	295,195.75
14	1,610.41	1,229.98	380.43	294,815.32
15	1,610.41	1,228.40	382.01	294,433.31
16	1,610.41	1,226.81	383.60	294,049.71
17	1,610.41	1,225.21	385.20	293,664.51
18	1,610.41	1,223.60	386.81	293,277.70
19	1,610.41	1,221.99	388.42	292,889.28
20	1,610.41	1,220.37	390.04	292,499.24
21	1,610.41	1,218.75	391.66	292,107.58
22	1,610.41	1,217.11	393.29	291,714.29
23	1,610.41	1,215.48	394.93	291,319.36
24	1,610.41	1,213.83	396.58	290,922.78
25	1,610.41	1,212.18	398.23	290,524.55
26	1,610.41	1,210.52	399.89	290,124.66
27	1,610.41	1,208.85	401.56	289,723.10
28	1,610.41	1,207.18	403.23	289,319.87
29	1,610.41	1,205.50	404.91	288,914.96
30	1,610.41	1,203.81	406.60	288,508.36
31	1,610.41	1,202.12	408.29	288,100.07
32	1,610.41	1,200.42	409.99	287,690.08
33	1,610.41	1,198.71	411.70	287,278.38
34	1,610.41	1,196.99	413.42	286,864.96
35	1,610.41	1,195.27	415.14	286,449.82
36	1,610.41	1,193.54	416.87	286,032.95
37	1,610.41	1,191.80	418.61	285,614.34
38	1,610.41	1,190.06	420.35	285,193.99
39	1,610.41	1,188.31	422.10	284,771.89
40	1,610.41	1,186.55	423.86	284,348.03
41	1,610.41	1,184.78	425.63	283,922.40
42	1,610.41	1,183.01	427.40	283,495.00
43	1,610.41	1,181.23	429.18	283,065.82
44	1,610.41	1,179.44	430.97	282,634.85

Figure 93: Annuity Amortization Payments

Notice: the actual principal amount remaining does not drop below $291,000—the amount you really borrowed—until the 24th payment (two years after you borrowed the funds). Nominally (based on the face of the loan), the first payment was $1,250 interest (5% of 300,000 divided by 12 months), and $360.41 was principal. Thus the amount due after one payment was the $300,000 nominally borrowed less the $360.41 principal payment: $299,639.59. Notice, the nominal interest portion of the second payment is 5% of $299,639.59 divided by 12, and the remainder of the $1,610.41 payment is allocated to principal. For tax and consumer finance law, those allocations are correct. The financial reality is more difficult to describe because the points are effectively a penalty for pre-payment. As such, the real interest rate changes each month, as the potential penalty amortizes. If the loan is outstanding for one month, the nominal interest rate would be 42.27%. If the loan is outstanding for 360 months, the nominal interest rate is 5.269%. It would be a different amount for each month in between, gradually dropping from 42.27%[1] to the stated *APR* of 5.269%.

To determine the 20-year payment amount for **Example 46** using a HP 10Bii™, input the following:

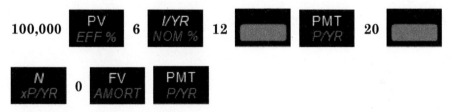

The display will read 716.43.

To determine the 15-year amount, do not clear the calculator after the above inputs. Press:

The display will read 843.86.

To determine the 10-year amount, press:

The display will read: 1,110.21.

---

[1] After one month, you would pay $1,610.41 plus the balance of 299,639.59 for a total of 301,250 on a loan of $291,000 for one month. That amounts to $10,250 interest for the month, with no real principal payment. Thus the interest would be 3.522337% for the month. Multiplied by 12, it would be 42.268% *NAI*.

———————

QUESTIONS

1.   You owe $100,000 in student loans. The stated interest rate is 6%. It contemplates monthly payments. How much are your payments if you pay it off over 10 years? 20 years?

2.   Suppose you owe the student loans in question 1. You decide to pay off the loan, using funds from a home equity loan at 4% *NAI* with monthly payments. Ignore any differing tax consequences involving home loans and student loans. What are you monthly payments if you pay off the home equity loan over 10 year? 20 years?

LESSON FOURTEEN

SINKING FUND

■ ■ ■

Lesson Objectives

1. Student will learn **how to** use the SINKING FUND CALCULATOR.

   - How to locate the Instructions.

   - How to find Definitions of each Function.

   - How and when to use the Begin and End Mode Functions.

2. Student will learn the **formula** for a Sinking Fund:

   > **Sinking Fund Payment:**
   >
   > $$\left[\frac{\left(FV \left(\frac{i}{100} \right) \right)}{\left(1 + \frac{i}{100} \right)^{n} - 1} \right]$$
   >
   > n = number of periods
   > i = nominal interest rate
   > FV = the future value

3. Student will learn **when** a lawyer would need to compute a Sinking Fund:

   - **As a lawyer, you would use this calculation if you or a client _know what is needed or owed in the future_ and you plan to save a series of _deposits_ . . . _i.e._, if you (or the other party) needs to know _how much to save_.**

4. Student will **work** some practical examples of situations in which a lawyer would need to compute a Sinking Fund.

———————

LESSON FOURTEEN covers a sinking fund. This calculation computes the amount needed in a series of payments to save a given amount. As a lawyer, you would use this calculation if you or a client desire to save (with level deposits) to pay a future debt or obligation. For example, you may want to save for your retirement, for a child's college education, to have funds for major plant and equipment replacement, to fund the anticipated mining clean-up costs in a few decades, or to have funds for decommissioning a nuclear power plant after its anticipated 40-year life. Of the six main financial calculations, this is probably the second _most useful_ for lawyers.

Figure 94 (**Figure 6** from LESSON THREE) shows the SINKING FUND CALCULATOR. You should remember: the term "sinking fund" is another term for an "annuity," albeit from the opposite direction. The sinking fund is the series of deposits (the annuity) that accumulates to a desired future value. In simple terms, you might own an annuity from which you receive payments. The other party to the transaction—the payor—is essentially amortizing the amount you paid for the annuity (or were entitled to receive in a lottery or tort settlement). Also, institution (perhaps a bank account or trust account) into which you deposit the sinking fund is essentially receiving an annuity from you.

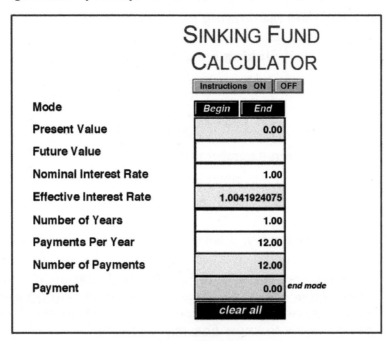

Figure 94: Sinking Fund Calculator

The major difficulties with a sinking fund involve the interest rate and the future value—the amount of savings desired. For example, a retirement sinking fund, if begun by a 25-year old, will likely span more than four decades. Anticipating how much one might need 40 to 60 years in the future is a daunting, though solvable, task. The same is true of anticipating interest rates over such a period. But, before we delve into those two hurdles, let's first work a couple *simple* problems.

EXAMPLE 48

Sinking Fund

You want to save $25,000 to replace your roof in five years. You are confident you can earn, after taxes, 4% *NAI* on monthly deposits. You want to begin saving today. How much does each deposit need to be?

Consider **Example 48**: saving $25,000 over five years, beginning today, with an assumed interest rate of 4% *NAI*. **Figure 95** illustrates the computation using the SINKING FUND COURSE CALCULATOR. Put the CALCULATOR in begin mode, insert $25,000 as the future value, 4% as the *NAI*, 12 as the payments per year, and 5 and the number of years. The answer is $375.87. If, instead, you were to begin saving one month from now, the answer would be $377.12. To compute this, simply click on End Mode on the SINKING FUND CALCULATOR after performing the above calculation. You do not need to re-enter the numbers or to clear the CALCULATOR. The deposits will produce the $25,000 at the given interest rate. Of course, the cost of the new roof could change over the five years. To partially compensate for this, you probably should modify the deposits annually by the actual inflation rate. Thus, if inflation turns out to be 3% during year one, the year two monthly deposits should be $387.15, an increase of $11.28 per month. Do the same each year and the modification should help approximate the inflation impact on the cost of the roof.

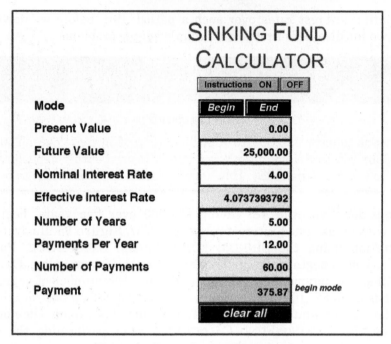

Figure 95: Example 48 in Begin Mode

To work **Example 48** using a HP 10Bii™, input the following (assuming the calculator is in end mode):

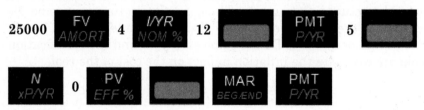

The display will read −375.83, which is 4 cents less than the amount computed by the COURSE CALCULATOR because of rounding differences. The negative number results because of the way HP treats cash-flows, as explained in prior LESSONS. If you were to then put the calculator into end mode and press payment, the display will read −377.08, which is also a four cent difference from the COURSE CALCULATOR—an immaterial amount.

We should now consider the two most likely uses a lawyer will have for a sinking fund: saving for a child's education and saving for retirement.

1. EDUCATION SAVINGS

EXAMPLE 49

Sinking Fund for Education

You want to save $100,000 for your child's college education. You are confident you can earn, after inflation, 4% *NAI* on monthly deposits. You want to begin saving today. How much does each deposit need to be?

Example 49 contemplates saving for a child's education. This example faces the reality of *speculative information*. You will not know what a college education will cost 18–20 years in the future, let alone inflation rates during that period. But you will have some very useful information:

- You will know the age of the child. In **Example 49**, the child is a new-born.

- You will know whether you want to start saving today—the day the child was born—or instead in the future. This helps you set the mode (begin mode if you start saving today and end mode if you start a month from now). This also determines the number of years—whether you save for 18 years for a new-born or for 12 years if you wait until your child starts first grade.

- You will know how frequently you want to make deposits, such as monthly.

- You will know whether you want to save for a state-school or private school education and whether you anticipate it lasting four years, or perhaps also for graduate school. That affects how much you want to save—the future value. You may feel you cannot make such a decision for a new-born; however, if you want to save for the child, *you* must begin with some assumptions—the baby certainly cannot.

- You will know whether you want to save sufficient funds to pay all costs, or whether you anticipate your child borrowing money or contributing through employment or scholarships. Realize, whatever you assume initially, you must consider modifying your assumption as time reveals reality. Perhaps the child is likely to work or perhaps not. You really cannot know for a new-born (though you can have hopes as all parents do), but you will have better information of what is realistic as the child ages. But, if changed assumptions result in increased needs, you will have less time to save, so be realistic and willing to re-evaluate.

- You will know the approximate amount you would need if the child were graduating from high school today, which is the present value of a four-year (or perhaps seven-year) education starting today (or within a few months). That will vary by geography, private versus public education, and lifestyle choices (do you expect your child to be frugal or extravagant?). Perhaps the best you can do is to estimate what you would want or need if you were 18 today and then assume your child will be similar to you.

- You will also know your own personal risk tolerance, which might range from a desire for zero risk (essentially U.S. Treasury securities) to a willingness to tolerate substantial risk (junk bonds).

- You will know that you can invest education savings in a tax-free account from which you can withdraw non-taxable funds.[1] You must, however, keep in mind that tax laws can and do change over time. Education funding also may change: perhaps a college education will be free for all persons by 2040. That is a political question/prognostication, but is nevertheless one you must make.

- You will know your current financial situation and investment skills, which will inform you regarding initial returns. In early years, when the amount accumulated is small, unless you have significant skill and likely significant other investments, you likely will not have sufficient capital to earn higher-than-typical returns, which should be approximately 2–3% plus inflation.

- You will also know, depending on your risk tolerance and other assets, that you likely will be willing to accept less risk, the closer your child is to high school graduation. For example, if the child is 10-years old and the investment markets enter a down period (a bear market), you have significant remaining time to modify plans (8 years); however, if the child is 17, you likely can ill-afford more risky investments because the need for funds is almost immediate.

In addition, you will know the history of education costs as well as the components. For example, for several decades, tuition costs rose faster than general inflation in the U.S. That trend appears to have slowed substantially. Also, perhaps half the cost of a college education involves items other than tuition: housing, transportation, utilities, clothing, travel, food, medical costs, and entertainment. While the prospect of tuition costs

---

[1]   IRC § 529.

mirroring general inflation may be speculative, the likelihood that general living costs follow general inflation trends in the future is strong. Thus, while future inflation is a substantial unknown, it is not completely unknown.

Example 49 anticipates you have considered the information you know and have decided that $100,000 would be an appropriate amount to have in an educational savings account if your child were graduating from high school today. That includes your likely expectation of additional savings during the education period. The example also anticipates significant investment confidence of a 4% *NAI* return, plus future inflation. Anticipating 5% *NAI* would be more aggressive and anticipating 2% plus inflation would be conservative. Returns outside that range for such an account are likely unrealistic, but are possible. As the years pass, you will have better information regarding your actual returns, actual inflation, and the educational prospects of your child in addition to your willingness to fund those prospects.

Figure 96 shows the computation using the SINKING FUND CALCULATOR. The required initial deposits are $315.86 using the above informed parameters. Keep in mind: you must monitor the account. You should annually adjust your monthly deposits by actual inflation. Thus, if inflation between your child's birth and first birthday is 10%, you would need to increase your monthly deposits by $31.59 (10% of the starting 315.86). Also, you would need to check to see if you actually earned 4% plus inflation (approximately 14%) on the funds during the prior year. Depending on your investment choices, that may be unlikely, as investment returns may lag sudden bursts of inflation, just as they may extend past substantial drops in inflation.

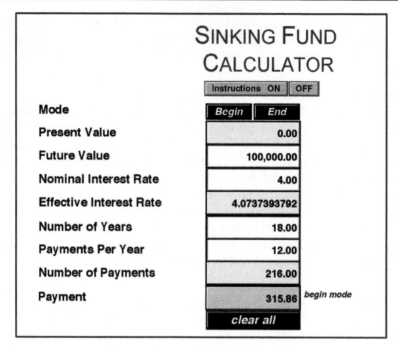

Figure 96: Example 49 Begin Mode

Additionally, you will need to account for new information as the years pass. For example, when I was born, parents would not likely have anticipated students living off campus, having their own automobiles, having television sets (which were then quite rare), jet travel, or microwave ovens, let alone air conditioning and access to automatic washing machines and dryers; however, they would have anticipated my needing a typewriter and a wristwatch—items which are almost quaint today. When my children were born, I did not anticipate cell phones or the internet, let alone the near universal use of laptop computers.

If, instead of starting the savings the day the child is born, you decide to wait one month, the amount needed, as shown in **Figure 97**, would be $316.91—an extra $1.05 per month for the entire 18-year period, also to be adjusted annually for inflation.

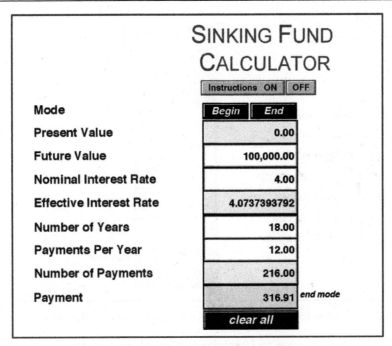

Figure 97: Example 49 End Mode

To be realistic, you may lack the $315.86 (or $316.91) when the child is born, as you will suddenly face substantial bills for diapers, child care, babysitting, health care, life insurance for you, strollers, clothes, a car seat, perhaps a larger car, an extra bedroom, and much more. You may also realize that $100,000 is likely insufficient to fund an education today; hence, you may want to save $150,000 or more, which increases the costs.

If you wait until the child is six before your start saving, you still have 12 years to save. Using the same assumptions ($100,000 needed and 4% *NAI* return), you will need to save $540.46 monthly starting on the child's sixth birthday (*adjusted upward for actual inflation during the prior six years*), as shown in **Figure 98**. At that point, you may, of course, have a second child and be facing $1,000 needed each month. If you desire a large family—as many people had within the last century—the costs can become almost prohibitive.

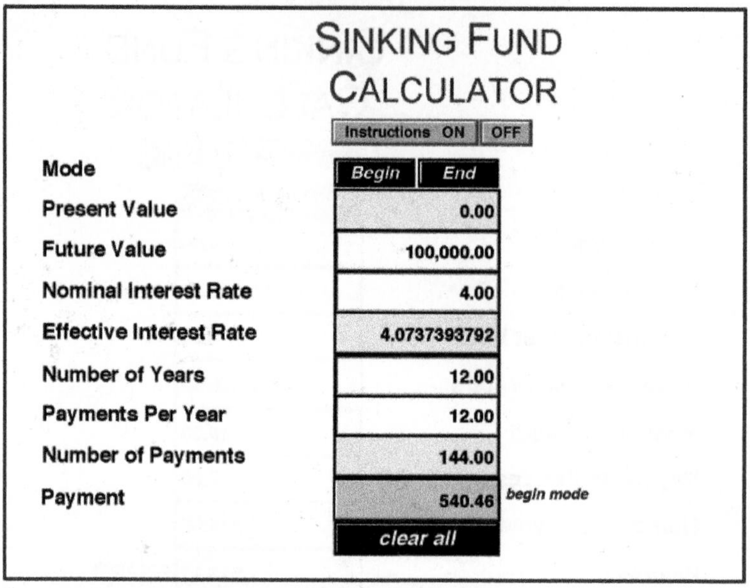

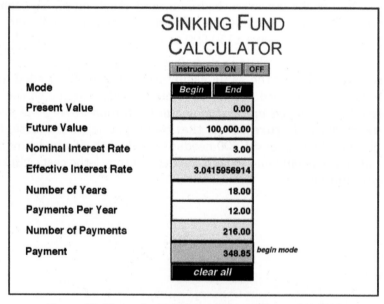

Figure 98: Example 49, Begin Mode, 12 Years of Savings

Or, you may choose to be more conservative and to assume you will consistently earn (at least using a *geometric average*) 3% *NAI* plus inflation. If so, you need $348.85 monthly starting the day the child is born, adjusted at least annually for inflation and new information, as shown in **Figure 99**.

Figure 99: Example 49, Begin Mode, 18 Years, 3% *NAI*

Assuming you are similarly conservative but you wait until the child is 8 years old, you will need $713.82 starting on the 8th birthdate, as shown in **Figure 100**. Once again, you must alter the savings annually for actual inflation. Further, if the $100,000 goal was the amount you estimated when your child was born, you would want to adjust that by actual inflation during the 8-year delay (or perhaps you would make a new estimate entirely).

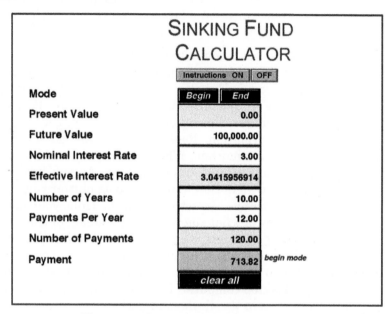

Figure 100: Example 49, 10 Years, 3% *NAI*

2. RETIREMENT SAVINGS

Next, let's use the same type of analysis for your own retirement. To simplify, assume you are saving merely for yourself (you neither have nor expect to have a spouse and you anticipate no children who will support you in your elder years, plus you anticipate nothing from social security or other government programs). How much should you save? The answer is a function of when you plan to retire and the lifestyle you want to have. Although traditionally, many workers retired at age 65, that number has increased significantly in recent years. You may, instead, plan on retiring at age 70 or even on a more advanced age. In addition, life expectancies have increased significantly over the past 50 years. You should pay careful attention to the life expectancy discussions in LESSON SIX-B.

Once again, you will have some solid information:

- You know your current age.

- For now, you know the age at which you hope to retire, though your anticipated retirement age may change during the next few decades.

- You have some idea of your risk tolerance—again, you will likely earn between 2% *NAI* plus inflation (conservative) and 5% *NAI* plus inflation (optimistic) over your saving years, with the understanding that early years may have fewer investment opportunities and later years may cause you to be risk averse.

- Although you do not know what amount of assets you will need in 40 or 50 years, you should have good information about what is required today to create the lifestyle you currently believe you will seek upon retirement. Perhaps examining grandparents or other older people you know can give you this information. Realize, people change in fairly predictable ways as they age. When young, you need housing and furniture, clothes and entertainment. As you age, you may find you have all of that and want to de-clutter your life, spending less on things attractive to youth. Thus, you should not think in terms of what _you_ want, but instead, of what _you being 65 or 70 or 75_ might want. Because the time frame is long, you will need to modify your plans regularly because of new stuff. When I graduated as an undergraduate, I had never seen a desktop computer, let alone a laptop, never seen a microwave oven or a cell phone, let alone the internet. Jet travel was common, but far from universal. Cameras had film. Long distance calls were expensive. Nearly everyone had indoor plumbing, but many did not. Things change. Items we easily lived without 50 years ago are now essentials. The same will likely be true for you. Also, tastes change. When I was an undergraduate, a cheap 50-cents-a-bottle-sweet wine was great. Today, I mostly want something that costs 50 to 200 times as much. Things you currently view as unnecessary or decadent may be exactly what you want when you are 65— especially if your parents or grandparents enjoy them or strive for them. Indeed, we often become our parents.

Thus, consider wisely as you plan. The child is the father of the man.[2] Perhaps you decide—as an educated and successful lawyer—solo

---

[2]   William Wordsworth:

My heart leaps up when I behold
A rainbow in the sky:
So was it when my life began;
So is it now I am a man;
So be it when I shall grow old,
Or let me die!

retirement at age 65 would require $4,000,000 for you to feel secure. If so, what amount of savings does that require? This is **Example 50**.

EXAMPLE 50

Retirement Sinking Fund

You want to save $4,000,000 for your own retirement. You are confident you can earn, after inflation, 4% *NAI* on monthly deposits. You want to begin saving today, your 25th birthday. How much does each deposit need to be?

Before we work it, consider how I obtained the number. I examined common lifestyles of 65-year-old retired and financially successful (but not hugely wealthy or extravagant) attorneys. I looked at life expectancy tables. Using a period-life table in 2020, a 65-year old male has a mean life expectancy of 18 years and a female 20.5 years. The medians are about 18.5 and 22 respectively. I increased the life to 25 years because I would not want to run out of funds: using the median, half the retirees would run out, assuming they spent all the funds, including investment income during retirement—a time when they may be risk-averse.

Assuming the $4,000,000 savings *plus* the proceeds of tax-deferred income on the savings will have the same purchasing power in 40 years that $4,000,000 would have today, the $4,000,000 will produce a 25-year taxable annuity beginning 40 years from now of about $21,045 per month (assuming it would continue to earn 4% *NAI* plus inflation), as shown in **Figure 91**. Arguably, that seems sufficient for a single retired professional 65-year old male, but perhaps low for a female because of her longer life expectancy. This assumes no social security and no other retirement funds or substantial assets. Likely, such a person *would* have other assets, but they must also recognize increasing life expectancies, flaws inherent in period life tables (which likely understate life expectancies), and whether they would want to leave a legacy to any family or charitable cause. In addition, the assumption in **Example 50** is for a 4% *NAI* return plus inflation, which is higher than commonly predicted real rates of return, as covered in LESSON SIX.

The Child is father of the Man;
And I could wish my days to be
Bound each to each by natural piety.

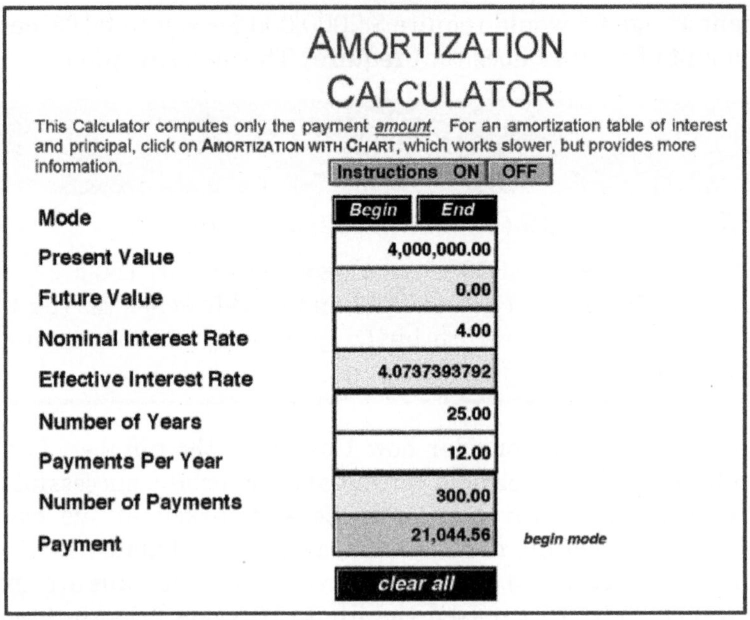

AMORTIZATION CALCULATOR

This Calculator computes only the payment *amount*. For an amortization table of interest and principal, click on AMORTIZATION WITH CHART, which works slower, but provides more information.

Instructions ON OFF

Mode	Begin	End
Present Value		4,000,000.00
Future Value		0.00
Nominal Interest Rate		4.00
Effective Interest Rate		4.0737393792
Number of Years		25.00
Payments Per Year		12.00
Number of Payments		300.00
Payment		21,044.56 begin mode

clear all

Figure 101: Amortization of $4 Million Retirement Savings over 25 Years

Thus the $4,000,000 number depends on factors personal to the saver (*you*): do you expect to have a partner to support or who can help support you? If so, you might seek to save more, or perhaps less (if that person is also saving). Do you expect to have descendants to whom you want to leave an inheritance or who might be able to help support you? Again, that cuts both ways, though it probably means you want to save more if you expect descendants. Do you expect to receive social security? Do you really expect to successfully earn, over six decades, a real investment return greater than commonly predicted for the U.S. economy? Do you expect a significant inheritance during your life that can provide some of the savings? The projected taxable annuity—$21,045 per month (**Figure 101**) for the projected life (which will vary by gender and other factors)—is certainly generous, though not generally considered wealthy (particularly depending on your state of residence). Would *you* be comfortable with this? Perhaps you seek more, or perhaps less. After answering those questions—now and regularly over your work-life—you should adjust the $4,000,000 figure appropriately to suit you, just as you will want to adjust your projected retirement age.

Using the **Example 50** assumptions, you need to save about $3,375 monthly, starting on your 25th birthday, as shown in **Figure 102**. You would need to adjust the deposits annually for actual inflation. Thus, if you save $3,375 per month for the first year and inflation during that year is 3%, the following year your deposits should be about $3,475 per month. You probably need about 10% more if you are female, or about 10% less if you are male (*depending on how you view the predicted lifestyle*).[3]

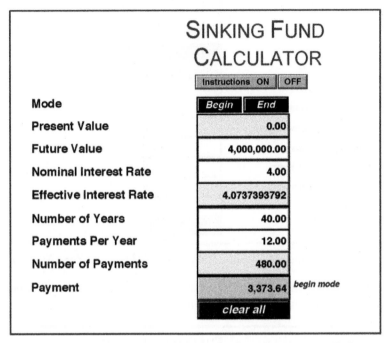

Figure 102: Example 50 40-Year Sinking Fund at 4% *NAI*

If, instead, you project a 3% *NAI* return (plus inflation) during the 40-years of savings, you should *also predict* the same return during the period of retirement (the 25 years). If so, the predicted $4,000,000 (in 2020 dollars) in 40 years will only produce a 25-year annuity of approximately $19,000 per month (2020 dollars) when you retire if you earn 3% *NAI* plus inflation. To generate the desired $21,045 monthly annuity for 25-year, you need to accumulate more as shown in **Figure 103**: $4,438,000 (which you may want to adjust for your gender).

---

[3]   If the projected lifestyle—one that $250,000 per year would provide in 2020—is sufficient for a female, then a male (who expects a shorter life) needs about 10% less ($3,600,000). Or, if that is what you perceive as the desired lifestyle for a male, then a female would need about 10% more ($4,400,000). Remember, the assumption is that you will be unmarried and without a partner or descendants who may needing financial help or who may be able to contribute. It also assumes no other savings.

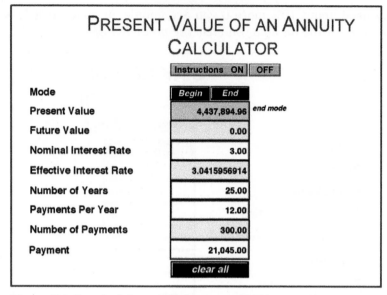

Figure 103: Required Accumulation at 3% *NAI* for a 25-Year Annuity

To accumulate this amount, your monthly savings would need to be $4,780 (adjusted annually for actual inflation), per **Figure 104**.

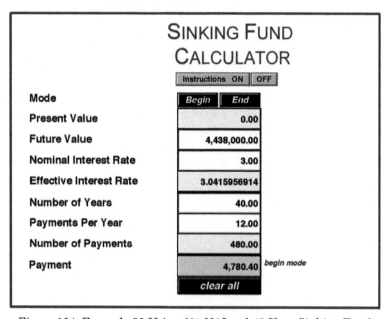

Figure 104: Example 50 Using 3% *NAI* and 40-Year Sinking Fund

If, instead, you project an optimistic 6% *NAI* return (plus inflation) during *both* the savings period (now until retirement) and *also* during retirement years, you need to accumulate about $3,266,000 as shown in **Figure 105**.

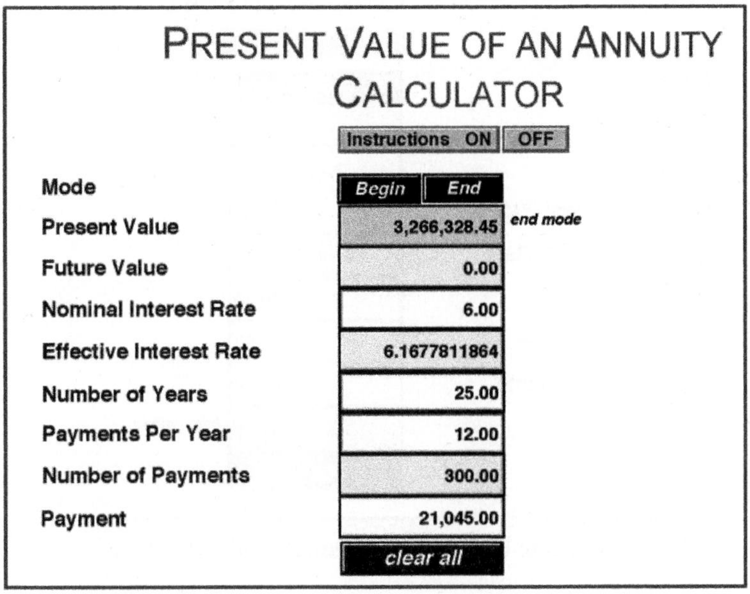

PRESENT VALUE OF AN ANNUITY CALCULATOR

	Instructions ON	OFF
Mode	Begin | End	
Present Value	3,266,328.45	*end mode*
Future Value	0.00	
Nominal Interest Rate	6.00	
Effective Interest Rate	6.1677811864	
Number of Years	25.00	
Payments Per Year	12.00	
Number of Payments	300.00	
Payment	21,045.00	
	clear all	

Figure 105: Example 50 Annuity Needed Using 6% *NAI*

To save that over 40 years, assuming the 6% *NAI* plus inflation return, you should save about $1,632 monthly (which you must adjust annually for actual inflation), as shown in **Figure 106**.

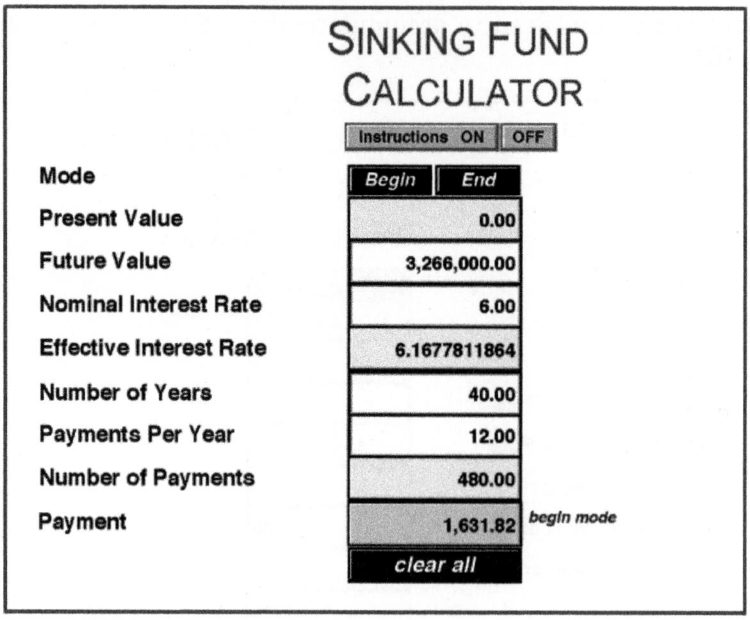

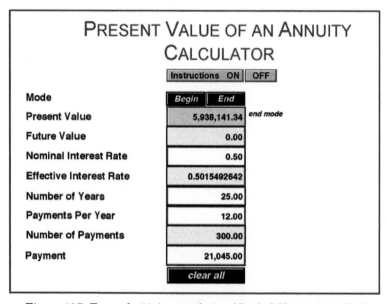

Figure 106: Example 50 Sinking Fund at 6% *NAI*

If you are more pessimistic and believe the projected real rate of return will be only about 0.5%—as argued by many economists (see LESSON FIVE)—you need to accumulate $5,938,000 by age 65 so as to generate the same $21,045 25-year retirement annuity, as shown in **Figure 107**. To save that, as shown in **Figure 108**, you need to begin saving about $11,168 monthly at age 25—a daunting task.

Figure 107: Example 50 Accumulation Needed Using 0.5% *NAI*

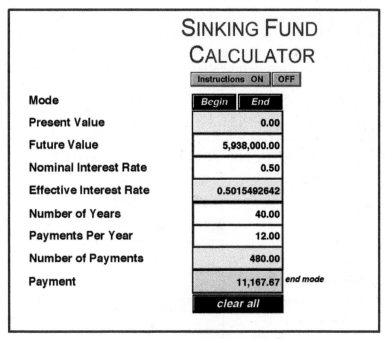

Figure 108: Example 50 Using 0.5% *NAI*

Arguably a more realistic scenario would assume retirement at age 70, as well as perhaps $1,000,000 in other assets (*e.g.,* a house and non-retirement investments) and some social security benefits.

EXAMPLE 51

Retirement Sinking Fund

You want to save for your own retirement, which you expect to be at age 70. You are confident you can earn, after inflation, 4% *NAI* on monthly deposits (for the next 65 years—from today until you are 90). You want to begin saving today, your 25th birthday. You anticipate Social Security benefits comparable to those provided a 70-year old retiree in 2020. You project having a net worth at age 70 of $1,000,000 (in addition to the retirement account) and you expect to be willing to liquidate it over your remaining life. You desire a lifestyle that would cost about $21,045 per month in 2020. How much does each retirement-account deposit need to be?

Example 51 uses the same $21,045 per month desired lifestyle used in **Example 50**. It delays retirement for five years (to age 70), but continues the assumption the retiree will live to age 90. It also assume social security benefits comparable to those of today.

In 2020, monthly social security benefits for a high-income 70-year old retiree are $3,790 per month. Assuming those continue at that level, adjusted for inflation for the next 65 years (you be the judge regarding whether that assumption is realistic), the required annuity drops $21,045 (in 2020 dollars) to $17,255. As shown in **Figure 109**, to produce that amount for 20 years, one would need about $2,850,000 (adjusted for inflation over the next 45 years).

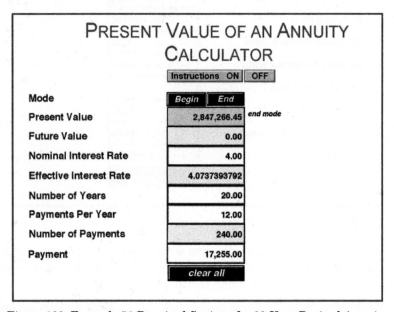

Figure 109: Example 51 Required Savings for 20-Year Desired Annuity

Example 51 also assumes you will have $1,000,000 in non-retirement net assets, using 2020 dollars, at retirement _and_ that you are willing to liquidate and consume those assets during the remainder of your life. With that assumption, you need only save $1,850,000 in the retirement account (again, to be clear, using 2020 dollars). Further, do not forget you should consider adjusting this amount depending on your gender, understanding current projections predict females with about a 10% longer life expectancy in 45 years. With all those assumptions (_which are arguably unrealistic_[4]), **Figure 110** shows what you need to save starting today, your 25th birthday: $1,221.79 per month, adjusted annually for actual inflation. That is substantially lower than the $3,373.64 projected need in **Figure 102**,

---

[4]   Many studies, including those from the Social Security Administration, predict substantial shortfalls over the next 45, let alone 65 years. A willingness to liquidate and to consume all assets by age 90 leaves the retiree with nothing but social security at age 90, a risk many people will be unwilling to take. The assumed 4% _NAI_ for 65 years is inconsistent with many reputable projections, as covered in LESSON SIX.

albeit with greater risks, as well as the separate need for savings outside of a retirement plan.[5]

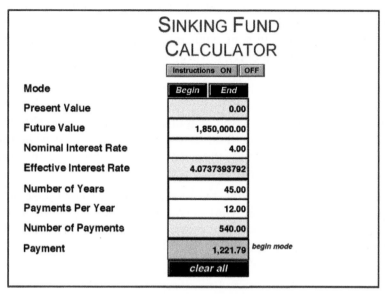

Figure 110: Example 51 Savings Required Assuming 4% *NAI* Return

Another issue to consider as you plan involves the assumption you remain single. Most people marry or have a partner. If that is your situation or plan, you (and your partner) combined need to save more for your joint retirements, but significantly less than twice the amount. Although supporting two people is more expensive than supporting one, a household of two has significant economies of scale: house maintenance, property taxes, insurance, the cost of furnishings, utilities and many other items vary little whether the household is one or two. Thus the required *per person* savings for *each* member of a two-person household would each be significantly less than the above numbers.

But, this being a course in finance *for lawyers*, we must consider other legal issues. A significant portion of those who begin saving for two will ultimately face a marital dissolution. Retirement and other accumulations (the house, furnishings and non-retirement investments) will, absent a marital agreement providing otherwise, either be community or marital assets. Upon dissolution, they will likely be divided equally. Because people saving for two typically do not save twice as much as people saving for one, each post-dissolution share will be less than would otherwise be needed by each.

---

[5] I did not adjust for projected taxes on the non-retirement account savings, which, based on current law, would produce more after-tax income per dollar than retirement accounting savings. That adjustment is beyond this course. It would reduce the monthly need for retirement savings by a few percent.

Perhaps using the above analysis, you decide (adjusting all variables except marriage and divorce) you, being single, need to save (in a retirement account plus accumulations outside such an account, such as home equity) about $2,000 per month starting at age 25. Perhaps you then marry and together decide that each must save $1,250 per month. That may be a great plan if you both continue to work and to save until age 70, you both live to age 90, and you remain married. But, if at age 45 or 55 or 65 you divorce and equally divide the retirement and other accumulations, you will each be 35–40% short of your anticipated needs because the economies of scale you anticipated evaporate in the divorce. If the marriage involves opposite genders, the female would likely be in worse shape than the male because she would typically have a longer remaining life expectancy and thus greater needs at retirement.

You could resolve all that by re-marrying someone else _who has adequate savings_. If, however, that is your plan, you may want to examine re-marriage-after-divorce statistics which vary significantly by age, gender, education, ethnicity, and financial situation.[6]

QUESTION

Your child was born today. You believe a proper college education costs $30,000 per year for four years if started today. You suspect that cost will change over time consistent with the general rate of inflation or deflation in the U.S. You would like to have adequate funds set aside for the entire four years when your child graduates from high school. You believe, in the alternative, you can earn 2, 3, 4, or 5% _EFF_ consistently in addition to actual inflation or deflation. You want to start saving today in a non-taxable account. How much should you save each month for the next 18 years?

------

6   https://www.pewsocialtrends.org/2014/11/14/chapter-2-the-demographics-of-remarriage/.

GLOSSARY OF FINANCIAL, TAX, ACCOUNTING, AND ECONOMIC TERMS *PLUS* RELATED ACRONYMS

Much of Finance, Accounting, and Economics involve definitions, as does much of law. If a reader fails to understand the proper meaning of a term, that reader will not understand the contract, obligation, agreement, statute, or instrument. As every lawyer knows, confusion[1] in financial and legal matters is a dangerous situation.

But, in an even _worse_ scenario, a reader may "think" he or she understands the terms, but actually does not. Remember this moral:

T'is best to know.
T'is second best to know what you do not know.
T'is worst to know what is not so.

Some financial terms are _terms of art_, *i.e.*, everyone agrees on their definition. Many other terms, however, are *not* terms of art; as a result, people—including lawyers—frequently disagree regarding them. An attorney may view this phenomenon from three angles:

1. ***Avoid Litigation*** (the *moral* angle): define all terms and ensure the other parties agree with your definitions, which should be prominent and clear. If your definition is unconventional, be clear about that, as well. If all parties do not agree on the definitions, you lack a meeting of the minds and you do not have a valid contract.

2. ***Take Advantage*** (the risky/zealous/*amoral* angle): use terms to your advantage. Use terms of art correctly. In particular, if you perceive another party misunderstands the term to his disadvantage, use the term and later insist on the proper meaning—even if that risks litigation. You should win, as a term of art, if clearly used in writing, is not subject to debate. For other terms, be precise, but not so clearly precise. For example, slyly alter compounding terms or periods or stated nominal rates when apparent small change actually result in large differences. If you do so openly—or if you are detected—concede another factor (which may appear large to the uninformed, but which is actually insignificant relative to your proposed change). The other party will believe

---

[1] Except, perhaps, for the Civil Law Doctrine of Confusion. In Civil Law, confusion refers to the Financial situation in which debtor and creditor become the same; as a result, the debt is confused.

he has won, when he actually has lost. Or, when using a non term-of-art, either slyly insert a definition which supports you, or—if you are in the stronger position—line up experts to testify to your definition and bully your way through the ultimate conflict.

To be very clear: I do not recommend this second approach; however, despite its moral deficiencies, it is probably acceptable under most state bar rules. At the very least, lawyers should be aware that others may use this approach.

3. ***Be Wary*** (the *smart* angle): if you ever detect a lawyer/banker/investment advisor using Angle B, never, ever trust him again and never do business with him again. If he will cheat you on one issue, he is likely cheating you on many others. Then practice Angle A.

The following are some common terms used in this course. This is by no means a complete—*or even nearly complete*—list of important terminology. Several good Financial Dictionaries are available.[2] You should have one available. You should, however, be familiar with at least the following terms.

Many free Finance, Tax Law, Accounting, and Economics dictionaries are available over the internet. Use them with *caution*. Most—probably all—define *non*-terms-of-art as if they have a fixed meaning. This is dangerous for lawyers. Also, many provide incorrect definitions for terms-of-art. That, too, is dangerous. Even the United States *Federal Reserve* website contains several erroneous or dangerously imprecise definitions.

In addition, Finance, Tax Law, Accounting, and Economics use many ACRONYMS. Lawyers should be familiar with these for several reasons.

1. Expert witnesses will use them. Lawyers need to be able to speak with their own expert, to cross examine an opponent's expert, and to translate to a judge or jury the terminology (including acronyms) used by an expert.

2. Financial, economic, and accounting reports may use these terms and acronyms. Lawyers need to understand them.

---

[2] Two examples are: John Downes and Jordan Elliot Goodman, DICTIONARY OF FINANCE AND INVESTMENT TERMS (BARRON'S 1995); John Downes and Jordan Elliot Goodman, FINANCE & INVESTMENT HANDBOOK (BARRON'S 1995).

3. Contracts will sometimes use these acronyms, with or
    without a clear reference. Lawyers need to be able to
    understand the terms, especially if the reference is unclear
    (which is an unfortunate situation, but a real possibility).

---

1. **Acid Test Ratio:** A commonly used accounting/financial ratio, this
    measures very short-term liquidity. Generally, the following formula
    represents it:

$$\left(\frac{cash + marketable\ securities}{current\ liabilities} \right)$$

In a very general rule, a one-to-one acid test ratio is good. A ratio much
higher indicates the entity may be overly liquid; it should therefore
consider more investment in operations. A ratio much below one-to-
one indicates *liquidity* problems in the near term; the entity should
therefore focus on raising more *working capital* so that it can satisfy
obligations as they come due.

One important point to remember about the *Acid Test Ratio* and the
Current Ratio: liabilities are fixed but assets other than cash are not.
Inventory can become worthless quickly as competitors produce a new
product. Accounts Receivable can become uncollectable as customers
become *insolvent*. Marketable Securities can quickly drop in value in
a *Bear Market*.

By itself, the *Acid Test*—or *Quick*—*Ratio* does not tell an analyst
much. But, in context of other *ratios* covering multiple years, as well
as quarters (so as to show trends) plus the *Statement of Cash Flows*,
an analyst can confidently predict short-term solvency.

2. **Accelerated Cost Recovery System:** *ACRS*: [pronounced **ak**-ris].
    Under *IRC* section 168, taxpayers may use rapid (accelerated)
    depreciation for various assets. Since 1986, this system has also been
    known as **MACRS** for *Modified Accelerated Cost Recovery System*
    [pronounced **mac**-ris].

Accelerated Depreciation for tax purposes is generally much more
rapid than permitted by *GAAP* for *financial accounting*; hence, it
results in a book/tax disparity. This is one reason tax returns are a
poor measure of income for legal purposes. Rapid depreciation through
MACRS—or even more rapid write-offs under *IRC* section 179—will
cause income to be significantly lower than justified. For tax purposes,
this is exactly what Congress intended; however, when lawyers use tax
returns for other legal purposes, the low income (and if the
depreciating assets were recently acquired, lower trending income)
will predict even lower income for the future. In reality, the person or

entity's ability to invest in productive assets predicts higher economic income—the opposite of what the numbers suggests.

Congress first adopted accelerated tax depreciation in the 1960s under the Kennedy Administration. The intention was to stimulate investment in assets and thus stimulate the economy. The policy was successful. This is an example of *fiscal policy*.

Lawyers should be wary of statutes and contracts which use income tax returns as measures of income. In some cases—such as for wage earners with few deductions, such returns may provide a good measure of income. In contrast, however, as suggested above, tax returns are often a very poor measure of income for small businesses. The use of accelerated depreciation is only one reason for this—it lowers income artificially fast. Other tax provisions are similarly distorting. That is not to say they are unreasonable: Congress can legitimately use the tax system to foster fiscal and social policy—at least in the eyes of many. However, the more Congress uses the tax system as a tool, the less accurate it becomes in measuring income for other purposes. Tax lawyers and accountants are often skilled at using such policy provision to manipulate income—particularly over the short run.

For example, suppose B's income is a function of A's income. If A controls the definition of income (*e.g.,* by choosing depreciation, inventory, and capitalization methods), A also has the legal ability to distort B's income. This can be very disadvantageous for B. Practical examples include:

- A and B are partners with A being the managing partner.

- A and B are married (but soon to be divorced) and A controls the family business and finances.

- A hires B in a recording/publishing/producing contract whereby B's income is a percentage of the total income from the activity.

- In each example, A has the power to manipulate B's results. While using such power may be abusive and amoral, it is probably not illegal. Indeed, many persons, including many lawyers may view such manipulation as appropriate, if not admirable and "cutting edge." Hence, B's counsel must be aware of tax and accounting tools which facilitate A and then be prepared to oppose them or to shed light upon them.

3. **Accounting Principles and Assumptions:** *GAAP* has eleven fundamental principles and assumptions. Lawyers, legislators, regulators, and judges should heed these fundamental principles and assumptions and should note the following:

*Any accounting system—such as <u>legal</u> or <u>contractual</u>
definitions of income or profit—without such
fundamental rules is inherently **<u>flawed</u>**.*

For example, lawyers often refer to income or profits in a contract or other legal document. Unfortunately, many fail to define those words adequately or by reference to adequate standards. Similarly, many statutes or court decisions use the terms—including income, assets, profit, losses, expenses, and liabilities—and also provide a definition for them. Almost always, however, they do so without reference to any fundamental standards, rules, principles, or assumptions. State family law references to income and assets for alimony, child support, or property division are a common and unfortunate example. The results are often unfair, subject to manipulation, wasteful in terms of unnecessary litigation, and distorting in terms of the economic impact they have on decision making.

Each principle, test, and assumption has its own definition herein.

- The *<u>Matching Principle</u>*.

- The *<u>Historical Cost Assumption</u>*.

- The *<u>Going Concern Assumption</u>*.

- The *<u>Monetary Unit Assumption</u>*.

- The *<u>Consistency Principle</u>*.

- The *<u>Revenue Recognition Principle</u>*.

- The *<u>Expense Recognition Principle</u>*.

- The *<u>All Events Test</u>* (*this formerly comprised the revenue recognition and expense recognition principles*).

- The *<u>Materiality Principle</u>*.

- The *<u>Separate Entity Assumption</u>*.

- The *<u>Time Period Assumption</u>*.

- The *<u>Full Disclosure Principle</u>*.

- The *<u>Conservatism Principle</u>*.

4. **Accredited Investor:** As explained by the *SEC*:

   Under the Securities Act of 1933, a company that offers or sells its securities must register the securities with the SEC or find an exemption from the registration requirements. The Act provides companies with a number of exemptions. For some of the exemptions, such as rules 505 and 506 of Regulation D, a company may sell its securities to what are known as "accredited investors."

The federal securities laws define the term accredited investor in <u>Rule 501 of Regulation D</u> as:

1. a bank, insurance company, registered investment company, business development company, or small business investment company;

2. an employee benefit plan, within the meaning of the Employee Retirement Income Security Act, if a bank, insurance company, or registered investment adviser makes the investment decisions, or if the plan has total assets in excess of $5 million;

3. a charitable organization, corporation, or partnership with assets exceeding $5 million;

4. a director, executive officer, or general partner of the company selling the securities;

5. a business in which all the equity owners are accredited investors;

6. a natural person who has individual net worth, or joint net worth with the person's spouse, that exceeds $1 million at the time of the purchase, excluding the value of the primary residence of such person;

7. a natural person with income exceeding $200,000 in each of the two most recent years or joint income with a spouse exceeding $300,000 for those years and a reasonable expectation of the same income level in the current year; or

8. a trust with assets in excess of $5 million, not formed to acquire the securities offered, whose purchases a sophisticated person makes.

http://www.sec.gov/answers/accred.htm.

5. **Accrual Method:** This has *two* distinct meanings, with four subparts and effectively three fundamental rules:

- For *Financial Accounting* purposes:

  o *Income recognition* is appropriate when *all events* have occurred such that the earner has a right to the item and the amount thereof can be determined with reasonable accuracy.

  o *Deductions* are appropriate when *all events* have occurred such the obligor must incur the item and the amount thereof can be determined with reasonable accuracy.

- For *Tax Accounting* purposes:

  o *Income recognition* is appropriate at the earliest of three events:

    ▪ When *all events* have occurred such that the earner has a right to the item and the amount thereof can be determined with reasonable accuracy.

    ▪ When the item is due.

    ▪ When the taxpayer has *received payment* of the item.

  o *Deductions* are *normally* appropriate at the later of two events:

    ▪ When *all events* have occurred such the obligor must incur the item and the amount thereof can be determined with reasonable accuracy.

    ▪ When *economic performance* of the item has occurred.

For *Financial Accounting*, both the *income* and the *deduction* rules are essentially identical: they require satisfaction of the *all events* test, which is fundamental to the *Matching Principal*.

For United States *Tax Accounting*, the *income* and the *deduction* rules differ dramatically in definition, but have essentially the same impact:

- The **income rule** often requires recognition *before* satisfaction of the *all events* test; as a result, it *materially* **increases** the effective tax rate on the affected items and it distorts the meaning of income.

- The **deduction rule** often requires recognition *after* satisfaction of the *all events* test; as a result, it also materially **increases** the effective tax rate on the affected items (by materially decreasing the effective tax benefit) and it, distorts the meaning of *net income*.

6. **Acquisition Premium:** *AP:* This is the amount by which a financial instrument's market price exceeds its stated or face value. A basic law of economics and finance is:

    As interest rates fall, bond values rise.

Similarly:

As interest rates <u>rise</u>, bond values <u>fall</u>.

Bond values and interest rates are thus inversely related.

Generally, *bonds, debentures* and other financial instruments have fixed, stated or coupon rates; hence, their internal or stated interest rates do not float or adjust as market interest rates change. Such market rates change continuously during trading hours. If the market rate for a particular instrument falls below the instrument's stated rate, the price of the instrument will naturally rise. Purchasers must therefore pay an *acquisition premium* for the instrument.

IRC section 1272(a)(7) provides a modified straight-line method for *amortizing acquisition* premium for tax purposes; as a result, taxpayers report—and pay tax upon—a more accurate amount of interest than the instrument itself will reflect. Treasury Regulation section 1.1272–2 provides an alternate—and even more accurate— method of amortizing *acquisition premium*. The Regulation method relies on a *constant yield to maturity* assumption and thus closely reflects the correct economic interest rate. The Code method, in contrast, permits taxpayers to defer recognition of some interest income because it relies on an arguably simpler formula. Well-advised taxpayers will typically adopt the less accurate Code method over the more accurate Regulation method because it defers income—and thus the taxes on that income.

Although the tax deferral of income possible though the purchase of bonds at a premium is small, it can be significant, particularly in conjunction with other tax deferral devices. Hence, lawyers should be wary of using tax return information as presumptive of economic income for legal purposes.

For *Financial Accounting*, the owner should amortize any acquisition premium using a *constant yield to maturity* (*CYM*) assumption.

7. **Active Foreign Business Income:** *AFBI*: *IRC* section 861(c)(1)(B) defines *AFBI* as:

> gross income which—
>
>> (i)   is derived from sources outside the United States (as determined under this subchapter) or, in the case of a corporation, is attributable to income so derived by a subsidiary of such corporation, and
>>
>> (ii)   is attributable to the <u>*active conduct of a trade or business*</u> in a foreign country or possession of the United

> States by the individual or corporation (or by a
> subsidiary.)

Emphasis added.

Active foreign business income results in different consequences than
does other types of foreign income, such as passive or investment
income.

8. **Active Conduct of a Trade or Business:** *See Passive Activity.* The
   phrase "active conduct of a trade or business" appears in twenty-six
   separate section of the Internal Revenue Code (as of 2011). The
   phrase's meaning is inconsistent and *not* clearly defined. For example,
   IRC section 167(j)(5) provides:

   > For purposes of this subsection, the rental to others of real
   > property located within an Indian reservation shall be treated
   > as the *active conduct of a trade or business* within an Indian
   > reservation.

   IRC section 335(b)(2) defines the term [titling itself a Definition]
   (albeit not particularly helpfully) as:

   > For purposes of paragraph (1), a corporation shall be treated
   > as engaged in the active conduct of a trade or business if and
   > only if—
   >
   > (A) it is engaged in the active conduct of a trade or business
   > . . . .

   One wonders what the term means for purposes other than paragraph
   (1) of subsection 335(b).

   The term "trade or business" appears frequently in the *IRC*; however,
   it has no consistent definition, although it generally connotes
   something involving "activity" rather than "passivity." As a result, the
   term "active conduct of a trade or business" may appear facially
   redundant, though in practical terms it certainly has meaning even if
   one cannot quite define it. In one provision, an entity is engaged in the
   active conduct of a trade or business if it merely reasonably expects to
   generate revenues within three years. Treas. Reg. § 1.45D–
   1(d)(4)(iv)(A).

9. **Additional Paid-In Capital:** *APIC:* This finance and accounting
   term has little meaning. It refers to the excess paid for shares over par
   or stated value. Par value has long lost most of its meaning. At one
   time, shareholders were liable for corporate debts to the extent they
   had not paid par value for their stock. For many years, however,
   companies have issues no-par stock or stock with an extremely low par
   value in states that retain the notion of par. The accounting line for
   APIC is part of owner's equity.

Some accountants refer to this as *EPIC* or *excess* paid-in capital.

10. **Adjustable Rate:** This is a contractual interest rate that changes over time, generally as a result of market changes. Often used for home mortgage loans—referred to as *Adjustable Rate* Mortgages (*ARMs*)—an initial *adjustable rate* may be artificially low such that the borrower may more easily qualify for the loan, based on outside conditions (such as those imposed by government programs). Contracts with *adjustable rates* require a reference rate. Many use a function of the *prime rate*, or the federal funds rate, or the *LIBOR* rate.

Consumers—and the lawyers who represent them—should be cautious of *ARMs*. They are useful for persons with reliably predictable income increases; however, they can be dangerous for persons with stable income. Adjustments can be large if market rates increase; as a result, the debtors may have great difficulty making the resulting high loan payments.

ARMs make sense when one can reliably predict falling interest rates; however, if one can reliably predict falling interest rate, one need not take this course, or even practice law for a living, as one must have a crystal ball. Reliably predicting income increases is more feasible. For example, college graduates often see substantial increases in pay in the early years of working. Others have contractual arrangements or trust arrangements which provide for secure increases. In contrast, the interest rate market can be very fickle.

11. **Adjusted Basis:** In general, for accounting purposes (after capitalization, amortization and depreciation), the historical cost basis of property can be increased or decreased.

For tax purposes, *IRC* section 1016 outlines the circumstances when basis adjusts. For example, depreciation reduces an asset's basis. Deprecation, which is a function both of what one did and what one should have done, will result in an adjusted basis that is lower than the cost basis for an asset. For all other purposes tax adjustments are a function of what one should have done.

For accounting purposes, basis adjustments should always be a function of what one should have recorded—shown by an extraordinary item on the financial statements if it is inconsistent with what one actually recorded. The adjusted basis is the basis upon which gains and losses are calculated at the time an asset is sold or disposed of.

A very simplified formula for adjusted basis is:

Adjusted Basis = Cost Basis + Capitalized
Expenditures − Depreciation (or amortization)

12. **Adjusted Gross Income:** *AGI*: This is a tax term or art defined by *IRC* section 62. In includes *Gross Income* (a tax term of art define by *IRC* Section 61), minus a list of "***above the line***" deductions. Most of the deductions are for ordinary and necessary *trade or business* expenses allowed by *IRC* section 162; however, the list also includes alimony deductible under *IRC* section 71 and moving expenses.

    Of significant importance, *AGI* does not include most employee business expenses, which are not only "***below-the-line***" deductions, but which are also subject to the 2% floor limitations of *IRC* section 64.

    Above-the-line refers to deductions allowable for purposes of *IRC* section 62 and *AGI*. *Below the line* refers to all other deductions. With few exceptions, above the line deductions appear on a tax return and benefit the taxpayer. *Below-the-line* deductions, however, are subject to several limitations and restrictions before they reach a tax return. Hence, whether a deduction is *above* or *below-the-line* can be very significant.

    Although taxpayers pay tax at their respective brackets on taxable income, the correct computation of *AGI* is important. Many deductions are a function of *AGI*: *e.g.,* medical expenses and charitable contribution deductions. Also, the statute of limitations, per *IRC* section 6501(e) can be a function of omissions from *AGI*.

    The *line* referred to in both *above* and *below-the-line* references is a line on a United States Form 1040—INDIVIDUAL TAX RETURN—which denominates the computation of *AGI* by requiring the addition and subtraction of the numbers above it. In accounting and financial reports, a *single line* indicates the need for addition and subtraction, while a *double line* indicates the net result of addition and subtraction.

13. **Adjusting Entry:** At the end of each period (which may be a month, a quarter, or a year) an accountant or bookkeeper makes a series of entries for non-transactional items. These include *depreciation* and *amortization*. In accounting parlance, they are *adjusting entries*, as they adjust for items which are not the result of events or transactions. Regular entries appear chronologically in the journal, but *adjusting entries* and *closing entries* appear at the end of a period.

14. **Affinity:** Relationship by Marriage. See *consanguinity*, which refers to relationship through a common ancestor. Spouses are related by *affinity*, as are in-laws. Blood relatives are related by *consanguinity*. Tax law has significant rules for related party transactions. Such transactions may result in imputed income, deduction disallowance, or even a collapse of the transactional steps into a single event or result. In some cases, accounting rules incorporate relationships, as well. Other legal areas—such as agency law, trust law, and family law—

also impute or define legal consequences at least partially from a consideration of the parties' relationships.

Hence, lawyers should have a clear understand of human relationships.

15. **After-Tax Interest Rate:** See LESSON EIGHT, which explains the concept of an *after-tax interest rate*. This is the appropriate statement of interest (*nominal, periodic,* or *effective*) computed after reduction for the income tax benefits resulting from deduction of the interest. For United States tax purposes, most business interest is deductible (although some must be capitalized); as is investment interest (subject to limitations) and some home mortgage interest. The tax benefits under *IRC* Section 163 can be substantial; hence, to reflect the true economic interest cost, planners should convert the *stated interest rate* to the equivalent *after-tax interest rate*. One must understand, however, that tax consequences often change over time, resulting in an *after-tax interest rate* being an *adjustable rate*.

The formula for an *after-tax interest rate* is:

$$atir = sir(1 - tr)$$

Where tr = marginal tax rate, $atir$ = after-tax interest rate and sir = stated interest rate.

A related concept is an ***after-tax cost***. In turn, this is related to the *True Cost of Ownership (TCO)*. Algebraically, the *after tax cost* is:

$$ATC = (1 - mtr) \times sp$$

Where ATC = after-tax cost, mtr = marginal tax rate, and sp = stated price.

Depreciable and deductible assets thus do not cost their *stated price*. For example, a $5,000 desk subject to *IRC* section 179 expensing at a 40% *marginal tax rate* (which is realistic considering federal and state income and employment taxes) has an *after-tax cost* of only $3,000.

$$\$3,000 = (1 - .4)(\$5,000)$$

or

$$\$3,000 = (.6)(\$5,000)$$

Another related concept is an ***after-tax value***. This one is more subtle than the other two and significantly less precise; nevertheless, it can be profoundly important. Far too often, lawyers and courts ignore the concept to the unfair detriment of some (and unfair benefit) of others.

To understand *after-tax value*, one must first understand *Fair Market Value (FMV)*, *Basis,* and *Minority Discount (MD),* as well as other discounting. All property has a *FMV* as well as a tax *basis* (generally cost). The difference between the two numbers is the potential or inherent taxable gain or loss in the property. Under the United States income tax system (which is also the case with most countries), the inherent gain or loss is not subject to tax recognition until the occurrence of a taxable event, generally a sale or exchange. Upon such an event, the owner must pay income tax on the gain (or he may deduct the loss subject to many deferral and disallowance provisions). The margin tax rate on the gain will vary depending not only on the owner's tax bracket, but also on the character of the property sold or exchanged. In many income tax systems, including that of the United States, *capital gain income* is subject to a lower set of tax rates than other types of income. The exact rate has varied substantially over the past nine decades of the U.S. income tax system.

But, if one owns property which one must value, one must consider the potential tax consequences of a disposition of the property. For example, if the *marginal tax rate* is 20% and the basis is zero, the property has an after-tax value of only 80% of the stated or nominal *FMV*, assuming an imminent sale. If the marginal tax rate is 40% and the basis is zero, the property has an *after-tax value* of only 60% of the nominal *FMV*, again assuming an imminent sale.

Dissolution of marriage—divorce in some jurisdictions—often involves the division of property. This can occur under a community property or equitable division statute, or as a result of the settlement of alimony rights. In any of these cases, for tax purposes, *IRC* section 1041 treats the transaction as a gift (hence no income or loss results from the transfer itself). But, section 1041 also transfers the property's tax *adjusted basis* (under *IRC* section 1016) to the recipient. High basis assets—and capital assets—potentially have a dramatically different after-tax value than low basis assets and ordinary assets.

For example, posit a soon-to-be divorced couple who together own four assets:

- Cash of $100,000.

- Securities with an undisputed *FMV* (after transaction costs) of $100,000 and with a *tax adjusted basis* of $1,000.

- Securities with an undisputed *FMB* (after transaction costs) of $100,000 and with a *tax adjusted basis* of $1,000,000.

- Inventory with an undisputed *FMV* (after transaction costs) of $100,000 and with a *tax adjusted basis* of $1,000.

Nominally, each asset has the same *FMV*: $100,000. Most state statutes and financial disclosure forms related to marriage dissolution do not require disclosure of tax adjusted bases or of the tax character of property. Hence, legally, each asset may have identical *FMV*s. But, assuming each would be sold immediately by the recipient, their relative after-tax values differ substantially. Assuming a 40% marginal tax rate (20% on capital gains), the after tax values would be:

- $100,000 for the cash.
- $80,800 for the appreciated securities.
- Up to $280,000 for the depreciated securities.
- $60,600 for the inventory.

The cash would have no potential tax consequences. The appreciated securities would likely generate long-term capital gains taxed at an assumed 20% rate. The depreciated securities would likely generate *long-term capital losses*, limited in deductibility by *IRC* sections 1211–1212, but potentially benefiting the owner/seller 20% (and possibly as much as 40%) of the loss. The inventory would likely generate *ordinary income* taxed at 40%.

With an *after-tax interest rate*, the computation is simple and reliable—the only variable being the deductibility of the interest and the rate of the payer—each of which could change, but each of which is nevertheless predictable with a high degree of certainty. Similarly, the computation of an *after-tax cost* is also simple and reliable because the transaction is current and thus subject to the current variable of the buyer's tax rate, which, again, is highly predictable (though it can change during the year).

But, computing an *after-tax value* requires information regarding the timing of the property disposition. If a sale is imminent, the computation is simple and highly reliable. If, instead, no sale is currently contemplated, the computation introduces a new variable— the likelihood and timing of a potential disposition. Eventually, an owner will dispose of all his property: at some point, he will die (remember we are considering humans in the process of a divorce). Statistical information is available regarding the typical ownership period of other property, be it securities or inventory or buildings. This requires informed speculation based on historical information regarding macro trends, as well as particular information regarding the particular property and the particular owner. With an assumed disposition date (be it imminent or postponed until death), an expert witness can compute an **after-tax present value**. The information will not be perfect, as it is subject to the speculative variable; however, the resulting computation is arguably more reliable than ignoring the inherent tax consequences altogether, as do most state statutes and courts.

Understanding that most property divisions result from *marital settlement agreements*, one should realize: clients with lawyers who understand the concept of *after-tax value* have a substantial advantage over clients with lawyers who do not.

16. **All Events Test:** This is one of the thirteen fundamental *accounting principles and assumptions*. It applies to the *accrual method* of accounting and is the cornerstone of the *Matching Principle*. See also the Revenue Recognition Principle and the Expense Recognition Principle.

    - *Income recognition* is appropriate when *all events* have occurred such that the earner has a right to the item and the amount thereof can be determined with reasonable accuracy.

    - *Deductions* are appropriate when *all events* have occurred such the obligor must incur the item and the amount thereof can be determined with reasonable accuracy.

    The *all events test* is irrelevant for the *cash method* of accounting.

17. **Alternative Minimum Tax:** *AMT*: Under *IRC* section 55, the *AMT* system is an alternative tax system to the general U.S. *income* tax system. Enacted in 1969, it originally targeted a small number of high income taxpayers who largely escaped income taxes because of investments in tax exempt securities. It now reaches many households with more modest income levels. For tax purposes, an inclusion in *AMT* is not the same as an inclusion in *gross income*, which affects some significant procedural rules.

    As more and more households have entered the reach of the *AMT*, the system has become *politically* controversial. Arguably, it raises significant revenue; however, arguably it also places too heavy a burden on households which are more middle class than upper class. When one computes an *after-tax interest* rate, an *after-tax cost*, or an *after-tax value*, one must consider the potential *AMT* consequences, which can be complicated.

    Lawyers who consider *Taxable Income* as relevant to the legal concept of *income* should pay heed to the *AMT* rules. In part, these rules add items to income which are otherwise excluded, such as tax exempt interest (*e.g.,* interest on state and local bonds). To be clear, *AMT* income is not necessarily a better measure of income than is *Taxable Income*, but it is certainly different and thus provides a different perspective.

18. **American Institute of Certified Public Accountants:** *AICPA*: According to the organization's mission statement:

The American Institute of Certified Public Accountants is the national, professional organization for all Certified Public Accountants. Its mission is to provide members with the resources, information, and leadership that enable them to provide valuable services in the highest professional manner to benefit the public as well as employers and clients.

In fulfilling its mission, the AICPA works with state CPA organizations and gives priority to those areas where public reliance on CPA skills is most significant.

http://www.aicpa.org.

Among other activities, it establishes ethical rules for public accountants. It also provides technical support to the *FASB*, which is responsible for *GAAP*. Further, it grants the *PFS* certification.

19. **American Stock Exchange: AMEX:** [pronounced *am*-eks]. This was one of the main stock exchanges in the United States from the 1920s until the late 1990s. Generally, it listed companies with capitalized values less than those on the *New York Stock Exchange*. In 1998, it merged with *NASDAQ*.

20. **Amortization:** This is the process of allocating a cost or a principal amount over time. An **AMORTIZATION CALCULATOR**—as explained in FINANCE FOR LAWYERS **LESSON THIRTEEN**—performs two important functions. First, it determines the amount of level payment required to reduce the principal amount of a loan to zero over a stated period, at a given periodic interest rate. Second, it determines—in an *amortization* schedule—the portion of each payment properly allocable to interest and the portion properly allocable to principal. For contracts with actual payments less than the determined interest component of each payment, *negative amortization* will occur: the principal amount will thus increase.

An *amortization* is either in *end mode* (payments occur at the end of each period) or *begin mode* (payments occur at the beginning of each period).

The **AMORTIZATION** calculation is one of the six basic calculations performed by a *Financial Calculator*. The formula for an *amortization* is:

$$PMT = \left[\frac{\left(PV \left(\frac{i}{100} \right) \right)}{1 - \left(1 + \frac{i}{100} \right)^{-n}} \right]$$

where i = nominal annual interest rate, n = number of periods per year, and FV = the future value.

Amortization has another important meaning. For accounting and tax law purposes, it involves the process of allocating *intangible* costs over time. Similarly, *depreciation* involves the allocation of *tangible* costs over time. Interestingly, for U.S. tax purposes, *amortization* generally follows a straight-line approach. *See, e.g., IRC* sections 195, 197, and 263 (with accompanying regulations). Occasionally, however, tax *amortization* properly follows an up-ward sloping curve. In contrast, tax and accounting *depreciation* generally follows a downward sloping curve per *IRC* sections 167 and 168. For real property, U.S. tax depreciation is straight-line—a graph of zero slope. Economically, the downward sloping curve would be most appropriate.

21. **Annual Percentage Rate: APR:** See **LESSON FIVE-C:** *Annual Percentage Rate.* In credit transactions not involving *points* or some other fees, the *annual percentage rate* equals the *nominal annual interest rate.* However, transactions involving *points* and some other fees have an *annual percentage rate* which reflects both the *nominal* rate and the *compounded* amortized effect of the points or other fees. United States Federal Law requires disclosure of this rate law for most credit transactions. *"APR"* is the typical abbreviation. The legal definition appears in federal statute, **15 U.S.C. § 1606. LESSON FIVE-** C explains the *APR.* Arguably the Truth in Lending Law requirement that lenders disclose the *APR* actually favors banks and mis-leads borrowers.

In credit parlance, a "point" is equal to one percent of the principal amount loaned. Thus on a $100,000 loan, one point equals $1,000 and two points equals $2,000. On a $200,000 loan, one point equals $2,000 and two points equals $4,000.

Of critical importance, the *APR* does not equal the *EFF* (*effective interest rate*) unless the obligation *compounds* annually. Financial Calculators always have an *EFF* function; however, they rarely have an *APR* function, as it is a legal rather than a financial term.

Other nations also use the term *Annual Percentage Rate* and abbreviate it as *APR.* Several of them define it differently than does U.S. law. Lawyers must therefore be careful when using the term contractually. They must define the meaning in relation to the law of a particular jurisdiction.

22. **Annual Percentage Yield: APY:** The term *Annual Percentage Yield* (*APY*) and its legal consequences appear in federal statute. **12 U.S.C. § 4302.** Specifically, the statute defines it as "the total amount of interest that would be received on a $100 deposit, based on the annual rate of simple interest and the frequency of compounding for a 365-day period. . . ." Advertisements for deposits generally must include a statement of the *APY.* The definition assumes re-investment of

periodic interest at the stated interest rate and a maturity of at least one-year. For deposits for which those assumptions do not apply, the *APY* is not accurate; nevertheless, federal law generally requires its disclosure.

23. **Annuity:** A series of payments. A fixed *annuity* is a series of payments for a fixed period. A life *annuity* is a series of payments for the remainder of a person's life. A joint life *annuity* is a series of payments for the remainder of the longer of two persons' lives.

For tax purposes, an *annuity* issued by an insurance company receives special benefits: internal accumulations in value are not taxable until disbursed.

Be careful when using the term *annuity*: to some people it inherently refers to an insurance product. While that is correct under one definition, it is not correct under the more general definition: an *annuity* is merely a series of payments.

For some legal purposes *annuities* receive preferential treatment. Examples include federal tax law (accumulations are tax deferred) and some state laws regarding garnishment (*annuities* are sometimes not subject to garnishment). In other cases, *annuities* receive detrimental legal consequences. An example commonly includes the determination of income for alimony or child support purposes. Many state statutes include "*annuity* payments" as income for these purposes. Such statutes are unfair to the *annuity* investor because—in most cases—the *annuity* is self-amortizing and thus the payments are part principal and part interest. Because family law definitions of income rarely define principal withdrawals as income, when they do so in relation to *annuities*, they are unfair.

24. **Annuity Due:** This is a reference to the *Mode*. Payments on an *annuity due* begin today, in contrast to an *annuity in arrears* for which payments begin one period in the future. Loan amortizations almost always use end mode to create an annuity of payments, because the first loan payment—for new loans—is typically one period in the future. Sinking funds—which are also annuities—use the begin mode, or annuity due format, if the creator wants to begin saving immediately.

25. **Annuity in Arrears:** This is a reference to the *Mode*. Payments on an *annuity in arrears* begin one period from now, in contrast to an *annuity due* for which payments begin today. Loans are almost always *annuities in arrears*: the first payment is due one period in the future; otherwise, the borrower would make the first payment simultaneously with borrowing the money. In such a case, he would merely be borrowing less. In contrast, loans with deferred payments—such as student loans—can effectively be annuities due. At the moment of

amortizing the loan, the first payment can indeed be due currently, as opposed to one period in the future.

26. **Annuity Trust:** This is a shortened reference to a *CRAT, or Charitable Remainder Annuity Trust.* It provides an annuity to the grantor for either a single or joint life with the remainder benefiting a charity. United States tax law provides significant tax benefits for annuity trusts—with the magnitude of the benefits a function of the grantor's income and asset levels. See the discussion on *CRAT* for more information.

27. **Applicable Federal Rate:** *AFR:* Internal Revenue Code section 1274(d) defines the *Applicable Federal Rate*—the *AFR.* Announced monthly, this rate forms the basis for many tax calculations, including *original issue discount* loan interest (OID per *IRC* sections 1272–74), *below market loans* (per *IRC* section 7872), and advanced or deferred payments for rent (per *IRC* section 467).

Under *Treasury Regulation* section 1.7872–13(a)(1)(i), the *IRS* annually announces a blended short-term rate for short-term obligations outstanding for the entire year, or a substantial part thereof. Some *IRC* provisions—*e.g.,* section 467—use a higher rate which is 110% or 120% of the *AFR.* These various rates are important for imputing current interest and other tax events for loans with deferred or understated interest.

IRC section 1274(d) provides:

    (1) Applicable Federal rate

        (A) In general

In the case of a debt instrument with a term of:	**The applicable Federal rate is:**
Not over 3 years	The Federal short-term rate.
Over 3 years but not over 9 years	The Federal mid-term rate.
Over 9 years	The Federal long-term rate.

        (B) Determination of rates

        During each calendar month, the Secretary shall determine the Federal short-term rate, mid-term rate, and long-term rate which shall apply during the following calendar month.

(C)　Federal rate for any calendar month

For purposes of this paragraph—

(i)　Federal short-term rate

The Federal short-term rate shall be the rate determined by the Secretary based on the average market yield (during any 1-month period selected by the Secretary and ending in the calendar month in which the determination is made) on outstanding marketable obligations of the United States with remaining periods to maturity of 3 years or less.

(ii)　Federal mid-term and long-term rates

The Federal mid-term and long-term rate shall be determined in accordance with the principles of clause (i).

(D)　Lower rate permitted in certain cases

The Secretary may by regulations permit a rate to be used with respect to any debt instrument which is lower than the applicable Federal rate if the taxpayer establishes to the satisfaction of the Secretary that such lower rate is based on the same principles as the applicable Federal rate and is appropriate for the term of such instrument.

The *AFR* is typically lower than market interest rates for comparable periods. That fact is particularly noteworthy. Taxpayers enter transactions with below market rates, or with deferred interest, because they want to escape, defer, or accelerate the tax consequences of market rates. By requiring use of the *AFR* in many situations, the *IRC* effectively precludes much of the intended manipulation: the escape, the deferral, or the acceleration. However, because the *AFR* is lower than market rates, it does not eliminate all the benefits of the affected transactions.

28. **Ask Price:** The ask price is the offer to sell price for items without a highly liquid market—*e.g.*, many stocks, bonds, debentures, or commodities. It contrasts with the bid price which is the offer to buy price. For securities listed on a major exchange, a "market maker" ensures the bid and the ask price come together. For other exchanges, the spread between the bid and ask prices exists until it does not, *i.e.*, until it "closes."

29. **Audit:** A *CPA* audits the financial statements of an entity or person. The audit consists of a plan, a management letter describing the audit, random sampling of various bookkeeping entries, and verification of

cash, receivables, liabilities, and other material items. It also includes an evaluation of the entity's *internal controls*. The auditor will suggest to management changes in *internal controls* or in bookkeeping procedures and policies, as appropriate. Ultimately, management prepares the *financial statements* and either follows the *CPA* auditor's advice or rejects it. Then the auditor expresses an opinion on the *financial statements*: whether they conform to *GAAP* and whether they present fairly the financial condition and operations of the entity for the period and as of the date stated.

Audit procedures follow *GAAS*. An auditor must make a variety of assumptions, including whether the entity is a going concern. If these assumptions are invalid, the auditor must so state and explain why.

Of significance, an audit does not certify or guarantee anything other than the fairness of the statements with the assumptions made and consistent with *GAAP*. If an auditor suspects fraud, he will conduct a more intensive fraud audit; or, he may withdraw from the engagement.

30. **Audit Committee:** Large, especially publicly traded entities, typically have an audit committee formed from the Board of Directors. This committee meets with the independent auditors, receives their recommendations, and reports to the general Board of Directors. The major purpose of an audit committee is independence from management. Along with management, they often have responsibility for ensuring proper *internal controls*.

31. **Auditor's Report:** This is the opinion of a *Certified Public Accountant* attesting to audit results. It follows a standard form under *Generally Accepted Auditing Standards (GAAS)*. It takes one of four common forms:

    • Unqualified Opinion

    • Qualified Opinion

    • Adverse Opinion

    • Disclaimer of Opinion

An unqualified opinion reflects the *CPA's* conclusion that the financial statements, including footnotes, fairly present the issuer's operations and condition for a particular period and at a particular time.

A *Qualified Opinion* follows the standard unqualified format; however, it conditions the opinion because of some irregularity. It does so in an "except for" paragraph explaining the condition. The irregularity is not one such that the auditor finds the statements to be unfair: that would result in an *Adverse Opinion*. Instead, the qualification may result from such things as:

- the inability of the auditor to examine a particular asset

- the necessity of the auditor's reliance on the opinion of another auditor not legally associated with the primary auditor

- a single deviation from *GAAP*, which does not affect the overall fairness of the statements.

A standard *Unqualified Opinion* follows the following format—and does not deviate from it significantly:

INDEPENDENT AUDITOR'S REPORT

Board of Directors, Stockholders, Owners, and/or
Management of ABC Company, Inc.
123 Main St.
Anytown, Anystate

We have audited the accompanying Balance Sheet of ABC Company, Inc. (the "Company") as of December 31, 20XX and the related statements of Income, Retained Earnings, and Cash Flows for the year then ended. These Financial Statements are the responsibility of the Company's management. Our responsibility is to express an opinion on these financial statements based on our audit.

We conducted our audit in accordance with generally accepted auditing standards. Those standards require that we plan and perform the audit to obtain reasonable assurance about whether the financial statements are free of material misstatement. An audit includes examining, on a test basis, evidence supporting the amounts and disclosures in the financial statements. An audit also includes assessing the accounting principles used and significant estimates made by management, as well as evaluating the overall financial statement presentation. We believe that our audit provides a reasonable basis for our opinion.

In our opinion, the financial statements referred to above present fairly, in all material respects, the financial position of the Company as of December 31, 20XX, and the results of its operations and its cash flows for the year then ended in accordance with generally accepted accounting principles.

Signature
Auditor's name and address
Date

A *Disclaimer of Opinion* is also the possible result of an audit or the engagement of a *CPA*. A disclaimer is appropriate if the limitations placed on the auditor were so significant that the *CPA* could not render an opinion.

Lawyers should never rely on statements accompanied by an *Adverse Opinion* or a *Disclaimer of Opinion*. They should be wary of a *Qualified Opinion* and should pay close attention to the "*except-for*" paragraph. Even an *Unqualified Opinion* will have many footnotes and explanations outside the actual opinion letter. Lawyer should be wary about relying on any *Financial Statements*—including those with an *Unqualified Opinion*—unless they are conversant with accounting terminology, financial ratios, and have comparative data.

32. **Balance of Payments:** This is an often-misunderstood measure of the payments between nations, generally on an annual basis. By definition, it must balance—just as a balance sheet must balance. Components of the measure, however, may be out-of-balance, depending on how one defines them.

For example, Country A can have an annual *trade imbalance* with Country B because Country A sold more goods and services to Country B than Country B purchased. Hence, the Trade measures between the two countries—as defined in terms of goods and services—will reflect a deficit for Country B and a surplus for Country A.

In terms of the *Balance of Payments*, however, a balance will result in every instance—although it may flow through multiple countries. For the above example, eventually the surplus country or countries—here Country A—will acquire currency, coin, government obligations, or assets in Country B (though with multiple countries, Country A may actually acquire surplus assets in Country C, which acquires surplus assets in Country B).

Hence no nation can have a *Balance of Payments* deficit or surplus, any more than a company's books can be out of balance. Imbalances, if they occur, are inevitably the result of recording or math errors, *e.g.*, a bookkeeper forgetting to enter a number or adding 2 plus 2 and getting 7. These things happen, but one should not place any greater significance on them other than people make mistakes.

Even in terms of *alleged* Trade Deficits, the numbers can be misleading for many reasons:

- The numbers may reflect *definitions* of trade which exclude material accounts. For example, if the United States buys 100,000 automobiles from Japan and sells the equivalent value of lumber and bricks to Japan, many *experts* suggest the trade accounts balance. However, if, instead, the United States exports nothing to Japan, but Japan instead purchasing a building in

Seattle comprised of those same bricks and lumber,
many experts suggest the United States would have a
Trade Deficit with Japan. Such a conclusion would be
accurate, but only by defining the sale of lumber and
bricks in Seattle as something other than Trade. Indeed,
it is not an export—but only if one defines exports in
terms of tangibles goods physically moving out of a
nation.

- The numbers may reflect inter-company transactions
  which, partially because of the *Separate Entity
  Assumption*, reflect misleading numbers.

For example, X Corporation—a multi-national entity
(but with substantial United States shareholders)—may
sell a beverage at a fast food establishment in
Gainesville, Florida. The $1.99 sale of a large Coke®
comprises many components: the cup (which includes all
the manufacturing parts of that cup), the ice, the
carbonated water, the syrup, the service of someone
filling the cup and accepting payment and
printing/providing a receipt, the provision of the building
or drive-thru window at the *POS*, and the use of the
name of the fast-food establishment. Probably, all the
manufacturing of the cup, ice, receipt, straw, napkin,
syrup, and window occurred within the United States.
Probably, none of it occurred in the Cayman Islands. But,
the trademark and trade name for the fast food company
may belong to an entity other than X Corporation;
indeed, that is very likely.

Under the Separate Entity Assumption, X Corporation
and Trademark Corporation have separate accounting
records. Trademark Corporation will charge X
Corporation for the use of the name, logo, and emblem on
cups, napkins, signs, sales personnel uniforms and other
such places. If the United States is a high tax jurisdiction
(which it tends to be in relative terms) and the Cayman
Islands is a low tax jurisdiction (which it tends to be),
then X Corporation has a strong incentive to place a high
FMV on the use of the trademark. This is particularly
true if the shareholders of X Corporation and Trademark
Corporation are identical, or if they overlap
substantially.

In the above example, perhaps $.25 of the transaction
involves trademark costs. If so, then the micro economic

accounting for the transaction will involve a *Trade Deficit* between the United States and the Cayman Islands—even though neither the customer nor the beverage has ever been in the Cayman Islands and no money (other than through an electronic transfer) ever appeared in the Cayman Islands. The alleged *Trade Deficit* is thus a *fiction* resulting from accounting assumptions and allocations. It has some reality in terms of tax consequences and share values and financial statements; however, is has no other economic value or reality.

If users of Trade Statements draw the wrong conclusions from the alleged resulting deficit, they risk making bad decisions. Similarly, if users of Financial Statements misunderstand their meaning—as lawyers often do— they, too risk making bad decisions.

- Many people assume *Trade Deficits* are bad and *Trade Surpluses* are good. While such assumptions have some validity, they also require a broader view.

First, numbers reflecting deficits and surplus are no better than the assumptions underlying the definitions of those terms. Because terminology is easily manipulation through misleading definitions, one should be wary of the numbers unless one fully understands the definitions—and, under the *Consistency Principle*—uses the identical definitions for any comparisons with other periods or nations.

Second, to the extent a *Trade Deficit* excludes the sale of currency, financial instruments, and domestic investments (e.g., the building in Seattle posited above), the alleged *Trade Deficit* is actually positive for the nation incurring it—at least in the short or mid-term. Think pragmatically: the deficit country has additional automobiles, computers, trinkets, oil, or whatever it imported. The surplus country, however, has additional paper currency and coin (neither of which has any intrinsic value) plus intangible obligations and some tangible property located in the deficit nation. Demand in the deficit nation is offset by increased supply (at no current cost other than paper) from the surplus country; hence, the deficit nation will have less inflationary pressures. The surplus nation, however, has increased demand (because of the sales and resulting profits) but decreased supply (which it exported); hence, the surplus nation will have increased inflationary pressure. Overall, the deficit nation has exported its inflation.

Admittedly, such *Trade Deficits* have a turning point: eventually—in the long run—the surplus nation will spend the excess currency reserves. It will thus export its own inflation to the deficit nation, which will suffer the unpleasant macro economic consequences of an <u>alleged</u> *Trade Surplus* (alleged because the definitions are so imprecise).

The United States has experienced annual, continuous *Trade Deficits* (as that term is traditionally defined by excluding paper, coin, and domestic investments) for many decades. Whether—and when—those turn into *Trade Surpluses* (using the same misleading definition as used for Trade Deficits) is unclear. In the long run, it is inevitable; however, as famed economist John Maynard Keynes once said, "Long run is a misleading guide to current affairs. In the long run we are all dead."

For an excellent discussion of trade and balance of payments, see commentary by Martin Feldstein, a former Chairman of the Council of Economic Advisors.

http://www.econlib.org/library/Enc/BalanceofPayments.html.

33. **Balance Sheet:** This is one of three important *Financial Statements*, the other two being the *Income Statement* and the *Statement of Cash Flows*. It presents a financial picture as of a particular date. Many users refer to it as a snapshot: it says a great deal about conditions at one moment.

The *Balance Sheet* lists assets on the left side and liabilities plus owner's equity on the right side. The two sides necessarily balance, as owner's equity results from the basic accounting equation:

$$(Assets - Liabilities) = Owners'\ Equity$$

or

$$Assets = (Liabilities + Owners'\ Equity)$$

Balance Sheet

Assets	Liabilities
	Owners' Equity
Total Assets	Total Liabilities plus Equity

A *single underline* on a *Financial Statement* indicates the column above it is being added or subtracted. A *double underline* indicates a sum.

34. **Balloon Payment:** Some loans provide for short-term partial *amortization* of the principal with the remaining principal due in a lump sum. This remainder is a *Balloon Payment*. The word arises from the notion of the payment amount suddenly ballooning or inflating to a large amount. Usually a balloon payment is a lump sum payment due at the maturity of a loan.

35. **Bankers Acceptance:** According to the *Fed*,

> *Bankers acceptances* are negotiable time drafts, or bills of exchange, that have been accepted by a bank which, by accepting, assumes the obligation to pay the holder of the *draft* the face amount of the instrument on the maturity date specified. They are used primarily to finance the export, import, shipment or storage of goods.

See the definitions of *negotiable instrument* and *draft* for fuller information.

36. **Basis:** In accounting and tax parlance, basis is the *historic cost* of an item, adjusted for subsequent events. Every asset has a *basis*, even if the amount is zero. A negative *basis* is impossible. Currency has, by definition, a basis equal to its face value.

The *basis* is essential for the determination of gain or loss on disposition of the thing. For example, if a chair has a cost basis of $500 and the entity sells it for $700, the gain is $200. Without knowledge of the *basis*, one could not measure the gain or loss.

For tax purposes, *IRC* section 1012 provides for a *cost basis* in all property. *IRC* section 1016 then provides for adjustments to *basis*. *Depreciation* and *amortization* result in downward adjustments. Similarly, improvements result in basis increases in the process called *capitalization*.

Because tax gains are taxable and tax losses are often deductible, an item's tax *basis* is a critical number in determining the item's **after-tax value**. For example, a tract of land with a *FMV* of $1,000,000 and a *basis* of $1,000,000 has no potential tax gain. It therefore has an *after-tax* value of $1,000,000. But another tract with a similar *FMV* but a basis of $1,000 has a built-in gain of $999,000. The owner of the second tract will be subject to income tax (at either ordinary or capital gains rates) upon the sale or other taxable disposition of the tract. Because that built-in tax gain may result in income taxes due in the amount of $150,000 or more, the *after-tax FMV* of the tract is significantly lower than the stated $1,000,000. Similarly, a third tract with a *basis* of $3,000,000 has a build-in loss of $2,000,000.

The owner may benefit from a substantial tax deduction upon a taxable disposition of that third tract; as a result, the *after-tax FMV* of the tract is significantly higher than the stated amount of $1,000,000.

Mostly, the legal system ignores tax *basis* for Family Law and other purposes. This refusal to consider important information results in some persons having substantial advantage over others. Lawyers need to be aware of this phenomenon. For example, in dividing property incident to marriage dissolution, the tax *basis* of a thing may be as important as the stated *FMV*. Too often, however, the parties ignore the tax *basis*.

A famous—and initially counter-intuitive—tax case defines tax *basis* in an arm's length taxable transaction as:

> *The Fair Market Value Received.*

Philadelphia Park Amusement Company v. United States, 126 F. Supp. 184 (Cl. Ct. 1954).

See also the definition of *Adjusted Basis*.

37. **Basis Point:** One one-hundredth of one percent. Thus 100 *basis points* comprise 1 percent. If a bond yield changes from 10% to 11% that is a change of 100 *basis points*, but also a change of 10% (1% is 10% of 10%). Lawyers need to be familiar with the terminology in stating *interest* rates as a function of an index.

    For example the *prime rate* may be 5%. A loan 150 *basis points* above *prime* would be 6.5%. That phraseology is clearer than referring to a loan 1.5% above *prime*: some readers may mistakenly view the 1.5% as a function of the underlying *prime rate* rather than a fixed addition to it.

38. **Bear Market:** This is a colloquial description of a period during which various stock market indexes are lower than during the immediately prior period. Generally, a *Bear Market* exists when an index is down 10% or more from his previous high. In contrast, a *Bull Market* is one in which stock indexes are generally higher and rising. To be *bearish* or a *bear* is to believe stocks will fall. In contrast, to be bullish or a bull is to believe stocks will rise.

    Investors who are *bearish* often *short* stocks or use *put options* to benefit from expected declines. Investors who are *bullish* tend to have *long* positions or use *call options*. An old saying worth noting is:

> *One can make money as a Bull and one can make money*
> *as a Bear, but one cannot make money as a Pig.*

Another version states:

Bulls make money. Bears make money. Pigs get slaughtered.

39. **Begin Mode: BM:** In *Begin Mode*, the first *payment* of an *annuity* (or for the *amortization* of a loan or for a *sinking fund*) is due today. In contrast, for *End Mode*, the first *payment* is due one period in the future.

Lawyers should be careful with the *mode* function. Mode mistakes are one of the more common errors in financial calculations. Unlike *P/YR* errors, *mode* mistakes do not result in profound consequences; hence, they are not obvious to most users. In contrast, compounding errors may result in large consequences; as a result, even the most inexperienced user should notice a problem. *Mode* mistakes are more subtle; nevertheless, they can be material.

The *Mode* is irrelevant in FUTURE VALUE and PRESENT VALUE computations. It is relevant for computations involving the FUTURE VALUE OF AN ANNUITY, the PRESENT VALUE OF AN ANNUITY, a SINKING FUND, or an AMORTIZATION.

40. **Below-Market Loan:** *BML:* For tax purposes, *IRC* section 7872 defines a *below-market loan* in two ways:

   - For demand loans, a *BML* is one for which interest is payable at less than the *Applicable Federal Rate (AFR)*.

   - For term loans, a *BML* is one for which the present value of all loan payments, *discounted* at the appropriate *AFR* is less than the stated *principal* amount of the loan.

Generally, *IRC* section 7872 imputes interest on *below-market loans* such that they reflect the *AFR*.

Employers often use *BMLs* as a form of disguised compensation to employees, particularly highly paid employees. *IRC* section 7872 forces the parties to recognize the economic reality of such loans, at least to the extent of the *AFR*. Corporations—particularly closely held ones—have also used *BMLs* as disguised distributions. Again, *IRC* section 7872 forces the parties to recognize the economic reality of such loans, at least to the extent of the *AFR*. Similarly, parents often use *BMLs* as disguised gifts to their children. Once again, *IRC* section 7872 removes most tax benefits from such transactions.

Below-market loans are common-place in many other types of transactions. For example, over the past several decades car companies have often offered low or zero-interest loans to buyers. Inevitably, these are in the alternative to a price reduction. Indeed, for tax purposes, such loans would have the consequence of a price reduction along with market interest. For financial accounting purposes, the same result should follow.

Accounting for such loans becomes difficult when the lender and the seller are different entities. Typically, however, they are substantially related entities, with common ownership. Hence the economic impact of the loan is that of a distribution from the lender to the seller of the present value of the discount, plus a rebate from the seller to the buyer of the *present value* of the discount (*i.e.,* a price reduction).

Marketing departments know that some consumers react to (are motivated by) lower prices, while others react to lower stated interest rates. Because money is fungible, the seller is indifferent whether it drops the price or the state interest rate, as the *IRR*—the *present value* of the cash flows—is the same. But, if offering two economically identical, but nominal different, prices helps to sell cars, then car companies are more than willing to join the charade.

Taxpayers enter transactions with below market rates, or with deferred interest, because they want to escape, defer, or accelerate the tax consequences of market rates. By requiring use of the *AFR* in many situations, the *IRC* effectively precludes much of the intended manipulation: the escape, the deferral, or the acceleration. However, because the *AFR* is lower than market rates, it does not eliminate all the benefits of the affected transactions.

41. **BEPS:** Base erosion and profit shifting. This is an international tax term which refers to a business shifting the "location" of income to a lower-tax jurisdiction through various accounting schemes. The "tax base" for the jurisdiction shifted from decreases, which results in loss of revenue.

42. **Beta:** In finance terms, an investment's beta indicates how volatile it is. A beta of 1 equals the general market. A beta greater than one suggests the investment has more volatile price swings.

43. **Bid Price:** The bid price is the offer to buy price for items without a highly liquid market—*e.g.,* many stocks, bonds, debentures, or commodities. It contrasts with the *Ask Price* which is the offer to sell price. For securities listed on a major exchange, a "market maker" ensures the bid and the ask price come together. For other exchanges, the spread between the bid and ask prices exists until it does not, *i.e.,* until it "closes."

44. **Blue Book:** This term has three very different meanings for lawyers. To most, it refers to THE BLUEBOOK: A UNIFORM SYSTEM OF CITATION (compiled by the editors of the Columbia, Harvard, and University of Pennsylvania Law Reviews and the Yale Law Journal). It provides a commonly-used (not universal, but close to it) system of authority

citations for law articles. It contrasts with the APA (American Psychological Association) format used by most social scientists.

The term also, however, has special meaning in tax law. It commonly refers to the report prepared by the staff of the Joint Committee on Taxation. The "Bluebook" appears after the enactment of tax legislation and thus is not "legislative history"; however, it provides contemporaneous information regarding the legislation. Some people suggest the point of view may be slanted by the party in power or by staff members subjected to lobbying; hence, the Bluebook may contain interpretations and constructions at odds with the legislation. Whether that cynical viewpoint is valid is unclear; however, it exists. In any case, the Bluebook is important in the study of U.S. tax law.

Further, the term often refers to the NADA Blue Book, which reports the value of used automobiles.

45. **Blue Book Value:** The value of a car in the *Blue Book*. This will vary based on the condition of the automobile and thus is not an absolute. It also varies depending on whether one is looking for a trade-in value or a used-car-dealer sales price or a consumer-to-consumer used car sales price. See *National Automobile Dealers Association* and *NADA*. The *Blue Book Value* of a car is not necessarily the *Fair Market Value* (*FMV*) of the automobile. Often one can purchase a car for less than *Blue Book Value*.

Be careful not to confuse the acronym *NADA* with the acronym *NASD*.

46. **Bond:** A *Bond* is a corporate or government obligation to pay money in the future. The term *bond* is **not** a term of art. Generally, it refers to long-term obligations (more than ten years), as opposed to notes (generally mid-term of approximately five to ten years) and commercial paper or bills (generally short-term obligations of less than five years). Often, people refer to secured obligations as *bonds* and unsecured obligations as *debentures*. Others, however, use the term *secured bonds* and then inter-change the terms *bond* and *debenture*. Almost always the term *debenture* refers, however, to an unsecured obligation.

Bonds may be registered or bearer (coupon). With registered *bonds*, the obligor remits interest to the registered owner; hence, the paper evidence of the *bond* does not by itself indicate ownership. In contrast, with *coupon bonds*, the obligor remits interest to whoever presents the interest coupon. For such bearer instruments, the paper itself reflects ownership. In recent years, almost all *bonds* have been in registered form because *coupon bonds* were commonly used to evade taxes.

The term bond also appears in relation to various obligations. For example, the issuer of a *Bail Bond* guarantees the presence of a criminal defendant. The issuer of a *Performance Bond* guarantees the obligation or contractual performance of another.

47. **Books:** In *financial accounting*, a set of books refers to:

- *Journals*: These are chronological entries of transactions. An entity may have a single journal. More likely, it will have multiple journals, including ones for cash receipts and disbursements, one for sales, one for inventory, and one for closing entries.

- *Ledgers*: These are topical entries of transactions. They include all journal entries, but in a different format. Often called *T-accounts*, ledgers group a period's transactions by type. For example, all debits and *credits* affecting cash will appear in the cash ledger. All *debits* and *credits* affecting supplies will appear in the supplies ledger.

Accountants maintain *journals* daily, as transactions occur. They then transfer the *debits* and *credits* separately to the appropriate *ledgers*. Both *journals* and *ledgers* provide important information. *Journals* show the timing of transactions while *ledgers* show the impact. *Journals* are continuous, although accountants separate them by periods. Some *ledgers* are continuous—those which are *balance sheet* items, such as assets, liabilities and equity. Accountants net them periodically, but the *ledgers* and their balances continue from period to period. In contrast, some *ledgers* are temporary—confined to a particular period. These are the income and expense, profit and loss *ledgers*, which are *Income Statement* items.

At the end of each period, accountants *close temporary ledgers* to a single *ledger* which produces the *Income Statement*. Accountants then close this *ledger* into *Retained Earnings*. A periodic *profit* will have a *credit* balance in the *income statement* ledger. The final *closing entry* will be a *debit* to the *ledger* and a credit to *Retained Earnings*, a permanent ledger (account). A periodic loss will have a *debit* balance in the *income statement* ledger. The final *closing entry* will be a *credit* to the ledger and a *debit* to *Retained Earnings*.

Management is responsible for keeping an entity's books. Internal accountants supervising bookkeepers perform this task. From the books, management will prepare the entity's *Financial Statements*: the *Income Statement*, the *Balance Sheet*, and the *Statement of Cash Flows*.

The external auditor—a *CPA*—will audit (check and verify, often using statistical samples), the *financial statements*. He will then issue an *auditor's opinion* regarding whether they are fair and consistent with

GAAP. He will base his audit on *GAAS*. The auditor neither prepares the books nor the statements.

Most entities will have multiple sets of books. Contrary to popular wisdom, not only is this appropriate, but it is required:

- *Financial Books*, consistent with *GAAP* for external reporting.

- *Tax Books*, consistent with the *IRC* for tax reporting.

- *Internal Books* for managerial and *cost accounting*.

- *Pro Forma Books*, for special circumstances which require adjustments to account for changed methods or assumptions. For example, a Bank may require special assumptions or depreciation or inventory methods. If so, the entity will re-state its accounts to conform to such contractual requirements.

Accountants must be able to reconcile the different sets of books. As one might suppose, this is not a simple process. Lawyers should be aware of the multiple sets of books and the multiple sets of *Financial Statements* which flow from them. In particular, lawyers who need to know an entity's income or *equity* must realize that these are not terms of art. Accountants have many ways of presenting income, expenses, assets, liabilities, and *equity*. Lawyers who request information about these terms should expect multiple answers—which may appear to conflict and which may be very different.

Also, too often lawyers accept a single set of *Financial Statements*, as if they are correct. An unfortunate example involves the common acceptance of tax returns as evidence of *income* for Family Law and other legal matters. Hence, lawyers who request, through discovery, financial information should request all of it, including tax statements, external accounting statement, internal accounting statements, and any *pro forma* statements used in loan or other applications or disclosures.

48. **Book Value:** This represents the value of an entity for financial reporting purposes. Because accounting uses several significant and conservative reporting principles, *book value* is not generally representative of *fair market value*. For example, accountants generally record items at historical cost and do not change that number unless the item has clearly lost value. Rarely would an accountant increase the value. Hence, *book value* is generally much lower than *fair market value*.

Lawyers need to pay special heed to *book value*. While *Financial Statements* are an important tool, they are not easily interpreted by non-accountants. Lawyers should not take numbers on *Financial Statements* literally without understanding the context of the numbers, the methods of accounting used, and the various assumptions made, as well as the *auditor's opinion*.

49. **Bretton-Woods:** In 1944, 44 allied nations met at the Mount Washington Hotel in Bretton-Woods, New Hampshire. They signed a monetary and economic agreement which eventually established the *International Monetary Fund* (*IMF*) and the *World Bank*. The agreement pegged the price of gold at $35 per ounce. The United States took itself off the gold standard in 1971, which resulted in undermining much of the *Bretton-Woods* agreement. Since that date, the U.S. dollar has effectively been the world's reserve currency and other currencies have floated exchange rates in relation to the dollar.

50. **Brokerage Accounts:** Brokerage investment accounts have three basic formats:

   - **Cash Management.** For this account, the customer deposits cash or securities. The broker-dealer executes trades as directed by the customer. The broker, however, exercises no discretion over the account; hence, he or she has a substantially lower duty owed to the investor than in relation to a discretionary account.

   - **Margin.** For this account, the customer may borrow funds (generally not more than 50% of the value) from the broker-dealer.

   - **Discretionary.** For this account, the customer grants authority to the investment advisor to execute trades on his behalf.

   See: http://www.sec.gov/answers/openaccount.htm.

51. **Broker/dealer:** Generally, a broker executes trades for a customer. A dealer executes trades on his or its own behalf.

   The *SEC* regulates brokers and dealers under the Exchange Act and requires them to register. According to the *SEC*:

   Section 3(a)(4)(A) of the Act generally defines a "broker" broadly as

   any person engaged in the business of effecting transactions in securities for the account of others.

   Sometimes you can easily determine if someone is a broker. For instance, a person who executes transactions for others on a securities exchange clearly is a broker. However, other situations are less clear. For example, each of the following individuals and businesses may need to register as a broker, depending on a number of factors:

- "finders," "business brokers," and other individuals or entities that engage in the following activities . . .

- investment advisers and financial consultants;

- . . .

- persons that operate or control electronic or other platforms to trade securities;

- persons that market real-estate investment interests, such as tenancy-in-common interests, that are securities;

- persons that act as "placement agents" for private placements of securities;

- persons that market or effect transactions in insurance products that are securities, such as variable annuities, or other investment products that are securities;

- persons that effect securities transactions for the account of others for a fee, even when those other people are friends or family members;

- persons that provide support services to registered broker-dealers; and . . .

https://www.sec.gov/reportspubs/investor-publications/divisions marketregbdguidehtm.html#II.

52. **Bridge Loan:** This is a temporary loan intended to "bridge" between two other loans—perhaps a construction period loan and more permanent financing.

53. **Bull Market:** This is a colloquial description of a period during which various stock market indexes are higher than during the immediately prior period. Generally, a *Bull Market* exists when an index is up 10% or more from his previous low. In contrast, a *Bear Market* is one in which stock indexes are generally lower and falling. To be bearish or a bear is to believe stocks will fall. In contrast, to be *bullish* or a *bull* is to believe stocks will rise.

54. **By-Pass Trust:** This is a United States *Estate Planning* tool used to minimize estate taxes. Typically, it involves joint planning by a husband and wife. Each leaves substantial assets to a trust which can benefit the survivor during the survivor's life, but which leaves the principal to others (often children at the survivor's death). The corpus

of the trust should maximize the *Unified Credit* to reduce or eliminate estate taxes.

55. **Calendar Year:** A year ending on December 31st. *Income Statements* are periodic (as opposed to *Balance Sheets* which focus as a snapshot of one point in time) and thus focus on operations over a defined period. Because the earth revolves around the Sun in a period we call a year, humans have customarily reported operations, life events, and many activities based on an annual calendar. The same is true of finance and accounting. This, naturally, requires a beginning point and an ending point. For most individuals (humans), the calendar year is ideal—beginning on January 1 and ending on December 31. For non-human persons, *fiscal years* are often useful—particularly for cyclical business which have lots of operations for part of the year and little for others. In such cases, a fiscal year ending during the slow season is sensible; indeed, splitting a normal business cycle between two years could be misleading. For example, many retail businesses have their dominant sales period between the U.S. Thanksgiving (the fourth Thursday of November) through Christmas, and then after-New Year's sales. Because such a business cycle fits together, the use of a *Calendar Year* for financial reporting would split the year in ways that generate distortions. Last year's after New Year's sales would join with this year's before Christmas sales, generating less than optimal information. A *fiscal year* ending in February or March would make more sense in terms of presenting annual operations.

Thus, lawyers should realize: every person must have an annual reporting period because of custom. The *Calendar Year* makes sense in most cases, but can be distorting in others. But, lawyers should heed the discussion in relation to the definition of a *Fiscal Year (FY)*—because the option of having multiple entities with differing years presents opportunities for manipulation of financial information.

56. **Callable:** This refers to a common feature of an obligation: one party—or both—can *call* the obligation due. If the obligor has this power, it has the right to pay off the obligation—such as a *bond*—early. Investors should be aware of whether *bonds* and other investments are *callable*. If indeed they are, then they cannot rely on earning the interest rate prevailing at purchase should general market rates decline. In such a case, the issuer might *call* the obligation, pay it off, and then issue new obligations at a lower fixed rate. Often, people refer to this as the "call risk" of the instrument. The *bond indenture* will describe the call rights, if any. They may be restricted to certain dates, periods, or circumstances.

If the lender has this power, it can *call* the obligation due and thus insist on current rather than deferred payment. From the lender's standpoint, this makes the obligation a *demand loan*. Contractually, the power may be conditional. For example, a lender may retain a *call option* triggered by the borrower's *insolvency* or some other defined economic condition. Contracts frequently have call provisions triggered by defined financial circumstances, such as an entity's *current ratio* falling below 1.5 or its *acid-test ratio* falling below 0.75.

57. **Call Option:** This refers to a contractual right to force another to sell something or to pay some amount otherwise owed in the future. For example, if A owns a *call option* on stock in XYZ Corp., issued by B with a call price of $50, A can force B to sell him the stock for $50. A will have paid for this option. He will exercise it if the price of XYZ exceeds $50 at the time the option is exercisable.

Call options—as well as *put options*—are often traded on public exchanges.

Options have three flavors:

- At the Money: the right to purchase the item at the current market price. This option has no current value other than that equal to fixing the price, i.e., the opportunity to gain without the opportunity of loss.

- In the Money: the right to purchase the item for a price below the current market price. This option has a measurable value separate from the opportunity for gain.

- Out of the Money: the right to purchase the item for a price greater than the current market price. This option has no value other than the gain opportunity minus the required price increase.

58. **Carry-Over Basis:** This is a tax term with no significant financial accounting meaning. Generally, it refers to a tax basis in property carried over to another at the time of death. A similar term—*transfer basis*—generally refers to the transfer of a tax basis in property to the recipient of a gift. *IRC* section 1014 generally provides for a transfer basis for gifts, as does *IRC* section 1041 for transactions between spouses or incident to divorce.

The concept of a *Carry-over Basis* appeared briefly in the *Internal Revenue Code* in section 1023. Enacted in 1976, the provision was repealed in 1977 because of its alleged complexity.

Currently, the United States uses a *Stepped-up Basis* for most property received from a decedent. While very popular with many taxpayers, this provision—*IRC* section 1015—substantially distorts economic decisions by many property owners.

59. **Capital:** This term has many meanings:

In finance it may mean:

- *Equity.*

- *Debt* plus *equity* to equal *total capital investment.* A common phrase refers to the cost of capital. This would compare common stock (which requires price support through the maintenance of an adequate rate of return on *equity* and dividends which are not deductible for tax purposes), *preferred stock* (which requires dividends which are not deductible for tax purposes) with debt (which pays interest which is deductible for tax purposes).

- Fixed assets and producing assets such as plant, land, and equipment, as opposed to inventory and consumables.

Many people also refer to *human capital*—referring to an entity's trained labor force—or *intellectual capital*, which might refer to highly trained persons or intellectual property.

A capital intensive industry is one which requires large investment in fixed assets for production. In contrast, a *labor intensive industry* may require little *capital* but a large labor force.

In tax law, one might refer to *capital income* as opposed to *ordinary income*. This would be short-hand for *capital gain* income.

In other areas of the law, one might refer to *capital income* as opposed to income from labor and industry. Such a reference would include passive investment income such as interest, dividends, and *capital gains*. This usage is vague; hence, lawyers should avoid it without a more complete definition.

60. **Capital Asset:** *For tax purposes*, this is a United States tax term of art. *IRC* section 1221 defines it as including all property <u>other than</u> items on an *exclusive* list. Section 1221 lists:

(1) stock in trade of the taxpayer or other property of a kind which would properly be included in the inventory of the taxpayer if on hand at the close of the taxable year, or property held by the taxpayer primarily for sale to customers in the ordinary course of his trade or business;

(2) property, used in his trade or business, of a character which is subject to the allowance for depreciation provided in section 167, or real property used in his trade or business;

(3) a copyright, a literary, musical, or artistic composition, a letter or memorandum, or similar property, held by—

   (A) a taxpayer whose personal efforts created such property,

   (B) in the case of a letter, memorandum, or similar property, a taxpayer for whom such property was prepared or produced, or

   (C) a taxpayer in whose hands the basis of such property is determined, for purposes of determining gain from a sale or exchange, in whole or part by reference to the basis of such property in the hands of a taxpayer described in subparagraph (A) or (B);

(4) accounts or notes receivable acquired in the ordinary course of trade or business for services rendered or from the sale of property described in paragraph (1);

(5) a publication of the United States Government (including the Congressional Record) which is received from the United States Government or any agency thereof, other than by purchase at the price at which it is offered for sale to the public, and which is held by—

   (A) a taxpayer who so received such publication, or

   (B) a taxpayer in whose hands the basis of such publication is determined, for purposes of determining gain from a sale or exchange, in whole or in part by reference to the basis of such publication in the hands of a taxpayer described in subparagraph (A);

(6) any commodities derivative financial instrument held by a commodities derivatives dealer, unless—

   (A) it is established to the satisfaction of the Secretary that such instrument has no connection to the activities of such dealer as a dealer, and

   (B) such instrument is clearly identified in such dealer's records as being described in subparagraph (A) before the close of the day on which it was acquired, originated, or entered into (or such other time as the Secretary may by regulations prescribe);

(7) any hedging transaction which is clearly identified as such before the close of the day on which it was acquired, originated, or entered into (or such other time as the Secretary may by regulations prescribe); or

(8) supplies of a type regularly used or consumed by the taxpayer in the ordinary course of a trade or business of the taxpayer.

Much litigation involves the category one phrase: *property held primarily for sale to customers in the ordinary course of a trade or business*. Such items often involve investment property which a person held as a capital asset but which the owner later converted to *inventory*. The change in tax rate can be very significant.

For United States (and many other jurisdictions) *tax purposes*, long-term capital gains result in a materially lower tax rate than do short-term gains or ordinary income. *Capital gains* result from the sale or exchange of a capital asset. The long versus short distinction has traditionally been at one year; however, it has been as short as six months and also longer.

IRC section 1221(2)—generally depreciable property—forms a category in between capital assets and ordinary assets, which generate ordinary income and losses. Those are *IRC* section 1231 assets, which very generally produce capital gains and ordinary losses—the best of both types.

For family law purposes, generally most states keep separate property brought into a marriage as separate. Many, however, consider such property converted to marital or community property status—either in whole or in part—to the extent marital labor and industry significantly impacts its value. The process of developing property—such as a tract of land—and thus converting it from a capital asset to *property held primarily for sale to customers in the ordinary course of a trade or business* is related to the *family law* status change. Indeed, the two separate legal consequences largely overlap: to the extent a person converts property for tax purposes, he likely also converts some or all of it for marital purposes. Of note, the tax consequences may result in an extra 20% of the value going to pay taxes. But, in contrast, the family law consequences may result in an extra 50% of the value going to the other spouse for property division, plus up to 10% going to child support and another significant percentage going to the other spouse for alimony. Hence, the classification of an asset as capital or not is very important for tax purposes; however, it is potentially profoundly important for family law purposes.

Similarly, *trust law* may be significantly impacted by an asset's classification. For the most part, capital gains and losses should belong to the principal beneficiary; however, ordinary gains and losses—such as those resulting from inventory or *property held primarily for sale to customers in the ordinary course of a trade or business*—should belong to the income beneficiary.

Another fuzzy distinction between capital gains and ordinary income involves *Retained Earnings*. Earning belong to the common shareholders. If distributed, they result in dividends. For tax purposes those are taxable to the extent of earnings and profits. For other legal purposes, dividends are almost always—if not always—income. Whether they constitute income from labor and industry—and thus marital assets in most states even if derived from separate property— depends on the degree of management, a question of fact. But, undistributed *Retained Earnings* economically result in share appreciation. This, in turn, results in capital appreciation or capital gains if the owner disposes of the shares. But, many jurisdictions consider such capital appreciation in separate property to retain its character as separate property, regardless of the degree of management. This is widely true for C corporate investors and also commonly true of S corporate investors. *See, e.g., Zold v. Zold*, 911 So. 2d 1222 (Fla. 2005).

For accounting purposes, one might use the term capital assets to distinguish them from inventory, supplies, and variously consumable assets. Such usage is not incorrect; however, it risks confusion with the important tax law terminology.

61. **Capital Gain:** *For tax purposes*, *IRC* section 1222 defines a capital gain as gain resulting from the *sale or exchange* of a capital asset. *Long term* gain—generally entitled to preferential tax treatment—flows from assets held more than one year. The *sale or exchange* treatment is essential for capital gain or loss treatment. Some code sections *impute* a sale or exchange for transaction which would not otherwise satisfy the definition of that phrase (which is not well-defined). Over the history of the Internal Revenue Code, the treatment of capital gains has varied. Often long-term (variously defined, but often a function of a holding period of more than one year) gains have triggered a substantially lower tax rate than ordinary income.

For family law and trust purposes, lawyers must play close attention to the character of gains and losses. While ordinary—non *capital*— gains and losses likely are marital (in the family law realm) and income (in the income versus principal beneficiary realm), the treatment of capital gains and losses is less clear. In family law, such gains on separate property may remain separate (depending on the jurisdiction and the level of management). For trust law, such gains typically belong to the principal beneficiary.

62. **Capital Lease:** For accounting purposes, both under U.S. *GAAP* and IFRS, a capital lease (also known as a finance lease) receives treatment as ownership. Thus the nominal lessee must record the property as an asset and must record all associated liabilities for the

balance sheet. Also, the substantive owner recognizes related expenses such as depreciation.

IAS17 and ASU2016–02 deal with this. One should compare capital leases to IRC section 461(h), to sale-leaseback and gift-leaseback transactions, as well as the substance over form and economic substance doctrines.. Also, one should distinguish a capital lease from an operating lease.

63. **Capital Loss:** *For tax purposes*, IRC section 1222 defines a capital loss as loss resulting from the *sale or exchange* of a capital asset. *Long term loss*—generally entitled to detrimental tax treatment—flows from assets held more than one year. The *sale or exchange* treatment is essential for capital gain or loss treatment. *IRC* sections 1211 and 1212 deal with capital loss limitations and carryovers.

A capital loss carryover—which exists for the remainder of the holder's life—can be a valuable asset. While that statement may appear counter-intuitive, it is not. The loss carryover represents a loss which already occurred, but which has not yet appeared on a tax return because of limitations. It thus is a positive tax attribute which may result in positive tax benefits in the future. It is thus a valuable asset.

One of the more difficult oddities for non-tax law experts to understand is:

> *Losses, including built-in losses, are attributes.*
> *Gains, including built-in gains, are detriments.*

Of course, one does not want to lose money and one wants to gain money. Hence, overall, losses are bad and profits are good. However, if I get the money and you get the tax consequences, losses are good and profits are bad. Lawyers need to understand:

> *Tax consequences and the money related to those*
> *consequences do not necessarily flow together.*

To the extent they do not, much room for manipulation or advantage (and disadvantage) exists. The horribly complex rules involving partnership taxation provide enormous room for separating income, gains, deductions, losses, and credits from the money or assets associated with them. See *IRC* section 704(b). While treasury regulations defining whether special allocations of such items have substantial economic effect sharply limit the ability of persons to allocate them for tax purposes, they say nothing about the ability of persons to allocate them for non-tax legal purposes, if only for the short-term. Lawyers unfamiliar with the intricacies of partnership allocations risk respecting them in non-tax legal areas without understanding the likely future tax implications, which may be years away—outside the time period being considered in the non-tax legal matter.

64. **Capitalization of Earnings:** This is a common method of valuing a business. It is quite similar to a *DCF* (Discounted Cash Flow) analysis.

The formula is:

$$FMV = \frac{projected\ future\ earnings}{discount\ rate}$$

Projected Future Earnings are typically a function of past earnings; although, information regarding new products or activities could involve non-historically based earnings. For many legal purposes, however—such as torts and family law—most jurisdictions will likely limit projected earnings to those which have an historical basis.

The discount rate includes an evaluation of the interest rate risk the investor is willing to accept, adjusted for projected earnings increases and inflation or deflation.

An alternate way of computing the FMV is to multiply the expected earnings by a factor, which is the inverse of the discount rate. For example, if the appropriate discount rate is 20% or 1/5, then the multiplier would be 5.

In a simple example, an appraiser would first determine average net earnings during a base period—perhaps the prior three years. He would then multiply that number by 5 (or whatever the inverse of the appropriate discount rate happened to be) to obtain the current business value. Hence, if a business had average net earnings of $100,000, it would (using 5 as the multiplier) have a fair market value of $500,000.

For publicly traded companies, P/E ratios (price to earnings ratios) are often in the 12 to 20 range (though they can certainly be as low as 4 or 5 and as high as 100). For smaller, more closely held companies, however, an earnings multiplier of 12 to 20 would historically be excessive.

65. **Capitalization of Interest:** For finance purposes, the process of *capitalizing interest* involves adding it to principal. This is also known as *negative amortization*. It occurs because periodic payments on a loan are less than the periodic interest accrued.

For tax purposes, it can have the same meaning as it does for finance, but it also has a separate meaning. It refers to the process of adding construction period interest to the basis (cost) of a project. Under this definition, the process of capitalization is distinguishable from the process of expensing or deducting an item or cost.

66. **Capitalize:** For both tax law and accounting purposes, "to capitalize" an expenditure means to add it to an asset account. For example, if expenditure is for an asset or service with a life greater than one year—and if it is material—one would typically add the cost to an asset account via a debit. The corresponding credit would be to cash or a liability. The resulting asset would be "amortized" over its useful life (typically straight-line) or "depreciated" over its useful life. Capitalization furthers the **Matching Principal of Accounting** by ensuring costs properly match with the income they produce. One would "expense" short-term or immaterial expenditures.

67. **Carrying Charges: Cost of Carry:** Holding an asset costs money—directly in terms of storage and insurance, as well as indirectly in terms of opportunity costs. When computing the rate of return on investments in physical assets—such as precious metals—one should include the cost of carry.

68. **Cash:** Generally this refers to currency, coin, and demand deposits (mostly checking accounts). The term mostly has meaning in relation to a *payment*. Whether the use of a credit card as *payment* is considered a "cash payment" is up to the parties. Lawyers should be careful in using the term *cash* in a contract: they should define the meaning, as it is _not_ a term of art.

69. **Cash Flows:** For *financial calculation* purposes, the term *"cash flows"* refers to the direction of *payments*. For example, cash may flow from A to B as a loan and then back from B to A as a *payment* to amortize the loan. For some *financial calculators*, one of these *cash flows* must be a positive number and the other a negative number; indeed, the mathematical formula for computing the loan amortization requires that opposite direction *cash flows* have opposite signs (positive versus negative). *Financial Calculators* manufactured by HEWLETT-PACKARD® typically have this feature. Many *financial calculators*, however, have built-in computer software which eliminates the need for the user to state the various opposing flows with opposite signs.

If two *cash flows* occur simultaneously, _all_ *financial calculators* will collapse them into a single net flow. Hence, mathematically, the *pre-payment* of interest is impossible, as it would be simultaneous with the borrowing of *principal* (or at least with the obligation to continue to owe *principal*). The interest and the *principal* necessarily would have opposite signs as they are opposing *cash flows*. Thus they necessarily collapse and the attempted pre-payment of interest becomes a *principal* payment—or more simply, a lessening of the amount loaned.

Despite the economic and financial impossibility of *pre-paid interest*, tax law oddly contemplates such an event. See *IRC* section 461(g):

(g) Prepaid interest

(1) In general

If the taxable income of the taxpayer is computed under the cash receipts and disbursements method of accounting, interest paid by the taxpayer which, under regulations prescribed by the Secretary, is properly allocable to any period—

(A) with respect to which the interest represents a charge for the use or forbearance of money, and

(B) which is after the close of the taxable year in which paid,

shall be charged to capital account and shall be treated as paid in the period to which so allocable.

(2) Exception

This subsection shall not apply to points paid in respect of any indebtedness incurred in connection with the purchase or improvement of, and secured by, the principal residence of the taxpayer to the extent that, under regulations prescribed by the Secretary, such payment of points is an established business practice in the area in which such indebtedness is incurred, and the amount of such payment does not exceed the amount generally charged in such area.

See the discussion of *pre-payments* for more information.

One of the three main *Financial Statements* is the *Statement of Cash Flows*.

70. **Cash Method:** This is a commonly used *Method of Accounting*. *GAAP* does not recognize it, as it does not normally clearly reflect income.

Under the *Cash Method*, a person has income when he receives *payment* for the item. He has a deduction when he *pays* an item. Naturally, those definitions are a function of the definition of the term *payment*, which is often imprecise. A significant issue in U.S. tax law concerns the definition of the term payment. The litigation centers on three important, controversial issues:

• How does a *payment* differ from a mere *deposit*?

• May one pay an amount using borrowed money?

• If one uses money borrowed from the creditor, can one pay the creditor?

Most United States taxpayers may use the *Cash Method* for reporting income and deductions—as opposed to the *Accrual Method*, or a hybrid method. See *IRC* section 446. As a result, for many people, tax return information does <u>not</u> clearly reflect income; hence, lawyers should be wary of federal tax return numbers.

Use of the *Cash Method* is common because of its simplicity. A basic check book register use the cash method: one does not record deposits until one deposits the money and one does not record checks until one writes the check. Most people can use the method with a high level of accuracy (to the extent the method is accurate). If a tax system required everyone to use the *Accrual Method*, the result would likely be hugely complex.

71. **C Corporation:** A corporation subject to Subchapter C of Subtitle A of the Internal Revenue Code of the United States. C Corporations are themselves taxpayers. They pay taxes on income generally at a rate of 34%. Dividends and Distributions from them are not deductible; however, taxpayers who receive dividends are subject to preferential treatment. Nevertheless, *C Corporation* income is subject to double taxation in the U.S.: once at the corporate level and once at the shareholder level. This is as opposed to income of an *S Corporation*, which is a *pass-through entity*.

As a general rule, large corporations and widely-held (generally publicly traded) corporations are C's. Most other corporations elect *S* status or they are LLCs (limited liability companies).

72. **Charting: Chartist:** Some investors pay close attention to the graphic images presented by investment price changes. A chartist is a trader/investor who concentrates on chart theory. Under chart theory, prices form common (sometimes very complex) patterns. A common example involves a consistent floor or ceiling: the graphed price keeps reaching a particular level, followed by a rise or drop. That level is a ceiling or floor. If the price ever breaks through that level, it tends to keep going until it reaches another floor or ceiling. Often, even numbers simplistically become floors and ceilings, *e.g.*, $100, or $75, or $25.

73. **Chicago Mercantile Exchange: CME:** Now part of the CME Group, a publicly traded company, the *Chicago Mercantile Exchange* has existed since 1898. Originally it primarily traded or facilitated trades of commodities, such as metals and grains. It now also trades currencies, as well as futures, options, and derivatives.

74. **Churning:** In a discretionary account, the investment manager may be tempted to trade excessively so at to increase commissions for himself. This is an inherent conflict of interest with the owner/investor.

75. **Circuit Breaker:** This is a system for halting trading in particular securities—or for an entire market—upon the occurrence of defined events. Triggers include substantial price drops, which might cause a trading halt for a short period, or, in some cases, a much longer period. The intention is to prevent or to slow down panic and rumors and to create a "cooling off" time for investors and traders.

76. **Certificate of Deposit: CD:** A *CD* is a time deposit with a financial institution. They often have terms as short as 90 days or up to five years. Longer term *CDs* generally bear higher interest rates. The *FDIC* insures bank *CDs*. Interest may accumulate or it may be paid to the holder. Typically, a penalty applies for early withdrawal of funds.

77. **Certified Financial Planner: CFP®:** According to the Certified Financial Planner Board of Standards, Inc.:

> CFP® certificants must pass the comprehensive CFP® Certification Examination, pass CFP Board's *Candidate Fitness Standards*, agree to abide by CFP Board's *Code of Ethics and Professional Responsibility* which puts clients' interests first and comply with the *Financial Planning Practice Standards* which spell out what clients should be able to reasonably expect from the financial planning engagement. These are just some of the reasons why the CFP® certification is becoming increasingly recognized.

Since 1993, to become a *CFP®*, one must pass the *CFP®* exam which lasts about 10 hours. This is not a state issued license; however, the designation carries some evidence of expertise.

78. **Certified Forensic Accountant: Cr. FA®:** This is a designation sought by some *Forensic Accountants*. It is not a state license. See the discussion of *Forensic Accountant* and *Forensic Economist* for more information.

79. **Certified Fraud Examiner: *CFE*:** This is a designation sought by some *Forensic Accountants*. It is not a state license. See the discussion of *Forensic Accountant* and *Forensic Economist* for more information.

80. **Certified Internal Auditor®: CIA®:** According to the Institute of Internal Auditors:

> The Certified Internal Auditor® (CIA®) designation is the only globally accepted certification for internal auditors and remains the standard by which individuals demonstrate their competency and professionalism in the internal auditing field. Candidates leave the program enriched with educational experience, information, and business tools that

can be applied immediately in any organization or business environment.

http://www.theiia.org/certification/certified-internal-auditor/.

81. **Certified Public Accountant: CPA:** To use the designation *CPA* or (in most states) public accountant, one must have passed the *Uniform Certified Public Accountant Examination*. One must also satisfy state imposed education and continuing education requirements to earn a *license* to practice public accounting.

Certified Public Accountants may express an opinion on audited financial statements.

An Independent *CPA* is one who is not employed by the client. He expresses an independent opinion on financial statements prepared by management. His duties are to the public, investors, and creditors, rather to the client who seeks his opinion. In most states, conversations between a client and a CPA are *not* subject to an evidentiary privilege.

The first-time pass rate on the *CPA* exam is historically low— sometimes in the single digits and often less than 25%. Many states require 150 credits hours of study (essentially a Master's Degree) as well as substantial work-experience before one can obtain a license as a *CPA*. *In some states*, being certified is separate from being licensed: all licensees must have a *Certificate*, but some persons with a *CPA* Certificate do not have a license or have an inactive license. Although CPAs cannot generally handle litigation, they are allowed to represent taxpayers before the United States Tax Court.

Contrary to popular wisdom, *CPAs* often have little special expertise in tax law. While most—if not all—accounting schools offer courses in tax law and tax return preparation, they are not the equivalent of a law degree or an LL.M. in tax law. While many *CPAs* are knowledgeable about many aspects of tax law, they are not lawyers (unless they also have a law degree or Bar membership). CPAs, however, may enroll to practice before the *IRS* and may appear before the Tax Court.

CPAs, as well as attorneys who are *CPAs*, may properly identify themselves with the designation *PFS* or *CFP*, if they have earned the designation. *See Ibanez v. Florida*, 512 U.S. 136 (1994) [majority approving the use of *CPA, CFA* designation by an attorney in advertising over the objection of the regulatory bodies for *CPAs* in Florida].

In most other countries, a licensed accountant is called a Chartered Accountant or something similar. The designation varies significant but "chartered" and "accountant" are often part of the terminology.

82. **Certified Security:** this is a security for which the issuer has issued a certificate—such as for a stock or bond. Uncertified security have no certificate, but are instead merely noted on the issuer's or transfer agent's records. The UCC refers to certificated securities and uncertificated securities.

83. **Charity:** This is _not_ a term of art. Generally, the term refers to an organization exempt from United States income tax under _IRC_ section 501(c)(3). Contributions to such organizations are generally deductible by the donor for income tax purposes under _IRC_ section 170(c)(2). In this sense, the term _Charity_ includes organizations benefiting the arts, religion, the under-privileged, education, public safety, and many other endeavors not traditionally considered "charitable."

    The term is _not_ synonymous with the term _non-profit organization_. Nothing in _IRC_ section 501(c)(3) requires an approved entity to be _non-profit;_ indeed, many charities make substantial profits (of course, depending on how one defines the term _profits_). Many state corporation statutes have provisions for Non-profit Corporations (or Not-for-profit Corporations); however, seldom (if ever) do such acts forbid profits, at least as one might typically define that term.

    The term _Charity_ is also not synonymous with _Tax Exempt Organization (TEO)_, a United States tax term of art (and also a term or art in many countries). _IRC_ section 501(c) lists more than two dozen ways an entity can be exempt from United States income tax; however, only those described in paragraph 501(c)(3) fit the common usage for the term _Charity_.

    Two sub-categories of charities exist in the United States:
    - Public Charities, which are subject to few federal tax law restrictions.
    - Private Foundations, which are subject to extensive federal tax law restrictions.

    The _Private Foundation_ category has several sub-categories, as well.

84. **Check:** A _check_ is a kind of _draft_, drawn on a financial institution account. It is a directive to the institution to pay a stated amount of money to the order of a person or the bearer. The "to the order of" language is critical and is part of what makes a check a negotiable instrument under the Uniform Commercial Code. Not all _drafts_ are _checks_, but all _checks_ are _drafts_. See the definition of _Negotiable Instrument_ for more information.

    In some countries—particularly the U.K.—the spelling is _cheque_. In many countries—particularly in Europe—_checks_ are largely a thing of the past, having been replaced by _ATM_s, electronic transfers or _giros_.

In the United States, on-line banking, *ATMs*, direct deposits, and direct debits have substantially reduced the usage of paper *checks*.

For tax purposes, the transfer of a *check* has the same effect as the transfer of cash: it reflects payment and receipt. This rule is subject to the *check* not being dishonored. *E.g., Kahler v. Commissioner*, 18 T.C. 31 (1952).

85. **Closing Costs:** These are costs, other than interest, associated with a loan. They include an application fee, an appraisal fee, a notary fee, a title insurance premium, and a private mortgage insurance fee. They often amount to one to three percent of the amount loaned. They may include *points*—which are a separate charge denominated as *pre-paid interest. Points* and some other closing costs receive interest treatment under federal law. As such, they form part of the *Annual Percentage Rate* (*APR*) disclosed in relation to the loan.

86. **Charitable Lead Trust:** *CLT*: This is a tax term of art. Generally, such trusts fit into two types:

- **CLAT: Charitable Lead Annuity Trust:** This must pay a fixed dollar amount at least annually to a charitable beneficiary. It then pays the remainder to the grantor. This would be a *Qualified Grantor Charitable Lead Annuity Trust* (*QGCLAT*). *IRC* section 170(f)(2)(B) provides:

  (B) Income interests, etc.

  No deduction shall be allowed under this section for the value of any interest in property (other than a remainder interest) transferred in trust unless the interest is in the form of a guaranteed annuity or the trust instrument specifies that the interest is a fixed percentage distributed yearly of the fair market value of the trust property (to be determined yearly) and the grantor is treated as the owner of such interest for purposes of applying section 671. If the donor ceases to be treated as the owner of such an interest for purposes of applying section 671, at the time the donor ceases to be so treated, the donor shall for purposes of this chapter be considered as having received an amount of income equal to the amount of any deduction he received under this section for the contribution reduced by the discounted value of all amounts of income earned by the trust and taxable to him before the time at which he ceases to be treated as the owner of the interest. Such amounts of income shall be discounted to the date of the contribution. The Secretary shall prescribe such regulations as may be necessary to carry out the purposes of this subparagraph.

- *CLUT*: **Charitable Lead Unitrust:** This must pay a fixed percentage of trust FMV at least annually to a charitable beneficiary. It then pays the remainder to the grantor. This would be a *Qualified Grantor Charitable Lead Unitrust (QGCLUT)*.

Under *IRC* section 170(a), the grantor receives a charitable contribution deduction (subject to section 170(f) limitations) for the **PRESENT VALUE OF AN ANNUITY**: the income interest benefitting a *Charity* (or some other permitted beneficiaries described in *IRC* section 170(c)). The term for this non-fixed annuity would be the life expectancy of the grantor.

The grantor, however, must *include* the trust income annually. Some people may view that as a disadvantage: the grantor will have annual income, but no receipts. An evaluation of whether such a trust is beneficial would compare the *after-tax* **PRESENT VALUE OF A SUM**: the current income tax deduction to the *after-tax* **PRESENT VALUE OF AN ANNUITY**: the annual income inclusion minus the *after-tax* **PRESENT VALUE OF AN ANNUITY**: the annual deductible charitable contribution of the income amounts. Important factors in the analysis include:

- The donor's expectation that he will live less than his life expectancy as determined by relevant actuarial tables.

- The donor's expectation of decreasing tax rates in general, or for him individually.

Charitable Lead Trusts may also be *non-grantor* trusts, which, in turn, may either be *qualified* or *non-qualified*. See the discussion of *Grantor Trusts* for a more complete explanation.

- A *Qualified Non-Grantor CLT* may fit either the *annuity trust* or the *unitrust* formula. Hence, they would be either a *QNGCLAT* or a *QNGCLUT*. Such a trust does not generate a charitable contribution deduction for the grantor; however, the trust may deduct the annual charitable contributions. Also, the donor will receive a partial gift tax deduction. Because the charitable deductions belong to the trust rather than to the grantor, they avoid the percentage limitations of *IRC* section 170(b). Also, because the trust is not itself a charity under *IRC* section 501(c)(3), it avoids *Private Foundation* status.

- A *Non-Qualified Non-Grantor CLT* need not fit either the annuity trust or the unitrust formula; hence, it may pay a percentage of trust income to charity. One may describe such entities as *NQNGCLT*. The trust will annually deduct charitable contributions; hence, the grantor avoids the section 170(b) percentage limitations. Also, *IRC* section 642(c) permits contributions to foreign charities, while *IRC* section 170(c) limits them; hence, the grantor also avoids those restrictions.

87. **Charitable Remainder Trust:** *CRT*: This is a tax term of art. Generally, such trusts fit into two types:

- **CRAT: Charitable Remainder Annuity Trust:** This must pay a fixed dollar amount at least annually to the income beneficiary. It then pays the remainder to a *Charity*. *IRC* section 664(d) provides:

    (1) Charitable remainder annuity trust

    For purposes of this section, a charitable remainder annuity trust is a trust—

    (A) from which a sum certain (which is not less than 5 percent nor more than 50 percent of the initial net fair market value of all property placed in trust) is to be paid, not less often than annually, to one or more persons (at least one of which is not an organization described in section 170(c) and, in the case of individuals, only to an individual who is living at the time of the creation of the trust) for a term of years (not in excess of 20 years) or for the life or lives of such individual or individuals,

    (B) from which no amount other than the payments described in subparagraph (A) and other than qualified gratuitous transfers described in subparagraph (C) may be paid to or for the use of any person other than an organization described in section 170(c),

    (C) following the termination of the payments described in subparagraph (A), the remainder interest in the trust is to be transferred to, or for the use of, an organization described in section 170(c) or is to be retained by the trust for such a use or, to the extent the remainder interest is in qualified employer securities (as defined in subsection (g)(4)), all or part of such securities are to be transferred to an employee stock ownership plan (as defined in section 4975(e)(7) in a qualified gratuitous transfer (as defined by subsection (g)), and

(D) the value (determined under section 7520 of such remainder interest is at least 10 percent of the initial net fair market value of all property placed in the trust.

- **CRUT: Charitable Remainder Unitrust:** This must pay a fixed percentage amount at least annually to the income beneficiary. It then pays the remainder to a *Charity*. *IRC* section 664(d) provides:

(2) Charitable remainder unitrust

For purposes of this section, a charitable remainder unitrust is a trust—

(A) from which a fixed percentage (which is not less than 5 percent nor more than 50 percent) of the net fair market value of its assets, valued annually, is to be paid, not less often than annually, to one or more persons (at least one of which is not an organization described in section 170(c) and, in the case of individuals, only to an individual who is living at the time of the creation of the trust) for a term of years (not in excess of 20 years) or for the life or lives of such individual or individuals,

(B) from which no amount other than the payments described in subparagraph (A) and other than qualified gratuitous transfers described in subparagraph (C) may be paid to or for the use of any person other than an organization described in section 170(c),

(C) following the termination of the payments described in subparagraph (A), the remainder interest in the trust is to be transferred to, or for the use of, an organization described in section 170(c) or is to be retained by the trust for such a use or, to the extent the remainder interest is in qualified employer securities (as defined in subsection (g)(4)), all or part of such securities are to be transferred to an employee stock ownership plan (as defined in section 4975(e)(7) in a qualified gratuitous transfer (as defined by subsection (g)), and

(D) with respect to each contribution of property to the trust, the value (determined under section 7520 of such remainder interest in such property is at least 10 percent of the net fair market value of such property as of the date such property is contributed to the trust.

Under *IRC* section 170(a), the grantor receives a charitable contribution deduction (subject to section 170(f) limitations) for the **PRESENT VALUE** of the remainder interest benefitting a *Charity* (or some other permitted beneficiaries described in *IRC* section 170(c)). The term for the **PRESENT VALUE OF A SUM** computation would be the life expectancy of the income beneficiary.

88. **Chartered Financial Analyst: CFA:** This is a designation granted by the *CFA* Institute. It is _not_ a state license. According to the Institute:

> To earn the CFA charter, you must successfully pass through the CFA Program, a graduate-level self-study program that combines a broad curriculum with professional conduct requirements, culminating in a series of three sequential exams. Level I exams are held in June and December. Levels II and III are only held in June.

The designation *CFA* is multi-national. The Institute and its predecessors have granted it since 1963. The three required examinations total 18 hours.

89. **Chartered Life Underwriter: CLU®:** This is a designation granted by the *American College*. It is _not_ a state license. According to the College:

> The Chartered Life Underwriter (CLU®) is the world's most respected designation of insurance expertise, helping you gain a significant advantage in a competitive market. This prestigious course of study helps advance your career by providing in-depth knowledge on the insurance needs of individuals, business owners, and professional clients.

http://www.theamericancollege.edu.

90. **Chief Executive Officer: CEO:** This is the head of a corporation or group of related corporations. He may also serve with the title of President.

91. **Chief Financial Officer: CFO:** This is the person in charge of a corporation's financial operations. He would oversee bookkeeping, records, internal and external audits, and the management of investments and working capital.

92. **Class Life:** This is a tax law term of art (with often modified statutory definitions) without a clear statutory definition. *IRC* section 168(i) provides:

> (i) Definitions and special rules
>
> For purposes of this section—
>
>> (1) Class Life
>>
>> Except as provided in this section, the term "class life" means the class life (if any) which would be applicable with respect to any property as of January 1, 1986, under subsection (m) of section 167 (determined without regard to paragraph (4) and as if the taxpayer had made an election under such subsection). The Secretary, through an office established in the Treasury, shall monitor and analyze actual experience with respect to all depreciable assets. The reference in this paragraph to subsection (m) of section 167 shall be treated as a reference to such subsection as in effect on the day before the date of the enactment of the Revenue Reconciliation Act of 1990.

IRC section 167(m), referred to in the definition, no longer exists, having been repealed in 1990.

For *depreciation*—either tax or financial—an asset must have a useful life—the period over which the owner allocates the depreciation expense. For tax purposes, *Rev. Proc. 87–56 (1987)* includes the old *class life* system numbers, which set a range of acceptable class lives for a great many types of property.

For current United States tax *depreciation* under *IRC* section 168 (*MACRS*), the taxpayer must know the *Applicable Recovery Period* for the asset under IRC section 168(c). *Applicable Recovery Period* is a function of the asset's *Classification*, as defined by *IRC* section 168(e). *Classification* is a function of the asset's *class life*, if any.

Because current *IRC* section 168 *Applicable Recovery Periods* are typically much shorter than the more economically realistic *class lives*, the tax *depreciation* deduction is accelerated faster than the more economically justifiable (but often still accelerated) financial accounting depreciation deduction. The differences result in complicated book/tax disparities, which provide room for manipulation of financial information by educated, but less than scrupulous persons, including lawyers. Congress permits the super-*accelerated depreciation* as a form of *fiscal* policy: accelerated deductions lower tax obligations for affected taxpayers, who—because they are price elastic regarding the subject property—invest more or spend more. The resulting increased consumption results in increased economic activity, which results in a stronger economy (at least in theory).

93. **Closing Entry:** At the end of each period, accountants and bookkeepers *close* the books. More specifically, they close all *temporary accounts*, which are the income and loss or expense accounts.

An income account would normally have a *credit* balance. To *close* it, the bookkeeper *debits* the account for the amount of the periodic balance and credits another temporary account called profit and loss summary (or some similar name). The income *ledger*—or *T-account*—will then have a zero balance; hence, it has *closed*.

After similarly *closing* all income and expense *ledgers* to the profit and loss summary *ledger*, the bookkeeper will then close that *temporary account*. If it has a credit balance, the entity had a profit for the period. If the account has a *debit* balance, the entity had a loss for the period. In either event, the bookkeeper will *debit* or *credit* the balance so as to cause the resulting balance to be zero. He will correspondingly *debit* or *credit* retained earnings for the profit or loss. As a result, all *temporary accounts* effectively transfer to the *Balance Sheet* in the form of an increase or decrease to *retained earnings*. From the profit and loss summary *ledger*, the bookkeeper and accountant can easily prepare the periodic *Income Statement*.

Remember: *Balance Sheet* accounts are permanent accounts, and *Income Statement* accounts are temporary accounts.

By *closing* the books with such *closing* entries, the accountant keeps each period's operations separate. He also, by transferring those operations to *Retained Earnings*—either as an increase or decrease—maintains a proper snapshot of the entity's cumulative operations.

94. **COBRA: The Consolidated Omnibus Budget Reconciliation Act of 1986:** [pronounced **koh**-br*uh*]. It primarily affects health care plans of employees.

According to the U.S. Department of Labor:

> The Consolidated Omnibus Budget Reconciliation Act (COBRA) gives workers and their families who lose their health benefits the right to choose to continue group health benefits provided by their group health plan for limited periods of time under certain circumstances such as voluntary or involuntary job loss, reduction in the hours worked, transition between jobs, death, divorce, and other life events. Qualified individuals may be required to pay the entire premium for coverage up to 102 percent of the cost to the plan.

COBRA generally requires that group health plans sponsored by employers with 20 or more employees in the prior year offer employees and their families the opportunity for a temporary extension of health coverage (called continuation coverage) in certain instances where coverage under the plan would otherwise end.

COBRA outlines how employees and family members may elect continuation coverage. It also requires employers and plans to provide notice.

http://www.dol.gov/dol/topic/health-plans/cobra.htm.

95. **Codification:** The Financial Accounting Standards Board (the *FASB*) began codifying *FASB* statements (later called FASs or Financial Accounting Standards) into a code in 2009. It is now the official statement of U.S. *GAAP*.

96. **COLA: Cost of Living Adjustment: Cost of Living Allowance:** The cost of living adjustment generally refers to an automatic increase in Social Security Benefits. Since 1973, it does not require legislation by Congress. Since its enactment, the reference measure for the increase has changed. Currently the Social Security Administration uses the *CPI*-W, or the core inflation rate for urban wage earners.

The term *COLA* also refers to a *Cost of Living Allowance* granted by the United States military to service personnel stationed in high cost areas.

97. **COLI: Corporate Owned Life Insurance:** This describes insurance owned by a corporate employer on the life of an employee—often, but not necessarily a highly valued or *key employee*.

98. **Comfort Letter:** This term has many usages.

For accounting purposes, it can refer to a letter written by an independent *CPA* (not one employed by the entity) reflecting the opinion that current, not-yet-audited, financial information appears to conform to *GAAP*. This may accompany an entity's prospectus for an *Initial Public Offering (IPO)*.

It can also refer to a *CPA's* letter to potential lenders or investors regarding the continuing solvency of the entity. Rules Regulating the Professional Conduct of *CPAs* have some impact on the propriety of comfort letters in varying situations. *CPAs* should heed those rules carefully.

For tax purposes, it can refer to a letter written by a charity's counsel to a donor reflecting the opinion that a proposed donation will not adversely affect the charity's tax status. Or, it may more generally refer to an opinion letter from counsel regarding the expected or projected tax consequences of a stated transaction.

99. **Commercial Paper:** These are notes—typically short-term (less than one year and as short as a few days)—issued by various entities. A well-developed market exists for issuing and trading paper. Some *paper* provides for regular interest payments, while most defers interest to maturity. Often, paper is in bearer format and typically has a term of 5 to 270 days.

100. **Commodity:** According to the CFTC, the term means:

> (1) A commodity, as defined in the <u>Commodity Exchange Act</u>, includes the agricultural commodities enumerated in Section 1a(4) of the Commodity Exchange Act, 7 USC 1a(4), and all other goods and articles, except onions as provided in Public Law 85–839 (7 USC 13–1), a 1958 law that banned futures trading in onions, and all services, rights, and interests in which contracts for future delivery are presently or in the future dealt in; (2). A physical commodity such as an agricultural product or a natural resource as opposed to a financial instrument such as a currency or interest rate.

101. **Commodity Futures Trading Commission: CFTC:** The U.S. Commodity Futures Trading Commission, created by Congress in 1974, is an independent agency headed by five commissioners appointed by the President and subject to Senate Confirmation. Initially, it regulated trading in commodities; however, over the years, its authority has broadened to include futures in other items, including government bonds, and derivatives. In some areas, *CFTC* authority overlaps with that of the *SEC*.

http://www.cftc.gov/index.htm.

102. **Common Stock:** This is a type of security (a term which includes stock, bonds and *debentures*) which has voting rights. Although a corporation may issues various classes of *common stock* with various voting rights and liquidation rights, generally *common stock* is at the bottom in terms of preference upon liquidation. As a result, all other obligations—secured and unsecured—plus *preferred stock* would normally receive full payment on liquidation before common stockholders received anything.

But, *common stock*, in case of liquidation, would also have no cap on what it received on liquidation; hence, common shareholders would receive everything left after senior debts and securities received satisfaction. Thus *Common Stock* is riskier than *preferred stock* or *debentures*; however, it also has greater opportunity for gain.

103. **Community Property:** This refers to property held in a Marital Property Regime used in most nations and in nine U.S. states plus Puerto Rico:

- Louisiana
- Texas
- New Mexico
- Arizona
- California
- Nevada
- Washington
- Idaho
- Wisconsin

Community property regimes vary regarding how they define terms. Generally, income from labor and industry during a marriage creates community property. Similarly, liabilities incurred during a marriage create community liabilities. In some jurisdictions, income attributable to separate property remains separate, while in other jurisdictions it becomes community.

The regimes apply for all legal purposes—ownership during marriage, ownership in case of divorce (each party receives one-half), or ownership in case of the death of one party.

In contrast, most separate property states have adopted *equitable distribution* regimes which define marital assets and liabilities, as opposed to community assets and liabilities. Three significant differences between the regimes exist:

- While *community property* regimes apply during a marriage, *equitable distribution* regimes do not—they keep property separate unless the parties' behavior (through gifts or commingling) provide otherwise.

- While *community property* regimes apply if one party dies, *equitable distribution* regimes do not. Spouses in such jurisdictions may have an elective share in the property of the other, but it is typically not an issue of family law; instead, that is an issue of probate law.

- While *community property* regimes provide for equal division of community assets and liabilities, *equitable distribution* regimes provides for equitable division of assets and liabilities in case of marriage dissolution or divorce.

Alaska has an opt-in system for *community property*. Other jurisdictions permit parties to enter pre-marital (*ante* nuptial) agreements, which can include the adoption of a *community property* regime at least for family law purposes. Jurisdictions vary regarding their rules for post nuptial agreements.

Community property regimes historically fit into two major categories:

- A community of movables. Historically, such regimes descended from the French system. Movable property—personal property in common law terms—owned by the parties formed the community. Real property did not.

- A community of gains. Historically, such regimes descended from the Spanish system. Gains—*aka* income or profits—during the marriage formed the community.

104. **Comparative Financial Statements:** Generally, *Financial Statements*—the *Balance Sheet*, the *Income Statement*, and the *Statement of Cash Flows*—appear in comparison with prior years, often three. Standing alone, *Financial Statements* provide useful, but incomplete information. Standing alongside prior periods, the statements provide information regarding trends. Trend analysis, along with *ratio analysis*, helps financial analysts predict the future.

Predicting the future is the fundamental purpose of financial statements. Users certainly are interested in knowing an entity's current situation, as well as what it has done. But, they primarily want to know how the entity will perform in the future: whether it will be profitable and whether it can pay its obligations. *Financial Statements*, with the use of *Ratio Analysis* and *Trend Analysis* help predict the *micro economic* future of the relevant entity.

105. **Complex Trust:** This is a tax term of art, although the Internal Revenue Code does not use the term. Such trusts may accumulate income. Under *IRC* section 661, the trust is a taxpayer for accumulated income. It receives a deduction for distributions up to the amount of *DNI* and the beneficiary is then taxed on the distributions.

Complex trusts have many characteristics common to *pass-thru entities*; however, they also have differences in that they are themselves taxpayers, at least until they distribute accumulated *DNI*.

The family law impact of undistributed *DNI* in a *complex trust* is unclear in most jurisdictions. To the extent accumulated income must eventually be distributed to a particular beneficiary (and possibly to the extent it likely will be), the amount arguably is income for the determination of alimony and child support obligations, as well as for the determination of marital assets. But, a contrary view is also reasonable. To the extent a trust accumulates income, the beneficiary may *never* receive it. Distribution may be discretionary or the deferral period may be substantial.

The notion of *payment* then becomes important. To the extent a legal definition—such as the family law or contractual definition of income—is a function of trust *distributions* or *payments*, it may have a legal meaning different from the tax definition of income or *DNI*. Risk of double inclusion is possible: in one year the parties (or court) may include accumulated income and then in a later year, they may include distributions. One of the fundamental *Principles and Assumptions of Accounting* is the *Consistency Principle*. Whether it applies, either in theory or in practice, to family law and other legal matters is unclear. Lawyers should be aware of the possibility of such inconsistencies.

Readers may want to contemplate the prior paragraph. Inconsistencies in accounting methods are not permissible for financial accounting. Typically, they are also not permissible for tax accounting, although the rules involving inconsistencies are very complex. One can imagine an educated—but unscrupulous—person taking advantage of the complexities. Such a person might create difficult-to-detect inconsistencies with the knowledge that feigned ignorance of the rules will pass muster in the unlikely event of detection.

To the extent, accumulated *DNI* does not comprise income for family law purposes, much room for manipulation and divorce planning (both pre and post marriage) exist. Unlike marriage contracts—which both parties sign and which typically involve full or fair disclosure—non-contractual divorce planning may be apparent only to the party involved in the planning. Whether that is good or bad depends on one's perspective.

106. **Compound Annual Growth Rate: *CAGR*:** This is a financial term which represents the average compounded return on an asset. It does not represent any one year in particular; instead, it averages—or smoothes—a return over time. One formula for it is:

$$CAGR = \left[\left(\frac{Current\ Value}{Beginning\ Value} \right)^{\left(\frac{1}{n} \right)} - 1 \right]$$

Where *CAGR* = Compound Annual Growth Rate, *Current Value* = FMV at the time of measurement or computation, *Beginning Value* = the initial investment, and *n* = number of years.

This formula differs from an arithmetic mean average of annual growth rates; hence, the reference to *compound*.

107. **Compounding:** This is the process of paying or charging interest on interest. For example, if interest compounds monthly at 1%, then after one-month a $100.00 deposit would be worth $101.00. After two months, it would be worth $102.01. In the second month, the deposit would earn 1% interest on the original $100.00 deposit plus 1% interest on the first month's $1.00 of interest. All interest compounds, which helps explain the term effective interest rate. The *EFF* reflects the result of compounding the periodic rate for one year.

Arguably, interest on an *amortizing* loan does not compound because the borrower pays it regularly (typically monthly). This is correct when viewed solely as it affects the borrower and lender together. Individually, however, the interest necessarily compounds because it either goes somewhere or came from somewhere. The lender who receives the $1.00 interest at the end of the first month does not later receive any additional interest on the $1.00 of interest from that particularly borrower because the borrower has paid his debt of the $1.00 interest. The lender, however, may then lend the $1.00 to someone else—and thus effectively earn compounded interest; or, the lender will spend the $1.00. In the latter case, the lender receives no compounded interest; however, he reduces what would otherwise be borrowing costs or reduces what would otherwise be income from his *capital* and thus experiences the same effect.

The same analysis applies to the borrower who pays his $1.00 interest obligation at the end of the first month. He does not owe or pay any additional compounded interest on that interest to that lender; however, the $1.00 he paid came from somewhere. If he took it from a deposit, he earns less interest. If he borrowed it from someone else, he pays additional interest. Thus, his effective cost expressed in terms of a year necessarily involves compounded interest.

108. **Compounding Period**: This refers to the frequency of compounding for interest. For example, the period may be a month, which would result in twelve instances of compounding per year. Or, the period could be a day, which would result in 365/66 compounds per year.

A critical rule of finance is: the compounding period and the payment period must be the same or it must be annual. The mathematical formulae for determining present and future values for sums and annuities require this rule. Of course, if the two are not the same, one can easily adjust the compounding period—and the resulting nominal interest rate—to reflect compounding consistent with the payment period.

109. **Consanguinity:** Relationship though a common ancestor. See *Degrees of Relationship* for a fuller explanation. See also, *affinity*, which refers to relationship by marriage.

110. **Conservatism Principle of Accounting:** Under this principle, when given reasonable choices, an accountant will tend to choose the more conservative: the lower valuation for assets and receipts, and the higher valuation for obligations and expenses. Properly applied, this principle results in financial information such as income and net worth being more likely understated than overstated.

The mere existence of this principle illustrates an important point often missed by non-accountants:

> *Accounting is not a science. It is more art. Financial Accounting is filled with many legitimate but materially different choices, methods, assumptions, and rules.*

111. **Consistency Principle of Accounting:** Under this principle, accounting statements must rest on consistent principles and assumptions from period to period. Such assumptions may include depreciation methods, inventory methods and valuation techniques, cost segregation rules, capitalization rules, timing of income recognition rules, and similar decisions. As explained in relation to the *Conservatism Principle*, Accounting is not a science. Lawyers who view it as a guarantee of precision do so at their peril.

Comparative Financial Statements are essential for financial analysis. If those statements do not rest on consistent principles, any comparison of them risks being misleading.

Because most people and most entities do not have an annual audit, they are free to be inconsistent in their accounting choices. Viewed in isolation, such inconsistency is unwise as it impairs the validity of year-to-year comparisons.

While such inconsistency-created comparisons may be *useless* for internal purposes, they may be *beneficial* for illicit external uses: they may materially distort income and equity, particularly in terms of how those items appear on a trend graph. Most people would view the presentation of such distortions in legal matters as dishonest; nevertheless, such inconsistencies may not be illegal or unethical or even a breach of contract. Lawyers should thus be very careful in viewing multi-period un-audited financial statements.

112. **Consolidated Financial Statements:** For both accounting and tax purposes, related entities may report consolidated Financial Statements. In these, the entities combine their statements—income, expenses, assets, liabilities, and such.

For accounting purposes, creating *consolidated statements* is a difficult process. Why? Because of the elimination of inter-company activities. For example, if Corporation A owns shares in corporation B, that value already appears on A's *Balance Sheet*. If A and B were to file consolidated statements, the investment of A in B would need to disappear, as it is implicit when B's Balance Sheet combines with A's. Similarly, if B owes money to A, B separately reports a liability and A reports an asset. Combined, neither an asset nor a liability exists because one cannot owe money to oneself. In a third example, if A sells inventory to B, the sale as well as any resulting gain must disappear. Viewed as separate entities, the transactions between A and B are real; however, viewed as one entity, the transactions have no meaning. Reporting them would inflate the affected *Income Statement* or *Balance Sheet* accounts.

Failure to report consolidated statements can be very misleading. In many cases, *GAAP* or *SEC* regulations will require such reporting. For unaudited companies, however, such reporting is voluntary or contractual. Lawyers should heed this carefully. If your compensation is a function of an entity's financial statements—either in terms of income or ratios—you must define the entity carefully and you must anticipate related party transactions. If you do not, the entity could easily manipulate its numbers by entering transactions with an affiliate. Those transactions can artificially inflate or deflate numbers to the entity's advantage and to your disadvantage. An expert viewing the related entities in isolation could truthfully testify as to their accuracy, even though many of the numbers lack real economic meaning. Lawyers should also be careful of the *cliff effect* used in deciding whether consolidated statements are appropriate. For example, clearly a wholly-owned subsidiary should combine with its parent for clear financial reporting. In contrast, an entity should not combine statements with another entity in which it has a negligible ownership interest. Somewhere between negligible and 100%, consolidated statements become important. Tax law has specific guidelines for this. For example, one part of *IRC* section 1504 becomes applicable at 80% ownership; however, if one wanted to avoid this application, one could decrease ownership to 79%: the difference would be slight in reality, but substantial in reporting.

For United States tax purposes, *IRC* section 1501 grants groups of *affiliated corporations* the privilege of filing consolidated returns:

> An affiliated group of corporations shall, subject to the provisions of this chapter, have the privilege of making a consolidated return with respect to the income tax imposed by chapter 1 for the taxable year in lieu of separate returns. The making of a consolidated return shall be upon the condition that all corporations which at any time during the taxable year have been members of the affiliated group consent to all the consolidated return regulations prescribed under section 1502 prior to the last day prescribed by law for

the filing of such return. The making of a consolidated return shall be considered as such consent. In the case of a corporation which is a member of the affiliated group for a fractional part of the year, the consolidated return shall include the income of such corporation for such part of the year as it is a member of the affiliated group.

IRC section 1504 defines the very complicated term *affiliated group*.

113. **Constant Yield to Maturity: CYM:** This term assumes a constant interest rate on a loan, as opposed to a variable rate. Internally, such a constant interest rate is common. Externally, however, interest rates vary frequently; hence, they affect the present value of the payments due under the obligation. Federal tax law uses a *Constant Yield to Maturity (CYM)* assumption for purposes of *Original Issue Discount* computations. *See, IRC* sections 1272 and 7872(b).

114. **Consumer Price Index: CPI:** According to the United States Bureau of Labor Statistics (*BLS*):

> The Consumer Price Indexes (CPI) program produces monthly data on changes in the prices paid by urban consumers for a representative basket of goods and services.

http://www.bls.gov/cpi/home.htm.

Many government programs and benefits, as well as many contracts have provisions which are partially functions of changes in the *CPI*. For example, a compensation agreement may provide for automatic wages increase to match the *CPI*—or perhaps the *CPI* plus or minus a stated amount (preferably stated in terms of basis points).

As further explained by the *BLS*:

> The BLS publishes thousands of CPI indexes each month, including the headline All Items CPI for All Urban Consumers (CPI-U) and the CPI-U for All Items Less Food and Energy. The latter series, widely referred to as the "core" CPI, is closely watched by many economic analysts and policymakers under the belief that food and energy prices are volatile and are subject to price shocks that cannot be damped through monetary policy. However, all consumer goods and services, including food and energy, are represented in the headline CPI.
>
> Most importantly, none of the prominent legislated uses of the CPI excludes food and energy. Social security and federal retirement benefits are updated each year for inflation by the All Items CPI for Urban Wage Earners and Clerical Workers (CPI-W). Individual income tax parameters and Treasury

Inflation-Protected Securities (TIPS) returns are based on the All Items CPI-U.

115. **Contra Account:** This is an account used to reduce another account. It carries a balance opposite to what would normally be seen for its type. It is an accounting term for what amounts to a negative asset or negative *equity* account in Balance Sheet terms, or negative income in Income Statement terms. For example, *accumulated depreciation* will have a *credit* balance; however, instead of appearing on the right side of the balance sheet as a positive number, it appears on the left side as a negative number. Similarly, *Treasury Stock* will have a debit balance; however, it cannot appear on the *Balance Sheet* left side, as it is not an asset. Because *Treasury Stock* is part of *Owner's Equity*, it appears on the *Balance Sheet* right side as a negative number reducing the *Capital Stock* account. On an Income Statement, Returns would have a negative balance and would appear as a reduction to Sales or Revenue. Consider the two illustrations in the *Balance Sheet* below:

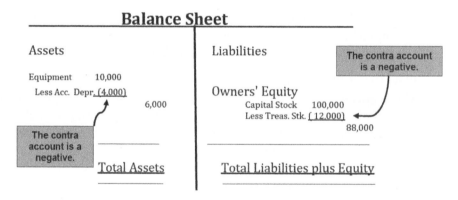

Balance Sheet

Equipment would appear at its *historical cost* of $10,000. Over time, the entity would have depreciated the equipment—in this example in the amount of $4,000. The depreciation journal entry—an *adjusting entry*—would have appeared as:

Depreciation Expense	$4,000	
Accumulated Depreciation		$4,000

No entry would affect the Equipment *ledger*, which would continue to appear as follows, along with the Accumulated Depreciation *ledger* (also a *permanent account*):

Equipment		Accumulated Depreciation	
$10,000			$4,000

Both would then appear on the left side of the *Balance Sheet*—the equipment *historical cost* as a positive number and the *Accumulated*

Depreciation as a negative number—as a *Contra Account*. The *temporary* account, Depreciation Expense, would have a $4,000 debit balance. Ultimately, the journal would have a closing entry crediting the depreciation expense for $4,000 and debiting a *Profit and Loss* account for $4,000. This would reduce *Retained Earnings*.

Similarly, if the entity purchased its own shares with the intention of holding them and later re-selling them, it would record the purchase as:

Treasury Stock	$12,000	
Cash		$12,000

If, instead, the entity intended to cancel the shares—thereby permanently reducing shareholder capital—the entry would be:

Capital Stock	$12,000	
Cash		$12,000

For Treasury Stock, the entity would maintain a *Permanent Account Treasury Stock ledger* with a *debit* balance. This ledger debit balance would not appear on the Balance Sheet left side, as do other permanent account debit balances. Instead, the Treasury Stock debit balance would appear as a negative number—a *Contra Account*—on the right side of the *Balance Sheet*.

Showing *Accumulated Depreciation* and *Treasury Stock* as negative numbers—*Contra Accounts*—provides useful information. For example, if the entity replaced the *Accumulated Depreciation credit* with an Equipment *credit*, the *Balance Sheet* would list Equipment with a $6,000 balance. While that number would be correct—and indeed, it is the same ultimate number shown above—it would fail to disclose the Equipment historical cost and the account of prior depreciation. Considering the potential, if not probable, inaccuracy of depreciation expense and accumulated depreciation, showing the accumulated depreciation number on the Balance Sheet reveals important information about potential inaccuracies. That Depreciation Expense appears annually on the *Income Statement* is insufficient: the accumulated number is also important.

Similarly, showing Treasury Stock on the Balance Sheet as a negative number reveals the expected temporary nature of the capital reduction.

116. **Contra Positive:** This is generally a math term, but can be useful in law and logic. It involves negating both the hypothesis and conclusion of a conditional statement and then reversing them. For example, consider the following statement: "If the moon is full, then the tides

are high." The contrapositive would be "If the tides are not high, then the moon must not be full."

117. **Converse:** This is a math or logic term. It involves switching the hypothesis and the conclusion in relation to a conditional statement. For example, "If the moon is full, then the tides are high." The converse would be "If the tides are high, then the moon is full."

118. **Controlled Foreign Corporation: CFC:** *IRC* section 957(a) defines a *CFC* as:

> any foreign corporation if more than 50 percent of—
>
>> (1) the total combined voting power of all classes of stock of such corporation entitled to vote, or
>>
>> (2) the total value of the stock of such corporation,
>
> is owned (within the meaning of section 958(a)), or is considered as owned by applying the rules of ownership of section 958(b), by United States shareholders on any day during the taxable year of such foreign corporation.

119. **Corpus:** This is generally a term for Trust Law. It refers to the principal of the trust. Derived from Latin, the word translates as *the body*.

120. **Correction:** *aka Market Correction:* This is not a term of art. Generally, it refers to a short-term drop in price of 5% to about 20%. At the upper range, some might refer to the trend as a *bear market*, or one trending downward. Corrections are common following sustained rallies or *bull markets*.

121. **COSO Opinion: Council on Sponsoring Organizations:** An auditor's opinion regarding the merits of internal controls.

122. **Cost/Benefit Analysis:** This is an accounting technique which weighs a project's costs with its benefits. If costs exceed benefits, the project is uneconomical. If benefits exceed costs, the project should proceed. *IRR* analysis and *TCO* analysis is similar.

Although the technique may appear simple—even common sensible— it is actually complex and fraught with room for manipulation.

For example, consider the term *cost*. Standing alone, the term has little meaning. It might include *direct costs*, *variable costs*, and *indirect costs*. It might rely on *full absorption costing*, or it might focus instead on *marginal costing*. Clearly, if one supports the project, one has a strong incentive—see *moral hazard*—to define costs narrowly. If one opposes the project, one would be tempted to do the opposite.

The term benefits are even more *elastic*. Some benefits are quantifiable—such as reduced expenses, and higher revenues. Other benefits are less clear and direct, such as longer life spans, which result in higher costs and are also less directly traceable to any particular project. For example, anti-smoking programs reduce expenditures for lung cancer, but they increase expenditures for Social Security and Alzheimer's treatments. Still other benefits are entirely non-quantifiable—such as a more beautiful landscape or more peace and quiet or more wolves or lizards or snail darters . . . or even more bald eagles which eat more black cormorant chicks. Species extinction is generally considered a cost; however, what if the species is HIV or Ebola or cockroaches or love-bugs? Do we add that to the cost or to the benefit column?

Cost benefit studies tend to make great headlines and wonderful fodder for politicians, but realist lawyers should remember:

The devil is in the details.

Or even better,

The devil is in the definitions.

123. **Cost of Capital:** see *WACC: Weighted Average Cost of Capital.* Capital generally includes both debt and equity. Each has a cost: debt costs the after-tax interest rate, and equity "costs" the expected dividend or return rate.

124. **Cost of Goods Sold: COGS:** This is an important function in inventory accounting. *Gross Profit* refers to:

$$Sales - COGS$$

In turn, *COGS* (in a periodic inventory system) refers to:

$$COGS = (BI + P - EI)$$

Where *COGS* = Cost of Goods Sold, *BI* = Beginning Inventory, *P* = Purchases, and *EI* = Ending Inventory.

Accounting for inventory costs is not as simple as the above equation appears. The term *"purchases"* includes *direct* costs of newly acquired inventory plus some *capitalized indirect* costs. Accountants and entities differ on which costs they capitalize into inventory; hence, the number is open to interpretation and manipulation.

Similarly, the numbers for Beginning and Ending Inventory require not only an annual physical count, but also an inventory method: LIFO, FIFO, average cost, or specific identification. The choice of method can have a substantial impact on the *BI* and *EI* numbers; hence, it can also have a substantial impact on *COGS* and *Gross Profit.* Such impacts are particularly significant in times of price instability, be it inflation or deflation.

Lawyers analyzing financial statements for businesses which maintain inventories should carefully scrutinize the numbers for *COGS*. They should ensure consistency of capitalization choices and inventory valuation (LIFO, FIFO, average cost, or specific identification). They may also want to question the choices, even if they are consistently made. While consistent treatment of inventory provides useful and generally dependable information for comparison of many periods, it may nevertheless provide distorted information for a single period or a few consecutive periods. For example, for the determination of compensation bonuses, valuation of a business through capitalization of earnings, or determination of alimony or child support obligations, inventory decisions can result in misleading numbers for the short run. LIFO can seriously understate income and asset valuations, which FIFO can do the opposite.

For United States tax purposes, *COGS* is not a deductible amount; instead, it is a reduction in Sales for purposes of determining Gross Income under *IRC* section 61.

125. **Cost-Plus Pricing:** This refers to various methods a producer may use to set his price to the customer. *CPP* is most common for activities with large variable costs which are difficult to predict. For example, it may be used in construction: rather than agree to an absolute fixed cost (which can be risky for the builder), the parties may agree to cost plus. Understandably, the builder is entitled to a profit. He may want to earn 30%, for example, as his mark-up. He would then contractually agree to charge his costs for all items or labor plus 30% of those costs.

As is true of many financial and accounting terms, however, the details are important. Lawyers must be very careful to define the term *costs*. Clearly *variable* costs are relevant; however, some or all fixed costs may be relevant as well—that is a matter of negotiation. One could legitimately argue that the 30% mark-up compensates the builder for its time and expertise plus a fair share of fixed or overhead costs. Under such an argument, no fixed costs should enter the equation. Or, the parties may agree the builder is entitled to allocate a portion of his fixed costs to the contract: as long as which costs are involved is clear, the parties may contract as they please.

Another issue involves the definition of a *variable* cost. Clearly, lumber used solely on the particular project is a *variable* cost of the project. However, transportation costs for the lumber—including depreciation on trucks and labor costs for the driver—also may vary by the project; or, they may not. Plus, the builder may legitimately combine transportation for various projects. That would be efficient, but it would also raise the accounting question of how to apportion the costs among projects. With regard to the *variable* nature of transportation, the fuel used is surely *variable*; however, the builder may maintain a fleet of trucks and drivers at a fixed cost (or partially fixed cost). Fairly, some of that cost should be allocated to the project, even if it does not vary by the project. These are fixed but direct costs, as opposed to fixed and indirect costs—such as electricity at the home office, which does not apply to any particular project.

The key message for lawyers is two-fold:

- Cost-Plus Pricing is common.

- Defining costs is difficult, subjective, and easily manipulated.

126. **Cost Recovery:** Cost Recovery has two basic meanings:

- The *accounting* method of allocating costs over time.

- A *tax law* rule affecting the timing of gain recognition.

For accounting purposes, one must allocate capitalized costs to the proper period under the matching principal of accounting. Three main terms encompass various methods:

- Depreciation: for tangibles.

- Amortization: for intangibles.

- Depletion: for minerals.

Some property—in particular, land—does not depreciate (at least not in traditional accounting and tax theory). For it, the owner recovers cost upon disposition by subtracting the land's adjusted basis from the amount realized.

For *tax law*, "cost recovery" sometimes refers to an accounting method for gain under which the seller recognizes no gain until he has recovered his "cost"—adjusted basis. This method, also known as an "open transaction" was more commonly used prior to *IRC* amendments in 1980 to section 453, which deals with installment sales. *See, Burnet v. Logan,* 283 U.S. 404 (1931).

127. **Cost Segregation:** *Cost Segregation* is an important—and controversial—accounting and tax law technique. It goes to the issue of what is an asset. For example, a building may comprise many separate assets: light fixtures, ceiling tiles, elevators, doors, windows and frames, wiring, and plumbing fixtures. The process of cost segregation does not change the total cost of a purchase; however, it places the cost in different assets subject to different depreciation or amortization rules. This can have a *material* impact on income.

128. **Coupon Bond:** Bonds are either registered or bearer. Bearer bonds which pay current interest have coupons attached to them. The bearer

must clip the coupon (cut it off with scissors) and submit it to the issuer to receive the interest earned. Traditionally, banks handle the submission for depositors.

Coupon Bonds are not common in the U.S. because of government restrictions. People have often used them to evade tax—which their bearer status facilitates.

Internal Revenue Code Section 1286 deals with the tax consequences of Stripped *Coupon Bonds*. A stripped bond is one for which the non-accrued coupons (those due in the future) are separated from the bond itself (the principal). The code apportions the owner's basis among the component parts based on their relative present values.

One of the most famous of all U.S. tax cases—*Helvering v. Horst*, 311 U.S. 112 (1940)—dealt with a stripped coupon bond. The owner gave the coupons to another but retained the principal. The Supreme Court found this act to be an unsuccessful assignment of income; as a result, while the donee received the interest payments, the donor had to pay the tax on the resulting income.

129. **Coupon Rate:** The *coupon rate* is the stated interest rate on a transferable instrument. Because interest rates change continuously with market forces, the coupon rate differs from the *current yield* on the instrument—which is traditionally a function of the instrument's current value. The issuer will pay the instrument owner interest based on the *coupon rate* times the face value, adjusted for the payment period. This is not a term of art, but it is a commonly used term. Compare to the *notional rate*.

130. **Credit:** this term has two very different, but equally important (and related) meanings:

- A *credit* is a bookkeeping entry on the right. It increases liabilities and owners' equity on the balance sheet and income on the income statement. It decreases assets and owners' equity on the balance sheet and expenses on the income statement.

- *Credit* also refers to one's ability to borrow money. A person with good *credit* can borrow at a lower interest rate than can a person with poor *credit*. A person's ability to borrow is generally a function of their "credit score."

The terms are related: for bookkeeping, a *credit* increases debt and in finance *credit* refers to debt. See the term *debit* for a fuller explanation.

131. **Credit Default Swap: CDS:** This is a *derivative* contract similar to insurance. It also has similarity to a _gamble_ or bet. The holder pays a fee to the issuer in exchange for the issuers promise to pay in the event

a financial instrument defaults. But, the holder need not own the referenced financial instrument, which causes it to differ from insurance. Also, United States and various state laws do not consider the issuer to be writing insurance for purposes of the swap; hence, the issue need not maintain any reserves (assets set aside) in case it must satisfy the promise.

Generally, *CDS*s are subject to *Mark to Market* Accounting. During the credit crisis of 2008–09, many holders of *CDS*s found their paper guarantees to lack much value. As a result, they had to right down the swaps. This, in turn, raised serious concerns about their own solvency, which caused swaps on their obligation to lose value, which impaired the capital of still other entities. Also, the issuers of *CDS*s suddenly found themselves obligated to pay far more than they anticipated, which resulted in defaults or expected defaults, which also led to a downward spiral in valuations.

132. **Crummey Trust Doctrine:** An important tax doctrine, this arose from a famous case: *Crummey v. Commissioner*, 397 F2d 82 (9th Cir. 1968). A *Crummey Power* grants a trust beneficiary the right to demand ownership of deposited property for a limited period. As a result, it is a <u>present</u> interest and thus excludable for gift tax purposes. It applies even if the beneficiary is a minor.

Five years after *Crummey*, the Internal Revenue Service promulgated Revenue Ruling 73–405 which essentially restated the case's holding:

> [A] gift in trust for the benefit of a minor should not be classified as a future interest merely because no guardian was in fact appointed. Accordingly, if there is no impediment under the trust or local law to the appointment of a guardian and the minor donee has a right to demand distribution, the transfer is a gift of a present interest that qualifies for the annual exclusion allowable under section 2503(b) of the Code.

The Ruling revoked a contrary 1954 ruling.

Eight years later, the Service again reviewed the *Crummey Power* factors. Specifically it found some donee rights illusory, resulting in non-excludable *future interests*. Revenue Ruling 81–7 hypothesized a donee who lacks a reasonable opportunity to learn of and to exercise a demand right before it lapses. The ruling grantor created the *Crummey Power* on December 29, did not inform the beneficiary, and provided for the demand right to lapse two days later. According to the Ruling:

> A trust provision giving a legally competent adult beneficiary the power to demand corpus does not qualify a transfer to the trust as a present interest eligible for the gift tax annual

exclusion under section 2503(b), if the donor's conduct makes the demand right illusory and effectively deprives the donee of the power.

In 1991, the Tax Court added further gloss to the *Crummey Power*. In *Cristofani v. Comm'r*, 97 TC 74 (1991), the court reaffirmed its support for the *Crummey* holding; however, it also addressed whether a demand power possessed by an individual with merely a contingent remainder trust interest qualifies as a *present interest* for purposes of the annual gift tax exclusion.

The taxpayer excluded trust gifts to her children and also to her grandchildren as secondary beneficiaries. The trust contained demand powers exercisable by the grandchildren who would benefit from the trust only if a child of decedent's died before decedent or failed to survive decedent by more than 120 days. The grandchildren ranged from three to thirteen years old. The demand power existed for merely fifteen days after the contribution.

According to the Commissioner, the only reason decedent gave her grandchildren the demand rights to withdraw was to obtain the benefit of the associated annual exclusion. The court disagreed with the Commissioner and held the decedent intended to benefit her grandchildren, if only remotely. Although the grandchildren never exercised the demand rights, they had a legal right to do so which satisfied the primary *Crummey* test. The court also found irrelevant the grantor's intention to obtain a tax benefit. Significantly, the entire Tax Court reviewed the opinion, with all 16 participating judges joining.

133. **Currency:** This comprises paper money issued by a government. A payment in "cash" would include a payment in currency or coin; however, a cash payment might also include use of a check, draft, or credit card. Currency and coin are thus only a small part of an economy's money supply.

134. **Current Assets:** Cash plus other assets easily converted to cash. It includes accounts receivable and similar items expected to be collected within one year. On a *Balance Sheet, Current Assets* appear separately from *Fixed Assets*. See the definition of *Working Capital* for a fuller explanation.

135. **Current Liabilities:** Liabilities which are due within one year. This includes the *current* portion of long-term liabilities. On a *Balance Sheet, Current Liabilities* appear separately from *Long-term Liabilities*.

136. **Current Ratio:** A commonly used accounting/financial ratio, this measures short-term liquidity. Generally, the following formula represents it:

$$\left(\frac{current\ assets}{current\ liabilities} \right)$$

The *current ratio* differs primarily from the *acid test ratio* in that it eliminates accounts receivable. Generally, a *current ratio* of two to one is ideal. Much less than that indicates near-term liquidity problems and much more than that indicates excess liquidity.

137. **Debenture:** An unsecured obligation. Some people refer to these as *debenture bonds*. Others inter-change the terms *bond* and *debenture*. As explained in reference to the definition of *Bond*, still others distinguish between a *debenture* (which is an unsecured obligation) and a *bond* (which, under their definition, is a secured obligation).

138. **Debit:** A *debit* is a bookkeeping entry on the left. It decreases liabilities and owners' equity on the *Balance Sheet* and income on the *Income Statement*. It increases assets on the *Balance Sheet* and expenses on the *Income Statement*.

Why *debits* are on the left and *credits* are on the right confuses many beginning accounting students. The answer is simple: that is how we define them. They have no other meaning. If one pictures a *Balance Sheet* (which is merely a complete *ledger*) as a *T-account*, one can see how the two sides should balance. Hence, for every entry on the left (a *debit*), one must have an entry on the right (a *credit*).

Balance Sheet

Debit	Credit

Often, the actual number of *debit* and *credit* entries does not balance because the bookkeeper uses summations for one or the other. For example, one could *debit* cash deposits $10,000 (which increases cash) and correspondingly *credit* ten different customer accounts for $1,000 each, reflecting payments from each of them. The single *debit* of $10,000 would balance the ten *credits* of $1,000 each: the totals are what are important.

From the business's point of view, it would *credit* each customer account to reduce the respective asset accounts called *Accounts Receivable*. From the customer's point of view, they would each—on their own books (in their own journals and on their own ledgers)—*debit* their respective liabilities called *Accounts Payable*.

139. **Debt to Assets Ratio:** This is a commonly used leverage ratio:

$$\left(\frac{total\ liabilities}{total\ assets} \right)$$

The appropriate number varies considerably by industry. For example, historically, some capital intensive industries were highly leveraged, often posting ratios of 80%. Other industries are not highly leveraged; however, debt is itself not a bad thing. A 50% ratio—in very general terms—is typically acceptable.

To the extent the ratio is a function of historical cost less depreciation—rather than *FMV*—it can be misleading. But, *FMV* is itself a soft number in that it depends on opinion and on the recent pricing and sale of things other than the thing being measured. If the thing being valued were the thing recently sold (so as to indicate market value), then the value stated would be cost value rather than fair market value.

140. **Debt to Equity Ratio:** This is a commonly used leverage ratio:

$$\left(\frac{total\ liabilities}{total\ equity} \right)$$

It will track the *Debt to Assets Ratio* because of the basic Accounting Equation:

$$assets = liabilities + equity$$

Clearly, creditors like to see a low debt to equity ratio, as it provides them with a larger cushion.

141. **Defined Benefit Plan:** This is a type of deferred compensation plan which defines the benefit to be received. Many people refer to this as a pension plan, although such plans need not involve retirement.

Defined Benefit Plans became very popular in the United States, particularly with larger employers and particularly after the adoption of *ERISA*. In more recent years, they have largely fallen into disfavor. Such plans must—for tax, regulatory, and financial accounting purposes—be actuarially sound. In other words, the *FMV* of their assets must equal or exceed the **PRESENT VALUE** of the expected pay-outs. Computation of the soundness involves the **PRESENT VALUE OF AN ANNUITY** or multiple annuities with indeterminate lives.

If a Plan is unsound, the creator—the employer in most cases—must make it sound. In a *bear market*, this can be very expensive. But, in a bull market, such a Plan may have such an excess of soundness, the employer may skip contributions. Temptation to raid such plans can be enormous. A less risky alternative is a *Defined Contribution Plan.*

Employers which offer Defined Benefit Plans typically also offer a plan through which employees may contribute funds as well. Such plans would immediately vest.

142. **Defined Contribution Plan:** This is a type of deferred compensation plan which defines the contribution to be made. It is not a traditional pension plan.

For example, a plan may provide for an employer to contribute the equivalent of 15% of each employee's wages or salary to the plan. Many plans provide for employee direction of investments. If the Plan performs well—as in a *bull market*—the employee benefits. In such a case, the employer must continue with contractually agreed to contributions. If, instead, the Plan performs poorly—as in a *bear market*—the employee suffers. In such a case, the employer has no obligation to provide extra contributions.

Most deferred compensation plans adopted in recent years have been *Defined Contribution Plans*. In addition, many employers have dissolved or discontinued *Defined Benefit Plans* in favor of *Defined Contribution Plans*. Employers that offer Defined Contribution Plans typically also offer a plan through which employees may contribute funds as well. Such contributions immediately vest. The two plans may merge as one or they may remain separate and be subject to different rules, *e.g.*, with regard to withdrawals and borrowing.

143. **Deflation:** This is an uncommon economic situation in which general price levels decrease. The opposite of *inflation*, it can seriously distort economic decisions. When consumers anticipate deflation, they will tend to postpone purchases, believing prices will fall. Collectively, such decisions depress demand, which further depresses prices, resulting in a downward cycle. One of the three main components of *interest* rates is inflationary expectation. In times of deflation, this component is negative.

144. **Degrees of Relationship:** This refers to relationships between and among persons. First *degree* is the closest relationship—it exists between parent and child. A second degree relationship is also close. It exists between grandparents and their grandchildren and also between brothers and sisters.

To count degrees, one can draw a family tree of descendants from a common set of relatives. Each step—from a parent to a child or the reverse—counts as one *degree*. Hence, for siblings, one travels one step up to the common parent and one step down to the sibling, for a total of two steps or *degrees*. First cousins are fourth degree relatives. One would count up two steps to the common grandparent and down two steps to the first cousin. The child of one's first cousin—a first cousin once removed—is a fifth degree relationship: two up to one's grandparents and three down to one's cousin's child.

Relationships are important in many areas. For inheritance, closer relatives typically inherit before more distant ones. Also, many jurisdictions prohibit marriage by persons related more closely than fifth (sometimes fourth) degree.

The following chart illustrates relationship degrees up to the tenth degree.

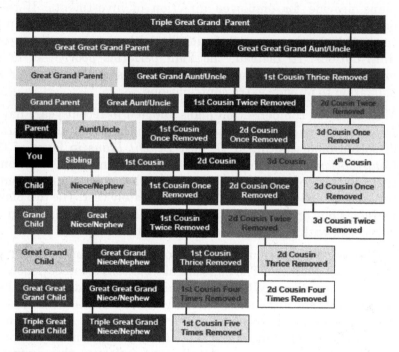

Red = 1 degree. **Orange** = 2 degrees. Yellow = 3 degrees. **Green** = 4 degrees. **Blue** = 5 degrees. **Purple** = 6 degrees. **Brown** = 7 degrees. **Grey** = 8 degrees. Light grey = 9 degrees. White = 10 degrees.

Common folklore often claims Franklin Roosevelt and Eleanor Roosevelt were cousins. People tend to be shocked by this revelation. Actually, according to the Franklin D. Roosevelt Presidential Library and Museum, they were fifth cousins. That would mean they had a common Quadruple Great Grandparent and were related in the twelfth degree—a quite distant relationship.

http://www.fdrlibrary.marist.edu/.

145. **De-Leverage:** This term refers to the process of reducing debt in absolute terms, or at least in terms of the *Debt to Assets Ratio*. An entity—or person—will want to de-lever when it has trouble satisfying obligations as they come due: debt payments are significant cash out-

flows. During the credit crisis of fall 2008, many persons—individuals and businesses—quickly began to de-lever as they feared a weakening economy. Generally, in times of expected deflation, one will want to de-lever. In times of expected inflation, one will seek leverage at fixed rates.

146. **Deposit:** This word has two significant legal meanings. The first is simple: it is merely the initial positive cash flow in a present or future value computation. Or, it represents the regular positive cash flow in an annuity computation. In that sense, it carries the same meaning as a payment.

In other legal arenas—particularly tax law—the distinction between a deposit and a payment is profound. Deposits create assets in the view of the depositor and debt in the view of the holder. In contrast, payments reduce debt in the eyes of both the payor and the recipient. Also, payments of obligations involved in income producing transaction result in gross income to the recipient and possible deductions to the transferor.

Many judicial opinions distinguish deposits from payments for tax purposes. Most of it is inconclusive and provides little predictive value. *See, e.g., Commissioner v. Indianapolis Power and Light*, 493 U.S. 203 (1990).

147. **Depreciation:** This refers to various cost recovery methods for tangible assets. Common methods include:

- Straight-line.
- Accelerated.
- Units of production or use.

Straight-line Depreciation allocates the asset's depreciable basis evenly over the recovery period, which is typically the asset's useful life.

Accelerated Depreciation allocates more of the asset's basis in the early years of its recovery period and less to the later years. Common methods of *Accelerated Depreciation* include:

- Double Declining Balance Method.
- 150% Declining Balance Method.
- Sum-of-the-Year's Digits Method.
- *MACRS* (for U.S. tax purposes).

Units of Production or *Use Depreciation* allocates an asset's depreciable basis as a function of the use of the asset. This is useful for assets which have a useful life which is a function of hours used, miles drives, or units produced. It is arguably the most accurate method of depreciation; however, most assets—such as a desk or chair—are not conducive to this method.

For financial accounting purposes, depreciation results in an *Adjusting Entry*:

Depreciation Expense	$xxxxx	
Accumulated Depreciation		$xxxxx

The Depreciation Expense debit affects a *Temporary Account* which closes ultimately to *Retained Earnings* and directly affects the *Income Statement*.

The Accumulated Depreciation credit affects a *Permanent Account* which appears on the *Balance Sheet* as a *Contra Asset*.

For both tax and accounting purposes, an asset's basis drops by the amount of depreciation expense. In addition, per *IRC* section 1016(1)(2), an asset's adjusted basis drops for tax purposes essentially by the greater of the amount allowed or the amount allowable; hence, if a taxpayer neglects to deduct depreciation expense on depreciable property, his basis drops anyway.

Lawyers analyzing financial statements for businesses which have depreciable should carefully scrutinize the numbers for depreciation expense. They should ensure consistency of capitalization choices, useful lives, salvage value, and depreciation method. They may also want to question the choices, even if they are consistently made. While consistent treatment of depreciation provides useful and generally dependable information for comparison of many periods, it may nevertheless provide distorted information for a single period or a few consecutive periods. For example, for the determination of compensation bonuses, valuation of a business through capitalization of earnings, or determination of alimony or child support obligations, d depreciation decisions can result in misleading numbers for the short run.

For United States tax purposes, taxpayers may choose to expense some purchased assets under *IRC* section 179. While the 179 expense is not technically depreciation, it has the same effects as depreciation—only it concentrates them into a single year. While appropriate for determining taxable income, section 179 expenses do not clearly reflect income and should not be used for non-tax legal definitions of income and expense.

148. **Depression:** An economic *depression* is a severe, prolonged downturn in a nation's or region's economy. Economists define it differently.

Some consider a 10% *GDP* decline as indicative of a *depression*, while others use a different measure.

In the 1930s, the United States experienced "The Great Depression," which resulted in unemployment rates as high as 25% and more than a 33% drop in *GDP* over several years.

Causes and cures for an *economic depression* are controversial. Conventional wisdom suggests increasing tax rates and restricting the supply of money will exacerbate rather than help an economic depression. Large increases in the money supply, however, risk causing inflation, which can be difficult to control. *Fiscal policy*—through government spending—is a typical governmental response.

It can result in rapid job creation and resulting consumer spending, each of which tends to improve economic measures. Arguably, such government action helps in the short run, but hurts in the long run as it distorts private economic activity by diverting resources.

President Reagan famously said, in 1980 while campaigning for office:

> *A recession is when your neighbor loses his
> job. A depression is when you lose yours.*

More directly, the difference between a bad *recession* and a *depression* is one of perception rather than one of definition or precision.

149. **Derivatives:** This is a broad class of assets whose value is a function of the value or cash flow of another asset. Futures contracts are common derivatives—their value is a function of the future value of some commodity or financial instrument. **Credit Default Swaps** (*CDS*) are a more recent type of derivative contract. In general, the use of derivatives transfers some underlying risk from an asset owner to another. For example, if a cereal manufacturer uses a substantial amount of corn and wants to avoid the risk of price changes in the value of corn, it can purchase corn futures contracts, essentially guaranteeing the price for the period involved. If the underlying corn price increases, the manufacturer can accept delivery of the corn purchased in advance, and the futures contract seller suffers the price increase. In contrast, if the price falls, the seller benefits either by delivering the corn at an above-market price or by settling the contract (essentially a bet) for the amount of the price drop. Complex derivative contracts can be highly volatile: they can produce large gains on small investments because the purchaser need not purchase the asset; instead, he merely purchases the right to the profit or part thereof. Also, such contracts can produce huge losses. For example, if A were to purchase a bushel of corn for $5.00 and the price dropped to $4.50, A would lose merely 10% of his investment. In contrast, if A were to

purchase a derivative which was a function of increased corn prices, A would lose his entire investment if the price dropped.

150. **Direct Cost:** *Direct costs* are those associated fully with a particular product or item. For example, the cost of lumber is a *direct* cost of furniture. *Direct* costs are also often *variable* costs in that they vary with more production. *Variable* costs, however, are either *direct* or *indirect*. The lumber cost of furniture is a *direct variable* cost. The electricity used in operating a manufacturing plant is an *indirect* cost that might be variable or fixed. it varies with production, but it is typically not traceable to a particular product; however, some portion is also likely fixed in that it occurs even if production is zero.

151. **Direct Tax:** Generally, this refers to a Capitation tax or to a direct tax on land. Per Article I, Section 9 of the U.S. Constitution, such taxes must be apportioned among the states by population. The Supreme Court invalidated an early income tax on individuals because it was not properly apportioned. *Pollock v. Farmers' Loan & Trust Co.,* 157 U.S. 429 (1895); *Pollock v. Farmers' Loan & Trust Co.,* 158 U.S. 601, 637 (1895). Later, in 1913, the 16th Amendment became part of the U.S. Constitution, permitting an un-apportioned income tax on income "from whatever source derived."

In contrast, *Indirect* taxes need not be apportioned under the Constitution; instead, they must be uniform. Examples include Excise Taxes, Duties, and Imposts.

Apportionment requires that the per capita amount of the tax be the same in each state. It does not require, however, that each person actually pay the same amount. States may decide themselves how to apportion a tax among its citizens.

152. **Discounted Cash Flow Analysis: DCF:** This is a method of valuing a project. It discounts the projected *cash flows* to the *present value.*

For investors, if the *present value* of projected cash flows exceeds the cost of investment, the project makes sense. Of course, the *discount interest rate* in such an evaluation is chosen by the prospective investor based on his desired return.

The model has many problems. First, it depends on projected cash flows. For investments such as bonds, that may not be problematic; however, for other investments, future cash flows from sales or rentals may be difficult to predict. Also, the model is highly affected by the choice of the discount rate: the higher the rate, the lower the present value.

If cash flows include everything—income, expenses, needed improvement costs, repairs, and residual value, then the *DCF* model is the same as the discounted value of profits.

Providing a formula for *DCF* analysis is not a simple matter because cash flows can vary in terms of amount, frequency, and direction. If all cash flows are in level, regular, and in the same direction, the formula is essential the sum of the **PRESENT VALUE OF AN ANNUITY** plus the **PRESENT VALUE OF A SUM**.

$$DCF = \left[FV \left(1 + \frac{i}{100} \right)^{-n} \right] + \left[\frac{\left[PMT \left(1 - \left(1 + \frac{i}{100} \right)^{-n} \right) \right]}{\frac{i}{100}} \right]$$

where i = nominal annual interest rate, n = number of periods per year, FV = the future value, and PMT = payment.

But, if cash flow amounts, frequency, and direction vary (as would be true of most businesses), the formula becomes essentially a series of *PV* computations, with each cash flow, time, and direction being entered separately.

153. **Discount Rate:** This term has three useful meanings:

- *Discount Rate* refers to the interest rate the *Federal Reserve Bank* or other Central Banks charge members banks for short-term loans.

- *Discount Rate* refers to the interest rate used in computing the present value of a sum or the present value of an annuity. In this sense, it has the same meaning as interest rate and requires a reference to a compounding frequency. For example, one might properly refer to a nominal annual discount rate compounded quarterly.

- *Discount Rate*, in reference to government bills and some instruments, refers specifically to the nominal annual discount interest rate on the instrument, without including any reference to compounding. For example, a Treasury Bill may sell for $950 and return $1,000 in one year. It would have a nominal discount rate of 5%, but an effective discount rate of 5.26316%. In this case, the 5% is a function of the principal plus the interest, rather than merely being a function of the principal, as is the typical case with statements of interest rates.

Because of the three different—actually, substantially different—meanings, a lawyer should be very careful in using the term *discount rate* and thus should always provide a clear definition.

154. **Distributable Net Income:** *DNI*: This is a tax law term under *IRC* section 643. It essentially reflects the taxable portion of a beneficiary's share of a simple trust's distributions. For tax purposes, a simple trust

(as opposed to a complex trust) is a pass-through entity. As such, the trust is not a taxpayer; instead, the income beneficiaries pay tax on the trust income, regardless of whether the trust distributes the proceeds.

155. **Domestic International Sales Corporation: DISC:** IRC section 992(a) defines a DISC as:

> a corporation which is incorporated under the laws of any State and satisfies the following conditions for the taxable year:
>
> (A) 95 percent or more of the gross receipts (as defined in section 993(f)) of such corporation consist of qualified export receipts (as defined in section 993(a)),
>
> (B) the adjusted basis of the qualified export assets (as defined in section 993(b)) of the corporation at the close of the taxable year equals or exceeds 95 percent of the sum of the adjusted basis of all assets of the corporation at the close of the taxable year,
>
> (C) such corporation does not have more than one class of stock and the par or stated value of its outstanding stock is at least $2,500 on each day of the taxable year, and
>
> (D) the corporation has made an election pursuant to subsection (b) to be treated as a DISC and such election is in effect for the taxable year.

156. **Double-Entry Bookkeeping:** This is an accounting system of *debits* and *credits*. All bookkeeping entries have both a *debit* and a *credit*; hence, books always balance absent recording errors.

Fundamentally, a *Balance Sheet*—which comprises all financial information (including the *Income Statement* closed to *Retained Earnings*)—is one large T-account. On the left are assets. On the right are claims on those assets—either creditors or owners. *Fundamentally*, that explains double entry bookkeeping: each entry ultimately affects property and the claim on that property. Of course, the actual entries are more complex that this fundamental model, but nevertheless the model is correct.

157. **Double Declining Balance Depreciation: DDB:** This is an arbitrary, but common method of allocating tangible asset costs over time. It allows a depreciation expense equal to twice the straight-line percentage as a function of the declining asset basis. Because the system relies on a fixed life for the asset, it switches to straight-line depreciation in the year in which that produces a higher number.

Most U.S. tax law depreciation under *IRC* section 168 uses *DDB* depreciation.

158. **Dow Jones Industrial Average: DOW:** [pronounced dou]. This is a stock index which is a function (but not simply an additive composition) of 30 large industrial companies traded on the New York Stock Exchange. Charles Dow, the founder of the Wall Street Journal and Dow Jones Company, originally created the index. From time-to-time, the index drops a company and adds a new one. Probably the most famous stock index, the *DOW* is not the best indicator of the state of the economy. Broader indexes, such as the *S & P 500* or the *NASDAQ* arguably provide better current information.

159. **Durable Power of Attorney:** A power of attorney (contractual grant of authority to act on another's behalf) which survives the incapacity of the grantor. In many jurisdictions—and at common law—a general or specific power of attorney ends on the mental incapacity of the grantor. Most jurisdictions now recognize a durable power through which the grantor specifically provides for some or all powers to survive the grantor's mental incapacity. In all events, however, such powers end on the death of the grantor.

A *Durable Power of Attorney* is an important tool for the elderly. It can grant authority to adult descendants to act on the grantor's behalf. Such powers typically include the authority to pay bills, provide for repairs, invest property, collect income, and often to sell property.

160. **Dutch Auction:** This is a special type of auction often used by the Treasury. The lowest bid price necessary to sell the entire amount of product offered becomes the price for all bidders.

161. **Draft:** A draft is an order to pay. Under Article 3–104 of the UCC it becomes a check under some circumstances and an instrument under others. See the definition of *Negotiable Instrument* for a fuller explanation.

An important rule to remember is:

All checks are drafts, but not all drafts are checks.

162. **Due on Sale: DOS:** This is a special—and common—*call option* pursuant to which the lender can *call* a loan due if the borrower sells the property securing the loan. In contrast, some loans are assumable; hence, the purchaser of the security can assume the obligation and the lender will release the original obligor. At one time, many home mortgage loans in the United States were assumable. More recently, almost all have a *due on sale* clause.

The almost universal existence of *DOS* clauses in residential mortgage loans is fundamental to the reason the disclosure of an *APR* is misleading for loans which have *points*.

163. **DSO: Days Sales Outstanding:** This is ratio which helps evaluate solvency and operations. It computes the average number of days between a sale and collection. Companies which sell for cash only, would have a *DSO* of zero. A higher ratio indicates credit sales.

$$DSO = \left(\frac{average\ accounts\ receivable}{sales} \right) n$$

Where n = number of days in the period (*e.g.*, 30, 90, or 365), and *sales* = total sales for the period.

Other presentations include:

$$DSO = \left(\frac{ending\ accounts\ receivable}{sales} \right) n$$

Where n = number of days in the period (*e.g.*, 30, 90, or 365), and *sales* = total sales for the period.

$$DSO = \left(\frac{ending\ accounts\ receivable}{credit\ sales} \right) n$$

Where n = number of days in the period (*e.g.*, 30, 90, or 365).

$$DSO = \left(\frac{average\ accounts\ receivable}{credit\ sales} \right) n$$

Where n = number of days in the period (*e.g.*, 30, 90, or 365).

164. **Earnings and Profits: E & P:** This is a United States tax term roughly equivalent to *Retained Earnings* for *Financial Accounting* purposes and *Earned Surplus* for Corporate Law purposes. It has significant differences from those other two terms, however, and thus is <u>not</u> interchangeable with them. A C corporate distribution is taxable to the recipient as a dividend to the extent of the corporation's *E & P*.

For a legal definition of *Earnings and Profits*, see generally *IRC* section 312. Generally, *E & P* includes taxable income (or losses) with several significant modifications, including:

- *IRC* section 453 installment sales deferrals are ignored.
- *IRC* section 179 expensing is instead amortized over five years.
- *IRC* section 168 *MACRS* depreciation is replaced with a modified system per *IRC* section 168(g)(2).
- Intangible drilling costs must be capitalized.
- The LIFO inventory method is effectively disallowed.

165. **Earnings before Interest and Taxes:** *EBIT*: [pronounced e-bit]. Used in financial analysis, this number provides useful information about a business' profitability. Essentially, it includes operating income by excluding interest and taxes. In some cases, users also exclude non-cash items such as depreciation and amortization. Because it is a function of earnings, it does not include (or, better, should not include) extraordinary items. Because the definition of extraordinary item—as well as the definition of interest—can be subject to some variation, lawyers should be careful with this term.

     As is true of many financial analysis terms, *EBIT* can be useful in a contract. For example, a contract provision may trigger specified consequences (acceleration of a loan, the change of an interest rate, more frequent disclosure or oversight) if *EBIT* falls below a pre-determined level.

     A related term is EBITDA: earnings before interest, taxes, depreciation, and amortization. Arguably this is a more useful number to measure current changes in liquidity in relation to loans because it excludes the artificial (non-cash flow) elements of depreciation and amortization.

     See IRC section 163(j)(6)(A) for a definition of "adjusted taxable income" which is comparable to EBITDA. Section 163(j) limits the deductibility of interest between related companies as a partial function of "adjusted taxable income." Many EU countries have similar rules which are a function of EBITDA.

166. **Earnings per Share: EPS:** While facially simple to compute, *EPS* can be a complex computation. At its simplest, *EPS* comprises a companies:

$$\left(\frac{earnings}{number\ of\ shares\ outstanding} \right)$$

     The term *earnings*, however, is open to definition. It may include all earnings; however, it may also exclude extraordinary items. Or, it may be *EBIT*.

     The number of shares outstanding is also open to definition. It may be as of a particular date, or it may be a weighted average over a period of time. Or, for partially diluted *EPS*, it may include convertible securities, options, and warrants, which—because of current conditions—are expected to be converted or exercised. Or, for fully diluted *EPS*, it would include all convertible securities plus all options and warrants regardless of the likelihood of exercise or conversion.

     A *PE* ratio—price divided by earnings—notes the relationship between a stock's market price and its *EPS*.

167. **Economic Benefit Doctrine: also, Secular Trust:** This is a United States tax law doctrine created by the judiciary. The *Secular Trust* name grew out of the *Rabbi Trust Doctrine,* which involved a successful deferred compensation arrangement which did not trigger the adverse consequences of the *Economic Benefit Doctrine.* The *Rabbi Trust* matter involved compensation to the Rabbi of a Synagogue. A *Secular Trust* is an unsuccessful attempted tax deferral for *non-qualified deferred compensation.*

Under the Doctrine, a *cash method* taxpayer has income when he receives the *economic benefit* of the proceeds. This occurs even if he lacks actual receipt, *constructive receipt,* or receipt of a *cash equivalent.* It results when the payor irrevocably places funds for the benefit of the taxpayer beyond the reach of the payor's creditors. *Sproull v. Commissioner,* 194 F.2d 541 (6th Cir. 1952). According to most authorities, the *Doctrine* applies only to service income and contest winnings; it does not apply to transactions involving the sale of property. The government has consistently, but unsuccessfully, disagreed with this limitation on the *Doctrine.*

168. **EDGAR: Electronic Data Gathering Analysis and Retrieval:** [pronounced **ed**-ger]. According to the Securities and Exchange Commission:

> EDGAR, the Electronic Data Gathering, Analysis, and Retrieval system, performs automated collection, validation, indexing, acceptance, and forwarding of submissions by companies and others who are required by law to file forms with the U.S. Securities and Exchange Commission (SEC). Its primary purpose is to increase the efficiency and fairness of the securities market for the benefit of investors, corporations, and the economy by accelerating the receipt, acceptance, dissemination, and analysis of time-sensitive corporate information filed with the agency.

> Not all documents filed with the Commission by public companies will be available on EDGAR. Companies were phased in to EDGAR filing over a three-year period, ending May 6, 1996. As of that date, all public domestic companies were required to make their filings on EDGAR, except for filings made in paper because of a hardship exemption. Third-party filings with respect to these companies, such as tender offers and Schedules 13D, are also filed on EDGAR.

> However, some documents are not yet permitted to be filed electronically, and consequently will not be available on EDGAR. Other documents may be filed on EDGAR

voluntarily, and consequently may or may not be available on EDGAR.

http://www.sec.gov/edgar/aboutedgar.htm.

169. **Effective Interest Rate:** *EFF*: Sometimes labeled an *EIR*, this is a compounded rate of interest. It is the *periodic* rate compounded for one year. It differs from the *nominal annual interest rate (NAI)* in that the *effective* rate is compounded while the nominal rate is not. All financial calculators have an *effective rate* function, as well as a nominal rate function. For financial calculations, a calculator uses the periodic rate; hence, the nominal rate—which is the *periodic* rate times the numbers of periods in one year—is useful. Given an *effective rate*, one can convert it to the equivalent nominal annual rate for a given compounding frequency; then, one can divide by the frequency to produce the needed periodic rate.

An effective rate (*EFF*) differs substantially from an *Annual Percentage Rate (APR)*, which is mostly a non-compounded rate. Federal law defines the *APR*, which generally is the nominal annual rate plus points and some other closing costs amortized for the stated life of the loan. In contrast, the *EFF* treats points as principal rather than interest and then produces a number different from the *APR* (assuming the loan includes points).

An *EFF* is arguably inapplicable to most consumer loans, which require current periodic interest payments. As such, they do not internally compound interest because the borrower pays all interest currently to the lender. But, externally, the funds for interest payments come from somewhere and end up somewhere. Hence, from the borrower's perspective, interest compounds to the extent the funds used to pay current interest are no longer available for other uses. Similarly, from the perspective of the lender, interest compounds to the extent the funds received in payment of current interest are either deposited elsewhere or expended (whereby they free-up other funds which are deposited or they relieve the need for other borrowing).

The formula for the *effective* interest rate:

$$eff = \left[\ 100 \left(\left(1 + \frac{pr}{100} \right)^{py} - 1 \right) \right]$$

where *eff* = effective interest rate, *pr* = the periodic rate and *py* = the number of periods per year.

170. **Efficient Market Hypothesis:** Arguably, the stock market is efficient: all relevant information is fully and immediately reflected in a marketable security's price. Variations on the theory range from inclusion of past information, to inclusion of public information, to inclusion of all information—public or private. The middle category is

probably the most common. Under this theory, an investor cannot obtain an extra or abnormal return because the price of all traded securities is correct. While no such perfect market exists, the theory provides a reference or basis point. Over long periods of time and including large numbers of investors, the hypothesis tends to be correct. Over short periods, or involving few investors, the hypothesis can be very wrong. In other words, the theory holds true in a macro-economic sense, but not true in a micro-economic sense.

171. **Elasticity:** This is an economic term that relates to the propensity for one item to vary as a function of another. High variance indicates high elasticity, while low variance—or stability—indicates inelasticity.

Price is often the variable. For example, many luxury goods—such as visits to a spa or filet mignon are highly elastic to price. If the price goes up, the quantity demanded will drop. Other items, however, tend to be price inelastic. For example, basic staples such as bread and milk are less price elastic than highly discretionary items because people need them regardless of price.

A manager setting the price of an item will tend to set it at the point just below where the demand becomes highly elastic. That way, he will tend to maximize revenue.

A basic economics graph illustrates the relationship of supply and demand. Both vary as to price. As price increases, supply will increase but demand will drop. At some point, they reach equilibrium. That will be the market price for the item.

An important related concept concerns government budgeting. Often government bases tax and other legislation on *static models*: consequences of a tax rate increase are a function of past economic activity. Such models, however, are seriously flawed. They assume inelastic behavior: that people will not alter their investments and consumption as tax rates change. The essence of Keynesian fiscal policy, however, is the ability of the government to influence behavior through spending and taxing policy changes. A superior budget model is *dynamic*: it attempts to predict behavioral changes which result from tax and spending changes.

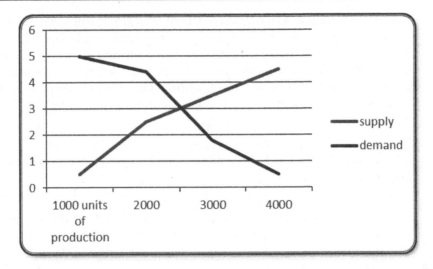

172. **Employee:** An employee—distinguished from an independent contractor—is a person whom an employer directs in terms of hours worked and manner of work. Largely, the distinctions appear in statutes, rules, and litigation under Subtitle C of the Internal Revenue Code: *Employment Taxes.*

Many areas of the law are functions of *employment* status or the lack thereof. These include:

- Social Security rules and taxes.
- Self employment tax.
- Unemployment compensation.
- Labor laws.
- Workers' compensation.
- Agency law.
- State and local laws requiring occupational licenses and work permits.
- Zoning rules regarding operating a business with employees in a particular location.
- Personal injury and tort laws regarding an employer's liability for acts of his employees.
- Deferred Compensation laws affecting qualified plans.
- Minimum wage laws.
- Employee benefits law.
- Insurance law regarding coverage of employees.

173. **Employee Stock Ownership Plan:** *ESOP*: [pronounced **ee**-sop].
This is a type of qualified deferred compensation plan permitted by
ERISA. The plan invests in stock of the founding company on behalf
of the employees. *ESOP*s have been popular with management
because they provide a source of capital. They have been popular with
employees because they provide an ownership interest in the
employer.

174. **Employee's Retirement Income Security Act:** *ERISA*:
[pronounced *uh*-**ris**-*uh*]. According to the United States Department of
Labor:

> The Employee Retirement Income Security Act of 1974
> (ERISA) is a federal law that sets minimum standards for
> most voluntarily established pension and health plans in
> private industry to provide protection for individuals in these
> plans.
>
> ERISA requires plans to provide participants with plan
> information including important information about plan
> features and funding; provides fiduciary responsibilities for
> those who manage and control plan assets; requires plans to
> establish a grievance and appeals process for participants to
> get benefits from their plans; and gives participants the right
> to sue for benefits and breaches of fiduciary duty.
>
> There have been a number of amendments to ERISA,
> expanding the protections available to health benefit plan
> participants and beneficiaries. One important amendment,
> the Consolidated Omnibus Budget Reconciliation Act
> (COBRA), provides some workers and their families with the
> right to continue their health coverage for a limited time after
> certain events, such as the loss of a job. Another amendment
> to ERISA is the Health Insurance Portability and
> Accountability Act (HIPAA) which provides important new
> protections for working Americans and their families who
> have preexisting medical conditions or might otherwise suffer
> discrimination in health coverage based on factors that relate
> to an individual's health. Other important amendments
> include the Newborns' and Mothers' Health Protection Act,
> the Mental Health Parity Act, and the Women's Health and
> Cancer Rights Act.
>
> In general, ERISA does not cover group health plans
> established or maintained by governmental entities,
> churches for their employees, or plans which are maintained
> solely to comply with applicable workers compensation,
> unemployment, or disability laws. ERISA also does not cover

plans maintained outside the United States primarily for the benefit of nonresident aliens or unfunded excess benefit plans.

http://www.dol.gov/dol/topic/health-plans/erisa.htm.

When spoken, the term *ERISA* is sometimes confused with the acronym *URESA*, which refers to the Uniform Reciprocal Enforcement of Support Act—an important family law measure. Clearly, they have nothing to do with each other. Hence, lawyers must be careful when pronouncing the two acronyms.

175. **End Mode: EM:** In *End Mode*, the first payment of an annuity (or for the amortization of a loan) is due one period in the future. In contrast, for *Begin Mode*, the first payment is due today.

Lawyers should be careful with the *mode* function. *Mode* mistakes are one of the more common errors in financial calculations. Unlike *P/YR* errors, *mode* mistakes do not result in profound consequences; hence, they are not obvious to most users. In contrast, compounding errors may result in large consequences; as a result, even the most inexperienced user should notice a problem. *Mode* mistakes are more subtle; nevertheless, they can be significant.

The *Mode* is irrelevant in **FUTURE VALUE** and **PRESENT VALUE** computations. It is relevant for computations involving the **FUTURE VALUE OF AN ANNUITY**, the **PRESENT VALUE OF AN ANNUITY**, a **SINKING FUND**, or an **AMORTIZATION**.

176. **Errors and Omissions Insurance: E & O:** Generally known as *E & O* Insurance, this covers members of a Board of Directors for mistakes they may make in their capacity as board members. Generally, it will not cover fraud or other criminal activity. A Notary Public may also purchase E & O insurance; indeed, state law may require it.

One would be very ill-advised to serve on a Board of Directors— including as a volunteer for a charity—that does not provide *E & O* insurance.

177. **Equitable Distribution (*ED*):** In contrast to a marital *Community Property* regime used by most nations, most United States jurisdictions have adopted a system of *Equitable Distribution* of Marital Assets and Liabilities upon dissolution of marriage. Ten States plus Puerto Rico use various forms of *Community Property*.

Typically, a states' *Equitable Distribution* statute applies for purposes of marital dissolution, but not for purposes of inheritance or even ownership during a valid marriage. In contrast, *Community Property* regimes typically apply for all three purposes, although they may have small varying rules within the three legal areas.

In an *ED* state, upon the filing of a petition for dissolution of marriage, the law fixes the status of assets and liabilities as either marital or separate (or mixed). State law definitions determine the reach of each category by using common financial and accounting terminology. Often, however, the family law usage differs from common financial or accounting usage. Also often, state law provides no definitions, leaving to courts the job of defining financial and accounting terms, some of which are terms of art and some of which are not.

Anecdotal evidence, as well as numerous reported court decisions, suggests parties often use United States federal tax returns as the basis for determining *income*, which is a component of any asset determination.

Some state statutes border on the ridiculous—*e.g.,* the Florida provision defining some *income* as an asset. *F.S. section 61.075(5)(b)(3).* Of course, *income results* in assets and rights to *future income constitute* assets; however, income itself is not an asset. *Debits* to income go to a *temporary account*, not a *permanent* asset *account*. Income is a matter for an *Income Statement* and assets are a matter for *Balance Sheets*.

The term *income* itself has little meaning in terms of a *Balance Sheet*. The *Balance Sheet* includes *Retained Earnings*, which result from *income*, but include only the portion *retained*. Without a reference to expenditures, consumption, and losses, the word *income* is undefined for *Balance Sheet* purposes. Nevertheless, lawyers dealing with *ED* must resolve such difficult-to-resolve issues. Because *ED* necessarily deals with assets and liabilities, it has a *Balance Sheet* perspective. In contrast, alimony and child support deal specifically with *income* and thus have an *Income Statement* perspective. With regard to the Florida statute's use of the word *income*, courts have yet to provide any clear guidance.

Another important financial criticism of *ED* statutes involves their relationship to alimony and child support. Most fail to explain the relationship clearly. For example, they typically fail to provide whether the *Present Value* of future alimony and child support obligations constitute a liability in terms of deciding whether the distribution and division of marital assets and liabilities has been equitable.

178. **Equity:** In finance and accounting terms, this is a net figure reflecting ownership. For example, on a balance sheet, owner's equity is the difference between Assets and Liabilities. It appears on the right-side of the *balance sheet*. It can be a negative number (which indicates balance sheet insolvency).

With regard to a particular asset, one might properly describe the owner's *equity* as being the difference between the fair market value of the asset less the liabilities encumbering it. In this sense, equity is not itself an asset and does not represent ownership. The owner owns 100% of the asset and the creditor owns nothing but a security interest in it (a preference right on liquidation or sale). The distinction is important in many legal areas. For example, for family law purposes, posit a person who has a house worth $300,000 subject to a mortgage securing $200,000 of debt. The person has an asset of $300,000 and a liability of $200,000. He does not have an asset of $100,000. In other words, his equity is not his asset and does not reflect his property interest. This matters in two ways. First, in a divorce, the court may allocate assets and liabilities differently; hence, the parties should ensure they denominate the categories correctly. Second, payment of the liability securing the asset increases the equity in the asset (assuming the asset retains its value or appreciates); however, payment of the debt does not enhance or increase the asset. Payment of the debt merely reduces the debt. In some jurisdictions, the enhancement of an asset has different legal consequences than does the payment of a liability. Hence, lawyers must clearly understand what *is* an asset and what *is not*. *Equity*—in finance or accounting terms—is not an asset.

The term *equity*, however, is a type of asset in corporate parlance. It refers to stock, both common and preferred, as opposed to debt, such as bonds or notes. Whether a particular instrument represents *equity* or debt is occasionally controversial. For example, the difference between non-participating, non-convertible preferred stock and unsecured notes may not be substantial.

179. **Estate Tax:** This is a tax imposed on the *Gross Estate*, less deductions, of a decedent. Subtitle B of the United States Internal Revenue Code imposes an estate tax. Under U.S. tax laws, an estate is a person and a taxpayer. The estate is primarily responsible for the tax; however, if the estate fails to pay the tax, the recipient heirs and legatees bear some liability, as well.

Many jurisdictions, including many states, impose *Inheritance Taxes*. These differ from an estate tax in that they apply to the heir or legatee, as opposed to the estate. Nevertheless, most *Inheritance Tax* regimes require the estate to collect and to pay over the tax prior to distribution.

The vast majority of estates in the U.S. are not liable for any *Estate Tax*. The actual percentage of estates liable for tax has varied over the past several decades, but has typically been less than 10% and often less than 3%.

The United States also imposes a *Gift Tax* under Subtitle B of the Internal Revenue Code. *Gift Tax* rule and rates effectively merge with *Estate Tax* rules. Each person has a *Unified Credit* against the transfer taxes. He may use it during his life, reducing liability for *Gift Tax*; or, his estate may use it to reduce its liability for *Estate Tax*.

For 2009, the Unified Credit was mathematically approximately the equivalent of either a $3,500,000 *exclusion* or *zero-bracket amount* (two other tax law terms used from time to time). Hence, persons with a net worth of under approximately $3,500,000 did not then need concern themselves with either a Gift or Estate Tax. Their heirs and legatees, however, may have been responsible for state *Inheritance Tax*.

For persons dying in calendar year 2010, the United States Estate Tax did not exist; hence, the Unified Credit did not exist. For years post 2011, the Unified Credit equals $5,000,000 in equivalent exclusion.

Estate Planning has many functions. Primary among them is the reduction—or *apparent* reduction—in the value of one's *Gross Estate* so as to reduce or eliminate liability for Estate Taxes. The word *apparent* in the prior sentence is critical: people reduce their worth in many ways:

- They give it away, which requires consideration of Gift Taxes.

- They consume it.

- They destroy or waste it.

- They define its value as less than its true value.

Rational self interest generally prevents the third option of destruction and waste. Consumption is something everyone does; however, consuming huge sums of value can be difficult. Investment is not consumption; thus the purchase of a valuable painting, expensive jewelry, or an obscenely large residence does not consume any value (unless one pays too much, which is waste). In contrast, travel, entertainment, eating, gambling, fancy cars and fancy clothing are forms of consumption which can reduce one's net worth.

Gifts are common estate planning tools—tempered by the Gift Tax. Gifts to Charities help, as well.

Probably, however, the most useful *Estate Planning Techniques* involve financial and accounting tools which cause an asset to lose *apparent* value without it losing *actual* value. See the discussion on *Family Limited Partnerships* (*FPL*). Because accounting is more art than science, such techniques abound, particularly in a self reporting system filled with *moral hazard*. Many people view such techniques as cutting edge. Others view them as magic tricks. Still others see them as abuse.

These *Estate Planning Techniques* have impact far beyond mere *Estate Planning*. Were they limited to that are, one might have little concern for them as they reduce revenues from a tax that generates a fairly insignificant amount of revenue in any event. But, life is not so simple. Such techniques impact other areas of the law. For example, a technique which successfully reduces one's apparent worth for *Estate Tax* purposes likely also reduces one's apparent worth for *Equitable Distribution* or *Community Property* division incident to marriage dissolution. *Divorce Planning*—and *Bankruptcy Planning*—are arguably both outgrowths of *Estate Planning*. They generally use the same methods and techniques. Instead of avoiding *Estate* or *Gift Tax*, uses avoid liabilities to creditors or to former spouses and children.

The Supreme Court found the pre-cursor of the Estate Tax and Gift Tax valid in 1900, as an excise under Article I, Section 8 of the Constitution, in *Knowlton v. Moore,* 178 U.S. 41 (1900).

180. **Estate Tax Freeze:** This is an estate planning technique by which the planner attempts to "freeze" the value of the estate assets.

For example, a wealthy person with several children may place his appreciating assets into a family limited partnership. His children may receive interests which will likely appreciate in value while he retains an interest in assets which will likely maintain a fixed value. As a result, the value of the estate freezes with all appreciation avoiding the U.S. estate tax. Other techniques involve placing appreciating assets into a trust such that the donor has made a "completed gift" for estate tax purposes—a term of art. He will then owe a current gift tax; however, the trust income and appreciation will avoid estate taxes. The donor may retain some incidents of ownership, but not much.

181. **European Central Bank: ECB:** According to the website for the "bank":

> The ECB is the central bank for Europe's single currency, the euro. The ECB's main task is to maintain the euro's purchasing power and thus price stability in the euro area. The euro area comprises the 17 European Union countries that have introduced the euro since 1999.

http://www.ecb.int/home/html/index.en.html.

Because the *EU* members retain substantial sovereignty, the "bank" cannot act with the same powers as the *FED*, which operates with the authority of the U.S. By late 2011, considerable doubt existed regarding whether the euro could continue as a common currency for so many sovereign nations and whether the *ECB* had the power and resources to keep the currency stable.

182. **European Community: EC:** Under the 2007 Lisbon Treaty, this will cease to exist and will officially merge into the European Union (*EU*). Until the treaty is fully in force, the *EC* is one of three pillars forming the *EU*: The *EC*, the Common Foreign and Security Policy, and the Police and Judicial Cooperation in Criminal Matters.

183. **European Union: EU:** This is an organization of 27 member states created by the 1993 Maastricht Treaty. Sixteen members have adopted the Euro as their single currency (**listed below in bold**). Others merely participate in a common market regarding trade, laws affecting commerce, and the movement of people, goods, services, and capital. The countries include:

- **Republic of Austria**
- **Kingdom of Belgium**
- Republic of Bulgaria
- **Republic of Cyprus**
- Czech Republic
- Kingdom of Denmark
- Republic of Estonia
- **Republic of Finland**
- **French Republic**
- **Federal Republic of Germany**
- **Hellenic Republic (Greece)**
- Republic of Hungary
- **Ireland**
- **Italian Republic**
- Republic of Latvia
- Republic of Lithuania
- **Grand Duchy of Luxembourg**
- **Republic of Malta**
- **the Netherlands**
- Republic of Poland
- **Portuguese Republic**
- Romania

- **Slovak Republic**
- **Republic of Slovenia**
- **Kingdom of Spain**
- Kingdom of Sweden

184. **Economic Value Added: EVA:** NOPAT minus capital times the cost of capital. See the definitions of NOPAT, capital, cost of capital, and weighted average cost of capital.

185. **Excess Paid-In Capital: EPIC:** This finance and accounting term has little meaning. It refers to the excess paid for shares over par or stated value. Par value has long lost most of its meaning. At one time, shareholders were liable for corporate debts to the extent they had not paid par value for their stock. For many years, however, companies have issues no-par stock or stock with an extremely low par value in states that retain the notion of par. The accounting line for *EPIC* is part of owner's equity.

   Most accountants refer to this as *APIC* or Additional Paid-in Capital.

186. **Excise Tax:** Generally, this term refers to taxes on activities, transactions, or the use of property. Typically, they are "pass on" taxes in that the obligor can pass on the tax to the consumer or user. Per Article I, Section 8 of the U.S. Constitution, Congress may impose excises, duties and imposts; however, each of these *Indirect* Taxes must be uniform throughout the country. The estate and gift tax systems are excises, as are the employer's share of FICA taxes, plus various levies on alcohol, tobacco, firearms, tires, telephone services, and many other items. In contrast, Direct taxes in the United States must be apportioned among the states by population per Article I, Section 9 of the Constitution.

187. **Exchange Traded Funds: ETF:** available in the United States since 1993, *ETF*s have traditionally been index funds. As such, they were mutual funds which tracked the value of a popular index such as the S & P 500 or the Russell 2000. Investors typically like the diversification offered by *ETF*s. They also like the ease of tracking the value.

   Since 2008, the U.S. has permitted managed *ETF*s.

188. **Expense Recognition Principle:** Per *GAAP*, an entity recognizes expense when incurred. Payment is irrelevant. Expenses break into three types:

   - Expenses recognized when revenue is recognized because the two are directly associated. An example would be the cost of goods sold.

- Expenses that will benefit the business over a period of multiple years. These must be capitalized and amortized over the relevant years. Depreciation is an example of the annual expense.

- Expenses that will benefit the business over a short period or which that provide no discernable future benefit. Research and development expenditures are often a good example. If management discerns a specific future benefit with regard to specific elements (such as a building or equipment) capitalization is appropriate. Otherwise, research expenditures are expensed. This is a substantial deviation from IFRS.

189. **Factoring:** This is the process of selling accounts receivable—often at a substantial discount—to a bank or other investor. Businesses factor *AR* to raise working capital and liquidity.

   Factoring is also an important algebraic tool for solving equations.

190. **Fair Market Value: FMV:** What a willing buyer would pay to a willing seller, neither under any special compulsion to buy or to sell at that particular time. For tax purposes, the amount realized in a taxable transaction includes the *Fair Market Value* (FMV) of any property or services received. At least a few lower court opinions have defined *FMV* in a personal sense, *i.e.,* at least partially as a function of the individual recipient's circumstances. For example, a person who won a first class trip to Brazil—but who seldom travelled and never first class—might have a *FMV* in the trip which is significantly less than would a more worldly winner. While authorities supporting such a viewpoint are few, lawyers should be aware of the potential "personal" nature of *Fair Market Value. See Turner v. Commissioner,* 13 T.C.M. (CCH) 462 (1954).

   See the definition of *Mark to Market* (*MTM*) and the *FASB* reference to *fair value* as opposed to *fair market value.*

191. **Family Limited Partnership: FLP:** This is a non-term-of art referring to a partnership owned by related parties—generally close family members. It would have some general partners and some limited partners. FLPs are useful in Estate Planning, as they can involve various allocations of risk, as well as gain potential. For example, a wealthy business owner may transfer his business to an FLP, allocating future gains to his children, but retaining substantial value for himself. With wise planning, the scheme can reduce or eliminate both gift and estate taxes in two ways:

- The future gain would not be part of the creator's estate for estate tax purposes and it may have minimal current value.

- The sum of the values of the various FLP interest will generally be substantially less than the value of the business when held by a single person. This value decrease results from valuation discounts attributable to minority interests.

192. **FDAP: Fixed or Determinable, Annual or Periodical:** This includes all income except: gains derived from the sale of real personal property and items of income excluded from gross income, without regard to the U.S. or foreign status of the owner of the income, such as tax-exempt municipal bond interest and qualified scholarship income. See, IRC sections 871a and 881a.

193. **Federal Deposit Insurance Corporation:** *FDIC*: According to the entity's website and mission statement:

> The *Federal Deposit Insurance Corporation (FDIC)* is an independent agency created by the Congress that maintains the stability and public confidence in the nation's financial system by insuring deposits, examining and supervising financial institutions, and managing receiverships.

Founded in 1933, the *FDIC* insures deposits at Banks. The limit is $250,000 per person per institution. Many entities such as insurance companies offer financial products similar to demand deposits at Banks or *CDs* at Banks. Such alternative instruments, however, are not insured by the *FDIC*.

194. **Federal Home Loan Mortgage Corporation: FHLMC: Freddie Mac:** According to the entity's website, its mission (which one should try to read without laughing) is (or was):

> Freddie Mac's mission is to provide liquidity, stability and affordability to the housing market.

> Congress defined this mission in our 1970 charter, which lays the foundation of our business and the ideals that power our goals.

> Our mission forms the framework for our business lines, shapes the products we bring to market and drives the services we provide to the nation's housing and mortgage industry. Everything we do comes back to making America's mortgage markets liquid and stable and increasing opportunities for homeownership and affordable rental housing across the nation.

Our mission strives to create:

- **Stability:** Freddie Mac's retained portfolio plays an important role in making sure there's a stable supply of money for lenders to make the home loans new homebuyers need and an available supply of workforce housing in our communities.

- **Affordability:** Financing housing for low- and moderate-income families has been a key part of Freddie Mac's business since we opened our doors. Freddie Mac's vision is that families must be able both to afford to purchase a home and to keep that home.

- **Liquidity:** Freddie Mac makes sure there's a stable supply of money for lenders to make the loans new homebuyers need. This gives everyone better access to home financing, raising the roof on homeownership opportunity in America.

Freddie Mac is an example of a *Government Sponsored Entity (GSE)*. Unlike *Ginnie Mae*, it lacks the full faith and credit of the Treasury for its obligations. Serious financial problems from the late 1990s until the fall of 2008 have raised substantial doubt about the continued viability of *Freddie Mac*.

195. **Federal Funds Rate:** This is generally an over-night interest rate at which banks lend to each other. Typically they do so through the *Fed* to maintain required reserves. The *Fed* sets the rate through the *FOMC*, which is one of its monetary policy tools.

196. **Federal National Mortgage Association: FNMA: Fannie Mae:** According to the entity's website (please read with a straight face):

Fannie Mae is a government-sponsored enterprise (GSE) chartered by Congress with a mission to provide liquidity and stability to the U.S. housing and mortgage markets.

Fannie Mae operates in the U.S. secondary mortgage market. Rather than making home loans directly with consumers, we work with mortgage bankers, brokers, and other primary mortgage market partners to help ensure they have funds to lend to home buyers at affordable rates. We fund our mortgage investments primarily by issuing debt securities in the domestic and international capital markets.

Fannie Mae was established as a federal agency in 1938, and in 1968 we were chartered by Congress as a private shareholder-owned company. On September 6, 2008, Director

James Lockhart of the Federal Housing Finance Agency
(FHFA) appointed FHFA as conservator of Fannie Mae. In
addition, the U.S. Department of the Treasury agreed to
provide up to $100 billion of capital as needed to ensure the
company continues to provide liquidity to the housing and
mortgage markets.

Fannie Mae has three businesses—Single-Family, Housing
and Community Development, and Capital Markets—that
work together to provide services, products, and solutions to
lender partners and a broad range of housing partners.
Together, these businesses contribute to the company's
chartered mission objectives, helping to increase the total
amount of funds available in America to make
homeownership and rental housing more available and
affordable.

http://www.fanniemae.com.

Fannie Mae is an example of a *Government Sponsored Entity* (*GSE*).
Unlike *Ginnie Mae*, it lacks the full faith and credit of the Treasury for
its obligations. Serious financial problems from the late 1990s until
the fall of 2008 have raised substantial doubt about the continued
viability of *Fannie Mae*.

197. **Federal Open Market Committee: FOMC:** The Banking Act of
    1935 created the Federal Open Market Committee (*FOMC*) to conduct
    open market operations OMO, which various Federal Reserve Banks
    had conducted without specific statutory authorization since 1923. As
    defined by the *Federal Reserve, open market operations involve*:

    Purchases and sales of government securities and certain
    other securities in the open market, through the Domestic
    Trading Desk at the Federal Reserve Bank of New York as
    directed by the Federal Open Market Committee (FOMC), to
    influence the volume of money and credit in the economy.
    Purchases inject reserves into the banking system and
    stimulate growth of money and credit; sales do the opposite.

Such *OMO*s, are one tool of the Federal Reserve by its it can affect
("influence" in its words and "control" in the words of others) interest
rates and the money supply (or vice versa). Lawyers should
understand these functions, as they—despite controversy regarding
their effectiveness and wisdom—clearly have short-term, if not long-
term, impacts on interest rate.

LESSON SIX covers *Why People Charge Interest*. It discusses three
main factors of interest, including risk. Although much of "risk" is
personal to the borrower, at least some of the factor is a function of *Fed*

behavior, including *FOMC* behavior. As a result, the measurement of risk is less a scientific study of the borrower than a well-educated evaluation of the borrower and a political and economic guess of future *Fed* and *FOMC* actions.

198. **Federal Reserve Bank: Fed:** [pronounced fed]. According to the Federal Reserve (Fed) website:

> The Federal Reserve, the Central Bank of the United States, provides the nation with a safe, flexible, and stable monetary and financial system.

In 1791, Congress created the first Bank of the United States under a twenty-year charter, which expired in 1811. In 1816, Congress created the Second Bank of the United States, again under a twenty-year charter, which expired in 1836.

In 1863, the National Banking Act effectively created the first national currency of the United States. Prior to then, various state bank notes were common. Because the 1863 Act taxed state, but not national, bank notes, the state notes became less common.

After a series of financial crises and much political debate, President Wilson signed the Federal Reserve Act in 1913. By late 1914, the nation had twelve regional Federal Reserve Banks.

The 1933 Banking Act, also known as the *Glass-Stegall Act*, created the *Federal Deposit Insurance Corporation* (*FDIC*). The 1936, separate open market operations from direct *Fed* control by created the *Federal Open Market Committee* as a separate legal entity. It also created 14-year terms for *Fed* governors and removed the Treasury Secretary and Comptroller of the Currency as members. This further removed the *Fed* from government control—or at least gave that appearance.

The 1956 *Bank Holding Act* gave the *Fed* authority to regulate Bank Holding Companies (entities who own more than one bank). The 1977 *Community Reinvestment Act* (CRA) "encourages banks to help meet the credit needs of their communities for housing and other purposes, particularly in neighborhoods with low or moderate incomes, while maintaining safe and sound operations." Arguably, this act and later actions consistent with it helped cause the *sub-prime* mortgage loan crisis of 2008.

The *Monetary Control Act* of 1980 further changed the role of the Fed and introduced a more modern banking system for the U.S. The 1999 *Gramm-Leach-Bliley Act* effectively overturned the *Glass-Stegall Act* and permitted banks to offers a variety of investment banking services.

For a more complete discussion, see the **FEDERAL RESERVE SYSTEM, PURPOSES & FUNCTIONS**.

199. **Federal Unemployment Tax Act: FUTA:** [pronounced **fyoo**-tə]. According to the *IRS*:

> The Federal Unemployment Tax Act (FUTA), with state unemployment systems, provides for payments of unemployment compensation to workers who have lost their jobs. Most employers pay both a Federal and a state unemployment tax. A list of state unemployment tax agencies, including addresses and phone numbers, is available in Publication 926, Household Employer's Tax Guide.

Only employers "pay" the tax. Unlike, *FICA*, no portion is deducted from wages. The tax is currently 6.2% of *FUTA* wages, which are $7,000. Employers receive a large credit of up to 5.4% for amounts paid to state unemployment funds, resulting in a federal tax rate of .8%.

The definition of an *employee* and *employer* can be complex. Essentially, an *employer* directs the activities of an *employee* but not those of an independent contractor.

When calculating the cost of an employee—or that which he produces—one must include not only his wages, but also any relevant *FICA* or *FUTA* tax as well as fringe benefits, contributions to deferred compensation and insurance plans, and other such items.

200. **Fiat Currency:** *Currency* printed or coined by a sovereign nation but not backed by valuable property such as gold or silver. Fiat *currency* is distinguishable from *commodity money*—such as actual gold or silver—or *representative money*—such as silver or gold certificates formerly issued by the U.S. Such certificates were redeemable in a stated amount of a commodity.

Some economists believe fiat currency is worthless and the United States should return to the gold standard: a system of representative currency. Others consider such views as folly.

The United States mostly ended its gold standard system in 1934. For several decades following that action, Americans could not legally own gold bullion. In 1973, the U.S. devalued the dollar and fully ended its agreement to redeem dollars for bullion.

201. **FIFO: First in First out:** [pronounced **fahy**-foh]. This is a common inventory system under which the user assumes the first inventory purchased was the first inventory sold. FIFO, in times of inflation, will understate *COGS* and thus overstate income. LIFO—as opposed to FIFO—better reflects inventory and replacement costs in times of

inflation. For tax purposes, LIFO is permissible only if the taxpayer also uses LIFO for financial reporting purposes. For purposes of computing corporate Earnings and Profits, IRC section 312 effectively requires the use of FIFO.

Inventories are an important part of many legal relationships. The use of LIFO versus FIFO inventory accounting can have a substantial impact on income and costs—particularly if the user changes from one method to another. While such a change of inventory method is an item that should always be reported or disclosed, life does not always work that way. Hence, inventory accounting is an area ripe for misleading statements. For example, if A must pay B a share of profits, A can affect his liability to B by adoption of one inventory method as opposed to another. Of course, B should be aware of this choice and should have some part in the choice; however, if B's lawyer is unaware of the meaning and the impact of LIFO and FIFO, then he is unlikely to make a wise choice.

Changing inventory methods violates the Accounting Principal of Consistency. As a result, if an audited entity were to change, it would need full disclosure in its statements, a notation in the *audit opinion*, and a clear reconciliation regarding the impact of the change.

Similarly, in other areas of the law dependent upon a definition of income—such as *family law* (for alimony and child support) and *trust law* (for measuring an income beneficiary's share of a trust)—the choice of an inventory method can have a profound effect. If one party has significant accounting and finance knowledge, while the other does not, the one with knowledge can take unfair advantage over the ignorant party. Whether such behavior is actionable varies. More importantly, if the ignorant party is unaware of the deception, he is unlikely to seek any reparation even if he is entitled to it.

202. **Financial Accounting Standards Board:** *FASB*: [pronounced **faz-** bee]. This is the entity that issues opinions or rules—called *FASB* opinions—on United States accounting issues and *GAAP*. These have also been called FASs (Financial Accounting Standards). Since 2015, they are part of the Codification.

203. **Financial Calculator:** This is a calculator which computes **Present** and **Future** values of either a sum or of an *annuity*. Necessarily, it will also have functions which **Amortize** amounts over time and which compute **Sinking Funds**. These latter functions mirror the present and future value computations of annuities.

One must distinguish a *Financial Calculator* from a *scientific calculator*, which has functions more useful for engineering. Some calculators have both types of function; however, most commercially available calculators are simple, financial, or scientific.

204. **FINRA: Financial Industry Regulatory Authority:** According to
the FINRA website:

> The Financial Industry Regulatory Authority (FINRA) is the
> largest independent regulator for all securities firms doing
> business in the United States. FINRA's mission is to protect
> America's investors by making sure the securities industry
> operates fairly and honestly. All told, FINRA oversees nearly
> 4,500 brokerage firms, about 163,470 branch offices and
> approximately 634,385 registered securities representatives.

> FINRA touches virtually every aspect of the securities
> business—from registering and educating industry
> participants to examining securities firms; writing rules;
> enforcing those rules and the federal securities laws;
> informing and educating the investing public; providing trade
> reporting and other industry utilities; and administering the
> largest dispute resolution forum for investors and registered
> firms. We also perform market regulation under contract for
> the major U.S. stock markets, including the New York Stock
> Exchange, NYSE Arca, NYSE Amex, The NASDAQ Stock
> Market and the International Securities Exchange.

http://www.finra.org/AboutFINRA/.

Typical broker/dealer or investment advisor accounts have clauses
providing for mandatory arbitration under FINRA rules. Those rules
also govern mediation involving such accounts.

205. **Fiscal Policy:** This involves government use of tax and spending to
affect the economy. In contrast, *monetary policy* generally refers to
government or Central Bank control of the *money supply* to affect the
economy.

ACRS and *MACRS* are examples of fiscal policy.

206. **Fiscal Year: FY:** This refers to a tax or accounting year which ends
on the last day of a month other than December. Generally, taxpayers
who use a financial *fiscal year* must use the same year for tax
purposes. An alternative is the use of a *calendar year*.

Cases in which a person controls multiple entities with different fiscal
years are ripe for manipulation. For example, consider one entity using
a January 31, 2011 *FY* and another using a February 28, 2011 *FY*. One
entity might pay the other in February. The payor, if on the February
28 *FY*, would deduct the cost for the year ending a few weeks later.
However, the entity receiving the item of income would not include the
income until the year ending January 31, 2012—eleven months later.
Further manipulation could occur if the first entity were itself a
reporting entity, but the second were a pass-thru entity such that it

distributed the income item to the owner during January, 2012. The owner—who would likely use a calendar year—would include the income for the year ending December 31, 2012, and the payor would report a net of zero for the *FY* ending January 31, 2012.

Ultimately, all income and all deductions would appear; however, they would appear in differing years. Often, legal consequences flow from income reported for a particular period, which might span a single year or several years. Manipulation with *FYs* would aim toward moving income and deduction items either into or out of the relevant period.

Depending on the types of entities involved and the degree of control the owner possessed, both United States tax laws and *GAAP* may require a restatement or consolidation either to prevent, or with the impact of preventing, the manipulation. However, most financial statements are not subject to *GAAP* because they are unaudited, and tax laws are themselves open to varying interpretation and manipulation.

Lawyers should be wary if their client's rights are a function of group of persons' income, particularly if those persons have common control and use different *fiscal years*.

207. **FTSE 100:** [pronounced **foot**-see]. This "acronym" actually no longer officially stands for anything other than the name of a widely followed stock index of companies traded on the London Exchange. FTSE International, Lmt.—the FTSE Group—is a joint venture of the Financial Times of London (hence the FT) and the London Stock Exchange (hence the SE).

208. **Forensic Accountant:** This is an accountant trained to reconstruct realistic financial statements. For example, a forensic accountant might work in marriage dissolution as an expert for a spouse who believes the other spouse has manipulated or wasted assets or income. Or, he might work in a labor law case for a union which believes management has understated its ability to pay higher wages. Just as forensic medicine focuses on the cause of death, forensic accounting focuses on the cause or reasons why a situation is what it appears to be.

According to the **American College of Forensic Examiners (*ACFE*):**

> Forensic accountants are professionals who use a unique blend of education and experience to apply accounting, auditing, and investigative skills to uncover truth, form legal opinions, and assist in investigations. Forensic accountants may be involved in both litigation support (providing assistance on a given case, primarily related to the

calculation or estimation of economic damages and related issues) and investigative accounting (looking into illegal activities).

http://www.acfei.com/forensic_certifications/crfa/.

The *ACFE* offers certification for *Forensic Accountants* through a program leading to a designation called Cr. FA®. This is not a state granted license.

Some Forensic Accountants specialize in fraud detection. Some seek the designation of **Certified Fraud Examiner (*CFE*)**. This is a designation offered through the Association of Certified Fraud Examiners (*ACFE*). It is not a state granted license. According to the *ACFE*:

> Globally preferred by employers, the Certified Fraud Examiner (*CFE*) credential denotes proven expertise in fraud prevention, detection, and deterrence. Members with the *CFE* credential experience professional growth and quickly position themselves as leaders in the global anti-fraud community.

http://www.acfe.com.

209. **Forensic Economist:** This is an economist trained to reconstruct realistic financial information. Such an economist performs tasks similar to those of a forensic accountant. Considerable debate exists whether economists or accountants are better trained for these endeavors.

According to the National Association of Forensic Economics (NAFE):

> Forensic economics is the scientific discipline that applies economic theories and methods to the issue of pecuniary damages as specified by case law and legislative codes. Topics within forensic economics include (1) the analysis of claims involving persons, workers, firms, or markets for evidence concerning damage liability; (2) the calculation of damages in personal and commercial litigation; and, (3) the development and use of generally accepted forensic economic methodologies and principles.

> NAFE's peer reviewed academic journal, the *Journal of Forensic Economics* (JFE), publishes articles of interest to economists, accountants, finance and business professionals, vocational counselors, lawyers, and actuaries engaged in such fields as business valuation, commercial litigation, employment litigation, and personal injury and wrongful

death torts. The JFE is indexed by major economic and social science indexing services . . . .

http://nafe.net.

210. **Free on Board: FOB:** This is a term relating to ownership of an item which is the subject of a sales contract. *Free on Board* suggests that ownership transfers when the seller places the item with a common carrier. *FOB* Destination refers to ownership transferring when the item reaches its destination.

Ownership of the item determines risk of loss and the duty to insure the thing.

211. **Full Absorption Cost:** This is a type of *cost accounting* which includes a portion of all costs—including *indirect* and fixed costs such as overhead—in the defined cost of an item produced. The resulting information is useful for some internal purposes; however, it is also potentially very misleading.

For example, a car dealer may say "we sell below cost"; however, that statement, without a definition of cost, in meaningless. One type of costing is incremental or marginal cost. Under such a system, the cost of the car sold would include the price the dealer paid plus any *direct costs* associated with it, such as incremental and variable transportation costs associated with that particular car. In contrast, under a *full absorption* system, the cost of the car would include a portion of fixed overhead—such as rent on the land and building, depreciation on office desk, annual tax preparation fees, and such. In reality, those extra costs exist regardless of whether the dealer buys and sells the particularly referenced car; hence, they are not fairly included in its cost. Also, management is unwise to include them fully in a pricing system. At some point, a business must cover all *fixed* and *variable costs*; however, with regard to a particular sale, it need only cover *variable costs*—anything extra received is profit on that item which helps cover fixed costs.

Cost accounting is an important and complex area of accounting. Lawyers who use the term cost should understand the term has little meaning standing alone. See the discussion of *TCO* for a fuller explanation.

212. **Full Disclosure Principle of Accounting:** This financial accounting principle—part of *GAAP*—requires *Financial Statements* to disclose all material information, particularly negative information.

For example, an *auditor* will traditionally request a statement from an entity's counsel regarding pending or possible litigation or liabilities. Counsel may be reluctant to provide such information, as it can be damaging from a litigator's perspective. Nevertheless, a *CPA* cannot say the *Financial Statements* fairly present the entity's financial condition if undisclosed liabilities exist. In many cases, such liabilities may be contingent or difficult to assess; nevertheless, proper and *Full Disclosure* requires the release of as much information as is fairly and reasonably available.

213. **Fungibles:** These are items which are identical, or essentially so; hence, one is as good or bad as another. For example, bushels of wheat are fungible—one is as good as another (yes, we know about the possibility of rye in the wheat, but stay with the point). Electricity is *fungible*. Arguably, to large law firms, associates are *fungible*.

For finance and accounting, an important rule is:

Money is fungible.

Thus, one dollar or euro is the same as another. Whether one pays with equity or debt, one has paid and the dollar does not care. Whether one pays from one bank account or another also is irrelevant (other than transaction costs and re-investment costs). Saving money and paying off debt are also essentially fungible: neither has an impact on equity, although the two transactions will impact several ratios differently (which tells you something about the validity of those ratios if they are so easily manipulated).

Interesting tax issues arise upon the exchange of *fungibles*, especially if time is a factor. Also interesting is the definition of *fungible* for tax purposes. *See, Cottage Savings v. Commissioner,* 499 U.S. 554 (1991).

214. **Future Interest:** Anyone who has studied law in a common law system has studied future interests. These are remainder interests in property following the expiration of a term of years or a life estate.

Civil law jurisdictions recognize no concept of future interests; indeed for them, all interests are present interests. The right to use property for a period—and to obtain its fruits—is a *usufruct*. That is a present interest in property. The remainder interest which exists at the end of the *usufructuary's* rights is a *naked ownership* interest.

In financial and economic terms, *future interests* are impossible. Everything is measurable in terms of present value. Anything subject to transfer is property. All property has a *Fair Market Value*, which is the *Present Value* of its future utility. The remainder interest following a life estate is itself a property right capable of being bought or sold or transferred by gift or inheritance. It is every bit a present interest as the current use of the underlying thing.

To illustrate what some common law lawyers might view as paradoxical, consider the following. Posit A who hires B to perform services for three years. In fulfillment of his obligations, A transfers a remainder interest in Blackacre to B at the beginning of the contract. Arguably, A has deferred payment to B. Or, has he? Just as arguably, A has currently transferred a property right—which B can sell or give away—in advance of B's performance. Thus A has pre-paid B. But, which is it—a pre-payment or a post-payment. It cannot be both . . . or can it be?

Consider the formulas for the **PRESENT VALUE OF A SUM** and *THE FUTURE VALUE OF A SUM*. Also compare the formulas for the **PRESENT VALUE OF AN ANNUITY** with the formula for the **FUTURE VALUE OF AN ANNUITY**. In each case, the formulas are algebraic equivalents. Of course they are the same. By definition, they are the identical. This is also true for pre-payments, post-payments, and current payments: they are all the same. *Accrual* accounting demands that this be so. Again, it is definitional. The numbers differ because the pre-payment is actually a loan from A to B and the post payment is a loan from B to A. Loans bear interest, which merely adds another transaction to the mix. But, the present values are identical to the *future values*. The *amortization* of the *present value* must equal the *sinking fund* of the *future value*. Both of these must equal the current payments. All of this is correct at any given, consistent rate of interest.

Once again, consider: does the Property 101 concept of a future interest make any sense?

215. **Futures Market:** A *futures market* trades *futures contracts*. These are agreements to purchase a specified quantity of a commodity at a set price at a specified time in the future.

The *Chicago Board of Trade (CBOT)* was the first real futures market in the United States. It opened in approximately 1820. It is now part of the CME Group, which include *CBOT*, the Chicago Mercantile Exchange, and the New York Mercantile Exchange (*NYMEX*). Most have standardized contracts for regular periods. For example, one can purchase a futures contract for 5,000 ounces of silver to be delivered on stated date in the future. Other contracts involve metals, grains, electricity and similar fungibles.

Typically, the holder of the contract does not actually take delivery; instead, he settles with the maker for a sum of money. Depending on the ultimate spot price, the money may flow from maker to holder or in the opposite direction.

Many companies use *futures* to hedge against unexpected price changes in essential commodities. For example, a maker of corn flakes may regularly purchase corn futures so as to ensure a stable, predictable price for corn. If the spot price increases, the company will accept delivery. If the price drops, the company will pay the difference, or will simply lose money. But, in so doing, it will have capped or limited its risk.

A famous tax decision—*Corn Products Refining Company v. Commissioner,* 350 U.S. 46 (1955)—dealt with the tax consequence of a company dealing in futures of an essential commodity. The Court held: *The IRC section 1221 list of non-capital assets is illustrative rather than exclusive.* Of mostly historical importance this decision found that property "integrally related" to a trade or business was not a capital asset. Common scenarios involving the <u>Corn Products Doctrine</u> involved investment in the securities of a critical supplier or customer. As "integrally related" to the business, any resulting gains were ordinary rather than capital. Losses, too, resulted in ordinary treatment and proved to be the most common application of the decision. As a result, the government regretted winning this decision. The Court subsequently severely limited the case in *Arkansas Best v. Commissioner,* 485 U.S. 212 (1988).

216. **Future Value of an Annuity:** *FVA:* This calculation computes the future value of a series of equal payments made at regular intervals, earning a constant interest rate. For example, $1,000 deposited at the end of each year for ten years earning 10% interest compounded annually, has a future value in ten years of $15,937.42. This calculation is particularly helpful in planning for retirement or saving for a child's education.

Such an annuity is either in end mode (payments occur at the end of each period) or begin mode (payments occur at the beginning of each period).

LESSON TWELVE explains the use of a FUTURE VALUE OF AN ANNUITY CALCULATOR.

The FUTURE VALUE OF AN ANNUITY calculation is one of the six basic calculations performed by a *Financial Calculator.* The formula for the *FVA* is:

$$FVA = \left[\frac{\left[PMT \left(1 + \frac{i}{100} \right)^n - 1 \right]}{\frac{i}{100}} \right]$$

where i = nominal annual interest rate, n = number of periods per year, and *PMT* = the periodic payment or deposit.

217. **Future Value of a Sum:** *FVS:* This calculation computes the future amount or value of a current deposit. For example, $1,000 deposited today, earning 10% interest compounded annually, will increase to $1,100 in one year. In two years it will increase to $1,210. In five years, it will be $1,610.51 and in 100 years it will be $13,780,612.34.

The **FUTURE VALUE OF A SUM** calculation is one of the six basic calculations performed by a *Financial Calculator*. The formula for the *FV* is:

$$FV = PV \left(1 + \frac{i}{100} \right)^n$$

where PV = present value, i = nominal annual interest rate, and n = number of periods per year.

218. *GAAP*: **Generally Accepted Accounting Principles:** [pronounced gap]. These rules form the basis of public accounting. In the United States, audited financial statements must conform to *GAAP* for them to receive an unqualified opinion of the auditors. Departure from *GAAP* is sometimes permissible—or even advisable; however, it will always raise a red flag of concern and thus necessitate a convincing justification.

   Unaudited financial statements need not conform to *GAAP*. Publicly traded companies must issue financial statements consistent with *SEC* (the *Securities and Exchange Commission*) accounting rules, which differ from *GAAP* in some instances. They must also issue *GAAP* conforming statements.

   Most nations other than the United States follow *IFRS* (International Financial Reporting Standards). The United States is considering the adoption of IFRS.

219. *GAAS*: **Generally Accepted Auditing Standards:** [pronounced gas]. Generally similar to *GAAP*, these are standards public accounting firms follow in conducting an audit. Part of the standard audit opinion refers to the audit having been conducted in accordance with *GAAS*. Since 2002, *GAAS* only applies for audits of non-publicly traded entities. For publicly traded entities, an auditor must follow standards issued by the Public Company Accounting Oversight Board (PCAOB). Prior to 3013, *GAAS* statements were called SAS's or Statements on Auditing Standards. Beginning in 2014, they are part of the Clarification (similar to the *GAAP/FASB* Codification) are have the designation AU (which stands for nothing). The PCAOB has, on an interim basis, adopted most of *GAAS*, but refers to it as PCAOB standards. It has issued some of its own standards with the designation AS.

220. **Generation Skipping Tax:** *GST*: This is a tax imposed by Chapter 13 of Subtitle B of the United States Internal Revenue Code. IRC section 2601 imposes the tax on Generation Skipping Transfers as defined in IRC section 2611.

   With the *GST*, Congress aimed to tax transfers which skip a generation. For example, a wealthy Grandparent may have a similarly wealthy son. If Grandparent devises his property to son, Grandparent's estate must pay an *Estate Tax*. Then, when son dies and leaves the property to grandson, son's estate must again pay an *Estate Tax* on the value included in the *Gross Estate*. To avoid this, Grandparent may use various devices to skip son and to devise or to give the property directly to grandson. A successful skip avoids the second *Estate Tax* on son's estate.

221. **Gift Tax:** This is a tax imposed by Subtitle B of the United States Internal Revenue Code. See the discussion of *Estate Tax* for a fuller discussion.

222. **Giro:** Akin to a direct debit, a *giro* is the opposite of a *check*. The creditor sends the *giro* to the debtor who presents it to his financial institution for payment. With a *check*, the debtor sends the instrument to the creditor who presents it to his financial institution for collection. *Giros* are commonly used in the *EU* and Japan.

A *giro* payment system has the advantage of eliminating bounced *checks*: if the debtor has insufficient funds, his financial institution will not process the giro. As a result nothing bounces. With *checks*, the creditor deposits the instrument with his institution which then sends it to the creditor institution, which may dishonor it for insufficient funds.

223. **Going Concern:** The *Going Concern Assumption* is one of thirteen important principals and assumptions of financial accounting: it assumes the business will continue operating for the foreseeable future. With that assumption, the book numbers on the *Balance Sheet* and *Income Statement* have predictive meaning. It that assumption, however, is invalid, the validity of the numbers change. Asset values likely drop as a non-going concern will need to sell them to liquidate obligations. Income, likewise, will drop as sale losses mount and customers become concerned about future service. Supplies will be wary to provide inventory except on a cash basis, so working capital will evaporate.

For tax purposes, the asset sale of a *going concern* is an important transaction: it is also a common transaction for commercial law. Generally, a buyer is uninterested in purchasing a small corporation: with such a purchase comes contingent, difficult-to-detect and possibly undisclosed liabilities (recent slip and fall accidents are but one common example). Hence, buyers tend to prefer asset purchases. But, with asset purchases of a going concern, a critical issue—perhaps the most important factor—involves allocation of the purchase price among the component parts. Generally, the *IRS* will respect an allocation agreed upon by the parties at arm's length: what it gains from one it loses from the other, so it is effectively a zero-sum for the government. *See, Williams v. McGowan*, 152 F.2d 570 (2d Cir. 1945).

For the parties, however, the allocation is all-important. Sellers will want to place large value on assets that generate no taxable gain or long-term gain, such as land and goodwill. Buyers, in contrast, will want to place high value on quickly recoverable assets such as inventory, or fast depreciating assets such as supplies or furniture. Buyers will want to place little value on non-deductible and non- or slowly depreciating assets such as land, buildings, goodwill, and *IRC* section 197 intangible (which take fifteen years to recover on a straight-line basis).

Lawyers who understand accounting, finance, and tax law—especially the concept of *basis* and the *character* of gains and losses—will prevail over lawyers who do not. The allocation of purchase price to the asset sale of a *going concern* is but one situation example.

224. **Goodwill:** *Goodwill* is an intangible asset comprised of a business' reputation, customer base, advantageous location, and similar qualities that cause the total value to be greater than the sum of the values of the individual parts.

Generally, *goodwill* is property in a 6th Amendment sense and thus is compensable if taken by the government. Similarly, generally it is property in a tort law sense and thus compensable. In family law, state and jurisdictions vary widely. Most consider business *goodwill* to be property, but personal *goodwill* not to be property. The difference can be slight. For example, a law firm partner in a very large firm may own substantial "*goodwill*." Because, for the most part, the value of the good will is not tied to the individual partner, it is relatively easy to value and widely considered an asset. But, a partner in a small firm may have goodwill of similar value; however, the process of valuing it is more tied to the individual. As a result, transfer of the *goodwill* is more difficult. Some jurisdictions do not consider it property for family law equitable distribution or community property purposes.

For tax purposes, *goodwill* is an intangible asset *amortizable* over 15 years per *IRC* section 197.

One of the more important issues in the sale of a going concern regards the allocation of purchase price to *goodwill*. From the view of the seller, a high allocation is generally preferable as the character of any gain is likely long-term capital for tax purposes. From the point of view of the purchaser, a lower allocation is generally preferable because of the long-term, ratable *amortization* required by section 197.

For financial accounting purposes, self-created *goodwill* is carried on the books at historic cost, which may be negligible. Until 2001, *GAAP* required purchased *goodwill* amortization over 40 years. Under FAS 142, purchased goodwill is no longer amortizable in the United States. Goodwill, however, is subject to an "impairment test." If, in the opinion of the CPA (who will have applied the complicated tests) the intangible asset's value is materially "impaired," the loss in value must be reported. As a result, in most cases, the present of Goodwill on a company's Balance Sheet will have no impact on its Income Statement; however, if the Goodwill becomes impaired, it can have a sudden negative impact.

Some European countries require the preparation of an Intellectual Capital Statement, which includes employee training, customer base changes, and similar items.

225. **Government National Mortgage Association: GNMA: Ginnie Mae®:** According to the entity's website:

> At Ginnie Mae, we help make affordable housing a reality for millions of low- and moderate-income households across America by channeling global capital into the nation's housing markets. Specifically, the Ginnie Mae guaranty allows mortgage lenders to obtain a better price for their mortgage loans in the secondary market. The lenders can then use the proceeds to make new mortgage loans available.

> Ginnie Mae does not buy or sell loans or issue mortgage-backed securities (MBS). Therefore, Ginnie Mae's balance sheet doesn't use derivatives to hedge or carry long term debt.

> What Ginnie Mae does is guarantee investors the timely payment of principal and interest on MBS backed by federally insured or guaranteed loans—mainly loans insured by the Federal Housing Administration (FHA) or guaranteed by the Department of Veterans Affairs (VA). Other guarantors or issuers of loans eligible as collateral for Ginnie Mae MBS include the Department of Agriculture's Rural Housing Service (RHS) and the Department of Housing and Urban Development's Office of Public and Indian Housing (PIH).

> Ginnie Mae securities are the *only* MBS to carry the full faith and credit guaranty of the United States government, which means that even in difficult times an investment in Ginnie Mae MBS is one of the safest an investor can make.

http://www.ginniemae.gov/.

Ginnie Mae® is an example of a *Government Sponsored Entity (GSE)*.

226. **Government Sponsored Entity: *GSE*:** This includes organizations chartered by Congress to conduct a particular activity. They *generally*

do not have the financial backing of the Treasury in that the Treasury does not owe full faith and credit for their obligations. *Fannie Mae, Freddie Mac, Ginnie Mae®,* the *FDIC,* and the *Fed* are examples. *Sallie Mae®* is a former *GSE.*

227. **Grantor Trust:** This refers to a trust in which the grantor retains a beneficial interest. In some cases, such grantors must report the trust income as their own. *IRC* Section 671 taxes grantors who are "substantial owners" of the trust. Section 678 provides instances in which a person other than the grantor is treated as a substantial owner.

Subpart E of Part I of Subchapter J of Chapter 1 of Subtitle A of the Internal Revenue Code deals with Grantor Trusts.

228. **GRAT: Grantor Retained Annuity Trust:** This is a device commonly used to avoid United States gift taxes. A grantor creates a trust in which he or she retains the right to income for a stated term. At the end, the remaining principle passed to a named beneficiary. A goal of the device is to use federal valuation methods such that the remainder has a zero value for gift tax purposes at the time of creation, thus resulting in no gift tax. A corresponding goal is for the remainder to have substantial value at the end of the fixed term, but to pass without subjecting the donor to a gift tax (because the gift occurred at creation and the gift value was "zero," no tax was owed then and no tax is owed at the end, because no "gift" occurs at that point, it having been made earlier).

229. **Gross Domestic Product:** *GDP:* This is the total amount of goods and services produced in an economy during a specified period.

$$GDP = MV$$

where *GDP* = Gross Domestic Product, *M* = money supply, and *V* = the velocity of money.

230. **Gross Estate:** *IRC* section 2031 defines this term for purposes of Subtitle B of the United States Internal Revenue Code:

The value of the gross estate of the decedent shall be determined by including to the extent provided for in this part, the value at the time of his death of all property, real or personal, tangible or intangible, wherever situated.

Per *IRC* section 2032, valuation occurs on the date of death or within six months of the date of death, if the executor elects the later date.

231. **Gross Income:** This is a United States tax term of art defined by *IRC* section 61. It comprises "all income from whatever source derived . . . ." The code definition of Gross Income mirrors the words of the

Sixteenth Amendment which permits Congress to tax "all income from whatever source derived."

232. **Gross Margin:** Usually stated as a percentage, this sales ratio indicates the percentage of each sale that is *gross profit*:

$$\left(\frac{sales - COGS}{sales} \right)$$

where *sales* = revenue from sales and *COGS* = cost of goods sold.

Some users refer to this as *gross profit margin*. Others interchange the term with *gross profit*.

233. **Gross Profit:** Gross Profit refers to:

$$sales - COGS$$

Where *COGS* = cost of goods sold.

234. **Hedge Fund:** This is not a term of art. It generally refers to unregulated, or lightly regulated, investment groups which focus on a particular investment strategy. The concept of hedging involves taking an economic or financial position opposite to another position, so as to minimize risk. For example, a fund might generally be long (own) specific investments, but also be short (short sell) other investments. What the fund gains on one, it may partially lose on the other, hence the notion of hedging or minimizing risk.

The term *Hedge Fund* has become almost generic in referring to management private unregulated funds. Many funds limit the number of investors and many require substantial contributions. Some do not involve significant hedging in a traditional sense.

Typically, a Hedge Fund will form as a limited partnership, an LLC, or a combination of the two. It will be exempt from *SEC* registration under the *Securities Exchange Act of 1934* if it has fewer than 500 investors.

Under the *Investment Company Act of 1940*, many *hedge funds* escape significant regulation if they have 100 or fewer accredited investors—those with a specified substantial net worth. Under the act, funds fit generally under section 3(c)(1) or 3(c)(7). *15 U.S.C. § 80a–3(c)(1), (7).*

For tax purposes, hedge funds are typically taxed under Subchapter K of the Internal Revenue Code as a partnership, which means they are *flow-thru entities*.

235. **Historical Cost Assumption:** This is one of the *Fundamental Accounting Principles and Assumptions*. For financial accounting consistent with *GAAP*, financial statements list assets at their original or historic cost. Some modification is permissible for depreciation and

amortization; however, those changes appear in *contra accounts* rather than as actual reductions of the affected asset. *Mark to Market (MTM)* and *Lower of Cost or Market (LCM)* rules permit limited changes in *Historic Cost*.

The definition of *cost* is subject to debate and manipulation, as it is not a term of art. Some assets include only *direct costs*, while others *capitalize* a portion of *indirect costs*. Valuation Methods—such as LIFO and FIFO—also affect the meaning of *cost*.

Cost Segregation is another important issue. It goes to the issue of what is an asset. For example, a building may comprise many separate assets: light fixtures, ceiling tiles, elevators, doors, windows and frames, wiring, and plumbing fixtures. The process of cost segregation does not change the total cost of a purchase; however, it places the cost in different assets subject to different depreciation or amortization rules. This can have a *material* impact on income.

236. **IASB: International Accounting Standards Board:** Run by the IFRS Foundation, this Board is responsible for creating and updating International Financial Reporting Standards.

237. **Income:** This is not a term of art; hence, it must be defined. For tax purposes, the Internal Revenue Code, Subtitle A defines Income. For external financial reporting purposes, *GAAP* defines Income. For internal accounting purposes, cost accounting systems define income. Various statutes also define Income. For example, all 50 states have adopted Child Support Guidelines which are a function of the parents' combined income. Such statutes themselves define income for these purposes. Similarly, most states have provisions for alimony post dissolution of marriage (divorce in some cases). Those statutes also define Income, although many of them do so very briefly.

Contracts frequently refer to *Income* or *Profit* in general terms or in specific terms relating to a particular venture or sale. Without a precise definition, the terms *Income* and *Profit* have little meaning.

238. **Income in Respect of a Decedent: IRD:** *IRC* section 691 defines *IRD*. It includes gross income items which, if received by the decedent, would have been includible in his gross income. For tax purposes, *IRD* is part of the gross estate for computing the estate tax. It also becomes gross income when the estate, heir, or legatee receives the item. Under section 691(c), the recipient who includes the *IRD* for income tax purposes is entitled to a deduction which is a function of the estate tax on the item.

Section 691(b) has provisions for *DID*, or *Deductions in Respect of a Decedent*.

IRD-type items have significant consequences in family law. For example, they may easily be forgotten on a financial statement filed incident to dissolution of marriage. Also, if disclosed, they probably constitute marital assets or community property. Per *IRC* section 1041 (as interpreted by the *IRS*), such items have a zero basis, but are nevertheless subject to the imputed gift provisions of section 1041. As a result, a spouse who receives *IRD*-type items incident to dissolution should value them in an after-tax sense. The later impact of the items on alimony and child-support obligations is also important.

239. **Income Statement:** This is one of three important Financial Statements, the other two being the *Balance Sheet* and the *Statement of Cash Flows*. It reflects a business' operation for a defined period— often a year or a quarter or month. The *Income Statement* first lists income from operations. It deducts expenses attributable to those operations, as well as overhead. It nets the items to determine the current net operational income. The statement then lists extraordinary (unusual) income and expense items, as well as taxes. The bottom line figure reflects the period's net earnings.

A closing entry then adds the net to (or subtracts it from) *Retained Earnings* on the *Balance Sheet*.

A traditional *Income Statement*, consistent with *GAAP*, uses the accrual method of accounting. The accompanying *Statement of Cash Flows (fka, the Statement of Changes in Financial Position)* essentially converts the *Income Statement* to the cash method of accounting by eliminating non-cash items.

240. **Indirect Cost:** These are costs not clearly associated with a particular product or project. Often called overhead, they include management fees, general office maintenance, many utilities, insurance, and security. Indirect costs can be *fixed* or *variable*.

241. **Inheritance Tax:** This is a common state-imposed tax on inheritance. Such tax systems differ from the United States Estate Tax, which applies to the estate itself primarily, and to heirs and legatees secondarily. An inheritance tax applies to the act of inheriting.

242. **IFRS: International Financial Reporting Standards:** Generally, they are less specific and more open to the judgment of the auditor than are U.S. *GAAP*. They were developed by the IASB, the International Accounting Standards Board.

243. **Imputed Interest:** *Money has value over time.* That is a basic principal of finance. Except in rare circumstances involving deflation, interest rates are positive. Nevertheless, some transactions label what is economically interest as principal: they do so to gain tax or other advantage. Imputed Interest rules restate such transactions to reflect

economic reality. They do so by "imputing" interest—by reclassifying a portion of a transaction as interest rather than principal. Section 7872 of the Internal Revenue Code includes such rules. It "imputes" interest on many "below-market" loans. Sections 483 and 1274 contain similar provisions. State trust laws also often "impute" income to underperforming assets so as to properly and fairly treat income and principal beneficiaries. State family law statutes—particularly for alimony and child support determinations—often provide for imputed income for under-employed spouses; oddly, however, such provisions rarely impute income on underperforming assets.

244. **Incremental Cost:** The increased cost from an action as compared to the costs which would occur without the specific action. This is as opposed to "cost" or full absorption cost. These terms are important in cost accounting, which is an arm of accounting aimed toward management and the setting of prices. The term cost by itself is misleading.

245. **Independent Contractor:** An independent contractor is a status in contrast to an employee. For U.S. tax purposes, employees and their employers must generally pay Social Security and Medicare taxes. Employers must also often pay unemployment and worker's compensation taxes or premiums with regard to employee wages.

Generally, an independent contractor directs himself with regard to the time and manner of performance. In contrast, an employer directs an employee as to time and manner of performance.

An important benefit to entities or persons utilizing independent contractor services involves tort liability: generally, an independent contractor is liable for his or her own torts and such liability does not transfer to the person paying for the services.

246. **Individual Retirement Account: IRA:** *IRC* section 408 creates and defines IRAs. Contributions to them—within specific and changing limitations—are tax deductible. Withdrawals constitute taxable income. Employees and self-employed individuals who actively participate in an employer-maintained retirement plan cannot make deductible IRA contributions unless their adjusted gross income is within specified dollar limits.

Some persons are eligible for a Savings Incentive Match Plan (SIMPLE) under which they can contribute—and deduct—contributions of up to $11,500 annually (2010) which they employer may match (without tax consequences to the employee).

247. **Industrial Revenue Bond: IRB:** Bonds issued pursuant to *IRC* section 103, insistent with *Treasury Regulation* section 1.103–7. For

tax purposes, these are Industrial Development Bonds. The interest on them *may* be excludible for income tax purposes.

248. **Inflation:** In economic or financial terms, inflation refers to a general increase in the level of prices for goods and services in a nation's economy. Expected inflation is one of three important factors in determining interest rates.

   The existence of *inflation* frequently becomes central to legal issues. For example, it is, as stated, one factor in interest rates. It may also be a factor in determining changes in legal obligations such as alimony or child support: significant inflation erodes the purchasing power of pre-determined obligations. As a result, substantial inflation may be sufficient to justify a modification of such obligations.

   Further, *inflation* distorts most income tax systems, which are not indexed for inflation. This occurs in two ways. One, the value of property may rise over time. To the extent it rises because of inflation, the increase is illusory—it is exactly off-set by the drop in the purchasing power of the underlying currency. Nevertheless, most income tax systems consider such inflation induced value to be gross income and thus taxable upon the occurrence of a taxable event. Similarly, interest income and to an extent dividend income includes an inflation component, which is, again, illusory wealth. Nevertheless, most income tax systems impose a tax on it. As a result, the property holder or interest income earner is worse off.

   Another legal impact concerns the use of and definition of the term income for legal purposes. In family law, one's income is an important factor in determining one's obligation for or entitlement to alimony and child support. Similarly, in trust law, income belongs to an income beneficiary while principal belongs to a principal beneficiary. But, as indicated above, to the extent income includes compensation for *inflation*, it is illusory and it more accurately represents principal.

249. **Initial Public Offering: IPO:** Generally called an *IPO*, this refers to the first sale of a corporation's stock to the public.

250. **Insider Trading:** This refers to illegal activities by which people with "inside" information (information not yet public) trade a corporation's securities.

251. **Insolvent:** This term is dangerous because it has two distinct meanings.

   - In one sense, the term *insolvent* refers to one whose liabilities exceed his assets. Such a person or entity has negative equity. This is the *Balance Sheet* definition.

- In another sense, the term *insolvent* refers to one's inability to pay what is currently due. Such a person or entity may have substantial positive equity, but little liquidity: his assets could be not easily marketable or his borrowing power may be limited. This is a *Cash Flow*— or in a loose sense—an *Income Statement* definition.

Both definitions are useful. Lawyers must be clear about which one they mean.

252. **Installment Sale:** This is a sale in exchange for a promise of *payments* over time. Such *payments* comprise an annuity. The stated sale price is the *present value of the annuity*. Also, the annuity reflects an *amortization* of the sale price.

For United States tax purposes, *IRC* section 453 provides for deferral of gain recognition by most taxpayers who sell non-inventoriable items on an installment basis. *IRC* section 483 provides for *imputed interest* on some installment sales with "unstated interest."

IRC section 453A(c) requires some taxpayers to pay what amounts to interest on the tax deferral. This *fascinating* provision is inconsistent with *IRC* section 461(h) which *fails* to compensate taxpayers for deduction deferrals and the **Schlude** case which fails to compensate taxpayers for early income accruals.

253. **Insurance Company:** What constitutes an insurance company and an insurance contract is mostly a matter of state law. Currently, states provide most regulation of insurance companies.

Subchapter L of the United States Internal Revenue Code provides the income tax consequences affecting income company income. Generally, insurance premiums are includible in an insurance company's gross income; however, the company may generally accrue a deduction for an amount equal to its expected liabilities under the contract. This treatment is very favorable when compared to the treatment given deferred liabilities of other entities by IRC section 461(h).

Holders of many insurance financial products receive favorable U.S. income tax treatment. In general, they may defer recognition of interest income until receipt; in contrast, holders of non-insurance financial products must often accrue interest income not yet received.

Thus, Lawyers need to understand the definition of an insurance company and an insurance contract for two main reasons:

- Insurance companies and their contracts are subject to significant state regulation.

- Insurance companies and their contracts receive substantial federal income and estate tax advantages.

254. **Interest:** the price charged for the use of money over time. LESSON
SIX explains *Why People Charge Interest*. The components are
liquidity, expected inflation or deflation, and risk.

For tax purposes, some *interest* is deductible, subject to limitations.
Because (for tax purposes) the character of *interest* income differs from
that of capital gain or service income, measuring what portion of a
payment is *interest* as opposed to *principal* or service income can be
very important.

At least one famous Ninth Circuit opinion defined—for some tax
purposes—compensation for the use of money over time as something
other than interest. The decision was both widely applauded and
widely ridiculed. Those who ridicule it have the better argument. *See,
Albertson's v. Commissioner*, 42 F. 3d 537 (1994).

255. **Interest-Only Loan:** This is a loan which does not *amortize*; instead,
the borrower pays only *interest* for the term of the loan. He is then
responsible for a *balloon payment* at maturity.

A person might borrow money on an *interest*-only basis if he cannot
afford the payments on an *amortizing* loan, but he expects both to be
able to re-finance the loan at maturity and to be able then to *amortize*
the *principal*.

256. **Interest Rate:** This term has no meaning.

To describe interest correctly, one must state it in one of three ways:

1)   as a *periodic rate* for a stated period;

2)   as a *nominal annual interest rate* to be compounded at a
stated frequency; or

3)   as an *effective rate*.

All three are identical ways of saying the same thing and are inter-
changeable (subject to rounding). Each of these methods includes the
effect of compounding and the frequency of compounding. The term
interest rate standing alone, however, does not; hence, it is inherently
non-specific and thus meaningless (or at least dangerous because of
vagueness). Using the term interest rate without modifiers reflecting
the compounding frequency is malpractice (or it should be).

257. **Internal Control:** This is a very important aspect of an entity's
operations. It refers to methods and procedures used to monitor
financial and accounting operations so as to minimize mistakes and
fraud. Some very simple examples include:

- The person who orders inventory should not be the same
person who pays for the inventory and who also accepts
delivery of the inventory.

- Employees must provide a printed cash register receipt for each transaction to the customer.

- Employees cannot accept returns in exchange for cash except under closely monitored conditions.

One of the first steps in an audit includes the *CPA's* evaluation of the client's internal controls. The *CPA* will discuss *Reportable Conditions* (apparent weaknesses in internal controls) with the audit committee and with management. Unless the entity corrects such deficiencies, the *CPA* may decide not to issue an *unqualified opinion.*

258. **Internal Rate of Return: *IRR*:** In *internal rate of return* calculation can be very complex. It represents the *discount rate* at which the *net present value* of all cash flows (inward and outward) equals zero. If an investment has cash flows in only one direction (other than the initial deposit or final withdrawal), the computation of an *IRR* is the same as the computation of the **PRESENT VALUE OF AN ANNUITY**, the **FUTURE VALUE OF AN ANNUITY** an **AMORTIZATION**, or a **SINKING FUND**, none of which is particularly difficult.

However, if the direction of cash flows varies—and particularly if the periods and amounts vary substantially, the computation is difficult. Most calculators which compute an *IRR*, do so through an iteration method: they guess at the answer, test it, re-guess, and continue until an answer of acceptable precision is achieved.

The formula for an *IRR* is:

$$NPV = \left[\sum_{t=0}^{n} \frac{C_t}{(1+r)^t} \right] = 0$$

where *NPV* = net present value, *n* = number of periods, *C* = cash flow, *t* = time or a particular period, and *r* = periodic interest rate.

Most lawyers will never need to compute an *IRR* other than the basic annuities, amortization, and sinking fund. Those involved with *M & A*, however, will need to understand the computation of an *IRR*.

259. **Internal Revenue Code: IRC:** Title 26 of the United States Code. It comprises nine subtitles, including Subtitle A for Income Taxes, Subtitle B for Estate and Gift Taxes, Subtitle C for Employment Taxes and Subtitle F for Procedural Rules. Referring to it as the *IRS Code* is incorrect.

Depending on the font size, the *IRC* is either very long or obscenely long. Traditional publications put it at well over 5000 pages. Treasury Regulations accompanying the *IRC* add an additional 15,000 to 20,000 pages, again depending on font and margin size.

Much of the *IRC* contains obscure cross references. A famous sentence appears in the flush language to IRC section 509(a):

> For purposes of paragraph (3), an organization described in paragraph (2) shall be deemed to include an organization described in sections 501(c)(4), (5), or (6), which would be described in paragraph (2) if they were organizations described in section 501(c)(3).

At some level, one must admire the conciseness of that sentence. At another level, one might want to injure the drafter.

Another famous sentence—one closely related to financial calculations—appears in IRC section 467, dealing with pre-paid and post-paid rent as well as the interest component of *non-qualified deferred compensation. IRC* clause 467(e)(1), defining a constant rental amount describes it as one with:

> *an aggregate present value equal to the
> present value of the aggregate payments.*

To a trained finance ear, that is sheer poetry. To others, it is typical tax nonsense.

260. **Internal Revenue Service: IRS:** A division of the Treasury Department responsible for assessing and collecting U.S. taxes. The person in charge is the Commissioner of Internal Revenue (*CIR*). Much tax litigation is styled as *Commissioner* versus Taxpayer.

261. **International Monetary Fund: IMF:** According to the *IMF* website:

> The International Monetary Fund (IMF) is an organization of 185 countries, working to foster global monetary cooperation, secure financial stability, facilitate international trade, promote high employment and sustainable economic growth, and reduce poverty around the world.

> The work of the IMF is of three main types. Surveillance involves the monitoring of economic and financial developments, and the provision of policy advice, aimed especially at crisis-prevention. The IMF also lends to countries with balance of payments difficulties, to provide temporary financing and to support policies aimed at correcting the underlying problems; loans to low-income countries are also aimed especially at poverty reduction. Third, the IMF provides countries with technical assistance and training in its areas of expertise. Supporting all three of these activities is IMF work in economic research and statistics.

In recent years, as part of its efforts to strengthen the international financial system, and to enhance its effectiveness at preventing and resolving crises, the IMF has applied both its surveillance and technical assistance work to the development of standards and codes of good practice in its areas of responsibility, and to the strengthening of financial sectors.

The IMF also plays an important role in the fight against money-laundering and terrorism

http://www.imf.org/external/about.htm.

262. **Inventory:** Inventory refers to merchandise held for sale to customers. Businesses that hold inventories must follow "inventory accounting" methods or systems. This involves deciding when to count inventory as well as how to value inventory.

For example, for financial accounting, a business with inventories must count the items either periodically or perpetually to keep track of them. See the discussion of Periodic Inventory System and the discussion of a Perpetual Inventory System. Generally, a periodic system counts inventory once per period (generally a year). In contrast, a perpetual system keeps track of each item sold (often with a bar code or UFID tag).

Businesses must also determine how to value inventory—both that which was sold and that which remains unsold. See the discussions of LIFO and FIFO inventory systems. Often, inventory is fungible; for example, a grocery store may have 100 cans of green beans, each of which is the same, but which it purchased at different times and with different costs. Deciding which can was sold and which remain involves LIFO versus FIFO systems. That affects the entity's cost of goods sold (COGS) and can have a large impact on income for a particular period.

Inventory Accounting for United States tax purposes is a specialized field. The internal revenue code distinguishes between "stock in trade," "inventory," and "property held primarily for sale to customers in the ordinary course of a trade or business." See IRC sections 1221, 1231.

State law also may tax inventory differently from other property. For example, a state may impose a tangible personal property tax on business assets, but exclude "goods" held for sale.

263. **Inverted Yield Curve:** This refers to a yields graph for instruments of varying maturities (but similar rating/risk/quality). Normally, shorter term instruments yield less than longer term instruments; hence, the yield-curve has a positive slope. In an inverted situation,

longer term instruments yield less than those of shorter terms. Most investors view this with some alarm, as it tends to predict lower economic activity or recession.

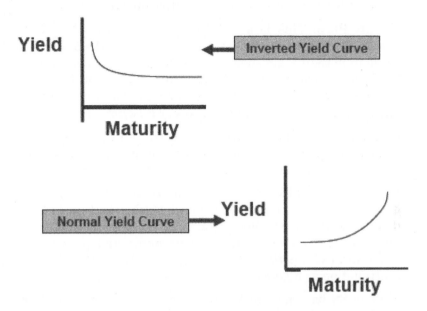

264. **Inverse:** Containing terms of which an increase in one results in a decrease of another. The **Multiplicative Inverse** (*aka* reciprocal) for a number x, denoted a 1/x, is a number which when multiplied by x yields the multiplicative identity. For example the multiplicative inverse of the number 5 is 1/5 and the multiplicative inverse of 1/4 is 4. Multiplied by each other, they produce the result of 1.

In contrast, the **Additive Inverse** of a number a is the number that when added to a yields zero. For example, the additive inverse of 5 is negative 5: added together they result in zero.

Lawyers should be careful in using the term "*inverse.*" They should specify whether they refer to the Multiplicative or the Additive Inverse, or perhaps some other usage. They must also be careful not to confuse the term with the similar-sounding term "*converse.*"

265. **Investment Advisor:** Defined in the Investment Advisors Act of 1940, any person or group that makes investment recommendations or conducts securities analysis in return for a fee, whether through direct management of client assets or written publications. In contrast, a Broker Dealer is a person or entity that is in the business of buying and selling securities for itself or on behalf of clients. Often, an investment advisor is also a broker dealer.

266. **Junk Bond:** This is a popular name for a lower grade, speculative bond. Because they carry significant risk of default, they have higher yields than investment grade bonds. Major ratings agencies consider bonds of BB and lower to be speculative, or *junk*.

267. **Keogh Plan:** This is a type of qualified retirement plan for self-employed and small business. Created in 1962, the plans derived their name from their main sponsor, Brooklyn Congressman Eugene Keogh. They are also known as HR 10 plans—after the House of Representatives Bill which created them. The plans take either the form of a *Defined Contribution Plan* or a *Defined Benefit Plan*.

More recent legislation has created SEP and SIMPLE plans for the self-employed or small businesses. In the opinion of many advisors, the new plans offer significant advantages over the older Keoghs.

268. **Key Employee: Key Employee Insurance:** Many small businesses have one or more employees who are very important to the business, if not essential. They may be the business founder or the creator of an important product. Generally, their name and presence contribute substantial *Goodwill* for the company. Without them, the company's continuation as a *going concern* may be in doubt.

If an entity has an employee who meets the above description, it may want to have *key employee insurance*. This would provide substantial benefits on the death of the employee, such that the company could locate a similar person or perhaps even liquidate. Valuation of a small business must account for *key employees* and whether any transfer of ownership would affect their continued employment and loyalty.

One insurance company which sells key employee insurance has a very good explanation of the term:

The untimely death of a key employee or business owner who is also a key employee can have a disastrous effect on a business. Some of the costs of such an event might include:

- A weakening of the company's credit rating.

- The financial cost (in time and dollars) to find, hire and train a replacement.

- The distraction of other employees, resulting in deadlines not met, deteriorating morale, or a higher level of personality conflicts.

- A need for cash to fulfill promises made to the deceased employee's spouse or family, such as salary continuation or deferred compensation.

- The inability to seize a business opportunity because cash reserves are being used to recruit and train the new employee.

- A loss of confidence among both suppliers and customers.

Additional problems (if key employee is an owner) might include:

- Disagreement between heirs and surviving business owners or key employees.

- Lack of cash to buy the interest of the deceased owner, requiring a sale of the business to an unknown "outside third party."

- Surviving owners may be forced to work with someone who is either not competent, or not motivated enough to make the business thrive.

- The business may have to be sold to pay estate taxes.

http://www.transamerica.com.

A *CPA* auditing a small business should inquire regarding the importance of various employees. While the definition of the term is often subjective, the *CPA* must exercise his or her judgment regarding whether disclosure of such information is necessary.

269. **Labor and Industry:** This is a commonly used term in family law regarding the type of efforts which generally create marital assets in Equitable Distribution states or Community property in other states. It connotes activity and efforts as opposed to passivity. For example, building a house by cutting the lumber and laying bricks is clearly labor and industry. Appreciation in value results more from the efforts at brick laying than from inflation affecting the bricks. Sitting back while undeveloped and used land appreciates is generally not labor and industry.

270. **Laffer Curve:** Named after economist Arthur Laffer, this graph illustrates the relationship of income tax receipts to income tax rates. At some tax levels—for example, a zero tax rate—revenue would be zero. Similarly, at a 100% tax rate, revenues would be zero as productivity would cease. In contrast, at other tax rates, revenues are positive. Rates higher than zero will produce increasing revenues to a point, at which further rate increases will result in decreasing revenues. The phenomenon occurs because income taxes discourage productivity. At low levels of tax, the economic discouragement is small and thus the increase in revenues is large. However, at high rates of tax, the economic disincentives become so large they outweigh any increases in revenue resulting from continued productivity. The

location of curve's zenith is debatable, but its existence is widely accepted. A common, simple depiction of a *Laffer Curve* is:

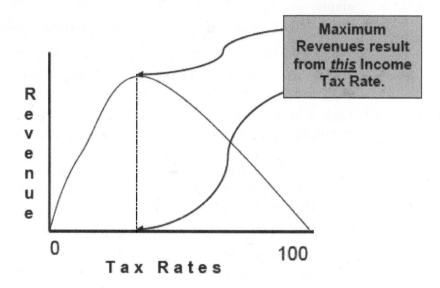

Clearly the zenith is greater than zero and less than 100%. Historically, total U.S. taxes have averaged within a few percentage points of 20%, although marginal rates have been as high as 94% as recently as the 1960s and as high as 70% as recently as the 1980s.

271. **Leverage:** This is a synonym for debt. See the various leverage ratios, such as *Debt to Assets*, *Debt to Equity*, and *LTV*.

272. **Leveraged Buy Out: LBO:** This is a type of entity acquisition which is highly leveraged—financed. Often, the assets of the target secure the debt, which may be without recourse against the acquiring entity.

273. *LIBOR*: **London Interbank Offered Rate:** [pronounced **lahy**-bohr]. This is an interest rate generally comparable to the *Federal Funds Rate*. Contracts which have an adjustable or floating interest rate usually have a benchmark. Many contracts use the prime rate plus or minus a stated number of points. Similarly, many other contracts use the *LIBOR* plus or minus a stated number of points.

274. **LIFO: Last in First out:** [pronounced **lahy**-foh]. This is a common inventory system under which the user assumes the last inventory purchased was the first inventory sold. LIFO—as opposed to FIFO— better reflects inventory and replacement costs in times of inflation. For tax purposes, LIFO is permissible only if the taxpayer also uses LIFO for financial reporting purposes. Use of LIFO, however, is not permitted for publicly traded entities.

Inventories are an important part of many legal relationships. The use of LIFO versus FIFO inventory accounting can have a substantial impact on income and costs—particularly if the user changes from one method to another. While such a change of inventory method is an item that should always be reported or disclosed, life does not always work that way. Hence, inventory accounting is an area ripe for misleading statements. For example, if A must pay B a share of profits, A can affect his liability to B by adoption of one inventory method as opposed to another. Of course, B should be aware of this choice and should have some part in the choice; however, if B's lawyer is unaware of the meaning and the impact of LIFO and FIFO, then he is unlikely to make a wise choice.

Similarly, in other areas of the law dependent upon a definition of income—such as family law (for alimony and child support) and trust law (for measuring an income beneficiary's share of a trust)—the choice of an inventory system can have a profound effect. If one party has significant accounting and finance knowledge, while the other does not, the one with knowledge can take unfair advantage over the ignorant party. Whether such behavior is actionable varies. More importantly, if the ignorant party is unaware of the deception, he is unlikely to seek any reparation even if he is entitled to it.

275. **Limited Liability Company: LLC:** An LLC is a type of state recognized entity. It operates much like a corporation in that it has shareholders and state granted limited liability. It is a person for purposes of bringing suit or being sued. For federal tax purposes, however, it is a partnership.

Such entities became very popular starting in the late 1980s.

An LLC operates essentially as a hybrid of a corporation and a partnership. An LLC is similar to a corporation because it has limited liability. It is similar to a partnership because it is a disregarded entity for U.S. federal tax purposes. LLC owners are called members; in contrast corporate owners are shareholders and partnership owners are partners and trust owners are called beneficiaries. Member-managed LLCs are those run by the member/owners; while manager managed LLCs are those run by a person selected by the owners. These distinctions have real legal consequences for issues such as liability, tax, and the determination of "income from labor and industry" for family law.

276. **Limited Partner:** All partnerships must have at least one General Partner, who is liable for partnership obligations. In most, if not all, jurisdictions, a partnership may also have many Limited Partners whose liability for partnership obligations does not exceed their investment in the partnership.

277. **Line of Credit:** An agreement between a bank and a customer under which the banks agrees the customer may maintain an outstanding loan up to the amount of the line of credit. Generally, the customer is responsible for paying current interest, but no principal on the loan. Such loans may be secured by a primary residence, in which case they are home-equity loans. Generally, such loans are callable, which places the borrower in a risky position. Credit cards are common examples of a line of credit.

278. **Liquidity:** This term has several important finance and accounting meanings:

    - The most common usage refers to the degree a person has available cash. For example a person who is very *liquid* would have substantial resources either in the form of cash or easily converted into cash.

    - *"Liquid Assets"* is an important category on a balance sheet. It includes cash deposits and other items readily convertible to cash. More generally, *"current assets"* includes not only items which are very *liquid*, but also inventory and accounts receivable, which generally turn into cash through sales and collections within one year.

    - *Liquidity* ratios are important tools for analyzing financial statements. The *current ratio* and the *acid test ratio* are commonly used liquidity ratios. Inventory turnover also provides information regarding liquidity.

    - As an element of interest rates, liquidity is a positive state for which people will pay money. A lender loses liquidity by exchanging cash for a promise to pay. In exchange, the lender will charge interest of approximately 2.5 to 3.5%. In addition, the lender will charge for risk and expected inflation.

279. **Living Trust:** This generally refers to a trust created during the life of the grantor with the grantor as the income beneficiary and others are the principal beneficiaries. Planned properly it will avoid the need for an estate or succession administration, as well as the need for a will regarding trust assets.

280. **Living Will:** This generally refers to a document pursuant to state law which provides instructions regarding the medical treatment wishes of the maker. It may provide, for example, that the maker does not want extraordinary measures taken to preserve his life in cases involving major injury or disease. Some people prefer a *Health Care Surrogate (or proxy)*, to whom they grant to power to make such decisions.

281. **Loan:** A *loan* is the lending of a valuable thing for a period of time. Typically, it involves money, but it need not. For example, one can loan the use of property. This is distinguishable from a gift of the use of a thing; while, that, too, would have value, it would not be a "loan" in the sense of this definition. Instead, that would comprise a gift of the use of property. A loan of the use of property essentially involves deferred rent.

One should also an exchange of the use of property for the use of other property. Two views of such a transaction are possible. From one perspective, each party lends or rents the use of one asset for another and each has rental income and a possible rent deduction. From another perspective, however, the use of a thing over time is a current property right. From that perspective, future interests in things do not exist—only present interests are possible. Hence, a transaction involving the use of property for the use of property or money is a current transaction or exchange rather than one over time. The difference may appear immaterial; however, it is not. The issue asks whether interest is a necessary component of time. If it is, then all transactions over time must involve interest, including the use of property . . . perhaps even the use of one's own property.

282. **Loan to Value Ratio:** *LTV*: This is a simple financial ratio used by lenders:

$$\left(\frac{loan\ principal}{fair\ market\ value} \right)$$

For example, a bank may offer a particular loan program and interest rate if the *LTV* is no more than 60%. In such a case, the owner would have 40% equity in the property.

Compare the *LTV* with the *Debt to Assets Ratio*.

283. **Long Sale:** This is the sale of a thing owned by the seller. It contrasts with a short sale, which involves the sale of a thing not owned by the seller, but instead borrowed from another. One should also carve out from the concept of *long sales*, those which involve *wash sales*—which are really not sales at all.

A *long sale* results from the disposition of a *long position*, or ownership of a thing. *Long* positions are distinguishable from short positions in which the party involved has sold a thing borrowed and thus has an existing obligation to *cover*, *i.e.,* to return the thing borrowed but sold. One completes such an obligation—*covers* it—by purchasing a similar (fungible) thing and then transferring it to the lender. One might refer to a person who holds a long position as having *gone long* with regard to the things involved, typically securities or commodities.

284. **Macro Economics:** This is the study of large groups, trends, their behavior and their consequences. It may be at a national or world level. What holds true in a *macro* sense, however, does not necessarily hold true in a *micro* sense.

285. **Matching Principle:** The most important principle of accounting, the *matching principle* provides:

> *An income statement must match income with the costs of producing that income.*

Without proper matching, an income statement would provide misleading information. For example, management needs to know whether a particular division is worth keeping, expanding, reducing, or eliminating. To evaluate the division, the manager would want to know how much income it produces. For that to be a meaningful number, the periodic revenue must match with (be reduced by) the direct and indirect costs of producing that particular revenue. Similarly, costs must match with the income they produce; otherwise, management could not evaluate whether the costs were justifiable.

The *accrual method* of accounting rests on the *matching principle*: income is recognized when *all events* occur such that the item has been earned and the amount can be determined with reasonable accuracy. The conditions of the all events test temper the *matching principle* of accounting with the conservatism principle of accounting: do not recognize income before it is earned and reasonably determinable. Thus an entity will accrue income in a period even if it has received nothing. Similarly it will defer advance receipts to the proper period in which they are earned. Also, an accrual entity will accrue expenses (costs) when they are incurred, regardless of whether they have been paid.

In contrast, the *cash method* of account does not follow the matching principle. Instead, a cash method user recognizes income upon receipt and expenses upon payment. This risks matching income from one operation with expenses from another. *GAAP* does not recognize the *cash method* because it violates the *matching principle*.

A reasonable criticism of statutory accounting in many legal areas is that it fails to provide basic principles, including the matching principle. For example, in Family Law, both alimony and child support are functions of income; however, most (perhaps all) state statutes defining income for alimony or child support fail to require adherence to the matching principle. Unless the parties or the court imposes matching—which would tend not to be the case—the resulting numbers risk being inaccurate, perhaps to a very large degree. Of course, a person who works for a regular salary, paid frequently, and who has few employee expenses or other accessions to wealth would provide similar numbers under both the cash and accrual methods of accounting. But, that scenario is probably a small percentage of the populace. For example, many salaried employees accrue deferred compensation, bonuses, overtime, and various fringe benefits which may be irregular or easily advanced or deferred. They also typically have a variety of employee and other business expenses, which are also subject to timing choices.

286. **Micro Economics:** This is the study of small groups or individuals and their behavior in an economy. What holds true in a *micro* sense, does not necessarily hold true in a *Macro* sense.

287. **Mark to Market:** *MTM*: This important term has varying meaning and significance:

A. In ***financial accounting***, consistent with *GAAP*, audited entities must follow *MTM* rules of *FASB* 115 and 157.

    FASB 115 provides:

    - If an entity has the positive intent and ability to hold debt securities to maturity, it must classify them as held-to-maturity securities and report them at amortized cost less impairment.

    - If an entity buys and holds debt or equity securities for the principal purpose of selling them in the near term, it must classify as trading securities and report them at fair value. It must include unrealized gains and losses included in earnings.

    - If an entity holds debt or equity securities not classified as either held-to-maturity securities or trading securities, it must classify them as available-for-sale securities and report them at fair value. It must exclude unrealized gains and losses from operating earnings; however, it must report such gains and losses in a separate component of shareholders' equity as other income.

    FASB 157 adds definitions and some other rules. Fair value is:

    > the price that would be received to sell an asset or paid to transfer a liability in an *orderly transaction* between *market participants* at the measurement date.

    Much criticism of these rules—and their application—appeared during the financial crisis of fall 2008. Banks and other financial institutions suddenly marked various sub-prime loans and other financial products to a rapidly decreasing market. This prompted serious concerns regarding the liquidity, solvency, and viability of the institutions. Arguably, no fair market existed for many of the financial instruments, as few *market participants* were available and *orderly transactions* were not occurring. Arguably, banks and other financial institutions over-reacted, *marking* many assets at fire sale prices far below their worth as *held-to-maturity* securities. Also, *FASB* 115 requires marking to *fair value* as opposed to *fair market value*, a more generally understood term.

B. For ***tax purposes***, *IRC* sections 475 and 1259 cover *MTM* rules.

Under *IRC* section 475, securities *dealers* must use *Mark to Market* accounting for tax purposes. Under subsection (e), commodities *dealers* may elect *Mark to Market* Accounting. Under subsection (f), securities traders and commodities *traders* may also elect *Mark to Market* Accounting. Subsection (a) requires *MTM* users to report affected property at *fair market value*. Nothing in the section, however, defines *fair market value*.

Under *IRC* section 1259, a taxpayer must recognize gain on the constructive sale of some property. Paragraph (c)(1) defines a constructive sale:

A taxpayer shall be treated as having made a constructive sale of an appreciated financial position if the taxpayer (or a related person)—

(A) enters into a short sale of the same or substantially identical property,

(B) enters into an offsetting notional principal contract with respect to the same or substantially identical property,

(C) enters into a futures or forward contract to deliver the same or substantially identical property,

(D) in the case of an appreciated financial position that is a short sale or a contract described in subparagraph (B) or (C) with respect to any property, acquires the same or substantially identical property, or

(E) to the extent prescribed by the Secretary in regulations, enters into 1 or more other transactions (or acquires 1 or more positions) that have substantially the same effect as a transaction described in any of the preceding subparagraphs.

288. **Margin:** This term has many important usages:

  • In financial terms, *margin* refers to debt. More specifically, assets bought "on *margin*" are assets purchased with borrowed money, at least in part. Generally, a lender will require a specific *Loan to Value* ratio for such debt. If the *LTV* drops below the pre-determined level, the lender issues a *"margin call."*

- In broader terms, *margin* refers to the difference between two numbers, either in relative or absolute terms. For example, a *profit margin* is an important financial ratio. It is:

$$(sales\ price - basis)$$

in *absolute* terms. Thus an item sold for $100 but with a basis (cost) of $60 would have an absolute margin of $40.

In *relative* terms, the *profit margin* is a percentage—either of the sales price or the basis (cost). The general formula, which is a function of sales price would be:

$$\left(\frac{sales\ price - basis}{sales\ price} \right)$$

For example, if an item with a basis of $60 sold for $100, the profit margin would be 40%. Of course, an important factor in this formula involves the term *cost* or basis. *Cost* is itself a fuzzy term: it can refer to *marginal cost* or it can include many other items under a *partial* or *full absorption method of costing*.

Another view of *profit margin* involves *mark-up*—the percentage by which the sales price exceeds the basis, as a percentage of the basis:

$$\left(\frac{sales\ price - basis}{basis} \right)$$

For example, if an item with a basis of $60 sold for $100, the *mark-up* would be 66.67%.

- The *marginal cost* of an item is also an essential finance, accounting, and economic term. This refers to the direct cost of one additional item. Under a common view of cost accounting, an entity should produce more items until the marginal cost equals the expected sales price. Such a policy would work well, however, only under conditions in which the seller can segment the market: sell some items at a high price so as to cover considerable overhead and other fixed, indirect costs. The seller could then produce more, but sell it at a lower price to other persons (perhaps under a different brand) as long as the marginal cost is less than the sales price.

- A *marginal tax rate* is also important. It refers to the tax rate imposed on the last dollar of income, considering not only the tax bracket but also collateral consequences such as deduction phase-outs or limitations triggered by the extra dollar.

289. **Margin Call:** A demand to a customer to deposit more money because his *Loan to Value* (*LTV*) ratio on securities has risen above a pre-determined level. *Margin Calls* are common in *Bear Markets*: many investors used borrowed money to purchase securities. In a *Bear Market*, those securities lose value, but the principal on the loan remains stable; hence, the *LTV* ratio deteriorates.

   Margin Calls can be self-reinforcing. A *Bear Market* occurs when demand for stocks is less than supply of stocks: the stock prices fall until a point of equilibrium—demand equals supply. But, a *Bear Market* triggers *Margin Calls*, which require investors to deposit money. But, in a *Bear Market*, investors may be *illiquid*; hence, they must often sell stocks to raise the money to cover *Margin Calls* on remaining investment. That increases the supply of stocks, but not the demand; hence, the prices fall further, resulting in even more *Margin Calls*.

290. **Market Discount: *MD*:** *Market Discount* results from increases in interest rates following the issuance of a debt instrument with a fixed interest rate. Because such a debt instrument is a series of cash flows—both the interest payments and principal payments—it has an easily computed present value. That *PV* drops as the relevant periodic interest rate rises. The *PV* drop is the *Market Discount*—the market, rather than the original issuer, has discounted the instrument.

   For tax purposes, holders of *MD* debt instruments have four options regarding the timing of interest income due to the discount. *IRC* section 1275 and 1276 explain the options.

   MD is the opposite of *Acquisition Premium*, which results from decreases in interest rates. *IRC* Section 1272 and the Treasury Regulations there under provide two methods regarding the timing of the negative interest income impact due to *AP*.

291. **Market Marker:** a Broker Dealer firm that accepts the risk of holding a certain number of shares of a particular security in order to facilitate trading in that security. Once an order is received, the Market Maker immediately sells from its own inventory or seeks an offsetting order.

292. **Market Risk:** This is the *risk*—danger—that an asset's value will change due to external factors such as:

   - General changes in securities markets.

- Changes in inflation different from expectations.

- Changes in currency exchange rates.

293. **Materiality Principal:** An important principle of accounting, this requires the reporting of material items only. Immaterial items may be expensed directly or even misstated without prompting a qualified opinion. Essentially, if something does not matter, it does not matter. Exactly what is material is situational. For example, for a small business, $1,000 may be a material amount, while it may be irrelevant for a large inter-national firm.

294. **Mean:** The word mean refers to a type of average. Traditionally, it contrasts with a Median (the mid-point on a list of numbers) and a Mode (the most common number or value in a group). A mean, however, has at least four significant forms:

- **Arithmetic Mean:** this is the sum of a group of numbers divided by the number of numbers. For example, 10, 15, 20 has an arithmetic mean of 15: 45 divided by 3. The arithmetic mean is the one we all learned in grammar school: add the numbers and divide by the number of numbers. A problem with it is that outliers (really large or very small numbers) distort it. That relates to life expectancies: the man who is expected at age 25 to live to 80, but dies at 26, has a big impact on the average, while the guy who lives to 81 or 82 has a very small impact (even though more of the latter exist). Each data point deserves (arguably) equal validity; however, the arithmetic mean over-weights the very short-lived person.

- **Geometric Mean:** A geometric mean multiplies the numbers (rather than adds them) and then takes the nth root of those numbers (if you have five numbers, take the 5th root). In finance, it makes sense because some years can have extraordinarily high or very low negative returns that can distort the "average." The geometric mean will be lower than the arithmetic mean if any of the numbers have a negative value.

- **Harmonic Mean:** The harmonic mean is the reciprocal of the arithmetic mean of the reciprocals of the various numbers. As I understand, it will underweight the highs and overweight the lows. It can, for example be used to compute average speeds (which may involve very high speeds, but low speeds cannot go below zero, thus lows deserve special attention because there is a limit to how low a low can be). It is also often used in finance, although I admit I cannot quite explain why it is sometimes thought to be more accurate than the geometric mean. In any event, it will likely be more conservative (lower) than the other two means.

- **Quadratic Mean:** Also called the root mean square (RMS) this is the square root of the arithmetic mean of the squares of a number set. It is used in electrical engineering.

295. **Merger:** Generally, a *merger* is the combining of two entities. Often, one entity acquires the other by issuing its stock to the shareholders of the target entity in exchange for their stock of the target. At that point, a parent-subsidiary relationship would exist. For an actual merger to occur, the parent would need to liquidate the subsidiary by transferring its assets and liabilities to the parent and by then cancelling the subsidiary's stock.

The term *merger* is not consistently defined; hence, lawyers should be careful about its use without a definition. For example, some people may define a *merger* in the truest sense: a combing of assets and liabilities from two formerly separate entities. Others may use the term more broadly, to include the *acquisition* of a subsidiary by a parent.

For United States tax purposes, *IRC* section 368 defines corporate reorganizations as including seven types. One—a Type A Reorganization—involves a "statutory *merger*" or traditional consolidation of two formerly separate entities into one new entity. A Type C Reorganization also involves a consolidation; however, it involves a continuing entity acquiring all the assets of another entity by the issuance of stock. A Type B Reorganization is better called an *acquisition*: a Parent acquires the stock of a subsidiary.

296. **Mergers and Acquisitions:** *M & A:* This is a term for the legal, accounting, and investment banking practice of handling both traditional mergers (usually consolidations) and parent-sub acquisitions.

297. **Method of Accounting:** This refers to various methods of allocating income and deductions among periods.

- For <u>audited</u> *Financial Statements*, only the *Accrual Method* is consistent with U.S. *GAAP*.

- For <u>unaudited</u> *Financial Statements*, most people use the *Cash Method*, which does not *clearly reflect income*.

- For *United States tax purposes*, taxpayers generally may use one of several methods—or even a combination of them—which include:

  o *Cash Method* (as specially defined for tax purposes).

  o *Accrual Method* (as specially defined for tax purposes, which is radically different from its definition for *Financial Accounting* purposes and *GAAP*).

  o *Installment Method*, to the extent permitted by *IRC* section 453.

  o Other special methods under *IRC* section 451.

Lawyers who refer to the term income for legal purposes need to be cognizant of the method of accounting used to measure that income. The various methods sometimes produce similar numbers; however, often they produce *materially* different numbers.

Lawyers should also be familiar with the *Consistency Principle of Accounting*, which requires an entity to use the same method of accounting from period to period. *Changes of Accounting Method* require complex adjusting entries and *pro forma Financial Statements* to ensure fairness and clarity. Lawyers must also recall the numerous intricacies of accounting methods: referring to the accrual method may sound clear, but it is not, as the Accrual Method prompts numerous choices and elections for matters such as capitalization, cost allocation, depreciation, and amortization. Hence, even one *Accrual Method* set of *Financial Statements* may not be consistent with—and therefore comparable to—another set of *Accrual Method* Statements from a separate entity. To a limited extent, *GAAP* requires specific rules which are at least comparable and consistent within industries, but even then it allows for many choices.

For United States tax purposes, a taxpayer cannot change from one method of accounting to another without permission from the Secretary of the Treasury. For many standard changes, permission is automatic; however, for others, it is not. Method Changes also necessitate *IRC* section 481 adjustments, which essentially subject the taxpayer to tax as if he had used the new method consistently since 1954 (the year of enactment for section 481).

What constitutes a Method of Accounting for tax purposes is a matter of significant controversy. Courts are divided on the issue. In particular, they disagree regarding whether an improper method of accounting is a method of accounting. According to the Treasury Department, consistent mistakes in multiple years may constitute a method of accounting; as a result, a taxpayer cannot, without permission, change to a proper method. With permission, he will be subject to *IRC* section 481 adjustments.

298. **Mill:** One-thousandth of a currency unit, as in one-tenth of a cent in the United States. Property taxes in the U.S. are often expressed in terms of millage, or the mill rate per dollar of value. For example, a tax of 10 mills would be one percent. On property with a value of $100,000, the tax would be $1,000. Often, property taxes are levied in fractions of a mill, sometimes to several decimal places.

299. **Minimum Gain Chargeback:** This is a United States partnership tax provision required to be in a partnership agreement in some circumstances. Such a provision would effectively reverse a special allocation of gain to a non-contributing partner in order to ensure substantial economic effect for the allocation.

Non-tax lawyers probably need not worry about the technicalities of a *MGC* provision; however, they should be generally aware of what necessitates one and of the consequences resulting from one. With a *MGC* provision, a partnership could allocate gains on property to non-contributing partners in some years. It would later need to allocate other gains to the contributing partner to make up for the non-economically real original allocation. As a result, the tax benefits would mostly evaporate. But, non-tax legal consequences from such an allocation could nevertheless be substantial. The original allocation would inflate the income of some partners and suppress the income of others. The chargeback would later reverse these consequences. However, if legal consequences flow as a function of the early years' income and not as a result of the later years' income, distortions are possible. Naturally, a non-tax law measurement of income should not rely on tax law provisions for its definition of income; however, in many instances that is precisely what occurs.

300. **Minority Discount:** A minority interest in a business—generally less than 50% of the voting power, is not as valuable as a controlling interest. Common sense would indicate this is correct. As a result, the *Fair Market Value* of a minority interest must include a *discount* factor—a percentage reduction—to reflect the lack of control and the existence of control in the hands of others.

But, that which common sense says is true is not always true: appearance can deceive. This concept forms the basis for much chicanery—legal, but of questionable morality (assuming that is a relevant inquiry for legal actions).

For example, much of estate planning practice involves breaking closely held entities into various ownership interests. This may include different classes of stock or merely the transfer of ownership to various family members. The person whose estate is the subject of the plan would traditionally retain only a minority interest. As such, his or her estate would traditionally value the retained interest at a substantial *discount* for federal estate tax purposes. Because the *marginal rate* on estate is 45%, this can result in significant savings.

The *minority discount* estate plan scheme, however, rests on the questionable notion that people intentionally destroy value in their property. For many observers, that proposition is not credible. More likely, in their opinion, the only persons who would use such a plan have families who will likely cooperate and who will likely put the pieces back together—at least in practical terms. Hence, the minority discount is arguably unwarranted. The discount, instead, would be appropriate for families with considerable hostility among the various factions; however, rational planners would not divide valuable property into competing hostile factions.

Despite much concern in the eyes of the government and many others, estate planning which rests on *minority discounts* tends to be successful.

301. **Mode:** The *mode* reflects the timing of the first payment in an annuity, an amortization, or a sinking fund. In *Begin Mode*, a calculator treats the first payment or deposit as occurring today—at the time of the calculation. In *End Mode*, it treats the first payment or deposit as occurring at the end of the first period (*e.g.*, month, quarter, or year).

Most *financial calculators* default to *end mode* because that is the most common feature of loans. One of the most common mistakes people make in using financial calculators involves forgetting to set the mode correctly. The consequences may be significant; however, they may not be noticeable. For example, setting the payment period or the term incorrectly can produce an obviously wrong—even ridiculous—answer. Setting the *mode* incorrectly, however, will not produce an answer which is clearly and obviously wrong to most users. Hence, the *mode* function is a dangerous one in that it results in many errors.

302. **Monetary Policy:** This involves government or Central Bank control of the money supply to affect the economy. In contrast, *fiscal policy* generally refers to government use of tax and spending to affect the economy.

303. **Monetary Unit Assumption of Accounting:** This important principle or assumption of accounting requires the use of a monetary unit—such as the dollar—to represent assets, liabilities, and equity. The assumption has two important consequences:

- Non-quantifiable items—such as emotional value—may be disclosed in footnotes; however, they cannot be disclosed directly on financial statements.

- The monetary unit has a constant meaning; hence, a dollar in 1950 is the same—for financial reporting purposes—as a dollar in 2010. Inflation and deflation are generally irrelevant for financial reporting, although their impacts may be discussed in footnotes and *pro forma* statements.

304. **Money Supply:** The money supply in the United States has several definitions, each of which has multiple components.

M1 includes:

- Currency
- Travelers' checks
- Demand deposits
- Other checkable deposits at banks
- Other checkable deposits at thrift institutions

M1 has ranged from a total of $138.8 Billion (of which $28.5 Billion was currency) in January, 1959, to $1,884.6 Billion (of which $844.9 Billion was currency) in March, 2009.

M2 (without M1) includes:

- Savings Deposits at Banks
- Savings Deposits at Thrift Institutions
- Small Denomination Time Deposits at Banks
- Small Denomination Time Deposits at Thrift Institutions
- Retail Money Funds

Non-M1 M2 has ranged from a total of $147.7 Billion in January, 1959, to $6,754.3 Billion in March, 2009. In addition, institutional money funds—which are not a component of M1 or M2, ranged from zero in January, 1959, to $2,492.4 Billion in March, 2009.

The Fed issues notices regarding the United States Money Supply weekly:

The H.6 release, published weekly, provides measures of the monetary aggregates (M1 and M2) and their components.

M1 and M2 are progressively more inclusive measures of money: M1 is included in M2.

M1, the more narrowly defined measure, consists of the most liquid forms of money, namely currency and checkable deposits.

The non-M1 components of M2 are primarily household holdings of savings deposits, small time deposits, and retail money market mutual funds.

Monthly data are available back to January 1959; for most series, weekly data are available back to January 1975.

The Money Stock Measure, which is the broadest Fed measure of money, including M1, M2, and money market mutual funds has ranged from a seasonally adjusted $286.6 Billion in January, 1959, to a seasonally adjusted $8,316.6 Billion in March, 2009.

The nominal *GDP* for the economy is the velocity of money times the money supply:

$$GDP = MV$$

where *GDP* = Gross Domestic Product, M = money supply, and V = the velocity of money.

305. **Money Market:** This is not an actual physical or even electronic market. Instead, it is a general term referring to the borrowing, lending, and trading related to short-term debt world-wide. Many *money market* funds exist—they are *mutual funds* which invest in *money market*-type obligations. Such obligations includes:

- Commercial Paper

- Certificates of Deposit

- T-Bills

- Bankers Acceptances

- Short-Term Municipal Notes Issued In Anticipation of Tax Receipts.

306. **Moral Hazard:** This is the consequence of risk insulation. If a person does not bear the risks of his actions, he will tend to behave with less concern for the risk. OPM—Other People's Money—is a more colloquial way of describing the phenomena.

Law, economics, and finance produce myriad examples. In insurance law, an insured with a very low deductible may take insufficient precautions to protect his property. In agency, an agent may succumb to temptation to cheat his principal who may not have sufficient information to prevent such behavior. In family law, a spouse with substantial knowledge of finance and accounting will be tempted to act to his own advantage—if he views any significant risk of marital failure—even if the action is to the collective disadvantage of the couple. In law school, mandatory grade curves and minimal risk of failure heap *moral hazard* onto students who lack the self-discipline to seek knowledge for its own sake: they shun work because the difference between a high score and a modest score is small and the risk of failure is essentially non-existent.

A capitalist economy works because of reward and risk—more crudely self interest and greed, tempered by a healthy dose of risk aversion. But, if government takes the risk away from the equation by providing too large a safety-net or too many bail-outs, greed may longer be controlled by risk and thus may (will?) expand out of control. The resulting economic distortions inevitably end badly. If government responds with greater regulation of greed—rather than with lesser protection from risk—additional distortions are inevitable.

A *Fed* definition of moral hazard is:

> The risk that a party to a transaction has not entered into a contract in good faith, has provided misleading information about its assets, liabilities or credit capacity, or has an incentive to take unusual risks in a desperate attempt to earn a profit before the contract settles.

307. **Mortgage:** This frequently mis-used term serves either as a verb or a noun.

- The verb form stems from the infinitive to *mortgage*, which means to grant or sign a *mortgage* on particular property to secure an obligation.

- The noun form refers to the security interest in the thing secured.

A *mortgage* is just a security device—and nothing more. It is not an asset and it (at least in most, if not all, jurisdictions) is not an ownership interest in the thing *mortgaged*. Instead, the holder of a *mortgage* has preference in bankruptcy over the proceeds of the sale of the thing *mortgaged*. This preference is for an amount up to the amount of the secured loan, but not more (except for foreclosure costs). One cannot "pay a *mortgage*." One can pay a debt secured by a *mortgage*. Similarly one does not owe a mortgage and one does not own a *mortgage*. Persons owe debts and own promises to pay—which may or may not be secured. The difference has substantial legal significance. For example, in family law, if one spouse improves separate property using marital funds, most jurisdictions would grant the other spouse an interest in the improvement to the extent of the marital funds used. What constitutes an improvement, however, is not always easy to discern. If one spouse uses marital funds to add a room onto a separately owned building, the addition is almost certainly an improvement. However, if one spouse uses marital funds to pay part of a loan (separate or marital) secured by the separate property, that does not necessarily improve or enhance the value of the property.

Courts differ widely on this issue, probably because they often
misunderstand the fundamental nature of a *mortgage.*

Related to this definition is the definition of equity. *Equity*, in one
sense, equals the *Fair Market Value (FMV)* of the property minus the
principal on a loan secured by the property. While that definition is
correct, it does not make equity an asset. It is not. *Equity*—in that
sense—is just a net figure . . . a number. The property is the asset and
it appears on the left side of the balance sheet. The debt is a liability
and it appears on the right side of the balance sheet. The two do not
net for accounting purposes and they should not net for legal purposes.

308. **Mutual Fund:** This refers to an investment company regulated by the
SEC. *See, 15 U.S.C. § 80a–3(a),* which codifies the *Investment Act of
1940.* It is a management company under 15 U.S.C. § 80a–4(3). Per
section 80a–5, management companies further divide into sub-
categories:

(a) Open-end and closed-end companies. For the purposes of
this title, management companies are divided into open-end
and closed-end companies, defined as follows:

(1) "Open-end company" means a management
company which is offering for sale or has outstanding any
redeemable security of which it is the issuer.

(2) "Closed-end company" means any management
company other than an open-end company.

(b) Diversified and non-diversified companies. Management
companies are further divided into diversified companies and
non-diversified companies, defined as follows:

(1) "Diversified company" means a management
company which meets the following requirements: At
least 75 per centum of the value of its total assets is
represented by cash and cash items (including
receivables), Government securities, securities of other
investment companies, and other securities for the
purposes of this calculation limited in respect of any one
issuer to an amount not greater in value than 5 per
centum of the value of the total assets of such
management company and to not more than 10 per
centum of the outstanding voting securities of such
issuer.

(2) "Non-diversified company" means any management
company other than a diversified company.

In more layman's terms, an *open-end mutual fund* issues new shares daily as investors purchase share. The fund also redeems shares daily as investors sell shares. A *closed-end mutual fund* has a limited number of shares which the share owners may themselves trade.

309. **NAFTA: North American Free Trade Agreement:** This is a trilateral treaty among the United States, Canada, and Mexico. It went into effect on January 1, 1994.

310. **National Automobile Dealers Association: NADA: Blue Book:** According to the organization's website:

> The National Automobile Dealers Association, founded in 1917, represents more than 19,700 new car and truck dealers, both domestic and international, with more than 43,000 separate franchises.

> NADA membership is open to any new-automobile or new-truck dealership holding a new automobile or truck sales and service franchise.

NADA:

- Provides counsel on legal and regulatory matters

- Represents dealers on Capitol Hill

- Develops research data on the automobile industry

- Operates training and service programs to improve dealership business operations, sales and service practices

The organization publishes a variety of pricing and value guides for new and used cars, motorcycles, recreation vehicles, and boats. These guides are available through nadaguides.com. Historically, they were known as the "Blue Book." Consumers and lenders often refer to blue-book value when referring to a used car.

311. **NASD: National Association of Securities Dealers:** See *NASDAQ*. Be careful not to confuse the acronym *NASD* with the acronym *NADA*.

312. **National Association of Securities Dealers Automated Quotations: NASDAQ:** [pronounced **naz**-dak]. According to the company website:

> NASDAQ is the largest U.S. electronic stock market. With approximately 3,200 companies, it lists more companies and, on average, trades more shares per day than any other U.S. market. It is home to companies that are leaders across all areas of business, including technology, retail, communications, financial services, transportation, media and

biotechnology. NASDAQ is the primary market for trading NASDAQ-listed stocks.

313. **Negative Amortization:** This occurs when *payments* on a loan are insufficient to cover current *periodic interest*. In such cases, the parties capitalize unpaid interest into *principal*. Thus, contrary to the traditional **AMORTIZATION** of a loan under which the principal drops over time, with negative amortization, the principal amount increases over time.

314. **Negative Interest Rate:** A negative interest rate is highly unusual. Prior to 2015, one might have thought it would impossible. In theory, it exists when expected deflation exceeds risk plus liquidity. For example, a particular borrower may have a personal risk factor of zero (generally the U.S. government or the *Federal Reserve Bank*). If expected deflation exceeds the traditional *liquidity* factor of 2.5 to 3.5 percent, then interest rates on government paper would be negative.

In practice, however, the theory initially seems to make little sense. Why would someone lend money to the U.S. government and demand less money in return after a period of time? Why would such a lender not simply maintain possession of the money? The answer involves a *liquidity risk*.

Generally, *liquidity* has value because the liquid person can spend the money while the illiquid person (the lender) cannot. This is why, as explain in **LESSON SIX**: *Why People Charge Interest*, the liquidity factor of interest typically ranges from 2.5% to 3.5%.

But *liquidity* also carries risk. Usually, this is tiny because someone who is liquid can park the funds in U.S. Treasury Securities or in insured demand deposits (such as a checking account or a *CD*). However, in times of considerable economic turmoil, such as faced in the United States and many countries during the Fall of 2008 through the Spring of 2009, many investors lost faith in many financial institutions, including banks. Hence, the risk associated with such deposits rose—sometimes beyond the inherent value of the liquidity. Other forms of liquid assets—such as gold, silver, and other commodities—also involve risk. Silver is bulky and thus expensive to store. One cannot typically store a great deal of silver at his home without increasing his risk of burglary. Similarly, gold—while less bulky than silver—has to be stored someplace. Storing it with a financial institution prompts both a fee and risk: what if the institution becomes insolvent?

For a short period—a few hours—some short-term interest rates on U.S. T-bills fell below zero during early November, 2008. For that time, one had to pay as much as $1,025,000 to purchase government securities that paid $1,000,000 thirty days later. While the notion of the lender paying interest to the borrower is strange, when viewed as a storage fee, it can seem rational. For that few hours at least, all other available options for those lenders carried so much risk, the lenders were willing to pay the Treasury to hold their money. Beginning in January 2015, many sovereign obligations in the EU began bearing or being issued at negative rates. By October 2015, some short-term U.S. obligations were selling at negative rates in secondary markets.

315. **Negotiable Instrument:** A negotiable instrument is a statutorily defined type of financial instrument. Under the Uniform Commercial Code, it creates a holder in due course. A negotiable instrument is necessarily transferable; however, a transferable instrument is not necessarily negotiable. Article 3–104 of the UCC provides:

(a) Except as provided in subsections (c) and (d), "negotiable instrument" means an unconditional promise or order to pay a fixed amount of money, with or without interest or other charges described in the promise or order, if it:

(1) is payable to bearer or to order at the time it is issued or first comes into possession of a holder;

(2) is payable on demand or at a definite time; and

(3) does not state any other undertaking or instruction by the person promising or ordering payment to do any act in addition to the payment of money, but the promise or order may contain (i) an undertaking or power to give, maintain, or protect collateral to secure payment, (ii) an authorization or power to the holder to confess judgment or realize on or dispose of collateral, or (iii) a waiver of the benefit of any law intended for the advantage or protection of an obligor.

(b) "Instrument" means a negotiable instrument.

(c) An order that meets all of the requirements of subsection (a), except paragraph (1), and otherwise falls within the definition of "check" in subsection (f) is a negotiable instrument and a check.

(d) A promise or order other than a check is not an instrument if, at the time it is issued or first comes into possession of a holder, it contains a conspicuous statement, however expressed, to the effect that the promise or order is not negotiable or is not an instrument governed by this Article.

(e) An instrument is a "note" if it is a promise and is a "draft" if it is an order. If an instrument falls within the definition of both "note" and "draft," a person entitled to enforce the instrument may treat it as either.

(f) "Check" means (i) a draft, other than a documentary draft, payable on demand and drawn on a bank or (ii) a cashier's check or teller's check. An instrument may be a check even though it is described on its face by another term, such as "money order."

(g) "Cashier's check" means a draft with respect to which the drawer and drawee are the same bank or branches of the same bank.

(h) "Teller's check" means a draft drawn by a bank (i) on another bank, or (ii) payable at or through a bank.

(i) "Traveler's check" means an instrument that (i) is payable on demand, (ii) is drawn on or payable at or through a bank, (iii) is designated by the term "traveler's check" or by a substantially similar term, and (iv) requires, as a condition to payment, a countersignature by a person whose specimen signature appears on the instrument.

(j) "Certificate of deposit" means an instrument containing an acknowledgment by a bank that a sum of money has been received by the bank and a promise by the bank to repay the sum of money. A certificate of deposit is a note of the bank.

316. **Net Operating Income:** *NOI*: Also known as NOP or net operating profit, this is generally another term for *EBIT*—earnings before interest and taxes; however, some users define it as earnings before interest but after taxes (some refer to this as NOPAT). It also represents an amount before *extraordinary* items. Some authorities interchange this term with "operating profit."

While finance and accounting authorities may quibble about whether *NOI* is a figure before or after taxes, lawyers should be more careful with the bigger picture. They must understand the distinction between "operating" income and "non-operating" income. Income from operations is an appropriate touchstone for managerial bonuses, valuation of business, and predictions of future income for child support and alimony. Non-operating items, however, generally should not figure into such calculations.

317. **Net Operating Loss:** *NOL*: For U.S. tax purposes, *IRC* section 172 defines an *NOL*. Taxpayers may carry-back an *NOL* for up to two years and carry forward an *NOL* for 18 years. Transferring an *NOL* to another person is complicated: a simple merger will not generally suffice. Hence, this is the subject of advanced tax courses.

A *NOL* has value, which may be non-intuitive to some: losses have value. To the extent a person can deduct the *NOL* for tax purposes; he will save his marginal tax rate, which may be upwards of 40%. Lawyers need to view such losses as assets, just as accountants would. For example, in relation to dissolution of marriage, an *NOL* can be quite valuable to the spouse entitled to use it. Similarly, a person with an *NOL* may be more attractive as a marriage prospect in the same sense that a person of wealth may be more attractive than a person who is poor.

For non-tax purposes, the term net operating loss refers to the same calculation as net operating income—it merely is a negative rather than a positive amount.

318. **Net Operating Profit After Taxes: NOPAT:** this is a realistic measure of income because it emphasizes *operating* profits, as opposed to profits (which include extraordinary gains and losses) and is *after* taxes. Whether it is after actual taxes paid or taxes accrued is important. A formula is:

$$(NOI)(1 - tr)$$

where NOI = net operating income and tr = the tax rate.

Whether "tax rate" is the "marginal rate" or the "effective rate" or the "average rate" depends on the user. Whether users consider all federal, state, local, and foreign income, excise, value added, and *ad valorem* taxes also varies. Be careful.

319. *NPV:* **Net Present Value:** This is the *present value* of all *cash flows* minus the initial investment. The number should be positive. If it is negative, the investment does not generate the assumed return.

320. **New York Stock Exchange: *NYSE*:** Also known as the *Big Board*, this is the major stock exchange in the United States.

321. **Non-Qualified Deferred Compensation:** For United States tax purposes, Deferred Compensation Plans and arrangements come in two basic formats: qualified and unqualified. Each format has sub-categories, as well.

Under Internal Revenue Code section 404, the payor of non-qualified deferred compensation may not deduct the amount of compensation until the year the recipient—whether an employee or an independent contractor—must include it in income. As a result, non-qualified plans do not have the substantial tax subsidy given qualified plans.

IRC section 467(g) arguably provides for current inclusion of any non-qualified deferred compensation plan earnings in the income of the beneficiary, *i.e.*, the interest component of the deferral. This section, however, has not been operative since its enactment in 1986.

See the definition below of "Qualified Deferred Compensation."

322. **Non-Recourse Debt:** This refers to debt for which the borrower is not personally responsible. In contrast, the borrower is personally responsible for recourse debt. Banks and other institutions have, at times, been willing to lend on a non-recourse basis because they are then able to charge a higher interest rate. A mortgage on substantial property typically secures non-recourse debt; otherwise, no one would be willing to lend in such a way. If the borrower defaults, the lender may foreclose on the security interest. If the security sells for a sufficient amount to satisfy the obligation, any excess belongs to the borrower. If, instead, the security is insufficient to satisfy the obligation, the lender suffers the loss and it cannot seek a deficiency judgment against the borrower.

Two of the most important United States tax cases involve the impact of non-recourse debt. According to the Supreme Court in *Crane v. Commissioner,* 331 U.S. 1 (1947), if a buyer acquires property subject to a mortgage securing non-recourse debt, the seller must include the amount of the debt in his amount realized regardless whether the buyer assumes the debt, agrees to pay it, or merely takes the property subject to it. In a critical exception, the Court (in the famous footnote 21) declined to apply its rule if the amount of the debt exceeded the fair market value of the security. Several decades later, however, the Court applied the *Crane Rule* to debt exceeding the security value. *Commissioner v. Tufts,* 461 U.S. 300 (1983).

Another important legal issue involving non-recourse debt focuses on the meaning of ownership. The owner of property has legal rights which differ from the rights of a secured creditor. The existence of non-recourse debt, however, blurs the economic distinctions between ownership and creditor status. An important factor in ownership involves the risk of loss; however, in non-recourse situations, the risk of loss falls on the creditor. Another important factor involves the opportunity for gain. In typical non-recourse debt situations, the nominal owner has the opportunity for gain. However, in some situations—such as complicate sale-leaseback transactions—the nominal owner lacks the opportunity for gain but retains the risk of loss. Whether such a nominal owner is legally the owner for tax law and other legal purposes varies from case to case. *See, e.g., Frank Lyon Co. v. United States,* 435 U.S. 561 (1978).

323. **Nominal Annual Interest Rate:** *NAI:* This is the *periodic interest* rate times the number of periods in one year. It is an uncompounded rate. Abbreviated as *NAI,* the nominal rate is an important key on all

financial calculators. The rate itself serves no purpose in computations; however, because humans tend to think in terms of one year, they typically multiply periodic rates times the number of periods in one year. The resulting *NAI* is a useful, albeit misleading, term for comparing financial instruments.

The formula for converting an *effective interest* rate to an *NAI* is:

$$\left[\, 100py \left(\left(1 + \frac{eff}{100} \right)^{\frac{1}{py}} - 1 \right)\right]$$

where *eff* = the *effective interest rate* and *py* = the number of periods per year.

324. **Notional Debt:** the stated nominal principal debt amount of which interest payments or accruals are a function.

325. **Opportunity Cost:** This measures what would have happened had a particular decision or choice not been made. It is the lost opportunity. For example, when one spends money to purchase a pair of shoes, one no longer has the opportunity to spend that money on a shirt or to invest the money. That analysis measures the *opportunity cost.*

326. **Option:** Options have three basic types:

- American Option. Holders may exercise the option at any time prior to the expiration.

- European Option. Holders may exercise the option on a particular date (the expiration date).

- Exotic (including Asian) Option. Holders may exercise the option based on a variety of factors, which sometimes include the average price of the underlying asset during a defined period.

Options also divide into Put Options (contracts to force someone to buy) and Call Options (contracts to force someone to sell).

327. **Order of Magnitude:** ten times. Thus the difference between one and ten is one order of magnitude. The difference between one and one hundred is two orders of magnitude.

328. **Original Issue Discount: OID:** Discount on a bond or similar instrument occurs in two ways:

- On original issue discount.
- As market discount.

For *original issue* discount, the maker defers payment of interest until maturity (which may include serial maturity—payments over time). For tax purposes, both holders and issuers of OID instruments must use the accrual method for reporting interest income or deductions.

Internal Revenue Code (*IRC*) Sections 1271 through 1276 generally provide the needed rules, along with subsection 163(e).

In contrast, *Market Discount* (*MD*) results from increases in market rates of interest. *Acquisition Premium* (*AP*) results from decreases in market rates of interest. Both of these affect the value of debt instruments after original issue and prior to maturity. They affect the instrument holder, but not the issuers.

The United States tax timing rules for OID, *MD*, and *AP* differ; hence, investment strategies must differ regarding the three interest effects, which are themselves mathematically the same.

329. **Organization for Economic Co-operation and Development: OECD:** An international organization which seeks to promote policies that will improve the economic and social well-being of people around the world. It focuses primarily on helping governments tackle economic, social, and governance challenges of a globalized economy.

330. **Other People's Money: OPM:** This is a slang term in financial circles. It generally refers to leverage, *i.e.*, borrowed amounts. It can also refer to government spending or expense account spending: arguably people are more conservative and more responsible when they spend their own money than when they spend OPM.

331. **Over the Counter: OTC:** Over the Counter trades refer to securities transactions which do not involve an established market, such as the *NYSE*, the *AMEX*, or the *NASDAQ*. Often these are very small issues which may trade for low amounts. Individual dealers—such as investment banks—handle the trades either themselves or through networks they join or create.

332. **Par Value:** This is largely an antiquated term denoting the original stated issue price of corporate shares. Historically, if an entity issued shares for less than par value, they were assessable for the under-paid amount. As a result, many companies issued stock with a par value of $1 per share, but charged an appropriate market price. The excess would be accounted for as "*APIC*" (additional paid-in capital) or "EPIC" (excess paid-in capital). Many states changes laws to permit a "stated value" rather than a "par value"; however, that change in terminology had no real meaning. States now vary regarding whether they require a stated/par value or permit it.

A bond issue for "par value" would be one issued for its "face value"—the stated amount on the bond, which is the amount due on maturity. Interest on a bond (the coupon rate) is a function of the "par value" of the bond. Bonds issued for more than par have "acquisition premium." Bonds issued below "par" have "original issue discount" (OID).

333. **Partner Capital Account:** Partnerships maintain capital accounts for each partner. Accounting for these is very complicated.

For United States tax purposes, proper maintenance of partner capital accounts is controlled by Treas. Reg. section 1.704–1(b)(2)(iv). For a partnership allocation to have substantial economic effect and thus be respected for tax purposes, the partnership must generally maintain capital accounts consistent with this treasury regulation. The rules are among the more complicated provisions in U.S. tax law.

The partner's capital account balance does not by itself reflect the value of the partner's interest in the partnership. To determine the value of a partnership interest, an expert would want to know the balance in the partner's capital account, whether the accounts are maintained consistent with the treasury regulations, the partner's inside basis in partnership assets, the partner's share of partnership liabilities, and the partner's outside basis. Such information would not be sufficient, as the expert would also want to examine all financial statements of the partnership.

334. **Partner Inside Basis:** A partner not only has an outside basis in his partnership interest, but he also has an inside basis in various partnership assets. One partner's basis in an asset may or may not equal another equal partner's basis in the same asset. Differences occur for many reasons, including the effect of asset contributions to the partnership as well as special allocations of various partnership items (*e.g.*, income, gains, losses, deductions, and credits).

Because U.S. partnership tax law is so very complicated, non-tax lawyers should be cautious when dealing with valuation issues involving partnership interests. While some such interests may be uncomplicated and simple to value, others may involve astonishingly complicated rules and allocations which can effectively hide substantial income and value.

335. **Partner Outside Basis:** Internal Revenue Code section 705 defines a partner's basis in his partnership interest. In tax parlance, this refers to the partner's outside basis. Section 705 provides:

> (a) General rule
>
> The adjusted basis of a partner's interest in a partnership shall, except as provided in subsection (b), be the basis of such interest determined under section 722 (relating to contributions to a partnership) or section 742 (relating to transfers of partnership interests)—
>
> > (1) increased by the sum of his distributive share for the taxable year and prior taxable years of—

(A) taxable income of the partnership as determined under section 703(a),

(B) income of the partnership exempt from tax under this title, and

(C) the excess of the deductions for depletion over the basis of the property subject to depletion;

(2) decreased (but not below zero) by distributions by the partnership as provided in section 733 and by the sum of his distributive share for the taxable year and prior taxable years of—

(A) losses of the partnership, and

(B) expenditures of the partnership not deductible in computing its taxable income and not properly chargeable to capital account; and

(3) decreased (but not below zero) by the amount of the partner's deduction for depletion for any partnership oil and gas property to the extent such deduction does not exceed the proportionate share of the adjusted basis of such property allocated to such partner under section 613A(c)(7)(D).

Per section 752, a partner's share of liability increases is generally treated as a contribution to capital which thus affects his outside basis.

336. **Passive Activity:** A federal tax term where generally an individual or entity will not be considered to have materially participated in the management or operation of a activity when the entity spends less than 500 hours per year on that activity. Passive activity losses can only be used to offset passive activity gains. An example would be a partnership that owns and leases out a beach house where one partner manages the property while the passive activity partner merely contributed money towards the purchase of the beach house but engages in no further activity in its management. *See* IRC section 469.

337. **Passive Foreign Investment Company: PFIC:** A federal tax term found IRC section 1297a. This is a foreign-based company that has one of the following attributes: 75% of its income derived from income that is deemed passive (dividends from stock ownership, income from rental property with a third party manager); at least 50% of the company's assets are investments that produce interest, dividends, and/or capital gains.

338. **Pass-Thru Entity:** For United States tax purposes, several types of *pass-thru entities* exist:

- *S Corporations* under Subchapter S.

- Partnerships under Subchapter K.
- *Simple Trusts* under Subchapter J.
- *REMIC* under Subchapter M.

An LLC under state law is a partnership for tax purposes and thus is also a *pass-thru entity*. In some senses, a cooperative under Subchapter T is quite similar to a pass-thru entity. Also, a *REIT* under Subchapter M has many similarities to a complex trust under Subchapter J and to *pass-thru entities* as a result. A defective or failure *Grantor Trust* collapses into a pass-thru entity. A common *Estate Planning* tool involves an intentionally defective *Grantor Trust*.

One might more generally speak of *pass through entities*, as well. The broader term refers to the following:

> Such entities are not taxpayers themselves (with some minor exceptions); instead, the owners must include their share of the entity income, distributed or not. Each *pass through entity* has its own set of rules defining income, shares of income, the consequences of contributions, distributions, the incurrence of debt and other issues.

The more narrow term, *pass-thru entity* appears in the Internal Revenue Code many times. Typically, the section using the term does not define it. No section defines the term for the code as a whole. Also, various sections which define the term do so inconsistently. For example, sections 170 (dealing with charitable contribution deductions) and 267 (dealing with related party transactions) both use the term *pass-thru entity*. Each defines it as including a partnership or an S corporation. In contrast, section 1281 (dealing with OID accrual on short-term obligations) has special rules for *pass-thru entities*. This section defines them as including not only partnerships and S corporations, but also trusts (not just simple trusts). A third example appears in *IRC* section 461 (dealing with the timing of deductions). A provision applicable for years following 2009 specifically targets partnerships and S corporations. The provision also grants the Secretary of the Treasury authority to extend the rule to "other *pass-thru entities*" by way of regulations. It does not define which other *"pass-thru" entities* it has in mind and no such regulations yet exist.

Lawyers need to heed the great complexities inherent in these various forms, as well as the frequent (annoying?) inconsistencies. While each is similar to the others in many respects, they also have substantial differences. State laws also differ on how they treat them. For example, an individual may have gross income from a trust or partnership, but may receive nothing in terms of a distribution. For tax purposes, the individual has income. But, does he have income for purposes of computing an alimony or child support obligation? For purposes of determining what is and what is not a marital asset or community property? That depends on state law, which is often inconsistent within the various states—which often treat different types of income differently—as well as from state to state. Does he have income for purposes of determining a contractual provision? That depends on how the contract defined *income*—or even whether it defined *income*.

339. **Patent Box (*aka* IP Regime):** This is **a** common international tax "colloquial term" referring to an entity existing to hold intellectual property (IP) such as a patent, copyright or trademark. Placed in a "tax haven" it can charge significant fees for licensing of its property and thus lower the taxable income of the user (almost certainly a related entity) without suffering significant tax itself.

340. **Payable on Death: *POD*:** This is a common way of holding a bank account: it is owned by one person, but payable on death of that person to another or others. For *FDIC* purposes, the account is insured as if it has multiple owners.

The acronym *POD* can also mean *Payable on Demand*.

341. **Payment: *PMT*:** The word *payment* has two very different meanings:

   - For *financial calculations*, the *PMT* button or function denotes the amount of the periodic cash flow for an *annuity*, *sinking fund*, or *amortization*.

   - For *tax purposes*, a *payment* is distinguishable from a *deposit*. Cash method taxpayers have income when they receive *payment* of an income item; also, they may take a deduction when they *pay* a deductible item. Similarly, *accrual* method taxpayers have income at the earlier of the date they earn an income item, receive *payment* of it, or when *payment* is due. For *accrual* method deductions, *payment* is a significant factor in determining whether a transaction satisfies economic performance under *IRC* section 461(h).

Exactly when *payment* occurs for tax purposes is not clear. At least three important tax ramifications of payment are important:

   - The Supreme Court considered the issue in *Commissioner v. Indianapolis Power and Light*, 493 U.S. 203 (1990); however, the decision arguably created more confusion than it resolved. The case involved the important distinction between a payment and a deposit. The same distinction—with different analysis—exists for

financial accounting. A payment affects an asset account
and a liability or expense account; however, a deposit
merely affects two asset accounts.

- Another important tax decision held that the transfer of
a check constitutes a *payment* for tax purposes. *Kahler v.
Commissioner,* 18 T.C. 31 (1952).

- A third important tax analysis of the term *payment*
involves the use of borrowed money. Typically for either
tax or accounting purposes, the source of the funds used
to satisfy an obligation is irrelevant. For example, A can
borrow money from C to satisfy an obligation to B. For
most United States tax purposes, A has paid B. If
payment is significant, then A has whatever tax
consequences flow from payment. Similarly, for financial
accounting purposes, A would have the following
bookkeeping entries:

Cash	1000	
Payable to C		1000

(to reflect a loan from C to A at x% *NAI* with y periodic
payments and a term of n years).

Payable to B	1000	
Cash		1000

(to reflect satisfaction of an obligation to B).

These two transactions would not impact A's *Income Statement,*
because payment is not an important factor in the accrual of an
expense; hence, if the obligation to B involved an expense, the item
would have been the subject of an accrual entry earlier in the Journal.

Similarly, the two transactions would not significantly impact A's
Balance Sheet because both cash and payables would have a net effect
of zero (although the term of the payable may change from current to
a longer term, which would affect A's ratios).

Also, the two transactions would not significantly impact A's
Statement of Cash Flows, although it would increase both in-flows and
out-flows.

But, the above analysis changes if A is related to either B or C, or B
and C are related.

If, for example, B and C are related, then A may not have paid
anything for United States tax purposes. Borrowing from B to pay B is
not a real transaction; hence, to the extent payment is an important

taxable event, such a transaction has no tax significance. Similarly, borrowing from C to pay B may lack reality if B and C are closely related. Just how closely related is too closely related is a difficult issue, beyond the scope of this dictionary. See, *Battlestein v. Commissioner*, 631 F.2d 1182 (5th Cir. 1980) *(en banc)*; *Burgess v. Commissioner*, 8 T.C. 47 (1947).

For *Financial Accounting*, borrowing from B to pay B or borrowing from C, who is related to B, to pay B is simply a re-financing arrangement. It typically has little or no real impact on the *Financial Statements* except to the extent the debt changes from a current liability to a longer-term liability, or vice versa.

If, instead, A is related to one of the other parties, then the economic reality of the transaction also changes from a true three-party transaction. One cannot truly owe money to oneself or pay oneself or borrow from oneself. Doing so may appear to inflate economic transaction which lack reality. As explained in relation to *Fiscal* and *Calendar* years and also in relation to *Consolidated Returns*, such related party transactions are a ripe area for misleading information and manipulation. Lawyers must be wary of them.

342. **Payments Per Year:** *P/YR:* This is the number of payments per year on a particular loan. Abbreviated as *P/YR*, it often serves the same purpose as the number of Periods Per Year. A basic rule of finance teaches us that the number of periods per year, also known as the compounding frequency, must equal the number of payments per year or it must be one.

LESSON FOUR: *Calculator Terminology* covers the term *P/YR*.

343. **PCAOB: Public Company Accounting Oversight Board:** Created in 2002, this non-government entity has authority to oversee audits of publicly traded companies in the U.S.

344. **P/E Ratio:** Price to Earnings Ratio: this is current market price of one share divided by the *EPS*:

$$\left[\frac{current\ market\ price}{\left(\frac{earnings}{number\ of\ shares\ outstanding} \right)} \right]$$

or

$$\left(\frac{CMP}{EPS} \right)$$

where *EPS* = earnings per share and *CMP* = current market price.

345. **PEG Ratio:** Price to Earnings Growth: a financial ratio that takes the price/earnings ratio divided by the growth rate. This ratio helps

determine a stock's value while taking the company's earnings growth into account. This is generally considered to provide a more complete picture than the P/E ratio. The ratio is the P/E ratio divided by the annual earnings per share (EPS) growth rate.

346. **Periodic Inventory System:** This is an inventory accounting system under which the business physically counts inventory annually (or sometimes periodically). Cost of goods sold in such a system represents:

$$COGS = (BI + P - EI)$$

Where $COGS$ = Cost of Goods Sold, BI = Beginning Inventory, P = purchases, and EI = Ending Inventory.

A Periodic Inventory System—as opposed to a perpetual system—requires little bookkeeping; thus, historically, it was very common. The system, however, does not distinguish between the cost of inventory sold and the cost of spoilage or theft: anything not included in ending inventory is part of COGS if it was available for sale (either part of BI or P).

In contrast, a *perpetual* system tracks each item of *inventory*. Users also physically count inventory annually; however, because of the tracking they can accurately determine theft and spoilage. The widespread use of bar codes, and more recently small implanted IDs, has caused many businesses to move from a *Periodic Inventory System* to a *Perpetual Inventory System*.

347. **Periodic Interest Rate:** This is the rate of interest earned in one period. The periodic rate is critical in all financial calculations. For simplicity, we often multiply the *Periodic Rate* times the number of periods per year—the *P/YR*—to produce the *Nominal Annual Interest Rate (NAI)*:

$$pr = \left(\frac{NAI}{P/YR} \right)$$

where pr = period interest rate, NAI = nominal annual interest rate, and P/YR = number of periods per year.

348. **Periods Per Year: *P/YR*:** This is the number of periods per year on a particular loan. Abbreviated as *P/YR*, it often serves the same purpose as the number of Payments Per Year. A basic rule of finance teaches us that the number of periods per year, also known as the compounding frequency, must equal the number of payments per year or it must be one.

349. ***PFS*: Personal Financial Specialist:** This is a designation awarded to *CPAs* who satisfy requirements defined by the *AICPA*. As explained by the *AICPA*:

CPAs who specialize in personal financial planning can earn a specialist's designation, the Personal Financial Specialist (PFS). This designation can only be acquired by CPAs who are AICPA members (binding them to the Code of Professional Conduct), have a minimum of 3,000 hours of financial planning business experience, in addition to continuing education within the last five years and a comprehensive and rigorous personal financial planning exam.

CPAs, as well as attorneys who are CPAs, may properly identify themselves with the designation PFS or CFP, if they have earned the designation. See, *Ibanez v. Florida*, 512 U.S. 136 (1994) [majority approving the use of CPA, CFA designation by an attorney in advertising over the objection of the regulatory bodies for CPAs in Florida].

350. **PITI: Principal, Interest, Taxes, and Insurance:** These are the four main components of *payments* on a home loan secured by a *mortgage*. The lender naturally expects interest plus *amortization* of the loan principal. Often, the lender also expects a regular *deposit* into an escrow account which will pay insurance premiums on the property plus property taxes when due. That way, the lender ensures the property is insured and the property taxes are *paid*.

351. **Points:** A *point* is one percent of the stated amount loaned. Borrowers "pay" points as "pre-paid" interest. For tax purposes, points "paid" on loans to purchase or improve a principal residence are deductible in the year "paid." As a result, taxpayer/borrowers have an incentive to "pay" points. Banks typically advertise the Nominal Annual Interest (*NAI*) on a loan, with the points stated separately. Federal truth in lending law requires banks to amortize the points over the stated loan term, resulting in an Annual Percentage Rate (*APR*) higher than the stated *NAI*. Banks thus like points because they can advertise an *NAI* lower than the later and lesser disclosed, but higher, *APR*. The *APR*, however, is itself a misleading figure for two reasons. One, it is an uncompounded rate (other than with regard to the impact of the points). Second, it assumes the loan will be outstanding for its stated term, which is generally unlikely. Because most people pay off home loans when they sell their house—typically in about seven years—and because *points* are actually a pre-payment penalty, banks are particularly fond of them. A more accurate rate on a loan is the *Effective Interest Rate* (*EFF*), which reflects the reality of compounding. The most significant and useful rate would be the *EFF* modified for the _expected_—rather than _stated_—life of the loan.

For example, if a loan has a stated principal amount of $300,000, one point would be $3,000, and two points would be $6,000.

352. **Point of Sale:** *POS:* This specifically refers to the place where a transaction occurs—a check-out line cash register is a common example. *POS* software allows companies to track sales continuously. Cash registers feed information about inventory to home offices and warehouses. Such *POS* operations substantially improve efficiency.

353. **Preferred Stock:** This is a type of security (a term which includes stock, bonds, and *debentures*) which typically has no voting rights. The name Preferred does not indicate anything about value or the wisdom of preferred stock ownership. Instead, it merely refers to the legal preference the stock has for dividends and liquidation over common stock. Normally, all other obligations—secured and unsecured—would receive full payment on liquidation before *preferred stockholders* received anything. Then *preferred stockholders* would receive full payment (including generally for accrued but unpaid *dividends*) before *common stockholders* received anything.

Preferred Stock typically has a right to a fixed *dividend*, which is similar to interest on a debenture. However, preferred *stock dividends* are not interest and thus are not deductible for tax or financial reporting purposes.

Often the differences between *Preferred Stock*—which is a type of *equity*—and an unsecured, *subordinated debenture*—which is debt—are slight. But, for tax and accounting purposes, the differences are substantial.

The rights of *preferred* stockholders appear in the indenture agreement that accompanied their issue, or in the corporation's articles. Preferred stock dividends may accumulate—which means they carry over if unpaid to future years. In such cases, common stockholders may not receive dividends until accumulated preferred dividends are paid.

Preferred Stock may also have limited *participating* rights—which means it can partially or fully participate in common stock dividends. Often, *participating preferred stock* does not receive a common dividend until the *common stock* dividend equal the *preferred stock* dividend. This is, however, a matter of contract.

Preferred Stock—and for that matter, bonds and debentures—may be convertible to common stock on the occurrence of a stated event. The existence of such conversion features has a significant impact on partially and fully *diluted Earnings Per Share* (*EPS*).

354. **Present Value of a Sum:** *PV:* This calculation computes the present value of a future amount. For example, $1,100 in one year, discounted

at 10% interest compounded annually has a present value of $1,000.00 today. Thus, if one owes $1,100 one year from now, he should be able to pay off the obligation with only $1,000, assuming the appropriate interest rate is 10% nominal annual interest compounded annually.

The **PRESENT VALUE OF A SUM** calculation is one of the six basic calculations performed by a *Financial Calculator*. The formula for the *PV* is:

$$PV = \left(FV \left(1 + \frac{i}{100} \right)^{-n} \right)$$

where i = nominal annual interest rate, n = number of periods per year, and FV = the future value.

355. **Present Value of an Annuity:** *PVA:* This calculation computes the present value of a series of equal payments made at regular intervals, earning a constant interest rate. For example, $1,000 deposited at the end of each year for ten years, earning 10% interest compounded annually, has a present value today of $6,144.57. Similarly, $6,144.57 deposited today, earning 10% interest compounded annually will produce a fund from which $1,000 could be withdrawn for ten consecutive years, beginning one year from today. This might be used to compute the payoff amount for a loan or to value lottery winnings.

Such an annuity is either in end mode (payments occur at the end of each period) or begin mode (payments occur at the beginning of each period).

The **PRESENT VALUE OF AN ANNUITY** calculation is one of the six basic calculations performed by a *Financial Calculator*. The formula for the *PVA* is:

$$PVA = \left[\frac{\left[PMT \left(1 - \left(1 + \frac{i}{100} \right)^{-n} \right) \right]}{\frac{i}{100}} \right]$$

where i = nominal annual interest rate, n = number of periods per year, and PMT = the periodic payment or deposit.

356. **Pre-Payment:** This refers to a *payment* in advance of the due date.

- For *accounting purposes*, a *pre-payment* actually constitutes a *deposit*. It creates an asset which the owner must *amortize* over the appropriate period. For example, if one were to pre-pay an insurance premium for three years, it would debit *pre-paid* insurance and credit cash. Then, over the three years, the entity would *amortize* the asset by debiting insurance expense and crediting the intangible "pre-paid insurance."

Whether the appropriate financial amortization should be straight-line, accelerated, or decelerated is open to debate. Generally, entities use a ratable (straight-line) method.

- For *tax purposes*, a *pre-payment* has a variety of consequences. For the recipient, it constitutes income if indeed the receipt constitutes a *payment* rather than a *deposit*. Few exceptions to this rule exist—even for accrual method taxpayers. *Schlude v. Commissioner*, 372 U.S. 128 (1963). For the transferor, the transaction generally results in treatment comparable to that of *financial accounting—capitalization* and amortization under *IRC* section 263 and the regulations there under.

  Under *IRC* section 467, however, a *pre-payment* of rent receives loan or deposit treatment if the total amount involves more than $250,000. This rule applies both to the lessor and the lessee. Both must impute interest on the "loan" from the lessor to the lessee and then annual rent with an opposite cash flow.

  For *tax purposes*, *points* on a home loan receive *pre-paid* interest treatment and are thus generally deductible when *"paid"* under *IRC* section 461(d). See the discussion on cash flows for more information.

- For *financial and economic purposes*, interest cannot be pre-paid. Any attempt to do so constitutes a principal payment by definition. All financial calculators deal with cash flows and interest accruing over time. Thus an attempted *prepayment* of *interest* cannot occur: it will always collapse into a *principal* reduction.

357. **Pre-Payment Penalty:** Loans are contracts. As do most contracts, they *may* contain penalty provisions which apply to those who fail to satisfy the contractual terms. Generally, loans do *not* have *pre-payment* penalty provisions; hence, a debtor may pay the *principal* to the creditor in advance of the contracted due date. In such a case, interest accrual stops.

Under some loan contracts, however, *payment* of *principal* in advance of the contracted due date triggers a defined penalty. This may amount to all or some of the interest which would have accrued under the loan had the advance *payment* not occurred.

Points on a home mortgage loan are essentially a contracted-for *prepayment* penalty. For *tax purposes*, they receive treatment as *pre-paid interest*. For federal *truth-in-lending* purposes, they receive *interest* treatment amortized over the contracted life of the loan. In reality, however, they constitute a penalty if the debtor pays off the loan early. Whether the preferable tax treatment outweighs the adverse economic effect of paying off a loan with *points* early depends on the tax bracket and on how early the pay off occurs.

358. **Prime Rate:** This is the base rate posted by 70% of the nation's largest banks.

> Effective December 16, 2008, the *WSJ* determines the Prime Rate by polling the 10 largest banks in the United States. When at least 7 out of the top 10 banks have changed their *Prime*, the *WSJ* will update its published *Prime Rate*.

http://www.wsjprimerate.us/.

The *prime rate* is a popular short-term rate. Many contracts reference it and float as the *prime* changes. For example, contracts may provide for an *interest rate* equivalent to the *prime* or *prime* plus or minus a specified number of *basis points*.

359. **Principal:** As is true of many terms, *principal* has varying meanings. It is not a term of art; hence, lawyers should always define it.

- *In relation to loans*, this is the amount borrowed or loaned. Interest accrues as a function of *principal*. In a **PRESENT VALUE OF A SUM** calculation, the *PV* is the *principal*. Similarly, in a **FUTURE VALUE OF A SUM** calculation, the *PV* is the *principal*. For an **AMORTIZATION**, the *PV* is the *principal*, as is a portion of each *payment*. For a **SINKING FUND** computation, each payment or deposit constitutes *principal*. The *FV* is the sum of *principal* plus capitalized interest.

  Unpaid accrued interest *capitalizes* into *principal*. This process involves *Negative Amortization* of the loan.

- *In relation to trusts*, the *principal* beneficiary effectively owns the underlying trust assets, while the *income* beneficiary owns the right to *income* from the *principal*.

  Much of trust law involves the proper allocation of items between *income* and *principal*. Lawyers should be familiar with state trust laws which define these terms. They should be aware of statutes and judicial doctrines which sometimes *impute* income on underperforming principal. Effectively, such income *imputation* moves items from the *principal* beneficiary to the *income* beneficiary.

Because the definition of *income* is imprecise—both for financial accounting and for tax accounting—lawyers should be careful with any legal relationship dependent upon income. Of necessity, a contract provision referring to *principal* also refers to *income*.

360. **Private Foundation:** This is a disfavored status for United States tax purposes. In other words, *Private Foundation* status is not generally preferred.

IRC section 509 presumes all charities (organizations described in IRC section 501(c)(3) to be Private Foundations. The organizations have the burden of proving *public charity* status.

For U.S. tax purposes, charitable contributions to Private Foundations are subject to greater reductions than comparable contributions to Public Charities. Also, the contributions are subject to stricter limitations. The Foundations themselves are subject to potentially onerous excise taxes under *IRC* sections 4940 through 4945.

Donors should consider alternatives to Private Foundation creation if the entity corpus is small—under U.S. $1 million. Donor-directed funds as elements of a Public Charity are one alternative, albeit with its own drawbacks.

361. **Private Placement:** The "opposite" of an Initial Public Offering (IPO), a private placement is a stock sale made to a relatively small number of select investors instead of the general public. The primary reason to do this is to raise money through equity without having to pay the expensive costs associated with an IPO.

362. **Private Placement Offering Memorandum: PPOM:** Whenever a Private Placement is made a company must include a PPOM with the offering. This document discloses the known risks that management is aware of an serves as a warning to investors that not all investments pan out and could result in a risk of loss up to the amount of the investor's investment.

363. **Producer Price Index: PPI:** This is a commonly watched index, used as a predictor of inflation or deflation. According to the Bureau of Labor Statistics, which compiles the index in the United States:

> The **Producer Price Index (PPI)** program measures the average change over time in the selling prices received by domestic producers for their output. The prices included in the PPI are from the first commercial transaction for many products and some services.

http://www.bls.gov/ppi/.

364. **Prospectus:** This is a legal document filed with the *SEC* in relation to the issuance of new *registered* securities. Unregistered securities may, consistent with Regulation D, need to file either a state-required registration document or a Private Offering Memorandum.

365. **Put Option:** This is an option contract under which the holder has the right to sell an item at a particular price to the issuer. Generally called a *"put,"* the contract might colloquially be understood as my right to "put it to you." If I am the holder and you are the issuer, I can make you buy at the *strike price*.

Essentially, the holder expects the price to drop while the issuer expects the price to rise. The holder of a *put* is in a similar position to the seller in a *short sale*; however, the difference is significant. In a short sale, the seller hopes the price will drop. If it rises, his exposure is unlimited. With a *put option*, the holder also expects the price to drop. If it does not, his risk is limited to the price he paid for the *put*.

A *put* is the opposite of a *call option*. Generally, most *put* and *call* options involve publicly traded equities; however, they can also involve other securities or commodities.

With a *naked put*, the holder does not own the underlying item. With a *married put*, he does.

366. **Q-TIP: Qualified Terminal Interest Property:** This is a trust commonly used by married persons to reduce potential estate taxes. The trust supports the surviving spouse during his or her life. Remaining property then passes to named beneficiaries.

Under *IRC* section 2056, the value of property passing to a surviving spouse escapes estate tax; however, generally, terminal interests do not qualify for the marital deduction. Section 2056(b)(7) provides an exception for Q-TIP trusts, the value of which indeed escape estate taxation when created (upon the death of the first spouse). The remaining property then becomes part of the survivor's estate for tax purposes.

367. **Qualified Deferred Compensation Plan:** For United States tax purposes, Deferred Compensation Plans and arrangements come in two basic formats: qualified and unqualified. Each format has sub-categories, as well.

A qualified plan must satisfy rules found in Subchapter D of the Internal Revenue Code. Generally, it must not discriminate in favor of highly compensated employees, it must provide for vesting within specified time periods, it must satisfy funding requirements, and it is subject to significant caps on the amount and percentage of income permitted to enter the plan.

In general, qualified plans are either Defined Benefit Plans or Defined Contribution Plans.

Per *IRC* section 404, contributions to a qualified plan are not included in the gross income of the plan beneficiary for United States income tax purposes. In addition, employer contributions to such plans are deductible by the employer for U.S. income tax purposes. This disparate treatment amounts to a substantial federal subsidy. Also, plan earnings are not taxable to the beneficiary until the beneficiary withdraws funds. This income tax deferral also amounts to a substantial federal subsidy in most cases.

Generally, a plan beneficiary may not withdraw funds without penalty before he or she reaches the age of 59 ½. Also, generally a plan beneficiary must begin withdrawals no later than the time he or she reaches the age of 70 ½.

368. **Rabbi Trust:** A transfer of funds for the benefit of a taxpayer which remain subject to the claims of the transferor's creditors does not trigger the *Economic Benefit Doctrine*. As a result, the taxpayer does not have taxable income—in the United States—from the transfer of funds to a *Rabbi Trust*. The doctrine arose from a fact pattern involving a synagogue and a rabbi. *See, Private Letter Ruling 8113107.*

369. **Random Walk:** Burton Malkiel coined this term in his book "A Random Walk Down Wall Street." According to the theory, stocks take a random and unpredictable path and that the past is no indication of the future.

370. **Ratings:** Various agencies rate bonds and similar debt instruments. Moody's, Corporation, Standard & Poor's (a Division of McGraw-Hill, Inc.) and Fitch, Inc. are common rating agencies.

Generally, they rate instruments as either *Investment Grade* or *Speculative Grade*. Within the two main categories, each rating agency has many sub-categories. Generally, the higher the rating on an instrument, the lower the instrument's risk (or vice versa); therefore, the lower the interest rate the instrument will command.

For *S & P* and Fitch, the highest grade is AAA. *Investment grade* ranges from AAA, AA+, AA, AA-, A+, A, A-, BBB+, BBB, and down to BBB-. Moody's has similar grades, but labels them Aaa, Aa1, Aa2, Aa3, A1, A2, A3, Baa1, Baa2, and Baa3.

Ratings from each agency similarly proceed downward through the B and C range, which are highly speculative. The D range is for instruments in default.

Lawyers should be familiar with the rating systems as many contracts are a function of the ratings. For example, a particular fund or foundation may limit its investments to a particular grade or higher. Or, a loan may have a provision under which the lender can accelerate (call the loan due) if the *rating* falls below a pre-determined level.

371. **Real Estate Investment Trust:** *REIT*: [pronounced reet or rīt]. In the United States, a *REIT* is a corporation, trust or even a mere association which invests in real estate and which distributes 95% or more of its income. *REIT*s often trade publicly. To qualify for U.S. tax purposes, a *REIT* must have 100 or more investors.

IRC section 856 defines a *REIT* as:

> For purposes of this title, the term "real estate investment trust" means a corporation, trust, or association—
>
>> (1) which is managed by one or more trustees or directors;
>>
>> (2) the beneficial ownership of which is evidenced by transferable shares, or by transferable certificates of beneficial interest;
>>
>> (3) which (but for the provisions of this part) would be taxable as a domestic corporation;
>>
>> (4) which is neither (A) a financial institution referred to in section 582(c)(2), nor (B) an insurance company to which subchapter L applies;
>>
>> (5) the beneficial ownership of which is held by 100 or more persons;
>>
>> (6) subject to the provisions of subsection (k), which is not closely held (as determined under subsection (h)); and
>>
>> (7) which meets the requirements of subsection (c).

The subsection (c) requirements are themselves complex.

372. **Real Rate of Return:** This is *not* a term of art, so lawyers should be careful with it. Generally, a *real rate of return* refers to the actual return on an investment adjusted for actual *inflation*. One should also adjust for taxes.

Even that definition is imprecise because the definition of *inflation* is itself imprecise. The *CPI* and other *inflation* measures represent broad segments of the economy, but they may not represent the individual.

The following formula is an acceptable representation of a *RRR*; however, it is not the only acceptable formula.

$$RRR = \left[\left(\frac{1 + eff}{1 + inf} \right) - 1 \right]$$

where RRR = real rate of return, eff = effective interest rate,
and inf = actual past inflation.

373. **Recession:** This term describes a declining economy. Generally, most economists define a recession as occurring after two consecutive quarters of negative economic growth. The National Bureau of Economic Research (*NBER*), however, states:

> The NBER does not define a recession in terms of two consecutive quarters of decline in real GDP. Rather, a recession is a significant decline in economic activity spread across the economy, lasting more than a few months, normally visible in real GDP, real income, employment, industrial production, and wholesale-retail sales.

http://www.nber.org/cycles/.

374. **Registered Bond:** This is a *bond* (or *debenture*) registered with the issuer. It is transferable only on the books of the issuer; hence, it is not bearer paper. The issuer will pay interest on the instrument to the registered owner. As a result, if a person purchases a *registered bond*, he must act to change the registration. In contrast, some bonds are in bearer form with coupons attached. While not used often in the United States, coupon bonds remain elsewhere. The issuer will pay interest on them upon presentation of the coupons. A transfer of ownership occurs upon the transfer of the paper evidencing the obligation.

375. **Registered Investment Advisor: RIA:** *See* Investment Advisor for a full definition. An RIA manages the assets of high net worth individuals and institutional investors. An RIA handles the buy side of the transaction.

376. **Regulation D:** According to the SEC:

> Under the Securities Act of 1933, any offer to sell securities must either be registered with the SEC or meet an exemption. Regulation D (or Reg D) contains three rules providing exemptions from the registration requirements, allowing some companies to offer and sell their securities without having to register the securities with the SEC.

> While companies using a Reg D (17 CFR § 230.501 et seq.) exemption do not have to register their securities and usually do not have to file reports with the SEC, they must file what's known as a "Form D" after they first sell their securities. Form D is a brief notice that includes the names and addresses of the company's executive officers and stock

promoters, but contains little other information about the company.

http://www.sec.gov/answers/regd.htm.

Regulation D has three broad exceptions:

- 504: Generally this applies if the offering is either registered in a State which requires an offering disclosure or if it is limited to "accredited investors." See http://www.sec.gov/answers/rule504.htm.

- 505: Generally this applies to the offering of "restricted securities" mostly sold to "accredited investors." It permits only very small offerings.

- 506: Generally this permits unlimited (in size) offerings mostly to "accredited investors" of "restricted securities." The restrictions and other requirements in this safe harbor rule are greater than under the 505 exception. See http://www.sec.gov/answers/rule506.htm.

377. *REMIC*: **Real Estate Mortgage Investment Conduit**: [pronounced re-mik]. This is a trust, partnership or even a corporation which holds notes backed by real estate mortgages. Typically, they pool instruments with similar grades and similar terms. The *REMIC* then issues securities to investors in what, for tax purposes, is a sale of assets rather than an issuance of debt. The *REMIC* is exempt from U.S. income taxes: it is a pass-thru entity, similar in that sense to an *S Corporation*, a partnership, or a simple trust. For tax purposes, *REMIC* rules appear in Sub Chapter M, Regulated Investment Companies and Real Estate Investment Trusts. The *REMIC* Rules appear in Part IV.

IRC Section 860D defines a *REMIC* as:

> For purposes of this title, the terms "real estate mortgage investment conduit" and "*REMIC*" mean any entity—
>
>> (1) to which an election to be treated as a *REMIC* applies for the taxable year and all prior taxable years,
>>
>> (2) all of the interests in which are regular interests or residual interests,
>>
>> (3) which has 1 (and only 1) class of residual interests (and all distributions, if any, with respect to such interests are pro rata),
>>
>> (4) as of the close of the 3rd month beginning after the startup day and at all times thereafter, substantially all

of the assets of which consist of qualified mortgages and permitted investments,

(5) which has a taxable year which is a calendar year, and

(6) with respect to which there are reasonable arrangements designed to ensure that—

(A) residual interests in such entity are not held by disqualified organizations (as defined in section 860E(e)(5)), and

(B) information necessary for the application of section 860E(e) will be made available by the entity.

378. **Research & Development: R & D:** This commonly used term is not clearly defined. Generally, it includes an entity's expenditures which do not contribute to current products and sales, but which, instead, may lead to future products. Much expenditure can involve both current and future products; hence, accounting for *R & D* expenditures can be subjective. Generally, *GAAP* requires the expensing of R & D, while *IFRS* tends more toward capitalization.

Generally, an entity with significant *R & D* relative to revenues, earnings, assets or equity is forward-looking.

$$\left(\frac{R \& D}{revenues} \right) \ or \ \left(\frac{R \& D}{assets} \right) \ or \ \left(\frac{R \& D}{earnings} \right) \ or \ \left(\frac{R \& D}{equity} \right)$$

Investors may be willing to forgo current revenues in exchange for future revenues from yet-to-be developed products. Pharmaceutical companies often have very large *R & D*. These and other industries or companies with high *R & D* ratio are risky investment because the results of *R & D* are speculative.

379. **Reserve Currency:** For many decades, the United States dollar has been the major *Reserve Currency* for the world. As a result, many commodities—such as oil—are priced in terms of dollars. Also, investors seeking a safe haven in times of economic or political instability tend to place their investments in dollar denominated accounts or instruments. The *Euro* also acts as a major reserve currency for many purposes, as does the Japanese Yen. Whether the U.S. dollar will continue as the primary *Reserve Currency* for the world is an important issue.

As the primary world *Reserve Currency*, the dollar—and thus the United States—obtains substantial benefits. Because many countries hold dollars in reserve to back their own currencies, to provide liquidity for themselves, or as investments, the U.S. money supply is effectively larger than it otherwise would be at the resulting price levels. If other countries moved dollar accounts into another currency, they would sell dollars, which would increase the supply of dollars and thus depress the value. The result would be inflationary for the United States.

380. **Responsible Party:** *AICPA* definition—the person who has a level of control over, or entitlement to, the funds or assets in the entity that, as a practical matter, enables the individual, directly or indirectly, to control, manage, or direct the entity and the disposition of its funds.

381. **Retained Earnings: RE:** This is an accounting term for the sum of an entity's net earnings minus its cumulative *cash dividends* paid and minus any capitalized *retained earnings* pursuant to the recordation of a *stock dividend*.

The term is generally comparable to *Earned Surplus*, which some corporate statutes use to reflect accumulated earnings minus cash dividends and capitalized *earned surplus*. Both terms are generally comparable to *Earnings and Profits*, a tax term also reflecting generally cumulative income minus cumulative dividends. See *IRC* section 312 for the computation of *E & P*.

Lawyers must be very careful not to inter-change the three terms, which have similar but significantly different meanings. While the differences may sometimes be small, they can be large.

A fuzzy distinction between capital gains and ordinary income involves *Retained Earnings*. Earnings belong to the common shareholders. If distributed, they result in dividends. For tax purposes those are taxable to the extent of earnings and profits. For other legal purposes, dividends are almost always—if not always—income. Whether they constitute income from labor and industry—and thus marital assets in most states even if derived from separate property—depends on the degree of management, a question of fact. But, undistributed *Retained Earnings* economically result in share appreciation. This, in turn, results in capital appreciation or capital gains if the owner disposes of the shares. But, many jurisdictions consider such capital appreciation in separate property to retain its character as separate property, regardless of the degree of management. This is widely true for C corporate investors and also commonly true of S corporate investors. *See, e.g., Zold v. Zold,* 911 So. 2d 1222 (Fla. 2005).

382. **Return on Assets:** *ROA:* This is a commonly used profitability *ratio*. It helps investors and creditors interpret an entity's financial statements. It combines analysis of the *income statement* and the

balance sheet. While analysts define it differently, a common definition is:

$$\left(\frac{net\ profit\ after\ tax}{total\ assets} \right)$$

If the *ROA* is less than the general cost of capital, the firm will want to consider expanding: it can borrow money at a lower rate than it can return through operations. For this analysis to be effective, the net profit figure should not include extraordinary items. One should not consider an *ROA* figure for a single year in isolation. It will provide more useful information in the context of multiple years and multiple ratios.

383. **Return on Equity: *ROE*:** This is a commonly used profitability *ratio*. It helps investors and creditors interpret an entity's financial statements. It combines analysis of the *income statement* and the *balance sheet*. While analysts define it differently, a common definition is:

$$\left(\frac{net\ profit\ after\ tax}{total\ equity} \right)$$

If the *ROE* is higher than the return on alternative investments, then equity holders should generally continue to hold their investment and may want to consider increasing it. If the *ROE* is less than alternative investment, then equity holders should consider selling their investment and choosing alternatives. One should not consider an *ROE* figure for a single year in isolation. It will provide more useful information in the context of multiple years and multiple ratios.

384. **Return on Investment: ROI:** This is another term for *ROE*.

385. **Revenue Recognition Principle:** This is the current terminology for was once the "all events test for income." It has four elements:

- Has delivery (per the contract) occurred or the service been rendered?

- Is the price fixed or determinable? [Arguably this has a "reasonable" element to it].

- Is collection reasonably assured?

- Is there persuasive evidence of an arrangement, *i.e.,* that a transaction has taken place?

386. **Reverse Polish Notation: *RPN*:** In *reverse polish notation,* the mathematical operation follows the operands. For example, to add the numbers 3 and 5 in normal notation, one computes:

$$(3 + 5) = 8$$

But in *reverse polish notation*, one would perform:

$$3,5 +$$

The comma represents the ENTER function. The calculator would have no equal sign, so one would not have that extra function. Early computers and calculators used this format. The HP 12C calculator still uses it and continues to be popular. Because the format does not require parenthesis and similar symbols, it can calculate some very complex functions more efficiently than standard notation.

Simple *polish notation* is the opposite: the operator appears first:

$$+ 3,5$$

The comma represents the ENTER function.

The term *Polish* dates from the creation of *Polish notation* by a famous Polish mathematician, Jan Lukasiewicz. The reverse method first appeared commonly in the 1960s.

Typically, lawyers have little use for *RPN*. They should be generally familiar with it because they will encounter many people—economists, real estate agents, and others—who use the HP 12C or similar calculators. As these people may be expert witnesses, a lawyer needs to understand their terminology and methodology.

387. **Risk:** This is a measure of the likelihood or probability that an investment's results will differ from the holder's expectations. *Risk* is one of three main interest components.

In terms of individual interest rates, *risk* assesses the probability of default in whole or in part (such as through payment deferral). Properly assessed, risk compensates for default. For example, a diversified investor might accept moderate *risks*, expecting some of his investments will fail, but most will succeed. If measured precisely, the *risk* premium would exactly compensate and the investor would earn no excess over risk-free investment.

In reality, investors cannot measure *risk* precisely because it is a prediction of future events. Hence, investors hope they are better at evaluating *risk* than their competitors. If so, they can earn an excess return.

388. **Roth IRA:** Under United States Internal Revenue Code section 408A, Roth IRAs are treated as IRAs in that the accounts are not taxable on their income. Contributions to such accounts, however, are not deductible—in contrast to contributions to IRA accounts.

389. **Rule of 72:** This is a simple method of calculating the time needed for money to double at a given *EFF*:

$$FV = 2PV \text{ in } y \text{ years when } y = \frac{EFF}{72}$$

For example, with an *EFF* of 8%, a deposit will approximately double in 9 years, which is 8 divided by 72. At an *EFF* of 9%, doubling will take approximately 8 years. At an *EFF* of 4%, doubling will take approximately 18 years. The short-cut formula is most accurate for interest rates less than about 20%.

390. **Sales Tax Clearance:** a government-issued certificate that verifies an entity has paid all its tax liabilities at the time that the entity ceases to exist or is transferred to a new owner. The use of such certificates varies from state-to-state. In jurisdictions where they are available, a purchaser of a business with inventories risks responsibility for unpaid sales taxes if the purchaser fails to obtain a **Clearance**.

391. **Salvage Value:** This is the residual value of a thing at the expected end of its useful life. The figure is useful in computing depreciation for financial accounting purposes. Typically, the depreciable basis of an asset is the cost of the assets minus its salvage value. For United States tax purposes, salvage value is usually irrelevant per *IRC* section 168.

392. **S & P 500:** A popular stock index, the *S & P 500* is:

> Widely regarded as the best single gauge of the U.S. equities market, this world-renowned index includes 500 leading companies in leading industries of the U.S. economy. S&P 500 is a core component of the U.S. indices that could be used as building blocks for portfolio construction. It is also the U.S. component of S&P Global 1200.

393. **Scientific Calculator:** A *Scientific Calculator* is one generally used to calculator trigonometric functions, such as sine, cosine, tangent, secant, cosecant and cotangent. They also typically compute logarithms. These functions are very useful in engineering and architecture; however, they are largely unimportant in the practice of law.

Most *scientific calculators* do not compute *financial calculations*, such as *present* and *future values, amortizations* and *sinking funds*—at least they do not do so conveniently. Similarly, most *financial calculators* either do not compute trigonometric functions, or they do so inconveniently. The reasons for this have less to do with memory chips than with button design. By itself, a financial calculator has many confusing and overlapping buttons—most of which serve two purposes. A typical *scientific calculator* is similar, often with buttons serving one main function and two shift functions. Adding financial functions to the interface is possible, but not convenient. Because the audience—scientists versus accountants and lawyers—does not overlap for the most part, the better part of wisdom suggests separate calculators for separate functions: scientific and financial.

394. **S Corporation:** A corporation subject to Subchapter C or Subtitle A of the Internal Revenue Code of the United States. C Corporations are themselves taxpayers. They pay taxes on income generally at a rate of 34%. *Dividends* and Distributions from them are not deductible; however, taxpayers who receive dividends are subject to preferential treatment. Nevertheless, *C Corporation* income is subject to double taxation in the U.S.: once at the corporate level and once at the shareholder level. This is as opposed to income of an *S Corporation*, which is a *pass-through entity*.

As a general rule, large corporations and widely-held (generally publicly traded) corporations are C's. Most other corporations elect *S* status or they are LLCs (limited liability companies).

An S Corporation is a type of *pass-thru entity*.

395. **Secular Trust:** *also,* **Economic Benefit Rule:** See the discussion of the *Economic Benefit Rule* and also the discussion of the *Rabbi Trust Doctrine*.

396. **Security:** This term has two broad but different meanings.

- Security for an obligation: This refers to the property that is the object of a security device such as a mortgage or pledge. For example, a mortgage on a house commonly secures a loan to purchase the house. The same is true of an automobile standing as security—through a mortgage—for a loan.

- A type of investment instrument: This typically refers either to equities—such as common or preferred stock (or options and warrants to purchase them—or to debt—such as bonds and debentures. The term may, depending on the jurisdiction or contract, refer to any transferable (tradable) financial instrument.

397. **Self Amortizing Obligation:** This is a traditional loan with regular *payments* of all current *periodic interest* plus a portion of *principal*. Typically, the *payments* are level; hence, the largest portion of the early *payments* are interest with very little being *principal*, and the largest portion of later *payments* being *principal* with very little being *interest*.

398. **Self Employment Tax:** United States Internal Revenue Code Section 1401—part of Chapter 2 of Subtitle A—imposes an income tax on self-employment income. This tax is generally equivalent to the social security and Medicare taxes imposed on employment income by Subtitle C. Self-employment refers to circumstances in which a taxpayer is not an *employee*. Generally, an employee is one who is subject to the direction and control of his employer. While the tax rate generally does not differ between the employment tax and the self-employment tax, other issues are critical. Employment taxes fall half upon the employer and half upon the *employee*, while self-employment falls entirely upon the earner. Also, the self-employment tax is an "income tax" imposed by Subtitle A and subject to all procedural rules applied to income taxes. In contrast, Subtitle C employment taxes are subject to different procedural rules.

399. **Separate Entity Assumption of Accounting:** One of the fundamental principles of accounting, this assumes an entity is separate from its owner. Hence, the entity has a set of books and financial statements, as does the owner.

400. **Shared Appreciation Mortgage Loan: SAM:** [pronounced sam]. This is a loan under which some or all of the interest is conditioned on appreciation in the property securing the loan. Arguably, it is more akin to equity rather than debt; however, for both banking and tax purposes, *SAM*s have generally received debt and interest treatment.

For example, in times of high inflation and high interest rates, some people may have difficulty qualifying for a home loan. The lender may also want to share in the expected appreciation of the property being financed. If so, the parties may contract for a relatively small fixed interest rate. In addition, they may contract that if the debtor sells the property within a specified period, the lender will receive a specified percentage of the increased value (which the contract should define with consideration given to the costs of sale). The contract may provide for appraisal of the property—and a payment of interest equal to a specified percentage of the increased value—if the debtor does not sell the property within a specified period.

The tax and other legal consequences of such an arrangement can be complex—and controversial. One must determine the period to which to allocate the conditional interest. One must determine whether the "conditional" interest truly represents interest or whether it represents a transfer of an ownership interest. One must determine whether the loan under which the debtor borrowed money was merely a loan with fixed and conditional interest, or whether it was a joint venture for the purchase of property, or even the sale of an interest in property.

For other legal purposes, one can sell appreciation rights in property separate from the property—at least in many jurisdictions. Stock appreciation Rights (*SARs*) are commonly bought and sold. Arguable, a SAM is more comparable to the sale of *SARs* than it is to a loan with conditional interest. The legal consequences of such a classification are substantial.

401. **Short Sale:** A transaction used by *bearish* investors, a *short sale* historically involved the sale of borrowed securities. The *bear* would borrow the securities from someone less bearish (someone who has a *long* position) and then sell them. The seller hopes the price will drop and he will then be able to cover (pay or satisfy) his obligation to return the borrowed stock by buying new stock at a lower price. The *short seller* would pay a small fee to the lender and would keep the remainder of the profit resulting from a price drop. Of course, if the price rises, the *short seller* loses money because he must purchase the securities at a higher price to cover his obligation.

Substantial *short selling* is mostly a *bearish* indicator because large numbers of investors expect prices to fall. However, it can also be a *bullish* indicator because it means the *short sellers* will have to cover their positions at some point, which will increase demand and thus prices.

402. **Simple Interest:** This term requires explanation in isolation as well as in the contextual usage of "simple interest rate," "simple-interest transaction" or "simple-interest obligation."

The term "simple interest" is not a financial or accounting term. Lawyers should understand no financial formulae or traditional financial calculators use the term; hence, it is undefined in the financial world.

The term "simple interest" is a legal term, used in federal and state statutes as well as regulations. Loan or deferred payment contracts also often use the term; hence, lawyers must understand its legal meaning. Further, they must understand how the term relates to similar financial terms of art.

As is true of many legal terms, this one is not defined uniformly by law and practical applications are not uniformly consistent. In contrast, the similar term "nominal annual interest rate" is a financial term with a specific meaning which forms part of the fundamental algebraic finance formulas. Definitions which different from that traditional meaning are wrong: they exist, but they are incorrect. "Simple interest" is not a term about which one can be so certain.

In most cases—perhaps close to all—one should be able confidently to substitute the term "nominal annual interest rate" for the term "simple interest rate." In that sense, the simple interest rate equals the periodic interest rate times the number of periods in one year. In some cases, one may find a reference; however, that equates the "simple interest rate" to the periodic rate. While that would not be common, it would also not be surprising. Thus lawyers should insist on clarity whenever the term appears.

For example, *12 U.S.C. § 4313* refers to:

> (3) ANNUAL RATE OF SIMPLE INTEREST.—The term "annual rate of simple interest"—
>
> (A) means the annualized rate of interest paid with respect to each compounding period, expressed as a percentage; and
>
> (B) may be referred to as the "annual percentage rate".

That statutory usage suggests the term "simple interest" or "simple interest rate" might be a periodic rate.

Section 226.17 of the Federal Truth in Lending Act provides:

> 2. *Simple or periodic rates.* The advertisement may not simultaneously state any other rate, except that a simple annual rate or periodic rate applicable to an unpaid balance may appear along with (but not more conspicuously than) the annual percentage rate. An advertisement for credit secured by a dwelling may not state a periodic rate, other than a simple annual rate, that is applied to an unpaid balance. For example, in an advertisement for credit secured by a dwelling, a simple annual interest rate may be shown in the same type size as the annual percentage rate for the advertised credit, subject to the requirements of section 226.24(f). A simple annual rate or periodic rate that is applied to an unpaid balance is the rate at which interest is accruing; those terms do not include a rate lower than the rate at which interest is accruing, such as an effective rate, payment rate, or qualifying rate.

This provision distinguishes the simple rate from the effective rate and the annual percentage rate (*APR*).

403. **Simple Trust:** This describes a *pass-thru entity* trust under *IRC* section 641. Such a trust is not a taxpayer; instead, the income beneficiaries must report their share of the trust income, whether distributed or not.

404. **Simple Yield:** The term *Simple Yield* is not a term of art; hence, lawyers should use it only with an accompanying definition. Most often it represents the following formula:

$$\left(\frac{NAI}{market\ value}\right)$$

> where *NAI* = the nominal annual interest rate. This results in a variable yield.

Some users interchange the term *yield* with the term *simple yield*. Both usages are common and neither is correct or incorrect.

LESSON FIVE-E: *Yield* covers the term simple yield.

405. **Simplified Employee Pension: SEP:** Under *IRC* section 408(k), an employer may contribute to individual or group IRAs of its employees. These form a Simplified Employee Pension Plan (SEP). Because the creation of such a plan is "simple," administrative costs tend to be low.

According to IRS Publication 4333:

> Simplified Employee Pension plans (SEPs) can provide a significant source of income at retirement by allowing employers to set aside money in retirement accounts for themselves and their employees. Under a SEP, an employer contributes directly to traditional individual retirement accounts (SEP-IRAs) for all employees (including the employer). A SEP does not have the start-up and operating costs of a conventional retirement plan and allows for a contribution of up to 25 percent of each employee's pay.

Also according to Publication 4333, advantages of a SEP include:

❑   Contributions to a SEP are tax deductible and your business pays no taxes on the earnings on the investments.

❑   You are not locked into making contributions every year. In fact, you decide each year whether, and how much, to contribute to your employees' SEP-IRAs.

❑   Generally, you do not have to file any documents with the government.

❑   Sole proprietors, partnerships, and corporations, including S corporations, can set up SEPs.

❑   You may be eligible for a tax credit of up to $500 per year for each of the first 3 years for the cost of starting the plan.

❑   Administrative costs are low.

406. **Sinking Fund: *SF*:** This calculation solves for the amount of the regular deposit needed, at a *stated interest rate* and period, to

accumulate a *future value*. This is the opposite of the calculation involving the *FUTURE VALUE OF AN ANNUITY*. For example, if you wanted to accumulate $25,000 in ten years and were willing to make ten equal annual deposits, beginning today, at an annual interest rate of ten percent, each deposit would need to be $1,426.03. Beginning one year from now, the necessary *deposits* would be $1,568.63. *Sinking Fund* schedules often involve the *begin mode* because savings plan deposits often begin at the inception of the plan, which would be the beginning of the first period. The *end mode* calculation, however, may also be used.

LESSON FOURTEEN explains the use of a SINKING FUND CALCULATOR.

The SINKING FUND calculation is one of the six basic calculations performed by a *Financial Calculator*. The formula for the *SF* is:

$$SF = \left[\frac{\left(FV\left(\frac{i}{100}\right) \right)}{\left(1 + \frac{i}{100} \right)^n} - 1 \right]$$

where i = nominal annual interest rate, n = number of periods per year, and FV = the future value.

407. **Slope:** The formula for the slope of a line is:

$$s = \frac{rise}{run}$$

The rise is the increase (or decrease) on the y-axis. The run is the increase in the x-axis. This is an important term for many areas of mathematics, as well as economics.

Lawyers must pay close attention to the difference between the slope of a line and its angle of change, which is a very different, but also important, factor. By altering the scale of either the x or y-axis, a graph user can dramatically alter the angle of change without affecting the slope. As a result, the user could "truthfully"—though misleadingly—testify that the graphed line presented the correct slope. While such testimony might sound impressive, honest, and helpful (and it might be), it could easily be misleading, distorting, and dishonest.

For example, lawyers often use income figures over a period of years to predict future income. In a tort case, this is useful to predict and thus value lost income for a victim. In business, a manager would use such information to analyze whether it should continue or cancel a particular project. In family law, such predictions of future income are useful in determining child support and alimony obligations. In the area of mergers and acquisitions, a potential purchaser will use such information to predict future income in deciding whether to purchase a target. In environmental law, a regulator would use such information in analyzing the predicted impact of rules and regulations.

Consider the following:

A's net annual income was:

2008	$500,000
2009	495,000
2010	485,000
2011	455,000

In this simple example, one can easily see—without a graph—the fairly gradual decline in income. Over the four-year period, income has fallen 9% and the rate of fall has increased. But, all four amounts are quite high and the change likely has little real impact on A's financial stability. Consider, however, three graphs of this information, each of which presents a line with the same slope, but a different angle of descent.

The first uses a truncated y-axis with an arithmetic scale crossing the x-axis at 450,000. The truncated axis amplifies the angle of descent. A casual observer might conclude that A's income is dropping at an alarming rate. To further mislead, albeit with "truthful information," the x-axis labels appear in large, bold type while the y-axis labels appear in smaller, less visible type.

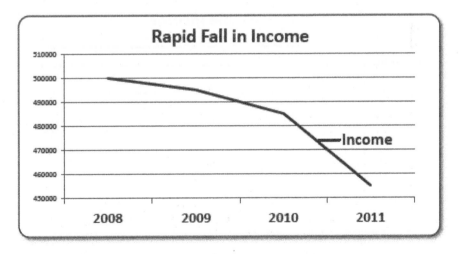

The second graph uses a non-truncated y-axis with an arithmetic scale crossing the x-axis at zero. It, however, uses a more elongated x-axis, which causes the income descent to appear even flatter. For the information provided, this is probably the most "honest" presentation in that it will likely lead a casual observer to the most accurate conclusions: A's income is falling, the rate is increasing, but over-all it is relatively stable.

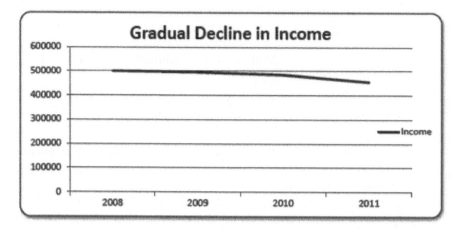

The third uses a non-truncated y-axis with a logarithmic scale crossing the x-axis at zero. The logarithmic scale minimizes the angle of descent, making the line appear very flat. While a logarithmic scale is often useful (*e.g.,* the Richter scale for measuring earthquake intensity), such a scale can present information in a way that would cause a casual observer to draw incorrect conclusions. In this graph, A's income appears very stable.

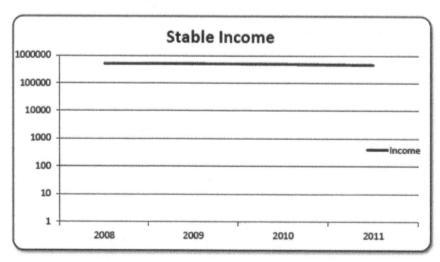

408. **Sovereign Wealth Fund:** A state owned investment fund investing in real and financial assets. SWFs are funded by revenues from commodity exports or from foreign-exchange reserves held by the central bank.

409. **Special Allocation:** This is a United States partnership law tax term under section 704(b) of the Internal Revenue Code. See the discussion of "substantial economic effect" for more information.

410. **Specie:** Coins, bullion, and commodity metals. This includes national coinage, as well as silver, gold, and platinum bullion. Not all national coins are struck from precious metals; indeed, since the 1930s, most are not.

   The word *specie* is generally unspecific by itself. When using the term, lawyers should specify whether they refer to items in the form of specific metals, and if so, the level of purity.

411. **Spot Price:** This refers to the current price of a commodity. In contrast, many quoted commodity prices refer to futures contracts for delivery in a month or six months or some other period. The spot price will sometimes vary substantially as a result of political, international unrest, or similar factors. Most commodity users, however, purchase supplies through the futures market and are therefore less subject to the volatility of the spot market.

412. **Substantial Economic Effect:** Under United States tax law, partnership may "specially allocate" items of income, gain, deduction, loss, or credit to particular partners. As a result, one partner may be allocated more capital gains, while another is allocated ordinary income. Or, one partner may be allocated gains while another is allocated losses. Naturally, the partners agree to such allocations because their relative financial and tax situations make them desirable, at least in the short term. For such "special allocations" to be respect for tax law purposes, they must have "substantial economic effect." *IRC* section 704(b) uses these three words. Treasury regulations spend approximately 100 pages defining the three words— which comprise perhaps the most complicated area of U.S. tax law.

   Of importance to lawyers is the impact of a special allocation which lacks substantial economic effect for non-tax purposes. Because the allocations result from contracts, they should be respected for other legal purposes, despite the lack of tax effect if they lack substantial economic effect. Lawyers dealing with definitions of income and loss for contractual, tort, or family law purposes should be wary of partnership allocations: in the short to midterm, such allocations may be contrary to economic reality and thus distorting. Even if they have substantial economic effect for tax purposes (because, for example, they result in an opposite future allocation through a minimum gain chargeback provision), they still may distort reality for non-tax purposes over a period of several years.

413. **Standard & Poor's Depository Receipt: SPDR: Spider:** These are Special Exchange Traded Funds (*ETF*s) which divide the S & P 500 into 9 sectors.

414. **Stated Interest Rate:** This refers to the given or *stated interest rate* on an instrument or financial obligation. While it may reflect the true interest rate—such as the current *effective rate* (*EFF*), it also may not. For example, it may fail to account for points or compounding. It also, by definition, does not adjust for external market forces which result in *market discount* or *acquisition premium*.

The term *stated interest rate* is thus not a term of art. Lawyers should use it only with a clear definition.

415. **Statement of Cash Flows:** Along with the *Income Statement* and the *Balance Sheet*, this forms a triad of fundamental *Financial Statements*. Essentially, the statement of cash flows is a cash method Income Statement. It eliminates accruals on un-paid expenses and receivables, as well as non-cash items such as depreciation, amortization, and bad debt write-offs. The statement does not comport to show accurate income; however, it does give a picture of an entity's liquidity or solvency and the direction or trend of liquidity.

416. **Statement of Changes in Financial Position:** Now known as the *Statement of Cash Flows*, this is one of the three principal *Financial Statements*.

417. **Statement on Financial Accounting Standards:** Issued by the *FASB* (Financial Accounting Standards Board), these are the actual opinions. They are also referred to as FAS number X.

418. **Stepped-Up Basis:** *IRC* section 1014 provides for a stepped-up basis for most property acquired from a decedent. Regardless of the decedent's tax basis, the heir or legatee will have a basis equal to the property's *FMV* at the date of death (or up to six months thereafter if the executor elects to use an alternate valuation date). Thus if a person owns Blackacre with a basis of $1,000 and a *FMV* of $1,000,000, his heir or legatee could receive the property upon his death and claim a basis of $1,000,0000.

In contrast, *IRC* section 1015 provides for a **Transferred Basis** for most property acquired by *inter vivos* gift. In the above example, if the property owner were to give Blackacre to his son, the owner's $1,000 *basis* would transfer to the son.

This important provision substantially distorts the economic behavior of many property owners. Elderly property owners have a strong disincentive to selling or otherwise developing their property, or to giving it away to the younger generation. If they were to sell it, they would suffer income tax on the resulting gain. If they were to give it to their children, the basis would transfer; hence, the children would have taxable gain when they sold the property. If, instead, the owner were to hold the property until his death, the heirs and legatees will receive a stepped-up basis to *FMV*. They can then sell the property without suffering any taxable gain.

For a brief period in 1977, the United States experimented with a **Carry-over Basis** system. Congress repealed the provisions within one year because of alleged complexities.

Be careful to distinguish this from the very different term: ***Adjusted Basis***.

419. **Sterling:** This has two main definitions:

- The British Pound Sterling, denoted by £. Originally, 240 British pennies weighed one troy pound. The British Pound equaled 240 pennies. The term pennyweight came from the old British penny.

- A level of purity in silver. Generally, *sterling silver* is an alloy of 92.5% silver and 7.5% copper (hence the tendency to tarnish). Most manufacturers stamp *sterling* products with the notation 925 or .925, indicating the level of purity.

Silver is a commonly traded commodity. Pure—fine—silver typically has a purity of .999 and is widely available in 100 *troy ounce* bars. Absolute purity is not possible with current metallurgy techniques. Coin Silver—which has nothing to do with coinage—has a purity of .9. Some older European silver had purity levels of from .800 to .875. Investors should be careful when valuing silver flatware or hollowware (trays and other non-utensil serving pieces). Silver coinage has traditionally had a fineness of .800, although the United States issued half-dollars from 1965 to 1970 with a fineness of .400, and silver nickels from 1942 to 1945 with a fineness of .350.

420. **Stock Appreciation Rights (SARS):** Stock appreciation rights are a portion of the bundle of rights which comprise the ownership of corporate shares.

The holder of the stock sells to another the right to all or a portion of the appreciation in the share value which will occur in the future. This can be the basis of a contract between individuals or companies; or, it may be a form of compensation to an employee.

The obligor would pay to the owner of the right the difference between the value of a share on the target date and the value of a share on the issue date.

The income tax consequences of a person issuing stock appreciation rights are complicated. Generally, it would result in an acceleration of ordinary income. Similarly, the income tax consequences of a person receiving SARS as compensation are also complicated. Generally, such a receipt results in ordinary income per IRC sections 409A and 83.

421. **Stock Dividend:** This refers to the distribution of additional shares to existing shareholders. Generally, it involves an increase in the number of outstanding shares by 20% or less. For (some) state and for financial accounting purposes, such a *small stock dividend* requires a bookkeeping entry to capitalize a portion of retained earnings (for financial purposes) or *eared surplus* (often for legal purposes). Such an entry debits contributed capital and credits *surplus* or *RE*. A *large stock dividend*—greater than 25% may not require such entries: that is open to the opinion of the *CPA* and attorney. A very *large stock dividend* is called a *stock split* and requires no bookkeeping entry.

For U.S. tax purposes, the receipt of a *stock dividend* does not result in income. *Eisner v. Macomber,* 252 U.S. 189 (1920). For tax purposes, the recipient of a *stock dividend* would apportion his basis among the pre-existing shares and the newly received shares by their relative *FMV*.

Whether a *stock dividend* represents income for <u>other</u> legal purposes is a matter of state law (which is often unclear if not conflicting) or contract. The issue can be significant in family law matters involving alimony, child support, and the division of marital or community property. If a *stock dividend* is income for those purposes, it will affect alimony and child support obligations. Similarly, if a spouse receives a stock dividend on separate property, the *dividend* portion may constitute income in the eyes of some courts—particularly if the spouse managed the separate property during the marriage.

The financial accounting treatment of *stock dividends*—requiring the capitalization of *Retained Earnings (RE)*—is consistent with the view that they constitute income. Effectively, financial accounting treats a *stock dividend* as a cash distribution of retained earnings following by a re-contribution of the distribution in exchange for more stock. Often, the effective income is a reality: the price of the stock either does not drop or drops to an extent disproportionately small when compared to the value of the stock.

According to at least some state courts, an increase in *Retained Earnings (RE)* does not produce income to the shareholder for purposes of alimony, child support, and apparently the determination of marital or community assets. This is true because the stockholder—unless he controls a majority of the shares—cannot force a distribution of the earnings. Whether that analysis holds for purposes of stock dividends is mostly an open question. In accounting terms, a stock dividend results in an entry changing the corporate capital structure. Under some state laws, it also results in such a change that effectively reduces the ability of the company to pay a *cash dividend* (which must come from *earned surplus* or *current earnings* in some states). In that sense, the stock dividend is an income item. But, an opposing view would recognize that despite the accounting entry, the total amount of stockholder equity does not change; instead, the entry merely moves it from one category to another. Hence a shareholder in a company with no stock dividend, but increased *RE*, is not in a substantially different position than a shareholder of a company that issues a *stock dividend* and then capitalizes some *RE*.

Lawyers must be familiar with *stock dividends*—small and large—as well as stock splits. They must understand the differences and the similarities. They must understand the financial and legal accounting issues and entries, as well. Failure to do so will result in adverse contractual or legal consequences from the incorrect or incomplete analysis of and definition of *income*.

422. **Stock Option:** Stock options, rights, and warrants are similar contractual rights. Generally, each grants the holder (owner) the right to purchase a fixed number of shares at a fixed price, often for a fixed period of time.

Generally, stock options are granted by an employer to an employee as a form of compensation. The U.S. income consequences of stock options granted to employees are covered, in part, by IRC section 83.

423. **Stock Rights:** Stock options, rights, and warrants are similar contractual rights. Generally, each grants the holder (owner) the right to purchase a fixed number of shares at a fixed price, often for a fixed period of time.

Generally, stock rights are granted by a corporation to its shareholders, who then have either the right to purchase additional shares at a fixed price or the right of first refusal on future share issues.

424. **Stock Split:** This is a very large *stock dividend*, often involving two shares in exchange for one, or even more. Typically, a *stock split* results in a price drop comparable to the increased number of shares outstanding. As a result, the market capitalization (stock price times the number of shares outstanding)

(stock price) times (number of outstanding shares)

does not change materially. For both tax and financial accounting purposes, this does not involve any book entry; instead, it merely requires a notation of the change in number of shares outstanding.

Corporations *split* their stock so as to provide greater market *liquidity*. For example, if a company has 1 million outstanding shares selling for $100 each, it could split the stock five for one, resulting in 5 million outstanding shares selling for roughly $20 each. Investors will arguably have an easier time buying and selling shares priced at $20 rather than shares priced at $100.

For legal purposes that are a function of *income*, a *stock split* should _not_ be considered *income*; instead, it is merely an exchange of *principal* for *principal*. This could affect Trust allocations of income and principal, a joint venture or partnership allocation of *"income"* from an asset, or the definition of a marital asset versus separate property in family law. Lawyers should be careful with this as the line between a stock split and a stock dividend is not bright; indeed, in the 20 to 25% range, it is quite fuzzy. Mostly, an increase of more than 25% is a split, and less than 20% is a dividend.

425. **Stock Warrant:** Stock options, rights, and warrants are similar contractual rights. Generally, each grants the holder (owner) the right to purchase a fixed number of shares at a fixed price, often for a fixed period of time.

Generally, stock warrants are granted to debt holders or preferred stock holders. They receive the right to purchase common share at a fixed price.

426. **Stripped Bond:** This refers to a *coupon bond* with the *coupons* detached prior to their maturities. The underlying bond represents the *principal* obligation while the *coupons* represent the *interest* obligation. The phrase also refers to U.S. treasury securities which have been severed among their component parts: the various promises to pay interest and the underlying bond.

IRC Section 1286 deals with stripped and severed bonds. It requires the holder to apportion the basis among the various components according to their relative *FMV*s.

One of the most famous tax cases dealing with the ASSIGNMENT OF INCOME DOCTRINE arose from a stripped bond. *Helvering v. Horst*, 311 U.S. 112 (1940).

427. **STRIPS:** This refers to the division of U.S. Treasury obligations into separate instruments representing principal and the various promised interest payments. They then trade separately as zero-coupon obligations. The stripped principal becomes one security and each of the separate interest obligations becomes other separately traded securities, as well.

IRC section 1286 requires the "stripper" to apportion the original cost basis among the various components. Each instrument then becomes subject to sections 1271 through 1277 for determination of the tax consequences for accrued interest, market discount, and acquisition premium.

428. **Student Loan Marketing Association: SLMA: Sallie Mae®:** According to the company's website:

> Sallie Mae®, the nation's leading provider of student loans and administrator of college savings plans, has helped millions of Americans achieve their dream of a higher education. The company primarily provides federal and private student loans for undergraduate and graduate students and their parents.
>
> In addition, Sallie Mae offers comprehensive information and resources to assist students, parents, and guidance professionals with the financial aid process. Sallie Mae owns or manages student loans for 10 million customers and through its Upromise affiliates, the company also manages more than $17.5 billion in 529 college-savings plans, and is a major, private source of college funding contributions in America with 10 million members and $450 million in member rewards. Sallie Mae employs approximately 8,000 individuals at offices nationwide.
>
> Sallie Mae was originally created in 1972 as a government-sponsored entity (GSE). The company began privatizing its operations in 1997, a process it completed at the end of 2004 when the company terminated its ties to the federal government.

http://www.salliemae.com/about/.

Note that *Fannie Mae, Sallie Mae®,* and *Freddie Mac* all began as government sponsored entities (*GSEs*); however, *Sallie Mae®* no longer fits that category.

429. **Supplemental Security Income:** *SSI*: According to the Social Security Administration website:

> SSI stands for Supplemental Security Income. The Social Security Administration (SSA) administers this program. SSA pays monthly benefits to people with limited income and resources who are disabled, blind, or age 65 or older. Blind or disabled children, as well as adults, can get SSI benefits.

http://www.ssa.gov.

SSI differs from general Social Security Benefits in several ways. The SSA lists some of them:

- Social Security benefits, SSI benefits are not based on your prior work or a family member's prior work.

- SSI is financed by general funds of the U.S. Treasury—personal income taxes corporate and other taxes. Social Security taxes withheld under the Federal Insurance Contributions Act (FICA) or the Self Employment Contributions Act (SECA) do not fund the SSI program.

- In most States, SSI beneficiaries also can get Medicaid (medical assistance) to pay for hospital stays, doctor bills, prescription drugs, and other health costs.

- SSI beneficiaries may also be eligible for food stamps in every State except California. In some States, an application for SSI benefits also serves as an application for food assistance.

- SSI benefits are paid on the first of the month.

- To get SSI, you must be disabled, blind, or at least 65 years old and have "limited" income and resources.

- In addition, to get SSI, you must:

  o be a resident of the United States, and

  o not be absent from the country for more than 30 days; and

  o be either a U.S. citizen or national, or in one of certain categories of eligible

430. **Supply/Demand Curve:** This is a basic graph in economics. It illustrates the convergence of two principles. First, as supply of a product increase, price will fall. Second, as the demand for a product increases, the price will rise. A graph of the supply curve superimposed onto a graph of the demand curve will have an intersection point, which is the optimum supply and the optimum price.

The following graph also appears in relation to the discussion involving elasticity. As price—the y-axis (left side) rises, demand (red) drops, as reflected in the units demanded because customers will buy less for a higher price. Also, as price rises, supply (blue) rises because produces will produce more for a higher price. At some point, the two cross, which reflects the optimum level.

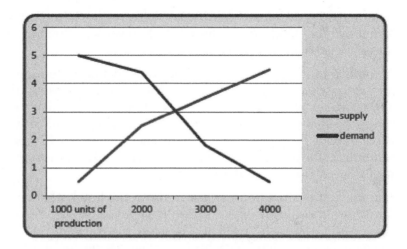

431. **TARP:** The *Troubled Asset Relief Program*, this was enacted by Congress during the fall of 2008. Initially, it involved plans for the Treasury to purchase sub-prime loans and other impaired (difficult to value) assets from banks. Later, the Treasury used substantial funds to purchase Preferred Stock in banks so as to infuse capital quickly. The bill was part of the Emergency Economic Stabilization Act of 2008, Public Law 110–343.

432. **T-Account:** Another term for a *ledger. See books/ledger.* These are called T accounts because they look like the capital letter T. *Debit* entries are on the left side and *credit* entries are on the right.

Asset and expense accounts/ledgers will normally have *debit* balances. Liability, equity, and income accounts will normally have *credit* balances. The aggregate *debits* will always equal the aggregate *credits*.

A *Balance Sheet* is actually one large *T-account* for all permanent accounts (plus all temporary accounts closed to *Retained Earnings*).

433. **Tax Account Transcript:** Shows basic data from an individual's tax return including marital status, type of return filed, adjusted gross income and taxable income. Also shows adjustments that were made after the return was filed. In contrast, a Tax Return Transcript shows the amounts on each line of a return. Neither constitutes the actual return.

434. **Tax Bracket:** The United States income tax system (and also most other systems), uses a graduated method of brackets. The first dollars of taxable income are subject to a low rate—recently 10%. Below that level, the rate is zero percent. Income above another level is subject to a higher rate—recently 15%, with the first dollars still subject to zero percent and 10%. Hence the 15% rate is a marginal rather than flat rate. Higher U.S. bracket in recent years have been 25%, 28%, 31%,

33%, and 35%. As recently as 1986, the highest U.S. bracket was 50%. As recently as 1982, the highest U.S. bracket was 70%. In 1961, the highest U.S. bracket was 94%.

According to many economists, a graduated tax system discourages productivity. Clearly, the higher the marginal rates, the more discouraging the system becomes. Other economists claim—in contrast—that high brackets actually encourage productivity: they leave producers with so little money, the producers will work harder to accumulate more. Little evidence supports the latter view which nevertheless is commonplace.

Other areas of the law work similarly to tax brackets. For example, family law dissolution matters effectively involve a tax: alimony, child support, and property division. The more income and assets one has, the more he must share with his former spouse on dissolution. Indeed, often the family law definition of income and assets parallel those of tax law. Often, the share percentage increases much like tax brackets. Indeed, one can view family law as just another tax system—only one with higher marginal rates and one in which the client has greater incentives. For example, consider how much a client will pay or do to pay less in tax to the government. Now consider how much a client might pay or do to pay less to a former spouse.

435. **10-K:** According to the *Securities and Exchange Commission*:

> The federal securities laws require publicly traded companies to disclose information on an ongoing basis. For example, domestic issuers (other than small business issuers) must submit annual reports on Form 10-K, quarterly reports on Form 10-Q, and current reports on Form 8-K for a number of specified events and must comply with a variety of other disclosure requirements.

> The annual report on Form 10-K provides a comprehensive overview of the company's business and financial condition and includes audited financial statements. Although similarly named, the annual report on Form 10-K is distinct from the "annual report to shareholders," which a company must send to its shareholders when it holds an annual meeting to elect directors.

> Historically, Form 10-K had to be filed with the SEC within 90 days after the end of the company's fiscal year. However, in September 2002, the SEC approved a Final Rule that changed the deadlines for Form 10-K and Form 10-Q for "accelerated filers"—meaning issuers that have a public float of at least $75 million, that have been subject to the Exchange Act's reporting requirements for at least 12 calendar months,

that previously have filed at least one annual report, and that are not eligible to file their quarterly and annual reports on Forms 10-QSB and 10-KSB. These shortened deadlines will be phased in over time.

http://www.sec.gov/answers/form10k.htm.

EDGAR publishes Forms 10-K along with other important information.

436. **TIN: Taxpayer ID Number:** This is a number assigned to all United States taxpayers. For individuals, it is the social security number. For others, as well as for sole proprietorships, it is an Employer Identification number, sometimes called an *EIN*.

437. **Time Period Assumption of Accounting:** Financial accounting, as well as *income* tax accounting, functions based on time. The arbitrary period used is one year, although many interim statements appear based on quarters or months.

See the discussion of a *Fiscal Year* and of a *Calendar Year* for a fuller discussion.

An alternative to the time period would involve transactional accounting. In such a system, one would report income, expenses, gains, and losses per transaction rather than per period. Many such systems exist:

- For *tax purposes*—at least from the consumer's perspective—excise taxes, sales taxes, VATs, gift taxes, estate taxes, and inheritance taxes are all transactional.

- For *financial accounting*, *GAAP* requires the time period assumption for regular Financial Statements; however, cost accounting—particularly for internal reporting— often functions on a transactional basis, or at least for groups of similar transactions.

- For *legal purposes*, many instances of transactional accounting exist. For example, a joint venture is often a single project or transaction. It would report financial operations for the venture, separate from activities and project involving other ventures. Similarly, partnership accounting has elements of transactional accounting, although it almost always is based on an annual period. Nevertheless, a partnership—which is not a legal entity—will prepare financial reports on a mixed annual and transactional basis.

  Family law also has elements of transactional accounting. While income for purposes of child support and alimony is typically based on a time period, financial reports for determinations of Community Property rules and Equitable Distribution rules are more transactional. That occurs because—in most jurisdictions—some transactions produce community or marital income while other transactions produce separate income. Oddly, under at least some regimes, some transactions which result in income from separate property affect marital property while those which produce losses from separate property do not.

Thus lawyers should be aware of the *Time Period Assumption*; however, they should also be aware that it is not universal.

438. **Total Cost of Ownership: TCO:** This is an element or method of *cost accounting* which reflects all costs associated with owning an asset. For example, if one were to purchase an automobile, the *TCO* would include all licenses, insurance, routine maintenance, parking, and similar costs. The analysis should help consumers and businesses evaluate a proposed purchase as it helps them understand the many necessary—or sometimes discretionary, but common—cost of having something. A very simple example would involve a dog. The animal itself may be free; however, it requires food, vaccinations, a license or tag, medications, check-ups, a bed, a dish, someone to watch it when the owner is away, and many other significant costs. When one budgets for a dog, or a car, or a college education, one should consider not just the direct costs associated with acquiring the thing, but also the *TCO*.

A complete *TCO* analysis is comparable to the calculation of an *IRR*: it would include the *present value* of all cash flows connected to the asset, from the original acquisition to the ultimate disposal.

439. **Trade or Business:** This important phrase appears in 271 separate sections of the Internal Revenue Code (as of 2011). It lacks a clear definition. Generally, it connotes business activity as opposed to investment activity. Trade or business expenses (per *IRC* section 162) receive more favorable treatment than do expenses for the "production of income" (per IRC section 212) or expenses in a "transaction for profit." More than two dozen sections further limit tax consequences to the *active conduct of a trade or business*. None, however, define that term, either.

440. **Transferable Instrument:** This is an *instrument* which can be transferred from one owner to another. It is distinguishable from a *negotiable instrument*, which creates a holder in due course.

A maker of a promise may destroy its transferability by providing merely a promise to pay a particular person but not his assignees.

Under the UCC, a non-transferable *instrument* would not actually be an *instrument*; instead it would merely be a promise.

441. **Transfer Pricing:** This is a profit allocation method used to attribute a multinational corporation's net profit (or loss) before tax to countries where it does business. It is the practice of setting prices among divisions within an enterprise. For example, Exxon owns an oil rig in Iraq, a refinery in Turkey, a shipping company in Greece, and is headquartered in the U.S. These subsidiaries act independently from each other except they are all subsidiaries of Exxon. The oil rig sells the oil it extracted to the refinery, the refinery then sells the oil to the shipping company and then the shipping company sells it to the headquarters. Transfer pricing determines at what price each of the subsidiaries sell the oil to each other.

Transfer pricing is also an important aspect of determining an entity's income or loss in a state within the U.S.

Often, transfer pricing results in significant distortions. For example, an entity will have a strong motivation to set a high price in low tax countries or states, which results in lower income or even losses in high tax jurisdictions.

442. **Treasury Inflation-Protected Securities: TIPS:** [pronounced tips]. Commonly known as *TIPS*, these are obligations of the U.S. Treasury. They earn a fixed rate of interest; however, the principal amount adjusts regularly as a function of changes in the *Consumer Price Index* (*CPI*). As a result, the coupon interest—which is based on a fixed rate—increases because it is a function of a greater principal amount. For U.S. tax purposes, both the interest and the inflation adjustment to principal are includible as gross income.

443. **Treasury Stock:** Corporations often purchase shares in themselves with the intention of selling the shares in the near future. Such shares are held as "Treasury Stock." They are never an asset; instead, they are a contra-equity account. Any "profit" or "loss" on the later sale must be closed to equity and does not appear on the income statement.

444. **Troy Ounce:** Most precious metal (*e.g.*, gold, silver, platinum) weights appear in *troy ounces*, rather than the more commonly used avoirdupois ounce. One troy ounce equals approximately 31.1034768 grams. Twelve troy ounces equal one troy pound.

One standard U.S. pound contains approximately 14.58 troy ounces as compared to 16.00 avoirdupois ounces. Hence, an ounce of gold weighs more than an ounce of feathers—the ounce of gold, whether noted or not—refers to a troy ounce. One troy ounce equals approximately 1.097 avoirdupois ounces.

One troy ounce also equals 120 carats or 155 metric carats, which is a commonly used weight for gems.

Lawyers and investors should be very careful in matters involving the weight of precious metals: while custom uses troy ounces, unscrupulous sellers may denote avoirdupois ounces or merely "ounces." For example, 16 ounces of gold—measured on a postal scale—would equal only 14.58 troy ounces. If the purchaser used the market value of gold (expressed in terms of troy ounces) but multiplied it by stated number of 16 ounces, he would pay approximately 10% too much for the metal.

445. *UBIT*: **Unrelated Business Income Tax:** This is a tax on exempt organizations imposed by *IRC* section 511. The highest corporate rate applies. Organizations exempt under *IRC* section 501—plus state colleges and universities—pay United States income tax on their *Unrelated Business Taxable Income (UBTI)*. The rules apply to all exempt organizations, not just *charities*.

Charities—and some other exempt organizations—with more than an *insubstantial* amount of UBTI risk losing their exempt status. The definition of insubstantial is not clear; however, many authorities place it at somewhere between 5% and 15% of the entity's operations or cash flow or activities. Most courts reject a percentage test; instead, they apply unclear subjective rules.

446. *UBTI*: **Unrelated Business Taxable Income:** This is the amount of income subject to the *IRC* section 511 tax. Several factors are significant:

- The activity producing the income must be unrelated to the reason the organization is exempt.

- The activity must constitute a trade or business.

- The activity must be regularly carried on.

- The income must not be within an *IRC* section 512(b) modification.

- The income must not be from an *IRC* section 513(a) excluded activity.

Generally, the *IRC* section 512(b) modifications include passive activities such as the collection of interest, dividends, rents, and royalties, as well as capital gains.

447. **Unified Credit:** This refers to a tax credit under *IRC* section 2010. It applies against either the United States Gift Tax or the U.S. Estate Tax.

448. **Uniform Gift to Minors Act:** *UGMA:* This is a uniform law adopted in some states to control non-trust gifts to minors. Drafted in 1956, most states adopted it, albeit with some variations. The act permits a custodian (typically a parent) to hold title to the property and to act on the minor's behalf until the child reaches the age of majority. While most states once adopted the *UGMA*, most have since replaced it with the *UTMA*.

449. **Uniform Reciprocal Enforcement of Support Act:** *URESA:* This is a uniform law adopted by all states to facilitate interstate collection of child support and alimony. The pronunciation of the acronym is easily confused with the pronunciation of *ERISA*, a wholly different act altogether.

450. **Uniform Transfer to Minors Act:** *UTMA:* This is a uniform law adopted (with modifications) in most states to control non-trust gifts to minors. It permits a custodian (typically a parent) to hold title to the property and to act on the minor's behalf until the child reaches the age of majority.

   The *UTMA* has replaced the *UGMA* in most states since 1986. Under the *UTMA*, contractual references to *UGMA* accounts are treated as references to the *UTMA*.

451. **Unitrust:** This is a shortened term for a *Charitable Remainder Unitrust (CRUT)*.

452. **Usufruct:** This is a civil law term. It refers to an ownership interest in the use and fruits of a thing. The usufruct term may be specified or it may be for the life of a person. The remaining ownership interest is the naked ownership.

   A usufruct is a present interest generally comparable to a term of years or a life estate in common law jurisdictions.

453. **U.S. Government Long Bond:** These are long-term obligations of the U.S. Treasury, also called *Treasury Bonds*. They earn a fixed rate of interest compounded semi-annually and typically have a maturity of thirty years.

454. **U.S. Government Note:** These are mid-term obligations of the U.S. Treasury (sometimes called *T-notes*). Typically, they earn a fixed rate of interest compounded semi-annually. Typically, they have maturities ranging from two to ten years.

455. **U.S. Government Series EE Bond:** According to the U.S. Treasury Website:

   > Series EE savings bonds are safe, low-risk savings products that pay interest based on current market rates for up to 30 years for bonds purchased May 1997 through April 30, 2005*.

You may purchase EE Bonds via TreasuryDirect or at almost any financial institution or through your employer's payroll deduction plan, if available. As a TreasuryDirect account holder, you can purchase, manage, and redeem EE Bonds directly from your Web browser.

*Series EE bonds purchased May 2005 and after will earn a fixed rate of return.

Under *IRC* section 454(c), a holder may elect to include Series EE bond interest as it accrues; or, a holder may elect to defer recognition of the interest until disposition.

456. **United States Real Property Interest: USRPI:** IRC section 897c. Ownership of property located in the U.S. and its disposition. This is a tax term that determines the treatment of a purchase or sale depending on whether the buyer/seller is a domestic or foreign entity.

457. **U.S. Government T-Bill:** These are short-term (less than one-year) obligations of the U.S. Treasury (hence the T in *T-bill*). Typically they have terms of 4, 13, or 26 weeks, roughly corresponding with one-month, three months, and six months. They are distinguishable from *Treasury Notes* and *Treasury Bonds*, which have longer terms.

458. **Value Added Tax: VAT:** [pronounced vat]. This is a widely-used consumption tax system. It is similar to a sales tax; however, it is also critically different.

Under a sales tax, the consumer pays the tax to the seller at the point of sale. The seller then remits the tax to the government. Such a tax is relatively easy to cheat, if both the seller and consumer are willing.

Under a *VAT*, each level in the manufacturing/distribution process pays a tax to the government on the value added to the product at that stage. Each stage charges the full *VAT* rate on the sales price, but remits only that portion attributable to the added value. Hence, ultimately the consumer bears the entire tax and the last seller has a strong incentive to collect it: because he paid a similar tax to his seller, he will want reimbursement from his seller for that amount.

For example, if a painter paints a painting, he will have paid *VAT* on his materials. When he sells the painting to a distributor, he would collect *VAT* on the entire price, retain the amount of *VAT* he paid for the materials, and remit the *VAT* attributable to his addition to the value of the painting. When the distributor sells the painting to a gallery, it collects VAT on the entire painting, retains the amount it paid to the painter, and remits the portion on its price *profit margin*. Lastly, the gallery will collect *VAT* on the entire sales price to a consumer. The gallery will retain the amount of *VAT* it paid to the distributor, and will remit to the government the portion of the *VAT* collected on its profit margin. Ultimately, therefore, the consumer pays the entire *VAT*. At each stage the seller has an incentive to collect the *VAT*, as it will retain a significant portion.

Consistent with *WTO* rules, a county may refund *VAT* on exports. A country may not, however, refund the portion of an export's value attributable to capitalized income taxes—such as corporate taxes. Hence, a system which relies more on *VAT* and less on corporate tax has a trade advantage over a system without a *VAT*. The United States stands alone among industrialized nations in not having a *VAT*. The various sales taxes charged by state and local government, however, generally receive *VAT* treatment from the *WTO*.

459. **Variable Cost:** As explained in relation to *Cost, cost accounting* is a very important—generally internal—function. It helps management understand whether a particular activity is profitable. For cost accounting to be effective, however, one must pay close attention not only to *costs*, but also to the meaning and classification of costs.

Variable costs do what their name suggests: they vary. They vary as a function of the activity being measured. For example, if management wants to produce an extra quantify of inventory, the *variable costs* would include:

- *Stock in trade* (inventory components)
- Additional labor
- Additional energy (electricity or gas)
- Additional wear and tear on machinery

Variable costs, however, would not include *fixed costs* such as management salaries (unless they include an extra bonus for production), insurance (unless extra is needed for the activity), interest on loans (unless extra borrowing occurs because of the activity), *depreciation* on fixed assets, and customary accounting or legal costs.

The total of *variable costs* would generally equal the *incremental cost* of the inventory or the *marginal cost* of the inventory.

460. **Velocity of Money:** This represents the frequency a given quantity of money changes hands in a given period of time, usually one year. The *velocity of money* is a factor affecting *inflation*. Generally, if the *money supply* increases without a general increase in productivity, *inflation* results because, as was said by Milton Friedman, more money is chasing fewer goods.

But, the *velocity of money* must also fit into the equation to determine *inflation* or *deflation*. If the *money supply* increases, but the *velocity of money* decreases, *inflation* will not result.

$$V_t = \left(\frac{nT}{M} \right)$$

where V_t = the velocity of money in all transactions for the economy, nT = the aggregate value of all transactions in the economy, and M = the total supply of money in the economy. The definition of M is not a static concept, but is open to interpretation and multiples methods of measurement. *GDP* (*nT*) likewise does not have a uniformly fixed definition.

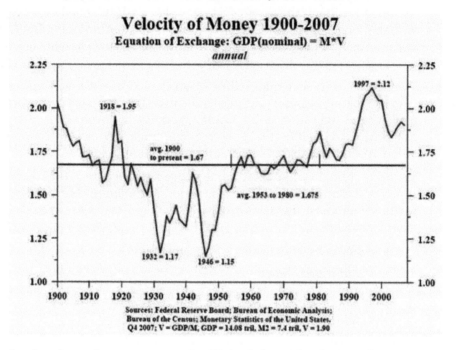

Velocity of Money 1900-2007

Equation of Exchange: GDP(nominal) = M*V

annual

Sources: Federal Reserve Board; Bureau of Economic Analysis;
Bureau of the Census; Monetary Statistics of the United States.
Q4 2007: V = GDP/M, GDP = 14.08 tril, M2 = 7.4 tril, V = 1.90

As the chart demonstrates, the United States' velocity of money has long hovered around 1.675. During the *Depression* years in the 1930s, the velocity dropped significantly, as it also did during the World War II years of rationing.

461. **Venture Fund:** An investment fund that manages money for investors seeking private equity stakes in startup of small and medium sized companies with prospects of strong growth. The fund is usually comprised of contributions from high net worth individuals that are looking to pool their resources in order to achieve high returns.

462. **Venture Capital:** A generic term that would include venture funds. Essentially any money contributed to a start-up company would be considered venture capital. There is a venture debt or equity but the characteristics of the recipient company would be the same. An early to mid-stage start up with an uncertain time horizon and a high risk of loss.

463. **Vesting:** This is the process by which rights become nonforfeitable. Vested rights are legal ownership of a thing or the right to a thing. Unvested rights are contingent or conditional. With Qualified Defined Benefit Deferred Compensation Plans, unvested interests are conditional on the passage of time and the employee continuing his employment for a specified period. IRC section 411 covers Minimum Vesting Standards for employer contributions. Generally, the section requires either full vesting in five years or a graduated vesting over a three to seven year period.

For several legal purposes, the existence of unvested rights is important. Such legal areas include the rights of creditors, contractual agreements concerning employment, contractual agreements concerning debt obligations, and family law. In a sense, an unvested right has no value; however, that view is simplistic. Certainly, while unvested, the right is valueless; however, many other legal rights accompany an unvested right. For example, an employee who is days short of vesting and who is then dismissed may have good cause to suspect improper treatment and the breach of good faith. Whether such causes are actionable depends on the specific facts; however, clearly the existence of unvested rights carries reasonable expectations of vesting absent misbehavior by the employee or unforeseen and unusual circumstances.

In family law, unvested rights constitute marital assets or community property in some jurisdictions, if earned during the marriage. Valuation of them is difficult. One must consider the absence of immediate value, coupled with difficult to determine expectancy value. One must also consider the cliff effect contribution. The last day of work prior to vesting is arguably the most important: without it, vesting will not occur. In a sense, therefore, all the value of the resulting vested rights belongs in the last day. Such a view is extreme, but not without some justification. An alternate view would place an equal amount of value in each of the days during the five year period (assuming five year vesting). But, that view, too, is unrealistic: many employees work for short periods and therefore never vest. One of the reasons deferred compensation plans require a vesting period is that it helps create loyalty by employees. Evidence of such loyalty—and arguably loyalty itself—increases during the five year period. Under that view, each day may legitimately receive some portion of the ultimate vested value, but in ever increasing amounts.

The financial calculations needed to apportion vesting value among various periods are not complex; however, they require some accounting principle to operate—straight-line value allocation, accelerated value allocation, or a cliff-effect (all at the end) value allocation are a few possibilities. Unfortunately, state laws provide little guidance.

464. **Vulture Fund:** A fund that invests in distressed and underpriced assets in hopes of making a large return on the investment. These funds had gone out of vogue for a while but cropped back up in 2009 when funds were put together to start snapping up homes that had gone into foreclosure.

465. **Wash Sale:** This is the loss sale and repurchase of substantially the same securities within 30 days. For United States tax purposes, the two transactions—if they occur within 30 days of each other—collapse into "no transaction" as if nothing happened. *IRC* section 1091 disallows the loss:

> In the case of any loss claimed to have been sustained from any sale or other disposition of shares of stock or securities where it appears that, within a period beginning 30 days before the date of such sale or disposition and ending 30 days after such date, the taxpayer has acquired (by purchase or by an exchange on which the entire amount of gain or loss was recognized by law), or has entered into a contract or option so to acquire, substantially identical stock or securities, then no deduction shall be allowed under section 165 unless the taxpayer is a dealer in stock or securities and the loss is sustained in a transaction made in the ordinary course of such business. For purposes of this section, the term "stock or securities" shall, except as provided in regulations, include contracts or options to acquire or sell stock or securities.

466. **Weighted-Average Cost of Capital: *WACC*:** *WACC* is the average of the costs of using debt and equity financing for a company. Debt and equity are weighted by their respective use in the given allocation. By taking a weighted average, a company can determine how much interest is paid for every dollar the company finances. The *WACC* computation also allows a company's managers to evaluate the economic feasibility of projects by determining whether the expected Rate of Return exceeds the *WACC* needed to fund the project.

WACC is computed using the following formula:

$$WACC = \left(\frac{(E)(Cost\ of\ Equity)}{V} \right) + \left(\frac{(D)(Cost\ of\ Debt)(1 - tax\ rate)}{V} \right)$$

E = fair market value of the company's equity; D = fair market value of the company's debt; $V = E + D$; E/V = percentage of financing that is equity; D/V = percentage of financing that is debt

A company uses all sources of capital in the computation of *WACC*. A company's goal is to maximize its Return on Assets (*ROA*) while minimizing the *WACC*. The goal of computing a company's *WACC* is to demonstrate the balance that maximizes of debt and equity that will maximize the return to stakeholders.

Many companies discount cash flows at *WACC* to determine the Net Present Value (*NPV*) of a project. Others may use a chosen *IRR* for the discount rate.

467. **Working Capital:** An important figure in the analysis of financial statements, *working capital* is:

$$working\ capital = (current\ assets - current\ liabilities)$$

This information—a *liquidity* "ratio"—indicates the ability of an entity to operate in the near term. Most businesses have regular needs for working capital to meet payroll, utilities, and similar obligations. They would likely maintain adequate amounts in highly liquid accounts. A sudden increase in the *DSO* ratio (days sales outstanding) could rapidly impair available working capital and liquidity. A localized or more general economic recession may occur when a substantial business faces a working capital shortage. It will be slow in paying bills, which results in increasing *DSO* ratios for its supplies, who in turn suffer *working capital* impairment, rising *DSO* ratios, and the cycle continues.

Cyclical businesses require a working capital budget that varies during the year. At some points, they may have large cash needs, while at other times, their needs are low. For example, a resort during the off-season does not need the same cash flow it requires during the high season. Similarly, a hospital in the resort community may experience substantial seasonal working capital variations.

468. **World Trade Organization: WTO:** Following World War II, the United Nations attempted to create the *ITO*, or International Trade Organization. This movement grew, in part, from the *Bretton Woods* conference. The attempt generally failed. It resulted, however, in *GAAT*, the *General Agreement on Tariffs and Trade*. This widely respected treaty attempted to reduce trade barriers for international transactions.

In 1995, the *WTO* replaced *GAAT*. It currently has over 150 members and several dozen observers. Organization headquarters are in Geneva, Switzerland. It began with the *Marrakech Agreement*, a conference and treaty signed in Marrakech, Morocco. Earlier, another series of international negotiations—called the Uruguay Round (started, not surprisingly, in Uruguay) set the parameters for the *WTO* and the *Marrakech Agreement*. More recently, the Doha Round of negotiations (begun in Doha, Qatar) has focused attention on third-world (very poor) nations.

469. **Yield:** The term *Yield* is <u>not</u> a term of art; hence, lawyers should use it only with an accompanying definition. Often it represents the following formula:

$$\left(\frac{EFF}{purchase\ price}\right)$$

where *EFF* = the effective interest rate. Others define it as:

$$\left(\frac{EFF}{market\ value}\right)$$

which results in a variable yield. Some users call this alternative definition the "*current yield.*" Both usages are common and neither is correct or incorrect.

Still other users impose the *NAI* as the numerator in one or the other above formulas:

$$\left(\frac{NAI}{purchase\ price}\right) \quad \left(\frac{NAI}{market\ value}\right)$$

Such usage interchanges the term *yield* with the term *simple yield.* Again, neither is correct nor incorrect, although the latter two are less common. In each of the formulas using "market price" in the denominator, one must determine whether the user considers the "asked" or the "bid" price to be the "market price" if firmer quotations are unavailable.

The *Fed* website has defined *yield* as:

> **Yield**—The return on a loan or investment, stated as a percentage of price.

The *Fed* defines *return* as:

> **Return**—The profit made on an investment.

Further, the *Fed* defines *profit* as:

> **Profit**—The return received on a business undertaking after all operating expenses have been met.

These three definitions are themselves <u>*disturbing*</u>—together they illustrate the dangers lawyers face with financial and accounting terminology. From the bottom up, the *Fed* defines *Profit* as a return *received* after operating expenses are *met.* The concepts of *received* and *met* suggest *cash method* of accounting, which is a <u>*bizarre*</u> assumption for the *Fed*: *GAAP* does not recognize the *cash method,* which does not clearly reflect income. Then the *Fed* defines *return* in relation to the term *profit,* which renders the two definitions circular. It then defines *yield* in relation to return, which is itself inadequately defined. Probably, the definition writer had *NAI* in mind for return, which would be consistent with one of the four common definitions of *yield*. But, even that definition fails to distinguish between the *yield* on a *discount* instrument from the *yield* on an instrument with current interest *payments*. It also fails to account for what the holder does with the interest paid. Ultimately, for the *Fed* to suggest that the term *yield* even has a firm definition is itself incorrect, as the term is unarguably imprecise.

470. **Yield to Maturity:** The term *Yield to Maturity* (*YTM*) is <u>not</u> a term of art; hence, lawyers should not use it without an accompanying definition. One statutory definition defines it in terms of a *yield*:

> *Definitions* (4) The <u>*yield to maturity*</u>, or <u>*yield*</u>, is the annualized rate of return to maturity on a fixed principal security expressed as a percentage.

70 FR 57437 (discussing 31 CFR Parts 356, 357, and 363, sale of T-bills, bonds etc.).

This particular definition has two problems. First, it assumes all interest received is re-invested at the stated rate. Second, it is a *nominal* rather than a *compounded* rate. Other users define the term *Yield to Maturity* using an *effective* or compounded rate.

471. **ZBB: Zero Based Budget:** This is a budgeting system under which the applicant for funds must regularly justify all items. In contrast, most budget systems work on additional fund requests: only increases necessitate intensive justification.

472. **Zero Coupon Bond:** This refers to a financial instrument with deferred interest. Also known as a Discount Bond, it would pay no current interest; instead, the issuer pays principal plus all the capitalized interest at maturity.

FINANCIAL, TAX LAW, ACCOUNTING, AND ECONOMIC ACRONYMS

The financial arena is replete with acronyms. Lawyers avoid familiarity with them at their peril. To be conversant in accounting and finance circles, lawyers should be familiar with the following acronyms for several reasons:

1. Expert witnesses will use them. Lawyers need to be able to speak with their own expert, to cross examine an opponent's expert, and to translate to a judge or jury the terminology (including acronyms) used by an expert.

2. Financial, economic, and accounting reports may use these terms. Lawyers need to understand them.

3. Contracts will sometimes use these acronyms, with or without a clear reference. Lawyers need to be able to understand the terms, especially if the reference is unclear (which is an unfortunate situation, but a real possibility).

Definitions of most terms appear in the **GLOSSARY**.

1. **ACRS:** Accelerated Cost Recovery System.
2. **AFBI:** Active Foreign Business Income.
3. **AFR:** Applicable Federal Rate.
4. **AGI:** Adjusted Gross Income.
5. **AICPA:** Association of Independent Certified Public Accountants.
6. **Aka:** Also Known As.
7. **ALF:** Assisted Living Facility.
8. **ALP:** Arm's Length Principal.
9. **ALS:** Arm's Length Standard.
10. **AMEX:** American Stock Exchange.
11. **AMT:** Alternative Minimum Tax.
12. **AP:** Acquisition Premium.
13. **APIC:** Additional Paid-In Capital.
14. **APR:** Annual Percentage Rate.
15. **APY:** Annual Percentage Yield.
16. **ARM:** Adjustable Rate Mortgage.

17. **ATAD:** Anti-Tax Avoidance Directive.

18. **B2B:** Business to Business.

19. **B2C:** Business to Consumer.

20. **BEPS:** Base Erosion and Profit Shifting (important in international tax or multi-state tax).

21. **BI:** Beginning Inventory.

22. **BIS:** Bank of International Settlements.

23. **BLS:** Bureau of Labor Statistics.

24. **BM:** No this is not what you are thinking. It stands for *Begin Mode* or *Below Market*, as in Below Market Loan (also, **BML**). It can also stand for *Bull Market*.

25. **BRICS:** Brazil, Russia, India, China, South Africa.

26. **CAFE:** Corporate Average Fuel Economy.

27. **CAGR:** Compound Annual Growth Rate.

28. **CbC:** Country by Country.

29. **CCCTB:** Common Consolidated Corporate Tax Base (or **CCTB** without the consolidated).

30. **CD:** Certificate of Deposit.

31. **CDS:** Credit Default Swap.

32. **CEO:** Chief Executive Officer.

33. **CFA:** Chartered Financial Analyst.

34. **CFC:** Controlled Foreign Corporation; or Chlorofluorocarbon.

35. **CFE:** Certified Fraud Examiner.

36. **CFO:** Chief Financial Officer.

37. **CFP:** Certified Financial Planner.

38. **CFTC:** Commodity Futures Trading Commission.

39. **CIA®:** Certified Internal Auditor; or, Central Intelligence Agency.

40. **CIF:** Cost, Insurance, and Freight.

41. **CLT:** Charitable Lead Trust.

42. **CLU®:** Chartered Life Underwriter.

43. **CME:** Chicago Mercantile Exchange.

44. **COBRA:** Consolidated Omnibus Budget Reconciliation Act.

45. **COD:** Cash on Delivery.

46. **COGS:** Cost of Goods Sold.

47. **COLA:** Cost of Living Adjustment.

48. **COLI:** Corporate Owned Life Insurance.

49. **CPA:** Certified Public Accountant.

50. **CPI:** Consumer Price Index.

51. **Cr. FA®:** Certified Forensic Accountant.

52. **CRAT:** Charitable Remainder Annuity Trust.

53. **CRT:** Charitable Remainder Trust.

54. **CRUT:** Charitable Remainder Unitrust.

55. **CTB:** Check the Box.

56. **DBA:** Doing Business As.

57. **DCF:** Discounted Cash Flow.

58. **DDB:** Double Declining Balance Depreciation.

59. **DJIA:** Dow Jones Industrial Average.

60. **DNI:** Distributable Net Income. Also, Director of National Intelligence, Director of Naval Intelligence, and Do Not Intubate. The first use is the financial use.

61. **DOS:** Due on Sale.

62. **DOW:** Dow Jones Industrial Average.

63. **DRT:** Dis-regard Tape.

64. **DSO:** Days Sales Outstanding.

65. **E & O:** Errors and Omissions Insurance.

66. **E & P:** Earnings and Profits.

67. **EBIT:** Earnings Before Interest and Taxes.

68. **EBITA:** Earnings Before Interest, Taxes and Amortization.

69. **EC:** European Community.

70. **ECJ:** European Court of Justice.

71. **EDGAR:** Electronic Data Gathering and Retrieval.

72. **EEOC:** Equal Employment Opportunity Commission.

73. **EFF:** Effective Interest Rate.

74. **EI:** Ending Inventory.

75. **EM:** End Mode.

76. **ENE:** Early Neutral Evaluation: proposed in BEPS.

77. **EPIC:** Excess Paid in Capital.

78. **EPS:** Earning per Share.

79. **ERISA:** Employee's Retirement Income Security Act.

80. **ESOP:** Employee Stock Ownership Plan.

81. **ETF:** Exchange Traded Funds.

82. **EU:** European Union.

83. **FAS:** Financial Accounting Standard.

84. **FASB:** Financial Accounting Standards Board.

85. **FATCA:** Foreign Account Tax Compliance Act.

86. **FBO:** For the Benefit of.

87. **FDAP:** Fixed or Determinable, Annual or Periodical.

88. **FDIC:** Federal Deposit Insurance Corporation.

89. **Fed:** Federal Reserve Bank.

90. **FERC:** Federal Energy Regulatory Commission.

91. **FHLMC:** Federal Home Loan Mortgage Corporation: **Freddie Mac**.

92. **FICA:** Federal Income Contributions Act.

93. **FIFO:** First in First out.

94. **FINRA:** Financial Industry Regulatory Authority.

95. **Fka:** Formerly Known As.

96. **FLP:** Family Limited Partnership.

97. **FMV:** Fair Market Value.

98. **FNMA:** Federal National Mortgage Association: **Fannie Mae**.

99. **FOB:** Free on Board.

100. **FOMC:** Federal Open Market Committee.

101. **401(k):** A qualified deferred compensation plan under IRC section 401(k).

102. **403(b):** A qualified deferred compensation plan under IRC section 403(b).

103. **FSA:** Financial Securities Authority (U.K.); also, the Farm Service Agency; Flexible Spending Account; Foreign Student Aid; Federal Student Aid; Full Speed Ahead.

104. **FTA:** Forum on Tax Administration.

105. **FTSE:** Financial Times Stock Exchange.

106. **FUTA:** Federal Unemployment Tax Act.

107. **FV:** Future Value (also **FVS** for Future Value of a Sum).

108. **FVA:** Future Value of an Annuity.

109. **FY:** Fiscal Year.

110. **GAAP:** Generally Accepted Accounting Principles.

111. **GAAR:** General Anti-Abuse Rule (international tax, but not in U.S.).

112. **GAAS:** Generally Accepted Auditing Standards.

113. **GAAT:** General Agreement on Tariffs and Trade.

114. **GDP:** Gross Domestic Product.

115. **GNMA:** Government National Mortgage Association: **Ginnie Mae**.

116. **GNP:** Gross National Product.

117. **GRAT:** Grantor Retained Annuity Trust.

118. **GSE:** Government Sponsored Entity.

119. **GST:** Generation Skipping Tax.

120. **HELOC:** Home Equity Line of Credit.

121. **IFRS:** International Financial Reporting Standards.

122. **IMF:** International Monetary Fund.

123. **INTL:** International.

124. **IOSCO:** International Organization of Securities Commissions.

125. **IPO:** Initial Public Offering.

126. **IRA:** Individual Retirement Account.

127. **IRB:** Industrial Revenue Bond; or Internal Revenue Bulletin.

128. **IRC:** Internal Revenue Code; *never* IRS Code.

129. **IRD:** Income in Respect of a Decedent.

130. **IRR:** Internal Rate of Return.

131. **IRS:** Internal Revenue Service.

132. **LBO:** Leveraged Buy out.

133. **LCM:** Lower of Cost or Market.

134. **LDC:** Lesser Developed Countries.

135. **LIBOR:** London Interbank Offered Rate.

136. **LIFO:** Last in First out.

137. **LLC:** Limited Liability Company.

138. **Lmt:** Limited.

139. **LOB:** Limitation of Benefits.

140. **LTV:** Loan to Value Ratio.

141. **M & A:** Mergers and Acquisitions.

142. **MD&A:** Management Discussion and Analysis.

143. **MD:** Minority Discount; or Market Discount.

144. **MLE:** Multiple Location Entity.

145. **MNE:** Multi-National Enterprise.

146. **MTD:** Month to Date.

147. **MTM:** Mark to Market.

148. **NADA:** National Automobile Dealers Association.

149. **NAFTA:** North American Free Trade Agreement.

150. **NAI:** Nominal Annual Interest Rate.

151. **NASAA:** North American Securities Administrators Association.

152. **NASD:** National Association of Securities Dealers.

153. **NASDAQ:** National Association of Securities Dealers Automated Quotations.

154. **NOI:** Net Operating Income.

155. **NOL:** Net Operating Loss.

156. **NOPAT:** Net Operating Profit After Taxes.

157. **NPV:** Net Present Value.

158. **NSF:** Not Sufficient Funds.

159. **NYSE:** New York Stock Exchange.

160. **OBO:** Or Best Offer.

161. **OECD:** Organization for Economic Co-Operation and Development.

162. **OID:** Original Issue Discount.

163. **OPM:** Other People's Money.

164. **OTC:** Over the Counter.

165. **PCAOB:** Public Company Accounting Oversight Board.

166. **PE:** Permanent Establishment (important in international tax).

167. **P/E Ratio:** Price to Earnings Ratio.

168. **PFIC:** Passive Foreign Investment Company.

169. **PFS:** Personal Financial Specialist.

170. π: Principal.

171. **PITI:** Principal, Interest, Taxes, and Insurance.

172. **PMT:** Payment.

173. **PO:** Purchase Order.

174. **POD:** Payable on Death.

175. **POEM:** Place of Effective Management (international tax term).

176. **POS:** Point of Sale.

177. **PPI:** Producer Price Index.

178. **PPOM:** Private Placement Offering Memorandum.

179. **PPT:** Principal Purpose Test (international tax).

180. **PV:** Present Value (also **PVS** for Present Value of a Sum).

181. **PVA:** Present Value of an Annuity.

182. **P/YR:** Payments or Periods per Year.

183. **Q-TIP:** Qualified Terminal Interest Property.

184. **R & D:** Research and Development.

185. **REIT:** Real Estate Investment Trust.

186. **REMIC:** Real Estate Mortgage Investment Conduit.

187. **RIA:** Registered Investment Advisor.

188. **ROA:** Return on Assets.

189. **ROE:** Return on Equity.

190. **ROI:** Return on Investment.

191. **ROTH IRA:** A Special IRA Under IRC Section 408.

192. **RPN:** Reverse Polish Notation.

193. **S & P 500:** Standard & Poor's 500 Stock Index.

194. **SAAR:** Special Anti-Abuse Rule.

195. **SAM:** Shared Appreciation Mortgage Loan.

196. **SARs:** Stock Appreciation Rights. This also refers to Severe Acute Respiratory Syndrome, so be careful.

197. **SEC:** Securities and Exchange Commission.

198. **SEP:** Simplified Employee Pension.

199. **SF:** Sinking Fund.

200. **SFAS:** Statement on Financial Accounting Standards.

201. **SIMPLE:** Savings Incentive Match Plan.

202. **SLE:** Single Location Entity.

203. **SLMA:** Student Loan Marketing Association: **Sallie Mae**.

204. **SPDR:** Standard & Poor's Depository Receipt: **Spider**.

205. **SSI:** Supplemental Security Income.

206. **T-Bill:** Treasury Bill.

207. **TCO:** Total Cost of Ownership.

208. **10-K:** SEC Form 10-K.

209. **TEO:** Tax Exempt Organization.

210. **TIN:** Taxpayer Identification Number.

211. **TIPS:** Treasury Inflation Protected Securities.

212. **TVA:** Tennessee Valley Authority.

213. **TVM:** Time Value of Money.

214. **UBTI: UBIT:** Unrelated Business Taxable Income or Unrelated Business Income Tax.

215. **UGMA:** Uniform Gift to Minors Act.

216. **URESA:** Uniform Reciprocal Enforcement of Child Support Act. Do not confuse with ERISA, which—when spoken—sounds similar.

217. **USRPI:** United States Real Property Interest.

218. **UTMA:** Uniform Transfer to Minors Act.

219. **VAT:** Value Added Tax.

220. **WACC:** Weighted-Average Cost of Capital.

221. **WTO:** World Trade Organization.

222. *y:* Income (generally an economic reference).

223. **YTD:** Year to Date.

224. **YTM:** Yield to Maturity.

225. **ZBB:** Zero Base Budget.